INSTRUCTOR'S MANUAL

LITERATURE

An Introduction to Reading and Writing

Fourth Edition

Edgar V. Roberts
Lehman College
The City University of New York

Henry E. Jacobs

PRENTICE HALL, Englewood Cliffs, New Jersey 07632

Cover photo: *Birch Tree*, Comstock © 1993

A Simon & Schuster Company
Englewood Cliffs, New Jersey 07632

ISBN: 0-13-123597-4

Printed in the United States

Contents

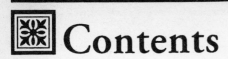

Poetry

Drama

To the Instructor

This manual is designed to help you in the practical tasks of teaching the various stories, poems, plays, and essay assignments in the fourth edition of LITERATURE: AN INTRODUCTION TO READING AND WRITING. For this reason, I encourage you to use the manual freely, in any way you wish, in classroom discussions. Above all, the conclusions in the manual should be used to encourage, never to dampen, student analysis. One problem encountered with questions in textbooks is that the questions are often mystifying. (I know that responses to many study questions take this approximate form: "What was on the author's mind on the day when he or she wrote the question?") I hope that this is not true of the study questions in the big book, but I have tried to make all the answers clear and unambiguous.

I do not claim perfection in these answers, nor do I expect that all instructors will find that they are adequate in all particulars. I have tried, however, to make the materials in the manual reliable both factually and logically. When there are points of varying interpretation I have offered possibilities for classroom discussion and disagreement.

For both the text and the manual, I would be grateful for suggestions for improvements and corrections of errors. Many people involved in the production of both text and manual have tried scrupulously to eliminate all mistakes. Please send both corrections of any mistakes you find, and suggestions for improvement (together with page numbers and locations of typographical errors) to me in care of Prentice Hall. If you have words of praise, these of course would be received with undying gratitude.

Thanks for assistance in the varying stages of the manual go to Alison Reeves, Phil Miller, Hilda Tauber, Andrew Roney, Gina Sluss, Lee Mamunes, and David Schechter, all of Prentice Hall. I am grateful to Nanette Roberts for helpful and penetrating advice. I am especially grateful to Jonathan Roberts for his never-failing creativity in fashioning the manual's handsome appearance.

— Edgar V. Roberts

Using This Manual

This manual is designed to help you in preparing to teach any of the works contained in the anthology, and also to help you in making assignments and in comparing individual works with other works. The chapters in the manual are therefore linked to the chapters of the big book. Each of the manual chapters begins with introductory remarks and interpretive comments about the works (stories, poems, plays) within the chapter of the big book. These are then followed by detailed answers for every single one of the study questions, question by question by question. Obviously our answers are not definitive but we offer them to give you a "launching pad" for your own classroom discussions. In addition, we have tried to be fairly complete in our answers, so that they might remind you of things that the classroom discussion might overlook or omit. Our goal in these answers is to provide you with as much assistance as possible.

In addition, to give you help in using the stories and poems in the *Additional Stories* and *Additional Poems* sections, we include brief general and thematic introductions and discussions of each of the works included there. In the "careers" chapters (11 and 24), we also provide a short working bibliography for further investigation and analysis.

Following the fiction section in the manual we provide a brief review of videotaped performances in *The American Short Story* series. Seven of the stories contained in the fiction section are included in this series ("I'm a Fool," "The Blue Hotel," "Barn Burning," "The Sky Is Gray," "Soldier's Home," "The Jilting of Granny Weatherall," and "The Greatest Man in the World").

Similarly, following the poetry section in the manual we provide a list of audiotapes available for 73 of the anthologized poets. For the third section, however, on drama, we include references to available videotapes and audiotapes in our introductions in the manual.

Works for comparison. In this edition of the Instructor's Manual, a new feature is included to help you in introducing comparisons of one work with others. This is the section entitled "Works for Comparison with . . . ." These "Works for Comparison" lists follow the "Writing topics" sections after each work discussed in the fiction and poetry sections (except for chapters 12 and 25). The works contained in the lists are all put there because they have points of comparison and contrast with the studied work. For example, the following entry appears for the story "Before the Firing Squad" by John Chioles (pages 138–142):

Works for Comparison with "Before the Firing Squad"

Hardy, *The Man He Killed*, 557
Laurents, *The Turning Point (film scene)*, 1588
Sassoon, *Dreamers*, 982
Zabytko, *Home Soil*, 403

The listed works are parallel because all of them concern violence and responses to it. The circumstances of the works are different but are similar enough to encourage a vigorous discussion of comparisons and contrasts. This method of introducing works for comparison is an additional way of providing you with the help that is contained fully in the Thematic Table of Contents. Please note that in the fourth edition we have removed the Thematic Table from the manual and now include it in the big book—as a second table of contents—immediately following the comprehensive chapter-by-chapter Table of Contents. For your convenience, the text pages of the listed works offer you quick referral to the locations of the works in the big book.

Finding locations within the manual. The chapters in the manual are designed to be connected with the chapters in the text. In paginating the manual we have assumed that you will be beginning with a story, poem, or play in the big book, and that you will therefore find it easy to locate sections in the manual by reference to the pages in the big book. We have therefore used the page numbers from the big book as a running head along the top of each page of the manual (e.g., Text Pages 93–112; Text Pages 88–130, and so on). If you are teaching Crane's "The Blue Hotel," for example, and are working up materials for the study questions on page 112, the "Text Pages" number will direct you to the right spot in the manual. In this respect, the big book offers immediate and accurate access to the manual.

The page numbers of the manual itself are located at the bottom of each page.

Writing Assignments and Workshops

One of the central goals of the fourth edition of **Literature: An Introduction to Reading and Writing** is to help students learn to write about literature effectively. To this end, we discuss writing processes and strategies in every chapter. We encourage you to have your students read the relevant section(s) of the text before they undertake any writing assignments.

Discussions of prewriting and writing in the text presuppose in-class or out-of-class assignments that will generate fully developed essays of 2 to 4 pages. (Students frequently pad longer papers on a single work because, under the pressure of extending their thoughts to the prescribed number of pages, they begin to retell stories and plots, and therefore abandon their thematic development.) The prewriting and writing discussions focus on the movement from the formation of ideas to the finished essay. In the classroom, this process can be analyzed in stages.

Short developmental assignments. As a way of assigning writing as you lead your class in the analysis and discussion of the total writing process, you may wish to make daily assignments. To avoid overburdening yourself with mounds of papers to be examined in great detail, you might use the pass-fail option for your grades. You might also make the assignments no longer than a single paragraph, which is an especially useful kind of assignment on most elements of literature. Such short assignments provide the advantages of constant writing and an ongoing monitoring of your students' skills. They can also, before class discussion, direct students to think about the material they are reading, thus leading to more productive and fruitful classes. Paragraph assignments can also serve as the building blocks for full-scale essays.

Writing assignments. Ideally, all assignments should be made in writing. This holds true for short paragraph assignments as well as full-scale essays. For a paragraph, a simple statement is probably enough, as long as your assignment is on a topic you have been studying with your students; e.g., *Write a paragraph about the character of Jacky (Pal) Smurch in Thurber's "The Greatest Man in the World"* (assuming that Chapter 4, on Character, has been the subject of discussion). This same formulation may be employed with reference to any topic or element. These sorts of assignments might even be listed in the course syllabus. In full-scale essay assignments, however, you will usually want to explain the task in more detail (both in writing and in classroom discussion).

Sequencing assignments. In many instances, the fourth edition of **Literature: An Introduction to Reading and Writing** will be used in courses where your students have had little experience in writing about literature. You might therefore want to organize the writing assignments so that they begin with a rather easy (and obvious) goal such as those in the first few chapters, and then go on to tasks that are progressively more difficult. In initial assignments, you might give your students a fully developed central idea of your own devising, and ask them to produce an essay based on this idea. Such a procedure cuts short the floundering stages of prewriting and enables students to focus immediately on the mechanics of organizing, writing, and revising their essays. As the course progresses, and as your students become more familiar with the stages of composition, you can provide less direction. Ultimately, you may give your students complete control of their own writing, including the freedom to select details, develop the thesis, and generally create their own individual essays.

In-Class Writing Workshops

If time permits, in-class writing workshops should be incorporated into your course. These can be useful to help students improve their writing. Three types of workshops are especially helpful: outlining, rough-draft workshops, and post mortems.

Outlining. In this type of workshop, you can establish a sample thesis based on a work that the class has just discussed. Then you might ask your students to outline a possible essay, paragraph by paragraph. The resulting discussion can be particularly effective in teaching organization and the selection of supporting details.

Rough-draft workshops. Time permitting, all out-of-class essays might be submitted in two stages: rough draft and final form. You can go over rough drafts quickly, and advise students about obvious problems. To provide further help in the early drafting stages, an actual rough-draft workshop can be effective. The idea is to get students to read, analyze, criticize, and edit the developing essays of their peers. Of course, such rough drafts should be in readable condition, if not fairly close to finished form. Students should be encouraged to treat the exercise seriously, since a competent job will obviously affect grades on the finished papers.

Mechanics. Students should be paired off to exchange papers. Using a checklist like the sample on the following pages, which we encourage you to reproduce and distribute to your classes, students should go through the papers carefully. Each student of the pair should then explain whatever problems she or he found in the other's essay.

Post mortems. This type of workshop involves an in-class evaluation of several essays in final form. You can select student essays that demonstrate the strengths or weaknesses that you wish to discuss. Sample papers may be duplicated (xerographed, dittoed) or projected.

Sample Guidelines for Student Editors in Rough-Draft Workshops

Before you begin working on your partner's draft, please study the questions in these guidelines. Then read through the draft carefully, as if you were reading it aloud. When you discover trouble in understanding your partner's sentences, or in following his or her meaning or reasoning, or when you think one of the questions below might be helpful in making an improvement, make a marginal note so that you can find the problem again. After you have finished your study of the draft, go over the trouble spots with your partner in light of the following fifteen questions. As you raise the issues with your partner, discuss how you may create improvements and modifications. Above all, don't do your partner's work. Ask questions; make suggestions; provide choices. In these ways you will be helping your partner make his or her own improvements.

1. Is the central idea clearly stated in the first paragraph?
2. Is the central idea followed and supported in the draft? Do all the paragraphs support the original idea, and do they hang together?
3. Does the draft have a strong and smooth introduction and a conclusion that closes the essay without being abrupt, misleading, or irrelevant?
4. Does the writer avoid the trap of retelling the story, restating the ideas in the poem or describing the actions of the play, while forgetting to make proper points in the essay?
5. Is the structure of the paper logical? Can you follow the thoughts and conclusions easily? Do the paragraphs follow each other logically?
6. Is there adequate transition between paragraphs?
7. Are the paragraphs correctly developed? Does each paragraph deal with one major thought or set of assertions? Should any paragraph be divided? How, and where?
8. Does the writer use enough quotation (but not too much) to support the central idea of the essay?

9. Does the writer avoid sentence problems? Check for the following:

   a. Sentences that are too long and confusing. Can they be broken into two or more shorter sentences?

      EXAMPLE: Thurber creates an interesting and ironic story in "The Greatest Man in the World" through the character of Jacky Smurch, a really low-brow kind of person who falls into the good luck of being able to fly an airplane around the world (at a time when airplanes flew only short distances), thus illustrating either his luck or his greatness, depending on how his character is interpreted.

      BETTER: In "The Greatest Man in the World," Thurber's interest and irony are focused on his major character, Jacky Smurch. Smurch is pictured as a lucky pioneer, for at a time when most airplanes could fly only short distances, he flies non-stop around the world. The irony is that Smurch, really a low-brow kind of person, is not great, but lucky.

   b. Run-on sentences or comma splices that link two complete sentences.

      EXAMPLES 1 AND 2: *Thurber's Jacky Smurch is not great but lucky he flies a plane around the world.*

      Thurber's Jacky Smurch is not great but lucky, he flies a plane around the world.

      CORRECTION FOR BOTH EXAMPLES: *Thurber's Jacky Smurch is not great but lucky; he flies a plane around the world.*

   c. Sentence fragments:

      1. A sentence fragment may be the result of groups of words missing a subject or verb (e.g., *This thought about a young woman who develops strength of character as a result of her responsibility.*)

      2. A sentence fragment may be the result of a word group beginning with a participle instead of a noun and finite verb (e.g., She is a lovely, aging woman. *Thinking about her past life and all the difficulties she has endured.*)

      3. A sentence fragment may be the result of the use of a dependent clause as a sentence (e.g., *Because the Duke of "My Last Duchess" knows that he has total power over the Count, his envoy, and his daughter.*)

4. A sentence fragment may be the result of the use of an object of a preposition as the subject of a verb (e.g., *Within this character thinks sympathetically and understandingly of the problems her friend has encountered on the lonely farm.*)

d. Awkward or ill-written sentences.

e. Sentences that are confusing because of grammatical errors or misplaced modifiers.

f. Short, choppy sentences that might be more interestingly combined to make one or two longer sentences.

10. Does the writer avoid agreement problems? Do nouns and pronouns always match up? Example: **When *one* reads this story, *we* see that Phoenix Jackson is very old, and *respect* her greatly.** Do verbs and nouns agree as to number? Example: **A *person* in these conditions *are* disposed to be overly imaginative.**

11. Does the writer avoid shifts in verb tenses? Example: **Phoenix *walks* through the woods and then *climbed* the steps of the hospital.** As a general principle, use the present tense exclusively when describing actions and speeches in any type of imaginative literature. Example: **The Prodigal Son *endures* great hardship for a long period, but when he *returns* home he *is welcomed* by his father, who *is delighted* to have him back.** See especially pages 27–28 of the text for a more detailed analysis and discussion of tense.

12. Does the writer avoid excessive repetition of particular words, phrases, or sounds, particularly in close proximity? (Use the example of this question, which repeats *particularly* four words after *particular,* and then uses the word *proximity,* which also begins with the *p* sound.)

13. Does the writer use words that seem inappropriate or out of place? Is a single level of diction maintained?

14. Does the writer spell words correctly, and make proper use of capital letters?

15. Does the writer use punctuation correctly? In checking punctuation, pay careful attention to commas, semicolons, and colons.

CHAPTER ONE
PAGES 1–44

Introduction: Reading, Responding, and Writing About Literature

Chapter 1 is a general introduction to literature and to the skills of writing about it. The chapter also includes one story which is used as the specimen for the various topics. In keeping with the introductory objectives, it proposes the most essential and basic of writing assignments: on likes and dislikes. All of these tasks may be somewhat imposing if taken in one large bite. You therefore may wish to assign pages 1–3 as a general introduction to the various genres, and then use "The Necklace" (pages 3–10) as the basis of your introductory discussion about characteristics of literature generally and fiction specifically.

For emphasis on writing, pages 3–37 (including "The Necklace") make up a unit centered around the procedure of reading a literary work, making marginal annotations, keeping a journal of all responses, and then going through the prewriting and writing tasks of preparing an essay. Along with the description of this process, there is additional material on the characteristics of good writing. You may wish to coordinate these passages with the assignment on likes and dislikes on pages 37–44.

You might use the writing section as a separate introductory unit, but we also hope that you will find these sections a convenient reference point for your students throughout your course. We believe that the section offers basic advice for students no matter where they may be as thinkers and writers about literature.

Please note the special sections in this chapter. These are (1) *Writing by Hand or by Word Processor,* on page 19; (2) *Use the Present Tense of Verbs when Referring to Actions and Ideas,* on page 27; (3) *Write with Your Readers in Mind,* on page 32; and (4) *Using the Names of Authors,* on page 34. These sections bring up points that need explaining when students first go about writing on literary topics. You might wish to introduce and discuss them as a special group early in the semester, when you make your first assignments.

The first section of **Literature: An Introduction to Reading and Writing**, on pages 1–3, is designed to get students thinking about the nature of literature. Classroom discussion should produce many questions and provide the chance to relate the general principles to works in the anthology and also to works that students know from other sources. The paragraph on the power and value of literature (pages 1–2) is an attempt to express briefly some of the ideas about reading that students certainly know, but which they themselves may never have articulated.

The definition of genres on pages 2 and 3 is designed as a quick introduction to the types. In discussing it, you might wish to refer quickly to the story on pages 3–10 to illustrate the generic qualities that otherwise may remain abstract in the minds of your students. In any event, the use of "The Necklace" is virtually mandatory in the use of the first chapter. The marginal notations accompanying this story demonstrate how responses embody both assimilation of the factual details and initial observations about character, situation, and meaning generally. The story thus illustrates the first phase of studying a literary text.

Although students are familiar with the word "study," they may not fully understand what studying is in actuality. Study is to be contrasted with the act of simple reading, and hence the subject of study is introduced on pages 10–18. This section attempts to explain the need for a regularized set of steps to be followed, more or less in the order suggested, in the process of developing not just a familiarity with literary works but also an understanding of them. Obviously, the key to study is the reinforcement to learning provided by the methodical keeping of a journal-notebook. It is surprising to learn that students sometimes have no clear notion of what to include. The marginal notations in "The Necklace" provide one type of response, while the specimen journal entries on pages 12–15 give a sense of the responses and observations that can form the basis for further thought and writing. Students who dislike marking up pages of books might include both types in their notebooks.

Writing Essays on Literary Topics, *pages 13 ff.*

The writing component of the introduction, beginning on page 13, is a most important section for students. Because it presupposes that students know "The Necklace," we stress once again that this story be assigned before the study of writing essays begins. The general definitions of an essay on page 13, for example, together with all the subsequent materials, will be meaningful only if students already have a good grasp of the story.

In the order of composition, once students have read the story assigned, and begin to create their own essays, the discussion of "brainstorming" outlined on pages 14–18 is an essential first step. Sometimes students hesitate to commit their first thoughts to paper during this brainstorming stage. If hesitancy or self deprecation is a problem, it is important to disabuse students of these feelings. You might emphasize that once something—anything at all—is on paper, students may work with it and develop it as a part of the essay that they are shaping. The special section on pages 19–20 is designed to stress the importance of getting something written, whether by hand, typewriter, or—especially for many of today's students—word processor. Even if students are uncomfortable with anything but a pencil or pen, however, it is worth emphasizing that writing is an essential aspect of thinking, because writing adds the dimension of vision to the process of thought.

Building on the brainstorming stage, and perhaps a part of it, is the process of establishing a central idea (pages 18–21). It is essential to the essay-writing process, because it enables students to focus their thoughts and to rewrite them in a clearly formed way.

The development of a central idea about a work is not a challenge that many students will have met before they get into your class. For this reason you may wish to devote a portion of classroom time to the discussion of thinking generally. A common misunderstanding you may need to overcome is that any kind of mental activity may be defined as thinking. Thus, the process of reasoning needed for developing a central idea should be distinguished from feeling, responding, daydreaming, planning a purchase (although such planning may involve some thinking), determining the day's activities, and so on. The process of abstract thinking will not come readily to the application of reading, however, unless the students can be shown that seemingly disparate details have some unifying, connecting theme. This process, involving the formulation of unifying themes in a work, is perhaps one of the major elements for you to stress in the initial stages of teaching writing about literary subjects.

The section from pages 21–24 concerns the mechanics of shaping an essay and of outlining. The central idea and thesis sentence separation, you will note, is an option presented as a way of dividing the thematic unity of an essay from the actual topics of the essay. Students often express nervousness about outlining. One of the most important assurances you can give them is therefore that a formal outline does not need to precede the writing of the essay. Instead, an outline is a constantly developing aspect of the composing process—one that can be provisionally established and then modified and reshaped as the student thinks and writes. Too often an outline is viewed as a preordained mold, into which the novice writer is expected to pour ideas. If the outline is used as a guide to thought and also as an incentive to develop further ideas, however, then it does not need to be such a frightening thing. This is not to say that outlines need to be neglected, but rather that they should be used for what they are—as an important part of the prewriting and freewriting processes leading to an advanced stage of composition—a means of giving shape to a writing process that is already well advanced.

The Two Sample Essays (pages 24 and 35). In this edition the two sample essays are separated by the discussion entitled "Revising the Essay" beginning on page 25. The intention of presenting this discussion here is to emphasize the actual process of writing that should occur after a first draft: analysis, correction, revising, and rewriting. The first essay (pages 24–25) is in a rough-draft stage which would probably be acceptable in many classes. The second represents a rethinking and a revision in light of the discussion on revising which extends from pages 25 through 35. Our hope is that students will benefit from seeing how the same topic material may be reshaped and rewritten to fit a central idea. Accordingly, the second essay introduces the way in which students should include details in their essays. In paragraph 2 of the first essay, for example, sentence 2, the detail is simply reported:

> The walls are "drab," the furniture "threadbare," and the curtains "ugly."

In the second essay, this same material, in keeping with the connection of setting to character, is given a stronger thrust:

> Though everything is serviceable, she is dissatisfied with the "drab" walls, "threadbare" furniture, and "ugly" curtains.

A further discussion, stressing how the second essay keeps the central idea foremost, should provide the chances to make clear the ways in which students should emphasize their central ideas as they introduce materials into their essays.

Revising the Essay, *pages 25–35*

This section is a brief introduction to the standards by which student essays (and more broadly, all writing) is to be judged. It has been developed over a period of many years in response to innumerable student inquiries about why grades have not been higher on submitted work. Perhaps the greatest problem of students is that they summarize works rather than analyze them. Thus the suggested changing of the order in an essay from the order in the work, for example (page 26), is only an elementary device that may free students from the trap of retelling a story. Also, the thought that the potential audience will already know the literary work may also help students focus on their own ideas in preference to summarizing. The idea that literary material is to be used as evidence (pages 26–28), in the writing of essays, is a way to help students break away from the narrative or logical order of the original.

For the section "keeping to your point" beginning on page 28, we have introduced an unfocused paragraph, and then shown how, with the aid of the line drawings (page 29), this paragraph may be focused in the light of the topic idea. Students would benefit from your pointing out to them the functional relationship of the underlined parts to the topic. Also, these underlined parts show that the writing of essays on literary topics should emphasize that the student writer take an interpretive, explanatory role with regard to his or her intended audience. There may be no other idea that is so important in the teaching of writing.

The final two parts of this writing section, "Checking Development and Organization" (pages 30–32), and "Using Exact, Comprehensive, and Forceful Language" (pages 32–35), are presented both as short-term and long-term goals. Because the need for accurate and forceful language will always be with everyone who ever takes up a pen or sits down in front of a word processor, you may wish to bring up the point whenever it becomes relevant as a result of student writing in your course. Indeed, many essential problems that students may encounter as they write may be addressed by reference to a number of the subtopics in this section. It is presented as a guide and set of goals to which students may always go for help when they need to conceptualize and execute any writing task.

Responding to Literature: Likes and Dislikes, *pages 37–44*

The reason for this type of writing assignment is that too often responses are ignored while the business of analysis and thought goes forward. Therefore this discussion, coming here as the first actual writing assignment described for students in the big book, is intended to remind students that their responses are important and foremost. Additionally, this first exercise in response might be related to the section on reader-response criticism discussed in Appendix D.

In relation to personal responses, it is important to consider the "de gustibus" argument that individual taste and opinion may take precedence over literary judgment. Thus we emphasize on pages 39–41 that responses of disliking may be modified upon thought to become the grounds for the broadened appreciation of literary works. We suggest that in teaching you might wish to stress this section as a reminder that the process of intellectual growth of students will be complemented by a corresponding development of taste. Of special note also is the list of possible reasons for liking a work and in addition the recommended practice of keeping a journal record of responses. With regard to first impressions, it is most important to stress the words "informed" and "explained" (see pages 37–38). The journal should be used as an incentive to the need for students to comprehend all aspects of the work being studied. Responses based on an inaccurate reading will not be valid, and this point should be stressed for their benefit.

Sometimes, however, despite full understanding, a reader will not like a work. On page 43, we treat this possibility, emphasizing that disliking, as with liking, must be grounded both in proper information about the work and also in a clearly defined standard of response.

Writing About Responses: Likes and Dislikes, *pages 41–44*

This assignment is visualized as an exercise in how students respond to a literary text. It is not to be a full-scale analysis, nor is it to be a reasoned defense of the literary merit of the piece being studied. Rather, the writing is to be based on a simple response: What in the work provoked positive or negative reactions? Thus, of the types of responses for the body of an essay described on pages 42 and 38–39, the most common one will be a list of things liked. The sample essay, pages 43–44, illustrates an essay-length treatment along these lines. You might wish to read parts of the essay with your students to demonstrate how each of Mathilde's good qualities is developed at paragraph length. Perhaps the most important point to emphasize here is that the reasons for liking are developed beyond the simple description of an abstract response of approval.

The other possible ways to develop an essay about likes and dislikes are not illustrated in the sample essay. You might discuss these with your students, noting that the second one described on page 42 is in effect a description of responses upon reading, and that the third and fourth possible essay developments are more fully considered on pages 38–41.

Questions for Guy de Maupassant, *The Necklace, pages 3–10*

Please note that in this edition the biographies precede the fiction selections, with the exception of this story, in which the biographical material is included in the footnote.

Questions for Study, together with Responses

(1) Describe the character of Mathilde. On balance, is she as negative as she seems at first? Why does Maupassant describe her efforts to help with the debt as "heroic"? How does her character create the situation that causes the financial penance the Loisels must undergo?

On balance, Mathilde is not negative, for in paragraphs 99–104, Maupassant describes the massive effort that she exerts to help pay the debt. The heroism that the speaker attributes to her suggests that readers are, finally, to admire her. The quality of character that is a first cause of the misfortune, however, is her refusal to accept the reality of her genteel poverty and her desire to use the borrowed necklace to appear prosperous.

(2) Are Mathilde's daydreams unusual for a woman of her station? How might a case be made that Maupassant fashions the ironic conclusion to demonstrate that Mathilde deserves her misfortune?

Her daydreams are not unusual. It is unlikely that Maupassant contrived the misfortune as a deserved punishment, particularly because Mathilde's good qualities are brought out as the story progresses. Also, the surprise ending indicates that the story is less concerned with showing how Mathilde gets her comeuppance than with evoking regret along with surprise. However, one might still claim that Mathilde deserves at least some acquaintance with reality, but certainly not the disaster that occurs. Thus Maupassant succeeds in directing sympathy toward Mathilde, together with whatever criticism she deserves because of her daydreams.

(3) What sort of person is Loisel? How does his character contribute to the financial disaster?

Loisel is a calm and complacent sort. He is satisfied with simple pleasures and is out of his depth at a formal social occasion. He is a hard, sincere worker, however, and sacrifices tirelessly for the sake of his integrity and honor. He contributes to the financial disaster by not insisting on confessing the loss of the necklace to Jeanne.

(4) Describe the relationship between Mathilde and Loisel as shown in their conversations. Does this relationship seem to be intimate, or is it less personal and more formal?

The conversations of Mathilde and Loisel in paragraphs 8–38 indicate that Mathilde pressures and manipulates Loisel. She seems to be less interested in him and in his needs than in her own. Loisel seems anxious to please Mathilde, but is unable to deal with her on a personal level. He buys her the dress, and suggests that she borrow the jewels, more to attain his own composure than to give her pleasure. There is no evidence in the story that the couple has a warm or loving relationship.

(5) The speaker states that small things save or destroy people (paragraph 105). How does "The Necklace" bear out this idea? What role might fate play in this scheme of things, or is chance the more important governing influence?

The story bears out the idea, for any number of things could be cited as the cause of the disaster, none of them by themselves of major significance: (a) the invitation, (b) the new dress, (c) the borrowing of the necklace, (d) the hurrying away from the party (paragraphs 55–59), (e) the failure of Jeanne to tell Mathilde that the necklace is only a cheap imitation. In a discussion about whether the story emphasizes fate or chance, one should probably emphasize chance, for the idea of fate implies a more systematic pattern of opposition than the circumstances working against Mathilde.

(6) To what degree does Maupassant illustrate a view that might be described as "economic determinism" in the story? That is, how does he relate economic status to happiness and character fulfillment?

Maupassant introduces the idea of "the horrible life of the needy" in paragraph 98, and his description of what happens to Mathilde under these circumstances may be construed as an illustration of economic determinism. In addition, the fact that Jeanne Forrestier is "always youthful, always beautiful, always attractive" can be read the same way inasmuch as Jeanne is "rich" (paragraph 6). The clear contrast, together with Maupassant's paragraph about "what would life have been like if she had not lost that necklace?" (paragraph 105), indicates that in this story at least Maupassant makes a connection between the economic condition of people and their happiness and character fulfillment. The discussion of economic determinism in Appendix D might profitably be introduced here, at least briefly.

Writing Topics. The character of Mathilde. The structure of the story, including the surprise ending. The use of symbols. The economic issues in the story. Tone and the irony of situation in the story.

Works for Comparison with "The Necklace"

Anonymous, *Lord Randal*, 913
Glaspell, *A Jury of Her Peers*, 155
Ibsen, *A Doll House*, 1466
Muske, *Real Estate*, 809

Part I — Fiction
Pages 47–543

Substitute Stories
for the Chapter Topics

To illustrate the topics of Chapters 3–10 on fiction, you may want to choose not only the stories specifically included for the various categories, but also others. Because any story may serve as the topic of a response (Chapter 1), a précis (Chapter 2), or a plot or structural analysis (Chapter 3), we have not classed stories according to the first three chapter topics. The lists are designed instead to assist you in making additional choices for the topics developed in Chapters 4–10. Thus, to focus on character, you will find that "Miss Brill" (from Chapter 5) and "The Chrysanthemums" (from Chapter 9), together with many stories from other chapters and also from the additional stories, will make suitable alternatives. The listing for point of view is designed to be a thorough analysis of all the stories in **Literature: An Introduction to Reading and Writing,** so that you may guide your students confidently through this very complex and subtle topic. In addition, we have included a few other classifications for some of the stories.

Character

✓A & P	✓Stand Here Ironing
A Jury of Her Peers	✓I'm a Fool
A Worn Path	Meneseteung
All Gone	✓Miss Brill
And Sarah Laughed	The Muse's Tragedy
✓Araby	The Other Two
Blue Winds Dancing	Rape Fantasies
Everyday Use	Roman Fever
Goodbye and Good Luck	Taking Care
Home Soil	✓The Chrysanthemums
How to Become a Writer	The Found Boat

The Horse Dealer's Daughter
The Story of an Hour
✓The Yellow Wallpaper
Young Goodman Brown

Point of View

◆ First Person

A – the narrator as a major mover

A & P
All Gone
Araby
Before the Firing Squad
Blue Winds Dancing
Everyday Use
First Confession
Goodbye and Good Luck
Home Soil
I'm a Fool
Rape Fantasies
Raymond's Run
The Sky Is Gray
The Yellow Wallpaper

B – the narrator as an observer and/or participant

The Hammon and the Beans
I Stand Here Ironing
Luck
The House on Mango Street
The Old Chief Mshlanga (*paragraphs 14–98*)

C – an unnamed narrator who is not a participant or an on-the-spot observer

The Masque of the Red Death
The Worker in Sandalwood

D – First speaker introduces and quotes the first-person narrative of another

Luck
The Widow of Ephesus

E – First-person narrative or discourse within a story

Meneseteung
The Muse's Tragedy (*final third*)

F – Narrator speaks of herself in the third person

The Old Chief Mshlanga (*paragraphs 1–13*)

◆ Second Person

How to Become a Writer

◆ Third Person

A – Limited Omniscient: A major character is the focus of the narrative, together with responses and thoughts of this character

And Sarah Laughed
Barn Burning
The Chrysanthemums
The Curse
The Found Boat
The Jilting of Granny Weatherall
A Jury of Her Peers
Meneseteung
Miss Brill
The Necklace
The Old Chief Mshlanga (*paragraphs 1–13*)
Pomegranate Seed
The Other Two
The Shawl
The Story of an Hour
Taking Care
A Worn Path
Young Goodman Brown

B – Limited Dramatic: a major character is the focus of the narrative, with few if any revelations of this character's thoughts

The Portable Phonograph
The Fox and the Grapes
The Myth of Atalanta

C – Omniscient: the All-Knowing Narrator

The Horse Dealer's Daughter
The Prodigal Son
A Very Old Man with Enormous Wings

D – Dramatic, or Objective

The Lottery
The Chaser
The Greatest Man in the World
The Blue Hotel

E – Third Person Frame: Speaker introduces the third-person narrative of another

The Prodigal Son

◆ STORIES ESPECIALLY NOTABLE FOR SPECIAL USES OF POINTS OF VIEW (INCLUDING STORIES ALREADY LISTED)

Everyday Use *(first person and dramatic)*
Goodbye and Good Luck *(first person narrator tells a story to a silent listener)*
Luck *(first person quotes a first-person speaker)*
The Muse's Tragedy *(two parts a third-person narrative, one part a first-person letter)*
The Old Chief Mshlanga *(speaker speaks of herself in the third person, then shifts to the first person)*
The Parable of the Prodigal Son *(narrator quotes a third-person narrative)*
The Widow of Ephesus *(first person quotes a first-person speaker)*
The Yellow Wallpaper *(first-person narrator seems to be writing the story surreptitiously over an extended period of time)*

A Futuristic Story

The Portable Phonograph

Setting

And Sarah Laughed
A & P
Araby
Barn Burning
Before the Firing Squad
The Chrysanthemums
Everyday Use
The Found Boat
Home Soil
The House on Mango Street
I'm a Fool
A Jury of Her Peers
Meneseteung
Miss Brill
The Necklace
The Old Chief Mshlanga
Pomegranate Seed
Rape Fantasies
Roman Fever
Soldier's Home
The Shawl
The Sky Is Gray
The Story of an Hour
Taking Care
A Very Old Man with Enormous Wings
The Widow of Ephesus
The Worker in Sandalwood
A Worn Path

Style

A & P
Araby
Barn Burning
Blue Winds Dancing
Everyday Use
How to Become a Writer
I'm a Fool
The Jilting of Granny Weatherall
The Lottery
Lullaby
Meneseteung
Miss Brill
Rape Fantasies
The Muse's Tragedy
The Shawl
Taking Care
The Worker in Sandalwood
Young Goodman Brown

Tone

And Sarah Laughed
Before the Firing Squad
Home Soil
Goodbye and Good Luck
A Good Man Is Hard to Find
A Jury of Her Peers
Luck
The Masque of the Red Death
Meneseteung
The Old Chief Mshlanga
The Other Two
Roman Fever
The Shawl
Soldier's Home
Taking Care
The Worker in Sandalwood
Young Goodman Brown

Humor

A & P
Everyday Use
First Confession
The Found Boat
Goodbye and Good Luck
The Greatest Man in the World
How to Become a Writer
Luck
The Other Two
Rape Fantasies
A Very Old Man with Enormous Wings

Symbolism and Allegory

A & P
Araby
Before the Firing Squad
Everyday Use
The Found Boat
The House on Mango Street

I Stand Here Ironing
The Lottery
The Masque of the Red Death
The Old Chief Mshlanga
Pomegranate Seed
The Portable Phonograph
Roman Fever
The Shawl
The Sky Is Gray
Taking Care
The Yellow Wallpaper
A Worn Path

An Absurdist Story

The Chaser

Idea or Theme

And Sarah Laughed
Blue Winds Dancing
First Confession
Home Soil
The Horse Dealer's Daughter
I Stand Here Ironing
The Lottery
The Muse's Tragedy
The Necklace
The Old Chief Mshlanga
The Other Two
The Prodigal Son
Rape Fantasies
The Shawl
The Sky Is Gray
The Story of an Hour
The Yellow Wallpaper

Fantasy and the Miraculous

The Myth of Atalanta
The Chaser
The Fox and the Grapes
The Lottery
The Masque of the Red Death
Meneseteung
Pomegranate Seed
A Very Old Man with Enormous Wings
The Widow of Ephesus
The Worker in Sandalwood
Young Goodman Brown

Fable and Parable

The Myth of Atalanta
The Fox and the Grapes
The Prodigal Son
A Very Old Man with Enormous Wings

Chapter Two
PAGES 47–87

Fiction: An Overview

The first half of this chapter, pages 47–59, is an introduction to the major characteristics and concepts of prose fiction. We therefore recommend that you assign it first before embarking upon any of the other chapters. The aim of the section is a general, while also fairly complete, coverage of fiction. Thus, point of view is just briefly introduced here (pages 55–56) so that students will have an overview of that topic as they study chapters such as plot, character, or symbolism. Should you not have time to use Chapter 5, which treats point of view in detail, you would still be assured that your students would know something about it from their introductory study here.

You may wish to expand upon the brief introductory explanations in this section. For example, pages 47–48 present a short definition and historical overview of fiction and narration, but you may wish to develop either of these topics in more depth. The same applies to the references to the beginnings of modern fiction (pages 48–49) and to the development of the short story (page 49). The addition of David's painting, *The Death of Socrates* (page 54), should provide the opportunity for connecting the narrative functions of art and fiction.

The key elements of fictional character (pages 51–52), plot (page 52), structure (page 53), and theme (page 53) are all developed more fully in later chapters, so that here you need to be sure only that your students develop familiarity with the concepts. Still, there will be questions that will need answering. We suggest that the four stories included in this chapter—"The Widow of Ephesus," "A & P," "Everyday Use," and "Taking Care"—may be used as references, because the problem in this introductory discussion will be maintaining concreteness.

The same will also hold true for your discussion of the major "tools" of fiction. Thus, narration (page 54), style (page 55), point of view (pages 55–56), description (page 56), dialogue (pages 56–57), and commentary (page 57) may all be discussed as they apply to the stories anthologized in the chapter, and may serve as reference points for discussions later in the school year. Tone and irony (page 58) and symbolism and allegory (pages 58–59) are mentioned in reference to stories included earlier and later in the book. Hence your discussion should maintain concreteness through continued references to the relevant sections. Obviously, as your discussion progresses, students may introduce references to fictional and real-life incidents and characters that they have encountered in your course and elsewhere.

GAIUS PETRONIUS, *The Widow of Ephesus, pages 59–62*

"The Widow of Ephesus" is, along with "The Banquet of Trimalchio" (a brief satire on conspicuous consumption), one of the best known sections of The *Satiricon,* a lengthy work which is attributed to Petronius. In effect, *The Satiricon* is like the picaresque type of fiction later developed by writers such as Cervantes and Fielding. Because the basic story concerns various adventures and travels, it enables the writer to vary the narrative fabric by introducing digressionary episodes and stories, of which "The Widow of Ephesus" is a famous example. There is much in the story that can be used in the initial approaches to literary study. For example, the Widow herself, within a short space of three pages, undergoes a change in her perspective—the change that characterizes the round or developing character (see pages 51–52). In addition, because the story is brief, it may be quickly studied, and perhaps may even be read aloud in class. In addition, it served Chekhov as the idea for *The Bear* (p. 1028), and it may profitably be discussed in relationship to this play.

As a practical matter, students may ask about how the Soldier might have, singlehandedly, put the dead husband on the cross. There seems to be uncertainty about the exact procedures of crucifixion, but apparently, ancient crosses were laid out on the ground, and they were not raised until the condemned persons were fastened to them either with spikes through the wrists and feet or with ropes. The Soldier could therefore have handled the job without too much trouble. Incidentally, crucifixion as a form of execution was outlawed in the Roman Empire during the fourth century, after Christianity became the official state religion.

Answers to the Study Questions, page 62

(1) The poet Eumolpus is the actual narrator of the story about the Widow and her Soldier, although the major narrator of the entire *Satiricon*

is Encolpius, the narrator of the first and sixteenth paragraphs. Eumolpus is therefore introduced by Encolpius as the narrator, and Encolpius actually quotes the words of Eumolpus. The circumstances are explained as having occurred in a moment of calm after a previous brawl-like encounter. We learn that Eumolpus is, at the very least, hostile toward women. His story of the Widow is designed to illustrate the inconstancy and hypocrisy he attributes to them.

(2) The responses by the listeners (sailors, Tryphena, Lichas) emphasize the dramatic situation of the narration. Their effect is that they provide a number of responses in addition to the expressed misogyny of Eumolpus. The story's final paragraph should therefore begin a lively classroom discussion.

(3) The Widow is known for her love and fidelity to her husband (paragraph 2). She demonstrates her resolution by going into the vault to stand vigil by her husband's coffin until she dies herself. In addition to this mental toughness, we learn about her capacity for taking charge of things. When she abandons her resolution in favor of the Soldier, she shows that her commitment to life and love is stronger than her vows to the dead (paragraph 14).

(4) Certainly the Widow's decision may be considered a joke, as Eumolpus intends. However, her explanation of her love for the Soldier makes the situation far more serious than it might at first appear (paragraph 14). Whether the story will be liked or not will depend upon individual students. Many might dismiss it as misogynistic and therefore dated. Others, however, may find that the portrait of the Widow rises above the ostensible debunking of her vow of self-sacrifice, and that this inadvertent sympathy makes her worthy of admiration.

Writing topics. The character of the Widow or the Soldier. Responses of like or dislike. Is the story more or less than a simple joke told at the expense of the Widow? Do the events of the story sustain Eumolpus's dislike of women?

Works for Comparison with "The Widow of Ephesus"

Bradstreet, *To My Dear and Loving Husband*, 920
Chekhov, *The Bear*, 1028
Wharton, *Pomegranate Seed*, 440

John Updike, *A & P, pages 63–67*

"A & P" is readily accessible to most students, with the possible exception of those for whom English is a second language. For them you might wish to focus on study question 2, on the topic of Sammy's diction (page 67). It is significant to stress his disregard of grammar at the opening, and his greater care at the end. Even the concluding word, *hereafter*, is notable in the context of his narration, for it is not of the same wordstock as most of the language he uses.

Answers to the Study Questions, page 67

(1) The exposition occurs simultaneously with the movement of the girls in the store. The essential character to learn about is the narrator, Sammy, and we find out much about him from his accurate and fascinated description of the girls' appearance, and from his observation of Stokesie and Stokesie's expression of doubt about the propriety of the girls' wearing swimming suits in the store (paragraph 9). As further exposition, the basis of the conflict is explained in paragraph 10, in which Sammy describes the Massachusetts town as a rather staid, respectable place. The conflict is thus created out of the contrast between the girls' inappropriate swimsuits and the conservative expectations of propriety.

The idea of fictional exposition is thus illustrated here, with enough material being introduced to make the conflict clear, but no more. The essential fact is that a story is not a sociological treatise; obviously a good deal more could be said about the town, and about Lengel as one of the "pillars of society." With a fuller treatment along these lines, however, the narrative elements of the story would be obscured. In other words, exposition is to be judged only in its relationship to story.

(2) From Sammy's language we learn that he has a strong sense of his own identity. His anger at the "witch" in paragraph 1, for example, indicates an awareness of his own worth when he is taken to task for what he thinks is an inadvertent mistake. His first response to Stokesie, *"Darling," I said, "Hold me tight"* (paragraph 8), indicates a sense of humor, camaraderie, and capacity for enjoyment. Throughout the story, which is presented in a spoken rather than written style as though Sammy is speaking to a sympathetic and friendly listener, Sammy talks himself alive as a person of perception, sensitivity, and understanding. He does, however, violate strict grammatical rules. He switches tenses constantly (see, for example, the beginning of paragraph 12), and utilizes slang expressions

("gunk" in paragraph 12, "juggled" in paragraph 5), inexact modifiers ("kind of" in paragraph 32 and elsewhere), colloquial phrases ("they all three of them" in paragraph 5, "but never quite makes it" in paragraph 2), misplaced modifiers ("Walking in the A & P ... I suppose ..." in paragraph 4). That Sammy also correctly uses a possessive before a gerund ("His repeating this struck me as funny" in paragraph 15), together with other passages of correct English, suggests that his violations of standard English are deliberate.

(3) Sammy's observations, such as "two crescents of white" (paragraph 1), suggest his extensive experience as a "girl watcher." Also, however, his references to his distaste for older women indicates that he has watched them, but not with approval. His remarks reflect his taste for youth and beauty, but also his own limited understanding of life as a boy of nineteen. His estimation of female intelligence in paragraph 2 about a "buzz like a bee in a glass jar" and his expressed lack of certainty about how girls' minds work indicate, under the guise of minimizing women, a lack of experience with women on an adult level. His gesture to quit his job is at odds with his patronizing estimate of women, for it shows more respect than he actually expresses.

(4) Sammy makes his sudden decision to quit for reasons that he does not articulate. Probably, however, his thinking (paragraph 21) is based on fears that he might eventually develop into a carbon copy of Lengel if he does not begin asserting himself on matters of principle. His explanation to himself is summed up in paragraph 31 with his observation that it would be "fatal" not to go through with his gesture. In other words, his sense of identity is on the line and he must maintain his integrity in his own eyes even if the girls know nothing about his action. He realizes that the world will be hard for him "hereafter" because people like Lengel may always be gaining economic or arbitrary power over him, and therefore he may feel future pressure to suppress his integrity.

Writing topics. A précis of "A & P." The plot and/or structure of the story. The character of Sammy. The theme of the story.

Works for Comparison with "A & P"

Anderson, *I'm a Fool*, 188
Faulkner, *Barn Burning*, 143
Henley, *Am I Blue*, 1403

Answers to the Study Questions, page 224

(1) The key to the story is the narrator-speaker, who reveals most about herself in the very last paragraph. We infer that she is a person who values life, and who has the diligence and interest to want to rescue something from the "rubbish" of time. We may also infer the character of this narrator from the powerful reconstruction she makes of the imagined life of Meda Roth. She utilizes ordinary details and then, from the hints she discovers, not only develops the outlines of Meda's quiet life, but also reveals this character's intimate secrets, such as her responses to the brawl outside her house, her noting of Jarvis Poulter's physical appearance, her feelings about finishing the grape jelly, and her musings about her own sanity. For the story itself, we are indebted to the curiosity and sensitivity of Munro's narrator.

(2) The "facts" presented by the narrator are the imaginary records of the time. The book of poetry is one of these facts (each of the sections of the story is begun with a selection from Meda's book of poems that the narrator describes in paragraphs 5–13), as are the photographs, the various reports in the town paper, the current condition of the town as witnessed by the living narrator, and the town graveyard where the heroine is buried. Although all the events of the story of Meda and Jarvis are imaginatively reconstructed, the narrator's first-hand experience with the location, the house, the local records, the streets, and the general "lay of the land" in Meneseteung makes for a haunting portrait of a ghostly but realistic past. From this imaginary factual location, the characters of Meda and Jarvis come alive.

(3) Paragraphs 14 and 16 mark a transition from the basic examination of local records, as brought out in the first thirteen paragraphs, and move into the real subject of the story, the life of Meda Roth. These paragraphs are characterized by the imposition of the present tense on the past, which enables the story of Meda to assume vividness. Paragraph 14 focuses on Meda, while paragraph 16 stresses the rough and tumble world in which Meda makes her life, with boisterous, noisy, primitive gangs of roving kids, together with the occasional cruelty and manifest stupidity of many of the town residents. Once this transition has created the focus on the imaginary life of Meda, paragraph 31 is an excursion into her mind, with her thoughts about Jarvis Poulter, and an explanation of the signals she would like to see from him. Here the narrator gives us one of the story's most intimate insights into Meda's consciousness. Paragraph

85 is a return to the story's beginning method of development, for it, along with paragraph 86, is an obituary notice from the local paper, the *Vidette*. Though the story from here to the end is objective about Meda, the narrator's exploration of the graveyard and her discovery of Meda's grave intensifies the interest and affection the narrator has created.

(4) The character development is that Meda, a woman of considerable sensitivity combined with a strong sense of independence, is led to a crisis point in which she opts for her own independence. Meda's poetry at first gives us a picture of a person of youthful enthusiasm, whose benign view of the world is not matched by her rough surroundings. Quotations from her verse beginning each of the sections of the story show a happy but contemplative spirit. Section VI, which quotes from Meda's poem "A Visit to My Family," shows a characteristic morbidity that apparently becomes dominant in her character after the ugly episode with the beaten woman. The circumstances of this beating episode also seem to bring home to Meda that she is unable to subject herself to the mastery of any man, for the vision of Jarvis in his dark trousers, unbuttoned shirt, wild hair, and unshaven face clearly depresses her, and determines her to remain single. In her relationships with men, her only experience has been with her father, whom she cares for during a period of twelve years. With him she had responsibility but no other demands. Clearly, she cannot contemplate submitting to the demands of Jarvis, and is unwilling to lose her independence.

(5) In paragraphs 72–73 the narrator briefly shifts the narration away from Meda, and limits it to the responses and thoughts of Jarvis Poulter. The key here is that the experience of dealing with the injured woman has brought him into intimate contact with Meda, an intimacy which the two have never before experienced. Previously Jarvis has been seen objectively, as Meda has seen him. But here, his "harsh joviality" indicates a dimension of which Meda has been unaware, and it is this dimension of reality, and potential force, that intrudes on her consciousness and which leads her to reject Jarvis's outward romantic signal of walking her to church. The information about Jarvis could have been integrated within the point of view limited to Meda, but the temporary focus on Jarvis enables readers to see Meda from the outside, as a woman of "agitation . . . foolishness . . . need." The shift in point of view is therefore integral to the story, for it provides an objective explanation for Meda's fear, which she manifests with the note she fastens on the front door.

WRITING TOPICS: The "documentation" from which the story is built. The character of Meda Roth. The character of Jarvis Poulter. The importance of the character of the narrator.

WORKS FOR COMPARISON WITH "MENESETEUNG"

Dickinson, *I Cannot Live with You*, 886
Lawrence, *The Horse Dealer's Daughter*, 393
Rossetti, *Echo*, 744
Steinbeck, *The Chrysanthemums*, 347

Writing About Point of View, *pages 224–229*

In the classroom use of this section, it is essential to emphasize that students are to write about point of view as a technique of narration. One of the most difficult aspects to get across to students is that a story's point of view is not about ideas and opinions, but rather about the narrative voice and the presentation of details (see the caveat on page 226). One of the best ways to bring out this fact, and hence also to provide students with the materials to be included in their essays, is to stress the various study questions dealing specifically with points of view of the stories and with the possibilities of approaching the material from other viewpoints. Once students have become familiar with the variations that might follow from differing points of view, they can undertake a specific assignment with confidence.

The sample essay on "The Lottery" (pages 227–228) will repay careful reading because the details included in each paragraph support the topic sentence there. In classroom discussion, you might stress that any one of the aspects treated so briefly in the sample might be more deeply analyzed and exemplified as the basis for an entire essay. Thus, an essay might be devoted to (1) the characterizations and the means by which these are brought out in the story (2) the possibilities of telling the story from other points of view, and the consequent results as contrasted with the dramatic viewpoint used by Jackson, or (3) the control over detail in the story. Above all, students will need to be reminded that the immediate purpose of an essay on point of view is to help them not so much to analyze topics such as an author's symbols and ideas, but rather to study her or his narrative technique.

Writing Topics about Point of View, *page 229*

(1) The first of these questions is creative, with the emphasis to be placed on the ways of looking at life that might be brought out through the words of secondary or minor characters in the stories.

(2) The second question should get students thinking concretely about other modes of narration than those used by the writer. An assumption of this assignment is that students may learn what the story is like by stressing alternative ways of presentation. It seems clear that the narrator of "I'm a Fool" might stress Meda's guilt about forsaking her opportunities with Jarvis Poulter, while the narrator of "The Lottery" might be less involved and less sympathetic with Meda than Munro's narrator is.

(3) The third may be an exercise not only in point of view, but in intellectual growth and tolerant understanding. Suppose, for example, a student as a child were playing with matches, and started to burn up a closet in the house. What would this child, now a mature college student, be able to say from the point of view of a parent discovering the fire and punishing the child?

(4) The fourth assignment is designed to be speculative, although if examples from student experiences were to be introduced, the conclusions could be greatly strengthened. Students who experience difficulty in beginning the assignment might wish to launch their discourse by analyzing words from some of their friends, assuming, of course, that names are not used and that all other circumstances are altered.

Chapter Six
Pages 230–263

Setting: Place, Objects, and Culture in Stories

The goal of this chapter is to define and explain the importance of objects, place, and time in fiction. While the various aspects of setting may be defined and discussed abstractly, it is important that classroom discussion be directed toward the uses of setting in the stories you assign for your students. "The House on Mango Street," "The Portable Phonograph," "And Sarah Laughed," "The Shawl," and "The Masque of the Red Death," present abundant materials for the study of setting. None of these stories could be told without their references to physical locations. "The House on Mango Street" is actually about locations and the meaning of locations to the aims of the narrator and her family and to the ones whom they meet. Clark makes "The Portable Phonograph" inextricable from the grim post-cataclysmic world that he deftly sketches at the story's beginning. The isolation of the farm home in "And Sarah Laughed" emphasizes how the characters are isolated by deafness. Ozick's story is both literally and symbolically imprisoned within its concentration-camp confines. Finally, the Poe story integrates the physical location of the rooms with the final action.

Sandra Cisneros, *The House on Mango Street, pages 235–236*

The House on Mango Street is perhaps not so much a group of short stories as a series of brief vignettes or impressions about the life of the narrator, a young woman named Esperanza Cordero, and those living near the poor little house on Mango Street.

Answers to the Study Questions, page 236

(1) It seems clear that the speaker is responding to the insecurity of her family's poverty, and that her unhappiness with the houses she has lived in results from shame. She therefore yearns for a house she can "point to," presumably with pride (paragraph 11). She also yearns for re-

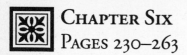

lease, and hence in a later impression (not anthologized here) entitled "Mango Says Goodbye Sometimes," she declares that the house on Mango Street is a "house I belong but do not belong to."

(2) The house is described in paragraph 5. The details clearly demonstrate the impoverishment of Esperanza's family. The windows are small, the steps tiny, the brickwork crumbling, the rooms few, the bathroom a common one for all six members of the family, and the bedroom also a common one for the family.

(3) The eleven paragraphs comprising the story do not provide extensive details from which we may infer the narrator's character. But we do learn of the things that pain her, namely the squalor of the previous apartments where the family has resided, the embarrassment caused by the physical details of the house on Mango Street, the even greater embarrassment and shame deriving from the house on Loomis, and the ironic conclusion at the story's end (paragraph 11). The result is that the narrator is demonstrated to be a person of good observational power, combined with strong feelings about her status and her wish to improve and to rise in the world.

Writing topics. Use of detail in the story. The implied comparison between the family's actual residences and the narrator's wished-for residences. The narrator's character, and her attitude toward her surroundings.

Works for Comparison with "The House on Mango Street"

Hughes, *Mulatto,* 1439
McKay, *The White City,* 967
Parédes, *The Hammon and the Beans,* 313
Salinas, *In a Farmhouse,* 980

Walter Van Tilburg Clark, *The Portable Phonograph, pages 237–241*

The central character in "The Portable Phonograph" is the "host," Dr. Jenkins. The speaker's giving him the title of "doctor" suggests that he is a medical doctor, although some students claim that he is a professor of literature since he thinks (paragraph 37) that he knows "all of Shelley by heart" (how many English professors would make such a claim?). He values literature and music most highly. His possession of the books, the phonograph, and the records, together with his management of his little cell, indicate a person of taste who is also practical enough to retain what he prizes most even under the worst conditions.

An interesting issue of interpretation arises in the reading of this story. If the protagonist of "The Portable Phonograph" is identified as the doctor, the antagonist might then readily be seen as the musician. If the story is viewed as a political tract or prognostication, the protagonist is civilization and the antagonist is warfare. Everyone in the story is then a victim of the antagonist; no one wins. Then too, the story may be read as a piece realistically depicting the precariousness of civilization. The protagonist would then again be the doctor and the music, while the musician would be the antagonist representing the force threatening the continuance of civilization. The story thus would be a parable about the need for eternal vigilance. In effect, the story ends during the crisis, and technically is unfinished. For this reason the resolution is Dr. Jenkins's recognition both of the threat and also of the need for continued watchfulness and preparedness.

The conclusion may require some attention. Even though the note for paragraph 15 (page 239) explains the nature of old-style wind-up phonographs, students in these days of compact-disk perfection may need some additional information so that the significance and uniqueness of the phonograph may be understood. A virtue of the old victrolas was that they operated without electric power, so that Dr. Jenkins and his group could listen to records any time they wished (granted that the records were on the verge of wearing out). In addition, students sometimes do not understand that the threat concluding the story is the musician. This uncertainty results from Clark's focusing of the point of view on Dr. Jenkins. What is described at the end is thus limited to what Dr. Jenkins can hear, and what he hears is vague and unclear. Clark's narrative technique therefore may need to be stressed and discussed.

Answers to the Study Questions, page 241

(1) The story is set in a bleak, cold, lifeless prairie that had once been a battleground. Heavy tanks have broken up the old pavement on the roads, and bombs have left large craters. The land has not yet regenerated itself, although there are "young trees trying again" (paragraph 1). The opening paragraphs convey a feeling of desperation and hopelessness, and an atmosphere of harshness.

(2) Adjectives such as *narrow, cold,* and *mute* have in common a

quality of stillness, constriction, emptiness, and fragility. They contribute to the impression of lifelessness and bleakness about the setting, and therefore characterize the world in which beauty and graciousness are no more than a dim memory.

(3) Dr. Jenkins's home is a *cell* (paragraph 3). The fire, dim as it is, is a kind of deception. The fire is *petty* and *acrid,* and the burning is *chary* (spare and meager), and is also *smoldering* (paragraph 4). Blankets are *old and dirty,* while the wrapping cord is home-made out of grass. Only a few utensils are mentioned, and those are of "tin," which in 1942 at least connoted cheapness and tawdriness. These details all suggest the spare, austere life lived by the few survivors in this devastated world.

(4) The men agree to hear Debussy's *Nocturne* for piano, primarily because it is selected by the musician (paragraph 44), whom they regard as an expert. The playing time of this piece, which is less well known than Debussy's three *Nocturnes* for orchestra and chorus, is about six minutes. Reactions of the listening men are described in paragraph 45. Three of the men perceive "tragically heightened recollection" while the musician listens more objectively, hearing "nothing" but what is there, but his response when the music ends indicates his heightened emotion and therefore his appreciation.

(5) After the group leaves, Dr. Jenkins hides all his valuables and rearranges his bed so that he may see any intruder, because he has heard noises outside and has seen a shadow indicating that the musician is waiting to enter his cell and steal the phonograph and the records. In effect, the doctor is being forced by the musician to return to a state of nature.

Writing topics. The setting of postwar devastation. The importance of scene, temperature, and darkness in the mood of the story. Setting and the characters of Dr. Jenkins and the musician. The setting as a symbol of destructive warfare. The use of artifacts. The integration of action and setting.

Works for Comparison with "The Portable Phonograph"

Nash, *Exit, Pursued by a Bear,* 664
Owen, *Anthem for Doomed Youth,* 630
Yeats, *The Second Coming,* 810
Zabytko, *Home Soil,* 403

Joanne Greenberg, *And Sarah Laughed, pages 242–250*

The time sequence in this story is particularly interesting because it begins at a central point of time, in effect *in medias res* or in the middle of things, then moves backward in retrospect, and finally moves forward. The point occurs when Sarah's son Abel and his new bride come home and create a new challenge for Sarah, who has the gift of hearing but whose family is deaf. Prior to this point, Sarah has made the difficult adjustment to her family's inability to hear and speak. The story's early paragraphs indicate how she learns to live with the deaf, first with her husband (Matthew) and then with her children (Abel, Rutherford, Lindsay, and Franklin Delano). We learn that she has taught her children to read her lips, and that at one point she put cotton in her ears to make her sympathetic to living without sound (paragraph 14). We also realize that this situation limits the connections that her family can have with the outside world (paragraph 25).

Once Janice appears with Abel, however, beginning with paragraph 32, Sarah is forced into a new situation requiring her adjustment, namely the use of sign language for the deaf. This new situation causes her to conclude that her life "had suddenly become . . . strange to her" (paragraph 35) because she finds "something obscene" about the signing gestures (paragraph 59). From this point the story's movement involves Sarah's realization that her family's happiness requires her assent to sign language and her involvement with it. The concluding paragraphs dramatically portray the power of her reconciliation and the love her family can give her through their only means of communication.

Answers to the study questions, page 250

(1) Sarah is characterized as a plain, serious, and decent girl who as a farm wife takes great pride in her personal circumstances and surroundings. Her concern for the appearance of the farm shows an almost compulsive need to make things "clean and orderly" (paragraph 2). But she also has a great capacity for adjustment, as is shown in her acceptance of her husband's deafness and her ability to communicate him through his reading her lips. Even so, she is starved for communication and exchanges notes with her friend, Luita (paragraph 8). This characteristic is her strongest, and the conflict she endures because of it is complex. Her adjustment to deafness gives her a certain amount of power over her family, and their wish to learn signs demonstrates a degree of individuality that in-

volves her letting them go. But there is a great, yearning hunger for expression, and Sarah's acceptance of that shows her love and her power of adaptation.

(2) Outside, the farm of Sarah and Matthew is in an almost painterly setting, covered with a blue and silent sky that is crossed with passing birds and bordered by a garden and a row of poplar trees. There is an orchard and a grape arbor. Inside everything is in order, and Sarah has developed a routine for serving meals to her family, including the preparation of "surprise" desserts like the shortcake she serves at the climax of the story (paragraphs 62–68). These details are included to demonstrate that the life of Sarah and her family is economically adequate but no more. The need is not for improved economic circumstances, but for communication, and it is this need that brings out her tears in paragraph 64). In addition, the farm is a location that separates the people from the outside world. People are distant, and thus not communicative, just as the deafness of Sarah's family isolates them—and also somewhat alienates them—from her.

(3) The fact of Matthew's deafness is not disclosed until the middle of paragraph 7. This delay enables readers to identify Sarah's life as involving the adjustment to normal life situations, such as the appearance of her son with his new bride. Abel's congenital deafness is made more poignant because Sarah does not realize it until the infant boy has been unable to hear the "madhouse of bells, horns, screaming sirens" of the fire engines racing to a nearby fire (paragraph 21). Her response is to cry bitterly and uncontrollably (paragraph 23).

(4) We realize that Sarah has adjusted to the deafness of her family and has been reconciled to it for twenty-five years. Janice's enthusiasm for signs has, in effect, rendered Sarah "the deaf one" (paragraph 64). We may judge Sarah's responses as being a mixture of jealousy, a loss of power, and an unwillingness to change habits fixed over her lifetime. Because such negative impulses are not in her character they constitute a crisis in her life. Sarah's first responses are grief and frustration, but her love for her family enables her to become reconciled and to accept the challenge of change. The title, derived from the Book of Genesis, suggests a parallel with the Biblical Sarah (Genesis 18:9–15), who laughed—probably in ironic disbelief—when she learned that she was destined to have a child in her old age. Students may wish to discuss the parallel situations of the two Sarahs, together with the effects of their responses.

Writing topics. The character of Sarah. The relationship of the farm surroundings to the life of Sarah and Matthew and their family. Problems that deafness (or other disability) creates for people within families.

Works for Comparison with "And Sarah Laughed"

Piercy, *Will We Work Together?*, 975
Pickthall, *The Worker in Sandalwood*, 341
Pound, *The River-Merchant's Wife*, 978
Williams, *Taking Care*, 74

Cynthia Ozick, *The Shawl, pages 251–254*

"The Shawl" is noteworthy because of its scrupulous control of its limited point of view, with the point-of-view character being the mother of a starving infant during the Holocaust. There is nothing in the story about the political conditions in Germany's Third Reich, which developed a policy of mass extermination of Jews, yet, within just a few pages, the story provides an inside view of the horror as it affected those who were the victims of this unspeakable policy. Students need to be reminded that the story requires great attention, for the details are not described objectively, but rather appear as they have been filtered through the suffering eyes and mind of the major figure, Rosa.

Answers to the Study Questions, page 254

(1) The details of the setting, important as they are, are not laid out according to any plan or scheme, as we receive the details about Prince Prospero's Abbey in "The Masque of the Red Death." We learn in the first four paragraphs that Rosa, along with her young daughter Stella and her infant daughter Magda, have been on a forced march, and that spectators have lined up along the way as the marching Jews have gone by. With paragraph 5 the scene shifts to the confines of a Nazi extermination camp, which is not named. Ultimately, a German guard throws Magda against an electrically charged fence of this camp, and kills her by this action. Ozick presents these details as the major character, Rosa, perceives them—not as she sees them and remembers them in outline, but as she receives impressions about them. The result is that we experience the setting as it affects Rosa. Unless she perceives it, it is not included in the story.

(2) The details in paragraph 15 are designed to heighten the story's irony. Outside the fence, one may see sun, butterflies, "placid, mellow"

light, green meadows, dandelions, violets, and tiger lilies. The irony is that the world outside is the way things should be, as contrasted with the horrors within which result from the political and military domination that turns life into hell for Rosa and the other prisoners, and destroys the innocent child, Magda.

(3) The center of narrative interest in the story is Rosa, the mother, who hides Magda within the shawl. She has been arrested by the Nazis and imprisoned because she is Jewish (paragraph 2). She has been so maltreated that she is losing touch with ordinary reality. For example, she hears voices in the surrounding fence, and also feels that she has become light as air. Her response to hunger is probably realistic, however, for with no food to satisfy her "ravenous" appetite she learns to "drink the taste of a finger in one's mouth" (paragraph 5), and at the story's end she has become like her lost infant, Magda, as she drinks "Magda's shawl until it dried" (paragraph 16).

(4) The more brutal details are included in paragraph 15, which reveal the true horror of life in the extermination camps. A short description of World War II and some of the facts of the Anti-Semitic policies of the Nazis may need explaining now that the war has been over for half a century. The story itself, however, provides a telling description of what the effects of these policies were, as the victims themselves were forced to experience them.

Writing topics. The setting of the story, as it was and as Rosa experiences it. The relationship of Rosa to her daughter Stella. The story's use of details about physical condition. Responses to various actions in the story.

Works for Comparison with "The Shawl"

Chioles, *Before the Firing Squad*, 138
Kernan, *Majdanek*, 957
Layton, *Rhine Boat Trip*, 961
Quasimodo, *Auschwitz*, 697
Zabytko, *Home Soil*, 403

Edgar Allan Poe, *The Masque of the Red Death, pages 254–258*

The central conflict of "The Masque of the Red Death" is Prospero's attempt to evade death. Prospero is the protagonist; Death or Fate is the antagonist. The climax of the story is in paragraph 13, when Prospero falls "prostrate in death." (The crisis begins in paragraph 8, on the first appearance of the masked figure.) The conflict is resolved with the revelation of the spectral nature of the figure and the instantaneous death of the guests.

One of Poe's major theories about literature was that the impact of a work was to transcend any attempt at using literature to teach or make a point. "The Masque of the Red Death" may be used as a test of this theory. Thus, Prospero's abbey is an impregnable fortress, totally capable of standing up against an army. The description helps readers understand that Prospero has absolute earthly power. The description also permits the conclusion that Prospero's thinking is anomalous when the opponent is not a human but rather a supernatural force. Students may wish to consider the importance of the idea embodied within the story, that death overwhelms all earthly powers.

You may find that students have trouble with Poe's diction: for example, words like *sagacious, seclusion, castellated,* and *impeded,* from only the first four paragraphs. For words like these, a dictionary assignment may be essential.

Answers to the Study Questions, page 258

(1) During the time of the story, a plague is devastating the countryside near Prospero's estates. The obvious historical parallel is the bubonic plague, the "Black Death," which ravaged Europe in the Middle Ages and again in the late seventeenth century. (The plague was called "black" because victims turned cyanotic from lack of oxygen as they died.) Students may need reminding that in 1842, when Poe's story appeared, the bacteriological causes of contagious disease were not understood. Louis Pasteur, who eventually made this discovery, was then only twenty years old. Disease was thus unexplained and unexplainable (one might cite similar mysterious outbreaks, such as Legionnaire's Disease and AIDS, even during our own medically enlightened times). During epidemics of plague, the common defense had been simply to flee the places where it was breaking out.

(2) Prospero's suite consists of seven rooms, a number which often figures in numerology (seven deadly sins, *seven* champions of Christendom, seven as the first roll of the dice, and so on). The rooms are, successively, blue, purple, green, orange, white, violet, and black with scarlet ("a deep blood color," paragraph 4). Light comes through tinted windows from fires blazing in braziers supported by tripods, so that the light in the

green room is tinted green, and so on. Poe's intention here is to evoke a mood of eeriness and unreality, except, perhaps, for the white light in the fifth room, for the monochromatic light reduces everything to the same color, and the revelers change as they go back and forth.

(3) The last, most awesome room is black with red trim on its window. These colors suggest the fusion of human blood and the darkness of death.

(4) The black room contains the large ebony clock, which is imposing in appearance and confounding in its hourly tolling. The guests are disconcerted, pale, confused, and tremulous at these sepulchral sounds (paragraphs 5, 7, and 8). The eerie black light together with the dull sound are sufficient to explain its effect of uneasiness.

(5) Poe does not describe the dress of the nobles in much specific detail. Instead (paragraph 7) he describes their garb impressionistically as being "grotesque," "arabesque," "beautiful," "bizarre," and "terrible." The "masked figure" is remarkable because he is decked out to resemble a corpse with its face "dabbled in *blood*" (paragraph 9), seemingly like a victim of the Red Death (see the description in paragraph 1). Prospero defies the figure and challenges him, commanding his servants to unmask him so that the person so costumed may be hanged the next morning (paragraph 11). The reaction of a host to anyone disturbing a party is natural, and therefore Prospero's anger is to be expected.

Writing topics. The setting. The symbolic and suggestive meanings of setting. The relationship of setting to action at the masquerade. Setting and Prospero's character.

Works for Comparison with "The Masque of the Red Death"

Dixon, *All Gone*, 475
Hawthorne, *Young Goodman Brown*, 330
Robinson, *Richard Cory*, 619
Stevens, *Dillusionment of Ten O'Clock*, 621

Writing About Setting, *pages 259–263*

The problem to confront in teaching this section is that of moving from the abstract descriptions of possible essays to the specific topics about which students will be writing. The most approachable topic on setting for most students will hence be the first one (page 260), on setting and action. With your guidance, students will quickly be able to determine this relationship and apply it to whatever topic you assign or they select. If you assign some of the other possible types, you may need to ask specific questions about stories to get your students to express their observations about the uses of setting. Types 4 and 5 will be the most difficult of the five listed (p. 260). The sample essay, based on Poe's "The Masque of the Red Death," is an illustration of the fourth type.

Writing Topics about Setting, *page 263*

(1) The first writing topic should emphasize the qualities of character brought out by adversity. One may presume that if the Doctor and the Musician had met during civilized times of prosperity, they would have had great rapport and friendship, because they have similar interests.

(2) The second question is one requiring a creative transplanting. More important than the transposition, however, is the analysis of the process that students might carry out, and their understanding of the various stories which they are studying.

(3) The third question is focused on the creative writing of a scene, but it might become a short-short story if a student wishes. Direction ***a*** focuses on the artistic connection between feelings, actions, and moods to conditions of light and atmosphere. Direction ***b*** might stem directly from a life-experience, so that one student might describe how a television program or a toy causes an argument, while another student might write about how the return of something found (say a set of car keys, or a book) brings about a new friendship. Whatever topic the student may choose, the important thing is to emphasize the relationship of setting to character and action.

(4) The fourth topic could become extensive if all five characters are chosen for discussion. It might therefore be reserved for assignment as the finishing writing task for a unit, or for an extended paper. The black-and-white reproductions of the Boucher and Hopper paintings (pages 232, 233) are intended to give artistic students the chance to relate art to literature. That these paintings graphically show differences of character perception might be especially useful in developing comparisons and contrasts between Meda Roth and either Miss Brill or Mrs. Johnson.

Chapter Seven
Pages 262–293

Style: The Words that Tell the Story

In teaching this section, you may find that students need assistance in understanding the examples. Thus, for instance, the passage from Munro's "The Found Boat," on page 270 (and also on page 265), may need in-class reading and analysis, with the use of the blackboard to illustrate the "they ..." sentences. Students may inquire what prevents these repeated patterns from becoming "boring," and you may need to respond that the sentences are of unequal length and content, and that therefore they illustrate the principle of variety—an important standard of excellence in style.

A good teaching approach, once you have covered the various concepts to your satisfaction, is to go to a story you have already read and discussed, and pick a passage at random for analysis. If you intermingle student comment with your own insights, such an impromptu consideration can build confidence in students about approaching their own analyses of style.

Ernest Hemingway, *Soldier's Home, pages 272–277*

The plot of "Soldier's Home" involves Krebs as the protagonist in conflict with the abstract antagonism of peacetime adjustment. Obviously, those around him expect him to have been the little boy he was, and to have been unchanged by the war. They therefore assume that he can begin life again, as though nothing has happened. The crisis of the story is his conversation with his mother, and the climax is his promise to be a good boy for his "Mummy" (paragraph 86). This portion of the story indicates that his disaffection is approaching total alienation, a condition that he rejects. The resolution, in his decision to go to Kansas City, and in his going to watch his sister play ball, suggests a compromise with his disaffection. Though he will continue to feel like an outsider, in other words, he will keep his reservations to himself, and will fit in, at least externally, with life at home.

In class, students may raise questions about Hemingway's meaning in the story. There is no ready-made, easy answer, except to respond by analyzing the difficulties, real and imagined, that Krebs experiences after returning to the ordinary home town of his childhood after living through the bitter fighting in France during the First World War. Hemingway is using Krebs to pose basic questions about life: Can people get back to everyday, ordinary normality after going through the worst possible experience that they can ever face, and if they can, what prevents them from doubting the value of such a life?

Answers to the Study Questions, page 277

(1) See page 267 of the text for a discussion about Hemingway's mixing of general and specific language, as shown in paragraphs 6 and 7 of the story. You might also wish to treat the question as it pertains to paragraphs 4, 11, 15, 16, and 95, where Hemingway uses a number of unspecific words to get at the uneasiness of Krebs as he attempts to adjust to life after the war.

(2) Generally, Hemingway uses short, almost clipped sentences, although, as in paragraphs 5 and 6, some of the sentences are fairly long and involved. Most of the words are short, but because of the topic of Krebs's difficulties a number of abstract words are introduced, such as *elaborately, actualities, reaction, apocryphal, exaggeration, complicated, consequences,* and *interesting.* Though Hemingway's sentences are brief, they are not necessarily uncomplicated. In paragraph 15, for example, one might notice the following sentence as complex even though short: "But the world they were in was not the world he was in." The last sentence in paragraph 5, involving the "who" constructions, is as complex as any to be found anywhere. Once the section of the story involving dialogue commences (paragraph 17), the words are short and specific, in keeping with the tensions within the family and also with the general inarticulateness of the speakers.

(3) In this story Hemingway is not describing actions as much as Krebs's displacement from battlefield to home. The details are therefore not profuse, being confined to no more than are essential and elemental (e.g., "he was sleeping late in bed," and so on). Some of the repetitious phrases and sentences sound almost childish, so easy are they (e.g., "He learned that in the army." [paragraph 13]). Hemingway introduces adjectives and adverbs only sparingly, in keeping with the spare nature of Krebs's

life at home. The descriptions are only minimal, and are not vivid. There are no details about the battles that Krebs experienced, for example, and we learn no more about them than that he was there.

(4) It is difficult to establish Krebs's true character because he is almost totally subdued and passive during the story. The only aspect of his life that seems to excite him is his encounter with books about the war, and this, we remind ourselves, is all in his past. Nevertheless he does undergo a change because of his decision to go to Kansas City (paragraph 95). Although he is neither deeply analytical nor articulate, he is trying to adjust to life back home. His adjustment for most of the story, however, takes the form of a general lassitude and a period of taking stock about his experiences during the war and also about his home and family. His integrity is shown in his good relationship with his sister and also in his regrets about the lies he has told. His integrity is additionally shown in his dissatisfaction with the thoughts about forming romantic attachments because of the additional lies he might have to tell and also because of the politics of establishing a love relationship.

Krebs is handicapped because he does not truly articulate his feelings. Most likely, however, he does not step quickly into the grooves of hometown life because he feels so changed by his war experience. He has gained a perspective which enables him to determine that many "lies" are essential for the habits of normal life, and he has likely concluded that the result of these lies is dissolution and war. He does not go to work immediately because he is unsure of what role he can honestly assume in his postwar world. In disavowing love for his mother (paragraph 73), he seems gratuitously cruel, but his remarks seem designed not to hurt her but rather to indicate his general unease and unhappiness.

Writing Topics. The conversational style of Hemingway's characters. The words used by the narrator to describe Krebs's feelings. The importance of the family in Krebs's thoughts. The difficulties of postwar adjustment as seen in Krebs. The structure of the story.

Works for Comparison with "Soldier's Home"

Hardy, *The Man He Killed*, 557
Northrup, *Wahbegan*, 971
Zabytko, *Home Soil*, 403

Alice Munro, *The Found Boat, pages 277–284*

Like many of Munro's stories, "The Found Boat" is set in Munro's imaginary small town of Jubilee, which is visualized as being in western Ontario, near her own home town of Wingham. The story's plot of may be seen as the conflicts or contrasts that young people experience at their time of growing sexual desires. The "Truth or Dare" game, for example, permits the young people to objectivize their private sexual wishes in a mixed friendly setting. Similarly, the discovery and repair of the boat offers the chance for companionship under the guise of cooperative effort. The high point of the sexual by-play is the collective decision to strip and run to the river, and Clayton's ejection of water from his mouth onto Eva's breasts. At the story's end, it seems that the girls will try to resume their lives as they were before, although their giggling suggests both their heightened emotions and their realization that they are moving toward adulthood.

In teaching the story, you may discover that the emphasis on budding sexuality comes as a surprise to many students who believe that the first half is more about the boat than the young people. It hence becomes necessary to study the first part of the story to demonstrate the many details of boy–girl relationships established there. You may wish to refer to pages 265 and 270 for further discussions of Munro's style in "The Found Boat."

Answers to the Study Questions, page 284

(1) The descriptive passages of "The Found Boat" are specific and accurate, but most of them introduce an element of human response and involvement. Paragraph 10, for example, demonstrates this movement from description to character. Also, paragraph 1 is less focused on details about the spring flood than on the reactions it produces in young and old.

(2) The level of diction among the boys is generally low, with contractions and interjections (paragraph 4), profanity (paragraphs 7, 8), and grammatical mistakes (paragraph 22). Eva's language is more at a middle level, as is Carol's, although Carol indulges in slang in paragraph 55, and Eva uses an insulting slang term in paragraph 12.

(3) Paragraph 10 suggests that Eva's imagination is strong, and that she yearns for magic worlds of romance. When she becomes the point-of-view character, the style is elevated to complement her brief romantic reflection. Her taunting of the boys in paragraph 12 is comically contrasted with paragraph 10.

(4) The last paragraph emphasizes the actions of the girls in getting out of the water and in bursting out in giggles. The action verbs and participles are *giggle, slapping, splashing, set about developing, showed, snort, start up, make, bend over, grab,* and *had.* Some of these are neutral, but many are graphic and vivid. The verb *snort,* which usually is used in reference to animals, is a perfect choice to describe the giggles.

(5) There are many details of setting in "The Found Boat." The lifestyle and artifacts of the people of Jubilee suggest a poor or working-class environment in the days before electronic entertainment. The town is graphically realized, as is shown in paragraph 47, where the recovery of winter's detritus is described. If the story is considered symbolically as an awakening of sexuality, the cold flood and the promise of warm water suggests the developing maturity of the major characters.

Writing Topics. The style of the descriptive passages. The use of colloquialisms and slang. The relationship of style to character. The style in a paragraph (such as the last one).

Works for Comparison with "The Found Boat"

Henley, *Am I Blue*, 1403
Joyce, *Araby*, 387
Olds, *35/10*, 854
Soto, *Oranges*, 992

Mark Twain, *Luck, pages 284–287*

The story moves forward in fairly easy order. The exposition is in paragraphs 1–9; the complication in 10–13; the crisis in 14. The climax occurs in paragraph 14, when Scoresby's blundering charge breaks the Russian ranks. The resolution (paragraphs 15, 16) emphasizes that "the best thing . . . that can befall a man is to be born lucky." In this way Twain ties together both the title and the resolution of the story.

Because there are two narrators, you might wish your class to consider their characteristics. The first narrator is fairly straightforward and not particularly noteworthy, while the second is much more conversational in manner and denunciatory in tone. He emerges as an individual.

Answers to the Study Questions, page 287

(1) From the example of this story, Twain includes only enough detail to make his concluding point clear, that "Scoresby's an absolute fool." He does not provide specifics about the "certain line of stock questions"

on Caesar's *Gallic Wars,* but he gives only the general detail that the narrator drilled Scoresby on them. In the battle description (paragraphs 14–16) the narrator is not interested in detail for its own sake, but gives only enough to show that Scoresby turns blunders into triumphs.

(2) Examples of humor in the story are the titles of Scoresby (paragraph 1), the fortuitous passing of the exams in Caesar and math (paragraphs 6, 8), the grown men crying (paragraph 12), and the clumsy victory in battle (paragraphs 14–16). Despite the truism that too much analysis chills humor, a study of any of these passages will show that the comic response is interconnected with Twain's arrangements of words.

(3) After the "look, and look, and look" phrase in paragraph 1, the language is elevated in an effort to inflate Scoresby as a recognized giant. Twain's obvious purpose is to use the rest of the story as an anti-climax to deflate Scoresby.

(4) The story about Scoresby is told within a narrative frame. An unnamed narrator (the "authorial voice") introduces the situation of confidential revelation in paragraphs 1–4. The second narrator, the clergyman, tells the story itself. This shift in point of view, from the unknowing narrator to the knowing counselor and friend (who is "a man of strict veracity" with a good "judgment of men" [paragraph 4]), is designed to authenticate the revelations about Scoresby's blundering career. The explanation of how Scoresby passed his exams, for example, depends on the clergyman's having been an instructor at Woolwich Academy and therefore having been familiar with the types of test questions usually asked (paragraph 5). In short, the clergyman narrator learns everything that he tells, first, because he was an observer and major mover, and, second, because he was an on-the-spot participant and observer.

Writing topics. Twain's stylistic purpose in the battle description, or in the opening paragraph. The ways in which Twain's style creates amusement and laughter. The differences in style between the two narrators.

Works for Comparison with "Luck"

Cummings, *next to of course god america i,* 929
Parker, *Penelope,* 826
Piercy, *A Work of Artifice,* 665
Field, *Icarus,* 833

Writing About Style, *pages 287–292*

Because writing about style must begin with the analysis of detail, the in-class work with style may be profitably developed from the "Questions for Discovering Ideas" on page 288. If you select a passage from any story, and show how the questions may produce materials that may be fitted into an essay, students may be guided to see that they, too, with these questions as analytical guides, may be able to produce materials suitable for their essays. Because the story chosen for analysis in the sample essay deals with only two paragraphs from Twain's "Luck," you may choose other paragraphs from this story as the basis of essay assignments in addition to any parts of the other stories, as you wish. You might also omit the two passages from "The Found Boat," on which there are illustrative commentaries. The sample essay may be longer than essays your students may write, but it is presented as an example showing how a number of aspects of style may be connected by a major central idea. Here the classroom reading of the sample, together with comments, would clarify the writing task for your students.

Writing Topics about Style, *pages 292–293*

(1) The first topic is designed to explore differences between two major speakers within the same story. Although there is less material from the first speaker than from the second, students should be able to develop enough details for a solid essay.

(2) The second topic is set up to permit students to explain the qualities of Hemingway's style through a contrast with the styles to be found in other stories. The contrasts are fairly obvious, particularly for Whitecloud (more articulateness) and Updike (detail and also slang). With a Faulknerian approach, there would probably be more detail about the father, and the story might end with Krebs leaving for Kansas City rather than going to the ball field to watch the sister play.

(3) This question gets at essential details about both "Soldier's Home" and "Luck." Obviously, Hemingway's portrait of Krebs is dramatic; Hemingway does not intend a full analysis of Krebs's uneasiness and alienation and therefore he leaves the job of interpreting to the reader. Similarly, Twain is trying to present Scoresby dramatically, and the narrator's comments represent his opinions and nothing more. With both stories, details like those presented by Munro and Crane would uncover subtle-

ties and create ambiguities that neither Hemingway nor Twain wishes to create. The style of "The Found Boat" and "The Blue Hotel" would therefore not be appropriate for either "Luck" or "Soldier's Home."

(4) This topic is designed, like all the creative-writing assignments, to help students in their critical understanding because of their hands-on experiences as writers. Once students have finished their sketches, they may be surprised to discover that they have made many unconscious word choices. An interesting variant on the assignment is therefore to ask for a revision, and then to ask students to describe their conscious choices as they make their changes.

(5) The idea of this topic is to cause students to think seriously about the adequacy of the portraiture and the probability of the actions in the stories. "The Found Boat" (page 277) may be interpreted as a story about youthful sexuality; "The Yellow Wallpaper" about mental deterioration in light of negative circumstances of life. Students may therefore find "The Found Boat" more immediately congenial as a writing topic, although some may be less inhibited in discussing "The Yellow Wallpaper." Of the two stories, "The Yellow Wallpaper" is likely to involve political as well as psychological discussions.

Chapter Eight
Pages 294–321

Tone: The Expression of Attitude in Fiction

The aim of this chapter is to introduce tone as a broad concept that includes literally everything that can make up a story. Tone begins with an attitude, and a study of tone should attempt to define and delimit the attitude. But then—this point is most important—the writer considering tone should analyze and explain how attitudes are rendered and made real. Hence students need reminding that to study tone is to consider how the story itself provides evidence of the author's awareness of the interdependence of speaker, character, circumstance, language, probability of action, and appropriateness of setting, together with evidence of how the author apparently views both audience and self—as nearly as these complex elements may be judged.

Margaret Atwood, *Rape Fantasies, pages 301–307*

"Rape Fantasies," excerpted from Atwood's 1977 volume entitled *Dancing Girls,* is noteworthy because of its "working-girl" speaker, whose manner is both individual and optimistic. In her imagination she turns constantly to conversation and sympathy as a civilized and sympathetic method of blunting the edge of potential violence. If one assumes, with her, that all persons have a similar bent, her concluding questions have great validity.

The plot of "Rape Fantasies" stems out of the reality and unreality of rape. Estelle provides continuity as the imagining protagonist, and the conflict results from her various ways of overcoming the rapists who are the antagonists. The crisis, if one may call it that, occurs when Estelle raises questions about the limits of sociability (paragraph 43), and the climax and resolution consist of her perplexity in the concluding paragraph. From the standpoint of the actual topic of rape, of course, there is no actual resolution, for the story treats an ongoing problem.

Answers to the Study Questions, page 307

(1) The comic elements in the various rape fantasies of Estelle develop out of her humanizing of the rapists of her imagination. By making the brutal situation normal and conversational through the everyday, matter-of fact way of describing it, Estelle provokes smiles and chuckles rather than horror. The rapists seem human, with ordinary human problems, and hence they may be approached through understanding and conversation. This contrast between the real and the imaginary provides the comedy of the story.

(2) Estelle's fantasies have in common that she is in control, and yet is involved with the rapists on a human level. Atwood controls the story's tone by the personalization and domestication of the experiences. Estelle has not had experience with violence, and thus does not permit violence in her imagination (paragraph 24). She is intelligent, pleasant, and comic, not analytical. Her background is that of an office worker, not of a criminologist, sociologist, or psychologist.

(3) The tone is intimate, conversational, personal, and chatty. This affects our perception of Estelle as being bright but superficial—vivid, lifelike, and comic (paragraphs 18, 23). Though Estelle is potentially analytical, Atwood confines her powers to the analysis of a misplayed hand at bridge (a misuse of the weak club opening, paragraph 3).

(4) From the extensive consideration of the subject matter we may conclude that Atwood is serious. The actual subject material she presents, however, keeps away from the dark side of rape—an aspect of life that most people find unbearable to face. Perhaps Atwood's symbol of the need for protection of women like Estelle is that the setting/location of the story, where Estelle is speaking to an unnamed listener about her fantasies, is the "nice place" where all the waiters know her and will protect her from molestation (paragraph 43). The actual violence and brutality of rape, in short, are unreal for her.

(5) The women around the bridge table deflect the seriousness by considering rape not as a problem of violence, but rather as an everyday matter, prompted by the article that Chrissy has read. The article speaks about the fantasizing aspects of rape, not about the horror or pain of it (as Estelle rightly observes, paragraph 24).

Writing Topics. The character of Estelle. The light, comic treatment of a serious topic. The tone of the story.

Works for Comparison with "Rape Fantasies"

Kate Chopin, *The Story of an Hour, pages 308–309*

Though brief, "The Story of an Hour" is a minor masterpiece of irony. The heroine's feelings are known only to herself, and those around her totally misunderstand her responses and feelings. Her death, to them, seems like a supreme act of wifely devotion, even though we as readers learn that it is not the shock of "joy" that kills her, but rather the shock of sudden and supreme disappointment.

Chopin's plot for the story is built up out of Louise's conflicting roles of bereavement and liberation. Louise herself, the protagonist, feels identified with liberation, while all the others in the story assume the status of antagonists because they project upon her the role of grieving widow. The crisis and climax both occur, almost simultaneously (in paragraph 21) when Brently Mallard enters the house and Louise falls dead of a heart attack upon seeing him. One might make a case that the climax has been already established by Brently's having escaped the train crash, for it has been stated right at the beginning of the story that Louise's heart is weak (paragraph 1), and therefore any sudden shock would kill her. The resolution is of course the reassertion of male dominance, as expressed by the doctors.

Answers to the Study Questions, page 310

(1) Louise's husband is portrayed as a good man, who always looked on her with love (paragraph 12). He himself has done nothing to justify her relief at the news of his death. Indeed, he, like Louise, is more acted upon than acting, but then, the traditional married state itself is the thing that has been giving her pressure. The context of the story, emphasizing as it does the onrush of Louise's feelings, guides our perceptions of her. She does not create the feelings, but rather they overwhelm her as she retires to her room.

(2) The details in paragraph 5 are more appropriate for love and joy than for grief. Words like "aquiver," "delicious," "singing," and "twitter-

ing" all create an ironic perspective on Louise's grief, and it is these words that make possible her sense of relief, which would have been almost unbearably cruel and insensitive if the author had created a backdrop of darkness and sobriety.

(3) The narrator's attitude toward marriage is one of disapproval, not because of the human affections that are brought out by the institution, but because of the control it gives men over women (see paragraphs 14 and 23). The relief that Louise finds in discovering newly found freedom (paragraphs 11–16) is an aspect of tone that stresses her previously unspoken dissatisfaction with her inferior status as a deferential wife.

(4) Both Josephine and Richards have great concern for Louise, and do everything they can for her. The irony is that they do not and cannot comprehend Louise's true feelings, and thus they are concrete embodiments of the traditional and expected views on marriage.

(5) The key phrase in the last paragraph is "of joy that kills." The irony is that the doctors assume that Louise's death is caused by a heart failure brought about by seeing her husband alive. They are right, but we know that the failure is caused by Louise's sudden and unexpected realization that her freedom was illusory. The doctors hence exhibit a comic shortsightedness brought about by their own masculine vanity.

Writing Topics. Irony in the story. The presentation of Louise's character. The plot of the story.

Works for Comparison with "The Story of an Hour"

Collier, *The Chaser*, 310
Gilman, *The Yellow Wallpaper*, 491
Glaspell, *Trifles*, 1038
Hardy, *The Workbox*, 683
Linda Pastan, *Marks*, 974
Wharton, *Pomegranate Seed*, 440

John Collier, *The Chaser, pages 310–312*

Collier's use of the dramatic point of view in "The Chaser" needs classroom attention, for the success of the story depends on the reader's objective judgments of Alan and the old man. The story demonstrates Collier's grim amusement, wry condemnation, and irony. With great subtlety, he exposes the folly of romantic possessiveness, and in this respect forces the reader to reconsider human relationships.

Students may wish to discuss the title, which is ironic because a chaser may be (a) a drink that washes down an earlier drink (b) one who pursues in love, and (c) one who hunts with a desire to catch or kill. The most important of these meanings is that the poison will be the "chaser" to the love potion. This meaning is made clear in the concluding ironic words, "au revoir." First, they mean "good bye," and, second, they refer to Alan's eventual return for the poison. This irony thus makes the title especially sinister.

Answers to the Study Questions, page 312

(1) The plot is based on the conflict between Alan and his romantic naiveté, on the one hand, and the cynicism of the old man. The poison (paragraph 7) kills without trace, and the love potion (paragraphs 23–37) commits the drugged woman to become a love slave to the man who gives it to her. The connection between the two potions, according to the insinuations of the old man, is that a man seeking the love potion will eventually demand the poison (the "spot remover" or "glove cleaner").

(2) The characters are representative and flat, for they do not develop. This characteristic permits the story to focus on the issue of love relationships. In addition, by keeping the characters undeveloped, Collier prevents the sympathy that readers might give round characters, and therefore he focuses negatively on Alan and the old man.

(3) The old man's room is poorly lit, dirty, and drab. Nothing is attractive; instead things are sordid (paragraphs 1–3). This dreariness underscores the secrecy and furtiveness of Alan's conspiratorial desire to control Diana. The darkness complements the old man's deceptiveness, which he disguises by his superficially sincere speech.

(4) The words are evocative, particularly because of the story's dramatic point of view. There are few direct responses by the characters; therefore, the existing ones should be viewed carefully. In addition, the old man's conversation should be studied closely to determine how Collier illustrates both the skillful and the diabolical nature of this character. For specifics, one could select words everywhere in the story, but in particular "nervous as a kitten" suggests Alan's youth and also belies his sinister motives (paragraph 1); "attempting a look of scientific detachment" (paragraph 20) indicates a degree of impatience but also hints that at a future time he will remember the poison; and "watching him fill it" (paragraph 42) suggests a sense of happiness in the possibility of gaining great power.

Words suggesting the calculating nature of the old man are "Bountifully, insistently. Everlastingly" (paragraph 19); the old man's final "Au revoir" demonstrates his cynicism (paragraph 45).

(5) The success of the story depends on the dramatic irony. Alan does not know where his desire to possess Diana will lead, but both the old man and the readers do. In addition, the old man's condition may be viewed as situational irony, for he victimizes others, but does so because he himself has apparently never understood that happiness might be gained from a good human relationship. The story thereby gains double irony, resulting from a victim who in turn victimizes others by preying upon their ignorance.

(6) "The Chaser" as already stressed, emphasizes that love cannot be coerced without destructiveness, that youth may succumb too easily to thoughtless desire and confuse it for love, and that desire may be destructive if it is not guided by understanding and toleration. The furtiveness and conspiratorial design of Alan and the old man negatively illustrate the need to fuse individuality with romantic commitment.

Writing topics. Because the sample essay (pages 319–320) of this chapter treats the tone of the story, it will be necessary to devise assignments that are not preempted. Some possibilities: The tone of the old man's speeches. The character of Alan. The use of irony.

Works for Comparison with "The Chaser"

Bradstreet, *To My Dear and Loving Husband*, 920
Browning, *How Do I Love Thee*, 923
Browning, *My Last Duchess*, 578
Wakoski, *The Ring*, 1004
Wharton, *Pomegranate Seed*, 440

Americo Parédes, *The Hammon and the Beans, pages 313–316*

"The Hammon and the Beans," first published in *The Texas Observer* in 1963, is first of all a poignant story about the death of the narrator's playmate, but in broader social and economic perspective it is also a portrayal of the plight of poor immigrants. One of the noteworthy aspects of the story is the narrator. He is apparently an adult recalling events that occurred in the 1920's. His advanced age at the time of his narration might be expected to produce understanding and perspective, but such a perspective is not apparent. Instead, the narrator recalls the events and responses only as they occurred to him as a child. The narrations in Joyce's

"Araby" (page 387) and Frank O'Connor's "First Confession" (page 520) are similar.

Answers to the Study Questions, page 316

(1) Parédes locates the grandfather's house near the fort, introducing the military and political background of a border town during the turbulence of early twentieth-century Mexico. Thus, the connection of the children with the soldiers is natural, and Chonita's dependence on them for food is logical. The dirty yellow of the narrator's home suggests that even the Mexican-Americans who are better off do not enjoy a luxurious existence. The shack in which Chonita lives with her family indicates their poverty (paragraph 12).

(2) Chonita is flat because she is a child and makes no choices. She does come to life, however, and seems real and lovable. She is described as a *scrawny little girl of about nine* (paragraph 14) who has a dramatic flair (paragraphs 16–17). Her behavior suggests great persistence (paragraph 7), along with incipient craving for recognition as a performer. She is also representative of her class of Mexican-Americans, for her death symbolizes the results of poverty and neglect. Dr. Zapata is in effect Parédes's *raisonneur,* or presenter, of these ideas (paragraphs 23–42).

(3) For Parédes's use of situational irony as a response to this question, please see the text, page 300. For further explanation of tone, one might consider the pathos exhibited in the sorry plight of Chonita as she receives a scolding before being given food (paragraph 11). Here the technique is the narrator's straightforward description, with no accompanying analysis or discussion. Dr. Zapata expresses indignation at Chonita's death. Parédes provides enough details for the doctor to substantiate his anger (paragraphs 21–33).

(4) That Dr. Zapata is a physician, thinker, and a caring person makes his anger credible. His declaration that he is not a political revolutionary is also consistent with his concern for the personal plight of persons like Chonita.

(5) The story is concerned with the problem of cultural assimilation (the attitudes expressed toward the soldiers), poverty (particularly that of Chonita and her family), inadequate health care (her death), and the Mexican revolutionary movements led by Villa and Zapata. In this political and economic context, Chonita's life and death are an example of what may happen on a broader scale to children raised in neglect.

(6) Clearly the tradition of Marion, the "Swamp Fox," as quoted from Bryant's poem, is of concern to all United States citizens, but the irony, as the story makes clear, is that the Mexican-American children are not taught anything about their own history and literature; therefore they become alienated from their own ethnic traditions.

(7) The women of Bryant's song are lovely and happy, but Chonita still wears her rags and speaks her pitiful English, even while the narrator describes his vision of her as a butterfly (paragraph 46). Though the narrator does not express his or her own feelings, it is logical that he or she would feel at least some indignation about Chonita's untimely death.

Writing Topics. Dr. Zapata and the story's tone. The tone and the economic and political situation. The irony in the education provided for the children of the town. The tone of the conclusion.

Works for Comparison with "The Hammon and the Beans"

Cisneros, *The House on Mango Street*, 235
Randall, *Ballad of Birmingham*, 775
Villanueva, *Day-Long Day*, 1002
Whitecloud, *Blue Winds Dancing*, 119

Writing About Tone, *pages 317–321*

In presenting writing tasks about tone in fiction, you will need to emphasize that the study of tone requires an analysis of how attitudes are shaped and controlled, not merely the identification of the attitudes themselves. This point needs constant stressing. Because there is a sample essay on Collier's "The Chaser" (page 319), you might assign this story beforehand, and use it as the reference point for your classroom discussion. Thus, in determining the tone of this story, you might stress how the reader's perspective is shaped by the way in which Collier shows the limitations of the two major characters.

The types of essays you choose to emphasize will be governed by what you might assign. With tone, however, it is probably good to go into detail about the particular plan to be followed. It is not out of order, either, to lead a general discussion of the story you have chosen, without dealing with the specifics of tone in the story. Such a coverage liberates many students to consider tone without needing also to create their own interpretations from scratch. Obviously, students who wish to maintain their own readings are always free to do so.

As further aid to students for this assignment, you might wish to set up paragraph-length exercises on particular spots in, say, "The Chaser." The benefit of these written exercises is that you can immediately address yourself to encouraging good approaches and correcting misperceived ones.

Writing Topics about Tone, *page 321*

(1) The first of these topics should get at the relative condition of powerlessness of the various female characters. Louise and Mathilde are both to be judged as traditional housewives who are confined to this station in life. Diana is clearly considered as potential property by Alan Austen. The most independent character is Phoenix, but she is being constrained by both poverty and age. A feminist consideration should get at the relationships of these characters to the politics of marriage and economics. Age is not as important an issue because it is outside the area of politics except as Phoenix's poverty makes her dependent on "charity" for the continued medication of her grandson.

(2) The idea of the second topic is to relate the conversational or narrative style of the speaker to the ways in which we as readers perceive it. Thus, in "I Stand Here Ironing" we are led to understanding through the narrator's clear awareness of her own shortcomings, from which she does not try to absolve herself. Similarly, we are led toward being impressed with the insights of the narrator of "Everyday Use" and also toward understanding the limitations of the narrator of "First Confession." Students might write on two stories, or three or more, for a comparison-contrast essay, should they wish.

(3) Estelle's attitude is conditioned by her expectation, or hope, that she would always be able to control the situation of rape. She is not vicious herself, and she expects humanity and even kindness of others. Therefore she is able to speak of rape as though it is an avenue toward friendship and even love. Obviously her attitude is shaped by her failure to understand the anger, hurt, guilt, rage, and viciousness of potential rapists.

(4) The fourth direction is perhaps more difficult to think about than to do. Students discover that the situation that they imagine (if indeed they exert a strong power of imagination) will govern their descriptions and word choices, so that irony is not as hard to bring out as it at first might seem. If they try to bring out verbal irony, of course, that will take more experimentation and experience.

Chapter Nine
Pages 322–360

Symbolism and Allegory: Keys to Extended Meaning

The aim of this chapter is to aid students in developing a working knowledge of these fundamental characteristics of literature. In teaching the subject, you may encounter uneasiness about symbols or allegorical patterns. For this reason you may wish to discuss a number of stories with the sole aim of determining whether and why certain elements and actions may be taken symbolically or allegorically. It is somewhat of a revelation for students to realize that picking out symbols may not be as impossible as it first seems. As long as they realize that they must make a good case for what they choose, they can soon become adept at discussing symbolism and allegory. Even so, the greatest temptation students face is to find symbols and allegories everywhere. If you keep stressing the need for explanations, however, this tendency may be controlled and creatively shaped.

Aesop, *The Fox and the Grapes, page 328*

"The Fox and the Grapes" is one of Aesop's best known fables. Because it has given us the phrase "sour grapes," you might begin by asking if any of your students knows the meaning of the phrase. From there it is natural to stress that the fable is applicable to the general attitude of people toward the unattainable.

Answers to the Study Questions, page 328

(1) The fox exhibits normal traits: He needs to satisfy his hunger, and knows that he can get the grapes only by leaping for them. He is also normal enough to maintain his own self-esteem by denigrating the prize when he fails. These traits are essential to Aesop's moral, because the fable genre depends not on exceptional but on average or normal human character.

(2) The plot develops out of the desire the fox has for the grapes, and

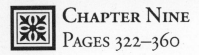

his inability to get them. The resolution is his minimizing the reward he cannot gain.

(3) Obviously the fox's claim is a rationalization. Students may miss the moral that human beings should not justify their own shortcomings by resorting to distortions and lies. Aesop is stressing the need to recognize the truth both about oneself and also about the world outside.

(4) The fable as a genre features animals with human traits who carry on a brief action illustrating truths about human beings. The need for animals as protagonists (and antagonists also) is to enable the fabulist to concentrate on the topic without any unnecessary complication.

Writing topics. The fox and the grapes as a symbol. The nature of the fable as a genre. The nature of the action in the fable.

Works for Comparison with "The Fox and the Grapes"

Faulkner, *Barn Burning,* 143
Frost, *The Oven Bird,* 900
Swift, *A Description of the Morning,* 730

Anonymous, *The Myth of Atalanta, pages 328–330*

This myth has been added in the fourth edition because of the obvious omission of an ancient myth in earlier editions. Even so straightforward an account of a mythical life as the story of Atalanta demonstrates just how important the understanding of myths really is. The study of myths rewards great scrutiny. It is possible, for example, to determine extensive meaning in every action and situation in a typical myth. Such meanings are suggested by the third question (page 330), which suggests eight topics of the Atalanta myth; each of these can serve as the basis of extensive interpretation and meaning. The most famous modern version of the Atalanta myth is Swinburne's poetic drama *Atalanta in Calydon* (1865), which deals with the episode of the Calydonian Boar and Atalanta's infatuation with Meleager.

Answers to the Study Questions, page 330

(1) Atalanta has abilities that in effect place her on an equal if not superior footing with men. She is a superb athlete and hunter, and leads a life of adventure (some accounts indicate that she actually did sail with Jason on the expedition of the Argonauts). She tries to preserve her independence by challenging potential husbands to a footrace, killing them if they lose.

(2) Atalanta vows to shun men because of a warning by the Oracle at Delphi. According to the Oracle, marriage would change her character totally. Needless to say, marriage would also inhibit the freedom she has enjoyed in pursuing her own way of life. It would seem that this awareness of her loss of freedom constitutes the principal meaning of the myth. The hatred of men that is mentioned in the retelling of the myth (paragraph 4) may be an expression of the idea that men and women have different interests, with women usually having to sacrifice theirs to serve those of men. That Milanion defeats Atalanta in their footrace because she picks up the dropped golden apples suggests that the security represented by gold is, mythically, the most usual way in which men overcome the interests of women. It is difficult to interpret the metamorphosis of the lovers into lion and lioness, but a strong suggestion is that uncontrolled passion does not lead to stability and is, further, a violation of divine propriety.

(3) The symbolic meanings of the various actions in the myth may be these:

a. Atalanta's name defines her invincibility. This meaning suggests the power of women, and the need for men to become even more powerful if love, birth, and family—in short, society—are to be established and maintained.

b. The golden apples symbolically represent the power of men to confer home and consequent stability so that women may be confined to their role of wife and mother.

c. The chopping off of the heads of losing runners obviously symbolizes the idea that "only the brave deserve the fair" (this is a phrase from Dryden's "Alexander's Feast"). A modern scientific interpretation of the destruction of the inferior suitors is that the victorious ones win the right of maintaining the strength of the human gene pool.

d. The father's abandonment the infant Atalanta represents an ancient way of maintaining property (usually a woman gave her goods and titles to the man who married her) and also a means of controlling population and inheritance through reducing the numbers of women. That Atalanta was suckled by a she-bear and reared by hunters is a common element in many ancient stories (see, for example, the accounts of Moses, Oedipus, and Romulus and Remus).

e. Presumably Atalanta hides the birth of Parthenopaeus, and exposes him to die, as a way of forestalling attempts by the family of Meleager to force her to return to their kingdom to bring up the child. In this respect, her abandonment of the infant is another phase of her desire to maintain her independent way of life.

f. Atalanta's rejection of the centaur, Hylaeus, symbolizes one of the means, along with the foot-race challenge, by which women control their own lives. Appropriately, Milanion wins the favor of Atalanta by protecting her when the rejected centaur attacks her. The myth therefore suggests another means by which men win women—through protection and, if necessary, sacrifice.

g. Atalanta presumably loses the race not through a lack of speed and power, but through a desire for the security represented by the apples. See also 3b.

h. The lovemaking in the holy grotto of Cybele, the Great Mother of Gods, probably represents a violation of holy ordinances. The underlying reasons for which promiscuous love was made taboo were likely economic. The offspring resulting from promiscuity would have tenuous claims to titles and inheritances. One might remember that the social structure in ancient Greece was tribal, and that therefore clear claims to parentage were essential in maintaining the social order.

WRITING TOPICS. The character of Atalanta. The symbolic or mythic meaning of her behavior. The importance of divine guidance on human affairs.

WORKS FOR COMPARISON WITH THE MYTH OF ATALANTA

Cummings, *she being Brand / -new*, 688
Marvell, *To His Coy Mistress*, 852
Paley, *Goodbye and Good Luck*, 531
Rukeyser, *Looking at Each Other*, 666
Shakespeare, *A Midsummer Night's Dream*, 1325

NATHANIEL HAWTHORNE, *Young Goodman Brown, pages 330–339*

In "Young Goodman Brown," the protagonist is the title character. The antagonist is ostensibly the devil, the spirit resembling his father (paragraph 13), although the antagonist might also be Brown's destructive sense of guilt—his projection of his own sinfulness upon others and his consequent damnation of them. The central conflict of the story, which seems lost even before it begins, is within Brown himself: an inner war of love and trust versus suspicion and distrust. The resolution occurs after Brown's climactic denial in paragraph 68. Brown's life is changed after this because his faith in others has been shattered, and therefore he alienates everyone around him.

Answers to the Study Questions, page 339

(1) The undeniable reality of the story is that Brown's journey is a dream, or nightmare. In psychological terms, Brown may be schizophrenic, because his view of others is distorted by his distorted convictions. It is probably best, however, to stress that his gloom results from religious fanaticism.

(2) Brown is a round character. Beginning as a seemingly good husband with a high estimate of the local minister (paragraph 21), his change into a foreboding, gloomy spirit marks a total alteration of character—for the worse, of course.

(3) The sample essay (page 357) discusses the topic of symbolism. There are additional symbols, such as the withering of the maple twigs (paragraph 38) and the fire at the forest meeting (paragraph 53), to name two. The symbols suggest death and hell. Ironically, though Brown disavows the devil (paragraph 68), it is his preoccupation with these diabolical symbols that ultimately governs his character and behavior.

(4) In Salem, the details of setting seem normal and ordinary: The threshold, street, church, meeting house, bed, pulpit, and grave are all a part of the town. The forest setting is provided with seemingly ordinary trees and a path which becomes increasingly unusual and symbolic. The woodland meeting place is characterized by the realistic details of the "dark wall of the forest," the altarlike rock, the blazing pines, the dense foliage, and the vague and sinful hymn, all bathed in red light. One can justify the forest setting as symbolic because it is a focus of Brown's preoccupation with sin, and because there the devil-like figure describes his awesome power (paragraphs 63–65).

(5) If one views the story allegorically, religious faith may be viewed both as a guide and as a dreg, and therefore the allegorical journey suggests the moral laxness and ambiguity into which people sometimes fall. The lesser characters belong both to Brown's journey into evil and also to his later life. Thus Deacon Gookin and Goody Cloyse meet Brown on the street (paragraph 70), and therefore they embody again the theme of Brown's disaffection with hypocrisy. At this point the narrator presents these characters as virtuous, however, and in this way Hawthorne emphasizes Brown's distorted vision. Ironically—and irony of situation is a

major aspect of this story—Brown becomes evil while pursuing good and supposed godliness. For these reasons together with a number of others, the forest journey justifies the claim that it is allegorical.

Writing topics. The story as allegory. The network of symbols. Setting and Brown's character. Brown as a symbol.

Works for Comparison with "Young Goodman Brown"

Blake, *The Tyger*, 636
Collier, *The Chaser*, 310
Jeffers, *The Answer*, 956
Wright, *A Blessing*, 597

The Gospel of St. Luke 15:11–32, *The Parable of the Prodigal Son, pages 340–341*

Luke's story of the Prodigal Son is told in the words of Jesus. You may therefore wish to claim particular respect for the text, because some students may take offense at scripture being interpreted away from their own churches. As long as the limits of the discussion are made clear, however, most students take a lively interest in a literary approach to the work.

Answers to the Study Questions, page 341

(1) The Prodigal Son is self-indulgent and improvident, but he is introspective and has the courage to admit his mistake and to confess unworthiness. He is round because he does indeed grow to recognize his error and to admit it. It is necessary that he also be representative of many human beings, because the religious promise of the parable is intended for all believers.

(2) The plot grows out of the conflict (contrast) between the forgiving parent and the headstrong son. The antagonism against the son is also his self-caused poverty and his recognition that he has ruined his life. The religious point of the parable is the father's speech (verses 31, 32), which he makes in response to the angry words of his other son. This older son represents the traditional "eye for an eye" punishment, and he therefore is to be contrasted with the all-forgiving father.

(3) The resolution is the father's acceptance of the Prodigal Son and his explanation of why he has rejoiced at his Son's return. There is no "they lived happily ever after" conclusion, because the parable highlights the character of the father, not the life of the son. This point is worth stressing as a means of illustrating the nature of the parable as a genre.

(4) The structure of the parable may be described in this way, according to the verse numbers: 11–13, exposition; 14–16, complication; 17–19, crisis; 20, climax; 21–32, resolution. These parts coincide with the development of the plot, except that the resolution takes up more than half the entire parable. It would not be incorrect, in fact, to label the resolution a second story that might be entitled "The Angry Older Brother," for this section has its own brief plot development with its resolution in the father's explanation. In purely technical terms, the Older Brother's anger might be considered a second complication of the parable, except that the resolution of the Prodigal Son's story has already occurred. It is best to think of the parable as a form, therefore, in which the structure is governed more by idea or theology than by plot.

(5) The point of view is limited omniscient in verses 12–21, with emphasis on the Prodigal Son. In verses 22–32 the point of view is dramatic, featuring the conversation of the older son and the father. In these last eleven verses, the Prodigal Son does not appear. This shift coincides with the shift in the structure of the parable.

(6) The parable, as a form, contains many characteristics of fiction: i.e., plot, character development, description, dialogue, and a relatively consistent point of view. The principal difference is that in the parable genre, literary characteristics are less important than theme and theology.

Writing topics. The Prodigal Son as a symbol. The parable as it allegorizes the possibility of forgiveness and a second chance. The shift in point of view in the parable.

Works for Comparison with "The Prodigal Son"

Greenberg, *And Sarah Laughed,* 242
Hayden, *Those Winter Sundays,* 950
Miller, *Death of a Salesman,* 1233
Roethke, *My Papa's Waltz,* 697

Marjorie Pickthall, *The Worker in Sandalwood,* *pages 342–346*

"The Worker in Sandalwood" exemplifies the deftness and exquisiteness of Pickthall's touch as a writer. The main occurrence in the story is not presented as a miracle that definitely happens, but rather it appears before us clouded, as though in a dream, from the distant past. Mysteriousness rather than certainty defines the detail.

Students may need some reminding about the master-apprentice system. Parents or guardians would bind a young boy like Hyacinthe (pronounced *hee-a-cent*) legally to the master, who from that time had the authority to control every aspect of the young boy's life, and also to exploit his talents. The arrangement was really a form of indentured servitude. If a master turned out to be kind, the apprentice was lucky, but Hyacinthe is unlucky because L'Oreillard is both cruel and arbitrary. In practice, short of running away (for which apprentices could be severely punished), Hyacinthe has no recourse against L'Oreillard's mistreatment.

Answers to the Study Questions, page 346

(1) The point of view is the first person. The speaker, who is not identified, does not claim to have been a witness to the events of the story. Rather, this speaker has apparently acquired his or her information directly from Hyacinthe and also from persons who would have heard about things soon after they happened—namely from the "Curé" and "Madame." The narrator knows more than might have been learned from these sources, however, because he or she fills in extra details (as in paragraph 15) that would probably not have been supplied by the relatively inarticulate Hyacinthe, who, after all, spoke "in wood, not in words" (paragraph 7). In addition, the speaker makes clear his or her belief that the visit by the young boy is truly miraculous. The stress on "long ago" is one of the devices the speaker uses to make unnecessary the need for total investigative "truth" that a more recent event would require.

(2) Hyacinthe is a deserving boy of fourteen who has great skill with wood but otherwise has no imagination. His daydreams are "dumb" and his fancies are "slow" and "reluctant" (paragraph 7). He has a strong sense of pride in perfecting his work (paragraph 11), and is generous with his possessions (paragraph 26). He is sensitive, however, and laments his loneliness and personal pain (paragraph 13). He accepts his cruel treatment as his normal lot as an apprentice who has had the ill luck to be controlled by an unkind master. Since the story is an allegory, the "strange child" with "quiet eyes" appears because Hyacinthe is one of those who labor and are heavy laden, for whom the promise of Christianity has been made.

(3) The narrator stresses the high quality of Hyacinthe's work to underscore the possibility that he did all the work himself, without any divine aid. The stress on the dream is consistent with this possibility, for a dream would not produce a superb job of cabinetmaking. Because of these alternative possibilities, together with the general indistinctness and

vagueness stressed by the narrator, the story is just realistic enough to prevent its being labeled as fantastic or sentimental.

(4) The setting of the woodworking shop on Christmas Eve is probably a symbol of religious hope. The hurt bird which the boy Jesus carries is a part of the symbol of healing power, as is the neighboring clause "where the wild does went to drink" (paragraph 17). These animals are not predatory, unlike the wolves mentioned in paragraph 23, but instead are prey, just as Hyacinthe is preyed upon by Pierre L'Oreillard. The symbolism refers to the poor in spirit and the pure in heart, who according to the Sermon on the Mount will receive the Kingdom of Heaven and will see God.

(5) The symbols associated with the stranger are all consistent with Jesus as described in the New Testament (Luke 2:42). The training as a carpenter suggests a realistic skill of construction as well as the healing skill of the servant of God, thus providing a scriptural base for the symbolism of the story.

(6) A strong case may be made that the story is an allegory describing the process of difficulty-despair-comfort provided by the mercy and love of Jesus or of any person who provides mercy and assistance. In such a reading, L'Oreillard represents forces of physical and emotional antagonism; Hyacinthe represents a deserving person in great need; and the stranger represents the belief that the faithful will receive hope and comfort.

Writing Topics. The story as allegory. Symbolism. The resonances of the strange child. Biblical allusion.

Works for Comparison with "The Worker in Sandalwood"

Blake, *The Lamb*, 612
Gaines, *The Sky Is Gray*, 367
Twain, *Luck*, 285
Wharton, *Pomegranate Seed*, 440

John Steinbeck, *The Chrysanthemums, pages 347–353*

In teaching Steinbeck's "The Chrysanthemums," you may encounter an initial difficulty that students have in determining what has happened. Here a stress on symbolism in the story may prove fruitful as explanation, for the "dark speck" on the road (paragraph 108) is of course the pile of earth in which Elisa has earlier placed the chrysanthemum shoots. Sometimes students claim to dislike Elisa, but if they can see the story as one about a difficult personal relationship, they can be persuaded to care about her and thus to find the story interesting. As always, understanding can overcome aversion.

Answers to the Study Questions, page 354

(1) For the most part, the narrator observes Elisa dramatically, and utilizes omniscience only in paragraphs 108, 109, and possibly also in 110. The advantage of this mostly dramatic rendering is that the reader is left to infer the nature of Elisa's elation and therefore the extent of her great disappointment. Steinbeck, by thus directing the reader's sympathy and understanding, creates a memorable character and a powerful story.

(2) The setting (paragraph 1) is symbolic because it complements Elisa's isolation as a woman. The time of the year is December, when things have ceased growing, and the foothills around the valley prevent the sun (a universal symbol of growth, intelligence, and fertility) from reaching the farm. The Allen ranch suggests that everything is finished and put away, with nothing more to do. These aspects of the setting are clearly designed to symbolize the bleak prospects for Elisa.

(3) Elisa's solitude may be taken to symbolize the isolation of women—or of anyone—cut off from free and voluntary communication with others. She is wearing clothes that mask and hide her femininity, such as the large apron, the gloves, and the hat. This clothing—worth discussing in detail—symbolizes Elisa's suppressed life on the ranch. A similar instance of such symbolism stemming from the isolation of rural life is Minnie Wright in Glaspell's "A Jury of Her Peers" (page 155).

(4) The central symbol of the story, the chrysanthemums, is stressed in paragraphs 6, 8, 12, 27, 50–71 (especially 71), and 108–109. These flowers symbolize Elisa's strong sexual and nurturing power. Her connection with dirt, which she handles skillfully, symbolizes an earth-mother force. Her description of proper care of the buds in paragraph 71 suggests her love and satisfaction in growing things. Because she has no children on whom to bestow this talent, she transfers her force to the flowers.

(5) In the washing and dressing scene (paragraphs 93–98) Elisa wishes to make herself pretty and sexually attractive. The pumice is a normal means of sloughing off dead skin cells and uncovering live ones. For this reason it is a symbolic means of causing her sexuality to emerge, just as her care with her dress indicates her desire to be attractive.

(6) Elisa's responses, including her foreknowledge, her hurt, her an-

ger, and her private despair, are described in paragraphs 108–121. The dumped flowers symbolize the truncation of her creative, sexual desires.

WRITING TOPICS. The symbolism of: (a) The chrysanthemums. (b) The setting. (c) The washing scene. Elisa's plight and the role of women within a rural setting.

WORKS FOR COMPARISON WITH "THE CHRYSANTHEMUMS"

Anonymous, *The Myth of Atalanta*, 328
Atwood, *Variation on the Word Sleep*, 915
Dickinson, *Wild Nights—Wild Nights!*, 883
Wharton, *Roman Fever*, 459

Writing About Symbolism or Allegory, *pages 354–359*

By the time you work on this section you will already have been discussing the symbolism and allegory in a number of stories, and therefore an assignment will not come as a surprise to your students. The biggest problem they will likely ask about is what to say once they have identified a thing, character, situation, or response as a symbol, or once they have identified a narrative (or part of a narrative) as an allegory. Here the schemes on pages 354 and 355 might be introduced as aids for the development of subtopics for essays. You might wish to encourage students to develop their own tables or graphs.

As you teach the various ways to structure possible essays, you might wish to use some of the stories in this chapter. Certainly the sample essay (pages 357–358) offers an approach for an essay based on a number of separate symbols. This structure is easiest for most students. You might also use the symbolism of the flowers in Steinbeck's "The Chrysanthemums." This story is a fine example for showing the extent to which a symbol may pervade an entire story. It also illustrates the relationship of symbol to character.

Writing Topics for Symbolism and Allegory, *pages 359–360*

(1) The first topic may come as a surprise to those students who know the various parables separately, but who have never considered them as a group. The likeliest way for students to begin is to establish the moral or theological purposes of two, three, or more of the parables. Then, with this as the basis of comparison, they may consider aspects such as length, amount of detail, explanations within the Biblical text, and so on.

(2) The second topic is essentially a comparison-contrast assignment (see Appendix B). The additional questions are directions to guide students in the development of their essays.

(3) The point that students should aim at for the third question concerns the fact that religious ideas, which are abstract, are probably best understood through the concrete medium of symbolism (and allegory). Human minds being what they are, in other words, a specific and concrete approach is better than abstract discussion.

(4) The material about male-female relationships in "The Myth of Atalanta" should be clear to most students. What should be emphasized in relation to this assignment, therefore, is that Atalanta's story is virtually as old as Western civilization. Some students might wish to make much of this truth.

(5) The fifth assignment might very well cause students to raise questions about the various universal symbols they live with in daily life. Sometimes students respond to "images," since these are made important in aspects of life such as politics, advertising, religion, and social issues. The suggestions about the flag, water, and the bomb should also prompt students to develop these or other universal symbols.

(5) An assignment that students find challenging, and particular instructive, is the sixth one. If a student is living away from home, perhaps a dog, a cat, or a particular street or store might prove to be the central contextual symbol in that student's short story about characters back home. One student developed the symbol of the family doing the dishes after the evening meal. Another wrote about auto trips that the family took together. The point is that anything, even something seemingly unimportant, can be made symbolic if the writer takes care to give it the proper emphasis and importance.

Chapter Ten
Pages 361–413

Idea or Theme: The Meaning and the Message in Fiction

This chapter aims at introducing students to the meaning of the words *idea* and *theme*, and to the means by which they are made significant in fiction. The earlier chapters have actually been, in their ways, introductions to the use of fiction as idea. Thus *point of view* (Chapter 5) is a means by which authors dramatize ideas and make them authentic, and *symbolism* (Chapter 9) is a concrete means of rendering ideas. In addition, if you have discussed poetry, you may also wish to consider Chapter 23 in conjunction with your discussions about ideas.

Teaching this chapter will involve a good deal of discussion about what exactly is meant by the word *idea*. Related words that might lend clarification are *concept, thought, opinion, belief,* and *meaning. Conception, interpretation, motif, analysis,* and *explication* might also arise, together with others that your students might contribute. What is most important is that ideas should be expressed as sentences or assertions, for stories are genuinely dramatic renderings in narrative form of a moving idea. Thus the complete sentence, or assertion, as a form (page 361) should be stressed as an initial stage in the perceptions of ideas.

Ernest J. Gaines, *The Sky Is Gray, pages 367–386*

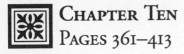

Although "The Sky Is Gray" is not a political document, but rather a story, it demonstrates a number of ideas. From the viewpoint of the child, the narrator, it dramatizes the problems that blacks face as a minority group: poverty, hunger, hardship, and systematic discrimination. It also dramatizes most of the views and solutions that have been raised about racial problems in the United States: passivity, evasion, religious refuge, and militancy. The elderly couple who shelter and feed the narrator and his mother demonstrate the idea that kindness and compassion are values that transcend political problems and solutions. Because the story contains so many perspectives, it should provoke extensive and thoughtful discussion among students.

Answers to the Study Questions, pages 386–387

(1) By using the eight-year-old child as the narrator, Gaines establishes a disinterested, innocent voice, who is able to report what he says and hears, but who is unsophisticated and who cannot therefore provide extensive commentary. A more mature narrator would feel compelled, in the light of the difficulties experienced by the boy and his mother, to explain, make comments, and generally become political or philosophical. The child, however, experiences things directly and reports them directly. With the child as the narrator, Gaines renders the situation, and therefore makes it a vivid experience for readers.

(2) The killing and eating of the birds is to be taken as a literal illustration that the impoverished and almost starving family needs the birds for food. James is unwilling to kill the creatures because he senses their innocence and inability to protect themselves, but his mother forces him to do so on the grounds that he, as an eight-year-old, needs to grow and therefore needs to do some of the unpleasant tasks required for maturity (paragraph 82). One might say that a major evil of poverty and hunger is that it forces people to act against their own wishes. Hence poverty demeans and enslaves the people who suffer it.

(3) After an introductory section about the life of the boy James and his family, the major action of "The Sky Is Gray" is the trip that James and his mother take to Bayonne to get treatment for James's toothache, together with the delay, pain, and kindness they find. In this way the story dramatizes a major example of their poverty and inequality. The delays in the dentist's office permit the exposition of the views of the minister and the young man, the negative experiences both outside in the sleet and inside in the hardware store and the café, and the positive experience with the elderly couple in their little store.

(4) The discussion in the waiting room brings out extremes of militancy, as represented by the young man, and patient endurance, as represented by the minister. After the minister leaves, the actual high point of this conflict is reached in paragraphs 220–230, particularly the young man's question to the nearby lady, "Name me one right that you have. One right, granted by the Constitution, that you can exercise in Bayonne."

It is this sort of radicalism, the story suggests, that may become a wave of the future. Certainly the young boy, James, immediately identifies with the young man's character and positions (paragraph 185). The minister's striking the young man demonstrates that anger and misunderstanding may keep people apart even when they should be allies (paragraphs 165–170). The young man's turning the other cheek therefore does not deter the minister from using force, but rather encourages it.

(5) The elderly couple in the little store, Helena and Ernest ("Alnest"), represent kindness and compassion. Helena recognizes that Octavia, James's mother, is a woman of spirit and pride, and therefore she does not phone the superior dentist. Helena wants to pursue her kindness to the point of giving Octavia an oversize portion of salt meat, but Octavia, insisting on her dignity, refuses it, accepting only the smaller portion. One may read this incident to say that blacks want no special favors, but only opportunity and fair treatment.

Writing topics. The meaning of the elderly couple in the store. The meaning of the discussion and conflict in the dentist's office. The dialect of the speaker. The character of the mother, Octavia.

Works for Comparison with "The Sky Is Gray"

Brooks, *Primer for Blacks*, 922
Hughes, *Harlem: A Dream Deferred*, 660
Hughes, *Mulatto*, 1439
Parédes, *The Hammon and the Beans*, 313
Whitecloud, *Blue Winds Dancing*, 119

James Joyce, *Araby, pages 387–391*

Much of Joyce's work has been called "fictionalized autobiography," a quality shown in "Araby," one of the stories in *Dubliners.* As a young child, Joyce lived on North Richmond Street, just like the narrator of the story. The bazaar which the narrator attends actually did take place in Dublin, from May 14 to 19, 1894, when Joyce was the same age as the narrator. It was called "Araby in Dublin," and was advertised as a "Grand Oriental Fete."

Students may wonder why the narrator expresses unexplained chagrin about himself at the end. This question cannot be easily answered without a discussion of the narrator's sense of guilt about his youthful feelings of love.

Answers to the Study Questions, page 391

(1) The idea is that youthful love is childish and foolish, but that it is also normal, overpowering, and creative. Ideally, memories like those the speaker is describing about his infatuation for Mangan's sister should be a cause for fondness, mingled perhaps with amusement. Much of the speaker's memory exhibits just such beauty. If the experience of the childhood "crush" produces unhappiness at the time it occurs, a mature understanding should be able to filter out and eliminate the childhood misgivings to achieve a celebration of time past. The speaker, however, does not indicate that this process has taken place, and hence Joyce is presenting a portrait of a narrator who is still a victim of childhood inhibitions.

(2) Before the narrator goes to Araby, this bazaar symbolizes for him his adoration of Mangan's sister and also an "Eastern enchantment" (paragraph 12) of mystic fulfillment of love. At the end it symbolizes unreality and unreachable hope which has been dashed by his adolescent lack of power and by the passive-aggressive and drunken uncle.

(3) From the first paragraph one might discover a good deal of submerged hostility toward home. For example, it is significant and also amusing that the speaker chooses the phrase "set the boys free" about the school, for these words are appropriate to a release from prison. The speaker almost literally endows the houses with a life that encourages decency, but which does not develop humanness and love. *Blind* is a normal word for a dead-end street, but it also is appropriate for a social group with no understanding of human impulses. The relationship of the first and last paragraphs is subtle but real, for the speaker demonstrates anger not only against himself, as at the end, but also against the culture out of which he came, as at the beginning.

(4) The narrator is an adult telling about events that occurred specifically to him when he was an early adolescent. If one considers the story as fictionalized autobiography, the time of the events can be determined as 1893–1894, with the narrator therefore being a boy of eleven or twelve. It is difficult to determine the age of the narrator at the time of the narration, except to note that he is not yet mature himself, for he still evidences embarrassment at his childhood feelings (see, for example, the end of paragraph 4). The effect of the age differential is to create detachment, if not total objectivity, about the events. The narrator, for example, seems distant enough from the prayerful "O Love" sequence to share the scene with readers despite the fact that it is amusing (paragraph 6; one

might assume that the narrator does not realize that the action is amusing). For comparison, a similar use of point of view may be found in Frank O'Connor's "first Confession" (page 520). See also Parédes's "The Hammon and the Beans" (page 313).

WRITING TOPICS. The point of view in "Araby." The ideas about love and inhibition. Setting and idea. The symbolism of the fair. The development of ideas. The idea of childhood love. The dead priest as a symbol.

WORKS FOR COMPARISON WITH "ARABY"

Keats, *La Belle Dame Sans Merci*, 806
O'Connor, *First Confession*, 520
Soto, *Oranges*, 992
Wharton, *The Muse's Tragedy*, 418

D.H. LAWRENCE, *The Horse Dealer's Daughter, pages 391–403*

"The Horse Dealer's Daughter" is typical of Lawrence's stories about the power of sexuality in life. Both main characters, Mabel Pervin and Dr. Jack Fergusson, have reached an impasse in their lives by themselves, and can go in new directions only when they realize their sexual needs. Despite their obvious reluctance and inexperience with their emotions, both Fergusson and Mabel realize that they need each other for their fulfillment. This realization gives them both confidence and doubt at the same time (see paragraphs 142, 150, 152, 158, 159, and 191). From paragraph 142 to the end, Lawrence takes great pains to emphasize their ambiguous feelings. As they approach change and growth, in other words, they also become apprehensive. Character development is not without cost.

Answers to the Study Questions, page 403

(1) By beginning the story with the breakup of the Pervin household, Lawrence stresses the idea that a central force is necessary for stability, and that instability and pain result once that force is gone (he could also be illustrating the need for young adults to establish their own ways of life independently of family ties). Some adjectives describing the scene are *desolate, desultory, dreary, strange, sullen-looking,* and *impassive,* all from paragraphs 2 and 3. These adjectives underscore the instability and pain being experienced by the brothers and sister in the disintegrating Pervin family.

(2) In paragraph 7, Joe Pervin, the eldest of the family, is compared to the massive draft horses. These are slow but strong (having a "slumbrous strength" [paragraph 6]), and are in harness, as Joe will be once he

marries the daughter of the steward of the nearby estate. In paragraph 20, Joe is also compared to horses because of his appearance when walking and speaking. In addition, another brother, Fred Henry (paragraph 11), is compared to horses, for he is under the control "of the situations of life," even though he masters horses easily. Because the horses, though strong, need the external control of reins, the idea seems to be that those without love are without the strength they need to guide their own destinies.

(3) Mabel is "rather short, sullen looking" with a face of "impassive fixity" (paragraph 3). We are to understand that she has felt the loss of her mother deeply, but has appreciated the power of being mistress of the household for the following ten years. She has developed no friendships with either women or men (paragraphs 95–97), and treats her brothers with contempt (paragraph 96). At the beginning of the story, she has nowhere to go, and has made no plans. Lawrence's speaker stresses that she has reached the end (paragraph 98). Apparently she does not want even temporary residence with her sister Lucy (paragraph 12). Her dilemma is that she does not know where to turn.

(4) In paragraph 103 the speaker notes "some mystical element" that touches Fergusson as he looks at Mabel in the cemetery. This power is further explained in paragraph 104 as having the strength of a drug. When Jack sees Mabel attempting to kill herself, he does not feel alarm, but fears the possibility that he might "lose her altogether" (paragraph 108). These two examples suggest that he is slowly realizing his emotional tie with her. The idea is apparently that love may develop even when (perhaps *especially* when) the individuals involved do not realize what is happening to them.

(5) Fergusson's rescue of Mabel is described in paragraphs 110–115. The setting is wetness, dankness, muckiness, and a foul smell (the smell is mentioned a number of times). To determine how this setting reinforces mood and idea, one must conclude that Lawrence, by the rescue, is suggesting that even though unpleasantness is necessary in life, and though at times the environment is ugly and threatening, there can nevertheless be good results.

(6) In paragraph 150, Lawrence's narrator emphasizes Fergusson's lack of intention about Mabel, and thus the story brings out the idea that love is overwhelming and irresistible. To live without love leads people, literally, to the dead end in which both Mabel and Jack find themselves in the first part of the story. Therefore, the discovery of love is a power that cannot be resisted, for without love there is no life.

(7) The reason for which Lawrence emphasizes the ambiguity of love is that he is not espousing any easy answers: All problems will continue, including many of the personal reservations that people have about each other and themselves. Love, however, is the Lawrentian basis of life. The sample essay (pages 406–408) deals further with this idea.

Writing topics. The idea about the barrenness of a loveless life as exemplified in the three brothers. The ideas represented by the horses and the harness. Lawrence's complex ideas about love as shown by the pond. The meaning of the wet, soggy, musty clothing in relationship to love.

Works for Comparison with "The Horse Dealer's Daughter"

Frost, *A Line Storm Song*, 895
Henley, *Am I Blue*, 1403
Joyce, *Araby*, 387

Irene Zabytko, *Home Soil, pages 403–408*

"Home Soil" centers upon the experiences and the guilt of a Ukrainian American, the narrator, and his son, Bohdan. The narrator committed a war crime in Ukraine during World War II, and he still replays "that scene in . . . [his] mind almost forty years after it happened" (paragraph 33). His son Bohdan, who has lost his Ukrainian roots (he prefers to be called "Bob" rather than "Bohdan" [paragraph 4]), has undergone some similar but undisclosed experience in the Vietnamese War.

The story itself takes place on a Sunday, the first section being in church (paragraphs 1–36) and the second at the narrator's home. The parallel experiences of father and son reach a climax in paragraph 36, when the narrator speaks of the impossibility of finding inner peace even though he is leading a totally peaceful and successful life. The son's tears (paragraphs 40–42) show that he feels the same loss of inner peace. Interestingly, there is no solution to the existence of guilt. As much as the narrator can say is "I don't die. Instead I go to the garden" (paragraph 37), an action that suggests the irrevocability of inhuman actions and the permanence of guilt.

Answers to the Study Questions, page 408

(1) The narrator is living in Chicago, and is doing well financially because he owns a restaurant and an apartment building. We learn that

he, as a young Ukrainian during the Nazi occupation of Ukraine after the 1941 invasion, participated in the Holocaust. He wrote pro-German propaganda and especially, on one occasion, forced a group of Jews into a cattle car to be taken to an extermination camp (paragraphs 31–36). This event remains fixed in his mind because even though he was young at the time he participated in an inexcusable atrocity.

(2) The question about the exercise of power during warfare has been constant as long as there has been war. The narrator confesses that "I enjoyed that power, until it seeped into my veins and poisoned my soul" (paragraph 33). Those who have been responsible for the deaths of others, even though they can lead outwardly normal lives afterward, can never escape the memory of the past. The narrator hence wishes that he had sought the family of the Jewish girl so that he could have confessed his responsibility to them. Even the thought that they might have condemned him is the only hope of absolution that he could ever hope to achieve.

(3) The complexity of the story is indicated by the tears of the narrator's son, Bohdan. The two, father and son, have obviously had parallel experiences with wartime atrocities, although we do not learn the precise nature of what Bohdan has been through. In light of the story's first-person point of view, we cannot learn what Bohdan has done because Bohdan does not speak to the narrator about his experiences. The parallel is made complete in paragraph 30, when the narrator observes that Bohdan may never tell him what happened in Vietnam. The narrator then confesses, "I never told anyone either." Some ideas that underlie this commonness of wartime experience are that fighting is never over, that people are called upon in warfare to engage in hostilities that produce death, that they can never forget that they have caused death even though they may find excuses for their actions, and that people and governments never learn from past experience to avoid the future guilt that state warfare creates in its citizens who participate in war.

(4) This statement suggests that maybe the narrator knows what it takes to crush someone's skull, and that in the story he has not told everything about his wartime experiences in Ukraine. There is a layer here, in other words, of something more sinister than the wartime action to which he confesses in paragraphs 31–36.

Writing topics. The ideas about warfare brought out in the story. The character of the speaker. The guilt that is clearly disturbing Bohdan. The apparent success of the narrator's new life in the United States.

Works for Comparison with "Home Soil"

Forché, *Because One Is Always Forgotten*, 943
Georgakas, *Hiroshima Crewman*, 944
Hardy, *The Man He Killed*, 557
Northrup, *Ogichidag*, 559
Northrup, *Wahbegan*, 971
Ozick, *The Shawl*, 251

Writing About Meaning in Fiction, *pages 408–412*

In the classroom use of this section, the brief examples of interpretive commentary on page 409 might provide a good beginning for analysis. Thus the very first example illustrates the method by which details of the text may be directly channeled into the discussion of ideas. You might stress here that the two sentences are designed as a model for the discussion of ideas in fiction. Obviously, a complete essay will be longer and more detailed. But students should be persuaded to see the interwoven discussion of (1) story content, (2) artistic presentation, and (3) interpretive commentary to explicate ideas.

The six models for the body of an essay, on pages 409–410, are designed to encourage student experimentation with the ways in which essays may be developed. The aim should be to use as many of these as possible and to query students on the material that might be included in a full-scale essay. The sample essay on pages 410–412 provides an example of how the first model may be developed. Should you choose to confine your students to a development based on one of the other models, it would be best to spend some time in class discussing the particular approach, for the models are designed to start processes of thought, not to demonstrate completeness of thought.

If you have enough time, you might discuss parts of the sample essay to show how story materials may be shaped in an essay to substantiate an idea. The fourth paragraph of the sample essay connects (a) Jack's common cold and his accidental seeing of Mabel to (b) his discovery of love and thus to being restored as an individual. It is instructive to emphasize how this paragraph illustrates a possible pattern of development like those which students themselves should try to establish in their own essays.

Writing Topics about Idea or Theme, *pages 412–413*

(1) This first assignment is designed to relate ideas to responses and to separate personal responses from intellectual ones. The problem in the assignment results from the difficulty that students—and all people, for that matter—have in being objective and impersonal about ideas and values which they may hold deeply. If students have difficulty in choosing a story to discuss, you might confine them to any of the stories in this chapter.

(2) This type of essay is one that students find particularly congenial because it introduces the concept of economic equality and applies it to a particular story. Students will have little difficulty in finding many examples throughout "The Sky Is Gray" which demonstrate the ill effects of adverse economic circumstances and their inhibitions upon human rights.

(3) The third question is designed for comparison-contrast, and would be best developed on the basis of a common theme or idea (as in "Home Soil" and "Soldier's Home," where the point of comparison might be a young man's return home after participating in war). Or, an essay might deal with a thread like the effects of marriage on a female character ("The Story of an Hour" and "The Yellow Wallpaper"), and so on.

(4) The final assignment is difficult because students, like most writers, begin a story with a specific event in mind, not a concept. The five possible topics might therefore need some fleshing out, for students can begin writing on these topics once they get some notion of how to proceed from the basic statement of the idea.

Chapter Eleven
Pages 414–468

A Career in Fiction: A Collection of Stories by Edith Wharton

A. Teaching Edith Wharton

The four stories by Edith Wharton lend themselves readily to a number of unifying topics. The major one is Wharton's perceptive depiction of character. In treating this topic you might find it helpful for students to review Chapter 4, on character. Another major topic showing Wharton's great skill is the complex intertwining of past life with present existence. Each one of the stories, to a greater or lesser degree, touches on this relationship. For example, the dead hand of the past reaches out literally to Kenneth Ashby of "Pomegranate Seed," to leave written reminders of his permanent ties with his dead wife. Similarly, the past touches every aspect of Mrs. Anerton's character in "The Muse's Tragedy," and, even though she would like to build a new life in the present, she ironically submits to the power of the past. To a similar degree, each of the other stories may be studied for this relationship.

Another unifying topic might be the irony with which Wharton invests her stories (see Chapter 8, on Tone). The conclusion of "Roman Fever" is perhaps the strongest example of irony, but "The Other Two" and "The Muse's Tragedy" are also heavily interlaced with irony.

Other possible unifying topics are these:

1. The relationship of men and women, with the most complex story being "The Other Two."
2. The social background of the stories (class, customs of travel, husband-wife behavior, work, habits).
3. The persistence of innocence and dedicated behavior within the fabric of experience.

4. The construction of a realistic world within Wharton's characters live, (especially "The Muse's Tragedy" and "The Other Two").
5. Wharton's use of dramatic dialogue and indirect discourse.
6. Wharton's treatment of women in their relationships with men and their connection with the world at large.
7. Wharton's use of allusions and symbols. These may be both literal (e.g., the Roman Forum, pouring coffee, a mysterious letter on a table, works by famous artists) and literary (the myth of Persephone, the works of a dead poet).

As a writing assignment, the extended comparison-contrast essay described in Appendix B provides convenient directions for dealing with a number of separate stories. Through the exploration of one of the topics just listed, as these topics are significant in Wharton's stories viewed as a group, students may achieve the goal of illuminating Wharton as a writer. In addition, if students find that they might reinforce their points about Wharton by referring to works by other writers, they should be encouraged to make these additional references (see also the sections below on "Works for Comparison . . .").

B. Answers to the Questions for the Four Edith Wharton Stories

The Muse's Tragedy, pages 418–427

This story is about a love that develops between two people of high culture, but, nevertheless, their love misses. The ingredients for love are there, and both people recognize their mutual attraction, but the pull of the past is too strong. The public image is so overriding that it suppresses private desires, and therefore the story is ultimately a sad one, like Wharton's story "Pomegranate Seed" (page 440) and the novel *The Age of Innocence.*

"The Muse's Tragedy" is also a fascinating exercise in point of view. It begins in the limited third-person, with the point of view character being Danyers, a young scholar and critic. The situation is highly complex, in keeping with Wharton's ability to create a complete and entire world in her fiction. Danyers becomes attached to Mrs. Anerton, the fabled "muse" of the writer, Vincent Rendle, whom Danyers admires above all writers. The things that Danyers learns, and that therefore we learn, come to us through his conversations with others and then through his conversations with Mrs. Anerton herself. We therefore see her and her relationship with Rendle as Danyers sees them. In keeping with this point of view, the observations in the story about the situation, such as the contrast between Mrs. Anerton as Sylvia, the private woman, and Egeria, the ancient symbol of the public, almost oracular woman (paragraph 39), are presumably taking place within Danyers's mind.

Wharton carries on two thirds of the story using Danyers as the central focus, but the final third marks a total shift into the first person of Mrs. Anerton, who expresses herself in the form of a letter to Danyers (page 423, paragraph 55). Readers may conclude that Wharton had created so complex a situation that she could no longer sustain describing it from a male perspective. The abrupt shift therefore marks a total change of insight, from the male to the female, for the story requires an "inside explanation" of matters that absolutely cannot be explained and hinted at, as they have been during parts I and II of the story.

Answers to the Study Questions, page 427

(1) Wharton successfully creates a fictional life for her characters, so much so that the reader wonders where reality ends and fiction begins. By introducing the young scholar, Danyers, Wharton introduces the topic of the great poet, Vincent Rendle, who had set the literary world ablaze with his *Sonnets to Sylvia*. Initially, Danyers is interested in Mrs. Anerton—the Sylvia of the poems—not because of herself, but rather because of what she can tell him, first hand, about Rendle.

As the story progresses, however, the interests of Danyers shift. From the first enthusiastic conversations about Rendle, Danyers slowly begins to appreciate Mrs. Anerton as a woman. The conclusion of the story's second section indicates that the two plan to meet in Venice to discuss the book that Danyers is going to write about Rendle, with Mrs. Anerton supplying the information and Danyers transcribing it to create a definitive volume on the great poet.

(2) Mrs. Anerton's character is most clearly revealed in the third section of the story, which is entirely taken up with her letter to Danyers explaining why she has left Venice and why she will not marry him: This is because, despite everything, she fears that she may have no more than a paper reality in his eyes, despite his declaration of love and proposal of

marriage. She does not want to become "a pretty little essay with a margin" (paragraph 77). She also explains that, to a degree, she has been using Danyers to test her own attractiveness to a real, living man, and not to an abstraction like Rendle. She explains her action with reference to her literary pedestalization by Rendle: Despite Rendle's acknowledged ardent sonnets to Sylvia, he never loved her. She has suffered because of this fact, because people suppose that her life has been rich with love, while she has had no love at all. Rendle's pursuit of the unnamed young woman, and his farewell poems to love (*Love's Viaticum,* paragraph 66) demonstrate that Rendle's idealization of Sylvia had no connection with his own interests. A poignant indication of Rendle's lack of love is shown in the way Mrs. Anerton prepared Rendle's letters for publication. She inserted asterisks to indicate where personal matters between Rendle and her have been omitted. She explains that she had included these to preserve the public fiction of love, but that this was all a sham because "*there was nothing to leave out*" (paragraph 63).

Finally, however, her having tested her power with Danyers has given her fulfillment. The test of her power—and of her capacity for love—is that never once, in their month together in Venice, did they speak about Rendle. Indeed, she has been particularly gratified to learn that Danyers has grown to hate Rendle. However, she has realized that her public image transcends her individual desires. For this reason she writes to Danyers explaining that she cannot marry him and is running away.

(3) Danyers at first seems to be interested in Mrs. Anerton only because of her role as the fictional, pedestalized Sylvia, but he develops genuine love for her as a real, living woman. His "dislike [of] Rendle's way of walking in unannounced" (paragraph 48) suggests his altered interests in her. At first, Mrs. Anerton is a living abstraction in his eyes, but she gains both reality and Danyers's love as a result of their real, actual being together.

(4) In the interval between sections II and III of the story, we conclude that Danyers and Mrs. Anerton were with each other for a four week period. Although the ostensible reason for the meeting was for Mrs. Anerton to tell Danyers about Rendle, we also conclude that the two never once discussed either Rendle or the book. Instead they learned about each other as persons, and the four-week period was climaxed with Danyers asking Mrs. Anerton to marry him.

(5) The shift (page 423) to Mrs. Anerton's letter—and hence the total shift to her first-person point of view—marks a climax of the story's

movement from the public Mrs. Anerton to the private one. In her letter she reveals herself as a complete person who totally understands the irony of her situation. Her experience with Danyers has given her a freedom she has never had before. Her decision to run away from him, and to keep on running, represents her choice about her dilemma: either to accept Danyers and to a degree give up her role as Sylvia, or to give up her newly found love but maintain her lifeless existence in the pages of Vincent Rendle.

At first, the shift to the letter is somewhat confusing, but it becomes more clear as it progresses, and it is, finally, successful, although students may wish to discuss their responses to the abruptness of the change.

(6) The nature of the muse's "tragedy" is that the fictional world of literature, in which people like Mrs. Anerton achieve an artificial reality, character, and immortality, destroys the real world of the present, or renders people in the present incapable of possessing lives of their own. In short, the tragedy is that the unreal existence of fiction and imagination becomes more real than the real-life people who have fashioned this existence. As Mrs. Anerton writes, the sonnets were "A cosmic philosophy, not a love poem; addressed to Woman, not to a woman!" (paragraph 62).

WRITING TOPICS. The story's changing points of view. The developing love of Danyers and Mrs. Anerton. What is the muse's "tragedy"? Wharton's use of dialogue.

WORKS FOR COMPARISON WITH "THE MUSE'S TRAGEDY"

Chopin, *The Story of an Hour*, 308
O'Shaughnessy, *A Love Symphony*, 693
Paley, *Goodbye and Good Luck*, 531
Rossetti, *Echo*, 744
Swenson, *Women*, 919
Whur, *The First-Rate Wife*, 679

The Other Two, pages 427–439

When "The Other Two" was published, in 1904, divorce was unusual, and sometimes scandalous, because adultery was the usual complaint in divorce cases (the complaint that Wharton had lodged against her husband, Teddy, in 1913). Although Wharton's narrator provides no more than intimations about the adulterous background of Alice's two earlier marriages, we may conclude that Alice's reputation rests on the wrongdoing—real or fictional—of her divorced husbands. Students may need reminding that divorce was usually not allowable in certain circles in the United States until relatively recently. It is commonly acknowledged, for example, that President Franklin D. Roosevelt, the creator of the New Deal, would have been ruined politically if his wife Eleanor had sued for divorce because of an early love affair. One of the causes for which Adlai Stevenson was not elected president in 1952 (and 1956) was that he had been divorced. It was not until 1980 that a divorced person was elected President of the United States. So, in 1904, divorce was unusual. People mostly were consigned to the private unhappiness of bad marriages in preference to public divorce.

It is in this context that "The Other Two" should be taken. The subject of divorce was serious. People often did not know how to treat divorced people (witness Waythorn's embarrassment when Varick first visits him in his office, paragraph 88), and sometimes divorced people underwent great difficulty in maintaining normal social relationships—an aspect that Wharton also treats in the novel *The Age of Innocence* and in the stories "Souls Belated," and "The Reckoning." As Newland Archer says in *The Age of Innocence*, "our legislation favors divorce—our social customs don't" (Chapter 12).

Answers to the Study Questions, page 439

(1) In "The Other Two," Wharton exploits the more comic aspects of divorce. She describes none of the anguish and grief of Alice's previous marriages, and, in fact, suggests that Alice may have exaggerated the previous unpleasantness. Indeed, once Alice announces to her third husband that her first husband must make a visit to her sick daughter, she is told to put all embarrassment out of her mind, which she promptly—and amusingly—does. In addition, the experience of Waythorn is in no way affected by his being the third husband of Alice. As he learns about the "other two," he finds that they are ordinary, pleasant human beings, not monsters, and he is able to get along well with both of them. The manners of the world which Waythorn inhabits prevents conversations from becoming personal and difficult, and hence he maintains cordial relationships with the other two.

It is for this reason that Wharton is able to preserve a wry treatment of the subject. Ironically, Alice forgets how Waythorn takes his coffee, and thus puts cognac into it for him in the way that Varick prefers his (paragraph 72). To avoid embarrassing Waythorn, Alice lies by denying that she had seen Haskett when he first comes to see Lily, her daughter. Wharton has Waythorn think of Alice as being " 'as easy as an old shoe'—

a shoe that too many feet had worn"—a domestic image that is comically reductive as it also points out that divorced people do not lose their humanity just because they get divorced (paragraph 143). Life itself overtakes custom because people themselves have common interests. Thus, Waythorn deals with Varick in an important financial venture that will be profitable not only to Varick but to Waythorn's firm. Haskett complains to Waythorn about Lily's governess, a matter of household employment in the Waythorn residence that Haskett has a concern in because of his interest in Lily. Life goes on.

In all these circumstances, Wharton creates humor with the contrast between what is ordinarily expected of a divorce situation—the strained relationships, the possible antagonisms, the renewal of mental injury and pain—and facts like the need that people have for tea at five o'clock. In short, the aftereffects of divorce are not terrible. The people involved are people, just like anyone else—no more, no less.

(2) As the story opens, Waythorn and Alice are newly married—they have been united for only a week—and Waythorn is still learning about his wife. He is an understanding man, and hence he draws conclusions about how Alice has been shaped for him by the other two: "he perceived that Haskett's commonness had made Alice worship good breeding, while Varick's liberal construction of the marriage bond had taught her to value the conjugal virtues; so that he was deeply indebted to his predecessors for the devotion which made his life easy if not inspiring" (paragraph 146). Despite his unusual circumstances, then, he accepts the values of the other two and eventually accepts the two men as well.

(3, 4) The most notable aspect of the point of view of "The Other Two" is the narrator's scrupulous establishment of observations and conclusions as Waythorn experiences them. Waythorn is newly married to Alice, and has learned about "the other two" through her. He has concluded, also from Alice, that the two men were offensive in ways that he does not fully learn. When he meets the others, therefore, he comes with negative presuppositions. But, with the point of view being limited to him, his own experience enables him to formulate his own opinions, and also the opinions of readers. Although Waythorn believes that he and Haskett live in different worlds, he develops strong faith in Haskett's inoffensiveness, honesty, and integrity, and great respect for the sacrifices that Haskett has been making for his daughter (paragraphs 125, 147). He feels a social kinship with Varick, finds Varick an obliging business associate, and notes that there is "something pleasant about his smile" (paragraph 90). These discoveries depend on the maintenance of objectivity about both Haskett and Varick, and on the explanations that Waythorn might give himself.

Writing Topics: The story's tone, particularly at the conclusion. Alice's character. Wharton's control of point of view. The situation of divorce, and implied attitudes toward it. The characters of the "other two."

Works for Comparison with "The Other Two"

Chekhov, *The Bear*, 1038
Muske, *Real Estate*, 809
Heaney , *Valediction*, 950
Petronius, *The Widow of Ephesus*, 60

Pomegranate Seed, pages 440–459

One of Wharton's favorite genres was the ghost story, in which she treated the coexistence of the unusual and "eerie" along with the ordinary. She wrote many such tales. In her critical work "Telling a Short Story," she explains that the goal of a ghost story is to grip the reader's throat with "fear, simple shivering animal fear." With this goal, the typical Wharton ghost story shrouds reality with vagueness and apprehension; clarity is shunned as much in this sort of story as it is sought in her other stories. In "Pomegranate Seed" Wharton features the appearance of mysterious notes and the strained behavior of the principal male character, concluded by a disappearance.

This disappearance is unexplained, but the story provides enough details to permit the conclusion that the major character, Kenneth Ashby, has been removed into another world, the world of the "eerie" (Wharton's word for the power of ghost stories). Even so, there is a suggestion that the disappearance is not an actual disappearance, but that the character himself will soon provide an explanation (paragraph 253). This conclusion is problematic, but should we presume that Wharton here is conjuring up a ghost world which releases its inhabitants for periodic visits among the living, just as the ancient god Hades permitted his half-time wife, Persephone, to return from the Underworld to the flowery fields of Enna?

Answers to the Study Questions, page 459

(1) The title of the story is partially explained by the excerpt from Wharton's letter quoted on page 440. This explanation, however, needs filling out. In ancient mythology Hades, the Lord of the Underworld, falls in love with Persephone and takes her into his kingdom, where she

becomes queen. When her mother Ceres, the Goddess of Corn and Harvests, learns of the abduction, she petitions Zeus to restore her daughter to earth and to life. The condition of return is that Persephone should not eat anything while in the kingdom of Hades. But the truth is that she eats some pomegranate seeds, and hence cannot be returned permanently. An arrangement is therefore made for her to spend one half the year on earth and the other half in the Underworld.

It was in this way that the ancients explained the seasons: When Persephone was in the Underworld, the earth was cold and barren, in accord with the sorrow of Ceres; when Persephone returned to earth, Ceres would be happy and make the earth warm, thus permitting the growth and harvest of crops.

It is somewhat difficult to fit the myth exactly to the story, but one may suggest some parallels: Kenneth Ashby is like Persephone, for his wife has died and he has undergone great sorrow. He could stay on earth, despite the pull toward death, as long as he doesn't remarry. But he does marry again—with Charlotte—and the marriage, like Persephone's eating the pomegranate seed, becomes the cause for the epistolary summonses that appear regularly on the hall table.

(2) It is in Wharton's use of comparisons and similes that she is most liberal in expressing the ghostly world that impinges on the everyday world. A few examples will suffice: "she felt that her husband was being dragged away from her into some mysterious bondage" (paragraph 144), "it was the clutch of a man who felt himself slipping over a precipice" (paragraph 149), "like an indistinguishable figure prowling on the threshold" (paragraph 173), "as she pushed about the familiar objects his own hands had so lately touched, they sent through her the icy chill emanating from the little personal effects of someone newly dead. In the deep silence of the room the tearing of the paper as she slit the envelope sounded like a human cry" (paragraph 212). While the confines of reality and probability restrict the story itself, Wharton has no such confinement with her comparisons. Therefore she freely uses the comparisons to imply that there are ghostly forces at work beyond our ordinary earthly perceptions.

(3) Because of the need to preserve a semblance of verisimilitude, Wharton does not reveal the content of the letters. They have been, after all, sent to Kenneth, and the story's point of view—with its focus on Charlotte—gives us an objective and dramatic view of Kenneth. His state of mind and his reactions to the letters are revealed to us only as Charlotte perceives them. Despite the difficulty of actually making out what

the letters say, it is clear that Kenneth can read them, and that they hold a terrible power over him. Charlotte recognizes their strength but can only guess about what they contain. When she and Mrs. Ashby try to read the last letter, however, Charlotte is unable to say anything more definite than this: "I can make out something like 'mine'—oh, and 'come.' It might be 'come' " (paragraph 222). It is likely that the letter, which Kenneth never sees, may be no more than a reiteration of an earlier command that Kenneth had received. In any event, the letters bring about his disappearance.

Of course, a fuller explanation of the letters would satisfy our desire to know the exact nature of what has been happening, but it would also destroy Wharton's mystery. In no way, therefore, would an explanation make the story superior.

(4) Because "Pomegranate Seed" is a ghost story, it is not Wharton's goal to develop the characters to any great extent. Nevertheless it is true that the story's effect depends on the characterizations of Kenneth and Charlotte. We learn that Kenneth's fidelity to Elsie, his dead wife, was deep, that her personality dominated his, and that his grief at her dying was great. This trait of deep love and strong bonding is important, because the letters would otherwise not have any power over him. Again, from "Telling a Short Story," Wharton states that the ghost story depends on what she calls "pathological conditions—conditions of body or mind outside the field of normal experience." What she presents of Kenneth, therefore, is enough to establish that his condition is truly pathological.

Charlotte is the fully developed character of the story, and her major characteristic is tenacity. Her affection for Kenneth, her suspicion about old entanglements, her confrontation with Kenneth, and her urging him to go away from the house—are all responses to a situation she cannot respond to in anything resembling a normal way. Her opening the letter is essential to our understanding that there are ghostly influences over Kenneth, but her decision to do so, with the consent of her mother-in-law, is also a high point in her desperate but tenacious search to discover what is happening.

(5) One might claim that the story is to be read symbolically and allegorically. As a symbol, the power that the dead Elsie has over Kenneth may be construed to refer to the traditions and conditions that cumulatively shape human life and character. In effect, the traits and habits of the hundreds, thousands, and millions of people who are long gone are continually influencing the present, just as Elsie maintains her hold over Kenneth. The discoveries and theories of previous generations have a simi-

lar governing influence over the ways in which we see and live, even though we may believe that we are constantly free in the things we do. For this reason, "Pomegranate Seed" is a brief allegory of life. Human beings constantly do something that is forbidden (e.g., eating pomegranate seeds, remarrying despite a previous commitment). Once the forbidden thing is done, the consequences—producing either conscious or unconscious guilt—are deleterious or even disastrous. Students might contribute additional interpretations about the symbolism and allegory of "Pomegranate Seed."

Writing Topics. Wharton's use of the "eerie" in this story. The importance of Charlotte's character in the mystery. The symbolic and allegorical value of the story. Wharton's use of point of view in "Pomegranate Seed." The relationship of the ancient myth to the story.

Works for Comparison with "Pomegranate Seed"

Chopin, *The Story of an Hour*, 308
Collins, *Schoolsville*, 547
García Márquez, *A Very Old Man with Enormous Wings*, 486
Pickthall, *The Worker in Sandalwood*, 341
Strand, *The Remains*, 996

Roman Fever, pages 459–468

"Roman Fever" is an ironic story about the past and present relationships of two women who are of "ripe but well-cared-for middle age" (paragraph 1). The two women, Alida Slade and Grace Ansley, have been rivals and then cordial friends. They are definitely not warmly attached to each other, but their manners permit them to carry on their normal societal relationship. The scene is Rome, overlooking the characteristic ancient tourist attractions, and the dialogue between the two women marks the climax of their long relationship. Their conversation is not so much a development of their characters as a set of spontaneous conversational decisions leading to a final explanation of hostile feelings that have simmered throughout a lifetime. Wharton comments on the irony of their situation thus: "So these two ladies visualized each other, each through the wrong end of her little telescope" (paragraph 24).

Answers to the Study Questions, page 468

(1) The title refers to malaria, a disease that until this century was attributed to "bad air," and not to the Anopheles mosquitoes that actu-

ally transmit it. The disease is important in the past of both women because one of them had contracted it when young, but the events both leading up to the disease and the aftereffects have lived on in the minds of both, and the revelations about their motives and feelings become clear as Wharton develops the story.

(2) The two widowed women have adult daughters, Jenny Slade and Barbara Ansley, who are leaving their mothers to themselves to go on an expedition with a number of eminently eligible Italian bachelors. It is expected that Barbara, who is "brilliant" (i.e., charming, popular), will return as the fiancée of the most eligible of the bachelors. Alida and Grace are left alone on the restaurant terrace, from which they can see the Palatine, the Forum, and the Colosseum. As the afternoon passes, they reminisce about their past life in both Rome and New York, where for many years they had been across-the-street neighbors. Their conversation discloses that Alida had married a man, Delphin Slade, whom Grace had also loved and wanted. In addition, we learn that Alida had been ruthless when young, for she wanted Delphin as hers alone. As a result, she had written a note to Grace, as if from Delphin, asking her to meet him at the Colosseum just after dark—a place where "Roman fever," or malaria, was a great danger (one recalls that Henry James's Daisy Miller dies as a result of malaria contracted at the Colosseum).

Alida confesses this ruse to Grace, defending her action by saying that she didn't want Grace to die, but only to be out of the picture long enough so that she could marry Delphin, with whom she was engaged. Certainly, this action demonstrates a vicious strain of jealousy, cruelty, and vindictiveness on Alida's part, if not criminal negligence (Wharton ironically calls her a "dark lady," paragraph 7). That she chooses to reveal her action to Grace at the time of the story may represent an affirmation of her vindictiveness, for she states that she envies Grace because she believes that Barbara, Grace's daughter, is superior to Jenny, her daughter. Throughout the story, Wharton lets us into Alida's character through silent, snideful comments, such as "Grace Ansley was always old-fashioned" (paragraph 10). In addition, Alida is also capable of surface insult, as when she wonders aloud to Grace how such apparently meek and innocuous ("exemplary") people as Grace and her husband, Horace, could have produced so vital and vibrant a daughter as Barbara (paragraph 36).

By contrast with Alida, Grace, who is small and pale, is portrayed as the embodiment of charm, distinction, sweetness, sympathy, and grace (her name) that Alida, so many years before, perceived as a threat in her relationship with Delphin. In the story, Grace emerges as a kind and tolerant woman. When Alida explains her ruse with the letter, for example, Grace's response is not anger but rather sorrow (paragraph 112). In addition, Grace also possesses determination and strength, for we learn that she actually had gone to meet Delphin Slade at the Colosseum, and that the two had made love. The irony in Wharton's portrayal of Grace's character is that Alida believes that Grace has lived her life on the pathetic memory of a letter from Delphin that Delphin never wrote. However, at the story's ending Grace reveals that Barbara—her daughter with Delphin, *not* Horace—is really the living embodiment of her memory. In other words, the joke is on Alida, not Grace, for it was Alida's deceit that brought Grace and Delphin together, though Alida had a totally opposite motive.

(3) The entire ironic situation between the two women is revealed as they sit together on the terrace overlooking the Colosseum (where Grace had conceived Barbara). Wharton plants many clues about the situation—Alida's jealousy of Grace, her public ridicule of Grace and Horace, her admiration of Barbara, her difficulty in believing that Grace and Horace could have had so "dynamic" a daughter, the way in which Grace herself had informed Alida about the vicious great aunt who had sent a rival sister to the Colosseum to get malaria (and die), the difficulty of getting into the Colosseum after dark, and Alida's "blind fury" in writing the false letter to Grace. The irony of the conclusion begins with Grace's explanations of her visit to the Colosseum, her two-month illness with "Roman fever," and her quick marriage to Horace so that Barbara had been born seven months after the marriage. The surprise, of course, is her statement that she had responded to the "letter" and that therefore Delphin had agreed to the meeting.

Writing Topics. The importance of setting in the story. The characters of Alida or Grace. Wharton's use of irony. Wharton's use of conversation to reveal past motives and actions. What is the nature of the Roman "fever"?

Works for Comparison with "Roman Fever"

Glaspell, *A Jury of Her Peers*, 155
Laurents, *The Turning Point* (film scene), 1588
Mansfield, *Miss Brill*, 202
Shakespeare, *A Midsummer Night's Dream*, 1325

Chapter Twelve
Pages 469–543

Additional Stories

Toni Cade Bambara, *Raymond's Run, pages 469–474*

The speaker of the story is "Squeaky" (Hazel Elizabeth Deborah Parker), who describes herself as "a poor black girl who really can't afford to buy shoes and a new dress you only wear once a lifetime cause it won't fit next year" (paragraph 14). Her narrative is an account of the events before and immediately after a Police Athletic League track competition in the fifty-yard dash, which she wins over her rival Gretchen, a new girl in the neighborhood.

Squeaky's speech is plain and colloquial, with many characteristics of Black idiom, such as, for example, "smart mouths" and "I much rather" (paragraph 2), "I never walks" (5), "me and Raymond" as a subject (13), and the just-mentioned "cause" for "because" (14). The situation of the narrative is that Squeaky is apparently speaking to an unnamed listener, probably the reader, who is present as though across a table or a room. In keeping with the colloquial manner, Squeaky is open and frank, describing her self-esteem, feelings, aims, likes, annoyances, and aspirations.

The plot grows out of the conflict between the childish influences acting upon Squeaky and the development of her adult awareness of the potential of others. Within the structure of her family, she has been assigned to a caring role for her brother Raymond, who is retarded because he was apparently a hydrocephalic. Her growth is marked by her realization that she would be able to help her brother become a fast runner, for Raymond evidences remarkable footspeed. In addition, she has been involved in a childhood antagonism against Gretchen and her gang of "sidekicks" (paragraph 6) who join Gretchen's antagonism. The crisis is the 50-yard dash (which Raymond, alongside a nearby fence, also runs, thus explaining the title, "Raymond's Run"). It is the crisis, even though Squeaky has been thinking of it as a climax, because it is the race that causes Squeaky to realize that she has more cause for affection and cooperation with Gretchen than antagonism. This realization, the smiles between the two girls, and Squeaky's thoughts about coaching Raymond—

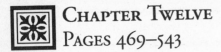

all demonstrate the theme that people need to be people, and that growth and mutual effort best lead to this goal.

Writing Topics. Squeaky's character. Her speech habits. The structure of the story. The major idea. The reality of the setting in Harlem.

Works for Comparison with "Raymond's Run"

Frost, *The Tuft of Flowers*, 894
Greenberg, *And Sarah Laughed*, 242

Stephen Dixon, *All Gone, pages 475–482*

"All Gone" is a prime example of cosmic irony, or irony of fate. Random violence occurs at the beginning, and, ideally, the guilty should be caught and punished, while the loved ones of the deceased should take up their lives again. Neither happens in the story. The protagonist, Maria Pierce, is determined to catch the killers, but finds nothing. When she learns later that the guilty ones have been arrested on another charge, she also learns that they almost entirely escape the sentences they deserve (paragraph 79). When she tentatively tries to take up her life again, she is also unsuccessful in that. In other words, life is in no way within the control of the major characters.

"All Gone" may be taken as a companion piece to "The Curse," by Andre Dubus, the story immediately following "All Gone" in the anthology. Both works involve a character in the role of Good Samaritan. In "All Gone" Eliot Schulter intervenes in the act of violence, and loses his life as a result. In "The Curse," on the other hand, Mitchell Hayes is prevented from intervening, and is forced to live with the guilt resulting from his inaction. In both stories, therefore, individuals are forced into a tragic dilemma: Either act and risk harm, or do not act and accept guilt. Students might find it fruitful to write about these comparable situations.

In "All Gone," Eliot is not the protagonist, for the subject of the story is really the responses of his woman friend, Maria Pierce, who tells the story from her first-person point of view. Maria is involved in two strands of plot. One is a suspense story about Eliot's murder and how the attackers are discovered. The other is her halting but steady effort to renew her interest in living. With both plots the solution is ambiguous and unsatisfactory. The conflict in the murder plot is to learn or not to learn the identity of the violent young men. In the Maria strand, the conflict is between her angry morbidity and her natural efforts to pick up the pieces and go on. The Eliot-murder aspect of the plot is resolved in the last three paragraphs of the story. There are no witnesses against the men—the girl whom the men molested cannot be found, and the elderly man has died—and hence they escape with a minor sentence. The Maria-Vaughn aspect (paragraphs 43–78) ends with paragraph 78, for Vaughn's interest in Maria has waned, and she does not believe that anything fruitful can come of pursuing things further. The story's title, "All Gone," describes the outcomes of both threads of the plot.

The first-person point of view of "All Gone" is, on the whole, successful. Maria uses an easy, neutral level of diction, mixing past tenses with present tenses, in accord with a conversational and easy speaking situation. The first-person point of view is not totally consistent, for from paragraphs 43 to 69 the action is presented objectively and dramatically. This shift represents a break in the narrative, inasmuch as a first-person narrator like Maria, knowing her own feelings and thoughts, could be expected to do more explaining than occurs in these encounters between her and Vaughn. But in paragraph 78, she does reveal her thoughts about Vaughn, and explains why she will not attempt to follow up their encounters. Paragraph 78 is therefore a superior example of writing from the first-person point of view. The point of view suggests an additional idea, however: The dramatic elements in Maria's first-person narration underscore the story's theme that people are not in control, that they are no more than witnesses even in their own lives, and that their wishes and feelings have little consequence in shaping their destinies.

In addition to the major strands of plot, "All Gone" contains a number of passages that stand out. The subway riders, for example (paragraph 38), use the pretext of the sudden stop, which is a matter of life or death for someone else, to "sue the city for . . . dizzy spells and sprained fingers and ripped clothes." The two young men guilty of Eliot's death plea-bargain for a reduced charge (paragraph 81). Finally, after Eliot is dead his personal belongings are "sold or given away or put on the street" (paragraph 31). One is reminded of Emily Dickinson's poem "The Bustle in a House."

Writing topics. The character of Maria Pierce. The irony of situation in the story. The first-person point of view. The dangers of trying to stop violence, in "All Gone" and "The Curse" by Andre Dubus (page 482).

Works for Comparison with "All Gone"

Dubus, *The Curse,* 442
O'Connor, *A Good Man Is Hard to Find,* 510
Whitman, *Reconciliation,* 759

ANDRE DUBUS, ***The Curse, pages 482–486***

The stories in Dubus's *Selected Stories* (1988), from which "The Curse" is selected, have a compelling force that develops out of topics touching on the darker areas of human existence. None of the stories is lacking in Dubus's ability to reveal the inner personalities of his characters. In "They Now Live in Texas," for example, a woman sees a horror ghost movie on her VCR, and then awaits her own demons. Another story, "Killings," concerns the anger and intensity of a man who commits an act of vengeance on the murderer of his son. In another, "Townies," a drifting, purposeless young man kills his girl friend, and achieves a curious serenity as he expects the police to arrest him. In "The Fat Girl," an overweight woman slims down, but becomes happy only when she returns to her original fatness, even though all other aspects of her life are ruined. In all such stories, Dubus succeeds in creating overpowering concern, suspense, and tension.

"The Curse" is not untypical of stories from the *Selected Stories.* It deals with violence and its aftereffects, and renders the deepest feelings of the major character. The setting in the Merrimack River area is a bar and the home of the bartender, Mitchell Hayes. There is nothing unusual or particular about the bar. It is summer, many of the "regulars" are at the beach, and Mitchell is alone and about ready to close. When five men on drugs come in to drink, Mitchell becomes the unwilling witness to their gang rape of a young woman who enters the bar alone. Though he makes an effort to stop the attack, the men threaten him and stop him entirely.

The story's plot, however, is concerned not with details about horror, but with Mitchell's responses. Between paragraphs 4 and 5 we learn that the rape has occurred, but the details are withheld until paragraph 43, and then these details are presented only as Mitchell remembers them. Much of the story's complication concerns the way in which Mitchell's family and friends respond to his claims that he should have stopped the violence. Without exception, his friends, his customers, the police, his wife, and his stepchildren all excuse him from guilt on the grounds that he could have achieved nothing and could have been injured or killed if he had intervened (paragraphs 8, 16, 29, 39). Despite such understanding, however, the story builds on his guilt, and the conclusion deals with "the curse" that the raped woman hurls at him after the assailants leave. In short, despite his knowledge of his powerlessness, the woman's reproach will always remain with him.

Though there is a fair amount of action and dialogue in the story, the crucial passages, in the third-person limited point of view, concern the inner workings of Mitchell's mind. His dilemma is in fact tragic: No matter what he does at the time of the rape, he cannot reach a satisfactory outcome. Either he can accomplish nothing, as he does, or else he can try to stop the men and probably suffer injury or death. The tragic resolution is of course not that Mitchell's life ends, as in a full-scale tragedy, or as with Eliot Schulter in Stephen Dixon's "All Gone" (page 475), but rather that he is imprinted with the guilt of the woman's curse. The story, especially in the last paragraph, succeeds in allowing us insight into the depth of Mitchell's anguish.

Classroom discussion of the story will revolve about the details of rape and the possible ways in which it might be prevented or deterred, but the discussion should also be redirected toward the meaning of Mitchell's responses: Can people who witness violence remain detached from it, or will their inadvertent involvement change them permanently? What is their responsibility? How much should they try to do? Should they consider the consequences of possible action? What will their future lives be like as a result either of action or inaction? These are serious questions that deserve thoughtful consideration.

Writing topics. The character of Mitchell. The purpose of the responses of the other characters. The meaning of the final paragraph. The point of view of the story. The treatment of violence in "The Curse" and in "All Gone" (by Stephen Dixon, page 475).

Works for Comparison with "The Curse"

Atwood, *Rape Fantasies*, 301
Dixon, *All Gone*, 475
Frost, *Acquainted with the Night*, 901
Zabytko, *Home Soil*, 403

Gabriel García Márquez, *A Very Old Man with Enormous Wings, pages 486–490*

The plot of "A Very Old Man with Enormous Wings" stems from the tension of supernatural happenings (magic), on the one hand, and the realism of everyday life, on the other. The supernatural is introduced in the very first paragraph with the angel's matter-of-fact appearance into the household of Pelayo and Elisenda. Other supernatural occurrences are the sudden cure of the infant child (paragraph 4), the acrobat with bat-wings (paragraph 7), the girl changed into a spider (paragraph 10), and the angel's miraculous and seemingly ubiquitous movements within the house (paragraph 12).

The story's complication concerns what can be done with the heavenly but only too real angel. He is old, dirty, smelly, threadbare, disgusting, and subject to illness (he gets chicken pox at the same time as the boy [paragraph 11]). Pelayo hence throws him into the coop with the chickens, which pick at the parasites on his wings; he speaks in a strange dialect that to the ignorant natives resembles Norwegian; Pelayo and Elisenda capitalize on his presence, and make a profit by exhibiting him to the locals; the doctor who examines him remarks about how well his wings are structured as a part of his body; the only thing the angel can finally eat, out of the things that are offered him, is eggplant mush (García Márquez seems to like making humor out of eggplant; in *Love in the Time of Cholera* a female character promises to marry a man if only he will not force her to eat eggplant). The crisis of the plot is that the angel is growing ill and weak, nearing death (paragraph 12), and the climax is that he gets better after a difficult winter (paragraph 13). The resolution is that the angel, after a period in Pelayo's household that may be as long as five or six years, soars away like "a senile vulture" after several bungling attempts at flying after being out of practice for so long.

The point of view of "A Very Old Man with Enormous Wings" is mainly dramatic and objective. There are some remarks that might be construed as omniscient, but these are reportorial rather than interpretive. The speaker relates everything in the same reportorial manner, as though there is nothing unusual about an angel in a chicken coop or a spider-woman on exhibition.

Within this narrative framework, the tone of the story takes on a wry and amusing cast. The most absurd thing is that the angel fails to complete his task of carrying the soul of the sick infant to heaven, but falls in the mud instead (paragraphs 1–3). Especially comic is Father Gonzaga, who pompously preaches about the wiles of the devil, and who grows suspicious about the authenticity of the angel because he does not respond to Latin, which, he declares, is "the language of God" (paragraph 5). Another comic thing involving the Father is the Byzantine procedure he describes for securing a Papal pronouncement about the nature of the angel (paragraph 5).

Although "A Very Old Man with Enormous Wings" is designed for diversion and amusement (it is subtitled "A Tale for Children") it is not without a thematic basis. Some ideas that you might deal with in class are (1) the fragility of life (as evidenced by the sudden recovery of the mortally ill infant [paragraph 4]); (2) the fact that human beings, almost by their very nature, reduce everything to their own levels of comprehension; (3) the curiosity that people show in unusual things, but also their fickleness when the novelty wears thin; and (4) the inevitable introduction of adaptation and opportunism for survival (as shown in Pelayo's getting rich by exhibiting the angel [paragraph 11]).

Writing topics. The setting of the story. The characteristics and habits of the human participants. The development of the plot. The tone and the humor. The nature of the speaker.

Works for Comparison with "A Very Old Man with Enormous Wings"

Hawthorne, *Young Goodman Brown*, 330
Pickthall, *The Worker in Sandalwood*, 341
Edgar Allan Poe, *The Masque of the Red Death*, 254
Serotte, *My Mother's Face*, 983
Stanton, *Childhood*, 592

Charlotte Perkins Gilman, *The Yellow Wallpaper, pages 491–502*

"The Yellow Wallpaper," was written early in Gilman's career, and is today the work for which she is best known. It is based on her own experience with the procedures for "rest cures" practiced by the famous Dr. S. Weir Mitchell. (The narrator has a young daughter, as Gilman herself did at the time of her breakdown, and Gilman had herself been subjected to Mitchell's cure.)

The point of view of "The Yellow Wallpaper" is first person, with the narrator sometimes describing things in the present tense—such as her observations about what her writing is doing to her, or about the condition of her room and the grounds around the house—and sometimes shifting into the past tense. The circumstances of the narration are that the narrator writes each episode of the story at a single sitting (see, for example, paragraphs 107–162) , and then hides the material, taking up her writing again only at a later time.

The total period of the episodes is three months, beginning when the narrator settles in the room and ending on the very last day of the lease period. You might want to raise with students the issue of how effective the narration is. At the end, for example, is it feasible that the narrator, writing in the present, could describe how she is crawling around the room, including how she climbs over her husband, who has fainted? Might this aspect of the narrative be more effective if told from a third-person limited omniscient point of view?

"The Yellow Wallpaper" is a story of fascinating complexity, for it may be read in either of two valid ways, which follow:

A. First, it may be construed as the revelations of a woman being overwhelmed by madness over a three-month period. Confined mainly in the top room of a mansion as a prescription to cure a nervous disorder, the narrator sinks into schizophrenia, characterized by her ultimate identification with a woman who has seemed to be clawing her way out of the grotesquely baroque yellow wallpaper adorning the room.

The power of this reading depends on the fact that the narrator describes some of the details without totally understanding their place in her increasing disassociation from reality. We learn in paragraph 32, for example, that some of the wallpaper in her room is torn. A natural conclusion is that she herself has torn it (for she tears it completely as the story progresses), but has begun doing so unknowingly—a symptom of her illness. Similarly, her bedstead has been bitten, and we learn in paragraph 230 that she has bitten it at least once. Is it fair to conclude that she has been gnawing the wood regularly during the period of her confinement? Additionally, she mentions the temptation to jump from the window (paragraph 240), but observes early in the story that the barred windows must have been placed in the room as a safeguard for small children (paragraph 31). Questions: Were the bars installed initially for children, or for her? Or was the room selected for her *because* of the bars?

Within the assumptions of the first reading, it is Gilman's realistic portrayal of oncoming insanity that makes "The Yellow Wallpaper" so chillingly powerful. One is reminded of Robert Wiene's film *The Cabinet of Dr. Caligari* (1919), in which the final words demonstrate that the protagonist is insane, although for most of the film we follow him, through his eyes, as though he is normal. Similarly, Gilman's narrator always seems in command of her pen, even as she becomes increasingly disturbed. At the end, of course, she has moved into another plane of consciousness. She notes (paragraph 192) that the woman behind the wallpaper has escaped, and soon the narrator speaks as though she believes that she herself *is* this newly freed woman (paragraph 245). The final paragraph is narrated matter-of-factly, just as the rest of the narration is presented, but it reveals her total loss of reality.

Still within the first reading, the title of the story raises the issue of the relationship of unfamiliar and oppressive surroundings to mental health. Is it possible that an ugly location may destroy an individual's sanity? In paragraph 67 the narrator speaks of how earlier in her life she had found shapes in inanimate objects: "I remember what a kindly wink the knobs of our big old bureau used to have, and there was one chair that always seemed like a strong friend." This is normal enough, for many persons would agree that one may see shapes in both internal and external objects. But the narrator, right at the start, speaks about the strangeness and even ghostliness of the "colonial mansion" in which she is being confined. Her suspicion that the house is haunted or perhaps cursed, which becomes more and more concrete as she perceives female figures behind the fantastic wallpaper (paragraphs 242–243), suggests that her sequestration in the mansion, away from the familiar objects of her regular home, may be producing not her cure but her madness. As she adjusts to the weird house and becomes obsessed with tearing off the wallpaper, in other words, she loses connection with the world outside, to the point where she is lost in her own world, unable to function anywhere else.

B. An alternative reading of "The Yellow Wallpaper" stems from the circumstances of the narrator as a woman—as a human being—desperately in need of self-sufficiency. In this reading, the story is about how the female narrator is driven into physical weakness and mental breakdown by what passes in her world as love, solicitude, and the best of medical care. Instinctively, she *knows* what she needs: work ("congenial work, with excitement and change," paragraph 13), freedom of movement and beautiful surroundings (a well-decorated room opening onto a garden, paragraph 26), and separation from her overmastering husband (the room she wants has no space for his bed, paragraph 27).

Instead, her doctor husband, like her doctor brother, prescribes rest and no writing, constant supervision (by her sister-in-law during the day, by her husband by night), and a room away from outside doors and also with barred windows, a gate at the top of the stairs, and ugliness (ugly furniture and torn and ugly yellow wallpaper)—all of which repel her. She is in a nursery because she is being infantilized, in the sense that she is not allowed to make any decisions for herself. The irony is that, because every suggestion she makes to help herself runs contrary to the medical and psychological knowledge imposed by males who live and move in the outside world, she is thrust into the impossible position of being unable to trust her own instincts. She therefore defers to her husband, persuades herself consciously that he is always right, and speaks again and again of her "dear" husband and sister-in-law who both have nothing but love and concern for her.

With so wide a dissonance between her own intuition about what she needs (work, freedom from John, freedom from her baby) and what she is told is good for her, the tension grows unbearable. She therefore finds the pattern of her distress within and behind the writhing, ugly wallpaper. Her vision of the woman clawing to get out suggests an imprisoned and caged animal, and she ultimately identifies herself entirely with this woman. Her ripping the wallpaper away thus suggests her own attempts to break herself free from her prison. The final stage in her liberation is that she herself creeps around and around the room, pushing against the walls that imprison her. Finally, her total rejection of what passes for ordinary reality lies in her lack of recognition of her husband (who has fainted), and over whose body she crawls again and again as she repeats going around the room.

Consistent with this reading, the many creeping women seen by the narrator (paragraphs 239, 240) symbolize the plight of women who, like the narrator, are stultified by the expectation that "a woman's place is in the home." Also symbolic is the open door, which the narrator cannot go through because she is tied within the confines of her room (tied literally, by her rope, paragraph 241). Living, for such women, is therefore an endless repetition of movements which go nowhere. Another symbol is her writing—that is, her work—which she must hide away from everyone concerned with her. Her husband, John, sees her imagination as being dangerous and destructive of her reason. For her, of course, writing could be just the opposite, but John "hates" to have her write. Does he dislike it because it makes her irrational or because it demonstrates her independence from him?

Without self-identity and independence, the narrator, like any kept or controlled person, is totally vulnerable. It is therefore not so much the narrator herself as the role of women in a masculine-dominated society that precipitates her mental deterioration. The story's major irony is that the narrator becomes free only when she moves into an existence which she alone can control—an existence which in the world is defined as total mental breakdown.

Writing topics. The narrator's obsession with the wallpaper. The use of the first-person point of view. The role of women as reflected in the story. The episodic nature of the story (shown by the spaces). The narrator's revelation of her madness. The complexity of the story: the view of mental health as understood by the husband and as understood oppositely by the narrator.

Works for Comparison with "The Yellow Wallpaper"

Glaspell, *A Jury of Her Peers*, 155
Rukuyser, *Myth*, 827
Steinbeck, *The Chrysanthemums*, 347
Swenson, *Women*, 919

Doris Lessing, *The Old Chief Mshlanga, pages 502–510*

"The Old Chief Mshlanga" is particularly powerful and moving, even though it may seem slow at first. The themes are those of the cruelty and insensitivity of colonial white settlers to the natives of southern Africa, the usurpation by whites of native land, the destructiveness and also the ugliness of colonial agricultural methods, the incommunicability of white and black cultures, and the monumental difficulties of effecting any change in the relationships between white colonialists and black natives.

To make these points, Lessing introduces a first-person narrator, a woman who recounts first her childhood and then her young adult experiences in Rhodesia. The story is unique, however, because the initial point of view is third-person limited, with the narrator obviously speaking about herself in the third-person before shifting to the first-person in paragraph 14. You might want to discuss this duality of point of view with your students. It would seem that the narrator, who is tolerant and who seems ashamed of many of the cruelties she describes in the narrative, thinks of her own early childhood as a period detached from her present consciousness, and that she therefore uses the third-person to convey this detachment, or even embarrassment.

It is clear that the narrator herself is one of the major subjects of the story. Her conflict is between her upbringing and her developing sensitivity. Her descriptions of her reading and of her inherited callousness about native people (paragraphs 9–13) establishes one pole of her personality. In contrast, her increasing tolerance and sympathetic growth are detailed in paragraphs 21, 31, 35, 38, 41, and 69. In addition to the subject of the narrator, the story of the Old Chief Mshlanga powerfully and poignantly dramatizes the case against white colonial cruelty and exploitation. The climax of this conflict occurs in paragraphs 85–95, in the confrontation of the Chief with Jordan, the narrator's father, and in the cruel and heartless decision to displace the Chief and his people to a "proper Native Reserve" (paragraph 96).

Aside from the narrator, who is a thoroughly drawn character, Lessing includes other skillful though brief characterizations. The narrator's mother is given only a few quotations (paragraphs 44–49) but her impatience and intolerance are made plain. The father is not just intolerant, but defiantly insensitive and pitiless. His decision to keep the goats of the Chief's tribe is of minor significance to him, but a death blow to the Chief's people (paragraphs 80–88). By contrast, Chief Mshlanga is shown sympathetically. He grows to the point of defying the narrator's father. Similarly, the Chief's son also grows by translating the Chief's words and then by leaving his ill-paying job in the Jordan household. A major achievement in Lessing's art of rapid and skillful characterization is the policeman (paragraphs 43–45, 95) who speaks of native government with derision, and who also discusses both the uprooting of a native habitat and a morning's tennis game as though these events were of equal importance.

The setting of the story in colonial Southern Rhodesia (now Zimbabwe) is the principal reason for the reality and power of the story. Lessing introduces colonial Dutch words to lend authenticity to the local places (*vlei*, *kopje*, *kraal*, *Kaffir*, and *mealie*). The descriptions of scornful meetings with natives, and the cruel harassment through the siccing of dogs, form a notable and unpleasant vision of the ways of life reflected in the story. Lessing also uses the setting symbolically, particularly in paragraphs 54–57 where the beauty of the unspoiled native area, as contrasted with the "harsh, eroded" white farmland, symbolizes the ugliness of colonialism.

Writing topics. The shift in point of view. The theme of anticolonialism. The growth of the narrator. The setting as reality and symbol. The effect of foreign words.

Works for Comparison with "The Old Chief Mshlanga"

Gaines, *The Sky Is Gray*, 367
Hughes, *Mulatto*, 1439
Lorde, *Every Traveler Has One Vermont Poem*, 962
Wheatley, *On Being Brought from Africa*, 1008

Flannery O'Connor, *A Good Man is Hard to Find, pages 510–520*

O'Connor's works combine flat realism with grotesque situations. Violence is encountered without apparent reason or preparation, and quite often her characters appear to be odd, eccentric, bizarre, and gratuitously cruel. She called some of them "rough beasts," a phrase made famous in Yeats's poem "The Second Coming."

In this respect "A Good Man is Hard to Find" is representative. The point of view is third-person limited (let us stress limited), so that all the characters are somewhat distant from the reader. The focal character is the unnamed grandmother, but she too is never appealing. The paragraphs in which the narrator permits us to enter the grandmother's thoughts are 1, 10, 29, 63, 65, and 69, although a study of these paragraphs will not reveal much about her thoughts or her personality. Essentially, she is portrayed by O'Connor as a contradictory, superficial, somewhat whimsical, manipulative, and forgetful person. After the Misfit and his henchmen appear, the point of view is almost totally dramatic or objective, but in the Misfit scenes the grandmother is still the center of the story.

The plot of "A Good Man is Hard to Find" is grounded in situational irony, a conflict between ordinary folks and both chance and evil. The forces of chance are built up by an almost overwhelming set of coincidences that lead in a straight line to disaster. These are:

a – the decision to go to Florida,

b – the decision of the grandmother to go too even though she says at first that she will stay home,

c – her hiding the cat in the car because she doesn't want to leave it behind,

d – her remembering the house she wanted to see, and exciting the children by making up a "secret panel" (paragraph 45),

e – her realization of her error just at the wrong moment,

f – her upsetting the basket with the cat in it,

g – the cat's jumping on Bailey's neck, thereby causing the wreck that makes the family vulnerable, and

h – the Misfit's being nearby when the accident occurs.

Evil is of course personified by the Misfit. He is a psychopathic killer, a person of mindless cruelty. Contradictions in his personality are shown in his apology for Bailey's language (paragraph 85) and in his apparent uneasiness at wearing no shirt (paragraph 99), even though he thinks nothing of killing the grandmother and having Bailey's family killed. If reasons for his evil are sought, his experience and preoccupation with

"first confession." In discussing the causes of laughter in the story, students should note the relationship of situations such as these to the Bergsonian principles of rigidity and incongruity. Thus Jackie in the communion class should be considering the state of his soul, but instead he demonstrates a little boy's concern for Mrs. Ryan's money (in this way fitting his rigidly childish perspective into a situation requiring thought and fear). In addition, sober and proper behavior is expected in a confessional; Jackie's antics, so clearly out of place, are funny.

Writing Topics. Mrs. Ryan as viewed by Jackie. Jackie as a narrator and character. The apparent religious views of Jackie as shown in his attitudes toward Nora, Mrs. Ryan, and the priest. The humor in the story. The plot. The structure.

Works for Comparison with "First Confession"

Donne, *Hymn to God My God*, 876
Joyce, *Araby*, 387
Zabytko, *Home Soil*, 403
Zimmer, *The Day Zimmer Lost Religion*, 1012

Tillie Olsen, *I Stand Here Ironing, pages 526–531*

The setting of "I Stand Here Ironing" is particularly significant and real. The year 1932, when the mother indicates that she herself was 19, was the time of the Great Depression, before the Roosevelt administration introduced the WPA (Works Progress Administration, 1935 and 1939) to aid families in need of welfare or relief. During this time talking movies were new, and a favorite child star was Shirley Temple (paragraph 35), who sang and danced to divert filmgoers from their real troubles. Many mothers of the time tried to model their daughters on Shirley Temple, and many other mothers regretted that their daughters resisted such molding. In World War II (1941–1945), wives and girlfriends were encouraged to write "V-Mail" (paragraph 45) to loved members of the armed services. From 1945 to 1952, many students developed a fatalistic attitude about atomic weapons (paragraph 53), before nuclear weapons became an even more ominous reality. In the 1930s a single parent like the narrator would have experienced just such difficulties with preserving a secure home as the narrator describes, and things would have improved during and after the war. All these aspects of setting make the story real, almost like genuine autobiography.

For this same reason, the story's point of view is authentic and convincing. The narrator is a woman of thirty-eight doing the common domestic chore of ironing clothes (in the days before permanent-press clothing). Her narration is not so much a story as a meditative recollection prompted by a presumably recent telephone call from a college counselor. One might also think of the narrative as an interior monologue or conscious musing, designed for a specific listener, but never heard or seen by him or her. At one point in the narrative (paragraph 16) the narrator becomes so affected by her recollection that she puts her iron down. At the end, she considers the iron again and it suggests to her a negative comparison with her daughter (paragraph 55). The narrator realizes that Emily is an individual with her own life and the capacity to make free choices, unlike the dress being ironed.

The mother is therefore, along with Emily, a major character who like most parents is vulnerable to doubt about the way she has raised her child. In the story the mother cites many occasions of regret—the separations, illnesses, instances of negligence and even neglect, and fears. Her narrative is laced with poignant memories of pain and helplessness (see paragraphs 9, 22, 24, 29, 30, and 35). It is these which make plain that the conflict in the story is the ideal vs. the actual upbringing of Emily, the daughter, with the complementary conflict being that the expected negative results do not occur but rather that Emily grows up to be a vital, talented young woman. The affirmative paragraphs near the end (46–50) are not totally negated by the moderately pessimistic concluding paragraphs (54, 55), for these last two may be considered a function of the anguish and self-doubt that never leave a caring parent. The mother, in this respect, is totally real.

Her daughter, Emily, is also real. The child's solitude (paragraphs 9, 12), her fear of separation (paragraph 14), and her humor (paragraph 15) are well portrayed. Her success as an entertainer in pantomime (paragraphs 18, 46) is anticipated in her silent but deeply-felt protests when as a child she is sent out for day care (paragraph 16). Her conversation with her mother as quoted in paragraphs 51–53 demonstrates her growing spirit and also illustrates the major theme of the story, namely that human character, unlike the symbolic rigidity of the clothes iron, is unique, resilient, and adaptable.

Writing topics. The first-person narrator as a character. The developing character of Emily. The depression and war years as setting. The point of view as part response and part meditation. The theme about the strength and adaptability of human character. The things a parent regrets. The relationship of mother and daughter.

Works for Comparison with "I Stand Here Ironing"

Cummings, *if there are any heavens*, 930
Gardner, *At a Summer Hotel*, 720
Henley, *Am I Blue*, 1403
Walker, *Everyday Use*, 68

Grace Paley, *Goodbye and Good Luck, pages 531–537*

The setting of "Goodbye and Good Luck" is the Yiddish theater of the lower East Side of Manhattan, which was supported by first- and second-generation Jewish immigrants from eastern Europe. Although some of these people knew a national language, most knew only Yiddish, and Yiddish was definitely their common bond. Children were brought up bilingually: They spoke Yiddish at home, and, as they were assimilated into American culture, they developed their knowledge of English. The strength of the Yiddish culture, however, enabled the Yiddish theater to flourish for many years. Though there is no longer wide support for it, it still exists to a degree in the lower East Side of New York, where it first grew and flourished.

The point of view of "Goodbye and Good Luck" is first person. Aunt Rose is the speaker, with her niece Lillie, her sister's daughter, as the listener. Only on one occasion, however, does Lillie enter into the discourse, when she has apparently taken exception to Rose's insinuation about the moral laxness of modern girls (paragraph 52). Otherwise, the story is a monologue in which Rose describes her lifelong love for Volodya Vlashkin, the principal actor in the Yiddish theater.

Rose's speech reflects the Yiddish idioms of her childhood. Presumably most of her communication with her mother, and also with Vlashkin and others connected with the theater, would have been in Yiddish. The English of the story, however, is her own, since she is speaking to Lillie, who is third-generation and mainly assimilated into American culture. Thus her language is laced with Yiddish rhythms. Students enjoy trying to describe the unique syntax resulting from the submerged Yiddish.

To a high degree, the tone of the story is shaped by the rhythms and, for want of a better term, "quaintness" of the language. With the speech being almost comic, it is difficult to stress the intense seriousness of the emotions that Rose would have felt. Thus the tone seems both warm and tranquil. When Rose thinks of a goodbye to Vlashkin, for example, she says to herself that he is a "dear friend" and "topic" of her life (paragraph

70). By such language Paley keeps the story light, and away from the edge from which it might possibly, in other circumstances, fall.

Though Rose admits that her being fat may have prevented her from having large numbers of serious suitors, she denies having been lonely in her life. Her character seems strong, patient, and resilient. As we have suggested, she does not admit to Lillie any of the grief she might have felt, but Paley suggests in a number of spots that her feelings nevertheless run deep. To determine the full range of Rose's character and feelings, you might wish to guide students in studying paragraphs 16, 30, 46, 53, 62, 70, and 94. These offer hints and suggestions, but not developments. One should stress that Rose is speaking throughout the story to her niece—who is not, one supposes, a person to whom she is accustomed to making confessions about her deepest feelings.

Rose's story is a normal enough plot of "Men and Women at Love." Her conflict is the opposition of custom and time. Vlashkin cannot marry Rose until he is free culturally to do so, and thus the relationship stretches out for many years. Ironically, it is Vlashkin's wife who sues for divorce, but her reason is a comic application of the old saying that a woman marries "for better or for worse, but not for lunch." Once Vlashkin is around the house full time, his wife chooses to use the grounds of adultery she could have used at any earlier point. The time that elapses in the story is not clear, but Rose's sister has been married for thirty years (paragraph 1) and Lillie has grown to adulthood while Rose has been unmarried. Thus the conflict is not the usual one of misunderstanding or intrigue, but rather is one of freeing the affection that has been restrained by difficult circumstances (Rose twice indicates that she does not see herself as a homewrecker (paragraphs 46, 94).

Writing topics. The style of "Goodbye and Good Luck." The setting of the Yiddish theater. Paley's control over tone. The character of Rose, as determined by both what she says and does not say. The plot as a love story. Rose as a first-person narrator.

Works for Comparison with "Goodbye and Good Luck"

Atwood, *Variation on the Word Sleep*, 915
Chekhov, *The Bear*, 1038
Donne, *The Canonization*, 871
Haines, *Little Cosmic Dust Poem*, 945
Lawrence, *The Horse Dealer's Daughter*, 393

Katherine Anne Porter, *The Jilting of Granny Weatherall,* pages 537–543

In "The Jilting of Granny Weatherall," Porter's analysis and insights into human character are shown at their highest level. Granny is on her deathbed, and significant events of her life are flashing within her consciousness. She sees the people around her with increasing vagueness, but is certain about her past. As she responds from morning to evening on her last day of life, Porter gives us an astoundingly complete account of her defeats, sorrows, resolutions, concerns, and triumphs.

The narration of "The Jilting of Granny Weatherall" may be compared with that of Mansfield's "Miss Brill" (page 202), where we go readily into the mind of the major figure, except that here the narration goes more deeply and fully into Granny's consciousness. In Porter's story, we are in the third person limited mode, and we constantly receive things exactly as Granny perceives and remembers them, almost literally in Granny's words. Thus, for example, we learn of Granny's great concern for Hapsy (paragraphs 41, 50, 57, 60), a favorite daughter whom Granny apparently expects to appear. But the narration does not tell us that Hapsy is present, and from this, together with Granny's vague memories, we are led to conclude that Hapsy died many years before, as a young woman, in childbirth. Briefly, therefore, because the narrator allows us to share everything going on in Granny's mind, we see both the surfaces and depths of Granny's character.

In an obvious sense, the plot is concerned with the conflict between Granny and death, which death wins at the story's end. In fact, however, the plot is more concerned with the lifelong conflict between Granny and adversity, beginning with her being jilted on her wedding day, and going on from there to the early death of her husband and her successful but solitary raising of their children. Although Granny has experienced great pain, which was particularly sharp because of her having been jilted as a young woman and also because of the deaths of her husband and Hapsy, she has come through triumphantly and with dignity.

Porter portrays Granny as a character of great determination, liveliness, nobility, and resilience. Though she is weak and on her deathbed, weaving in and out of consciousness and hallucinating much of the time, the story makes plain that she possesses, or possessed, great strength. Her concern for life extends even beyond her earthly existence, for one of her dying concerns to make "Sister Borgia" six bottles of wine for a stomach ailment, and wishes to give her daughter Lydia a gift of forty acres as a hedge against her husband's shiftless ways.

In a number of places throughout the story (paragraphs 27, 29, 51, 61), Granny is associated with light, and is portrayed as a giver of light. These references suggest her qualities of guidance, strength, and leadership. Her death is described as a metaphorical blowing out of light, thus indicating, even at the end of her life, that her existence is coincidental with the power and identity she gives to others. Her deathbed weakness may of course be taken as being atypical of her character even though she still maintains much of her power. Her observations about John, her long-dead husband, seem quite perceptive, but her oncoming weakness disturbs and distorts her perceptions of both her doctor and her daughter Cornelia.

In explanation of the title, we learn that George is the lover who jilted Granny when she was young. Obviously her memory of him is acute because she felt publicly humiliated by the desertion. Her concern with George indicates first of all her sensitivity and inability to forget the deep pain (paragraphs 49, 61), but it also indicates her sense of recovery and self worth, inasmuch as she wishes that George be told (paragraphs 42, 56) that she got along well without him.

Throughout the story the jilting, and the parallels between the earthly and heavenly bridegroom, are linked in Granny's mind (see especially paragraph 61). The metaphor of Jesus as a bridegroom is established in various New Testament passages (e.g., Matthew 9:15, Mark 2:19, Luke 5:34), and the desire for a sign is denied in Matthew 12:39. That the bridegroom appears on neither her wedding nor her death days is, with this linking, an extreme disappointment—both an earthly and a spiritual jilting—especially because a priest is present in the house on both occasions to witness the pain and embarrassment of her humiliation. Although it is not given to teachers and classes of literature to make final judgments about Divine Disposition, it would be hard to avoid concluding that Granny has earned a heavenly reward because of her long life of struggle and devotion.

Writing topics. Granny's relationship with her children. The nature of Granny's memory. The formal structure of the story. The character of Cornelia and of Dr. Harry. The place of religious metaphor in the story.

Works for Comparison with "The Jilting of Granny Weatherall"

Hardy, *The Walk*, 583
Heyen, *Mantle*, 768
Kennedy, *Old Men Pitching Horseshoes*, 808
Keller, *Tea Party*, 1050
Millay, *What Lips My Lips Have Kissed*, 967
Shakespeare, *That Time of Year*, 730
Tennyson, *Tithonus*, 998

The American Short Story Series

Seven of the stories in the fiction section of the anthology have also been filmed and are available on videotape in "The American Short Story" series. If you are able to use these films for your classes, they can be helpful in deepening understanding and appreciation of the stories. The films generally adhere closely to the originals; where there are departures, questions (like those included in the following brief discussions) may be raised about the differences between fiction and drama. Obviously, the films should not be a substitute for reading and discussion, but they have the major virtues of providing images of reality for the stories and of fortifying the idea that literature is about reality and the problems people face in their lives.

In addition, the films may be used, like the stories, to illustrate the development of life in America, as brought to life, for example, in the small-town, plains setting of "The Blue Hotel," the agricultural setting of "The Jilting of Granny Weatherall," and the increasing urbanization and mechanization exhibited in "The Greatest Man in the World." A brief discussion of each film follows:

In conjunction with discussion of any of these films, you might wish first to assign Chapter 30 in the text, on film.

- **Anderson, *I'm A Fool*** (1976). *Host,* Colleen Dewhurst. *Screenplay,* Ron Cowen. *Producer,* Dan McCann. *Director*, Noel Black. *Starring* Ron Howard *and* Amy Irving.

This version of the story compresses the two racing seasons in the story to one season, in which the hero rides the circuit as a swipe. The episode with Lucy Wessen is therefore seen as part of a day that he takes to go to the races as a spectator rather than as a participant. Of considerable interest are the images of the travel and scenery, the track, the races, and the estate of Walter Mathers. Questions to consider are why the time is compressed, why the protagonist is not filled with self-reproach until the end, why the conversations in the stable are added and developed, and why the romantic episode with Lucy is comparably less developed than in the story.

- Crane, ***The Blue Hotel*** (1974). *Host,* Colleen Dewhurst. *Screenplay,* Harry Mark Petrakis. *Producer,* Ozzie Brown. *Director,* Jan Kadar. *Starring* David Warner *and* James Keach.

The longshot scene at the opening, together with the street scene of the small town as the men walk toward the blue hotel, creates an authentic image of how a prairie town must have appeared almost a century ago. The screenplay, which is quite faithful to Crane's story, brings up the topic of Crane's use of vivid, pictorial detail. How much of the descriptiveness of the story is brought out in the film? It would be interesting to compare Kadar's version, so close to the text, with Rosenblum's film version of Thurber's "The Greatest Man in the World." Topics to discuss about "The Blue Hotel" are the use of the hotel room as the setting in which the Swede is killed as opposed to Crane's use of a bar in another building; the subdued light; and the effectiveness of the opening and closing scenes at the train station.

- Faulkner, ***Barn Burning*** (1980). *Host,* Henry Fonda. *Screenplay,* Horton Foote. *Producer,* Calvin Skaggs. *Director,* Peter Werner. *Starring* Tommy Lee Jones *and* Shawn Whittington.

The life of the Snopes family on the mule-drawn wagon is of particular vividness in this film, as is the life in the log cabin (especially interesting, for example, is the patching of the outside wall), the beginning of the plowing, and the trip to the blacksmith-wheelwright. All of this is authentic Americana. Topics to discuss are the view of Abner Snopes and his articulation of his ideas of justice, his behavior in the trial scenes, and his preparations to burn the barn; the scornfully gratuitous maltreatment of the rug; the way Sarty learns about his father's background; the treatment of Sarty's character; and the concluding scene in daylight the day after the burning of the De Spain barn.

- Gaines, ***The Sky Is Gray*** (1980). *Host,* Henry Fonda. *Screenplay,* Charles Fuller. *Producer,* Whitney Green. *Director,* Stan Lathan. *Starring* Olivia Cole *and* James Bond III.

Granted the length of "The Sky Is Gray," this intelligently selective teleplay effectively supplements the story. Particularly strong are the scenes of the killing of the birds, the bus going to town, the dialogue in the waiting room, Olivia's thanking Helena, and Olivia's final advice to James.

The waiting-room scene successfully conveys the story's conflict between passive and radical thinking, but because the film shows less hurtful violence than the story, it somewhat abates the story's underlying anger. Discussion might begin with the effect of the street scenes being filmed in sunshine rather than in sleet or rain, particularly because of the story's title.

■ **Hemingway, *Soldier's Home*** (1976). *Host,* Colleen Dewhurst. *Screenplay,* Robert Geller. *Producer,* David Appleton. *Director,* Robert Young. *Starring* Robert Backus *and* Nancy Marchand.

Quite interesting in this film is the opening footage of World War I scenes and the posing group of young men, showing the transition from life to photograph. The part about the photograph is authentically derived from Hemingway's story. The costuming is particularly noteworthy, and the vintage automobiles give authenticity to the setting. For discussion, one might query why the production shows Krebs making a pass at the girl, and also why the friend seems angry. Other topics might include the comparative importance of Krebs's sister, the confrontation with his mother, and the concluding scene in which he leaves town. Perhaps most important are the ways in which story and film versions bring out Krebs's sense of alienation and disaffection with life in the small town after the action and excitement of the War. Does the line quoted by Colleen Dewhurst, about how to keep young men on the farm "after they've seen Par-ee," explain Krebs's feelings?

■ **Porter, *The Jilting of Granny Weatherall*** (1980). *Host,* Henry Fonda. *Screenplay,* Corinne Jacker. *Producer,* Robert Geller. *Director,* Randa Haines. *Starring* Geraldine Fitzgerald and Lois Smith.

Of great interest in this film are the scenes and artifacts of the farm of Granny Weatherall. It is doubtful that many of today's students have seen a butterchurn, a wind-up floor-standing Victrola, or a "scratch" cake (in this age of premixed cake flour), or have seen how to lift a hen to recover eggs. The scenes reflect a period of the 1920s, although a 1937 Ford is driven in, and the farm has benefited from the introduction of Rural Electrification (earlier than it reached many farms). Topics to discuss are why Granny's early liveliness is followed so quickly by her quick failure and demise, her philosophy of work, the way in which her recollections are introduced as dialogue rather than memory, the two males around the farm, her visions of George and Hapsy, and the effectiveness of her dying moments and the receding figures of her loved ones.

■ **Thurber, *The Greatest Man In The World*** (1980). *Host,* Henry Fonda. *Screenplay,* Ed Wanchel. *Producer,* Ed Lynch. *Director,* Ralph Rosenblum. *Starring* Brad Davis, Howard Da Silva, and William Prince.

Thurber had trouble with his vision, and one might consider this fact in comparing story with film. Students will be interested in the scenes with the airplane, especially the landing. The question of tone is of great importance in a comparison of film and story. To what degree does the film agree with or differ from the story as Thurber has given it to us? What similar and different roles do the reporters take in the story/film? How does this role create a difference in perception? How does the film present Jacky Smurch? Is it possible to render Smurch realistically and still preserve the quality of Thurber's presentation? What is the effect of introducing the "sweet patootie" as a real, living woman with sensitivity and responses (she is only spoken about in the story)? What impression does the film create about the officials and their reaction to Smurch? What is the mood created by the presidential direction to hurl Smurch from the window? How alike are the effects of the film and the story? How unlike?

PART II
PAGES 547–1012

Poetry

Coverage of the Manual

We provide information and suggestions for every poem in **LITERATURE: AN INTRODUCTION TO READING AND WRITING** except for some of the poems that are discussed extensively in the text. For each poem with study questions in a chapter, we provide a brief overview and introduction, some observations on teaching, the answers to the study questions, and one or more suggested topics for writing. For poems without questions in the text, such as those in *Chapter 25: Additional Poems*, we provide brief observations that might serve as the basis for classroom discussion, and for *Chapter 24: Poetic Careers*, we provide questions together with answers. You may use as much or as little of the material here as you like; it is not our intention to tell you how to teach poetry. All the following material simply suggests some approaches; others are equally valid and rewarding. As with the rest of the manual, the material is designed to help (where necessary) rather than to prescribe.

Using the Chapters in the Poetry section of the Text

We do not expect you to use every poem in a chapter or even every chapter. The material in any given chapter may be taught using only a few of the included poems, or even poems from other chapters or from the "Additional Poems" section. Nor do we expect that you will use the chapters in sequence; the text is designed so that the chapters may be taught in almost any order and number. To ensure that such a reordering of material will not confuse students, we have provided many cross-references and a glossary of technical terms. In addition, we repeat crucial information and guidelines where such material will be helpful.

Organization of Each Poetry Chapter

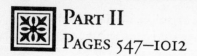

Although there is much variation, each chapter in the poetry section follows the same general plan. Each begins with an introduction to the aspect of poetry under consideration. This material may be assigned as outside reading and reviewed in class or not, as time permits. Along with this introduction, or at its close, a poem (or several poems) may be discussed in detail.

In each chapter, the introductory material is followed by poems for study that may be used to illustrate the characteristics and issues raised in the introduction. The number of these poems may vary; in addition, most chapters include much variety so that you may select poems that you prefer.

The poems in each chapter are followed by a discussion of writing. This section treats prewriting activities and strategies, questions for discovering ideas, formulations of central ideas, the identification of supporting details, and suggestions for organization. It also provides a sample essay and a brief commentary, followed by a number of topics for writing, including many creative-writing assignments. The sample essays deal with one of the poems in the chapter. For chapters in which you are not assigning an essay or a writing exercise, you may wish to omit the writing section. The sample essays, however, might still serve as examples of how to treat the topics of the various chapters.

Texts and Titles of Poems

The texts for all poems are drawn from standard editions or standard anthologies. Where a poet has provided a title, it has been included. Untitled poems are identified in the text, index, and manual by their first lines. Poems that are often identified by number, such as Shakespeare's Sonnets or Donne's Holy Sonnets, carry both the numbers and the first lines as titles (in the manual, some first lines are shortened to the first few key words).

Spelling and Punctuation

Many poems from the Renaissance and the late medieval period of the popular ballad were spelled originally in ways that are classed as "old spelling." Sometimes the old spelling includes letters used in outdated ways, such as *j* for *i*, *v* for *u*, and *u* for *v*. In the interests of providing a uniform text, and to avoid making reading any more complex than it needs to be, we have silently modernized these old spellings. American poetry is reproduced with American spelling; British poetry retains some of the qualities of British spelling, such as *honour*, or *centre*. Punctuation is left as is in the texts we have used. Interested readers may note that the punctuation in many of Shakespeare's sonnets is derived from the 1609 text. Ben Jonson's "Drink to Me, Only, with Thine Eyes," includes commas that we might not prefer today. In all cases, we have avoided extensive editorial textual-intervention, and have sought to present the poems in the best versions available.

Glosses and Notes

The poems in the text feature both side glosses and (when necessary) explanatory notes. In the side glosses, we attempt to find a reasonable middle ground between glossing all "hard" words and glossing only foreign or obsolete words. Our aim is to be as helpful and as unobtrusive as possible. Students will still benefit if they read all poems with a dictionary close by and if they check out words that are not immediately clear. We use the explanatory notes to give various kinds of relevant information, including extended definitions, explanations of allusions, and identification of many historical, mythological, and literary figures and events. Occasionally, we use the notes to explain a possible meaning of a difficult phrase or line; for these occasions, we try to give a straightforward (rather than interpretive) reading. Also, in the interests of helping clarify a reading, we use the explanatory notes to change syntax, adding words in brackets when necessary, so that students may see a difficult line laid out in easy order.

Suggestions for Teaching Poetry

There are many helpful strategies for teaching poetry. One effective way is to begin by reading aloud; you or a student might read the poem aloud, sentence by sentence. The class may discuss (or you may ask questions about) the sense and the effect of each sentence. Questions about specific topics, such as those included following the poems, will allow students to see how the poem's ideas are presented, and these questions may provide data about the poem that you can put together, along with the class, to develop a larger view.

Analysis of this type can be followed by synthesis: A set of questions designed to allow the class to pull the whole poem back together into a coherent moment of experience, thought, and emotion. Again, by using questions and allowing responses (or insisting on them), you give your students the chance to follow your methods and thereby to learn the process of interpretation and understanding. At the close of discussion, you might have a student (perhaps the same student) read the poem aloud again. Let us hope that this second reading will reflect the intervening process of discovery and experience.

As in the guide for the fiction section, we have included the "Works for Comparison . . ." lists at the end of each selection in Chapters 13–23. These, it is hoped, will furnish an abundance of topics for both study, discussion, and writing.

Chapter Thirteen
pages 547–568

Meeting Poetry: An Overview

This chapter introduces students to poetry and to the processes of analysis, interpretation, and explication. The opening pages raise some issues that you may want to discuss briefly in class. The high point of this opening material is the set of four reading objectives (pages 551–552) that can be used at any stage in the study of poetry, to be augmented by specific topics as students become more informed and adept.

The chapter contains poetry that many students will be at least partly familiar with already, and this knowledge should help set them at ease. Indeed, many students may think that they already understand most of these poems, at least to some degree. Further reading and classroom discussion should help these students clarify and reappraise the understanding they already possess.

Early in the chapter, a number of poems are discussed in some detail. In your classroom discussion of these poems, you may wish to go over the explanations, and use these to illustrate the processes of reading, learning about details, analyzing them, and discovering meanings and relationships—all of which constitute the heart of reading poetry.

Billy Collins, *Schoolsville, pages 547–548*

The questions about this poem are treated on pages 548–549. Question 4, requiring a comparison of Roethke's "Dolor" (page 620) and the Collins poem, might bring out that the realistic details in "Dolor" point toward a mood of dreariness, while the realistically based but also fanciful details in "Schoolsville" are shaped to create that amusement which we find in recognizing allusions and exaggerations. One might remark that adding "-ville" at the end of a word creates a slang expression indicating qualities and making observations about the word. Thus, to be from "Joysville" is to be happy, and to be from "Schoolsville" is to be imbued with the knowledge and customs of educational institutions.

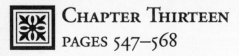

WRITING TOPICS. The tone of the poem. The transition between reality and fantasy. The imagery.

WORKS FOR COMPARISON WITH "SCHOOLSVILLE"

Smith, *Not Waving But Drowning*, 989
Maura Stanton, *Childhood*, 592
Mark Strand, *Eating Poetry*, 621

RANDALL JARRELL, *The Death of the Ball Turret Gunner, page 550*

See pages 550–551 for a brief discussion of this poem.

WRITING TOPICS. The tone. The accuracy with which the fate of the Gunner is portrayed. The anti-war theme.

WORKS FOR COMPARISON WITH
"THE DEATH OF THE BALL TURRET GUNNER"

Eberhardt, *Fury of Aerial Bombardment*, 616
Forché, *Because One Is Always Forgotten*, 943
Gay, *Let Us Take the Road*, 656
Georgakas, *Hiroshima Crewman*, 944

ANONYMOUS, *Sir Patrick Spens, pages 553–554*

See pages 554–555 for a brief discussion of this poem.

WRITING TOPICS. The use and omission of detail in the ballad form. The motivations of the various characters. Why is Spens sent to sea at a dangerous time?

WORKS FOR COMPARISON WITH "SIR PATRICK SPENS"

Dickey, *The Performance*, 930
Emily Dickinson, *Because I Could Not Stop for Death*, 555
Lowell, *Patterns*, 963

EMILY DICKINSON, *Because I Could Not Stop for Death, pages 555–556*

This poem presents an extraordinary perspective on death and the process of dying. It can be taught almost as a story, dealing with the narrative details in the order in which they occur. In the 1980s, composer John Adams set this text to music in his work "Harmonium," which was nominated for a Grammy award in 1985.

Answers to the Study Questions, page 556

(1) The speaker is characterized as having been preoccupied with her own self-importance. She was therefore too busy to stop for anything, as though the hustle-and-bustle of life ruled out anything new or different. There is a note of self-directed irony or mockery here. In the last stanza, we discover that the speaker is long dead, and that she is speaking from a perspective that has stretched out time. She also has given up her commitment to being busy, for she asserts (line 22) that her life in eternity has seemingly been passed swiftly.

(2) Death is characterized as gracious and polite; the key words in this portrait are "kindly" (line 2) and "civility" (line 8). This characterization is unconventional, for Death is not accompanied by pain, war, and sickness—Death is not the "grim reaper"—but rather Death is seen as a quiet, pleasant, and normal force that extends life into another dimension.

(3, 4) The carriage might be considered a hearse, the house a grave or vault. More abstractly, the carriage and the house suggest a movement from earth to heaven, in whatever conveyances take people there. On its journey to the grave, the carriage passes a school, children playing at recess, fields of grain, and the setting sun. The sun passing Death and the speaker in the carriage apparently suggests the ending of the speaker's time on earth. In any event, lines 12 and 13 together indicate movement away from earthly perspective to a more heavenly one.

Writing topics. The attitude toward death in the poem. The characterization of Death. The comparison between life and death.

Works for Comparison with "Because I Could Not Stop for Death"

Justice, *On the Death of Friends in Childhood*, 847
Poe, *The Masque of the Red Death*, 254

Robert Frost, *Stopping by Woods on a Snowy Evening, page 556*

Frost's most familiar poem dramatizes a number of alternatives that students may not readily see: life versus death, action versus contemplation, involvement versus withdrawal. Life, action, and involvement are embodied in "promises"; death, contemplation, and withdrawal in the dark, cold, silent woods and the snowfall. In teaching the poem, you can open some of these darker and less accessible ideas through questions that focus on speaker, setting, and situation.

Answers to the Study Questions, pages 556–557

(1–4) The speaker is in familiar territory; he is riding through the woods during an evening snowfall and has stopped to watch them "fill up with snow." There is nothing particularly noteworthy in the speaker's decision to stop, for falling snow is lovely to watch. On a deeper level, however, the stopping may signify a reluctance to move forward, a fear of the future, and so on. The speaker apparently feels embarrassed by the stopping, for he notes that the "little horse" *must* be taking exception to the action. The speaker seems to be projecting onto the horse his own ideas that we must be busy every second of our lives. In addition, the speaker has a sense of invading someone else's property, for the "though" of line 2 suggests that he would not stop if the owner were present to observe him. Some commentators have asserted that the house in the village is a church, and that therefore the woods belongs to God. The implications of this reading raise many speculations in a classroom full of students with varying religious convictions.

(5) In the last stanza, the alternatives are brought into sharp contrast: the woods vs. the promises and the miles. The speaker opts for responsibility, involvement, and action; all this is embodied in the single word "but" in line 14.

(6) Technically, the poem lends itself to classroom considerations of sound and rhyme. Alliteration on the *s* and *w* sounds (lines 11–12) reinforces the silence and the sweep of the wind. The sounds are comforting and attractive; they seemingly invite withdrawal. The rhyme scheme is *a a b a, b b c b, c c d c, d d d d.* It provides for linking or interlocking each stanza with the next. To end the poem, Frost uses the same rhyming sound throughout the last stanza and repeats the last line.

Writing topics. The implications of the setting and the situation. The alternative attitudes or courses of action implied in the poem. The effects produced through sound, rhyme, and meter.

Works for Comparison with
"Stopping by Woods on a Snowy Evening"

Finch, *To the Nightingale*, 690
Moore, *Poetry*, 853

Thomas Hardy, *The Man He Killed, page 557*

The questions on pages 557–558 are considered in the two sample essays on pages 563 and 565–566. With regard to question 5, both "The Man He Killed" and "The Death of the Ball Turret Gunner" alike describe the deaths of men in war. Jarrell's poem is told first-person by the dead man, who describes how his awakening in life corresponds to a death-dealing nightmare, while Hardy's poem is told by the man who killed an enemy in battle. Both alike are antiwar poems, but Jarrell's reveals war's senseless brutality while Hardy treats its anomalous breakdown of normal human relationships.

Writing topics. The irony of the speaker. The speaker's character. His diction, and his probable situation. Hardy's view of warfare as manifested in the poem.

Works for Comparison with "The Man He Killed"

Chioles, *Before the Firing Squad*, 138
Whitman, *Reconciliation*, 759

A.E. Housman, *Loveliest of Trees, page 558*

This lyric, from *The Shropshire Lad*, may be Housman's most famous. It has been memorized by many students, and has been read at many interpretive reading competitions. Sometimes readers have queried the meaning of "white" in line 4, and "snow" in line 12, and also, the age of the speaker has been questioned. But the season of cherry blossoms should not occasion doubt, and the correct subtraction of twenty from threescore years and ten makes the speaker's age unequivocal. The poem is in the "carpe diem" tradition, although the movement toward life is vitality and appreciation, not seduction.

Answers to the Study Questions, page 558

(1) The time of year is spring, when the cherry trees are filled with spring blossoms. The speaker is twenty years old, for the math he performs indicates that he has fifty more to live, granted that he will fill out the traditional seventy years suggested in Psalms 90:10. Because he has fifty remaining, he has already lived twenty years of his allotted time.

(2) Even though the speaker is young, he has lived long enough to acknowledge the speed with which time passes. The words "only" (line 7) and "little" (line 10) indicate his perspective, for both words suggest shrinkage and diminution.

(3) The idea about time, beauty, and life is that these things pass quickly. The seasonal setting—spring and the Easter season—suggests

that even at the beginning there is an awareness that things will eventually end. Because of this fact, people should celebrate their existence when they are able, and "see the cherry hung with snow" now in the light of inevitable change and impermanence. If life is not lived now, it will be lost.

WRITING TOPICS. The speaker's age, and his resolution about life. The meaning of the references to "white" and "snow." Reasons for enjoying life now, as expressed in the poem.

WORKS FOR COMPARISON WITH "LOVELIEST OF TREES"

Frost, *Birches*, 897
Frost, *The Tuft of Flowers*, 894
Kennedy, *Old Men Pitching Horseshoes*, 808
Stevens, *The Emperor of Ice-Cream*, 995

LOUIS MACNEICE, *Snow, pages 558–559*

"Snow" repays careful study, for the circumstances of the snow against the window pane develop powerful significance by the poem's end.

Answers to the Study Questions, page 559

(1) The speaker is apparently inside a room, watching the snow accumulate outside against the window pane, before which is standing a bouquet of pink roses. The roses are warm and colorful, and signify human relations and love. The snow, on the other hand, is cold; if it were to penetrate the glass, it would kill the roses. The scene is important because it represents so well the slender difference between the cold, hostile universe and the delicate fragility of civilization.

(2) Words expressing the nature of snow are *spawning, incompatible, suddener, incorrigibly plural, various,* and *gay.* These words are all abstract and impressionistic, in keeping with the speaker's idea that nothing is simple in the world (universe), and that human beings are unable to explain and define the diversity of life.

(3) This is a puzzling line that students may enjoy speculating about. Briefly, the glass may be interpreted symbolically to indicate the cumulative history of humankind, the many ways of life, discoveries, customs, and institutions that enable us to continue our civilization against great odds. On the other hand, some students might claim that the glass symbolizes the ways in which our civilization separates us from our roots in the natural world. Good discussing.

(4) Between Frost and MacNeice, Frost is more precise in his visual-

ization of the outdoor scene, and his speaker speculates briefly and then continues his tasks. MacNeice sees things from inside, and speculates about the difficulty and sometimes the irrationality of life—the good and the bad, the civilized and the uncivilized, which MacNeice characterizes as "more spiteful and gay than one supposes."

Writing topics. The symbolism of the snow and the roses. The speaker's ideas about the worlds inside and outside. The use of abstract and impressionistic words.

Works for Comparison with "Snow"

Hopkins, *Spring*, 641
Whitecloud, *Blue Winds Dancing*, 119

Jim Northrup, *Ogichidag, page 559*

Today's students may need some explanation of the wars cited in the poem, from World War I ("WW One," line 3) to some future war (line 21). You may thus need to assist students in answering the first study question.

Answers to the Study Questions, page 560

(1) In the first World War, chlorine gas was used by the German armies in Ypres, in Belgium. Guadalcanal is a Pacific Island which was the location of fierce fighting between Japanese and American forces in 1943. The North African campaign was chiefly between German and allied forces (led by the German Rommel and the British Montgomery) in 1943. The Battle of the Bulge occurred in Belgium during the winter of 1944–45. The Korean War, between North Korea and United Nations forces (principally American), occupied the first years of the 1950s. The "Cuban Missile Crisis," which was caused by the attempt to introduce Russian missiles into Cuba, occurred in 1962. The Vietnamese War (of which Da Nang was a part) lasted from 1965 to 1975. The poem, in short, covers all the major wars in which the United States has been engaged during the twentieth century.

(2) The speaker states that he learned about the battles second hand from old men, uncles, and cousins. Then he experienced battle first hand because of his participation in the fighting in Da Nang. The method of acquiring information is thus personal. The speaker concludes the poem in this immediate way by referring to wars in which his son might be engaged.

(3) There is a progression of information in the poem, developing from the words of "old men" (line 2) to himself and his son. The ques-

(3) A common thread in the three war poems is the death of men in combat. Two of the poems treat death individually ("Ball Turret Gunner" and "The Man He Killed"). The third ("Ogichidag") treats the subject more distantly. Each poem is unique in that one is specifically about the man who is killed; the second is about the man who does the killing; and the third is about the general experience of going to war.

(4) The "creative-writing" poetry assignment is designed to get students to explore, at both first and second hands, the essential connection between speaker, attitude, and situation. The differing situations, involving differing presuppositions, will create entirely different poems. There are many later such assignments for students to write poems of their own. In these, and in this assignment, the second half, in which students turn critics and analyze their own creative needs and responses, is most essential. To the degree that the students can reflect upon their own creative experiences, they will become more skilled as disciplined readers.

(5) This sort of assignment is designed to connect the experience of poetry with the personal experience of students. Of great importance, therefore, is the last sentence of the assignment: Students should use their own experience to get into the poem or poems, and should stress the poetry first and their experience second.

Chapter Fourteen
Pages 569–603

Character and Setting: Who, What, Where, and When in Poetry

The goal of this chapter is to demonstrate the importance and interrelationships of character, situation, and setting in poetry. Unlike fiction, poetry usually does not trace the growth of a character through all the interactions and changes that bring about "roundness" and development. Rather, in poetry, characters are at a crisis or climax, making a decision, reflecting about the past, or pointing in a new direction. Place and situation (*what, where, when*), then, are significant because of the bearing they have upon characters (*who, whom, whose*) at important moments and crossroads in their lives.

As a practical consideration, it is important to emphasize that there is a difference between the poet and the speaker; students have a strong tendency to conflate the two. Poems like "The Passionate Shepherd" (page 587) and "The Nymph's Reply" (page 589) are ideal to make the distinction, because Marlowe was certainly not a shepherd and Raleigh was not a nymph. Once students understand that the speaker of a poem is no less fictional and no less a character than the narrator of a short story, they will be better able to understand poetry and discuss it in class.

With regard to setting in poetry, students usually find it easy to describe the places, periods, and artifacts that are mentioned. Indeed, some may be able to provide actual sketches. It is harder to get them to recognize how character and attitude are shaped by the objective surroundings described in poems. You may therefore find it essential to emphasize that the setting is important because the poet introduces it to clarify and develop the responses, attitudes, and thoughts of the various characters and listeners who people the lines of poetry.

Western Wind, When Will Thou Blow?, page 570

The speaker of this poem speaks about love and warm spring days (nurtured by the misty fertilizing rains), so that he and his love may celebrate their affection in his bed. The loved one is absent, and the weather is presumably still cold, but the speaker's yearning is strong and his hopes are high.

WRITING TOPICS. The situation of the speaker. The poem as a celebration of desire. The connection between season and love.

WORKS FOR COMPARISON WITH "WESTERN WIND"

Bishop, *Rain Towards Morning*, 657
Burns, *Green Grow the Rashes, O*, 613
Frost, *A Line Storm Song*, 895
Haines, *Little Cosmic Dust Poem*, 945

Bonny George Campbell, page 571

This poem illustrates the swiftness of narration and the inclusion of speech to be found in traditional ballads. The repetition (e.g., *toom home, Saddled, and bridled*) is one of the characteristics of the ballad form. Additionally, the poem focuses attention upon the reality of the permanent, unchangeable absence of the leader of the family. The version included here is assembled from the various states included in the Child collection of ballads.

Answers to the Study Questions, page 571

(1) The three characters in the poem are Campbell, his mother, and his wife. None is described in any detail. Although we may conclude that the family is well-off and perhaps noble, details do not seem to matter; the poem focuses only on the climax of a series of actions.

(2) George Campbell is clearly dead, having ridden away expectantly to an unspecified battle—probably a border skirmish. He has been killed in the fighting, and his horse returns home without him. We may infer that his comrades, too, were also killed, because if they had survived they would have brought the corpse home. The ballad leaves us to imagine these events, first of all, because our discovery deepens our awareness and our involvement with the poem, and second, because the ballad is a short form, at its best when it touches the main details without superfluous explanations.

(3) The quotation marks indicate a speaker, most likely Campbell's wife, although some observers have suggested that the speaker may be Campbell's ghost (because of the unbuilt barn). If the wife is indeed the speaker, all her major supports of life are gone with Campbell's death.

WRITING TOPICS. The effect of the reader's emotional detachment. The riderless horse. The repetition of the "never came he" refrain.

WORKS FOR COMPARISON WITH "BONNY GEORGE CAMPBELL"

Anonymous, *Sir Patrick Spens*, 553
Dickinson, *The Bustle in a House*, 888
Dixon, *All Gone*, 475
Tennyson, *The Passing of Arthur*, 731

BEN JONSON, *Drink to Me, Only, with Thine Eyes, page 573*

This song is Jonson's most famous because of the lovely music to which it is sung. Those who have sung both stanzas, however, may be unaware of the wit and complexity of Jonson's handling of the dramatic situation.

Answers to the Study Questions, page 573

(1) The speaker is a young swain who demonstrates great wit because he shows the capacity for merging compliment with irony. He also shows a working familiarity with ancient mythology, and we may therefore conclude that his level of education is high.

(2) Before the poem the situation was this: The speaker had sent the lady a "rosy wreath" (line 9), which she sent back to him (line 14) in apparent rejection of his offer of love. He has decided to try again, and hence he is writing the poem to make the lady really take notice of him.

(3) The tone of the second stanza is particularly important. A strong case may be made that the speaker is demonstrating his ingenuity rather than simply complimenting his lady. He succeeds in complimenting her breath (stating that it is comparable to that of the rose), but he also qualifies his reasons for sending the wreath (line 10). It is clear that he wishes to draw attention to his own wit, but also to cause the lady to observe that he is persistent in his attention.

WRITING TOPICS. The situation of the poem. The tone of the second stanza. The nature of the speaker's compliments.

WORKS FOR COMPARISON WITH "DRINK TO ME, ONLY"

Donne, *A Valediction: Forbidding Mourning*, 658
Wakoski, *Inside Out*, 668
Waller, *Go Lovely Rose*, 1006

BEN JONSON, *To the Reader, page 574*

The voice here is a persona that Jonson employs in much of his poetry: the positive-minded critic who tells his readers how his poems should be read.

MATTHEW ARNOLD, *Dover Beach, pages 576–577*

"Dover Beach" is Arnold's best-known poem, for many reasons, not the least of which is the powerful conclusion. Arnold perceived a loss of absolute religious faith in his time, and hence he stressed the need for an intensive search to recover absolutes—an indefinite time of searching, inquiry, and what he called "criticism." "Dover Beach" reflects the loss of faith, while at the same time it stresses the need for integrity.

Arnold's speaker is unnamed. He (most likely) is an educated, thoughtful person, fully attuned to the intellectual (and particularly the religious) currents of the time. The speech begins as a kind of soliloquy, but by the middle of the first stanza the speaker is addressing another person, someone dear enough to be called "love" in the last stanza.

Answers to the Study Questions, page 577

(1) Words used in establishing the setting include "sea," "moon," "straits," "cliffs of England," "window," "night," and "pebbles." The time is evening, the place a room overlooking the sea and the beach. Because the night is clear and moonlit, one can see all the way across the English Channel to the French coast. The reference to the withdrawal of the Sea of Faith places the poem in the mid-nineteenth century, when European Protestantism in particular was reeling under the combined effects of scientific developments and the application of new scholarly techniques and discoveries to Biblical texts and religious teachings.

(2) The speaker and the listener are in a room in Dover overlooking the English Channel directly across from France. They can see the sea and the cliffs, and also the moon-blanched land, and can also see a light on the French coast. They can hear the constantly pounding surf.

(3) The speaker's eye moves from distant (the sea and the French

coast) to near (the English shore), and finally to the room and to the situation of the two persons in the room.

(4) To Sophocles, the speaker says, the Aegean was a reminder of the "ebb and flow / Of human misery" (rather like Wordsworth's "still, sad music of humanity" in the "Tintern Abbey" lines). By comparing Sophocles's thoughts to the present, the speaker suggests the timeless and inevitable unhappiness of the human condition.

(5) The faith that remains is personal fidelity, based on love between people. Nothing else is sure; the beauty, joy, and other human experiences which we wish were certitudes—all these are illusory. The private world of the little room assumes the full weight of human life and freedom. Therefore, what remains is the commitment that individuals make to fidelity, and this commitment enables people to conquer all that is vulnerable and transient.

Writing topics. Structure and setting. The importance of location and philosophy on the speaker's thoughts about life. The pounding surf and the influence of its sound. The faith that remains amidst uncertainty.

Works for Comparison with "Dover Beach"

Frost, *Misgiving*, 901
Williams, *Taking Care*, 74
Zimmer, *The Day Zimmer Lost Religion*, 1012

William Blake, *London, page 577*

Blake was distressed because he believed that the human spirit was being suppressed by custom and politics. His idea was that humanity could flower if institutions could be eliminated or at least redirected. The poem may be considered revolutionary because it stresses the need to correct the misery the speaker describes. Those who are degraded should be healthy and wholesome. By contrast, we are reminded of privilege, soldiers, and palaces, all of them aspects of oppressive authority. *Songs of Experience,* from which "London" is taken, was a collection of poems on this basic theme. Blake published the work in 1794 (the French Revolution was only five years old at the time) with his own engravings.

Answers to the Study Questions, page 578

(1) London represents a fallen world. Every person the speaker observes has been blighted or plagued, and the midnight streets heighten the darkness, misery, and danger.

(2) The speaker mentions cries, both of adults and children, public pronouncements, the cry of the Chimney Sweep, the sigh of the Soldier, and the curses of young prostitutes. These are sounds of sorrow, rage, poverty, and debasement; they symbolize the political degradation of human beings.

(3) *Chartered* suggests the privilege of those who can hire the river Thames itself for their use and whose lives contrast with the misery of the poor. It also suggests that all of this is *charted* (i.e. mapped), and thus the city itself has violated natural beauty by creating artificial streets, and by consigning even the river to commerce and ownership. *Marks* in line 4 means permanent marring of people's faces by grief; in line 3 it simply means *observe.* In stanza four the reiteration of the *bl* sound gives each word emphasis, as does the position of this sound in stressed syllables.

(4) The poem purports to be based on the personal observation of the speaker, the "I" who has observed these abuses and horrors. Having made these observations, the speaker is qualified to speak from experience. The inclusion of the poem in *Songs of Experience* is therefore natural.

WRITING TOPICS. The use of actions and sounds as setting, The destructiveness of the political system on human character. The relationship of the setting to the mood of indignation.

WORKS FOR COMPARISON WITH "LONDON"

Halpern, *Summer in the Middle Class,* 947
Sandburg, *Chicago,* 981
Williams, *Landscape with the Fall of Icarus,* 832

ROBERT BROWNING, *My Last Duchess, pages 578–579*

(See the sample essay on pages 601–602.) Although Browning did not invent the dramatic monologue, he specialized in it and made his poems in the form memorable. The Duke and his most recent Duchess are portrayed in the poem (discussed in the sample essay) as widely diverging characters. Students sometimes assert that the Duchess must have been guilty of something more than inappropriate smiles or blushes. They usually suspect infidelity. If this point arises, it can be an effective point of discussion, because it leads naturally to the characteristics of both Duchess and Duke.

WRITING TOPICS. The character of the Duke. The place of his wealth in his view of others. The symbolism of the works of art. The picture the poem leaves us of the Duchess: Could she have ever done anything right to satisfy the Duke?

Works for Comparison with "My Last Duchess"

Thomas Gray, *Elegy Written in a Country Churchyard, pages 579–583*

Gray's "Elegy" is one of the major lyrics of the eighteenth century, and one of the representative poems of the "graveyard school" of poetry, a major theme of which was the need for living a sensible, good life in view of the inevitability of death. As a biographical note, you might point out that Gray himself was the only one of his parents' twelve children to grow to adulthood. A concern with death and how to take life is therefore not an unexpected aspect of his art.

Answers to the Study Questions, page 583

(1) The time of day of the poem is twilight. The cattle are heading back to the barn to be milked, the farmer is returning from the fields, the sun is setting, and the curfew bell is ringing from the church tower. For much of the poem, the speaker seems to be addressing no one in particular, but in line 37 he does address "ye proud," and in 93 he seems to speak to a buried person (see question 4).

(2) The people buried in the church graveyard are humble, rural folk. Yet the speaker asserts that they are not contemptible because of their simplicity; instead he emphasizes their "useful toil" and "homely joys," pointing out that death is the great leveler, and that "the paths of glory lead but to the grave." Some of those buried here might have made great rulers, musicians, defenders of human rights, or poets. But the speaker balances the missed opportunities for good buried here by pointing out that the people never had the chance to do evil either. In short, the churchyard is the occasion of reflection on the need for goodness and piety, and the inevitability of death is cause for people to live their lives to their fullest potential.

(3) The setting (the rural landscape with its animal sounds, the churchyard and cemetery, the closing of day and the tolling of the bell) establishes immediately a mood of intensity, heightened by the approach of night with its overtones of dying. Times of passage and change (dawn, nightfall, festivals marking changes of season) are often viewed as mo-

ments when the natural and supernatural are most open to one another.

(4) The "thee" of line 93 is the author of the "frail memorial . . . erected high" which in unlettered fashion attempts to record and honor those buried here. He was the natural poet, a loner, lover of nature and its beauties, one not quite at home in life, perhaps "crazed with care, or crossed in hopeless love" (line 108). He too has died, and is buried here.

Writing topics. Time of day and the passage of time. The setting in the graveyard. The effect on life of the presence of death and the dead in cemeteries.

Poems for Comparison with Gray's "Elegy"

Brodsky, *In Memory of My Father*, 921
Ransom, *Bells for John Whiteside's Daughter*, 979
Thomas, *Do Not Go Gentle*, 781
Thomas, *A Refusal to Mourn*, 1000

Thomas Hardy, *The Walk, page 583*

"The Walk" represents Hardy's mastery, within a short compass, of deeply felt dramatic situations. His long experience as a novelist had sharpened his skill at perceiving human interactions, a capacity he also exhibits with great skill in, for example, "The Workbox" (page 683). In "The Walk," he captures the sadness and poignancy of love, age, and encroaching death.

Answers to the Study Questions, page 583

(1) The relationship between the speaker and the person being addressed appears to be long-standing, for the second person's failure to join in the walk has been going on for some time ("of late"). They are close enough for the speaker to know the state of the other's health.

(2) The companion is "weak and lame." The speaker, at least at first, appears unaffected by the other's absence, saying "I did not mind" (line 7).

(3) The final two lines give the poem its intriguing ambiguity. All has proceeded as is customary—the speaker walks alone as he or she has now frequently done—until these final lines, when the powerful thought of "the look of a room on returning hence" brings home to the speaker the reality of the changed situation. Their old walking place is now closed to the homebound companion, and a part of life is ended for both of them. The poem thus seems to be saying that age or illness will inevitably affect a relationship, although if one member resists thinking of the other "as left behind," there is a sense in which they are still together.

Writing topics. The idea of emotional unity amid physical parting. The use of setting as a symbol of aging and separation. The effect of the concluding lines.

Works for Comparison with "The Walk"

Albee, *The Sandbox*, 1431
Moore, *Believe Me, If All Those Endearing*, 968
Porter, *The Jilting of Granny Weatherall*, 538
Frost, *Nothing Gold Can Stay*, 900
Tennyson, *Tithonus*, 998
Yeats, *Sailing to Byzantium*, 1011

Thomas Hardy, *Channel Firing, page 584*

Readers might expect a poem about warfare, written immediately before World War I and "spoken" by a skeleton, to be thoroughly depressing. Surprisingly, this poem is rather amusing until we stop and think about its implications; then it becomes depressing indeed. The references to the locations of Stourton Tower, Camelot, and Stonehenge expands the poem's time frame from the immediate present back through history (Stourton Tower) and legend (Camelot) to the dim past of prehistoric Britain (Stonehenge). Because these places are all gone, the implication is that our present civilization, too, may vanish if warfare continues and if red war continues to get redder.

Answers to the Study Questions, page 585

(1) The speaker has been long buried in the local churchyard. The noise of guns, being fired out at sea in distant target practice, has awakened him, along with all the other skeletons in the cemetery.

(2) The *your* of line 1 could refer to us, the listeners, who support the existence of armaments with our resources, or to the Naval Commanders who direct the guns.

(3) The guns have awakened the speaker and his companions (a play on the phrase that something [i.e., the sounds of the guns] is loud enough to waken the dead). The mistake—and the joke—is that the speaker thinks that Judgment Day has come.

(4) The other three voices are God, another skeleton, and Parson Thirdly. Their traits are revealed through the qualities of their individual speeches. God is scornful, ironic, and amused, but he is also nevertheless somewhat understanding. The other skeleton is disillusioned. Parson

Thirdly is regretful about his life of piety, and wishes he had enjoyed himself when he was alive rather than preaching for forty years.

(5) This question is a good one for both writing and discussion. Essentially, the poem suggests that humanity may be powerless to stop war, for human beings are indifferent to suffering and ignore those who try to do good. There is a restlessness or madness driving us to war, and we may not be able to stop this drive until we have "rest eternal" (line 24).

WRITING TOPICS. The dramatic situation. The vision of human character. The traits of God as presented by Hardy. The other corpses. The poem's structure. The effect of the concluding references.

WORKS FOR COMPARISON WITH "CHANNEL FIRING"

Eberhart, *Fury of Aerial Bombardment*, 616
Georgakas, *Hiroshima Crewman*, 944
Nash, *Exit, Pursued by a Bear*, 664
Yeats, *The Second Coming*, 810

RICHARD HUGO, *Degrees of Gray in Philipsburg, pages 585–586*

This poem is typical of many of Hugo's works, concentrating, as it does, upon a "derelict" or ghost town. With this subject matter, Hugo, who lived in Montana for the last eighteen years of his life, dwells upon themes of economics, psychological stability, and the interdependence of life.

Answers to the Study Questions, page 586

(1) Philipsburg is a virtual ghost town. The economic boom which gave it its reason for being is over, the young people have left or are leaving, and all of its promises have petered out. The past was a boom caused by the mining of silver, which supported bars, hotels, businesses, and churches. But for some reason the demand for silver dropped (line 16), and the town's prosperity vanished. The "you" is the speaker, in stanza one and throughout, speaking to himself or herself.

(2, 3) The speaker calls "rage" the town's present principal business-rage against the mines, the mill, the repeal, and the absence of the pretty girls who have left town. Life is boring and empty, without much hope. By contrast, a living town would not live on rage. The pretty girls would stay, and there would be "blondes, good jazz, and booze" (line 30).

(4) The color gray relates to the color of all the items listed as a part of graying and fading Philipsburg, suggesting depression, sameness, and

a lack of spark or excitement. It symbolizes the diminution of the town and of the human hopes needed to build it. There is a cyclic aspect of this deterioration. Life is high when economic conditions are good, but when things get bad, particularly in a one-industry town, people leave and conditions deteriorate. For these reasons, one might make much of the poem as an expression of ideas about politics and economics.

WRITING TOPICS. The specifics of the setting. The ghost town setting and the relationship to human character. The use of "gray" in the title. The things necessary for community and urban life.

WORKS FOR COMPARISON WITH HUGO'S "DEGREES OF GRAY"

Cummings, *Buffalo Bill's Defunct*, 763
Jeffers, *The Purse-Seine*, 805
Shapiro, *Auto Wreck*, 986

C. DAY LEWIS, *Song, page 586*

Obviously, this poem is to be compared with the two poems by Marlowe (page 587) and Raleigh (page 589) elsewhere in the chapter. Marlowe's was of course, followed by Raleigh and, later, by Lewis.

Answers to the Study Questions, page 587

(1, 2) Lewis's poem parodies Marlowe's "The Passionate Shepherd." It reflects the conditions of contemporary life, complete with poverty and pollution, thus being like Raleigh's "The Nymph's Reply" (pages 589–590).

(3) The speaker—a man—invites the listener—a woman—to share the pleasures that "chance employment" might provide. The life that he offers is meager and uncertain, full of care, pain, toil, and hunger.

(4) Lewis's diction underscores the ironic uncertainty of modern life. Phrases like "dainties on the docks" and "a wreath of wrinkles" undercut the pastoral, Arcadian assumptions of Marlowe's poem. Instead of "having" summer frocks or "hearing" madrigals, as in Marlowe, Lewis's speaker offers only the chance to "read" about dresses and the "hope" to hear songs. The "chance employment" suggests the difficulty of modern persons who depend on wages which may be lost when they are laid off.

WRITING TOPICS. The view of modern life. Human relationships in the light of modern insecurities. The political implications of Lewis's poem.

WORKS FOR COMPARISON WITH LEWIS'S "SONG"

Marlowe, *The Passionate Shepherd to His Love*, 587
Raleigh, *The Nymph's Reply to the Shepherd*, 589

CHRISTOPHER MARLOWE, *The Passionate Shepherd to His Love, page 587*

This is an ideal poem for the speaker-listener relationship since both are named in the title.

Answers to the Study Questions, page 587

(1, 2) The title identifies the speaker as the "passionate shepherd" and the listener as "his love." The poem is a speech of persuasion in which the shepherd asks the lady to join him in love. Since the speaker is trying to persuade, we may assume that the lady has resisted his advances up to this point.

(3) The shepherd offers the lady a world of "valleys, groves, hills, and fields" where they can watch "shepherds feed their flocks" and listen to "melodious birds sing madrigals." In this Arcadian, ideal world, the young "dance and sing" each "May morning." The world being offered is therefore one of total "delights."

(4) In portraying the idealized world, the shepherd almost ignores the reality of everyday life. He does slip, however, when he mentions "cold" in line 15—his only acknowledgment that spring and May are not eternal.

WRITING TOPICS. The relationship of the shepherd and his lady. The shepherd's view of the natural and artificial world. The nature of reality/unreality in the poem.

WORKS FOR COMPARISON WITH "THE PASSIONATE SHEPHERD"

Raleigh (589) and Lewis (586)
Donne, *The Sun Rising*, 871
Frost, *A Line Storm Song*, 895
Lawrence, *The Horse Dealer's Daughter*, 393

JAMES MERRILL, *Laboratory Poem, page 588*

This is an excellent poem for showing that poetry need not be confined to "poetic" images and situations. The vivisection of living turtles to experiment with their hearts is a long way from the proverbial "hearts and flowers" that are often associated with poetry.

Answers to the Study Questions, page 588

(1, 2, 3) The poem is spoken in the third person. The speaker is outside, detached, and uninvolved, although he or she has access to Charles's thoughts. The two characters, Naomi and Charles, are lovers (line 18). Naomi, the scientist, is cutting open living turtles, removing their hearts, and experimenting with "solutions tonic or malign" on the heart muscles to evaluate the effects. Charles, a philosopher rather than a scientist, gags at the blood and the "blind twitching," and is appalled by her experiments (lines 14–16).

(4) The poem is set in a research laboratory and offers a dramatic situation. Merrill uses diction, metaphor, and pun to make the language exact and to broaden meaning: "Taking heart" (line 1) can refer to the experiments, to courage, or to love. The heart becomes the central image, and it comes to embody science, human endeavor, love, and courage. Charles's meditation establishes these possibilities, for he considers that the heart leads people into "exquisite disciplines" and, if the turtles' hearts are any indication, they are all fated to expire.

WRITING TOPICS. The characters of Charles and Naomi. The importance of the setting to the individual responses. The symbolic value of the heart. The conflict between science and humanities in the poem.

WORKS FOR COMPARISON WITH "LABORATORY POEM"

Dickinson, *I Cannot Live with You*, 886
Drayton, *Since There's No Help*, 936
Haines, *Little Cosmic Dust Poem*, 945
Minty, *Conjoined*, 663

MARGE PIERCY, *Wellfleet Sabbath, pages 588–589*

Marge Piercy is well known as a novelist, and in addition to her many novels she has published a number collections of poetry. Three of her poems may be found elsewhere in the anthology ("A Work of Artifice," "Will We Work Together?" and "The Secretary Chant," pages 665, 975, 974).

Answers to the Study Questions, pages 589

(1, 2) While elsewhere one may note tones of irony or even anger, and also tentativeness, in Piercy's poems, here the dominant mood is one of satisfaction. Among words for the outdoors that suggest calm and serenity are "softly feathered," "sailing free," "purrs and rolls over," and "fresh clean night," for these indicate a metaphorical aura of benign Nature and domesticity. One need look no further than the fourth stanza for the same interior mood. Dinner candles flicker between the phlox (a bouquet) and the roast chicken, illumined also by shining red wine. The key word is "Shekinah" (see the note, page 589) suggesting that the divinity manifesting itself in the external world (of the summer day in Wellfleet) is also present in the internal world of the Sabbath where the presence of divinity is being celebrated.

(3) The speaker is apparently in a dining room, just before the Sabbath meal, and everything seems orderly and calm. No specific person is being addressed, and the reader is therefore invited to share the serenity of the moment. The original insights provided by the poet's metaphors (such as the water being gray like a dove, and the sky being barred like the sand after the tide is out) indicate that both speaker and reader may view life with wonder and love.

WRITING TOPICS. The poem's observations about the external and internal world. How does the poet achieve a reverential mood? The relationship of the mood to animals and objects like hawks, doves, sparrows, chicken, balloons, and cats.

WORKS FOR COMPARISON WITH "WELLFLEET SABBATH"

Dickinson, *This World Is Not Conclusion*, 890
Pickthall, *The Worker in Sandalwood*, 341
Warren, *Heart of Autumn*, 1006
O'Connor, *First Confession*, 520

SIR WALTER RALEIGH, *The Nymph's Reply to the Shepherd*, *pages 589–590*

This poem was intended as a reply to Marlowe's poem, and students enjoy making the comparison. Marlowe's shepherd is passionate, supplicating, and sly; he knows that spring and youth do not last, but he avoids dwelling on this detail. Raleigh's nymph is honest, realistic, and cynical; she ruthlessly exposes the flaws in the shepherd's argument.

Answers to the Study Questions, page 590

(1) As in Marlowe's poem, the speaker and the listener are identified in the title. The speaker is the "nymph" pursued by the shepherd; the listener is the shepherd, although he may not wish to listen to the end.

Raleigh's poem imitates the situation, rhythm, rhyming words, and stanza form of Marlowe's poem. Both offer six four-line stanzas, and rhyme on the word "love" at the beginning and end.

(2) The nymph's rejection of love is based on her realistic awareness of love and the world, as contrasted with the ideal world portrayed by Marlowe's shepherd. Time consumes all; flowers fade; storms rage; the world is full of cares, and so on.

(3) A parody is an imitation of an artistic form for purposes of ridicule (either the form or the topic of the original). Because Raleigh uses the same form as Marlowe, and introduces many of the same details (but with an opposite view), the poem qualifies as a parody. In this respect, it is also a refutation of the unrealistic, head-in-the sand views of life that may do more harm to relationships than the more realistic view of the nymph.

(4) The nymph's refutation may be schematized in a logical pattern: *1. If A, then B. 2. Not A. 3. Therefore, not B.* The *1* is "if the world were young, etc., then I would live with you" (brought out in stanza 1). The *2* is all the negative detail in stanzas 2–5. The *3* is the final stanza, in which she draws the conclusion of the previous stanzas. The world is not eternally young and pleasant, and therefore she rejects the shepherd; in fact, however, even if the world were perfect, she does not concede to the shepherd that he would be her choice ("my mind *might* move," line 24).

WRITING TOPICS. The speaker's argument, schematized and considered. The character of the speaker. The connection between the natural world and human activity. The dramatic situation of the poem.

WORKS FOR COMPARISON WITH "THE NYMPH'S REPLY"

Herrick, *Corinna's Going A-Maying*, 952
Shakespeare, *My Mistress' Eyes*, 643
Wyatt, *I Find No Peace*, 670

CHRISTINA ROSSETTI, *A Christmas Carol, pages 590–591*

This poem is also one of the famous Christmas hymns, with music by Gustav Holst (1874–1934) whose best-known orchestral composition is *The Planets* (1914–1916). You may be fortunate enough to have students who know the tune of *A Christmas Carol* and who also have the bravery to sing it.

Answers to the Study Questions, page 591

(1) The time is Christmas day, here shown as in the coldest depths of

winter, the place allegedly Bethlehem. Yet Rossetti is describing an English winter (frozen ground, snow falls, ice stony hard, etc.). The bitterness and bleakness contrast with the warmth and glory of the event.

(2) The location—stable, manger, adoring Magi, shepherds, and animals—is part of the story of Jesus' birth as presented in the Biblical books of Matthew and Luke, and as legend has embroidered it. The simplicity is essential, theologically, to present the human vulnerability of the God/Man and yet to remind readers (most of whom, at least in Rossetti's day, would have known Christian teaching) that the person born in such poverty was the King of Kings.

(3) Both angels and the mother are present to love and honor the child (stanza 4). They stress human involvement in the event, and therefore prepare us for the speaker's own poverty and humanity in the final stanza.

(4) The speaker considers the gifts (gold, frankincense, myrrh, and, presumably, a lamb), which were offered by poor and rich alike. Being "poor," she opts for the gift of herself. Since the heart is both the traditional location of emotions and also the center of one's whole being, her gift is total; no one could offer more.

Writing topics. Winter and warmth. Historical and legendary scenes of the birth. The connection between the speaker's adoration and the scene she describes. The structure of the poem, leading to the climactic last line.

Works for Comparison with "A Christmas Carol"

Pickthall, *The Worker in Sandalwood*, 341
Crashaw, *On Our Crucified Lord*, 639
Donne, *A Hymn to God the Father*, 876

Jane Shore, *A Letter Sent to Summer, pages 591–592*

This poem could only have been written by a poet living in a temperate zone. It surely represents a mood that people experiencing winter have often felt. On certain cold, snowy, windy days, the yearning for summer occurs, even allowing for some of the summer's unpleasant aspects. "A Letter Sent to Summer" is notable for its negative as well as positive details about summer, and for this reason it avoids the excessive romanticization often found in popular songs, such as "White Christmas" and "Autumn in New York," that extol the various seasons.

Answers to the Study Questions, page 592

(1) The speaker is obviously a creative person who evidences strong powers of observation. Line 14, for example, assumes that the "hapless rabbit" is hibernating and therefore also wishes the summer to come so that "Desire" may "return." The speaker also evidences a sense of humor, as shown in the many inventive images (such as inviting summer to "wallpaper" her bedroom, and describing winter's snow as "buckets of whitewash").

(2) Summer, to the speaker, means a return of natural pleasantness, as shown in the friendly "baskets of flowers" that summer leaves, just "like an old friend." The bugs and monsoons, in addition to plums and the rose, show that the speaker's views are balanced, and that she recognizes summer's negative as well as positive aspects. Despite these, warm weather and summer provide the incentive for the speaker toward action, unlike winter, which causes her to "curl back into . . . [her] blizzard of linens" (line 19).

(3) The phrase "always snowing" suggests an admission that the speaker's moods correspond to the seasons. She admits to a permanent degree of lassitude or even depression (she says "it is always snowing" inside her head), particularly in winter, but that this feeling is lessened by the sights and flora of summer.

WRITING TOPICS. The positive and negative images of summer. The speaker's sense that summer is an antidote to negative moods. The various personifications of summer in the poem.

WORKS FOR COMPARISON WITH "A LETTER SENT TO SUMMER"

Keats, *To Autumn*, 661
MacNeice, *Snow*, 558
Scott, *Snow*, 791

MAURA STANTON, *Childhood, pages 592–593*

This poem is based on a fancy that "all the world's turned upside down." The phrase is commonly applied to situations in which the unexpected and unusual happens. In the poem, the speaker assumes that gravity is somehow suspended and that therefore her world is governed by life on the ceiling. If one grants this fanciful supposition, what would the world down on the floor, where gravity applies, be like?

Answers to the Study Questions, page 593

(1) The first four lines describe a normal enough type of daydream

in which the speaker admits to imagining that she could walk on the ceiling of her house all by herself. Perhaps not everyone has had such a daydream, but most people have had, at one time or another, similar wild fancies that are fun to pursue to their logical extensions.

(2) The world as seen from the ceiling is accurate and well imagined. The lines "I liked to walk across the swirling plaster / Into the parts of the house I couldn't see" (10–11), for example, are applicable to walkers in a house whether on the floor or on the ceiling. The rooms described from above (lines 13–17) contain the normal clutter of a house that is lived in by a normal family.

(3) Line 20 is a pivoting line that shifts the poem from its fanciful base toward a consideration of serious issues. In light of the title, the subject seems to be that of growth. As a child one accepts all the circumstances and situations of living in the family, but as one gets older, one becomes more distant and disconnected from childhood. If we accept such a proposition about the purpose of the final thirteen lines, the line "How do I ever get back to the real house" takes on a serious and almost plaintive tone.

(4) The speaker is obviously brilliant and imaginative. She is also expressing the concerns of a young person growing out of childhood, moving out of the confines of home, and trying to become established in life. A change in the line "I strive to look down" to "I strive to look back" clarifies the idea that the poem reflects a transition from childhood to adulthood. Of course, the line "I strive to look down" is infinitely better because it is so vibrantly consistent with the concept and imagery of the poem.

Writing topics. The meaning of living on the ceiling. The shift that line 20 brings about in the poem. The accuracy of life on the floor, as seen from the ceiling. The meaning of the title.

Works for Comparison with "Childhood"

Collins, *Schoolsville*, 547
Henley, *Am I Blue*, 1403
Olds, *35/10*, 854
Olsen, *I Stand Here Ironing*, 526

William Wordsworth, *Lines Composed a Few Miles Above Tintern Abbey*, *pages 593–597*

A critic once said that writers of the Romantic movement wrote poetry, not poems. "Tintern Abbey" fits this description. Note that Wordsworth himself describes the work as "Lines," implying that he did not have specific limitations of form in mind when he composed it. "Tintern Abbey" also illustrates the Romantics' idea that the source of poetry was mysterious and also virtually holy. Thus Wordsworth says that the poem came to him as he was completing a walking tour in 1798. He says that when he wrote it down, he changed nothing, thus observing the sacredness of his own inspiration.

Answers to the Study Questions, page 597

(1) The speaker visualizes the scene as taking place in the present moment. He is lying beneath a sycamore on the banks of the Wye River, surrounded by steep cliffs and an agricultural landscape. In the distance there are farm houses from whose chimneys come "wreaths of smoke." The scene is specific because the speaker describes it as he sees it, and locates it clearly at a particular place near Tintern Abbey. During the past five years he has often been in towns and cities, and there, in his lonely rooms, the memory of these scenes has given him great pleasure.

(2) The speaker believes that experiences of natural beauty, and the pleasure they give both as they occur and as they are remembered, directly cause human beings to be moral, kind, and loving. He clearly finds in nature a transcendent experience, a "motion and a spirit," that unites all created things with the unseen and mysterious life force of the universe.

(3) The speaker believes that this experience will be "life and food for future years" (lines 64–65).

(4) The speaker's argument is subtle. He believes that a spirit both in and beyond nature speaks to human beings at special or heightened moments. It is a two-way street: The individual must be willing both to see and listen, knowing that eye and ear also help create the experience which allows the speaker to find this "presence" in the world. The setting is therefore fully integrated into the speaker's philosophy. Without the two-way relationship (the speaker bringing his thoughts, experiences, and responsiveness to the scene; Nature providing the beauty from which many of his intellectual and emotional responses spring) the philosophy would not have its coherence and emotional power.

(5) Nature, the speaker believes, has the power to create scenes of beauty which, in their overwhelming power and effect upon the mind and senses, bring the receptive viewer to a state in which "we are laid asleep / In body, and become a living soul," (lines 45–46) and penetrate to the essence of reality and life itself. The "cheerful faith" (line 133), shared by

the speaker and his "friend," is that nature will never fail to give this joy if people continue to love her; that with the strength given by this happiness they can withstand life's disappointments or human betrayals, and that everything around them is "full of blessings" (line 134).

Writing topics. The setting as an actual perceived place. The effect of setting upon the speaker's ideas. The contrast between remembered, present, and future perception.

Works for Comparison with "Tintern Abbey" Lines

Dickinson, *Some Keep the Sabbath*, 884
Pickthall, *The Worker in Sandalwood*, 341
Piercy, *Wellfleet Sabbath*, 588

James Wright, *A Blessing, pages 597–598*

Wright's "A Blessing" demonstrates a flat, common portrayal of experience. The skill of the poem is its restraint in the rendering of action, and its sudden, climactic expansiveness at the end. In this respect "A Blessing" may be compared with Virginia Scott's "Snow" (page 791).

Answers to the Study Questions, page 598

(1) Just before the narration begins, the two ponies have come out of the woods, as if to welcome the two representatives of another order of beings (the speaker and friend). The present tense gives the poem immediacy, so that the greeting appears to be happening before the speaker's eyes.

(2) The setting is specific: The event is located in place and time, moving from physical concreteness into the speaker's more intense but less easily described feelings of satisfaction and happiness.

(3) The realization which overtakes the speaker is that of the kinship, perhaps even the "oneness," of living things. Filled with love for the animals, the speaker delights in the feel of the pony. At that point the speaker realizes that, could he or she transcend the human body and its limitations, the true expression at the moment could only be a transformation into a burst of blossoms.

(4) The first 21 lines are essential because they bring the reader along into the speaker's experience. The care with which the landscape is drawn, the description of events in the present tense, the shift from what the ponies do to how the speaker is responding—all this gives an immediacy which sets the stage for the speaker's concluding revelation.

Writing topics. The importance of the details about natural setting. The structure leading up to the last lines. The significance of twilight and darkness in connecting speaker, animals, and natural scene.

WORKS FOR COMPARISON WITH "A BLESSING"

Dickinson, *There's a Certain Slant of Light*, 883
Frost, *The Strong Are Saying Nothing*, 902
Walker, *Revolutionary Petunias*, 1005

Writing About Character and Setting in Poetry, *pages 598–603*

In assigning an essay for this chapter, you should emphasize the interactions of character with time, place, and circumstance. Traits are not brought out over an extended time, as in fiction, but rather the immediate circumstances and traits merge to create attitudes or decisions. In Hardy's "The Walk," for example, the life full of living together has already taken place between the speaker and the listener, and the speaker is now exhibiting loving traits combined with sorrowful perceptiveness about life's shortness and approaching death.

Similarly, the sample essay (pages 601–602) illustrates the treatment of a character in the midst of a situation. The Duke's various traits are brought out because of what he tells us of his past, and the evil quality of his character is clearly to be applied in his present negotiations with the envoy of the Count. It is the interactions of character and circumstance, in this way, that should be emphasized.

Writing Topics about Character and Setting, *page 603*

(1) The first topic requires the comparison of three poems that fall together naturally because of authorial intention—a rare circumstance in the study of literature. Making the comparisons is in a great sense the attempt to show how the later poems follow Marlowe's original in form, detail, and development.

(2) The poems by Blake, Arnold, and Wordsworth are, respectively, political, philosophical, and almost mystical. They all center upon responses to change. Blake's, however, seems to point toward political changes. Both Wordsworth and Arnold emphasize how individuals should use what they can of the past in order to move into the future.

(3) Students may express embarrassment about trying to create an

autobiographical poem. For this reason they might be glad to resort to the anonymity of a using a third person, even if they themselves are still the subject. What is important here is that they use details about events and places as a means of developing the topic of character: qualities, responses, resolutions, and decisions.

(4) All five of the poems base their religious conclusions upon a concrete situation, from twilight near the water to ponies in a field. It is difficult to determine what students will conclude as a result of their analyses, but the connection between the reality of place and the vitality of religious experience should be stressed with all the poems.

Chapter Fifteen
Pages 604–626

Words: The Building Blocks of Poetry

This chapter introduces students to the importance of individual words and of word order in poetry. In teaching the concepts, you can stress the relatively heavy load that each individual word must carry in a poem. In teaching denotation and connotation (pages 610–612), you may want to call on your students to provide more examples of words that have acquired negative or positive connotations. The analysis of advertisements, both printed and dramatized on television, can be a gold mine for strongly connotative words.

The discussion of diction (pages 604–608) may also be expanded in the classroom with a call for student examples. This can be especially effective with jargon and slang. A good illustrative field here is computer jargon, which is quickly moving into "mainstream" English. Jargon is especially important in discussing the poems by Reed and Eberhart

In teaching syntax (pages 608–609), your problem may well be how to stop. It is unlikely that many students will have thought much about syntax beyond their awareness of the differences between declarative and interrogative sentences. For examples, you might select the line "Yet morning smiles the busy race to cheer / And new-born pleasure brings to happier men" from Gray's "Sonnet on the Death of Richard West" (page 617), and ask students to lay it out in an order more in line with today's speech ("Yet morning smiles to cheer the busy race [of human beings] / And brings new-born pleasure to happier men"). The examples in the discussion about parallelism and repetition should be sufficient for establishing the relationship of syntax to rhetorical patterns.

Robert Graves, *The Naked and the Nude, page 611*

This poem, discussed briefly on page 612, dramatically shows the impact of denotation and connotation, not only on language and poetry, but also on human behavior. The first study question (page 612) invites the student to associate *naked* with its origin in Old English, and *nude,* with the elevation and tendency toward abstraction of many words that have come to our language from French and Latin. This point may be buttressed with the examination of English-Latinate pairs of words like *live* and *reside, hearty* and *cordial, live* and *reside, house* and *mansion, cow* and *beef,* and *think* and *ponder* (one may exempt words like *joy, law, porch, flower*, and so on, all of which are straightforward and specific).

Writing topics. Denotation and connotation in the poem. The importance of word selection in conveying the right meaning. The nature of the speaker.

Works for Comparison with "The Naked and the Nude"

Dove, *Ö*, 935
Keats, *Ode on a Grecian Urn*, 848
MacLeish, *Ars Poetica*, 851
Moore, *Poetry*, 853
Strand, *Eating Poetry*, 621

William Blake, *The Lamb, pages 612–613*

This poem is useful for discussing the effects of simple diction and repetition in creating tone and meaning. The childlike diction reinforces the simplicity of the speaker and the listener, and emphasizes through connotation the poem's portrayal of a Creator with loving and mild attributes. The first stanza asks the poem's central question four times: "who made thee?" The diction implies an answer; words like *lamb*, *delight*, *softest*, *wooly*, *tender*, and *rejoice* suggest a loving and cherishing creator. The second stanza answers the question, equating God with both the lamb and the child (lines 13–18).

Answers to the Study Questions, page 613

(1) The speaker is a child and the listener a lamb (line 20); they are linked in their mildness, simplicity, and symbolic value as alternate images of the Creator (Jesus as a child and the Lamb of God, the agnus dei).

(2) The repetition (the rhetorical device *anaphora*) stresses the speaker's innocent, childlike qualities and makes the structure of the poem simple and clear.

(3) The diction is neutral and concrete, in keeping with the speaker's childlike character, and appropriate for the concept of a beneficent and peaceful God.

(4) The Creator, like the lamb and the child, is meek and mild, loving and gentle, simple and caring. The words all connote the most direct, least complicated view of God that is possible.

(5) Blake's idea of God in this poem from *The Songs of Innocence* is that God is a God of peace and love, not the God of Donne's "Batter My Heart" who is an active warrior ready to break down the barriers that people erect through their spiritual impiety, negligence, and defiance.

Writing topics. The effect of diction and repetition in the poem. The image of the creator. The speaker's character. Good poems for comparison are listed immediately above in the discussion of Donne's "Batter my Heart."

Works for Comparison with "The Lamb"

Frost, *Desert Places*, 764
Kumin, *Hello, Hello Henry*, 618
Roethke, *Dolor*, 620
Zimmer, *The Day Zimmer Lost Religion*, 1012

Robert Burns, ***Green Grow the Rashes, O, pages 613–614***

This poem is one of Burns's most famous. It is included here for this reason and also because of its use of dialect. With only a few side notes, students can recognize the words that otherwise might be obscure (such as *han'* and *war'ly*), and they can readily appreciate the relationship between the rhythmical lines and the content.

Answers to the Study Questions, page 614

(1) The speaker is clearly an individual who is celebrating his love of women. He is unabashed in his pronouncements but there is no reason to take his remarks as anything but serious, despite his use of hyperbole in praising women.

(2) The speaker claims that he has spent his "sweetest hours" among "the lasses." He also seeks to corroborate his attitude by claiming that the "wisest man the war'l e'er saw" was also a person who "dearly loved the lasses." He is uncomplimentary toward sober people who might sneer at his pronouncements (lines 17–18).

(3) There are two Biblical versions of God's creation of humankind. In the first (Genesis 1:27) men and women are created simultaneously. In the second and more recognized version, (Genesis 2:20–23) God fashions woman out of one of the man's ribs. Because of Burns's stanza 5, in which

man is only the work of Nature's apprentice hand, with woman being the presumed product of Nature's master hand, it is likely that people in 1787 would have felt shocked if not outraged. One might also note that Burns's speaker attributes the creation of humankind not to God but to "Nature."

Writing topics. Burns's use of Scottish dialect. The speaker's reasons for praising women. The nature of the speaker.

Works for Comparison with "Green Grow the Rashes, O"

Jonson, *Drink to Me, Only, With Thine Eyes*, 573
Marlowe, *The Passionate Shepherd to His Love*, 587
Rukeyser, *Looking at Each Other*, 666

Lewis Carroll (Charles L. Dodgeson), *Jabberwocky, pages 614–615*

This poem shows that we can understand poetry to some extent without knowing the meanings of all the words. Like Alice, we can get the drift without being able to pin down the exact meaning of any lines. To make the poem as clear as it is, Carroll depends on the suggestions that sounds create for meaning. More importantly, however, he uses key words to give us the essential idea (such as "Beware," "sword," "through and through," and "dead"), and he also scrupulously observes the proper syntax, so that we may imagine meaning for some of the nonce words. Ironically, perhaps, some words that Carroll made up for this poem have entered the language, to such an extent that computerized spell-checkers do not flag them as misspelled.

Answers to the Study Questions, page 615

(1) The "tale" of this short, ballad-like poem is that an unnamed hero goes forth, defeats the monstrous Jabberwock, and returns home victorious.

(2) The unpacking exercise can work very well in class, especially if you ask the students to prepare something in writing beforehand. When you make the assignment, you might ask the students to consider how they can tell what part of speech (noun, verb, adjective) a specific word is supposed to be. The answer, of course, is that Carroll's syntax defines the role of each *portmanteau word* absolutely. Here are some of the more obvious unpackings you might offer as examples: *slithy* = slippery + slithering + lively + lithe; *toves* = toads + doves; *gimble* = gambol + nimble;

manxome = maximum + noxious + fearsome; *galumphing* = galloping + lumbering + lump; *chortle* = chuckle + snort ("Chortle" has become a standard word.)

Writing Topics. Why "Jabberwocky" works, despite the made-up words. How the ballad-narrative tradition helps us understand the poem.

Works for Comparison with "Jabberwocky"

Hall, *Scenic View*, 946
Morgan, *The Computer's First Christmas Card*, 774
Strand, *Eating Poetry*, 621

John Donne, *Holy Sonnet 14: Batter My Heart, Three-Personed God, pages 615–616*

This sonnet is a meditation on the speaker's sinfulness and his desire that God purify him. Of great interest are Donne's verbs of violence—the metaphor being that the speaker's soul is like a fortress, or a woman "betrothed" to another man; paradoxically, neither will be free and pure unless God defeats them. The central quatrains are based on traditional metaphors. In lines 5–8, the speaker compares himself to a town captured by evil forces, the governor (Reason) having failed to defend it for the king (*You,* God).

Answers to the Study Questions, page 616

(1) The "three-personed God" is the Trinity; the active verbs in the first quatrain suggest that God is a being with awesome, overwhelming power.

(2) *Knock* and *break* can be associated with God the Father, *breathe* and *blow* with the Holy Spirit (*spiritus* = spirit, breath, wind, blowing), and *shine* and *burn* with God the Son (the pun lurking here is the traditional play on *son* and *sun*).

(3) The effect of the altered word order is to throw emphasis on the *me* as the object of the verb *defend* and, similarly, to put *fain* into a position of stress so that the speaker may show that his will is to love God, but that his character is such that he is weak, and cannot follow his own will without the control of God.

(4) In lines 9–14 the speaker becomes the bride, Satan the *enemy* to whom the speaker is engaged, and Christ the bridegroom who must "break that knot again." The couplet states the clinching paradox; the speaker will never be *free* of sin unless God enthralls him and he will never be

chaste (cleansed of sin) unless God ravishes him. *Enthrall* means both *enslave* and *captivate; ravish* means both *seize by force* and *fill with joy.* Spiritually, of course, both suggest their opposites; to be enthralled or ravished by God implies freedom from sin and absolute purity.

WRITING TOPICS. The way that the diction creates a specific image of God in this poem. The speaker's conceptualization of his own spiritual state. The use of sexual imagery.

WORKS FOR COMPARISON WITH "BATTER MY HEART"

Blake, *The Lamb*, 612
Blake, *The Tyger*, 636
Eberhart, *The Fury of Aerial Bombardment*, 616
Hardy, *Channel firing*, 584
Herbert, *Love (III)*, 951
Piercy, *Wellfleet Sabbath*, 588

RICHARD EBERHART, *The Fury of Aerial Bombardment, page 616*

Eberhart's poem, like Hardy's "Channel Firing" (page 584), uses the occasion of war to consider questions about God and humanity. In class, you might begin by asking your students to describe the differences they see between the first three stanzas and the last.

Answers to the Study Questions, pages 616–617

(1) The speaker, as we discover in the last stanza, is a military instructor ("late in school"); the "you" can be the reader, an unspecified person who might be present, or humanity in general.

(2) The diction of the first three stanzas is general and abstract. The speaker asks unanswerable questions: Why does humanity continue to wage war? Why doesn't God put a stop to it? Is humanity stupid? Is God indifferent? Is warfare the only "eternal truth"?

(3) In the last stanza, the speaker shifts to specific and concrete terms and names: *Van Wettering, Averill, list, lever, pawl.* He also shifts from abstract considerations ("infinite space," "eternal truth") to specific facts: the names of young soldiers who have "gone to early death" (notice the ironic contrast between the "*early* death" and "*late* in school"). This shift does not answer the earlier questions, but it does focus the poem and bring it to an effective conclusion. The jargon in this closing stanza works perfectly; it provides the concreteness of objects and weaponry even if we cannot identify the objects.

(4) Both poems bring out strong anti-war sentiments. Hardy vividly brings out the character of a scoffing, jesting God and also the disillusioned Parson Thirdly, while Eberhart does not develop any characters. Both poems raise the same questions, though Eberhart attributes war more to God than to humankind, unlike Hardy's attribution of war to nations striving to make "red war yet redder." A thorough comparison could become fairly extensive. One might also compare Reed's poem, "The Naming of Parts" (page 618) as another anti-war poem with a teacher-student similarity to "The Fury of Aerial Bombardment," but with a less ironic and bitter tone.

Writing topics. The tone of the last stanza. The view of God, and the questions about God. The view of humankind. The specific names.

Works for Comparison with
"The Fury of Aerial Bombardment"

Crane, *Do Not Weep, Maiden*, 928
Dickinson, *My Triumph Lasted Till the Drums*, 888
Hardy, *Channel Firing*, 584
Seeger, *I Have a Rendezvous with Death*, 982
Weigl, *Song of Napalm*, 1007

Thomas Gray, *Sonnet on the Death of Richard West, page 617*

This poem was Gray's poetic response to the death of his good friend, Richard West, in 1742. It is notable here primarily because Wordsworth used it as the basis for criticizing the diction of the previous age while defending his own concept of poetic diction. For today's students the poem is of interest because of the diction and also because of Gray's relatively unfamiliar syntax.

Answers to the Study Questions, page 617

(1) A good case can be made that the speaker's subject is himself. It is only in the thirteenth line that the subject ("him that cannot hear") is mentioned, but for the rest of the poem the speaker concentrates on his own responses and makes no effort to praise the dead friend.

(2) See the special discussion, page 607, for a discussion of the concept of decorum and poetic diction. Gray's phrases all have an element of accuracy about them, as with "redd'ning Phoebus," which refers to the ruddy appearance of the sun when it first rises. Certainly the phrases are

not common, and their use keeps the references distant from the reader rather than immediate.

(3) The characteristic of these line is that objects and modifiers are not placed in the order that students today are accustomed to seeing. Thus, line 6 may be inverted to read "These eyes do require a different object." Similar rearrangements may be carried out with the other lines. Students may ask why the poet has written such lines. The obvious answer, of course, is that Gray assumed that his audience had been schooled in Latin, and that word order is less significant in that language than English is.

(4) The revolution in language that Wordsworth sought to carry out required that poetry should contain words that were to be middle, not high, and that they should be appropriate for both prose and poetry. By this standard many of Gray's lines fell short. The lines Wordsworth noted contain none of the elaborate phrases, such as "smiling mornings," to which he objected. Students may want to debate the issues Wordsworth raised; likely they will agree with Wordsworth.

WRITING TOPICS. The meaning of many of Gray's phrases. The reasons for Wordsworth's objections. The topic of the poem.

WORKS FOR COMPARISON WITH "SONNET ON THE DEATH OF RICHARD WEST"

Cummings, *Buffalo Bill's Defunct*, 763
Dryden, *To the Memory of Mr. Oldham*, 763
Robinson, *Richard Cory*, 619

MAXINE KUMIN, *Hello, Hello Henry, page 618*

This poem by the Pulitzer Prize winner is one of a series featuring the character of the speaker's country neighbor, Henry Manley. Henry is a person out of the past: individualistic, cantankerous, stubborn, slow to change, and generally representing the lifestyle of a vanishing period of American life. Kumin's poems about Henry contain a mood of mild amusement mingled with genuine respect and affection.

Answers to the Study Questions, page 618

(1, 2) The language is studiously specific. The result is that the poem seems to be about the real world, the outside one affected by world leaders like Stalin, Roosevelt, and Churchill (the "Big Three"), and the local one lived in by the likes of Henry, who slowly have been assimilating the artifacts and conveniences of the twentieth century. The implication is that the more real of the worlds is the one that ordinary people, like Henry and the speaker, inhabit. Because world politics are remote, and unreachable, a reasonable response is interest in the activities of real, ordinary folks.

(3) The speaker is unidentified, but seems to be a reasonable, observant sort, whom we may presume to be a woman, also wishing for her own identity and space. The third stanza indicates her desire for privacy and individuality, and also suggests why she is friendly and sympathetic to Henry.

(4) The listener is apparently someone with whom the speaker has been involved. She has tried to sever her connection with him, but he still calls her and lets the phone ring all afternoon, an action which she regards not as a pleasure but as a "summons" (line 15). The listener's response indicates her strong wish to be herself and to be free.

Writing topics. Kumin's use of specific language. The nature of Henry's character and circumstances. The meaning of the telephone to Henry and to the speaker.

Works for Comparison with "Hello, Hello Henry"

Dickinson, *The Soul Selects Her Own Society*, 884
Halpern, *Summer in the Middle Class*, 947
Nemerov, *Life Cycle of Common Man*, 970
Sexton, *To a Friend*, 832

Henry Reed, *Naming of Parts, pages 618–619*

Reed's ironic anti-war poem, which balances the parts of a weapon against an altogether different set of parts in nature, works well in class. The two sets of parts named in the poem are pieces of a weapon and objects in nature, such as the Japonica, the branches, blossoms, and the early bees. In addition, an overtone in the speaker's meditations is that he is also thinking about the parts of a woman. The ideas explored here are neither profound nor cosmic; the poem suggests that young men in spring would prefer to follow their natural instincts rather than listen to boring military lectures. Some students may not immediately perceive the poem's layers of ambiguity. The contrast between the lecture and the out-of-doors is fairly easily understood, but the application to lovemaking may not be perceived quite as readily.

Answers to the Study Questions, page 619

(1) The two voices that we hear in the poem are the instructor's lecture and the recruit's musings about nature and the garden. Ask your

students to establish exactly when (or where) one voice stops and the other begins in each stanza.

(2) The setting is apparently a lecture room in which recruits are attending a weapons lecture as a part of their basic training. A group leader is likely standing in front of a drawing which lays out the parts of a rifle, which he is explaining. He does not, however, have an actual gun as his example, and things are dull. It is a lovely spring day, there are nearby gardens, and one thoroughly bored recruit's mind keeps slipping away from the lecture to consider the burgeoning fertility of the spring.

(3, 4) The recruit "slides" one set of words into another in his mind as he picks up words and phrases from the lecture and applies them to the garden and also to himself in the sense of sexual activity. Phrases like "easing the spring," "point of balance," and "rapidly backwards and forwards" do not require an exhaustive explanation to determine that they may refer equally to the operations of firearms and sexual parts.

Writing topics. Ambiguity in the poem. The setting. The tone, particularly about war and also about young people. The organization.

Works for comparison with "Naming of Parts"

Atwood, *Rape Fantasies,* 301
Cummings, *she being Brand / -new,* 688
Seeger, *I Have a Rendezvous with Death,* 982

Edwin Arlington Robinson, *Richard Cory, pages 619–620*

This poem is discussed in the sample essay (pages 624–625). Even if you choose not to use the writing material in this chapter, you may want to assign the essay in connection with the poem. The repetition of *And* at the beginning of six of the lines keeps the poem moving rapidly, driving us on from line to line, and suggests that all Richard Cory's qualities are connected. Students may be interested in being reminded (or being told) that Paul Simon made a musical adaptation of "Richard Cory" in 1966 (compiled in Simon & Garfunkel's *Collected Works,* Columbia, C3K 45322).

Writing topics. The characterization of the speaker. Contrasts between appearance and reality.

Works for Comparison with "Richard Cory"

Dickinson, *After Great Pain,* 884
Dickinson, *The Heart is the Capital of the Mind,* 888
Frost, *Acquainted with the Night,* 901

THEODORE ROETHKE, *Dolor, page 620*

In this poem, Roethke combines general and abstract words for sadness or grief with concrete and specific words that describe the details of day-to-day life in the offices or institutions of the modern world, in this way asserting that lives lived in such places are empty and unhappy. In teaching the poem, it will be useful to let your students separate the two classes of words and let them see that the specific-concrete terms define and focus the general-abstract ones.

Answers to the Study Questions, pages 620–621

(1) "Dolor" refers to pain, suffering, and grief. Words generally related are *sadness, misery, desolation,* and *pathos.* The details objectifying the word are made objective through a linkage with concrete and specific words and images, such as *pencils, pad, paper-weight, dust, nails,* and *pale hour.* The linkage is done with the object and an aspect of dolor. *Misery,* for example, is linked to "manila folders and mucilage," just as *sadness* is associated with "pencils." One may compare this aspect of the poem with Eliot's detail in "The Love Song of J. Alfred Prufrock" about measuring out one's life in coffee spoons (page 938, line 51). A contrast might be Billy Collins's "Schoolsville" (page 547), particularly the detail about chalk dust (line 5).

(2) The poem resembles a sonnet, though it is not rhymed, and is not molded into any dominant rhythmical pattern. Unity is achieved through rhythmical cadence groups and alliteration (e.g., *misery of manila ... mucilage*). The most notable break with the sonnet form is that there are ***thirteen*** lines rather than fourteen. One might claim that thirteen, often considered an unlucky number, is appropriate for the poem's ideas and tone.

(3) Although the poem is not specific about the institutions characterized by dolor, we may assume that Roethke is referring to places such as business offices, reception rooms, administrative offices, schools, and anywhere else where business is carried out and where files are kept. All such places have in common a certain sameness in which procedure takes precedence over life and spontaneity.

(4) For a discussion of this question, please see page 609 in the text.

WRITING TOPICS. Specific–general and concrete–abstract words. The meaning of dolor. The tone of the poem. The structure.

Works for Comparison with "Dolor"

Eliot, *The Love Song of J. Alfred Prufrock,* 938
Collins, *Schoolsville,* 547
Piercy, *The Secretary Chant,* 974

Wallace Stevens, *Disillusionment of Ten O'Clock, page 621*

The poem contrasts the colorless lives and imaginations of the townspeople of an unidentified town (the white nightgowns) with the vivid and exotic life and imagination of the drunken sailor. In teaching the poem, you might begin by discussing this contrast.

Answers to the Study Questions, page 621

(1) The time of the poem is evening, as indicated by *nightgown* and *dream.*

(2) Stevens's strategy in lines 3–11 is negative; he tells us that the townspeople *do not* have the experience or imagination to dream of anything beyond their own average lives, nor do they have the flair to wear anything green, purple, yellow, multi-colored, or ringed; instead, they wear only their white nightgowns.

(3) The people in the sleeping town are contrasted in lines 12–15 with the "old sailor" who has what the townspeople lack: the extensive experience which has supplied his imagination with some of the wonders contained in the world, so that his dreams are rich even though he is old.

(4, 5) All the vivid colors, bizarre images, lace socks, beaded ceintures, baboons and periwinkles disassociated from the townspeople in these lines are ultimately linked to the old drunken sailor who dreams of catching tigers in *red weather.* The lace and beaded ceintures suggest finery (wealth, a sense of fine living, exotic foreign places, different ways of life, a different mentality, and a broad outlook on the world). The baboons hint at distant ports and jungles, and the periwinkles evoke the sea.

(6) The disillusionment of the title may refer to the absence of illusions (dreams, imagination) or to the poet's revelation that the people in white nightgowns lack any imaginative life.

Writing topics. The dominant tone of the poem. The contrast between the people in white nightgowns and the drunken sailor. Stevens's use of color and connotative words.

Works for Comparison with "Disillusionment of Ten O'Clock"

Hugo, *Degrees of Gray in Philipsburg,* 585
Lightman, *In Computers,* 961
Heather McHugh, *Lines,* 966
Shelley, *Ozymandias,* 778

Mark Strand, *Eating Poetry, pages 621–622*

Usually writers indicate the acquisition of learning and poetry by referring to difficult and tiring actions like "burning the midnight oil" and "hitting the books." "Eating Poetry" is unique, however, because it emphasizes the pleasure and joy of learning. Indeed, the poem is an intellectual romp, just like the dogs coming up the stairs (line 9) to devour more poems. Poetic allusion in the poem may be seen in the phrase "eyeballs roll," an overstatement to indicate the throes of passion which is used by Pope in "Eloisa to Abelard." In addition, the phrase "bookish dark" (line 18) recalls Frost's "pillared dark" in the poem "Come In." In Frost, the pillared dark is like an invitation to come in and change the speaker's life. Here Strand uses the phrase similarly, for the "bookish dark" has effected such a change in the ebullient speaker.

Answers to the Study Questions, page 622

(1) Obvious indications that the poem is not to be taken literally are the ink running from the corners of the speaker's mouth and the eating of poetry. The image developed in the poem is that the speaker has been emptying the shelves of books in the way dogs would empty shelves of dog food.

(2) The serious topic undergirding the poem is suggested by line 2, "There is no happiness like mine," and line 16, "I am a new man." These lines clearly suggest that learning is accompanied with joy.

(3) With the exceptions noted in question 2, almost all the words indicate the comic topic. The sad eyes, the poems being gone, the rolling eyeballs, the stamping of the librarian's feet, the licking of the hand, the screaming—all are clearly a part of the poem's comic scene.

Writing topics. What does it mean to be "eating poetry"? The contrast between the poem's comic mode and its serious intent.

WORKS FOR COMPARISON WITH "EATING POETRY"

Bradstreet, *The Author to Her Book*, 687
Finch, *To the Nightingale*, 690
Keats, *Chapman's Homer*, 650
Moore, *How to Become a Writer*, 205
Nash, *Very Like a Whale*, 969

Writing About Diction and Syntax in Poetry, *pages 622–626*

This assignment might prove difficult for those students who are not used to thinking about words and the possibilities of various shades of meaning among them. The material here should help solve at least part of the problem. The opening discussion considers ways to begin this sort of investigation, to discover ideas, and to formulate a central idea for an essay. In preparing your students to write an essay about words, you might wish to take them through the investigative and thesis-formation processes in class, using the model of a specific poem. You could then have them write about that poem or any other in the text. The sample essay on "Richard Cory" (pages 624–625) illustrates many of the principles and processes discussed in the chapter. These are highlighted once again in the commentary on the essay (page 625).

Writing Topics for Diction and Syntax, *page 626*

(1) This topic, requiring the analysis of four separate poems, can be difficult unless the students can lay out their materials so that they can see them at a glance. For this, separate sets of cards, or separate columns, are necessary. Ask students to study Appendix B, on the Extended Comparison-Contrast Essay, for ideas about how to develop their essays without making their papers too long.

(2) The second question involves another careful look at "Jabberwocky," together with some of the ideas explored in the study questions and in the appropriate part of this manual.

(3) To write the short poems suggested in the third writing topic, students will need to exert their imaginations energetically. Yet today, with all the television and film fare analyzing crime from the standpoint of criminals, they may have precedents for seeing things in that way. What is important is that they are able to explain why different choices of words, both favorable and unfavorable, stem naturally out of the differences in approach to the particular "crime" they write about.

Chapter Sixteen
Pages 627–648

Imagery: The Poem's Link to the Senses

This introductory section acquaints students with the various types of images—visual, auditory, olfactory, gustatory, tactile, kinetic, and kinesthetic—all of which account for the appeal and validity of poetry. Real images in a poem lend reality to the poem's assertions. The logic of understanding imagery is this: Readers have seen many of the same things that poets describe (sun, moon, stars, ocean), and have also perceived many similar things (roses, boats, fish, sweethearts, boats, singers, songs, jewels, hair, and so on). Therefore, references to these things create a bond of perception authenticating the presuppositions, responses, attitudes, thoughts, and ideas of poetry. The use of the black-and-white reproduction of the Herkomer painting (page 629) may help as a visual demonstration of the relationship between the viewer–reader and the artist–poet's depictions of the world.

John Masefield, *Cargoes, pages 629–630*

"Cargoes" is a fascinating image-picture, analogous to a triptych in art, in which things are almost graphically rendered in poetry. Students respond easily to the language. Indeed, the poem's great value is that its diction, being so real itself, leads naturally into a general discussion of degrees of reality as represented by language.

Answers to the Study Questions, page 630

(1) Stanza 1 provides images which are exotic and splendid. They represent color and oriental grandeur, as well as the values of a world now long gone. All the objects are appropriate to Solomon's time, whether as gifts to be used to amuse the court or as building materials. They evoke the nostalgia with which we view this lost world. Stanza 2 and the values it contains are closer to our world. Finally, stanza 3 shows us what it has all been for—so that a dirty coastal ship can carry fuel and cheap prod-

ucts for sale in the modern world. Gone are the splendor, the color, and the beauty; utility and trade are all.

(2) The images are primarily visual. Almost all suggest colors and textures, though some also suggest aromas (cedarwood, cinnamon) and some suggest smells (smoke stack, coal). The blazing colors of stanza 2 are preceded by somewhat less color in stanza 1 and followed abruptly by an almost unrelieved gray-brown-black palette of color in stanza 3. There is little stress on auditory images, except that one may imagine the apes chattering and the peacocks calling.

(3) The use of the participles intensifies the impression that the poem is a word, or image, picture. It is not a description of action but a verbal rendering, almost like a painting of ships. *Rowing* suggests human action, and one visualizes the unified motions of men and oars; *dipping* suggests flight, like that of a bird; *butting* suggests struggle, and the determined action of a stubborn and tough animal like a mule or a goat.

(4) The supposition is possibly accurate, but Masefield obscures that line of thought by his choice of verbals and word pictures.

WRITING TOPICS. Masefield's images of sight. The relationship of image to mood. The allusiveness of the imagery.

WORKS FOR COMPARISON WITH "CARGOES"

Nemerov, *Life Cycle of Common Man*, 970
Pound, *In a Station of the Metro*, 642
Stevens, *Disillusionment of Ten O'Clock*, 621

WILFRED OWEN, *Anthem for Doomed Youth, pages 630–631*

Wilfred Owen was killed in France in 1918, a week before the Armistice that ended World War I. Today he is considered one of the foremost anti-war poets. Benjamin Britten set "What Passing Bells" for tenor and orchestra in his *War Requiem* (1962). The band "10,000 Maniacs" recorded a version of this work, and *Dulce et Decorum Est,* on *Hope Chest* (Elektra 9–60962–2).

Answers to the Study Questions, page 631

(1) The predominant images in the octave are those of sound. Lines 1, 4, 5, 6, and 8 refer to sounds of peace, while 2, 3, and 7 ironically displace these peaceful sounds with sounds of war. Thus the "passing bells" are not bells but gunfire, and the prayers ("orisons") are made up of rapidly rattling rifles. In line 8, the sound of bugles from "sad shires"

suggests the solemnity of military burials. In the last six lines the images are primarily visual—held candles, shining eyes, pale brows, flowers, and the repeated drawing of window shades. It is as though a cease-fire calm had descended.

(2) The contrast and tone are set in the first line, where the image of the death of cattle stands for the death of men in combat. The image suggests that the men are not valued as human beings. Similarly, the metaphorical comparisons of rifle fire to prayers, and the wailing of shells to the sounds of demented choirs, underline the monstrous lack of dignity with which these men died.

(3) There is a progression of images in the poem, all having to do with those who are left behind—family, sweethearts, parents. The "holy glimmers of good-byes" suggests how light from altar candles shines in the tear-filled eyes of those who mourn. The grief of sweethearts is suggested by the "pallor of girls' brows." The consolations of philosophy and the privacy of grief are brought out by the "tenderness of patient minds" and the "drawing-down of blinds." All the images share in depicting the unutterable grief of those whose loved ones are now dead.

Writing topics. The auditory images. Images conducive to sorrow. The use of irony or ironic reversal in the images.

Works for Comparison with "Anthem for Doomed Youth"

Jarrell, *The Death of the Ball Turret Gunner*, 550
Northrup, *Ogichidag* 559
Owen, *Dulce et Decorum Est*, 681
Seeger, *I have a Rendezvous with Death*, 982
Zabytko, *Home Soil*, 403

Elizabeth Bishop, *The Fish, pages 632–634*

With its stress on vivid details and flat, scrupulously plain diction, "The Fish" has been a particular favorite among lovers of Nature and the environment. It was so often requested for anthologies that by the early 1970s Bishop did not grant permission for it to be printed, on the grounds that she wanted readers to learn the wider range of her poetry.

Answers to the Study Questions, page 634

(1) The actions imaged in the poem are (a) the catching of the fish and holding him out of the water by the speaker, (b) the fish's absolute

passivity (line 7), (c) the movement of his gills as he breathes, (d) the speaker's careful observation of this trophy, (e) the fish's tiny eye movements, (f) the expansion of the speaker's sense of triumph, (g) the development of the rainbow colors in the boat, and (h) the release of the fish. The images are both ordinary and unusual, since it is the internal motion (the growth of the sense of victory) which pulls the reader into the poem's movement and excitement.

(2) The fish is very ugly. It is described in such detail to give us a sense of its identity and therefore its value.

(3) The fish has been caught before and has, on five previous occasions, broken the line and gotten away. It is a fish of almost legendary prowess in the battle with its human enemies.

(4) The rainbow is a floating oil stain, but to the speaker it represents the shimmering excitement of victory.

(5) The action is abrupt, but in the light of the fish's unusual passivity (a fish hooked and pulled out of water fights and wiggles desperately) and its almost Olympian refusal to meet its captor's eye, release is the only appropriate act. Letting the fish go signifies both the speaker's respect for this old fighter and the speaker's realization that to have caught the fish is victory and achievement enough.

Writing topics. The fish and the rainbow as symbols. The kinesthetic images. Images of endurance and indomitability.

Works for Comparison with "The Fish"

Wright, *A Blessing*, 593
Jeffers, *The Purse-Seine*, 805
Lightman, *In Computers*, 961
Whitecloud, *Blue Winds Dancing*, 119

George Herbert, *The Pulley, pages 634–635*

"The Pulley" is an excellent poem for the illustration of imagery because of its graphic title and emblematic comparison of mechanics and salvation. Students who are artistic may be able to draw a sketch of a pulley for the benefit of your class. If any students of physics know about the mechanical advantage of pulleys, you may be able to call on them to furnish the literal basis of the image.

Answers to the Study Questions, page 635

(1) The dramatic scene of the poem is apparently The Garden of

Eden or somewhere on earth at the time of the Creation. God is deciding what blessings to bestow. God decides to withhold rest or repose, fearing that we human beings will otherwise have all we need and will have no reason for divine reliance. Herbert may be thinking of the frequent Biblical references to the need for rest (e.g., Lamentations 5:5; Revelation 14:11), and particularly to Matthew 11:28 ("Come unto me, all ye who labor and are heavy laden, and I will give you rest.")

(2) These blessings include strength, beauty, wisdom, honor, and pleasure. All are blessings because they give joy and happiness as corollaries of living.

(3) Herbert is building the poem on the faith that God accepts humankind unconditionally; his phrase "repining restlessness" (line 17) describes the anxiety prior to this acceptance. Herbert emphasizes "weary" and "weariness" here as the accompanying condition of the search. Weariness is a recurring Biblical word and concept. See, for example, Isaiah 28:12 ("give rest to the weary").

(4) The dominant image of the pulley is unusual and ingenious, but it is also brilliantly right. When we realize that pulleys are mechanical devices, that they hold exceedingly firm, and that they sustain and lift great weights, we may see the appropriateness of the image.

Writing topics. The image of blessings as part of a liquid. Allusiveness. The metaphor of the pulley (how does it connect the various parts of the poem?).

Works for Comparison with "The Pulley"

Dickinson, *A Word Made Flesh*, 889
Hopkins, *God's Grandeur*, 722
Porter, *The Jilting of Granny Weatherall*, 538

William Blake, *The Tyger, page 636*

"The Tyger" is one of Blake's best-known poems, to be contrasted with "The Lamb" (page 612). The large predator as a symbol of evil is readily understood; our tradition abounds with fearsome images of wolves, foxes, bears, and so on. Some students today, newly enlightened and firmly aware of the ecological need for the preservation of the predator-prey relationship and also of the endangered state of the world's predators, regret Blake's choice. In all other respects, however, Blake's poem is timely.

Answers to the Study Questions, page 637

(1) *Burning* suggests heat, brightness, danger, and the capacity to spread and engulf all. The fire is bright at night and, like everything else, seems more dangerous then. That night has "forests" makes it all the more wild and dangerous.

(2) Creation is a kinesthetic image; other such images include burning, flying, seizing, twisting, hammering, and grasping. These images, including that of the blacksmith, suggest powerful muscularity.

(3) The question posed in the poem is whether God is the source of both good (the lamb) and evil (the tyger) in the world, and the poem therefore raises the issue of how an allegedly all-powerful and beneficent creator permits evil at all.

(4) The word "could" suggests the simple ability to do something, while the word "dare" implies a willingness to accept a challenge to perform an action without a primary concern about the outcome.

WRITING TOPICS. The meaning the tyger and the lamb. The kinesthetic imagery of creativity. Darkness and night as images.

WORKS FOR COMPARISON WITH "THE TYGER"

Eliot, *Preludes*, 640
Van Duyn, *Advice to a God*, 1001
William Butler Yeats, *Leda and the Swan*, 822

SAMUEL TAYLOR COLERIDGE, *Kubla Khan, pages 637–638*

This poem is a virtuoso piece in every major respect, even though we have only a fragment of a much longer work that Coleridge was in the process of writing. We can only regret that the fatal knock on the door, which drove the rest of it from Coleridge's mind, did not occur several hours later. As "Kubla Khan" exists, however, it possesses its own unity, being a perfect representation of the Romantic theory of inspired composition that attributed the source of creativity to a "penetralium of mystery," to use Keats's phrase. Of particular note is the indulgence in sound. Lines 17–24 form a unit that illustrates the device of onomatopoeia, and so also do lines 25–28.

Answers to the Study Questions, page 638

(1) Many of the imagined scenes are panoramic, especially those in stanzas one and two. They could be sketched or visualized, although the

sounds of the mighty fountain would be missing, and they are essential to a full sense of the excitement and splendor of the scene. The damsel with the dulcimer is a close-up image, as is that of the wailing woman. The romantic setting of the poem is a fictitious and exotic locale (Xanadu), complete with palace, deep caverns, a sacred river, gardens, incense, and greenery.

(2) The auditory images convey excitement, sorrow, danger, and supernatural involvement in the action of the poem.

(3) The poem does not seem unfinished, although the abrupt switch at line 37 from landscape description to the far more simple, human, and quiet image of the damsel points in a new direction that Coleridge did not complete. Yet, as an argument for completion, one might note that Coleridge's speaker is asserting that inspiration, whether it be from a vision or from the milk of Paradise, is essential to the development of creative energy like that which shaped Khan's palace and its gardens and landscapes.

(4) "Miracle" and "rare" suggest wonder and scarcity, something widely out of the ordinary, and therefore remarkable. Sun and ice together appear to be contradictory, but to combine them as sources of pleasure suggests a mysterious union, beyond everyday reality.

(5) To the speaker, the magical union is represented by the image of the singing maid; she is an incentive to him to aspire to goals that he has not yet seen but has only imagined. The poem concludes with the image of a group of persons, who are in awe of the person of inspiration, who dance around the speaker three times to protect themselves through ritual. The kinesthetic images recall the earlier images of motion, but here they have brought the movement into human terms.

Writing topics. The visual imagery. Images appropriate to natural scenery. The effect on the poem of auditory imagery and onomatopoeia. The image of the Abyssinian maid and the speaker.

Works for Comparison with "Kubla Khan"

Dickinson, *I Died for Beauty*, 890
Keats, *Ode on a Grecian Urn*, 848
Shakespeare, *Not Marble*, 560

Richard Crashaw, *On Our Crucified Lord, Naked and Bloody, page 639*

Characteristic of seventeenth-century religious poetry, the sanguinary imagery here is heavily allusive. In addition to Mark 15:24 and 15:17, interested readers may also see John 20:23 and Matthew 27:28. In lines 2–4, the image refers to the Roman soldier who speared Christ in the side after he had died (John 20:34 alone includes this detail).

Answers to the Study Questions, page 639

(1) The poem is built on contradiction and irony: The idea is that the speaker wishes that Jesus would not have been beaten and crucified, but unless he had been so treated, he would not have risen. Then, however, there would be no Christian religion, and the speaker would not be worshipping him. In the first line, therefore, the speaker refers to the clothing taken away from Jesus before the scourging, and asserts his wish that the Lord could have been left naked rather than undergoing crucifixion. The speaker laments the crucifixion personally, though he worships the divinity that Christ assumed through it.

(2) These words refer to the horrors of the flagellation and crucifixion of Jesus. "This garment" in line two refers to the blood which covered his body as a result of the thorns, sticks, fists, whips, and sword. "Thee with Thyself" (line 3) refers to the Lord's own blood which covered his body, which itself becomes a garment. To consider blood in this way is ironic and contradictory, since it would neither warm, protect, nor conceal. But the speaker asserts that Jesus is so rare a being that no human garment could be fine enough to clothe him except for his own blood.

(3) Although the emphasis on blood may seem excessive, the concern is appropriate to the Christian tradition which has always seen the blood of Christ as life-giving.

WRITING TOPICS. The double meaning of *robe* and *garment.* Color imagery. Allusiveness. Images as causes of worship.

WORKS FOR COMPARISON WITH "ON OUR CRUCIFIED LORD"

Donne, *Hymn to God My God*, 876
Hopkins, *Pied Beauty*, 955
Pickthall, *The Worker in Sandalwood*, 341

H. D. (HILDA DOOLITTLE), *Heat, page 639*

"Heat," like Pound's "In a Station of the Metro" (page 642) exemplifies imagism in poetry. Through image and analogy, it shows how a simple topic may be understood not through the intellect but through the senses. "Heat" was published in *Sea Garden* (1916), Doolittle's first collection of poems.

Answers to the Study Questions, pages 639–640

(1) The speaker presents heat as being solid and palpable, as strong and as oppressive as heavy canvas that can be moved only by a powerful, shredding wind.

(2) The oppressiveness of this heat is such that it lies like a solid weight, pushing on soft things like fruits and putting them out of shape.

(3) In the plow image we see soil (as in a farmer's field) being cut apart to open a furrow. Again, the poem is stressing the solidity and resistance of the heat.

(4) The poem thus catches those days of suffocating summer heat in which one longs for a wind (remember that in 1916 there was no air conditioning). It presents an unusual and yet extremely effective series of images, all the more effective because the poet does not push the images too far, and also because she keeps the poem brief.

WRITING TOPICS: Visual images. Images rendering sensations of heat. The images of cutting, rending, and plowing.

POEMS FOR COMPARISON WITH "HEAT"

Dickinson, *I Taste a Liquor*, 882
Frost, *Birches*, 897
Milton, *O Nightingale!*, 968

T. S. ELIOT, *Preludes, pages 640–641*

This poem reflects Eliot's early poetry in the imagist tradition. Eliot presents little vignettes almost cinematically, as though he had selected them through the process of montage. Because these vignettes represent the reverse side of life, the anti-heroic nature of modern urban existence, they cause "Preludes" somewhat to resemble the view of city life presented by Swift in "A Description of the Morning" (page 730).

Answers to the Study Questions, page 641

(1) The images of evening in stanza one are derived from locations just outside buildings. In the second stanza the early morning images move into the thousands of furnished rooms in which urbanized human beings spend their lives. The third stanza focuses on one of these rooms in the morning, and a woman in the room is dozing before getting up to begin the day.

(2) We may presume that the "you" is female because of the image of

the curled papers in the hair. The images associated with this woman are "sordid," and a terribly damnatory statement is that her "soul" is "constituted" out of a thousand such images; in other words, the negative pictures of life are more prominent than the positive. The things she sees are the shutters, the gutters, soiled hands, and the yellow soles of feet. There is nothing pretty or idealistic here.

(3) The identity represented by "his" is not clear. We may assume that a general person is intended, one of the representative ones who live in one of the thousand furnished rooms, one of the faceless persons in the crowd. The meaning of "blackened street" seems to be that there is much that is bad in the urban environment (it is "blackened"), but that it too needs to be active. There is a direction in the impatience to "assume the world," but it is all in the anti-heroic direction.

(4) There are not many references to the human body. The feet are muddy, the hand is raising a dingy shade, the hair is rolled with papers, the soles of feet are yellow, and the fingers are short and square. Images of the urban scene are more abundant. Both are equally discouraging about the development of human possibilities.

(5) The idea of the fifth stanza is that there is a power somewhere which may be able to make sense out of the urban images, who through suffering may be able to redeem the people who are consigned to the dreariness of the city. The last stanza moves from this note of hope to a final note of resignation. Have your beer, wipe the foam away, and have a good time, because the world goes on in its own way despite anything anyone can do. This idea is not dissimilar to the *carpe diem* tradition, but it provides a twist on the theme because of the poem's emphasis on dreariness, not on mortality.

Writing topics. A characterization of the urban images. The development of the poem's stanzas. The meaning of the concluding unnumbered stanzas.

Works for Comparison with "Preludes"

Swift, *A Description of the Morning*, 730
Kennedy, *Old Men Pitching Horseshoes*, 808
Williams, *The Red Wheelbarrow*, 1009

Gerard Manley Hopkins, *Spring, pages 641–642*

"Spring" is a poem of celebration—celebration of the time of year, the existence of the world and the universe, the glorious sounds of English words, and the Resurrection. Like "Kubla Khan," it is a virtuoso piece of sound. Even students who are not particularly perceptive about sounds can appreciate the repeating segments, as in patterns like "weeds, wheels," "long and lovely and lush," and "strikes like lightnings," to quote just a few of the many ringing examples.

Answers to the Study Questions, page 642

(1) Images supportive of the beauty of spring include lushly growing weeds, bird songs, blue skies, and leaves and flowers. Except for the weeds, they are not unexpected. What seems unusual is the language of movement in which the speaker expresses them.

(2) Imagery of motion is the thrush song "like lightnings," the leaves brushing "the descending blue," the blue being in "a rush," and the lambs racing. These are dynamic images, suggesting that the speaker is surrounded by a season of moving color and sound.

(3) This pristine beauty is like Eden before the fall, and is equally at risk because of sin (line 12). But for now it is all new and lovely.

(4) For many readers, the references to Christ, and the assertion that this Edenic world is worthy of him, may make the poem seem nothing more than an intellectual exercise. But the loveliness of the first eleven lines is fully accessible to all who respond to color, movement, and word painting.

Writing topics. Images of nature. Visual images. Images of motion. Allusiveness.

Works for Comparison with "Spring"

Herbert, *Easter Wings*, 761
Keats, *To Autumn*, 661
MacNeice, *Snow*, 558
Piercy, *Wellfleet Sabbath*, 588

Ezra Pound, *In a Station of the Metro, page 642*

This poem, an example of poems of the "Imagist School" that heavily influenced modern sensibility and taste in poetry, is an experiment because it does not embody traditional form or even traditional grammar. The impression, the image, is what Pound expresses, on the presupposition that poetry exists in the transference of mood from the poet to the reader through the creation and apprehension of strong and direct images.

Answers to the Study Questions, page 642

(1) The image of the petals is complex: Are they part of a full blossom? Have they dropped off the flower? Are they sticking temporarily to the wet bough? Do they suggest that, even in rain and clouds, some remnants of beauty are still visible in human experience? If they were petals on a sunny tree they would be positive and less ambivalent.

(2) Another aspect of ambivalence is the word "apparition," which is usually a ghostly figure, but which may be simply an unexpected sight.

(3) Short as the poem is, it is still a poem because it works entirely in images, not logical development. It is, in effect, in the tradition of the Japanese *haiku* (see page 754).

WRITING TOPICS. The poem as image. Imagery and mood.

WORKS FOR COMPARISON WITH "IN A STATION OF THE METRO"

Kennedy, *Old Men Pitching Horseshoes*, 808
McHugh, *Lines*, 966
Williams, *The Dance*, 782

WILLIAM SHAKESPEARE, *Sonnet 130: My Mistress' Eyes Are Nothing Like the Sun, page 643*

This sonnet, from the 1609 edition of the sonnets, is one of those (numbered from 126 to 152) which supposedly refer to a "dark lady," about whom there have been many attempts at identification. More to the point of the sonnet is that in it Shakespeare openly ridicules some of the sonnet conventions that the English inherited from the Italian, Petrarchan writers. Students may be interested to note that the popular singer Sting entitled one of his records "Nothing Like the Sun."

Answers to the Study Questions, page 643

(1) The speaker makes the following comparisons: eyes to the sun, lips to coral, breasts to snow, hair to wires, cheeks to roses, breath to perfume, voice to music, and walk to the progress of a goddess. Then he concludes that no part of the lady can properly be compared to the object chosen. The negative comparisons are visual, olfactory, auditory, and kinesthetic.

(2) Shakespeare is mocking a style of hyperbolic comparison and rhetoric popular in his time. The point he makes by puncturing this particular balloon is that a human woman, who "when she walks, treads on

the ground," is, for a real lover of flesh and blood, better than any remote and non-existent ideal.

(3) The images are not insulting because so many of the comparisons are preceded by "if . . . be . . . then" and so on, although in current English (but not in Shakespeare's English) the word *reeks* carries unfortunate connotations. The point is quite the contrary, for the conclusion stresses that the mistress has attributes which are rare.

(4) Although there is a good mixture of images in the poem, the poet relies most heavily upon visual images, such as ordinary and unsunlike eyes, lips unlike red coral, dun rather than white breasts, black wires for hair, and so on.

(5) The point made about love poetry is that it usually concerns the speaker's enthusiasms about a loved one rather than any objective descriptions. The idea is that a relationship built upon reality and the recognition of truth is more solid and enduring than one in which the lover pedestalizes the woman (a modern word, but an old situation).

WRITING TOPICS. The nature of the images. The reversal of convention in Shakespeare's images. Humor and seriousness as a result of the images.

WORKS FOR COMPARISON FOR "MY MISTRESS' EYES"

Donne, *The Flea*, 874
Merrill, *Laboratory Poem*, 588
Paley, *Goodbye and Good Luck*, 531

DAVID WOJAHN, *"It's Only Rock and Roll But I Like It": The Fall of Saigon, pages 643–644*

" 'It's Only Rock and Roll But I Like It' " is one of the powerful poems from the Vietnamese War era. The images, both of vision and sound, are vivid and graphic. The title is taken from the title song of an album by The Rolling Stones (CBS disk CK 40493). It may be difficult to determine just exactly what the lyrics are, but one might question Wojahn's "indeed" in line 7. The words sound more like this: "I know it's only Rock and Roll, but I like it; like it, like it, yes I do."

Answers to the Study Questions, page 644

(1) The poem records an actual historical event, the final evacuation of Americans as they are lifted by helicopter from the roof of the United States Embassy in Saigon (now Ho Chi Minh City) in 1975. The poem

itself explains the major actions. The Saigonese man clinging to the airborne skis is clearly afraid of being killed if he remains behind, and he is willing to risk his life by holding on to the landing apparatus.

(2) The three major images of sound are the noise of the helicopter, the music of The Rolling Stones, and the fists of the marine beating time on the fuselage. These images of noise are to be contrasted with the great seriousness of the military evacuation.

Images of sight are plentiful, and, as the speaker says, "The camera gets / It all." Some of the sights the poem refers to are the arabesques of dust, the bonfires of official records, the helicopter straining to lift off, and the pathetic Saigonese holding on but then "giving way."

(3) The title is little more than a major line in a popular rock and roll song. The content of the poem concerns life and death. The apparent lack of concern of the marine beating time to the music is only the final element of irony in the poem.

(4) The images all involve personal concerns. There is nothing said about the purpose of the war or about the political reasons for the withdrawal. The actual scene is one of "artful / Mayhem" of the lost war and the evacuation. The clear implication is that the war is irrelevant to the personal interests of those who are involved in the evacuation.

Writing topics. The poem's irony. The imagery of sight and sound in the poem. The contrast between the poem's title and the subject matter.

Works for Comparison with
" 'It's Only Rock and Roll' "

Chioles, *Before the Firing Squad*, 138
Hardy, *In Time of 'The Breaking of Nations'*, 801
Jarrell, *Death of the Ball-Turret Gunner*, 550
Northrup, *Wahbegan*, 971

Writing About Imagery, *pages 644–648*

The aim of this section is to provide guidance for students who otherwise might not know what to do with an assignment on imagery. Of course, the major principle is that students deal with what they find in the poem they are studying, and then develop their essays in the light of their findings. Thus, for example, the poem "Cargoes" may be the basis of a type 1 essay (page 629) stressing images of sight, just as a major image of sight may be discussed in "In a Station of the Metro." By contrast,

Doolittle's poem "Heat" highlights kinetic imagery, and a type 1 essay would put this imagery foremost. Also appropriate for type 1 would be Shakespeare's Sonnet 130. "Cargoes" is an obvious example connecting images and mood, and "The Tyger" could be the subject of a similar essay. For type 3, the text (page 645) cites six poems which might be fitted.

Writing Topics about Imagery, *page 648*

(1) The images in "I Have a Rendezvous with Death" are ones of gentleness in which the narrator imagines himself participating. The images of home in "Anthem for Doomed Youth" are those of the people back home expressing silent and helpless grief to the news of battlefield death. The deaths of the poets of course have nothing to do with the poems as such, but the poems take on a special poignancy in light that the deaths actually occurred.

(2) For the second writing direction, it would be best for students to lay out their observations in parallel columns, from which they might extract the details and conclusions they wish to bring out in their essays. In addition, students might profitably consult the second part of Appendix B, on the Extended Comparison-Contrast essay, for developing an approach to this topic.

(3) Suggestions for the essay on Eliot's "Preludes" may be developed from the answers responding to the study questions. Comparative poems might be Swift's "A Description of the Morning," already suggested (page 730), or Roethke's "Dolor" (page 620).

(4) The fourth direction gives a number of possibilities for a short poem, to which students may add after consultation. As with most creative-writing assignments, it is best for students simply to write the poems, and turn critics of themselves only after they have completed a fairly advanced draft of their work.

(5) This assignment requires that students be able to work with the painting's images (page 629). Although the black-and-white minimizes much detail, the painting's principal images are clear (e.g., the tired couple, the long road, the emptiness of the distance ahead). These images may be contrasted with the view of spring in Hopkins's poem and the very brief but depressing observation of people walking in the train station in "In a Station of the Metro."

Chapter Seventeen
Pages 649–677

Rhetorical Figures: A Source of Depth and Range in Poetry

This chapter introduces students first to the concepts of metaphor and simile, and second, to a number of other rhetorical figures essential in poetry. Most students are familiar with similes, and can usually identify one when they see one, but they have difficulty recognizing metaphors. Thus the use of many examples, together with accompanying explanations, will be fruitful.

The other figures are often omitted by instructors who in a one-semester course are pressed for time. Because it is important that students know at least some of the figures, however, we have structured this introductory section so that you may assign as many of the figures as you think important or for which you have time. Each of the discussions is self-contained: Students may benefit from as many of them as you assign. The "other" figures, with pages, are these:

Thus, for example, if you wish to assign paradox, personification, and the pun only, there should be no confusion about either the location or the extent of the discussions.

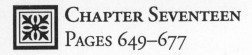

JOHN KEATS, *On First Looking into Chapman's Homer, pages 650–651*

Students may be interested to learn that Keats had trained not as a poet or writer, but as an apothecary-surgeon. In the year of this poem, 1816, he received his license to practice, but he gave it up to pursue a life of reading, thinking, and writing. The excitement he describes in this poem explains that decision. One of the rhetorical figures usually associated with Keats is *synæsthesia,* the metaphorical mingling of references to different senses. In line 7 of this poem, the word "serene" is both a political and ecological metaphor, referring both to clear air and the majesty of Homer's poetry. To "breathe its pure serene," by synæsthesia, equates breathing with reading and also with understanding.

Answers to the Study Questions, pages 651

(1) Keats uses the metaphors of demesne and discovery to indicate that he is experiencing the power of the ancient poet Homer. The unknown, in short, is becoming known. Students may testify to the universality of Keats's discovery by bringing out some of their own experiences with learning something for the first time.

(2) The metaphor suggests that literature, like travel, takes us to new places, with all the acquisition of knowledge and experience that seeing new places implies. Keats uses the metaphors of "realms of gold" "goodly states and kingdoms," and "western islands," to illustrate the metaphor.

(3) The similes in lines 9–10 and in 11–14 convey the thrill of being the first person to see an unknown planet or an unknown ocean. With that thrill comes the awareness that the universe is larger and more amazing than had been dreamed. Keats has found exactly the right similes for this enlarged sense of the world.

(4) The metaphor of *swims* suggests that the planet is active, engaged in its own purpose in the universe. The other words, as metaphors or similes, would suggest a vaguer, less purposeful mission. The comparison of course is apt, since the vehicle is the power of Homer, who in *The Iliad* and *The Odyssey* was an intentional and deliberate poet.

WRITING TOPICS. Keats's similes of discovery. The value of reading as expressed in the metaphor of Homer's territory as a ruler. The metaphor of fealty and the condition of the writer.

Works for Comparison with "On First Looking Into Chapman's Homer"

Shakespeare, *Not Marble*, 560
Shelley, Ode to the West Wind, 776
Strand, *Eating Poetry*, 621

Robert Burns, *A Red, Red Rose, pages 652–653*

Burns wrote this poem for the *Scots Musical Museum,* which was a collection of old and new Scots songs in the eighteenth-century traditions of William Thomson's *Orpheus Caledonius* and the poems of the elder Allan Ramsay. Students can understand the poem with a minimum of annotation, for the diction is not overburdened with localisms, and the sentiments and expressions are clear and easy.

Answers to the Study Questions, page 653

(1) The initial two similes of the poem, and much of the rest of the speaker's language, are commonplace. The speaker is obviously male, an energetic and fanciful man who does not mind exaggerating a bit in the interests of wooing his sweetheart and impressing his listeners. His situation is that he is declaring his love for his "bonnie lass" (line 5), vowing his love's continuation, bidding her good bye, and promising to return. The charm of the poem lies in its evident sincerity and boldness, even if the language is unexceptional. This situation is like that in Donne's "A Valediction: Forbidding Mourning" (page 634), except that Burns's speaker does not have the wit or sophistication of Donne's speaker.

(2) The first stanza of Burns's poem may be regarded as a brief general statement to whoever may be near, including the speaker's lass. In stanza two, and in the remainder of the poem, the speaker addresses the lass directly, explaining to her that even though he must travel, she will always be foremost in his thoughts, inasmuch as he attributes to her the beauty of both flowers and music.

(3) The speaker asserts that seas must dry and rocks must melt before his love will end. These are both figures of hyperbole, and they suggest a strong commitment. More serious as a figure is the metaphor of the "sands o' life," which compares life to an hour glass which will eventually run out of sand. Though the concluding metaphor of lengthy travel (we might remember that at the time a trip of ten thousand miles might have taken three or four years) is also hyperbolic, the sands metaphor suggests

that the speaker, underneath his exaggerations, is not without his serious side.

WRITING TOPICS. The rose as a simile. Structure. Hyperbole. A comparison with Donne's "Valediction."

WORKS FOR COMPARISON WITH "A RED, RED ROSE"

Frost, *A Line Storm Song,* 895
Haines, *Little Cosmic Dust Poem,* 945
Paley, *Goodbye and Good Luck,* 531
Wyatt, *I Find No Peace,* 670

JOHN KEATS, *Bright Star, pages 654–655*

This is a personal poem in which Keats's speaker describes the wish to be a "steadfast" lover like the "bright star" which is a distant witness to the earth's waters and snows (i.e., the changing seasons). The most steadfast star that we know in the northern hemisphere is of course the North Star, or the Pole Star, and we may presume that this is the star that Keats has in mind for his metaphor of stability and permanence.

Answers to the Study Questions, page 655

(1) The topic is the speaker's love. The comparison of speaker and star is the implicit one that the speaker, being human and therefore changeable, is as impermanent as the waters and snows. The contrast with the star is that the speaker wants to remain close to his love ("pillowed upon my fair love's ripening breast [line 10])" and not remain aloof in "lone splendor" (line 2).

(2) The qualities the speaker attributes to the star are steadfastness (line 1), patience (line 4), sleeplessness (line 4), and attentiveness ("gazing," line 7). He seems to assign to the star the role of guard or watcher, thus suggesting that the star is like a divine presence, neither slumbering nor sleeping because of eternal guardianship over the children of God.

(3) The words "forever" and "ever," combined with the attribution of the star's being "steadfast," provide a backdrop of permanence for the speaker's love, which he wishes would remain forever firm and steady. Granted the comparative permanence of the stars, the choice of the star as subject is quite appropriate.

WRITING TOPICS. The use of the star as a metaphor for a lover. The comparison of universal permanence and human impermanence. The character of the poem's speaker.

Works for Comparison with "Bright Star"

Atwood, *Variation on the Word Sleep,* 915
Shakespeare, *Let Me Not to the Marriage,* 757
Spenser, *Amoretti 75 (One Day I Wrote),* 856

John Gay, *Let Us Take the Road, page 656*

The questions on page 656 are discussed on page 657. You may wish to amplify some of the points, like the work of the alchemists. In addition, the first-line word *road* referred to grand theft that occurred on the open highways of eighteenth century England. Even today we still use the phrase "highway robbery," which originated in this aspect of eighteenth-century life. The song is sung by the gang of thieves to the music of George Frederick Handel's march from the opera *Rinaldo* (1711), and, in its time, the music became more closely associated with *The Beggar's Opera* than with the original opera.

Writing topics. The imagery appropriate to thievery in the poem. The use of puns. The use of rhyme.

Works for Comparison with "Let Us Take the Road"

Cummings, *Buffalo Bill's Defunct,* 763
Dickey, *The Performance,* 930
Frost, *Fire and Ice,* 900

Elizabeth Bishop, *Rain Towards Morning, pages 657–658*

This poem, which is personal, impressionistic, and symbolic, may be contrasted with Bishop's much more specific "The Fish" (pages 632–634). Both poems speak of "freeing" living creatures, but the effect of the liberations is different: In "The Fish" the cause is love for Nature. In "Rain Towards Morning" the freeing of the birds signifies the solution of a problem or difficulty.

Answers to the Study Questions, page 658

(1) The poet does not allow us to know any specific details about the situation, except to say that the liberation of the birds has brought about a release of intense feelings.

(2) The overstatement of the million birds suggests the magnitude of the previous unhappiness or frustration. The "kiss" of line 8—a simple action, and not an overwhelming act of love of extensive duration—sug-

gests that simple things produce great results. Both overstatement and understatement are equally effective.

(3) The "great light cage" can only be taken suggestively or impressionistically. It likely indicates a publicly known problem of a suppressive or enslaving nature ("great ... cage"). The "puzzle" may refer to the sometimes paradoxical, contradictory, and incomprehensible attitudes and motivations of a human being.

(4) The synecdoches of "face," "kiss," and "hands" suggest that another person is involved, who has been hostile, mysterious, or otherwise alienated, but that this person, through a kiss, has opened up and freed the relationship.

(5) Rain usually accompanies gloomy moods. Once the character (is it the speaker?) has been freed from worry and anxiety, however, even rain seems to be brightening (no longer "frightening") and cheerful.

Writing topics. The personal meanings. The use of paradox. The use of overstatement and synecdoche.

Works for Comparison with "Rain Towards Morning"

Heaney, *Valediction*, 950
Wakoski, *Inside Out*, 668
Wyatt, *I Find No Peace*, 670

John Donne, *A Valediction: Forbidding Mourning, pages 658–659*

It is impossible to date this poem, and hence all we can do is surmise that it may have been inspired by an occasion of a trip, when the poet found a need to answer objections that might have been raised to his going. Students brought up in the jet age may wonder why a trip should be a cause of consternation or grief. They might need reminding that even a short trip in the days of horse and sail would require an absence of at least several weeks, and perhaps several months. More to the point here is the extensive use of metaphorical language, together with the renowned concluding metaphysical conceit, or simile, about the relationship of lovers to a geometric compass. It is of course important to explore this simile in some detail, for whenever students of literature refer to the "metaphysical conceit" they invariably turn to this poem and this comparison.

Answers to the Study Questions, page 659

(1) The situation of the poem is a valediction, literally, a saying of farewell. The speaker is speaking to his lady, to whom he is married or

affianced, and who has apparently been "mourning" at the idea of the speaker's departure. The poem is developed as a set of statements and arguments to distract the listener from crying and mourning.

(2) The first two stanzas form a simile developing the following idea: *Let us part the way virtuous persons die, quietly and easily.* The phrases "tear-floods" and "sigh-tempests" are designed to tease the listener out of weeping, and then to emphasize the remaining parts of the poem, which are quite serious.

(3) The simile about the dying men sets a serious tone, and makes clear that the parting is genuinely painful, both for speaker and listener.

(4) The metaphor of stanza three refers to parting and disruptions: Earthquakes destroy earth and the dwellings on it. Trepidation of the spheres disrupts the smooth, circular movements of heavenly bodies. Both these metaphorical equations may be considered less harmful than the parting of lovers because they are distant, inanimate, and non-feeling. To pursue the metaphors, however, we may conclude that these cosmic movements do no permanent harm, and that they are therefore "innocent." How, in comparison, can the smaller parting of lovers do any harm?

(5) The basis for the speaker's claim in lines 13–20 is that the love of ordinary lovers ("sublunary," line 13) is only physical, and that for this reason they cannot retain their love at a distance. By contrast, the love of the speaker and the listener is not just a physical love, but is also an interaction of minds; therefore a separation of the physical does not imply a separation of the mental.

(6) The subject of the simile about metallurgy begun in line 17 is the refining of gold, in which all dross and impurities are removed and only the purest and most valuable gold remains. The speaker also refers to the malleability of gold to suggest that even when lovers are apart they are still united, just like a sheet of delicate gold foil (line 24). This metaphor supports the conviction that this love is deep and lasting.

Writing topics. The apparent dramatic situation occasioning the poem. The extended simile of the compass. The concept of love as evidenced in the poem. The cosmological metaphors.

Works for Comparison with "A Valediction: Forbidding Mourning"

Burns, *A Red, Red Rose,* 652
Haines, *Little Cosmic Dust Poem,* 945
Waller, *Go Lovely Rose,* 1006

T. S. Eliot, *Eyes That Last I Saw in Tears, page 660*

This poem is not one of Eliot's reputation poems (such as *Prufrock, The Waste Land, Preludes,* etc.), but it is unusual in his work because it is considered to be quite personal, likely a reflection of the pain he apparently experienced in his marriage.

Answers to the Study Questions, page 660

(1) The word *eyes* as a synecdoche stands for a person who was obviously in close communication and in an intimate relationship with the speaker. The word *tears* as an instance of metonymy is a substitute for the emotions of grief and sorrow.

(2) The tears result from "division," in other words, a rupture of the relationship. The meaning of eyes outlasting tears is apparently that people cannot sustain deep emotion. Eventually they go on to do other things, and, though they do not forget causes of sorrow, the emotions become less painful. The eyes holding "us in derision" (line 15) do so perhaps because hurt feelings can lead to anger. Perhaps, also, the speaker is here expressing guilt for having caused the tears. The meaning of the eyes being of "decision" (line 9) suggests that the grieving person has made personal choices that will lead to a new way of life. It is in the nature of these references that they cannot be expressed too specifically.

(3) The "eyes but not the tears" is paradoxical because the speaker seems to be remembering the eyes, without tears, as in a "golden dream;" that is, he thinks of the person as she was *before* the "division" occurred. The paradox is that the relationship seems over, but the fond memory is not. The "affliction," about which the speaker remarks in lines 6 and 7, is apparent inability to close off the memory.

(4) The entire poem might be considered a paradox because of the complex awareness of the speaker; he sees a "golden vision" but knows it is a dream; he knows of the tears but cannot see them when he recalls the eyes; he looks forward to less division in death than he experienced in life, but expects that ultimately all human beings ("us") will be held "in derision" by persons for whom all former arguments are now irrelevant. He would like reconciliation but knows that there can be none.

(5) The references to the two kingdoms of death are obscure and likely allusive. They may be explained perhaps as allusions to classical states of dreaming and death. Thus Homer (*Odyssey,* 19: 562) explains that an ivory gate opening to the region of dreams permits the issue of

false dreams, while a gate of polished horn is the entry way of true dreams predicting the future. Death is viewed not as an end but a continuation of consciousness. The kingdom of death, ruled by Hades, was reached through an entrance, or door.

Writing topics. The personal topic matter. Paradox and contradiction. The meaning of "eyes" and "tears."

Works for Comparison with "Eyes That Last I Saw in Tears"

Anonymous, *Barbara Allan*, 912
Dickinson, *I Cannot Live with You*, 886
Minty, *Conjoined*, 663

Langston Hughes, *Harlem, pages 660–661*

This is perhaps Hughes's best known poem, principally because of the memorable second line, which was used by Lorraine Hansberry for her play *A Raisin in the Sun* in 1959.

Answers to the Study Questions, page 661

(1) The idea is that the goals and ideals as defined in the Declaration of Independence and the Constitution enunciated a great dream that has never been equally applied to African Americans. See also Hughes's poem "Let America Be America Again," in which the line "It never was America to me" is repeated almost as a refrain (page 723).

(2) The initial question (line 1) is answered by additional questions from lines 2 through 7. The interval of two lines offers one answer—namely that blacks will do nothing. The final line, however, resumes the predominant structure of questioning. This concluding line, 11, because of the implied answer that an explosion will be forthcoming, is one of the most powerful in all of Hughes's writing.

(3) The images all refer to things spoiling and rotting, with those in lines 4 and 6 being particularly bitter and ironic. The last comparison (line 11) suggests how deferring a dream is like nurturing the fuse of a powerful explosive.

(4) The shift to the metaphor in line 11 involves a shift from similarity to actuality. The idea is that the suppression of African Americans is creating not an *impression* of explosive hostility, but is creating *real* explosive hostility.

Writing topics. The negative imagery in the poem. The power of the images as symbols. The structure of rhetorical questions in the poem. The meaning of the final line.

Works for Comparison with "Harlem"

Imamu Amiri Baraka, *Ka 'Ba*, 917
Emanuel, *The Negro*, 720
Randall, *Ballad of Birmingham*, 775

John Keats, *To Autumn, pages 661–662*

Because this poem is so successful and so lovely, readers may sometimes be oblivious to the many figures that Keats employs. Indeed, the poem is loved by many persons who would wonder if knowledge of the figures can add anything to their appreciation. The fact remains, however, that Keats created the figures as an integral part of the poem, and therefore to understand them is one way of following the processes of his poetic art.

Answers to the Study Questions, page 662

(1) In the first stanza, Autumn is presented in his prime, actively "conspiring" with his "close bosom-friend," the sun, to "load" and set budding all growing things. Here is Autumn the busy, active producer of the copious harvest. In the second stanza, Autumn is a laborer who sometimes forgets the task of gleaning and making cider, and sits down instead to doze in the midst of the work day. The change suggests the passage of time: The actions of stanza one produce the crops, stanza two is concerned with reaping them and the resulting fatigue.

(2) The poem progresses in accord with qualities or powers given to Autumn. In stanza one Autumn is an internal force, expanding and making the world grow. In two, Autumn is manifested in human beings, replete and satisfied in the security of the harvest. In three, Autumn is a bringer of sounds and evening songs, all heard through the air illuminated by the rosy sun. There is a twist on convention here, for autumn in the tradition of pastoral poetry is a time of decline which leads to the death of winter. Keats's emphasis on the fruitfulness of the season therefore illustrates the security provided by Autumn as personified as the grower and harvester.

(3) Keats uses both synecdoche and metonymy in each of these two stanzas. Specifically, however, the metonyms in stanza one are the thatch-

eaves, which represent the people who live in the houses so protected, and the clammy cells of line 11, which, because they are the location of honey, stand for the honey itself and the sweetness of the season. In stanza two, synecdoches are *hair* (line 15), which figuratively represents the dust of harvested grain and therefore the grain itself; *laden head* (line 20), which represents the persons working in the autumnal harvest both as laborers and as planners of the season; and *oozings* (line 22), representing specifically cider but generally the substances made from the year's produce. These figures give insights into the intricacy of growth, harvest, and manufacture, and also along with the personification of autumn, the intention of Nature and life to nurture human beings.

(4) The metaphors throughout the poem suggest ripeness, harvest, rest, and beauty after labor. The trees are loaded with apples; the machinery (cider press, reaping hook) is that which is used at the time of harvest; the light is red and mellow—rosy—and is seen over plains of cut grain; and the sounds are those of twilight and night—not threatening but restful.

WRITING TOPICS. The structure of the poem. Metonymy and synecdoche. Metaphors of ripeness and fullness. Personification and apostrophe.

WORKS FOR COMPARISON WITH "TO AUTUMN"

Shore, *A Letter Sent to Summer,* 591
Snodgrass, *These Trees Stand,* 990
Twichell, *Blurry Cow,* 1001
Wordsworth, *Daffodils (I Wandered Lonely),* 858
Wordsworth, *Lines Written in Early Spring,* 1009

HENRY KING, *Sic Vita, page 662*

"Sic Vita" is virtually a tabular arrangement of metaphorical language, and is memorable for this reason.

Answers to the Study Questions, pages 662–663

(1) There are six similes in lines 1–6, ranging from the objects in the night sky to drops of dew on leaves and grass. All are comparisons from nature, and all describe motions which come to an end.

(2) In lines 7 and 8, human life is presented as light, so that night comes to represent death. Human light or life is borrowed, and can and will be called in for payment; that is, death. The source from which life is borrowed is God or Nature.

(3) Lines 9–12 are not logically essential, but without them, lines 7

and 8 would have to bear the weight of the poem, and the balance would be skewed. By adding these lines, King not only underscores his point, but does so in rhythms which give the poem stateliness, importance, and closure.

(4) The poem emphasizes the mutability and brevity of human existence, but similes like that of the falling star and the rippling of water suggest that life is also beautiful, desirable, and admirable, despite its shortness.

Writing topics. The philosophy of the poem. The development of the similes. Borrowed light in relationship to life.

Works for Comparison with "Sic Vita"

Eliot, *The Love Song of J. Alfred Prufrock,* 938
Haines, *Little Cosmic Dust Poem,* 945
Jeffers, *The Answer,* 956
St. Luke, *The Parable of the Prodigal Son,* 340

Judith Minty, *Conjoined, page 663*

Alert students will notice the irony in the poem's subtitle, "a marriage poem." Like Eliot's "Prufrock" (page 938), which is supposed to be a love song but ironically has nothing to do with love, this poem's subtitle suggests a celebration about marriage, but instead expresses great misgiving if not hostility.

Answers to the Study Questions, page 663

(1) The "us" and "we" of lines 10 and 11 refer to the speaker and the spouse, those who have just been married. If the poem were to be taken as an interior monologue, then the plural first-person pronouns could refer to the body and soul of one person (since to cut them apart might kill [line 13]), but husband/wife is more plausible. The paradoxical subordination-freedom idea of love and marriage in this poem may be compared with that in Wyatt's "I Find No Peace" (page 670).

(2) In the figures of the onion, the twins, and the calves, the three were intended to be separate, but instead they are freaks of nature, monstrous accidents that allowed them to live but to live abnormally. The speaker suggests that this situation is like marriage. In lines 12–13, the speaker suggests that freedom (divorce, separation) might kill one partner, as it sometimes kills a Siamese twin. Note that the one who might

not survive is not specified. The metaphor thus represents a recognition of reality and both a reluctant concession and a decision to adjust.

(3) An increasing number of men now "slice onions," but men, more often in charge of power and money, usually lay out the grounds of a relationship. Hence it is often asserted that women must be alert to hidden dynamics (body language, looks) to protect themselves emotionally, while men may be more direct and less subtle.

Writing topics. The irony of the subtitle. The view of the marriage bond. The figures of the onion, the Siamese Twins, and the calves.

Works for Comparison with "Conjoined"

Broumas, *Circe*, 824
Keats, *La Belle Dame Sans Merci*, 806
Lawrence, *The Horse Dealer's Daughter*, 393

Ogden Nash, *Exit, Pursued by a Bear, page 664*

"Exit, Pursued by a Bear" is more serious than one usually expects Nash's poetry to be, expressing, as it does, the destructiveness of a nuclear war. At the poem's end, the *fireball* refers to the explosion of a nuclear bomb. The idea is that nuclear war has no limits; once it begins, because of the politics of escalation, it must go on and on until there is nothing left. Some students may claim that the easing of East-West tensions may date the dangers that Nash warns about in the poem. If such a claim is put forward, it should occasion energetic discussion.

The source of the idea about animals overrunning places of former wealth is Fitzgerald's translation of *The Rubaiyat of Omar Khayyam,* which Nash directly echoes in lines 17 and 21 (please see the explanatory notes).

Answers to the Study Questions, page 665

(1) The allusion to Shakespeare's stage direction as the title of the poem creates the emphasis of irony and understatement. The bear of course refers to the bear that roars at and then eats up Antigonus in Act III, scene 3, line 58 of *The Winter's Tale,* and it can also refer to the danger added to the world by the proliferation of nuclear weaponry by potentially hostile countries.

(2) The location described in the poem is one of extreme wealth—likely a private home as evidenced by the artifacts contained there, all suggested by the identifying names as metonyms. The home is now vacant, for the owners are presumed to have been killed as a result of warfare.

(3) Because the building is no longer maintained, animals have gained entry and now use the artifacts for their lairs. The situation has apparently lasted for a long time, for mold has had a chance to grow on the rare and expensive books (line 15).

(4) One paradox in the poem is that the collector's items, usually not used by people because of their value, are used indiscriminately by animals once the people are gone. Another paradox is that the people who took such good care of the collector's items did not take enough care to negotiate for their ultimate security—the elimination of the nuclear threat.

Writing topics. The use of the names of museum pieces and collector's items as metonyms. Setting. Allusion. Paradoxes.

Works for Comparison with "Exit, Pursued by a Bear"

Chioles, *Before the Firing Squad,* 138
Hardy, *Channel Firing,* 584
Quasimodo, *Auschwitz,* 697

Marge Piercy, *A Work of Artifice, page 665*

This poem embodies a deeply effective metaphor which is straightforwardly detailed and applied, and a tone that one student described as "controlled fury."

Answers to the Study Questions, pages 665–666

(1) The bonsai tree—a major metaphor of the poem—is a tree that has been traditionally cultivated, particularly in Japan, to remain small, even though it is otherwise capable of reaching great height. For the first sixteen lines, the apparent subject of the poem seems to be the tree itself, though after this it is clear that the subject is really women. The metaphor is apt granted the poem's view that traditional attitudes toward women do not encourage their development. A full growth ("eighty feet tall," line 3) could result only from equality of opportunity.

(2) In lines 12–16, the gardener's song represents society persuading women to be content with being dwarfed and feeling fortunate when and if they find "a pot to grow in" (a home) and a singing gardener (a husband). Note the implication that it is the gardener (i.e., the controlling class of males) that does both the stunting and the brainwashing.

(3) At line 17 the poem switches to a number of metaphors on the topic of women dwarfed in their growth. Thus distorted, they are concerned with their looks (curlers), they have allowed their minds and abili-

appealing to one of the greatest figures in the English tradition. It is likely that Wordsworth is thinking as much of Milton's connection with the causes of freedom developed during the revolution and interregnum (1642–1660) as of *Paradise Lost.*

(2) His claim is that the church (*altar*), the military (*sword*), the intelligentsia (*pen*), home and family life (*fireside*), and the legal establishment (*hall and bower*) have all lost the sense of meaning and direction that is their heritage (*have forfeited their ancient English dower*).

(3) The hyperbole of the *fen / Of stagnant waters* and the broad brush leveled against the institutions described in question 2 are clearly intended to make clear Wordsworth's sense of alarm, not to describe each individual in the country. Wordsworth therefore dramatizes his point that the country does definitely need new thinkers, and new guidance, in the tradition established by Milton.

(4) The claims Wordsworth makes for Milton is that the great epic poet was a special person, in tune with God and Nature, but that he was also a person who lived in "life's common way." Therefore he combined the intelligence and compassion necessary in a national leader. The metonyms of *soul* and *heart* refer to Milton's spirituality and humanity.

WRITING TOPICS. Wordsworth's use of hyperbole, metonymy, or overstatement (or all three). Wordsworth's judgment of Milton. The qualities of leadership as envisaged in the sonnet.

WORKS FOR COMPARISON WITH "LONDON, 1802"

Blake, *London*, 577
Sandburg, *Chicago*, 981
Shelley, *Ode to the West Wind*, 776

SIR THOMAS WYATT, *I Find No Peace, page 670*

This poem is one of the most famous for exploring the figure of paradox. It is by no means easy, and beginning students especially may need to be guided closely, line-by-line, in an examination of the ideas. It would be difficult within a fourteen-line limit to bring out more of the conflicting states that people in love sometimes experience. The poem should be placed in the context that love is often considered the solution of all problems, the "happy-ever-after" idea of a life without difficulty and doubt. The speaker is aware, however, of all his future needs for adjustment, and therefore his apprehension is the cause of the many paradoxes in the poem.

Answers to the Study Questions, page 670

(1) The speaker is referring to the paradoxical nature of his love. On the one hand, he wants to love deeply, but on the other he approaches the situation of love expecting that it will change his life completely. Thus, he describes both anticipation and also trepidation. In expressing these opposing feelings, he brings in a number of metaphors and similes, such as those of peace and war (line 1), burning and freezing (line 2), flying like a bird (line 3), and wealth and poverty (line 4). All these paradoxical metaphors, if well considered, are successful in bringing out the contrary states of the speaker's feelings.

(2) A count reveals fifteen separate paradoxes in the poem. Lines 5 and 6 provide just one paradox, but lines 9 and 12 each give us two. The total effect of the paradoxes is to stress the conflicting emotions elicited by love. The point is made about as strongly as it can be, from the global paradoxes in lines 1–4 to the more political and personal ones in lines 5–8. The logic of turning the love of another to hate for oneself (line 11) is difficult to follow unless the line refers to the speaker's inability to express his love or to pursue it successfully. The assertion that the speaker's "delight" causes all the "strife" (line 14) is easier to follow. We may suppose that the speaker had established a regular way of life which has been upset by the changes required and anticipated by his having fallen in love.

(3) Wyatt's many paradoxes, as expressed in this personal poem are the expression of a person who cannot communicate all his feelings with the loved one. The poem implies that the love may be forbidden in some way, or that the speaker has not yet had the opportunity to speak extensively with the loved one. Presumably, in a courtship in which the two lovers have unlimited freedom of expression, all the feelings might be aired, but in a courtship hemmed in by custom and inhibition, the speaker's expressions seem perfectly natural.

Writing topics. The effect of the first line. The number and nature of the poem's paradoxes. Possible reasons for the heavy reliance on paradox in the poem.

Works for Comparison with "I Find No Peace"

Marvell, *To His Coy Mistress*, 852
Piercy, *Will We Work Together?*, 975
Shakespeare, *My Mistress' Eyes*, 643

Writing About Rhetorical Figures, *pages 671–676*

It is unlikely that you would want to assign full-length essays on a number of separate figures. Rather, we presume that writing assignments will be confined to just one major figure, such as metaphors or similes. With the other figures, as well, it is probably best to use just one figure per writing assignment. For these reasons, we have envisaged a paragraph-length treatment as shown in the sample paragraph on page 674. Because of its brevity, such a paragraph could be done for in-class writing exercises, just as it might also be a model for examination questions.

The more common assignments will likely concern metaphors and similes. Accordingly, we have supplied a number of suggestions for development (pages 671–673). Most students will probably model their essays on 2a, with perhaps some reinforcement from 2b, as is shown in the sample essay on pages 674–675. The third type of essay (2c, page 673), because it attempts to select characteristic metaphors, may be most useful if students study more than a single poem by a particular author (see Chapter 25, or consult the index under the names of individual poets, for such materials). The fourth development (2d, page 673), in addition to being a study of metaphor generally, also brings in tone.

The second sample essay (pages 674–675) is useful as a guide to any of the suggested writing topics for this chapter because, throughout, it stresses the topic of metaphor. In such an essay it is easy to get diverted from the rhetorical figures and begin a general discussion. Students should concentrate on the assigned topic of this or any essay.

Writing Topics about Rhetorical Figures, *pages 676–677*

(1) The first of these assignments can be readily done by those with a compass at hand. If students have left this equipment at home, however, a blackboard drawing, or a duplicated drawing, might serve as well. An interesting question is whether Donne himself, in writing the poem, had a compass in front of him, and worked out his extended simile as he changed the positions of the instrument.

(2) The second question depends of course on the figures selected by the student. In developing the essay, students will need to pay particular attention to the meaning of the word "effective." You might suggest clarifying words such as *clear, forceful, thought-provoking, emphatic, appropriate,* and so on.

(3) The third question might best be made concrete by reference to

some of the questions following specific poems, such as those on pages 670, 658, and 668. Of all the writing topics, this one might require the greatest guidance from you, either in class or in individual conference.

(4) The last writing direction is designed to get students into the act of developing their own rhetorical figures in poems of their own. For this assignment, it is more important that they concentrate on their governing metaphor or simile than that they worry about the absolute best word choices and rhythms (this could, of course, come later). An important part of the exercise is the section in which students write about how they, as poets, decided to develop their poems.

Chapter Eighteen
Pages 678–702

Tone: The Creation of Attitude in Poetry

Tone is both easy and difficult. It is easy because the beginning and ending of a discussion of tone is the formulation of attitudes present in a poem, or a statement about the appropriateness of diction, imagery, or metaphor to the content. Usually these judgments are readily described.

It is difficult, however, because a full discussion requires not only the formulation of an attitude but also the analysis of how the poem permits the reader to draw conclusions. Thus, any investigation of tone is complex, requiring students to show the interaction of poet, material, reader, situation, word choice, fairness, completeness of development, truthfulness, and structure, together with anything else that might have a bearing on the proper interpretation of attitudes. When you ask students to describe the dominant tone in a poem, they may respond by saying "irony," "humor," "phoniness," "indignation," "pathos," or a number of other descriptive terms. The problem for them then becomes explaining the means by which the poem enables them to make these assessments. The reproduction of Léger's *The City* is included as a graphic complement to the study of literary tone, for Léger's arrangements, distortions, and partial views demonstrate the control he exerts to communicate a negative attitude toward city life.

Cornelius Whur, *The First–Rate Wife, pages 679–680*

The commentary on the poem (page 680) addresses many of the study questions.

Writing topics. The nature of the speaker. The tone with respect to women and men. How good (bad) is the poem?

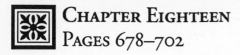

Works for comparison with "The First-Rate Wife"

Bradstreet, *To My Dear and Loving Husband,* 920
William Shakespeare, *My Mistress' Eyes,* 643
Edmund Spenser, *Amoretti 75 (One Day I Wrote),* 856
Wakoski, *The Ring,* 1004

Wilfred Owen, *Dulce et Decorum Est, page 681*

The text, page 682, deals with the subjects of the study questions on pages 681–682.

Writing topics: The tone of the speaker toward the listener. Attitudes about warfare. The irony of the title.

Works for Comparison with "Dulce et Decorum Est"

Eberhart, *Fury of Aerial Bombardment,* 616
Hemingway, *Soldier's Home,* 272
Jarrell, *Death of the Ball-Turret Gunner,* 550

Thomas Hardy, *The Workbox, pages 683–684*

See pages 684–685 for a brief discussion of "The Workbox."

Answers to the Study Questions, page 684

(1) The speaker is mainly the husband, a village cabinet-maker. The tone develops here as much in the rhyme scheme and rhythm used—variations on the ballad form—as in other devices. Here the poem tells a story, and though there is no refrain there is a parallelism of actions or words stressing the poem's concerns (e.g., "look white," line 21; "wan," line 37; face held or turned aside, lines 22 and 38; the intimate address of "little wife" and "my dear," lines 1 and 21). Thus the form suggests that a significant drama will occur, and that the poet wants us to be attentive, for much is suggested and not made explicit.

(2) The dialogue in lines 21–40 indicates that the wife knew the dead man, John, and had established a close relationship with him. She denies the previous connection because she had never told her husband about it before. She hence is covering up an earlier lie. The last stanza (lines 37–40) insinuates that in some way she had knowledge of the causes of John's death. The mystery is preserved about the death (lines 12 and 40) so that the irony of the poem may be maintained.

(3) The irony of the little workbox is that it is in effect a miniature

coffin, and what the husband meant as a gift of love becomes its opposite—an occasion for pain each time the wife begins to sew.

(4) A more sinister possibility, of course, is that the husband knows the full story, or more likely that he suspects it, and has deliberately fashioned the workbox either as a test or as a punishment for his "little wife." The deeper irony is therefore that the husband, by his suspicions, is probably destroying forever any possibility of future truth and intimacy with his wife. The wife's rejection of the husband's suggestion that she is "shocked" is also ironic. Whether she makes the denial to preserve her mystery or to defend herself from further probing is part of the poem's intriguing ambiguity.

(5) The opening speech of the narrator establishes the dramatic situation of the poem. Of the narrator's concluding four lines, the first two are dramatic, and the last two (lines 39–40) indicate his own conclusion about the wife. These lines could possibly be eliminated because they are not consistent with the objective viewpoint of the rest of the poem. Better lines would be descriptive ones, more like lines 37 and 38.

Writing topics. The use of irony in "The Workbox." The problematic nature of the wife's relationship with the dead man. The irony of situation. The role of the narrator.

Works for Comparison with "The Workbox"

Glaspell, *A Jury of Her Peers,* 155
Browning, *How Do I Love Thee,* 923
Browning, *My Last Duchess,* 578

Alexander Pope, *Epigram from the French, page 686*

(Questions 1–3) This epigram may also be described as a squib, lampoon, or barb because of its shortness. The rhetorical structure in lines 2 and 4 is *chiasmus* or antimetabole: *poet, fool; fool, poet.* The characteristics of satire are the qualities of (a) attack, and (b) humor. Insult alone is not enough to create interest in such a poem, but with the wit shown in the speaker's attack, the poem captures the involvement and assent necessary for successful satire.

Writing topics. The speaker's nature. The speaker's attitude toward the listener. The poem as a brief example of satire.

Alexander Pope, *Epigram, Engraved on the Collar of a Dog which I gave to His Royal Highness, page 686*

(Questions 1–2) This barb is an even more brief illustration of satiric technique, yet it accomplishes much within this shorter space. Students who have had acting experience might be able to mimic the superciliousness of the speaker, and thereby demonstrate the skill with which Pope has brought this canine to life. Here, satire is illustrated *within* the speaker himself or herself: The speaker embodies the attitudes being satirized.

Writing topics. The speaker as subject of satire. The use of satire to attack attitudes. The dramatic situation.

Anne Bradstreet, *The Author to Her Book, page 687*

Anne Bradstreet's brother-in-law had arranged for publication of her manuscript poems in 1650, and did so without her knowledge and corrections (see lines 3–6). The volume, entitled *The Tenth Muse,* was the first poetic publication in England by anyone living in colonial America. Apparently a second and corrected edition was considered in about 1666, and "The Author to Her Book" was composed in this expectation as a prefatory poem. The new edition did not appear, however, until after Bradstreet's death in 1678.

Answers to the Study Questions, pages 687–688

(1) The tone of the speaker's references to her friends eager to publish her work is one of both disapproval and disavowal, but at the same time she acknowledges their fidelity by labeling them "true" (line 3). The negative aspect of the tone is governed by the words "snatched," "less wise," and "exposed," all of which are ambiguous.

(2) The speaker's excuse for issuing the poems is stated in lines 11–12, where she talks of amending "blemishes"; that is, she wishes to have her reputation depend upon corrected and accurate copies of the poetry. The tone is conducive to humor because of the continuing metaphor of the child. Thus, the images of washing off spots, stretching joints, and improving clothing are all comic. The concluding application of the metaphor, in effect equating the birth of the poems with the birth of a bastard, is amusing. Thus the tone throughout makes the collection of poems—the "book"—seem like an external object, to be laughed about by both poet and reader.

(3) The author's portrayal of herself is not unconventional: She de-

clares herself as being both a busy and harried but also affectionate mother, trying to amend the appearance of a difficult child, thereby encouraging an amused response. Along with amusement, however, the details are arranged to promote understanding and sympathy.

(4) In dealing with the metaphor of the bastard child (lines 11–18), a metaphor appropriate for a female voice, the speaker demonstrates a degree of self-depreciation (she also says that the book is "ill-formed," suggesting shame). The metaphor is also developed elsewhere in the poem (e.g., lines 8, 22–23, among others).

WRITING TOPICS. The speaker's attitude toward herself and to her work. The attitude toward the well-meaning friends. The tone of the metaphor of the bastard child.

WORKS FOR COMPARISON WITH "THE AUTHOR TO HER BOOK"

Keats, *On First Looking Into Chapman's Homer,* 650
Moore, *How to Become a Writer,* 205
Shakespeare, *Not Marble,* 560

LUCILLE CLIFTON, *homage to my hips, page 688*

This is a poem that surprises by its frankness. The line lengths are uneven and free, perhaps suggesting a swaying, dancelike motion. The structural development is also free and spontaneous. In lines 1, 5, 8, 11, and 12, new units begin with the phrase *these hips*. Elsewhere, the structure is governed by the repetition of *they.* These structures all suggest movement. The freedom and informality suggested by the motion is also complemented by the poem's lack of capitalization.

Answers to the Study Questions, page 688

(1) The topic of the speaker's hips is not the usual subject material of poetry. The attitude expressed here is not only that the speaker speaks freely about her hips, but demonstrates total delight in them, without embarrassment but with pride and the memory of delight and power.

(2) These words reflect a union between mentality and physicality. The hips are free, not enslaved, and do their own bidding. The speaker's philosophy is to move with the hips, and in no way to restrain the life, involvement, and memory that they bring.

(3) Words like *free, mighty, magic,* and *spin* often belong to other contexts, such as those of politics, power, incantation, and physical me-

chanics. Because they are put into the context of hips, they take on new meaning, and therefore produce smiles and laughter. This is a happy poem.

WRITING TOPICS. The poem's subject. The function of varying lines and absence of capitalization. The relationship of diction to the poem's tone.

WORKS FOR COMPARISON WITH "HOMAGE TO MY HIPS"

Cummings, *she being Brand / -new,* 688
Gardner, *At a Summer Hotel,* 720
Wakoski, *Inside Out,* 668

E. E. CUMMINGS, *she being Brand / -new, pages 688–689*

This poem is characteristic of Cummings in many ways. It demonstrates his use of popular material, in this case the breaking in of a new car. It also shows his frankness, sexual explicitness, and sense of fun, together with his poetic arrangement of poetry as unusual arrangement on the page. Modern students, accustomed to cars with self-starters, may not know that in 1926, the date of the poem, cars were started with a hand-crank (lines 9–10), gears did not always engage smoothly when the foot clutch was released (line 12), and the spark and choke were worked by levers (line 16) that were moved up and down, to be held in place on a heavily notched dial.

Answers to the Study Questions, pages 689–690

(1) The sexual *double entendre* of the poem depends on the equation of "breaking in" a new car and a first experience with sex. Once this premise is admitted, most students are adept at determining the extensive double meanings in the poem. The excitement and discovery invariably cause students to remark that the poem is enjoyable and fun, although this aspect of the poem should probably not be emphasized if there are students who express any dismay about it.

(2) Cummings's spacing and alignment assist in the visualization of the experiences both of sex and of driving a new car. The slowness caused by the specific line ["again slo – wly; bare, ly nudg. ing (my"] is appropriate to the tentative nature of testing new apparatus. Similarly, the run-together word "greasedlightning" suggests that once working, things may move smoothly. Need we be more explicit with regard to the double meaning?

(3) The poem is better called "frank," "open," or "happy" rather than "bawdy" or "off color." The narration of the poem—the difficulty of

breaking in the car—preserves a surface innocence. The frankness develops from the verbal irony and ambiguity.

WRITING TOPICS. The poem's frankness and joy. The *double entendre.* The spacing, alignment, and punctuation, and their effect on the tone.

WORKS FOR COMPARISON WITH "SHE BEING BRAND / -NEW"

Anonymous, *Western Wind,* 570
Herrick, *Corinna's Going A-Maying,* 952
Munro, *The Found Boat,* 277

ANNE FINCH, COUNTESS OF WINCHILSEA, *To the Nightingale, page 690*

The nightingale is one of the popular birds because of the sweetness of its call. Perhaps because of the associations with night, the bird has also symbolized the mysteriousness of poetic inspiration, also treated by Keats in the "Ode to a Nightingale" (page 770). If students are curious about what a nightingale sounds like, Ottorino Respighi's *The Pines of Rome* contains a recording of the bird's call.

Answers to the Study Questions, page 691

(1) The speaker is ambiguous about the nightingale, which is "sweet" in line 1, but a "trifler" in line 27. The tone is therefore mixed.

(2) The speaker praises the bird's song for its wildness (line 7), spontaneity (line 8), feeling (line 13), division or harmony (line 23), and superiority to human song (line 25). The tone of the description in lines 14–25 is built up out of the envious notion that the poet cannot find words as easily as the bird can sing. The speaker's censure in lines 26–29 therefore reflects both anger and envy. The apparent intention is to represent human imperfection.

(3) The tone of the connection between the nightingale's song and poetry is one of yearning—the poet's desire to imitate in words the song that the bird expresses naturally. The idea underlying this wish is that the poetic spirit is both difficult and mysterious, a function of a "spirit of the brain" (line 20).

(4) The metaphor of the thorn causing song is that the poetic spirit is brought out best through the experience of pain, and, by extension, deep feeling. The implication is that the speaker too is best inspired when she feels pain, even though she does not detail her personal circumstances.

(5) In lines 30–35, the speaker concludes the poem on a note of self-

reproach, the idea being that those who cannot reach perfect expression envy those who can. The speaker makes the generalization about "we poets" in order to include her own judgments within a broad range of human response.

WRITING TOPICS. The bird as a model for the poet. The tone of admiration. The tone of envy. Structure and development.

WORKS FOR COMPARISON WITH "TO THE NIGHTINGALE"

Bridges, *Nightingales*, 921
Eliot, *Sweeney Among the Nightingales*, 799
Keats, *Ode to a Nightingale*, 770
Milton, *O Nightingale!*, 968

LANGSTON HUGHES, *Theme for English B, pages 691–692*

(Questions 1–4, page 692) See the sample essay (pages 700–701) for a discussion of the tone of this poem.

WRITING TOPICS. The character of the speaker. The connection that the speaker establishes with his reader, the teacher.

WORKS FOR COMPARISON WITH "THEME FOR ENGLISH B"

Angelou, *My Arkansas*, 912
Bontemps, *A Black Man Talks of Reaping*, 920
McKay, *The White City*, 967

X. J. KENNEDY, *John While Swimming in the Ocean, page 692*

This poem is selected from the poet's collection entitled *Brats.* Perhaps this is a fitting commentary on the unfortunate protagonist. One may compare "John While Swimming" with the satiric barbs of Pope (page 686).

Answers to the Study Questions, page 693

(1) The idea of a person's putting suntan lotion on the backs of sharks is ridiculous, and actually attempting to do it is impossible on the surface (not to mention under water).

(2) *Ocean* and *lotion* as rhymes are trochaic, and rhythmically they complement a comic mood. Also, the comparative sizes of *ocean* and *lotion* are so distinct that the juxtaposing of the two in rhyme causes the humor of anticlimax. To rhyme *John's* with *bronze* is unusual and good, and in the context marvelously funny.

(3) A characterization of the poem's attitude toward beach culture would be disapproval, at the very least.

Writing topics. The poem's use of rhyme. The ludicrous nature of the action. The poem in relationship to Pope's short satiric poems (p. 686).

Works for Comparison with "John While Swimming in the Ocean"

Anderson, *I'm a Fool*, 188
Frost, *Desert Places*, 764
Parker, *Resumé*, 974

Arthur O'Shaughnessy, *A Love Symphony, page 693*

This poem ties the subject of romantic adoration to the images of flowers, birds, and sea—topics which are often included separately but not often all together. Those who wish to speak about the so-called "pathetic fallacy" may wish to use the poem in illustration, although the tone of the poem makes the comparisons seem true and genuine, not sentimental. The flowers in stanza one are all appropriate to the purpose of praise. With regard to the second stanza, both the thrush and the linnet were birds that for many decades had been associated in songbook and miscellany collections with the beauty of nature. In this scheme, the blackbird is problematic.

Answers to the Study Questions, page 693

(1) The "symphony" of love is the blending of all colors and sounds to make up a song that in the speaker's fancy speaks of praise for the listener. The tone is conditioned by the selection of locations and appropriate flowers and harmonies. Thus the "bindweed" (line 6) becomes a means of complimenting both the beauty and personal care of hair. If these references were more fully developed they might fall over the edge into sentimentality, but here, because of the directness and simplicity, they work, particularly because of the "you were more" formula of lines 8 and 16.

(2) The tone of the phrase "ancient mystery ..." (lines 19–20) is designed to reflect the amazement of the speaker at the paradox that love is both old and past, on the one hand, and ever present, on the other. On mysteriousness, all three poems, by Donne, Finch, and O'Shaughnessy, use the concept of religious mystery to describe the power and force of love. Here, O'Shaughnessy uses the idea as a straightforward descriptive statement. Anne Finch uses the idea to contrast the often expected state of married people (coldness and indifference) with the state of her speaker's marriage. The mystery makes Finch's couple draw inward toward their

own private world. In Donne's "The Canonization," the mystery is both sexuality and love, with the idea moving from a playful pun on "die" to the seriousness of the canonized union. Both Donne and Finch therefore treat the concept more fully than O'Shaughnessy.

(3) Lines 23–24 suggest not closeness but admiration and praise, not intimacy, but worship and adoration. The phrase "fled back to your feet" suggests the distance of a statue, with the concluding location of the speaker at the statue's feet.

Writing topics. The meaning of the "symphony" of love. The speaker's attitude toward the listener. The idea of love as a religious mystery, as expressed by O'Shaughnessy alone, or as contrasted with Donne and Finch.

Works for Comparison with "A Love Symphony"

Joyce, *Araby*, 387
Moore, *Believe Me, If All Those Endearing*, 968
Piercy, *Will We Work Together?*, 975

Alexander Pope, *From Epilogue to the Satires, Dialogue I, pages 694–695*

Because of the ways in which "An Essay on Man" is contrasted with Voltaire's *Candide*, Pope is often denigrated as an apostle of the idea that everything is for the best in this best of all possible worlds. This denigration, first of all, results from a misreading of his idea that "Whatever is, is right," which would be better construed as "Whatever is, is, and it won't change, so we had better do the best we can." Second, the misconstruction ignores the fact that Pope was a satirist during his entire poetic career. The fragment contained here, from Dialogue I of the *Epilogue to the Satires*, is a self-contained unit illustrating the scope of Pope's satire, and the concluding line should dispel the misinterpretations from which Pope often suffers.

Answers to the Study Questions, page 695

(1) In light of the fact that Pope often uses the dialogue form in his satires, the designation *P* may be construed as a representation of Pope's own views. The final couplet surely is a personal statement, at least a statement of Pope's own sense of outrage at some of the actions he satirizes in the poem.

(2) Pope's satire is couched in general terms in this excerpt, but elsewhere he used generalized names to refer to reprehensible qualities. He

skated a fine line in his satire, for if he named names, those who were not named would feel absolved. If he did not name names, people could claim that they were not intended for criticism. Here, Pope criticizes the importation of continental customs as opposed to English ones, corruption in "soldier, churchman, man in power," and the public admiration of people who were noted not for their virtue but for their outrageousness.

(3) The tone of the excerpt rises from the opening to line 160, "That 'not to be corrupted is the shame.'" From there it sustains a strong level of invective, climaxing with line 170, "'Nothing is sacred now but villainy.'"

(4) Students might enjoy discussing this question, and might bring in copies of some of the current tabloid publications which seem to thrive on scandal and misdeeds. The question about these publications is whether people read them to revile the actions they describe, or to enjoy learning about these actions. Lively discussion, in any event, should result.

Writing topics. The objects of Pope's satiric criticism. The tone of the satiric excerpt. The voice of the satirist in the poem.

Works for Comparison with Pope's "Epilogue"

Eliot, *Sweeney Among the Nightingales,* 799
Frost, *A Considerable Speck,* 902
Pastan, *Ethics,* 855
Swift, *A Description of the Morning,* 730

Salvatore Quasimodo, *Auschwitz, pages 695–696*

(Please see the explanatory notes about Auschwitz on pages 695 and 696.)The poem "Auschwitz" is a searching and agonized poem in which the speaker describes a visit, with his "love," to the camp and attempts to explain its meaning. But answers are not easily found. The use of the imagery of transformations is hence appropriate, for those who are living must find meaning out of the hundreds of thousands of deaths that took place in the Auschwitz gas chambers.

Answers to the Study Questions, pages 696–697

(1) The first ten lines describe negative images of rust, tangled fencing, rain, funeral cold, and general lifelessness, all of which produce a sense of depression, "hurt," and hopelessness. The concluding six lines have shifted away from the depressing images in the poem to a positive resolution: "never from the pit of ashes / to show itself [i.e., the horror,

the atrocities] again." These lines supply at least some answer to the question about "the meaning of our destiny" posed in lines 9 and 10.

(2) These lines, 13 and 14, affirm the need for life in the light of "every No" that took place at the camp. In other words, the contemplation of the many exterminations at Auschwitz makes the speaker firmly resolved to take the actions that prevent such atrocities in the future. From death, in other words, there must arise life.

(3) The references to ancient myths of transformation, particularly to the stories of Alpheus and Arethusa (which Milton refers to in his elegy "Lycidas," where they also signify the continuation of life despite the reality of death), are intended to bolster the speaker's thoughts and also those of his listener. The specific transformations in lines 25–43 are those of the dead who have gone back into the earth. Many of the personal possessions of the victims, testifying to the reality of their suffering, are still displayed at the camp (lines 37–40). This visual testimony, in the speaker's judgment, should create a transformation of the people who visit the camp, a transformation through which people dedicate themselves not to military coercion but rather to ethical and political solutions of problems.

Writing topics. The use of realistic, physical imagery in the poem. The meaning of the transformation myths described in the poem. The sense of resolution in the concluding six lines.

Works for Comparison with "Auschwitz"

Kernan, *Majdanek*, 957
Layton, *Rhine Boat Trip*, 961
Ozick, *The Shawl*, 251
Zabytko, *Home Soil*, 403

Theodore Roethke, *My Papa's Waltz, page 697*

As is brought out in question 3 on page 702, "My Papa's Waltz" might arouse a certain amount of controversy among students. One view is that the speaker considers the "waltzing" father as a pleasant association of childhood. Another view is that the experiences were not pleasant at all. Students may find justification in the poem to take either position. An attempt to achieve a balance is made in the following answers.

Answers to the Study Questions, page 697

(1) The opening description of the father is conducive to the speaker's boyhood sense of ambiguity and anxiety. The phrases "like death" and

"such waltzing" are opposed; either one or the other is inappropriate, or else the speaker is being ironic. In the context of "like death," however, the term "waltzing" is likely an understatement. The tone then suggests apprehension and anxiety, although the assertion that the father's whiskey breath could make "a small boy dizzy" is a tempering (but not a temperance) overstatement.

(2) The "waltz" is an understatement describing a drunkenly boisterous mock dance done by the speaker's father, with the speaker as a boy being the partner. The tone of the description suggests the mixture of emotions conveyed in the opening stanza. The roughness and grossness of the father is brought out in the references to his battered knuckle, his lack of coordination, the scraping his buckle gives the speaker's ear, the tattoo on the boy's head, and the dirt-caked palm. The lack of control is made mildly amusing by the sliding of the pans and the frowning mother. The potential pain and fright that might be experienced by the boy are mitigated by the light iambic trimeter and the trochaic rhyme of lines 10 and 12.

(3) "Countenance" is an instance of overstatement in line 7 because the word is inconsistent with the diction in the rest of the poem. In context, and along with the use of "unfrown," the word "countenance" suggests the mother's annoyance and disapproval but not outright anger or fear.

(4) The tone of the speaker's treatment of the father suggests the speaker's sense of powerlessness accompanying his memory. Whatever pain he experienced is not mentioned in the poem, even though the descriptions indicate that he would have felt at least some (such as having time beat out on his head, his right ear scraping the buckle). Thus the speaker's recollection emphasizes that he is attempting to understand and reconcile himself to his memory of his father, with the less pleasant aspects being diminished.

Writing topics. The attitude towards the father. Overstatement and understatement. The speaker's attitude toward the memory. The function of rhythm and structure.

Works for Comparison with "My Papa's Waltz"

Cummings, *if there are any heavens,* 930
Hayden, *Those Winter Sundays,* 950
Serotte, *My Mother's Face,* 983

Writing About Tone in Poetry, *pages 697–702*

In teaching this section you will need to remind your students that tone can be a slippery topic if they do no more than describe the attitudes they find in the poem. Always, it is important to emphasize that to write about tone is to explain how the attitudes are built up. Just to determine and describe the attitudes is not enough.

Therefore, the strategies for organizing ideas suggested on pages 698–699 may be stressed as providing ways for students to explore tone. The sample essay on pages 700–701 illustrates that the approaches are by no means mutually exclusive. Thus a discussion of tone emphasizing the poem's situation will invariably include a section on diction, as the sample essay does in paragraphs 5 and 6. Probably the best thing to stress in teaching is that students should be prepared to adapt their approaches for their essays to the circumstances of the poems on which they will write. Once students are so forewarned, they should be able to control their handling of tone in poetry.

Writing Topics for Tone in Poetry, *page 702*

(1) These poems all share the topic of love, though they treat it very differently. In "A Love Symphony" the stress is on the ways in which beautiful things lead the speaker to increased devotion; in "she being Brand / –new" the stress is on merry sexuality; in "The Workbox" on secrecy, surreptitiousness, suspicion, and unhappiness; and in "The First-Rate Wife" on (unwitting) pompousness and condescension.

(2) From a feminist viewpoint, each of the poems assumes that women will be in an inferior position. Students will want to offer their own ideas about how to judge the poems as a result of these assumptions.

(3) "My Papa's Waltz" has aroused differences of opinion. You might consult the discussion in this manual as a point of departure for your students.

(4) The task of poetry writing here should underline for students the absolute need for imagination and thought in the molding of just the right tone for a poem. An additional idea: There are always elections going on either nationally or locally during fall semesters. As an exercise for students preparing to write a poem emphasizing tone, you might assign a political speech or political controversy, and ask for an analysis of the tone of the various office-seekers. By way of criticism, students might

write short poems as either corrective or corroborative ways of treating the topics being brought up in the campaigns.

(5) Léger's painting should probably be discussed by the class as a group (or by small groups interested in working on this question) before anyone undertakes to write. The poems referred to in the question have mainly negative views of city life for comparison with the painting. "Chicago" is the only one of these poems that presents city life at all sympathetically.

(6) All the mentioned attitudes are to be found in the Quasimodo poem, but the development of a sense of resolution and firmness is probably the major attitude that emerges. This development governs the structure of the poem, from the negative images at the outset to the transformational myths introduced as the poem progresses.

Chapter Nineteen
Pages 703–748

Prosody: Sound, Rhythm, and Rhyme in Poetry

Students may not need everything in this section to carry on a competent discussion of prosody. Some students can easily perceive light and heavy stresses and also the distinctions between sound and spelling; they may therefore produce good essays with no further instruction. Many students have difficulty, however, and therefore they may need to go back to basics about the syllable (page 704) and also about segments (pages 703–704). Many students quickly recognize both regular and rhetorical substitutions. If they have difficulty, however, you may wish to have them study the section on these matters (pages 710–711). Also, the section on the various feet and types of measures is longer than you perhaps will have time for in a one-semester course. As a result, the most essential material on the two-syllable feet (pages 706–708) will serve most students first becoming acquainted with prosody. If students become genuinely interested in the complexities of rhythm, they may profit from pages 708–709, including the shaded box describing the less common meters.

In teaching the caesura, you may encounter surprise again about the rôle of pause and spacing in the development of meaning and rhythm. Most students understand junctures and use them properly. The problem comes when they are first asked to systematize their knowledge, and then to determine the effect of juncture or caesura in poetic rhythm. Punctuation is a great help here, for students will usually pause naturally at a comma or period. The problem will come in the determination of where internal open junctures and caesuras coincide. It may take much practice for many students to perceive caesurae occurring in these circumstances. Here, as elsewhere, practice, together with your supervision, will help.

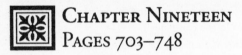

A very basic and important idea which students should establish is the distinction that must often be made between pronunciation and spelling (page 704). You may discover that some of the students, even against their own hearing, will identify sounds on visual rather than spoken evidence. It is therefore good to select a poem or short passage and have the class analyze the written words for the sounds themselves. Some students might truly believe that the < s > in *sure, silver,* and *resemblance* spell out the same sound. You will need to raise consciousness about the differences in these and in other words. Sometimes students have a special problem with digraphs, identifying the < t > in *the* with the < t > in *type,* the < t > in *thick,* or the < t > in *Betty.* The principle of the differences is not difficult, but it is often difficult for students to distinguish between what they see and what they hear.

Because rhyme is the aspect of poetry with which students are most familiar, the technical material in this chapter is limited and straightforward, and should be relatively easy to teach. Brief in-class explanations of exact rhyme, rising and falling rhyme, and slant and eye rhyme might be helpful. The section on rhyme schemes (page 717) is a bit more demanding since it presupposes that students already understand the concepts and applications of meter. Of course, you might allow your students to define rhyme schemes simply by reference to the sounds (i.e., *abab, cdcd,* etc.). If you do use the whole formulation in class, be sure to remind students to look for the dominant meter and not to be misled by variant lines.

As exercises in segments, the following nonce sentences might prove useful for your students. You may add to these as you wish, or omit them. Students sometimes enjoy creating exemplifying lines of their own.

VOWEL SOUNDS

He sees deep fields of green freaks.

Palely made cakes are aided by savory flavors.

Swift Camilla skims the pillowed plinths.

The fresh fellow offended Ted's sense of method.

Afterward, a lanky lad ambled by with angular ankles.

Often he saw faults that caused awe.

She told of opposing foes openly loading goalposts.

Puny new tunes are few in the pews on Tuesdays.

The stupidly fooling troupe coolly sat on stools.

I find the sky quite high in my mind's eye on the ninth of July.

He announced, avowed, and avouched that he found
    the brows of cows to weigh one ounce.

His foible was joining in toil, not to foil but to spoil.

CONSONANT SOUNDS

The beau in the bed was bored with his beard and his billboard.

The dark darter daringly dashed from the den
to the dappled dawn.

The kiln cooked while the king courageously counseled quiet.

The pen pals panted palpably and probably panicked.

His task was tasting tangy but tart tangerines.

The game was to glide gallantly in galloping galoshes.

The ocean shore shifted the nation's passions.

Azure closures measure beige rouges.

Chinese chimpanzees chirped cheerfully in chimneys.

George generally enjoyed judging jellies and jams.

With special skill, Smith smashed several small smelt.

Zebras and zephyrs zigzagged in the zoo zones.

Phil fancied fabulous financial finds following
funny but fantastic failures.

Vales of vexatious vampires vanish in vapors of vinegar.

He was thumped and throttled thoroughly by the
thin but thriving thresher.

In the withering weather, the other brother then
went thither to bathe the feather.

Nervous neighbors need nice new nutrition.

Mobilized manufacturers modestly make moccasins.

Red railroad ramps recede roaringly and raucously.

Limber and loose loops loom locally, linking linnets to limes.

Gwendolyn Brooks, *We Real Cool, page 718*

Winner of the Pulitzer Prize for Poetry in 1950, Gwendolyn Brooks in later years has stressed the topic of race. "We Real Cool," with its strong pathos, is a part of this emphasis.

Answers to the Study Questions, page 718

(1) The major idea of the poem is that an aimless existence leads nowhere. The speakers are young men whose life pattern is based on diversionary and fruitless activity. They do not mention any obligation toward constructive service, but speak glowingly of enjoyable but destructive habits, which they describe as "cool." The last sentence is a climax because it recognizes the outcome of the way of life depicted in the poem. The poet's attitude is clear because of the poem's situational irony: The opportunities for those who waste their lives at the Golden Shovel should be improved in all respects.

(2) The rhythmical stresses on all syllables are strong. The absence of weak stresses, making the poem totally strong-stressed, is achieved because all the words are of one syllable, and because there are no definite or indefinite articles, and no prepositions. Thus, every word counts as a subject, verb, object, or predicate adjective or adverb.

Writing topics. The use of strong stress in the poem. The relationship between the metrical beat and the main idea.

Works for Comparison with "We Real Cool"

Emanuel, *The Negro,* 720
Evans, *I Am a Black Woman,* 942

Emily Dickinson, *To Hear an Oriole Sing, pages 718–719*

This poem beautifully illustrates Dickinson's power of compactness and dramatic expression. It contains, in little, the substance of an extensive aesthetic discussion and argument. Though the topic is the song of an oriole, the bird has little to do with the poem after the first line. Rather, the subject spreads out to beauty and how we perceive it.

Answers to the Study Questions, page 719

(1) In classroom discussion, it helps to identify the speaker and the listener, and their positions, as quickly as possible. The listener ("The Skeptic") argues that the "Tune is in the Tree" (line 13). The speaker, who presents virtually a whole aesthetic theory in fifteen lines, asserts that the tune (music, poetry, art) is "In Thee!" (the ear of the listener, the mind of the perceiver). Simply put, this poem exemplifies the adage that "beauty is in the eye of the beholder." Those who are interested may wish to relate the poem to Bishop Berkeley's ideas about perception and understand-

ing, but too extensive a discussion along these lines would create a course in philosophy rather than literature.

(2) The poem is written in triplets, rhyming *aaa, bbb, ccc,* and so on. The rhymes coincide with the various shifts in topic and situation. Only the rhymes in the fifth stanza are exact throughout; the rest contain at least one slant rhyme (the fourth contains two).

(3) Only the rhymes in the fifth stanza are exact. The rest contain at least one slant rhyme, with the fourth containing two. The slant rhymes emphasize and illustrate the various things that people might consider beautiful. If the slant rhymes work at all as rhyme, it is because our ears (eyes, imaginations, perceptions) make them work.

(4) The rhymes are developed according to a pattern of contrast or reinforcement. The first variation ("divine"), for example, is ironic, particularly because it is preceded by the word "only," as if divine things are less important than common ones (or is the entire world to be considered as a miracle?). The final stanza emphasizes the speaker's position, and hence this stanza is the only one with exact rhymes.

Writing topics. The rhymes. The degree to which the rhymes of the poem reflect and reinforce the poem's theme.

Works for Comparison with "To Hear an Oriole Sing"

Engels, *Naming the Animals,* 942
Hall, *Whip-poor-will,* 845

T. S. Eliot, *Macavity: The Mystery Cat, pages 719–720*

Eliot, often considered a hyper-serious poet of either negative or religious themes, published *Old Possum's Book of Practical Cats* in 1939. He was what is called by cat-fanciers a "cat person." There is a 1928 photo of him with a cat named "George" (George V was king at the time), and among some of his other cats were "Wiscus" and "Pettipaws." There were many other cats, no doubt, which he owned or with whom he was friendly or acquainted. His poems about felines achieved popular fame in 1981, with the musical play *Cats,* freely adapted from *Old Possum's Book.* In July, 1994, *Cats* was still running on Broadway.

The poem illustrates the "nonsense" lyric developed to its highest potential. Eliot admired the nonsense verse of Edward Lear (1812–1888), who is perhaps best known for "The Owl and the Pussycat." In writing "Macavity" and the other poems in the *Old Possum* Book, Eliot tried to achieve enjoyment as a major standard of poetic achievement. However, students might also note that "Macavity" is a well-formed poem with an introduction, characteristics of the "hero," accomplishments, refrains, and a climax. There are allusions to large matters of criminal law and international politics, and throughout there is a constant use of overstatement and anti-climax. Thus the nonsense is tightly controlled, showing that poetic craft is essential for all poems, regardless of subject.

Answers to the Study Questions, page 720

(1) Macavity's "crimes" are detailed from lines 21 to 34. The speaker expresses fear and amazement at the crimes, which in a human being would indeed have been heinous. The misdeeds occasion humor, however, because they are part of the overstatement on which the poem is built: To attribute felonious behavior to a cat (a felonious feline) is automatically incongruous and therefore comic.

(2) The line length, according to a conventional scansion, is heptameter or the septenary, with iambic feet as the norm but with occasional lines commencing with anapaests (e.g., lines 9, 10, 12, 19, etc).

(3) Once one begins reading and getting into the swing of the lines, however, the dipodic foot takes over, so that each line contains four major stresses accompanied by a number of minor stresses, as in, "He always has an alibi, and one or two to spare." In this line, the dipodic feet put heavy stress on "al," "al," "one," and "spare," even though more formally the line contains seven iambic feet. Because the poem is really on a "nonsense" theme, the transformation of the serious verse form into the bouncier, thumping rhythm adds to the ridiculousness that Eliot is creating.

WRITING TOPICS. The dipodic foot. The development of humor. Macavity as a normal cat. Macavity as a "villain."

WORKS FOR COMPARISON WITH "MACAVITY: THE MYSTERY CAT"

Eberhart, *The Groundhog*, 937
Kyger, *Destruction*, 960
Tate, *The Blue Booby*, 997

JAMES EMANUEL, *The Negro, pages 720–721*

This poem is even more cryptic than the dramatically presented "We Real Cool" of Gwendolyn Brooks. In classroom discussion, students can bring out the ideas of the poem, but they may need some leading questions to do so.

Answers to the Study Questions, page 721

(1) The attribute of the black described in lines 1–4 is "invisibility." In other words, the black is not visible because he has never had a chance to develop knowledge, character, and identity. Lines 5 and 6 bring out the traditional servile role in which blacks have been cast. Lines 7 and 8 refer to the wasteful and destructive ways of life pursued by many blacks because they were denied more fulfilling opportunities.

(2) "The-ness" in line 9 (with the definite article) refers to the definite and circumscribed role of the black. "A-ness" in line 11 (with the indefinite article) refers to freedom and the opportunity to grow as an individual without the restrictions imposed by race.

(3) The predominant metrical foot of the poem is the trochee, with the concluding light stress missing in lines 2, 4, 10, and 12. The trochee, with falling rhythm, is here suitable to the poem's irony of situation. A rising foot, specifically the iamb, would suggest a more complete, fulfilled life than the poet is dealing with here.

WRITING TOPICS. The main metrical foot of the poem. The use of metrical variation. The use of short dramatic quotations in lines 5–8 to symbolize the condition of blacks.

WORKS FOR COMPARISON WITH "THE NEGRO"

Brooks, *Primer for Blacks,* 922
Giovanni, *Nikki-Rosa,* 766

ISABELLA GARDENER, *At a Summer Hotel, page 721*

Gardner's short poem is an instance in which rhyme and sound contribute to an ironic portrait of a speaker. The issues in the poem are serious, but the poem demonstrates that the speaker can probably do nothing about them, and that life cannot be held in check when it is bursting in its bounty.

Answers to the Study Questions, page 721

(1) The speaker here is a mother at a "summer hotel" by the sea with her daughter, who is apparently attractive and nubile. The mother is passive; she sits "on the veranda" and worries. The daughter is active and immersed in nature ("gold in the sun," "bold in the dazzling water"). The speaker wants to relax, but the "beautiful bountiful womanful" daughter causes anxiety in her. The source of the speaker's anxiety is revealed in the

closing allusions to Europa, Persephone, and Miranda, for all three fictional women attracted violent sexual attention.

(2) The *b* sound, like the repetitive "ful" and the *r* sounds in "roused by these roses roving," emphasizes the fullness and life of the daughter, and therefore serves as a lively view of the daughter in opposition to the speaker's apprehensiveness.

(3) Internal rhyme, as in "gold–bold" (line 3), "roses–roving" (line 2), and "blond–sand" (line 4), both helps to hold the lines together and produces a slightly comic effect.

(4) The end rhymes also create a certain amount of humor, and enable us to view the speaker in the perspective of being an overly protective mother. "Child–wild" is an exact, rising rhyme that neatly captures some of the daughter's qualities and the mother's anxiety. "Water–daughter" and "veranda–Miranda," however, are falling (trochaic and amphibrachic) rhymes that ring in the comic. Like the first rhyming pair, "water–daughter" captures some of the speaker's anxiety, especially if we see the water as even faintly sexual. "Veranda–Miranda" can only be amusing, as rhymes.

WRITING TOPICS. The effects of rhyme, alliteration, and repetition. The character of the speaker. The presentation of the daughter. The poem's use of allusion.

WORKS FOR COMPARISON WITH "AT A SUMMER HOTEL"

Adamé, *My Grandmother Would Rock Quietly,* 910
Serotte, *My Mother's Face,* 983

ROBERT HERRICK, *Upon Julia's Voice, page 722*

This poem is one of Herrick's poems on the qualities of generalized, conventionalized women, including also Corinna (page 952). The idea of the poems is not so much to describe specific details about a woman as to demonstrate the poet's sharpness and skill.

Answers to the Study Questions, page 722

(1) The speaker praises Julia's speaking voice, but commends it for its "melodious" qualities. "Silv'ry" and "amber" are euphonious words as well as rich commodities, therefore reflecting the speaker's high opinion.

(2) The "joke" of the poem is that Julia's voice is beautiful enough to overcome the devil's power of torment, so that damned souls would stop their screams of pain from hell fire to listen to her.

(3) The alliterations are *s* ("so smooth," "so sweet," "so silv'ry"), *n* ("no noise"), *m* ("melting melodious"), and *l* ("melting," "melodious," "lutes"). The *m* sounds complement the praise for the voice, for *m*, being a bilabial nasal continuant, brings the mouth into obvious use.

Writing topics. The poem as a compliment. The use of alliteration and euphony.

Works for Comparison with "Upon Julia's Voice"

Joyce, *Araby*, 387
Moore, *Believe Me, If All Those Endearing*, 968
O'Shaughnessy, *A Love Symphony*, 693

Gerard Manley Hopkins, *God's Grandeur, page 722*

If one did not read the poem word by word, but merely looked at its form, it would seem to be a traditional Italian sonnet, with an extra iambic foot in line 3. An oral reading, however, dramatizes the tension between the formal and the actual rhythms caused by Hopkins's use of "sprung" rhythm. He achieves the vigorous spoken effect through the frequent juxtaposition of single-syllable words together with alliteration. Thus the regular light stresses are replaced by stronger stresses, which "spring" out of the lines.

To stress God's grandeur and power throughout all creation, Hopkins speaks of God as living everywhere in the universe, as ruler and as all-pervasive Holy Ghost who resembles traditional images of angels (with "bright wings"). To show divine omnipresence, he uses metaphors of electricity or flame, the freshness of creation, the dawn, and guardianship.

Answers to the Study Questions, page 722

(1) The first four lines praise God, concluding with a question about human disobedience. The second four lines contain a brief review of the speaker's judgment that human beings are enslaved by commerce. The sestet develops from this octave because it stresses the world's beauty, and suggests the possibility that improvement, like a new dawn, is awaiting those who are open to God's power.

(2) There are many alliterative patterns in the poem, which coincide with positions of rhythmical stress and therefore also with important words and ideas. See, for example, line 2, which emphasizes *f* in "flame" and "foil" and *sh* in "shining and "shook," and line 7, with its *sm* pattern in "smudge" and "smell."

(3) For assonance and internal rhyme, see, for example, lines 4 and 5: "men," "then," "reck," and "generations," where the eh sound predominates. There are other internal rhymes: "seared," "bleared," "smeared"; and "wears," "shares."

Writing topics. Hopkins's use of a–alliteration, b–assonance, c–internal rhyme, d–the Italian sonnet form, and e–"sprung" rhythm.

Works for Comparison with "God's Grandeur"

Arnold, *Dover Beach*, 576
Pickthall, *The Worker in Sandalwood*, 341
Piercy, *Wellfleet Sabbath*, 588

Barbara Howes, *Death of a Vermont Farm Woman, page 723*

Do not let the title mislead. The poem is not about death, but rather is about an individual and a way of life. It is a brief but touching expression of a moment in a life that his been lived to the fullest. The speaker is a sixty-year-old farm woman whose life has been a constant struggle for survival. She has worked the farm, given birth four times, outlived three of her sons, and now looks for peace (perhaps death). The setting is established in the opening lines. It is late July, and fall is approaching.

Answers to the Study Questions, page 723

(1) The fields, like the speaker, are old but still productive, a state that is germane for all women and all persons approaching advanced age. For the speaker, the "long green evenings" will delay death for both the fields and herself, even though the shift towards winter (and death) is inevitable. We are reminded of the next winter by the speaker's recollection of the last (lines 6–9). She may have thought that her death was approaching then, but she "was wrong." In the last stanza, the speaker looks back over her whole life; it seems short and difficult. Now she seeks rest, and asks, "Is it time now?".

(2, 3) There are only three rhyming sounds, *ay*, *-ong*, and *ow*. The rhyme scheme is *aabba, aabc, aabbac.* Most of the lines end with the ***a*** or ***b*** rhyme, thus creating a unifying network of repeated sounds. The third rhyming sounds in lines 9 and 15 isolate the speaker's central question. The repetition of sounds may emphasize the constancy and repetitiveness of the speaker's life.

(4) Within the rhyming pattern, the double use of *long* (lines 4 and 13) does not weaken the poem. Quite the contrary, it stresses the sense of

age, struggle, and exhaustion linked to the speaker. Similarly, the repetition of *now* as the *c* rhyme emphasizes the speaker's readiness for peace and rest in the present.

WRITING TOPICS. The character of the speaker. The setting. The seasonal imagery. The use of rhyme, and their relationship to topic.

WORKS FOR COMPARISON WITH
"DEATH OF A VERMONT FARM WOMAN"

Halpern, *Summer in the Middle Class,* 947
Hardy, *The Walk,* 583

LANGSTON HUGHES, *Let America Be America Again, pages 723–725*

Today the timeliness and the greatness of Hughes's work is becoming widely recognized. His poem *Harlem* (page 660) is the best known poem, with its powerful phrases *dream deferred* and *raisin in the sun.* Other Hughes poems may be found on pages 956, and 691. His play *Mulatto* is on page 1439.

Answers to the Study Questions, page 725

(1, 2) The first sixteen lines contain a statement of an ideal, and thus the quatrains followed by the repetition in lines 5 and 10, with rhyming words in lines 15 and 16, form a unit both topically and rhythmically. The remainder of the poem may be considered a critique of how the ideal has been neglected and corrupted, and hence the units take on irregular lengths, much as in the free form of the ode. Although there are powerful rhymes in the stanzas after line 17, they are not regular, in keeping with the idea that the poet is describing a yet unrealized dream. It is not until line 71 that the poet repeats the line "America never was America to me." Once this theme is reestablished, the remainder is an exhortation to fulfill the dream the poet associates with the founding of the country.

(3) There are many examples of alliteration throughout the poem. Phrases such as *land of love, kings connive, ancient endless chain, grab the gold, sailed those early seas* and *great green*—all invite an incantative recitation and a consequent strong emphasis on the ideas brought out by the phrases. The alliteration hence contributes the poem's effectiveness and assertiveness.

(4) Assonance, rhyme, internal rhyme, and slant rhyme are all employed throughout. One of the prominent rhymes is the use of *ee* in the

words *be, free, me, liberty, lea*—a rhyme which appears a number of times. Another prominent set is *again, plain, chain, gain, pain, rain*, and *stain. Again* may be a slant rhyme in this pattern, depending on how one chooses to pronounce it, but it opens the poem (lines 1 and 3) and concludes it (lines 79, 81). Assonance may be seen, for example, in the first stanza on the words *be, dream, be, he*, and *free*, and later (lines 64–66) on the words *me, steel, freedom*, and *leeches*. One might consider this pattern to be also part of the poem's internal rhyme, with the pattern of *ee* rhymes. Slant rhyme is not prominent, but one may see it in the words *dreamed* and *scheme, become* and *home* and *came*, and *pain* and *rain* and *again*. As with the regular rhymes, these features underscore the poem's assertiveness. Because the dream is unfulfilled, perhaps the idea is that a time might come when all rhymes, like making America America again, will be true.

Writing topics. The varying stanzaic patterns. The use of rhyme. The use of regular meters and free rhythms. The effect of the repetition of the phrase "America never was America to me."

Works for Comparison with "Let America Be America Again"

Gaines, *The Sky Is Gray*, 367
Sanchez, *right on: white america*, 980

Edgar Allan Poe, *The Bells, pages 726–728*

"The Bells" evokes the connection between sound and mood. If students come to the poem searching for ideas as such, they will be disappointed. Instead, in "The Bells" the idea is mood, or rather the separate moods evoked by Poe's descriptions. In making this stress upon emotion as a mode of knowledge, this poem, noisy and percussive as it is, is not unlike Emily Dickinson's "There's a Certain Slant of Light" (page 883). Dickinson, remember, speaks about the "heft" of cathedral tunes.

Answers to the Study Questions, page 728

(1) The stanzas discuss (a) silver sledge or sleigh bells, (b) golden wedding bells, (c) brass alarm bells, and (d) iron funeral bells. The metals are appropriate because of their colors and textures. Certainly silver and gold suggest happiness and security, while brass and iron are more suitable for the fearsome, somber, and bizarre uses to which Poe puts these bells. The stanzas, particularly the third and fourth, become longer because the situations of alarm and death being described are more far-

reaching and complicated than sleighrides and weddings, and perhaps more congenial to his temperament.

(2) In stanza one, the major assonance is the short *i*, and there are a number of repeated t and d sounds in alliteration. For the wedding bells in stanza two, there is more of a mixture of sounds. Thus one may note assonances in "*eh*" (mellow, wedding), "*oh*" (molten, golden), short *i* (liquid, ditty, listens), and a number of "*oo*" sounds (through, tune, euphony, voluminously, future). There are more nasals ("*m*" and "*n*") here, and liquids ("*l*") than in the first stanza, so that brittleness gives way to something more like the "mellow" sounds to which Poe refers in line 15. The third section introduces a number of "*r*" sounds to emphasize the noise of terror (as in "scream out their affright"). In the first part of the stanza there is also the plosive "*t*," and the "*k*" sound is introduced in line 53. The fourth stanza, about funeral bells, introduces the fricatives "*s*" and "*sh*," presumably to imitate sounds of sighing and weeping. From line 89 to the end, however, the poem moves from the suggestion of sorrow and shivering into a bizarre, mad dance by a King of the Ghouls. The repetition here is principally on the word "bells," which is a percussive counterpoint to sobbing, moaning, and groaning, which the bells also are doing.

(3) The word *bells*, used sixty-one times in the poem, as a refrain and as the repeated word in lines, is a one-syllable word that begins with the voiced stop b and then moves to *eh*, *l*, and *z*. It suggests a constant hammering and ringing sound. Musical notation (because several lines can be laid out simultaneously) would be better able to capture Poe's desired effect than lines of poetry alone can do.

(4) The pattern of rhymes is complex throughout the four stanzas, but all the stanzas begin and end with "bells" and words that rhyme with it.

Writing topics. The relation of segments to content (any stanza). The progress or change in sounds in the poem.

Works for Comparison with "The Bells"

Eliot, *Macavity: The Mystery Cat,* 719
Thompson, *To a Snowflake,* 733

Edwin Arlington Robinson, *Miniver Cheevy, pages 728–729*

This portrait illustrates the futility of seeking an escape into the romanticized and idealized past. The poem's subject is a failure and a drinker. One might think of him as a perfectionist who, because he cannot achieve perfection, gives up on everything and loses the ability to function. An effective classroom strategy for teaching the poem might be to focus on 1–the portrait of Miniver, 2–the speaker's attitude toward him, and 3–the poetic techniques that Robinson employs to make Miniver all the more ludicrous.

Answers to the Study Questions, page 729

(1) The speaker uses rhyme to emphasize disgust and amusement at Miniver's pathetic silliness. For example, by rhyming ordinary, trite words like "old" and "bold" in the second stanza ("In days of old, / When knights were bold," as a well-known obscene poem begins), the speaker stresses the futility and inaccuracy of Miniver's visions of what life should be. There is also the echo of the legendary "Purple Cow" rhymes ("see one" and "be one") in Robinson's lines 18 and 20:

I've never seen a purple cow.
I hope I'll never see one.
But I can tell you here and now
I'd rather see than be one.

(2) The use of "Miniver" at the beginning of each line recalls the word "minimal" (which Miniver's name echoes), and also stresses the idea of littleness and ineffectiveness. The "thought, and thought," phrases of lines 27–28 stress the inconsequentiality of Miniver as a thinker and a person.

(3) Through sound, the falling (trochaic) rhymes in the second and fourth lines of each stanza underscore Miniver's ridiculous situation.

WRITING TOPICS. The use of trochaic rhymes. The use of repetition. The use of irony in the portrait of Miniver.

WORKS FOR COMPARISON WITH "MINIVER CHEEVY"

Anderson, *I'm a Fool*, 188
Swift, *A Description of the Morning*, 730

WILLIAM SHAKESPEARE, *Sonnet 73: That Time of Year, page 730*

"That Time of Year" is one of the best known of all the sonnets. Students should memorize it and be able to quote it.

Answers to the Study Questions, page 730

(1) The topics of the quatrains are these: lines 1–4, autumn; lines 5–8, sunset and night; lines 9–12, a dying fire. The common link is diminution or dying. The concluding couplet is tied to the previous twelve lines

by the demonstrative pronoun "This," which begins line 13, and which turns the thought to the need for strengthening love.

(2) The spondees create emphasis by slowing the speech and thereby thrusting the ideas into prominence. Also, the frequency of spondees in this sonnet suggests the heaviness of a slow march or respectful walk appropriate to a funeral procession. The phrases "those boughs" (line 3) and "that well" (line 14) should be added as spondaic substitutions.

(3) Line 2 connects to line 1 because it begins a subordinate adverbial clause, just as line 3 begins an adverbial-prepositional phrase in which the headword "boughs" is modified by the adjective clause "which shake against the cold." The completeness of each line is hence caused by the pause produced between the verbs and the modifying elements. Much the same is true from line 5 to line 6; here, however, the modifying element in line 6 is an adjective clause modifying the noun "day" (or is it "twilight"?).

(4) The caesurae in the lines are placed as follows: Line 2, after syllables 4, 6, and 8. Line 5, after syllables 2 and 7. Line 6, after syllable 5. Line 9, after syllables 2 and 7 (the same as line 5). These pauses cause emphasis or continuity where they appear. In line 2, the effect is one of slowness and heaviness. In lines 5 and 9, which are grammatically and rhythmically identical, the similarity is a means of tying together the two four-line units describing the setting sun and the dying fire. Line 6 is regular, divided medially by the caesura. This regularity throws emphasis on the eternal sameness of the setting sun. In the last two lines, the rising caesurae (in both 13 and 14, after the fourth syllables) stress the positive qualities of the love which is the subject of the lines.

Writing topics. The use of spondees as the main substitute foot. The relationship of caesurae to the ideas in the poem. The repetition of rhythms (e.g., the use of the "in me" patterns, and the adjective clauses).

Works for Comparison with "That Time of Year"

Porter, *The Jilting of Granny Weatherall,* 538
Olds, *35/10,* 854
Tennyson, Tithonus, 998

Jonathan Swift, *A Description of the Morning, pages 730–731*

During the period from 1701–1714, Swift lived in England as a special envoy of the Irish church and also as a writer for the Tory government. This poem was one of many satiric pieces that he wrote during the time.

Answers to the Study Questions, page 731

(1) All the images are anti-heroic, being derived from seamy and unromantic aspects of life, such as the lazy apprentice, the dirty kennel's edge, and the noisy charcoal seller. Mention of "his lordship" is sarcastic; the lord symbolizes form without substance.

(2) Alliteration may be found in lines 1 (*h*), 2 (*p*), 3 (*b* and *f*), 4 (*s*), 7 (*m*), 8 (*s*), 9 (*wh* and *w*), and 16–18 (*l, s*). The effect generally is emphasis, as in *softly stole* in line 4, which stresses by sound the furtive quality of Betty's movement to her own room.

(3) Assonance may be found in lines 2 and 4 (*o*), 3 (*eh*), 7 (*aw*), 9 (*oo*), 10 (*eh*), 12 (*ih* as in "shriller"), 15 (*er* in "turnkey," "returning"), 17 (*ay*), and 18 (*æ* as in "lag"). Because the poem is in couplets, these closely connected patterns (at least nine of them) create unity of sound and therefore emphasis within this brief scope.

(4) The anti-heroic subject matter cast within heroic couplets emphasizes Swift's realistic view of London in the morning, and it also underscores his satire against phonies like the lord and the prison keeper.

Writing topics. The use of segmental devices in the poem. The negative images of life. The use of realism. Satire.

Works for Comparison with "A Description of the Morning"

Eliot, *Preludes*, 640
Nye, *Where Children Live*, 972
Williams, *The Dance*, 782

Alfred, Lord Tennyson, from *Idylls of the King: The Passing of Arthur*, pages 731–732

One of Tennyson's preoccupations was the legendary King Arthur. He began publishing *Idylls of the King*, consisting of twelve connected poems on Arthurian topics, in 1857, and added more as time went by. The completed version was published only in 1891, the year before his death.

Answers to the Study Questions, page 732

(1) The poem's action produces a mood of depression. Bedivere carries the dying Arthur from a series of ridges to the water, where a barge awaits. Arthur is then taken aboard to the lamentations of three queens. Tennyson develops the mood of depression by including images of cold,

darkness, shrill winds, dust, and, primarily the simile of a shattered column. The column may be construed as an allusion to Samson, whose death was brought about when he shattered the columns of the building in which he was imprisoned.

(2) The first sample essay analyzes segments in the section from lines 349–360. Further study could produce additional patterns, such as "dark," "scarf," and "stem," "stern" (line 362); "were," "ware" (line 363); "decks," "dense" (line 364); and "dream," "these," "three," "queens" (lines 365–366). These patterns of assonance and alliteration unify these passages and render them particularly suitable for spoken delivery.

(3) The onomatopoeia in lines 349–360 is discussed in the first sample essay (pages 741–743). The content of lines 369–370 concerns the sounds of lamentation being likened to shrill winds in an empty land. Here Tennyson uses a number of syllable-lengthening consonants, principally "*l*," "*n*," and "*m*," to enable the words to be extended in virtual imitation of wind. Words thus stretched are "lamentation," "wind," "shrills," "land," "one," and "comes." In lines 380–383, Tennyson emphasizes the tears of the tallest queen falling upon Arthur, and also the streaks and spots on him as a result of his mortal battle wounds. Tennyson achieves onomatopoeia here through the use of one-syllable words to emphasize the individual drops (line 380, for example, consists of ten one-syllable words) together with the use of stop sounds which also emphasize the drops (in the words "striped, "dark," "blood," "greaves," "cuisses," "dashed," and "drops"). When he describes Arthur's face he uses words with fewer stop sounds ("face," "white," "colorless," "withered," "moon," "springing"), which when mingled with the monosyllabic words succeed in creating a vivid word picture.

Writing topics. Tennyson's use of assonance and alliteration in a selected portion of the fragment. The means by which Tennyson creates onomatopoeia.

Works for Comparison with "The Passing of Arthur"

Anonymous, *Bonny George Campbell*, 571
Howes, *Death of a Vermont Farm Woman*, 723

Francis Thompson, *To a Snowflake, page 733*

If poetry can be thought to dance, the lines of "To a Snowflake" dance. The topic of God the Shaper is heavy and serious, but the created object—the snowflake—is light and beautiful. The speaker, either the authorial voice or an indefinite person who is perceptive and sensitive, is speaking to an individual snowflake, who is personified to reply in lines 11–22. The metaphor dominating the poem is God as a skilled sculptor and metalworker. The poem may hence be considered a religious tribute because God, rather than producing a heavy statue, delicately creates the lightest and most fragile of things—the snowflake.

Answers to the Study Questions, page 733

(1) The dimeter, a short, light line, is appropriate to the subject because a snowflake too is small and light.

(2) The most common foot in the poem is the amphibrach, although there are many trochees intermixed for variation. These feet are appropriate to the subject of snow because they both end on lightly accented or falling syllables.

(3) Theoretically, rising rhyme would be less appropriate than the predominant falling rhymes because rhymes placed on stressed, heavy syllables would create a heavier, slower effect. An exclusively rising rhyme scheme would likely therefore be more overtly philosophical than "To a Snowflake" actually is. In the last three lines of the poem, however, Thompson switches the amphibrachic-trochaic norm of the poem to an iambic-anapaestic pattern. The effect is that our attention is shifted from the lightly dancing snowflake to the more enduring power of God.

(4) In comparison, "To a Snowflake" is more like "The Lamb" than "The Tyger," although all three raise questions of created things about their Creator. Both the snowflake and the lamb are alike because they represent the lighter, less sinister parts of creation, while the tyger is used as a symbol of evil in the world. "To a Snowflake" is not like either of the Blake poems in the respect that there is no complication or irony about the snow, which is clean and innocent, without qualification.

Writing topics. The use of falling rhythms in the poem. The use of dimeter. The metaphor of God the Creator in the poem.

Works for Comparison with "To a Snowflake"

Frost, *Stopping By Woods on a Snowy Evening*, 556
MacNeice, *Snow*, 558
Scott, *Snow*, 791
Shore, *A Letter Sent to Summer*, 591

David Wagoner, *March for a One-Man Band, pages 733–734*

Wagoner has been extremely productive both as poet and novelist. This poem, "March for a One-Man Band," is a short virtuoso piece, which mixes iambs and anapæsts together to work up an infectiously rhythmic but also slightly chaotic tetrameter.

Answers to the Study Questions, page 734

(1) The speaker enjoys the one-man band being described: not with awe or respect, but with amused acceptance of a "fun" situation. The noise is so outlandish that "irrational" is a better word than "national" to describe the anthem he plays.

(2) The words italicized in the poem are all echoic; that is, they are onomatopoeic or imitative in origin, having sound-effects as their meaning. The accompanying rhythms are swinging, bouncing, or thumping, designed to imitate and illustrate in words the noisy, desperate motion and sound of one person working all the instruments with hands, feet, knees, and mouth–a frantic, wild spectacle of sight and sound.

(3) At the end of the speaker's description, the *bang* recalls the so-called "button" note which punctuates the second beat of the last bar of a march (hear, for example, the conclusion of Sousa's "The Stars and Stripes Forever"). The one-man band's *bang* (try saying that fast) presumably ends the national anthem, creating an amusing sound where none at all ought to be, a sound that is not at all inappropriate if one considers how "The Star-Spangled Banner" is sometimes excruciatingly performed at many sporting events and public spectacles.

Writing topics. Onomatopoeia in the poem. Rhythm. Poe's "The Bells" and Wagoner's "March for a One-Man Band."

Works for Comparison with
"March for a One-Man Band"

Kumin, *Hello, Hello Henry,* 618
Poe, *The Bells,* 726
Tennyson, *The Passing of Arthur,* 731

Writing About Prosody, *pages 734–747*

In teaching the essays on rhythm, segments, or rhyme, you will need to stress accuracy. If students make no errors in their prosodic analyses, then their essays will go forward well. If there are mistakes, however, then the essays will go astray. With normal analytical essays, errors are not quite as crucial, for students may make a good argument even for a misinterpretation. In the study of prosody, however, it is not easy to make a well-reasoned discussion compensate for a mistake.

It is therefore important to stress that students work up a correct and thorough worksheet (see pages 738–740 and 744–745) in the prewriting stages of their essays. You may need to give students classroom time so that their observations may be checked. Have they correctly recorded the sounds? Do they have any doubts or questions about proper rhythms? About rhyme schemes? Especially important is that students have not confused spelling with sound. If, in the poem you have assigned, there are any possible chances for confusion, you may wish to use selected lines as the basis of exercises and queries. Invariably, you will find students who will set up incorrect correspondences of sound and sense. The best time to make corrections and clarify understandings is at those times when students can see where they are likely to be going astray.

When you use the sample essays, it is important to note the comparative modesty of the claims there between content and prosody. Only in the section on onomatopoeia is there a graphic, almost pictorial connection, and here the assertions go no further than can be supported by Tennyson's descriptions.

Also, when you use the sample essays as possible models or examples for your students, you might profitably direct them to the strong connection between the central idea and the development. Thus in paragraph 5 of the second sample essay the thematic development is stressed by the following words: "echoes," "major echoing word," "which appears six times," "repeated systematically," "repeats," and "echoes." No matter what central idea students may develop about the rhythm, segments, or rhyme of their assigned poems, the same need for overall thematic unity will prevail.

Writing Topics for Sound, Rhythm, and Rhyme, *pages 747–748*

(1) The first assignment requires a close analysis of Shakespeare's Sonnet 73 (page 730). The questions are clear, and if students analyze their worksheets closely, they can produce perceptive and worthwhile essays.

(2) Both "The Bells" and "March for a One-Man Band" are designed as bravura pieces, and they therefore furnish a fertile field for a student wishing to bring out connections between sound and topic. In

both poems, the echoic words transmit real sound to the printed page. Wagoner of course uses more variety than Poe, for while Poe speaks only of bells, Wagoner mentions drums, cornet, harmonica (the "wheeze"?), cymbal, whistle, and perhaps a few other "instruments" thrown in for good measure. Since Poe's poem is so extensive, students may wish to confine their comparisons to only one of the stanzas.

(3) The comparison of the three poems should bring out that "Barbara Allen" (page 912) is inherently serious and that it is designed to be sung, while both "Miniver Cheevy" and "At a Summer Hotel" become serious because of their underlying irony.

(4) Writing limericks can be fun, and the fourth assignment should be approached as fun. The key to the job, however, is to put the topic matter from the limerick into iambics and anapaests. The resulting comparison should make the students realize, from their own experiences in poetic creativity, the important connection between rhythm, form, and effect.

(5) A wise person said that it is more difficult to be funny than to be serious, and that clarity in humor is much more essential than in ordinary statements (clarity is always essential). Nevertheless, some surprisingly clever poems can result once students get going. Distortion of words is totally acceptable in the interests of humor, such as "I drove to Schenectady / And got into a wrecktady," "I asked for a hot dog / But got a broiled wart hog," "His jokes were insupportable; His expenses unaffordable," or "I went to Chanhassen / With all of my classen." Play of this sort, here, is an object. If some students come up with such rhymes, and some other students groan a bit, that isn't so bad.

Chapter Twenty
Pages 749–788

Form: The Shape of the Poem

This chapter introduces students to the connection of poetic form and structure. It makes no attempt to describe or define every possible traditional form; such an undertaking would require an entire book. Your students may come to the idea of form in poetry with some degree of reluctance or skepticism. They may assume that all closed forms are artificial, and, as such, have been invented by poets in collusion with teachers. While in this century there may be some justification for this claim (poets invent forms, we identify them), it by no means was true before literature was taken up as a disciplinary study in the late nineteenth century. A quick look at several ballads or lyrics written when there were almost no colleges in existence will reveal the natural and organic connection between singing, memory, patterns of repetition, and form. More sophisticated students might condemn all closed forms as too restrictive, or all open forms as too sloppy and disordered. Classroom discussion and emphasis can deal with these positions.

The key distinction in this chapter is between closed and open forms; this central distinction can be reiterated in class. At the same time, you can encourage your students to consider the ways in which the two forms share qualities. Closed-form poets seek the greatest freedom and innovation within rigid structures. Open-form poets undertake an equally difficult task; they must impose order, shape, and meaning in new ways. Encourage your students to appreciate each type of form for its strengths.

The discussion of the building blocks of closed form (pages 749–752) considers one-, two-, three-, and four-line units. The one-line unit (blank verse) is exemplified by a speech from *Hamlet* (a sample essay explicating this passage is in Chapter 26). Other poems in the text you might use to illustrate blank verse include Tennyson's "Tithonus" (page 998) and Wordsworth's "Tintern Abbey Lines" (page 593).

Couplets are illustrated by excerpts from two poems (pages 750, 751) and by the epigrams. Other useful poems that exemplify couplets of various lengths include "My Last Duchess" (page 578), "The Destruction of Sennacherib" (page 926), "Very Like a Whale" (page 969), "Macavity: The Mystery Cat" (page 719), "We Real Cool" (page 718), and "Ars Poetica" (page 851).

The three-line unit (triplets, tercets) is exemplified by "The Eagle" (page 751), "Ode to the West Wind" (page 776), and Thomas's villanelle "Do Not Go Gentle into That Good Night" (page 781). Two other poems that illustrate the usefulness of the tercet are Dickinson's "To Hear an Oriole Sing" (page 718) and Roethke's "The Waking" (page 979), another villanelle. Poems that illustrate the versatility of the quatrain can be found throughout the text; they are far too numerous to mention.

The discussion of types of closed-form poetry (pages 750–757) deals with some of the major forms that have remained popular for centuries and a few minor forms. Most of the closed forms introduced here are exemplified by one or two poems later in the chapter. Beyond these, examples of most closed forms are scattered throughout the text. Here are some alternate examples for teaching:

- **Italian or Petrarchan Sonnets:** Keats, *On First Looking into Chapman's Homer,* page 650; Wyatt, *I Find No Peace,* page 670; Wordsworth, *London, 1802,* page 669; Hopkins, *God's Grandeur,* page 722; Yeats, *Leda and the Swan,* page 822; Browning, *How Do I Love Thee,* page 923; Millay, *What Lips My Lips Have Kissed,* page 967; Hacker, *Sonnet Ending with a Film Subtitle,* page 945.
- **English or Shakespearean Sonnets:** All sonnets by Shakespeare; Keats, *Bright Star,* page 654; Cullen, *Yet Do I Marvel,* page 929; McKay, *The White City,* page 967. For modifications of the form, see Donne, *Batter My Heart,* page 615; Owen, *Anthem for Doomed Youth,* page 630; Spenser (the Spenserian sonnet), poems on pages 856 and 994.
- **Ballads:** *Sir Patrick Spens,* page 553; *Bonny George Campbell,* page 571; *Barbara Allan,* page 912; *Lord Randal,* page 913; Keats, *La Belle Dame sans Merci,* page 806. See also Carroll's *Jabberwocky,* page 614.
- **Common Measure:** Many of Emily Dickinson's poems (Chapter 25).
- **Songs and Lyrics:** Housman, *Loveliest of Trees,* page 558; Rossetti, *Echo,* pages 744–745; Herrick, *To The Virgins,*

PAGE 846; DONNE, POEMS IN CHAPTER 25; SHAKESPEARE, *Fear No More the Heat o' the Sun,* PAGE 984; WILBUR, *The Sirens,* PAGE 1008.

- ODES: KEATS, *Ode on a Grecian Urn,* PAGE 848, *To Autumn,* PAGE 661, *Ode to a Nightingale,* PAGE 770; HUGHES, *Let America Be America Again,* PAGE 723.

ALEXANDER *Pope, Epitaph on the Stanton-Harcourt Lovers, page 755*

SAMUEL TAYLOR COLERIDGE, *What Is an Epigram?, page 755*

These epigrams share brevity, wit, and satiric thrust. Pope's epitaph is part of a set of three commemorating the deaths of Hewet and Drew. The other two that he wrote are longer, more decorous, and mock-heroic. This one is terse, witty, and bawdy. Coleridge's epigram is a superb definition of an epigram. Epigrams are related to heroic couplets and to the couplets that end Shakespearean sonnets in that they clinch ideas with a very rapid poetic thrust. Couplets and epigrams contain whole thoughts put with economy and skill. Two additional epigrams by Pope are included on page 686.

ANONYMOUS, *Limericks, page 756*

You should not have to say much about limericks in class beyond noting the usually observed rules on page 755. The limerick is a popular form no matter what the subject matter, although most are bawdy. Indeed, a collection edited by G. Legman (New York: Bell, 1969) entitled *The Limerick* includes 1700 limericks, all of which are bawdy. As an exercise, you might ask students to write a few topical limericks; such an assignment can serve as a pleasant introduction to the task of writing verse within a fixed form.

E. C. BENTLEY, *Two Clerihews, page 756*

Clerihews are almost always humorous or satirical; they attack or at least mock the figure named in the first line. The form has relatively few requirements: four lines rhymed *a a b b;* the first line must name a famous character or literary figure. Like limericks, the clerihew is a closed form that most students can handle reasonably well. You might have your students write a few as an exercise, and share them in class.

ANTHONY HECHT, *Nominalism, pages 756–757*

Double-dactyls, also called *Higgledy-Piggledies,* were in vogue in the late 1960s. Like epigrams and clerihews, they are usually humorous or satirical. The form is rigid and demanding, requiring two quatrains. The first line must contain two rhyming nonsense dactylic words; the second consists of a name (or title and name) that can be read as two dactyls (e.g., *Moses Maimonides, Judas Iscariot, Emperor Oedipus*). The third, fifth, and sixth or seventh lines much be two dactylic feet, while the fourth and eighth lines must be short (a dactyl and one stressed syllable) and rhyme. Finally, the fifth or sixth line must be a single word that scans as two dactylic feet (e.g., *antepenultimate, octogenarian, quasi-theistically*). These are not easy to write. Nevertheless, you may want to have your students give it a try. The exercise will give them a stronger sense of the difficulty of writing in closed forms.

WILLIAM SHAKESPEARE, *Sonnet 116: Let Me Not to the Marriage of True Minds, page 757*

Please see the discussion of this poem in the text, pages 758–759.

WRITING TOPICS. Imagery and meaning. Form and meaning.

WORKS FOR COMPARISON WITH
"LET ME NOT TO THE MARRIAGE OF TRUE MINDS"

Burns, *A Red, Red Rose,* 652
Wakoski, *Inside Out,* 668

WALT WHITMAN, *Reconciliation, pages 759–760*

This poem, discussed in the text (page 760), may be compared with Hardy's "The Man He Killed" (page 557). In addition to contrasting open and closed form poems on the same subject, there is clear contrast in speakers and tones. Whitman's speaker is more sophisticated and clear about his own feelings. The two poems make a good comparison-contrast writing assignment. The focus of such an essay could be form, tone, speaker, imagery, diction, or meaning. Ralph Vaughan Williams, in *Dona Nobis Pacem* (1936), which is based on poems from Whitman's *Drum Taps,* set this poem to gorgeous music for baritone, chorus, and orchestra.

WRITING TOPICS. The nature of the speaker. The use of variable line lengths in the poem.

Works for Comparison with "Reconciliation"

Hardy, *The Man He Killed,* 557
Sassoon, *Dreamers,* 982
Zabytko, *Home Soil,* 403

George Herbert, *Easter Wings, pages 761–762*

This splendid and skillful example of shaped verse is well worth class discussion. Teaching can be organized around questions of content and then shape or structure. The ideas are expressed in four movements: humanity's fall, personal salvation, personal fall, and personal flight. The poem takes the form of a petitional prayer, in which the speaker asks the Lord to permit him to sing praises and to feel the joy of the Easter victory over sin. The connection between this desire and the title is that Easter is the celebration of this victory. That the speaker wishes to rise like a lark (line 8) and also like a falcon (lines 19–20) is comparable visually to the Resurrection.

Answers to the Study Questions, page 762

(1) When viewed straight on, the poem's shape resembles two hourglasses (suggesting elapsed personal and cosmic time, the end of time, and also suggesting spiritual thinness and the need for unity with God). When turned sideways, the shape does suggest wings, whether of an angel (visually suggesting grace, Christ, resurrection, salvation), or of a bird. Each line also visually reflects its own meaning through its length (by a diminution or expansion, according to the spiritual stage being described).

(2) The typographical arrangements follow the sense closely, with both stanzas narrowing to a central point, as with lines 5 and 15, and then, as the emotion surges, expanding to the approximate beginning widths.

(3) The first five lines show, both graphically and assertively, how humankind has been spiritually diminished as a result of the choice of the first disobedience (the "fall," line 10). The speaker reiterates the same conclusion about himself in lines 11–15, and the lengths of these lines match those of 1–5.

Writing topics. The visual connection between form and content. The reasons for the shortening and lengthening lines. The importance of the larks and the falcon.

WORKS FOR COMPARISON WITH "EASTER WINGS"

Dickinson, *A Word Made Flesh*, 889
Frost, *Misgiving*, 901

E. E. CUMMINGS, *Buffalo Bill's Defunct, page 763*

This poem exemplifies the importance of how the printed form affects comprehension of a subject. It has a conversational ring, and an ambiguous, mocking tone, considering that the famous Buffalo Bill had actually transformed himself from an individual to a business or a myth. Cummings's form is worth extended discussion.

Answers to the Study Questions, page 763

(1) Lines made up of single words or names (1, 5, 7, 11) depend on typography and space to emphasize the images/ideas. *Buffalo Bill's* and *Mister Death,* as the opening and closing lines/names, are balanced and opposed against one another.

(2) The run-on words create an initial difficulty in reading on the page, and they also emphasize the activity of Bill and the sounds of the speaking voice. You might remind students that spaces between words are one of the major conventions of writing.

(3) *Defunct* is a Latin word originally meaning "non-functional"; that is, dead. It is to be found in the Latin Mass for the Dead, and there it is quite serious ("*Libera animas defunctorum*"). In English, however, it is a comic, overblown word. "Dead" is the straightforward English word, while *deceased* has a formal and somewhat obnoxious ring to it.

(4) This poem can lead to a spirited class discussion. It is certainly a portrait, but your students will have to decide if it is admiring, mocking, or something in between.

WRITING TOPICS. The spatial relationships on the page. The relationship of these to Cummings's ideas in the poem. The tone. The image of death.

WORKS FOR COMPARISON WITH "BUFFALO BILL'S DEFUNCT"

Dickinson, *The Bustle in a House*, 888
Nemerov, *Life Cycle of Common Man*, 970

JOHN DRYDEN, *To The Memory of Mr. Oldham,* PAGES 763–764

This short poem commemorates the death in 1684 of the young poet

John Oldham, whose major contribution to literature was a satire against the Jesuits (1679, a time of great anti-Catholic feeling in England). In 1684, Dryden had not yet switched his religious allegiance to Catholicism, and therefore he was still supportive of Anglicanism. Dryden's most memorable line is the last one, which, being an alexandrine rather than a pentameter, effectively summarizes the poet's view of the finality of death.

As Dryden presents the consolations of early death here, they are pagan and classical, not Christian and redemptive. The speaker asserts that Oldham might have improved by writing smoother lines (*numbers*) had he lived longer, but that the "rugged" verse he actually wrote was all right for satire (condescending?). *Marcellus* (line 23) implies that Oldham would have succeeded as a brilliant poet; the *laurels* suggest that he had already achieved greatness. Rhymes are useful in clinching ideas and linking concepts; you might ask your class about pairs like *thine/mine, shine/line,* and *prime/time/rhyme* (the triplet). See if your students think the repetition of the *young/tongue* rhyme (lines 13–14, 22–23) helps or hurts the poem.

One might compare this poem with other poems on death, such as Gray's "Elegy," Frost's "Out, out—," and Cummings's "buffalo bill's defunct." Most such poems stress the lost potential of the dead person, and conclude on a note of reconciliation, even if that reconciliation is to raise questions about the fairness of life.

Answers to the Study Questions, page 764

(1) The poem is in the closed form of heroic couplets (iambic pentameter: *aa, bb,* etc., with a triple rhyme in lines 19–21). The couplet form is a self-enclosed unit of development, giving the poet the opportunity to shift ideas quickly when needed (as in line 22, the beginning of the last unit of the poem), and also bestowing upon the poem a dignified and stately tempo appropriate to its elegiac tone. Dryden uses an *alexandrine* (line 21) to slow the poem still further before its final "hail and farewell." The couplet form, also used by Oldham himself, was particularly important in the late seventeenth century because the developing admiration for science created a pressure for poets to develop their thoughts in a pithy, axiomatic form analogous to the conclusions and generalizations of science.

(2) In the opening ten lines, the speaker describes his affinity with Oldham, noting that their souls were *near allied* and that they both wrote verse satire. The allusion to *Nisus* (line 9) puts the friendship in a classical and poetic context.

(3) The classical *ethos* also dominates lines 11–25, where the speaker attempts to explain that dying young may not be all bad. The idea is that one's full power comes early, and that age merely "mellows" the achievement of an older person. Therefore, Oldham did reach his full power, and time would not have granted him additional strength for further contributions.

WRITING TOPICS. Form, rhyme, diction, or allusion in connection with character or meaning.

WORKS FOR COMPARISON WITH "TO THE MEMORY OF MR. OLDHAM"

Brodsky, *In Memory of My Father*, 921
Gray, *Sonnet on the Death of Richard West*, 617
Plath, *Last Words*, 976

ROBERT FROST, *Desert Places, pages 764–765*

Frost employs repetition, alliteration, and rhyme in this lyric to create a network of related images and sounds that reinforce meaning. Reading the poem aloud in class may help your students pick up the repetitions of *snow*, the alliteration on *f* (*falling, fast, field, few*) and the web of sounds/words linked to *loneliness.*

Answers to the Study Questions, page 765

(1) The poem is a four-stanza lyric (iambic pentameter, *aaba, ccdc, eefe, ffgf*).

(2) The setting and situation are that snow is falling on a field and covering everything in a monochromatic white. The snow affects the landscape, the animals, the field, and, through metaphor, the universe and also the speaker himself.

(3) Even though at the time of the poem, astronomers were learning that the universe was incalculably more vast than anyone had ever supposed, the speaker asserts that the mind-boggling distances of the universe, and the virtually infinite emptiness, are less important and frightening than the "desert places" within his own spirit.

(4) The falling rhymes in the last stanza—*spaces/race is/places*—do not lighten the poem's tone; they add a twist of grim irony.

(5) In stanzas 1 and 2, the snow covers and isolates, turning the earth into a *desert place.* The speaker is included in this loneliness *unawares*

because he is too "absent-spirited to count." In the third stanza, the speaker begins to meditate on this desert of loneliness, and implies that there is nothing within or without (*nothing to express*) to mitigate the desolation. The snow, landscape, speaker, and nature are all *benighted.*

WRITING TOPICS. An analysis of form, repetition, rhyme, or sound in connection with tone, speaker, or meaning.

WORKS FOR COMPARISON WITH "DESERT PLACES"

Frost, *Acquainted with the Night*, 901
Frost, *Fire and Ice*, 900
Larkin, *Next, Please*, 850

ALLEN GINSBERG, *A Supermarket in California, pages 765–766*

This tribute to Walt Whitman imitates several features of Whitman's style, including his poetic cadences, enumerative lists, and long sentences.

Answers to the Study Questions, page 766

(1) The speaker is alone at night looking for *images.* The *neon fruit super market* is the contemporary (1955) America of conspicuous consumption and wealth; the Whitmanesque lists reflect this abundance.

(2) Lorca and Whitman (both poets and homosexuals) are the speaker's spiritual progenitors. The speaker, like the Whitman presented in the poem, is an outcast on a journey without a destination. For all these complementary figures, the key terms are *childless, lonely, solitary,* and *silent.* Whitman's journey to death (*Charon, Lethe*) is as silent and lonely as the speaker's journey through the night.

(3) The enumeration of various elements is consciously mentioned by the speaker in lines 5–6. The detail is a tribute to the concreteness of Whitman's poetic style, and might also be considered particularly American because of the sense of abundance.

(4) Even though the individual lines are long, the poem should not be considered prose because it is not expansive. In addition, the rhythms produce more strong accents than in prose, and there are a number of repetitive "I walked," "I went," and "I heard" structures—more characteristic of a poetic than a prose style.

WRITING TOPICS. The impact of setting, form, diction, or imagery. The link between the speaker and Whitman. The ideas about modern America and its values.

Works for Comparison with "A Supermarket in California"

McHugh, *Lines*, 966
Jeffers, *The Answer*, 956
Kennedy, *Old Men Pitching Horseshoes*, 808

Nikki Giovanni, *Nikki-Rosa, pages 766–767*

Giovanni is a poet whose reputation has coincided with the development of African-American consciousness and pride. Often her material is political, although a strain of the personal may also be found in her work, as in this poem, which is selected from the 1968 volume entitled *Black Feeling, Black Talk.*

Answers to the Study Questions, page 767

(1) Short lines and cadences alternate with longer ones here to punctuate ideas; conjunctions at the opening of lines speed up the tempo.

(2) The poem is full of positive and loving images of childhood, even when they are linked with hard times. Some of these images are the big tubs, the meetings, and the togetherness of the family. The speaker shows an attitude of self-awareness and assurance about herself, and a sense of identification with Blacks. Her expectation is that she will be successful enough so that someday someone will write about her.

(3) The assumption attributed to whites by the speaker is that poverty, fighting, and drunkenness must automatically make a child unhappy. She denies this assumption, asserting instead that she was quite happy because, whatever her sorrows, she always felt a sense of Black identity. The speaker's central assertion is in the last four lines; he or she claims that *no white person* will ever understand that *Black love is Black wealth.*

Writing topics. The use of detail. The variable lines and the free form. The contrast between the speaker's good memories of childhood and the assumptions that the speaker claims they (biographers, line 6) will make about the childhood.

Works for Comparison with "Nikki-Rosa"

Evans, *I Am a Black Woman*, 942
Stanton, *Childhood*, 592
Wheatley, *On Being Brought from Africa*, 1008

George Herbert, *Virtue, pages 767–768*

This wonderful lyric explores the differences between transient worldly things and the immortal soul. The poem is discussed at some length in the sample essay in this chapter (pages 786–787).

Writing topics. Form and meaning. Rhyme and meaning. Meter and meaning. The imagery (especially the *day, rose,* and *spring*).

Works for Comparison with Herbert's "Virtue"

Arnold, *Dover Beach*, 576
Crashaw, *On Our Crucified Lord*, 639

William Heyen, *Mantle, page 768*

Heyen, a highly versatile poet, is introduced into this volume for the first time. His fresh and original shaped poem was written only recently. The other poem we include, on a more serious subject, is "The Hair: Jacob Korman's Story," on page 953.

Answers to the Study Questions, page 769

(1) This poem is designed to resemble a curve ball. The last stanza represents the ball going over the plate. The mark of the great major league hitter, of course, is the ability to hit curve balls. Mickey Mantle, the subject of the poem, hit curve balls, and he also hit fast balls, sliders, and changes. He did confess once, however—and probably on many occasions—that he had trouble with a high inside pitch.

(2) In the poem Mantle is a symbol of the loss of youth and the need to carry on after the shouting stops. Housman's poem "To an Athlete Dying Young" (not in the anthology) is a comparable poem, but Housman's athlete's life is over, and he therefore does not need to face the circumstance in which "the name" dies "before the man." After Mantlequit playing baseball, he advertised bread and hair cream on TV, operated a restaurant, and attempted in other ways to capitalize on his fame.

(3) George Herman Ruth ("Babe" Ruth, the "Sultan of Swat"), Lou Gehrig (the "Iron Man"), and Joe DiMaggio (the "Yankee Clipper") were all New York Yankees and were awesome power hitters. All set records. Ruth's record of 60 homers was broken in 1961 by another Yankee, Roger Maris. Gehrig's record of playing in consecutive games is being approached by Cal Ripkin, Jr., of the Baltimore Orioles. However, DiMaggio's record of hitting safely in 56 straight games in 1941 has not been threatened. Both Ruth and Gehrig died young. DiMaggio has spent his later career

in throwing out balls at season openings, and also advertising on television for a bank and a coffee-maker. They are all like Mantle because of their ability and successful baseball careers. DiMaggio is closest to Mantle, however, in living in the shadow of former greatness.

Writing topics. The relationship between the poem's shape and its subject. The major idea in the poem.

Works for Comparison with "Mantle"

Frost, *Nothing Gold Can Stay*, 900
Frost, *The Oven Bird*, 900
Millay, *What Lips My Lips Have Kissed*, 967

John Hollander, *Swan and Shadow, page 769*

Answers to the Study Questions, page 770

(1, 2, 3, 4) This poem works as shaped verse, but not quite as well as Herbert's "Easter Wings" (pages 761–762); there is no multiple image here, and every line length does not reinforce meaning. The poem is about perception, memory, and time; the swan is only a convenient example. The image awakens recognition in the beholder, creates illumination in the mind, and then fades into memory. The relation of swan to shadow is parallel to present and past, image and reflection, perception and memory. Typography and shape produce some interesting effects. The *what when where* (lines 10–12) are all answered in the same lines of the body. Line 18 divides swan from shadow, present from past, perception from memory. It is the "perfect sad instant now." A single rhyme (*light/sight*) frames and emphasizes the transition. At the close, Hollander introduces a visual-verbal pun. The "swan / sang" is an allusion to the *swan song*, the myth that a swan sings once in its life immediately before dying. The single word *sang* visually embodies that dying and fading away, a last glimmer of memory.

Writing topics. The relationship of shape to meaning. The limits of spatial poetry.

Works for Comparison with "Swan and Shadow"

Herbert, *Easter Wings*, 761
Solt, *Forsythia*, 779
Swenson, *Women*, 780

John Keats, *Ode to a Nightingale, pages 770–772*

This poem is one of Keats's most important, written in his last, "living year" of great poetic creativity. It is by no means easy, and may require some explanation of Keats's idea of "negative capability." That is, the person of great creative power, being a kind of receiver of divine information much like the ancient Biblical prophets, is satisfied with recording the results of creative impulses without seeking explanations and without erasing what comes from the "penetralium of mystery" that constitutes the source of inspiration. The poem develops through a comparison of the song of the invisible nightingale with the everyday, here-and-now life of the speaker, and it may be construed as a statement of faith that there is a force in the universe that can reach us through the imagination of the poet. Needless to say, these ideas need discussion and exemplification.

Answers to the Study Questions, page 772

(1) The stanza form Keats employs throughout is a truncated Italian sonnet (iambic pentameter, *abab cde 3cde*).

(2) The first stanza establishes the speaker's mental and emotional state; he is unhappy and pained. Key metaphors relate this condition to poison (hemlock) and narcotics (*opium*), but it is the nightingale's song that has produced the lethargy.

(3) The speaker (in stanza 2) thinks of drinking wine (vintage, warm south, Hippocrene, inspiration, spirit) so that he can join the nightingale and vanish "into the forest dim." His wish is somehow to escape the sickness, age, loss of power, and death that constitute living in the world.

(4) In stanzas 4 and 5 the speaker's tone changes. He claims that he will join the nightingale through the power of poetic inspiration/imagination ("the viewless wings of Poesy"). In his imagination, he transfers himself to the nightingale's green, fragrant, murmurous, and dark world. The sensual images here are visual, olfactory, and auditory.

(5) In the seventh stanza, the heart of the ode, the speaker establishes the transcendent, symbolic meaning of the nightingale's song, which has been heard throughout human history by emperors, clowns, and even spirits ("in faery lands"). The bird's song, in other words, symbolizes something more permanent than the short lifespan of individual human beings. After this climax, the speaker describes the loss of his visionary insights, claiming that his "fancy," or imagination, may have cheated him. Characteristically, and perhaps paradoxically, it is this sort of questioning

and chiding ("deceiving elf") that is the essential quality of everyday, ordinary (boring) existence, and the speaker concludes on the question of his uncertainty about the state of his waking consciousness. His assertions may thus reflect more hope than certainty.

Writing topics. The organization of the poem's ideas or argument through form. The impact of rhyme or diction. The ideas about the world, poetry, or imagination.

Works for Comparison with "Ode to a Nightingale"

Bridges, *Nightingales*, 921
Frost, *The Tuft of Flowers*, 894
Hopkins, *God's Grandeur*, 722
Wordsworth, *Lines Written in Early Spring*, 1009

Claude McKay, *In Bondage, pages 772–773*

McKay was born in Jamaica, emigrated to the United States in 1912, and settled in Harlem in 1914, where he became an important poetic voice in the Harlem Renaissance.

Answers to the Study Questions, page 773

(1) "In Bondage" is a Shakespearean sonnet (iambic pentameter, *abab, cdcd, efef, gg*). McKay uses the three quatrains and the couplet to organize his ideas. In teaching, it is important to get your students to see the radical shift (or disjunction) between the hypothetical (lines 1–12) and the actual (lines 13–14), indicated by *would* and *but.*

(2) In lines 1–8, the word *would* signifies the hypothetical nature of a world of freedom, leisure, fairness, and time.

(3) The third quatrain (lines 9–12) draws back from this world and explains its importance: Life is more important and enduring than petty and short human conflict.

(4) All this is sharply undercut by the couplet, which jerks us back to the reality of Blacks in the United States during McKay's life. Here, the rhyming words—*grave/slave*—pound home the image of what *is* instead of what should be.

Writing topics. The relation of form to meaning. The ideas explored about life, reality, humanity. The effects of rhyme, especially in the couplet.

WORKS FOR COMPARISON WITH "IN BONDAGE"

McKay, *The White City*, 967
Harper, *She's Free!*, 949

JOHN MILTON, *When I Consider How My Light is Spent, page 773*

This sonnet is one of Milton's most famous, having been for many years, in many schools, a requirement for memorization. The concluding line, "They also serve who only stand and wait," is quoted as often, if not more often, than any other Milton lines.

Answers to the Study Questions, pages 773–774

(1, 2) In this Italian sonnet (iambic pentameter: *abba, abba, cde, cde*), Milton employs the octave-sestet structure to organize the poem's movement and meaning.

(3) In the octave, the speaker complains about his failures and frustrations, only one of which is blindness. More significant is the crisis of faith in which the speaker expresses uncertainty about God's expectations, and assumes that he will be rejected. The speaker *almost* asks if God exacts "day-labor, light denied" (*light* here means sight, faith, inspiration), and he admits that it is a foolish question. The problem is resolved in the sestet, where the speaker's (personified) Patience prevents him from asking the question by explaining God's expectations. Patience makes it clear that God is self-sufficient, not needing either "man's work or his gifts." The *best* service to God is to "bear His mild yoke," and that can be done by those "who only stand and wait" (*wait* suggests a series of actions connected with service, including *wait on, wait for, attend,* and *expect*).

(4) In a limited sense, the *one talent* refers to the speaker's skill at poetry and political writing (Milton was a brilliant propagandist for the Puritans during much of the Interregnum). As an allusion to the parable in *Matthew,* however, *talent* refers additionally to the active and energetic preparation for the Lord's return.

WRITING TOPICS. The connection between form and meaning. The character of the speaker or of Patience. The image of God.

WORKS FOR COMPARISON WITH
"WHEN I CONSIDER HOW MY LIGHT IS SPENT"

Donne, *Batter My Heart,* 615
Herbert, *Love (III),* 951

Edwin Morgan, *The Computer's First Christmas Card, page 774*

Answers to the Study Questions, pages 774–775

(1, 2, 3, 4) The poem looks like a column of words generated at random by a computer; the typeface is reminiscent of Courier type in computer printers. As a poem (if your students will accept it as one), the words provide interesting linked sound effects and images we might associate with Christmas. Combinations like "jollymerry" or even "boppyjolly" might work, but those like "hoppyBarry" or "moppyjelly" wander pretty far afield. Nevertheless, sound holds the entire list together until the end, when the "computer" goes completely off the subject and generates "`asMERRYCHR/YSANTHEMUM.`"

Writing topics. The reasons why this can (or cannot) be considered a poem. The effects of sound produced in the work. The extent to which the poem makes fun of Christmas cards, computers, and/or poetry.

Works for Comparison with "The Computer's First Christmas Card"

Herbert, *Easter Wings*, 761
Solt, *Forsythia*, 779
Swenson, *Women*, 780

Dudley Randall, *Ballad of Birmingham, pages 775–776*

In 1965, Randall founded the Broadside Press, an important and valuable publisher of modern Black poetry. One of the first poems he published as a **broadside** (a single sheet, often political in topic matter) was this ballad. The poem demonstrates that the ballad survives as an effective and moving poetic form.

Answers to the Study Questions, page 776

(1) The poem is traditional in form and subject matter. The rhyme scheme (*xbxd,* etc.) and meter (iambic tetrameter and trimeter) reflect medieval practice, as do the use of quotation and the sensational and disturbing events.

(2) The quoted speaker in stanzas 1 and 3 is the child; the mother is quoted in stanzas 2, 4, and 8. This dialogue slows the ballad down and delays the climax.

(3) The story of the bombing is told through dialogue and third-person narration. The speaker is dispassionate; emotion is conveyed

through description and dialogue. The daughter wants to join a freedom march; the mother, considering this too dangerous, instead sends the daughter to safety in church. The irony here is complex. The mother is ironically wrong about safety. American society is also presented in an ironic light; in the world of the ballad, it is safer to face "clubs and hoses, guns and jails" than it is to go to church. The little girl's shoe (line 30), like the hats of Sir Patrick Spens's crew (page 553), is a more gruesome and ironic symbol of death than the actual body would be.

(4) All three poems share a narrative structure with speeches added to increase dramatic tension. They also share the common subject matter of death, with the causality being either directly or indirectly political.

Writing topics. The relation of form to impact, the characters, tone, and ideas about society. The character of the mother, daughter, and/or speaker.

Works for Comparison with "Ballad of Birmingham"

Anonymous, *Barbara Allen*, 912
Anonymous, *Bonny George Campbell*, 571
Anonymous, *Sir Patrick Spens*, 553

Percy Bysshe Shelley, *Ode to the West Wind, pages 776–778*

Like Keats's ode, this poem may present difficulties, and we therefore recommend a careful stanza-by-stanza approach. The poem shares with "Ode to a Nightingale" a focus on the need for poetic inspiration, but, unlike Keats, Shelley stresses the practical, political, and ultimately revolutionary results of what the poet says.

Answers to the Study Questions, page 778

(1) The ode is in five fourteen-line stanza of iambic pentameter terza rima concluded by a couplet, as follows:

aba, bcb, cdc, ded, ee
fbf, bgb, ghg, heh, ee
iji, jkj, kck, cec, ee
ele, lml, mnm, non, oo
pqp, qrq, rsr, sts, tt

The terza rima interlocks and unifies each stanza through sound; the repeated *b, c,* and *e* rhymes help unify the entire ode.

(2) The three *e* couplets tie stanzas 1–3 together and separate 4 and 5,

although the initial repetition of the *e* rhyme in 4 creates a bridge. The stanzaic structure rigorously organizes the poem's ideas: Stanzas 1–3 deal with the West Wind and nature, stanza 4 with the speaker's problem, and stanza 5 with a solution.

(3) In stanza 1, the wind blows the leaves and seeds; it is both a destroyer and preserver, and the images reflect death and rebirth. In the second and third stanzas, the wind similarly drives clouds and waves. In each instance, the wind represents power, movement, death, and rebirth.

(4) In the fourth section, the core of the poem, the speaker presents his problem; he wants to be affected by the wind just as he was in his "boyhood." Life and change have destroyed this ability; maturity and time have *chained and bowed* him. The speaker wants to be lifted as a leaf, wave, or cloud; he wants to become the wind's lyre (voice, stanza 5).

(5) The movement progresses from a sense of death and despair to one of optimism. Though the speaker may never see the rise of a spring of happiness for humankind, his ideas nevertheless may "quicken a new birth" and, through political means, create happiness after he is gone.

(6) The West Wind symbolizes the force of creativity, that imaginative power that enables the poet to express strong and moving ideas that can ultimately influence people and politicians to change society and create a new social and political order. Keats's song of the nightingale is quite similar to the West Wind in the respect that both refer to the unexplainable source of expressive and artistic beauty. Shelley is more political in his views, while Keats is more inward, more aesthetic.

Writing topics. An analysis of the interconnection between form and meaning. The symbolic value of the wind. The character of the speaker. A comparison of Shelley's poem and Keats's "Ode to a Nightingale."

Works for Comparison with "Ode to the West Wind"

Finch, *To the Nightingale*, 690
Moore, *How to Become a Writer*, 205
Wordsworth, *London, 1802*, 669

Percy Bysshe Shelley, *Ozymandias, pages 778–779*

When Shelley wrote "Ozymandias," the science of Egyptology was in its infant stage. Scholars could not yet read Ancient Egyptian, although Jean François Champollion (1790–1832) was making breakthroughs and published a guide in 1821. Shelley's choice of topic, in short, was timely. The sonnet is one of the many poems dealing with the topic of change and mutability. Shelley implies that the *lone and level sands* will in time cover everything—artifacts like the colossal statue, and also the memory of the power of persons like Ozymandias. Ironically, however, the ancient artist's skill still endures.

Answers to the Study Questions, page 779

(1) This is a modified Italian sonnet (iambic pentameter: *abab, acdc, ede, fef*). The modified rhyme scheme has an effect similar to that of Spenser's adaptation of the Shakespearean sonnet; through sound, it allows each unit to be interconnected with the next.

(2) The octave-sestet structure organizes the poem's images and ideas. The statue, or its remains, are described in the octave, the inscription in the first triplet of the sestet, and the surrounding desolation in the second triplet of the sestet.

(3) The image of the face and the inscription convey Ozymandias' arrogance, pride, and vanity. There are three remaining parts of the statue: the head, the legs, and the pedestal containing the inscription. The effect of distributing the parts throughout the poem is to emphasize the fragility and impermanence of human works. Thus, the sonnet illustrates the vanity of human tyrants and the power of time and change. The artist, who recognized this vanity, mocked both the king's vain passions and the pompous heart that "fed" the king's yearning to seem grandiose.

Writing topics. The relation of form to meaning. The ideas explored about tyranny, time, and art.

Works for Comparison with "Ozymandias"

Cummings, *next to of course god america i*, 929
Hugo, *Degrees of Gray in Philipsburg*, 585
Stevens, *Disillusionment of Ten O'Clock*, 621

Mary Ellen Solt, *Forsythia, page 779*

Students from areas where forsythia is not winter-hardy should perhaps be told that the bush makes a spectacular display of yellow in early spring. One of the most joyful sights imaginable after a drab winter is the budding forsythia along roadsides and in hedges.

Answers to the Study Questions, page 780

(1, 2, 3, 4) This is an example of concrete poetry; words give way to image completely. The image on the page evokes forsythia; the yellow background (in the original printing) reinforces the visual effect. The dots and dashes between the letters are Morse Code for "forsythia." They also reinforce the "telegram" concept in the (minimal) text.

Writing topic. Is this a poem?

Works for Comparison with "Forsythia"

Herbert, *Easter Wings*, 761
Heyen, *Mantle*, 768
Swenson, *Women*, 780

May Swenson, *Women, page 780*

One of Swenson's objectives is to create a position for poetry in space as well as time (poetry, like music, being understandable only when moving through time or else being read in the order of lines on a page). The result is exemplified in this poem, which suggests some of the qualities of movement and character to be attributed to her topic, women.

Answers to the Study Questions, pages 780–781

(1) This poem is open-form rather than shaped or concrete; the typography is suggestive, but is does not displace the words in importance, nor does it form a specific image like wings or like a swan. The poem can be read at least two ways: down the left column and then the right, or in ten-line two-column units divided at lines 10 and 20; the second method may provide a more coherent reading.

(2) The undulating typography suggests curves, movement, and pliancy—all consistent with the textual images of women "moving to the motions of men" as "rocking horses rockingly ridden." If the poem were in straight lines it certainly would be less noticeable visually.

(3) The devices of repetition and alliteration move in sympathy to the poet's ideas. For example, "ridden / rockingly / ridden until / the restored ..." provides a rhythmic undertow to the sexual references being described by the poet.

(4) The poem asserts that women may be envisioned as "pedestals moving to the motions of men, " as "painted rocking horses," and as "immobile," always "waiting willing to be set in motion"; they are the "gladdest things in the toyroom." These images are sexual and ironic; women are ironically presented as passive objects (toys) to be used and then abandoned by men ("the restored egos dismount and the legs stride away"). The speaker's irony suggests that the social/sexual formulation is

wrong. The poem also implies that those men who accept this view of women are really perpetuating their own childhood. Indeed, the social structure depending on this view is itself immature, for by stereotyping women it denies the rights of freedom and individuality to all.

Writing topics. The various ways to read the poem. The suggestiveness of the poem's shape. The irony of the view of women. A defense of an opposing view.

Works for Comparison with Swenson's "Women"

Herbert, *Easter Wings*, 761
Heyen, *Mantle*, 768
Solt, *Forsythia*, 779

Dylan Thomas, *Do Not Go Gentle into That Good Night, page 781*

In the 1980s, the musician John Cale set "Do Not Go Gentle" and other poems by Thomas to music as part of his *Falklands Suite* (found on *Words for the Dying*, Opal/Warner Bros. 9 26024-2).

Answers to the Study Questions, page 781

(1) The villanelle is a form borrowed by English poets from the French, who originally acquired it from the Italian. Traditionally it contains five tercets rhyming *aba,* and it concludes with a quatrain rhyming *abaa,* as is shown by Thomas in this poem. The first line of the first tercet is repeated as the last line of the second and fourth tercets, and the last line of the first tercet is repeated as the last line of the third and fifth tercets. Both these lines, in addition, conclude the poem as the eighteenth and nineteenth lines. Although the form has been used as the vehicle for lighter subject matter, Thomas here illustrates its potential for the most serious of topics. Roethke, in the villanelle "The Waking" (page 979) also illustrates the use of serious and also personal topic matter, with the repeated lines developing an increasing weight of meaning as the poem evolves. Both poems exhibit the same mastery over form and subject.

(2) The poem reflects the speaker's dismay at his father's emotional and physical decay (Thomas's father had been a strong and authoritarian teacher; in his eighties, however, he became blind and ill). The speaker addresses the poem to this father (line 16) as an incentive to maintain his courage in the face of blindness.

(3) The speaker wants his father to emulate "wise men" (lines 4–6),

"Good men" (7–9), "Wild men" (10–12), and "Grave men" (13–15), all of whom have raged against death, and have not gone "gentle into that good night."

(4) The poem is enlivened by puns on *good night* (dying and "farewell") and *grave* (serious and dead—a pun made famous by Mercutio in Shakespeare's *Romeo and Juliet*). Connotative words and phrases are "close of day" (i.e., dying), "bright" (a result of the activity of vigorous life), and "gentle" (well-bred, and also passive).

Writing topics. Use of the villanelle form. The function and meaning of the repeated lines.

Works for Comparison with "Do Not Go Gentle"

Frost, *Nothing Gold Can Stay*, 900
Millay, *What Lips My Lips Have Kissed*, 967
Olds, *35/10*, 854
Porter, *The Jilting of Granny Weatherall*, 538
Rossetti, *Echo*, 744
Shakespeare, *That Time of Year*, 730

Jean Toomer, *Reapers, page 782*

Toomer was born in Washington, D. C., studied at five colleges, and eventually settled in the Black community in Sparta, Georgia. An important voice in the Harlem Renaissance, his only book, *Cane*, was published in 1923.

Answers to the Study Questions, page 782

(1) "Reapers" is in iambic pentameter rhymed couplets that are enjambed rather than end-stopped. The enjambment, especially in lines 1–2 and 7–8, moderates the effect of the couplets and keeps the poem moving quickly.

(2) The auditory images of the poem contrast the silence of reaping to the *sound of steel on stones* and the *squealing* of the field rat. The visual images form a linked chain that related to death: *black reapers, scythes ... silently swinging, black horses,* the bleeding field rat, and the *blood-stained blade.* Like the squeal, the blood (lines 6–8) shocks by contrasting vivid red with the dominant black of the poem.

(3) Alliteration on the *s* sound links together the various images. One might particularly notice the similarity of the *s* to the actual hissing of a scythe cutting through "weeds and shade." In addition, the *b* sound

in the concluding lines links the inanimate mechanism of the blade to the belly of the dying animal.

WRITING TOPICS. The impact of the rhymed couplets on meaning. The reapers as metaphorical images of life or of death. The play of colors (especially black and red) in the poem.

WORKS FOR COMPARISON WITH TOOMER'S "REAPERS"

Lessing, *The Old Chief Mshlanga*, 502
Toomer, *Reapers*, 782
Villanueva, *Day-Long Day*, 1002

WILLIAM CARLOS WILLIAMS, *The Dance, page 782*

Williams captures in verse the movement and energy rendered visually in Brueghel's painting (page 783). The key question for class discussion is how Williams recreates the essence of the painting in the poem. Since the painting is reproduced below the poem in the text, students may study both poem and image.

Answers to the Study Questions, pages 782–783

(1) The repetition of the first line at the close creates a circular movement; the poem could start all over again. The identical lines also create a frame, like the edges of an artist's canvas.

(2) The repetition of sounds, syllables, and words drives the poem rapidly forward, and forms internal connections (notice, for example, the web created by "round ... round ... around ... round ... impound ... sound"). Williams employs onomatopoeia to suggest/duplicate the sounds of the instruments (*squeal, blare, tweedle*). While end-rhyme is lacking, internal rhyme (*around/impound* or *prance/dance*) pulls different parts of the poem together and speeds up the movement. The participles (*tipping, kicking, rolling, swinging, rollicking*) suggest the confusion and energy of ongoing activity.

(3) The poem capitalizes only the first words of two sentences, and the other capitals are placed at the beginnings of proper nouns. The absence of capitals elsewhere, particularly at the line beginnings, produces a steady pace, a visual enjambment, much in keeping with the constant round of activity in the painting.

(4) Williams avoids a regular meter. Instead he juxtaposes accented and unaccented syllables, almost randomly, to develop the rapid and dancing cadences of anapaests and dactyls. Similarly, the unstressed or split

words that end lines (*and, the, thick-, those, such*) push the reader on from line to line.

(5) Readers must judge the success of Williams's efforts themselves. A close look at the painting, however, shows that he captures the boisterousness of Brueghel's figures. The selection of an open form is appropriate to convey some of the random, hustle-and-bustle movement in the painting.

Writing topics. The absence of capitals. The use of verbals. The use of alliteration. The repetition of the first line at the end.

Works for Comparison with "The Dance"

Wagoner, *March for a One-Man Band*, 733
Williams, *Landscape with the Fall of Icarus*, 832
Wojahn, *"It's Only Rock and Roll, But I Like It"*, 643

Writing About Form in Poetry, *pages 783–788*

Although the sample essay (pages 786–787) deals with a closed-form poem, the discussion on writing about form provides approaches that will work effectively for either closed or open poems. In assigning an essay on form, it is important to stress the need to consider the relationship between form and content (speaker, idea, tone, meaning) rather than form itself or idea itself. The questions for discovering ideas on page 784 will be helpful in furnishing the basic ideas from which to organize and develop essays on the topic.

In selecting a poem on which the essay is to be based, choose one in which form makes a significant impact on content. Closed- and open-form poems lend themselves equally well to this sort of assignment.

Writing Topics for Form in Poetry, *page 788*

(1) The first topic introduces a comparison-contrast of poems by Shelley and Keats. Students may wander away from the topic of form and produce instead a comparison of ideas. It is therefore important to stress that students should bring out the relationship of form to content.

(2) The four poems offer differing treatments of the topic of death. As with many essays on more than two works, the problem here is keeping within reasonable limits. Ask students to study Appendix B, on Extended Comparison-Contrast, for using groups of poems as the basis of the comparison.

(3) To write a visual poem may at first seem difficult. You might suggest that students first create the shape they wish the poem to take, and then start working out their lines to fill in the shape. Once they get the "hang" of pouring words into shapes, they will discover that the technique is not considerably more difficult than writing a poem, say, in a given number of iambics. The real challenge of this assignment is to relate the line lengths not only to the shape, but also to the actual topic itself (see Herbert's "Easter Wings" for a successful example).

(4) The writing of haiku has been a favorite assignment for many years in schools throughout the country. The virtue of haiku is that they are short, and that students discover the need for short, specific, and concrete words rather than long and abstract ones. It is interesting to shorten the lines, for this exercise also enables writers to achieve even greater clarity, and often more pointed imagery.

(5) This topic would be best controlled either through the participation of the entire class, or of the group of students who would like to undertake the assignment. Students would not need to select each of the poems for analysis. They might wish to confine themselves to just those poems which either portray action ("The Dance," "March for a One-Man Band") or relative calm ("Swan and Shadow").

Chapter Twenty
Pages 789–816

Symbolism and Allusion: Windows to a Wide Expanse of Meaning

If you have already taught symbolism in fiction (Chapter 9), you may wish to use this introductory section simply as a review. If you omitted Chapter 9, however, there will be much here that is new. Particularly important is that poetry, being more compact than fiction, does not go into as much detail with symbols as one is likely to find in fiction. Students should thus be sensitive to the rapidity with which symbolism is often rendered in poems, through words, actions, setting, character, and situation (pages 793–794).

Allusion (pages 794–796) is sometimes difficult for students because they may not have built up the background needed for recognition. Even with good explanatory notes, they need guidance, so that they may understand the context and therefore the meaning of allusions.

On pages 796–797 we address one of the perennial problems of students: how to recognize symbols and allusions. Often we ourselves may take these things for granted, but students are less sure of their ground. A frank discussion about how students may try independently to determine the presence of symbols and allusions will hence be much appreciated.

Virginia Scott, *Snow, pages 791–792*

The matters raised in the questions about this poem are considered on pages 792 and 797. Writing topics may deal with any of the questions.

e. e. cummings, *In Just-, pages 797–798*

This poem is one of the more joyful that Cummings wrote, although students may be perplexed at first about the appearances of the balloonman. Sometimes they may need some prodding to see that the poem is about development and sexual growth, for the subject may superficially seem like a nostalgic memory of childhood. Here the change of the balloonman is important, for he alters from a colorful salesman to a symbolic, Pan-like figure representing spring and ritual fertility.

Answers to the Study Questions, page 798

(1) As symbols, *mud-luscious, marbles, puddle wonderful,* and *hopscotch* all signify the excitement and joy of childhood. Spring symbolizes growth, and also incipient sexuality. The whistle, at first not more than a realistic sales-call of the balloonman, by the end of the poem symbolizes the urges and needs of sexuality.

(2) At first the balloonman suggests the joy and color of childhood discovery. Once Cummings introduces the goat feet, however, the connection with Pan and symbolic sexuality is plain.

(3) Beyond the "wee," or "we," who may be an unidentified first-person plural group, the four characters are Betty, Isbel (or Isabel), Eddie, and Bill. Cummings runs their names together to stress their common identity as children, and, additionally, to symbolize their growth as sexual beings.

(4) The spacing and alignment definitely influence one's perception of the poem. Students may wish to experiment in spoken delivery. Interestingly, many students prefer the poem on the page, as a visual, seen artifact alone, rather than a poem to be read aloud or heard.

Writing topics. The use of symbols. The relationship of spring to sexuality. The effects of spacing, alignment, and lack of capitalization.

Works for Comparison with "In Just-"

Collins, *Schoolsville,* 547
Joyce, *Araby,* 387
Soto, *Oranges,* 992

T.S. Eliot, *Sweeney Among the Nightingales, pages 799–800*

This poem is one of Eliot's early "quatrain poems" published by Virginia and Leonard Woolf. Students experience difficulty with it because the narrative is obscured and because of the allusiveness. Some of the difficulty can be removed, however, if you point out that Eliot embodies an idea about the complexity of experience: One event does not happen in isolation, but is a part of world and even universal history. Thus the broadness of references is designed to show the integration of life—the current reenactment at one place of things that have happened in the past and are happening elsewhere.

Answers to the Study Questions, page 800

(1) Sweeney symbolizes the broad, coarse, unthinking mass person of drives and instincts devoid of thought. The animal attributes accentuate these gross features. As the epigraph, Agamemnon's outcry demonstrates the continuity of human brutality from ancient to modern times.

(2) The constellations, one of which refers to a mythic hero who was killed (Orion), suggest the galactic and even universal scope of brutality. Corvus, the crow, also signifies ill fortune. All the references, both real and mythical, are a universal setting for evil and violence.

(3) In stanza two, the moon is associated with lunacy, thus symbolizing madness or depravity. The direction west, where the sun sets, traditionally symbolizes death. The raven symbolizes rapacity and greed. The horned gate is the entrance to the underworld through which true dreams emerge; hence this gate seems here to symbolize the reality of evil.

(4) Rachel in line 23 is animal like because Eliot conceives of her as living on an inhuman level, without morality or the capability of remorse. The selection of the name "Sweeney," an obvious allusion to the Irish hero, seems intended as a disparagement of Irish traditions.

(5) In lines 33–34, the host and the indistinct person are conversing about something undisclosed, but from the context we may conclude that they are making an agreement about robbing Sweeney and harming or killing him.

(6) Nightingales are usually praised and admired because their songs symbolize the beauty of the universe. In lines 39–40, however, Eliot suggests that they turn their backsides and defecate upon the shroud of Agamemnon. This ironic reversal seems to be applicable to both modern life and to ancient.

Writing topics. Sweeney as a symbol. The other symbols in the poem. Eliot's use of allusion. The poem as an ironic commentary on both ancient and modern life.

Works for Comparison with "Sweeney Among the Nightingales"

Blake, *The Tyger*, 636
Dubus, *The Curse*, 482
Frost, *Desert Places*, 764

Isabella Gardner, *Collage of Echoes, page 801*

In her lifetime, Gardner acted, edited *Poetry* magazine, taught, published four volumes of poems, and gave frequent poetry readings. This poem, "Collage of Echoes," is from her final volume, which appeared two years before her death.

Answers to the Study Questions, page 801

(1) Granted the allusiveness, the poet clearly assumes that readers have the knowledge to recognize the total context upon which she is drawing.

(2) Gardner's many echoes truly make the lines resonate, for the poem would have little meaning without the lexical strength of the allusions.

(3) The phrases all suggest weariness, a feeling of having fulfilled obligations and borne many cares. Because the originals are easily recognized, they might be considered comic in this new context. The "collage" of quotations is therefore a different and totally new application of something well known (a collage is usually thought of as an assemblage of cuttings and pastings, often by children in the early grades). "Witty" is perhaps a better description of the allusions than "comic."

Writing topics. The integration of the echoes. The meaning and application of the allusions.

Works for Comparison with "Collage of Echoes"

Keller, *Tea Party*, 1050
Millay, *What Lips My Lips Have Kissed*, 967
Porter, *The Jilting of Granny Weatherall*, 538

Thomas Hardy, *In Time of "The Breaking of Nations," pages 801–802*

With this poem, students may wish to discuss whether the topic is politics or people. Another interesting subject is whether such a poem could be written today, with the threat that nuclear warfare could penetrate even the remotest corners of earth to destroy maids and their wights.

Answers to the Study Questions, page 802

(1) The man and woman are easily recognized as a universal symbol of love. The man and the horse are also a universal symbol. The smoke coming from the grass, however, is contextual; the poet must arrange the stanza to make the smoke symbolic. As images, these symbols refer to sight, sound (whispering) and smell (smoke).

(2) Hardy emphasizes the symbolism of the phrase "breaking of nations" by speaking of dynasties and war's annals in lines 7–8 and 11–12. The Biblical allusion adds the sense that wars and political changes have been going on for millennia, but that human life has been predominating and will prevail, because strength is in human affection, not anger.

(3) Stanza one is descriptive, whereas in stanzas two and three only the first halves are descriptive. In developing his assertions, Hardy refers to these halves as "this" (line 7) and "their story" (line 12).

(4) Hardy's speaker makes his evaluation by citing the quietness and permanence of his pictures of life among the people, the folk. He dismisses the great business of war and dynastic change by relegating it to the second parts of the stanzas, and by negating it in favor of common life.

Writing topics. The visual symbols. The importance of the Biblical allusion and the quotation marks in the title.

Works for Comparison with "In Time of 'The Breaking of Nations'"

Haines, *Little Cosmic Dust Poem*, 945
Strand, *The Remains*, 996
Sexton, *Three Green Windows*, 983

George Herbert, *The Collar, pages 802–803*

Herbert's poems, which dramatize his conflicts about God before becoming a priest, were not published during his lifetime. "The Collar" describes one of these conflicts. Herbert's speaker cites the following reasons for pursuing his own secular goals: freedom, impatience, earthly reward, capacity and opportunity to do other things, independence, and possible adventure. The sole reason in favor of the clergy role is God's call (line 35), and this is overwhelmingly persuasive.

Answers to the Study Questions, page 803

(1) At the beginning the speaker describes a moment when in frustration he beat a table and began the train of inward debate contained in the rest of the poem. The speaker is thinking about accepting a calling to divine service, and for most of the lines he cites reasons for which he should resist it.

(2) The title of the poem is a multiple symbol, because it involves an elaborate pun. It represents the speaker's anger (choler) against what he considers the yoke (collar) of service for which God (the caller) is calling

him, and also the power of service because the clerical collar is round and therefore enveloping and enclosing. Because of the way the poem concludes, the calling by God and the collar as an enclosure are dominant.

(3) The symbols of the poem may be classed as follows: a– Positive religious symbols are thorn, blood, wine, and the parent-child relationship. b– Positive secular symbols of independent self-fulfillment are bays, flowers, and garlands. c– Negative religious symbols (prompting the speaker's anger or "choler") are cage, the death's head, and the rope of sands (symbolizing the many complex, endless, and never-to-be-finished duties of the clergy).

Writing topics. The use of "collar" as a symbol and as a pun. The conflicting symbols. Herbert's use of allusion.

Works for Comparison with "The Collar"

Williams, *Taking Care*, 74
Donne, *Batter My Heart*, 615
Herbert, *The Pulley*, 634

Josephine Jacobsen, *Tears, pages 803–804*

This poem is a unique reflection on the subject of tears. Crying, the poet states, is a purely human condition. The power to feel pain and to respond with tears, and to sympathize with the plight of others and to cry for them, are human characteristics. Without the capacity for tears, the poet states, we lose our humanity.

Answers to the Study Questions, page 804

(1) As a symbol, tears signify the immense suffering, agony, and cruelty that the human race has experienced since its beginnings. The memory of past tears has vanished, however, just as the tears themselves have vanished without trace. Symbolically, the tears thus suggest that each generation of humanity must go through the same experiences, even though one would hope that generations would benefit from the sufferings and persecutions of the past.

(2, 4) The poem applies the symbol to past civilizations (Ur, Persepolis), to other cultures ("in some countries, openly, in others, not"), to the future (line 31), and to literature (Shakespeare, Thomson). All these allusions are introduced to demonstrate that grief, together with the human causes of grief, throughout all times and all societies.

(3) It would appear, from the poem, that tears are a response to

suffering in its various forms, both past, present, and to come. Animals, however, have no recorded history, and live primarily in the moment. The last two lines refer to the fact that many human beings, in their desire for power and control, forsake their capacity to understand and sympathize with suffering, and hence their eyes become figuratively dry as they pursue their goals. In essence, they give up their humanity as they give up their ability to sympathize and to shed tears for others.

Writing topics. The use of tears as a symbol in the poem. The meaning of the final two lines. The nature of the speaker.

Works for Comparison with "Tears"

Quasimodo, *Auschwitz*, 695
Serotte, *My Mother's Face*, 983
Stern, *Burying an Animal on the Way to New York*, 995

Robinson Jeffers, *The Purse-Seine, pages 805–806*

One of Jeffers's major themes is the capacity of human beings to self-destruct. Out of the destruction, however, may come a restoration of the pristine beauty of the natural world. "The Purse-Seine" deals with this theme, although in the poem Jeffers is not concerned with the potentially positive aftermath.

Answers to the Study Questions, page 806

(1) A purse-seine contains floats at the top and a draw-cable at the bottom. When drawn, the net does not permit any fish to escape. In the second stanza the speaker responds to the seining by claiming that it is terrible because of the certainty of capture, but he also stresses details about the beauty of the fish as they struggle to free themselves.

(2) In stanza three, the speaker shows the symbolic nature of the purse-seine by equating it to the inability of industrialized humanity to survive independently. He points out that the draw cable may take the form of dictatorship, revolution, repression, anarchy, or mass disasters, from which there is no escape. The sardines hence symbolize the present world population, and the seine symbolizes destructive political forces.

(3) Both Jeffers and Yeats agree that a sinister force will soon become powerful. To Yeats, however, things happen in 2,000-year cycles, with the possibility of a better cycle replacing the evil one now approaching. Jeffers is less systematic than Yeats, for Jeffers makes plain that repressive political processes are destroying world civilization.

(4) The concluding assertion (line 31) about death as the end of life is both a recognition and an acceptance. Because the fish are described as "caught" (line 9), the poem does not offer the possibility of escape for human beings. The speaker is clearly concerned, if not fearful, about the loss of beauty represented by the city and its lights (line 17).

(5) The sighing watch of the sea lions in line 12 may be seen as a symbolic lament for the loss of the freedom and natural beauty represented by the fish. The "you" of the concluding lines is the reader being drawn in to the scene of the poem as a virtual witness, who would need to be insensitive not to sigh at the prospects of destructiveness symbolized in the poem.

WRITING TOPICS. The symbolism of the purse-seine. The symbolism of the lighted city and the fish. The cataclysmic views of Jeffers and Yeats compared and contrasted.

WORKS FOR COMPARISON WITH "THE PURSE-SEINE"

Bishop, *The Fish*, 632
Kumin, *Woodchucks*, 959
Tate, *The Blue Booby*, 997
James Wright, *A Blessing*, 597

JOHN KEATS, *La Belle Dame Sans Merci, pages 806–807*

Because of Keats's letters, we know the precise time when he wrote the first version of this poem (April 21, 1819) and also the circumstances (soon after he had taken care of the personal effects of his dead brother, Tom). Critical biographers have tried to demonstrate the influence of this situation on the poem, together with Keats's own uncertainty about his love for Fanny Brawne. Despite the wealth of information about the circumstances of composition, and also despite attempts to relate the poem to a linkage of death and life in the poet's psyche, "La Belle Dame Sans Merci" has an independent existence that defies categorization. All poems of course require great perception and care. With this poem, special care is needed.

Answers to the Study Questions, page 808

(1) The first three stanzas contain the first speaker's questions. The remaining eight stanzas contain the knight's narrative about his encounter with the lady, the "Belle Dame." The knight's narrative is structured according to the meeting, the first loving, and the magical journey (stanzas 4–7). In stanzas 8–11, the knight goes with the lady to her grotto; they make love and the knight falls asleep and dreams the ghostly dream, only

to awake on the hill's side. The last stanza (12) is the knight's answer to the speaker's question in the first stanza. The source of the knight's information about his thralldom is only his own dream, his own imagination.

(2) That the knight's narrative is a dream requires that it be read as a symbol. The meaning, however, is not certain. Is it disillusionment with love? A sense of doom about life itself? A disparagement of the regrettable power of the human imagination to misconstrue and negate positive experiences? Sorrow about the hauntingly brief nature of happiness? Your students might wish to discuss any or all of these possibilities.

(3) Relish, honey, and manna are all magical, unreal symbols. Manna, particularly, is the food provided by God to the ancient Israelites (Exodus 16). Keats probably intends by it no more than a magical nourishment. The pale kings and warriors symbolize powers of doubt and negation.

(4) The multiple setting of withered sedge, the meadows, the herbs, and the grotto all symbolically complement the knight's dazed state of mind.

Writing topics. The narrative structure of the poem. The puzzle of the meaning of the poem's major symbols. The nature of the fairy lady, apart from the knight's perception.

Works for Comparison with "La Belle Dame Sans Merci"

Dickinson, *I Cannot Live with You*, 886
Drayton, *Since There's No Help*, 936
Wyatt, *I Find No Peace*, 670

X. J. Kennedy, *Old Men Pitching Horseshoes, page 808*

Although this poem invites a symbolic reading, it makes no overt claims about being symbolic or profoundly meaningful. The title is totally descriptive: Four men are playing a game of horseshoes. One man throws a horseshoe and misses, but his second one is a ringer. While his side cheers, his opponents mutter. After this, the four men change sides, and continue the game. Yet the poem suggests that such actions are as old as the ages, as old as human civilization itself. The poem therefore is an example of how a work may be contextually symbolic.

Answers to the Study Questions, page 808

(1, 2) The symbolic nature of the game is brought out not so much by the description of the action, but by the permanence suggested by the diction. *Dirt-burnished iron*, for example, is an observation about a horseshoe that invests it with a long-term connection with the earth. Words like *congregate, appraising, inhabits, extended, outpost, withered, worn path of earth, sheaves of air, warm distortions,* and *force* all together support the idea that the single game of horseshoes is like all previous games, like all games to follow, and like all games of all sorts. As long as there are people, in short, there will be old men pitching horseshoes, an activity in which they engage after their years of work and service are past, and they retreat into the recreational years of retirement.

(3) Eliot's poem concludes with the image of "ancient women gathering fuel in vacant lots." The image is one of effortful work, gleaning energy and continuing life under unpromising conditions. Kennedy's characters are old men, and his location is a recreational area set aside for play. Kennedy's poem therefore suggests a world of greater stability and security than Eliot's. Or do the roles assigned to men and women in both poems suggest that women must always work, even in age, while men ultimately reach a state in which they may afford to spend their time in relaxing games?

WRITING TOPICS. The poem's symbolism. The use of descriptive and abstract diction.

WORKS FOR COMPARISON WITH "OLD MEN PITCHING HORSESHOES"

Eliot, *Preludes,* 640
Howes, *Death of a Vermont farm Woman,* 723
Porter, *The Jilting of Granny Weatherall,* 538

CAROL MUSKE, *Real Estate, page 809*

"Real Estate," has a number of personal or private allusions, and for this reason students may find it difficult. Hence the reading must rely upon the suggestiveness and meaning of the references themselves, even though the exact applications may not be clear. It is not important, for example, to learn the identity of the "paid escort," or to know about the family's "real estate." Instead, what is needed is an understanding of how these things function within the poem itself.

Answers to the Study Questions, pages 809–810

(1) The speaker is apparently a woman uneasy about her future, addressing herself in the second person. She is alert and knowledgeable, thinking of her own need for power and self-determination. She assumes that people normally use sex to gain power and status. Her advice to herself

is to buy land, which offers the only security and power she can have.

(2) As a symbol, the "teen-age pharaoh" means that death comes to everyone, powerful and weak alike. The modern set of objects suggest the same: Rich things or poor things, they all end up being useless for a dead person, and they therefore symbolize the futility of human acquisitions.

(3) The "paid escort" symbolizes the need of some single females to appear desirable. The "old trombone" is a phallic symbol. These symbols indicate a disaffection with conventional male-female role-playing.

(4) Lines 25–27 are ambiguous because they may refer either to the control of land or to the stance of women with regard to men. The idea is that a woman in an inferior position accepts a man (the "river") out of necessity, while with independence she is worthy of dignity and respect. These lines must be considered symbolically because the specifics cannot be exactly known.

(5) Frost in "Build Soil" advises the entire nation to develop its collective natural resources. Muske's advice is similarly applicable, though it pertains in the poem to the role of a specific woman.

Writing topics. Muske's use of symbols. Criticism of past assumptions about the economic, social, and sexual roles of women, and suggestions for change. Allusion as symbolism.

Works for Comparison with "Real Estate"

Steinbeck, *The Chrysanthemums*, 347
Bogan, *Women*, 919
Rukuyser, *Myth*, 827
Swenson, *Women*, 919

William Butler Yeats, *The Second Coming, page 810*

The issues in the questions are treated in the notes, and also in the sample essay on pages 814–815. In 1991, singer Joni Mitchell wrote a musical adaptation of this poem, entitled "Slouching Toward Bethlehem" (on *Night Ride Home,* Geffen GEFD–24302).

Writing topics. The structure of the poem. A major symbol in detail (e.g., the gyre, the rough beast).

Works for Comparison with "The Second Coming"

Frost, *'Out, Out—'*, 899
Jeffers, *The Purse-Seine*, 805
Nash, *Exit, Pursued by a Bear*, 664

Writing About Symbolism and Allusion in Poetry, *pages 811–816*

In teaching this section, you will probably need to stress the strategies for organizing ideas described on pages 812–813. Questions that your students raise about these patterns may be sufficient for your discussion. However, you might additionally need to go over the material in detail. It is best, always, to combine a discussion of essay forms with the reading and interpretation of a specific poem that is relevant to the forms. If you assign approach 2, for example, you might use Isabella Gardner's "Collage of Echoes" to illustrate how a poem may be shaped by allusion. Or you might find that Eliot's "Sweeney Among the Nightingales" is effective in illustrating approach 1, the meaning of symbols. In your use of the sample essay (pages 814–815), it would be best also to teach "The Second Coming" as a base from which to show students how they, too, may apply an interpretation of symbols and allusions to the task of writing.

Writing Topics for Symbolism and Allusion, *page 816*

(1) The symbols of capture are love and sex (Keats), dedication and guilt (Herbert), and the net and the consequences of civilization (Jeffers). In context, all these symbols are totally appropriate.

(2) All these poets are highly allusive in their respective poems. Finch, Cummings, and Eliot refer heavily to material from the classics, while Yeats, also using classical references, adds Christian apocalyptic allusions and combines them with his own specific system.

(3) The third direction should produce some interesting poems featuring major symbols. Students, always, may select their own subject, but be sure that they consult you before doing so. The self-analysis is of course an important aspect of this assignment, as with all other such assignments made in the writing topics.

(4) As with the third direction, this fourth one, involving the use of allusions, is designed to get students thinking about people, activities, governments, and publications in the world around them, and, through allusion, determining how these things have both direct and indirect influences on their own lives. You might indicate that students might make allusions through names, quotations, and situations.

Chapter Twenty-two
Pages 817–838

Myth: Systems of Symbolic Allusion in Poetry

This chapter has the double aim of giving students a quick introduction to mythology and a longer consideration of the ways in which poets employ myths as symbolic allusions that add layers of meaning and resonance to their poems. The introductory discussion of mythology (pages 817–820) seeks to establish the importance of myth to humanity and to emphasize the symbolic nature of myth. "Mythology and Literature" (pages 820–821) takes up the essential differences between the two, and the ways they can intersect. The Ansel Adams photograph (page 819), may serve as a touchstone for a discussion of the relationship of mythology and perception.

Problems may arise when you deal with the subject of myth and poetry. Some students may question the relationship of myth to revealed religion. It is important to respect this question, and carefully to establish the boundary lines between the two. Additionally, it is often difficult for students to recognize the mythic aspects of a poem at the outset of their reading. This process often idealistically assumes a high level of familiarity with a variety of mythic systems, including Buddhist, Hindu, American Indian, Norse, and Chinese myth. We have tried to avoid this problem by limiting the mythic systems evoked in the poetry here to the system familiar and accessible to most students—Greco-Roman myth. In addition, the section entitled "Mythological References in Poetry" (page 821) should guide students to undertake the research necessary for their understanding of a particular mythic system.

Besides the poems in this chapter, the text contains many others that lend themselves to an exploration of the impact of myth in poetry. These include Tennyson's "Tithonus" (page 998, Greco-Roman myth), Gardner's "At a Summer Hotel" (page 720, Greco-Roman myth), Keats's "La Belle Dame sans Merci" (page 806, folk mythology), Yeats's "The Second Coming" (page 810, Christian tradition and private mythology), T. S. Eliot's

"Sweeney Among The Nightingales" (page 799, Greek), Cummings's "In Just" (page 797, Greco-Roman), Plath's "Last Words" (page 976, Egyptian and Babylonian myth), and Silko's "Where Mountain Lion Lay Down with Deer" (page 988, Navajo Indian myth).

William Butler Yeats, *Leda and the Swan, page 822*

The poem is explicated in the text (pages 822–823). In class discussion, you might begin with myth and meaning, but meter, rhyme, and form are also worth class time. Yeats employs iambic pentameter with substitute feet to stress important words and ideas (e.g., the spondee on great wings in line 1 that produces three heavy beats in a row). The Italian sonnet form organizes the poem's argument and ideas; rhymes present some elegant and suggestive connections (e.g., *thighs/lies, up/drop*).

Margaret Atwood, *Siren Song, pages 823–824*

The adventure with the sirens is an important episode in Homer's *Odyssey*. Always a lover of danger, music, and temptation, Odysseus fills the ears of his crew with wax to prevent their hearing, while he himself is lashed to the mast so that he will not throw himself overboard and kill himself when cast under the spell of the sirens. Students are interested in discussing the views presented in the poem about male-female relationships. Atwood may be suggesting that males will always succumb (because of sexual attraction, their egos, their interest and love?). She may also be implying that some women may find the pattern of interaction boring, inevitable, predictable, and repetitious.

A famous musical version of the sirens is the nocturne for orchestra and women's voices, *Sirènes,* by Claude Debussy (1898). David Bedford composed a musical impression of the sirens in 1976 ("The Odyssey," Caroline-Blue Plate CDOVD444 • 7243 8 39574 22).

Answers to the Study Questions, page 824

(1) In the mythology as told by Homer, the sirens were a trio of bird-women in Greco-Roman mythology who enchanted sailors in passing ships with their beauty and songs. The sirens' singing was so alluring that the captivated sailors inevitably forgot their native land, lost their will to go on, and landed (or wrecked themselves) on the island where they starved to death. The shores around the sirens were therefore covered with bleached bones.

(2) Atwood focuses on the sexual allure of the sirens—their seductive power which undermines masculine resistance. Atwood's speaker is a contemporary siren who is tired of being with her two sisters. Her colloquial language brings her into the present, as does her claim that she is trapped in a bird suit (line 12).

(3) In lines 1–9 the speaker defines her song; it is irresistible and unknown (to what extent is it this very poem?). This is the hook that the siren speaker uses to get *you* (the reader, men) interested. In lines 10–18 the siren offers what appears to be an offer that cannot be refused: She will reveal the secret/song if *you* will help her escape. The listener is drawn in deeper. Finally, the speaker appeals to the listener's (male) ego: "I will tell the secret to you, / … only to you" and "Help me! / Only you, only you can, / you are unique" (lines 19–24). But of course *you* are not unique because the song (poem, seduction) *works every time.*

Writing topics. The speaker or the listener, language, tone, or form. The irony and humor of the poem.

Works for Comparison with "Siren Song"

Herbert, *The Collar*, 802
Wharton, *Pomegranate Seed*, 440
Wilbur, *The Sirens*, 1008

Olga Broumas, *Circe, pages 824–825*

The myth of Circe is told not only by Homer, but also by Hesiod (*Works and Days*) and by Ovid (*Metamorphoses*). Like Parker in Penelope, Broumas looks at the myth not through the male eye, but through the female. Bedford's "The Odyssey" also includes a musical representation of Circe based on a modulation of the Sirens' song into a minor key.

Answers to the Study Questions, page 825

(1) Circe is a sorceress in Greco-Roman mythology who has the power to turn men into pigs. Her most famous encounter is with Odysseus and his crew (*Odyssey,* Book 10). She transforms half of Odysseus's men, but Hermes fortifies Odysseus against her spells, and Odysseus forces her to restore the men. Circe then honors Odysseus and gives him her love. He spends a year with her on her island. Like the sirens, Circe symbolizes the power of female sexuality.

(2) The title identifies the speaker as Circe. Her sexual power here, as in the myth, can turn "men into swine" (line 25).

(3) While Homer presents the Circe myth from the point of view of the male, Broumas here presents it from the point of view of Circe. The speaker and poem thus symbolize the resentful attitude of women who are often used or even victimized in the relationships between the sexes. Circe's mythical power consisted of her herbal potions. Here her power seems to be venomous and spiderlike.

(4) The *charm* and the *fire* (lines 1–5) represent both Circe's power and her desire to use the power. *The Anticipation* (lines 6–15) sets up the social and sexual context in which Circe's power can work. *They* are men, society, and the followers and enforcers of social custom; they court (weave, entrap, tie up) the speaker (Circe, women) and, in doing so, create the situation (the spell) that will undo them. The *courting hands* (limitations, customs, boundaries, demands) of the men are balanced against Circe's *spiderlike* waiting and knowledge that she has the power to change them. *The Bite* (lines 16–26) presents anew the transformation myth. The speaker is confident, powerful, self-satisfied, joyful, and *divine.*

(5) After line 21 the scene shifts to modern settings, and Circe is an individual woman who is watched by nearby construction workers and by men hanging out at local bars and stores. The men's responses to her make them little different from animals; indeed, women may testify that the whistling and grunting they hear are truly "wild" sounds that one might expect of "swine" (lines 26, 25). The repetition of *corner* (lines 22–23) stresses the point of turning or transformation that both the speaker and the men experience. Classroom responses to this poem should be vigorous.

WRITING TOPICS. Male-female relations as portrayed in "Circe." The ambiguity of location in the poem. The spell-like powers of Circe.

WORKS FOR COMPARISON WITH "CIRCE"

Anonymous, *Barbara Allan*, 912
Anonymous, *Lord Randal*, 913
Keats, *La Belle Dame Sans Merci*, 806
Lawrence, *The Horse Dealer's Daughter*, 393

W. S. MERWIN, *Odysseus, pages 825–826*

This poem draws on the mythic associations of Odysseus as a wanderer and adventurer to suggest that such a life can become redundant and meaningless. A good approach to teaching the poem is to ask students to comment on the words *same* in lines 1–2 and *identical* in line 5. When they determine the idea that Odysseus's life has become repetitive and boring, they will have a good perception of the poem's tone and central idea.

Answers to the Study Questions, page 826

(1) The aspects of the myth concern the life of Odysseus after his return from his wanderings. Like Tennyson's Ulysses, Odysseus must go in quest over and over again, to the point where his life becomes confused, purposeless, and monotonous. The speaker (outside the poem, detached) suggests that it is "As though he had got nowhere but older" (line 3). Beginning at line 5, the speaker reviews Odysseus's adventures, blending them through the use of unspecified allusions and Odysseus's own confusion into a repeated pattern of betrayal and abandonment.

(2) The originality and surprise of the poem is that Odysseus is lost as the traditional symbol of going out on the quest, and instead becomes a symbol of desertion and infidelity. He abandons the women he lives with and encounters, including Penelope, Circe, and Calypso. The last six lines suggest that Odysseus can no longer distinguish these women from one another or keep Penelope fixed in his mind. Odysseus's life becomes almost meaningless; "it was the same whether he stayed / Or went" (lines 11–12).

(3, 4) The poems by Merwin, Tennyson, and Parker in the *Poems for Study* section form a triad based on the same mythic material; they demonstrate the ways that poets can evoke the same myth for differing purposes. Merwin's Odysseus is the reverse side of the coin of Tennyson's Ulysses (page 828). Parker, who makes Penelope the central figure in her view of the myth, ignores the career of Odysseus while focusing on the woman left behind (page 826). The result is that Parker throws the King's adventures into the class of dereliction of responsibility. Progressively, therefore, Odysseus's restlessness and adventurousness moves from the positive with Tennyson to the totally negative with Merwin and Parker.

WRITING TOPICS. A comparison of the poems by Merwin, Tennyson, and Parker. Merwin's view of the adventurer. Varying concepts of heroism and lengthy life.

OTHER WORKS FOR COMPARISON WITH "ODYSSEUS"

Field, *Icarus*, 834
Heyen, *Mantle*, 768

Dorothy Parker, *Penelope, page 826*

(1, 2) This short lyric, the subject of the chapter's sample essay (pages 836–837), also gains resonance from its evocation of myths in the *Iliad* and the *Odyssey.* Here however, the focus is on Penelope, Odysseus's wife. The ironic conclusion is a testimony to the fact that the heroic quest depends on the sacrifices of loved ones and dependents, and that therefore this quest may very well be characterized as juvenile as well as heroic.

Writing topics. The use of myth in the poem. The view of war and wandering from Penelope's side of things. The irony of the poem.

Works for Comparison with "Penelope"

Piercy, *A Work of Artifice*, 665
Whur, *The First-Rate Wife*, 679

Muriel Rukeyser, *Myth, page 827*

For background on this poem, see *Oedipus The King* together with the introduction (page 1082).

Answers to the Study Questions, page 827

(1, 2, 3, 4) Briefly, Oedipus's solving of the Sphinx's riddle—he answered "man"—freed Thebes from the terror of the Sphinx. In return, he was rewarded with the throne and the recently widowed queen, Jocasta. Class discussion can focus on the form of the poem and on Rukeyser's tricky use of the word *myth.*

Rukeyser, like Atwood and Broumas, employs mythic material to comment on a contemporary (and perhaps universal) aspect of the relationship/difference between men and women. At one level, the word *myth* refers to the story of Oedipus and the Sphinx. At another, however, it refers to Oedipus's assertion that "When you say Man ... you include women / too. Everyone knows that" (lines 10–11). The Sphinx's reply exposes the linguistic and sociological problem with the myth; it suggests that exclusion rather than inclusion has been the order of language and society for eons.

Writing topics. Rukeyser's modern application of the ancient myth. Humor in the poem. The characterizations of Oedipus, or the Sphinx.

Works for Comparison with Rukeyser's "Myth"

Anonymous, *The Three Ravens*, 914
Bogan, *Women*, 919
Sophocles, *Oedipus the King*, 1082

ALFRED, LORD TENNYSON, *Ulysses, pages 828–829*

Tennyson's "Ulysses" (Latin) and Merwin's "Odysseus" (Greek) allude to the same mythic and literary hero of Homer's Odyssey. Odysseus was ruler of the island kingdom of Ithaca, husband of Penelope, and father of Telemachus. In myth, he is characterized as shrewd, intelligent, crafty, and eloquent. He spent twenty years away from Ithaca and family—ten at Troy during the Trojan War, and ten trying to return home. It was he who brought about the end of the war by developing the strategy of the Trojan Horse

Odysseus's return home took an additional ten years because he was opposed by Poseidon (Neptune), God of the Sea, even though he was favored by Athena, Goddess of Wisdom. During the time, Odysseus confronted ghosts, sirens, monsters, and gods, and had amorous interludes with Circe and Calypso. When he finally arrived home, he found his palace full of greedy suitors seeking to marry Penelope and take his crown. With Telemachus' help, Odysseus destroyed all the suitors and regained authority in Ithaca.

Answers to the Study Questions, page 829

(1) Tennyson's dramatic monologue (in blank verse) is spoken by Ulysses many years after his return. In the poem, Ulysses represents a commitment to the active life and the continual search for new experiences. The poem draws on the mythic figure's intelligence and symbolic value as an adventurer and wanderer.

(2, 3) Students may debate what Ulysses wants: adventure, knowledge, death, or escape. The speaker, Ulysses, establishes his attitude toward life in Ithaca (lines 1–5) with phrases like *little profit, idle, still hearth,* and *barren crags* that are images of waste and boredom. He has nothing in common with the people he rules; they do not know him. At line 6, he considers his attitudes toward life; he wants to live it to the fullest, for one life is almost not enough. He notes that it is dull to "pause … make an end … rust … not to shine" (lines 22–23). His past adventures (lines 7–17) have become part of his present (line 18) and this pushes him onward to "that untraveled world whose margin fades / Forever and forever." He contrasts his need to move (explore, discover) with his son's complacency (lines 33–43). Telemachus will be a good and happy king, but Ulysses has other work. His quest is for knowledge (line 31), and his journey westward will be a new experience. He admits that he and his men are old and weak, yet he affirms that they are "strong in will" The poem thus absorbs the features of the myth of Ulysses as adventurer, and expands on them, turning the mythic figure into a symbolic affirmation of the life that never yields to habit or decay.

Writing topics. The problem of settling down after an exciting period of life (e.g., war, expeditions, athletics). The character of the speaker of "Ulysses."

Works for Comparison with Tennyson's "Ulysses"

Auden, *The Unknown Citizen*, 916
Frost, *The Road Not Taken*, 898
Hemingway, *Soldier's Home*, 272
St. Luke, *The Parable of the Prodigal Son*, 340

The "Icarus" Poems, *pages 830–834*

The story of Daedalus and Icarus is told most fully by Ovid in the *Metamorphoses* and the *Heroides*. The reproduction of the Brueghel painting (page 834) provides a graphic interpretation of the story, and also are the base of the poems by Auden and Williams.

In general, the mythic figure of Icarus symbolizes pride, ambition, arrogance, striving, and daring as well as recklessness, foolishness, and suffering. The myth presents the outline of a tragedy in microcosm; the striving toward the sun is heroic, while the fall into the sea is tragic (or at least pathetic—there is no explicit self-knowledge attained). The various poets use the figure of Icarus to embody a series of different qualities and ideas. As with the poems based on Odysseus and Penelope, these illustrate the way the same mythic figure can be employed to very different ends by writers.

Stephen Spender, *Icarus, page 831*

Stephen Spender was a close friend of W. H. Auden's, and his reputation as a poet reflects the tendency to compare the men's work. This poem, published in *Poems* (1933), evokes both the daring flight and the tragic fall. It is often read as a description of the flight and crash of a World War I aviator; you can try this suggestion with your students and see if it changes their perception of the poem. The Icarus figure in the poem is proud and arrogant; he is described as *aristocratically indifferent* to those beneath him (hawk, men, eagles). The first ten lines focus on his flight and pride, his *War on the sun* (line 10). The last two focus on the fall; the figure is shattered into *Hands, wings*—an image that stresses the destruction and finality. Spender uses the whole myth (flight and fall) with most of its symbolic overtones intact; the focus remains on Icarus. Other things to consider in class: 1– the shift in verb tense (*will, had, are);* 2– the speaker (external, detached) and his attitude toward the Icarus figure; 3– the form (uneven couplets) and its impact on meaning.

W. H. Auden, *Musée des Beaux Arts, pages 831–832*

Auden's open-form poem uses the figure of Icarus (portrayed in Brueghel's painting, page 834) to explore ideas about suffering and the world's reaction to suffering. In teaching, you can focus on the way Auden moves from a general point to specific instances. In lines 1–13, the speaker asserts that the *Old Masters* (painters) were right about suffering; the victims always suffer alone while others remain indifferent and life goes on. He cites two unnamed paintings (one of the nativity and the other possibly of the crucifixion) as examples. Each presents a momentous event and a victim surrounded by indifference: the children, dogs, horse. The last eight lines focus on the example of Brueghel's "Icarus" (you may need to point out to your students the legs entering the water at the right just below the ship).

The myth of Icarus operates in this poem at second hand; Brueghel's treatment of the myth (rather than the myth itself) is the focus. The painting ignores the heroic aspirations of the mythic figure, dealing only with the fall. Auden, in turn, uses Brueghel's placement of the figure (the legs) to underscore his point that people like the plowman and like those on the ship (and also like the sun above and the natural world generally) go about their business, indifferent to the falling and dying young man.

Auden illustrates his idea by making the mythic figure seem insignificant. The effect only works, however, if the reader brings the whole symbolic impact of Icarus to the poem. We must assume the heroic and tragic stature, so that we can see how it is ignored by the figures in the painting, the painter, the speaker, and the poet.

Writing topics. The ideas of suffering in Auden and Brueghel, and also in Frost's "Out, out–" (page 899) The poem as an accusation about human indifference to others.

Anne Sexton, *To a Friend Whose Work Has Come to Triumph, page 832*

Sexton's sonnet (*abab cdcd efgf hh,* with many slant rhymes) focuses on the heroic triumph of Icarus's flight. Icarus *acclaiming the sun* is contrasted with his *sensible daddy* (Daedalus) and with other things on earth (*trees*) and air (*starlings*). The fall, mentioned in line 12, is dismissed; it is secondary to the image and the fact of the flight. The tone—familiar, admiring, a bit condescending—undercuts the heroic presentation; it is established through diction and understatement. Note especially *sticky* (line 1), *little tug* (2), *quite well* (7), and *sensible daddy* (14).

Writing topics. The figure of Icarus. Icarus contrasted to Daedalus. Diction and tone. Sexton's use of mythic material.

William Carlos Williams, *Landscape with the Fall of Icarus,* pages 832–833

Like Auden's, Williams's treatment of the Icarus myth is once removed, filtered through the pictorial medium of Brueghel's painting (page 834). Unlike Auden, however, Williams does not explore a separate issue such as human suffering; rather, he's interested in recreating the painting in verbal images. As in "Musée," the mythical Icarus is secondary but essential to this poem.

We must bring all the mythic associations to the painting and the poem to appreciate the effect of displacing the figure from center stage to the lower right-hand corner. Williams recreates this effect in the poem by relegating Icarus to the opening (line 2) and the close (lines 14–20). The center of the poem, like the painting, focuses on the landscape rather than the fall. The speaker "pans" the painting from left to right, noting the *farmer,* the regeneration of nature, the *edge of the sea* and the sun. In lines 16–21, Williams focuses on the *splash quite unnoticed* of *Icarus drowning,* and also observes how insignificant the event was to the world at large in the painting. Icarus's fall frames the poem, even though most of the poem turns away from the event and the figure.

Writing topics. The importance of the Icarus myth to the poem. How does the poem recreate the effect of the painting? The ways that form contributes to this recreation.

Edward Field, *Icarus, page 834*

In contrast to Auden and Williams, Field directs his attention squarely to the mythic figure of Icarus. Even here, however, there is a displacement; the heroic and tragic values in the myth make ironic the central figure's descent into the average, boring world of suburban commuters. Like Atwood and Broumas, Field uses colloquial language to underscore this transformation. The poem explores the idea that the mythic, heroic, and tragic can be reduced to the ordinary, common, and pathetic in the modern world.

In the first stanza, the speaker reviews the disaster, reduces it to the *usual drowning,* and rewrites the end of the myth; Icarus has *swum away* and come to the city, *where he rented a house and tended a garden* (line 9). The remaining stanzas explore Icarus's feelings and his place in this unexciting existence. The mythic figure in the suburban world of *neat front yards* and *commuter trains* embodies alienation and despair.

"Icarus" may be compared with the Odysseus poems beginning this chapter. All the poems more or less deal with the hero who goes on living long after the moment of glory, and who is puzzled, bored, and unhappy with the drabness of the uneventful life.

Writing topics. The way the mythic figure is undercut in the poem. The problem of Icarus in the modern suburban world: Why does Icarus, as an alienated figure who *wishes he had drowned,* seem to illustrate that the modern world can accommodate neither heroic aspiration nor tragic fall?

Writing About Myth in Poetry, *pages 834–838*

The key point here is that myth must be explored and written about in connection with some other aspect of the poem, such as speaker, tone, or meaning. Your students will be tempted to write a merely descriptive essay, noting and explaining in series the mythic allusions in a poem. When you assign an essay about myth in poetry, warn them to avoid such an exercise in description. The sample essay on Parker's "Penelope" (pages 836–837) illustrates how myth material may be connected with character and meaning.

Writing Topics for Myth, *page 838*

(1) The five poems illustrate a wide divergence of treatment. Students will thus find more material for differences than similarities. The task will be to relate these differences to similar topics (e.g., the wandering figure of excitement, the woman left behind, the yearning for adventure, the dismay at a life without danger, etc.) Use Appendix for help with the extended comparison-contrast.

(2) The topic of Icarus is somewhat different, because it brings out the plight of those experiencing misfortune and the responses of those who are not directly involved. For this subject, it is also essential to refer to the reproduction of Brueghel's painting.

(3) Rukuyser's "Myth" brings up the topic of feminism and inclusive language, a topic that goes far beyond the subject of Oedipus's misfortunes. Students undertaking to write on this question should make a special point to keep referring to "Myth" as they make their various points.

(4) The fourth direction suggests a freedom of selection of topic, which you might wish to limit, or about which you may want to confer. There are many examples of poems in the chapter which should give students guidance for transforming old materials within a contemporary context. As with most of the creative-writing assignments, it is important for students to turn critics of their own works, and try to recall and analyze how and why their treatments have taken the form they have created.

Chapter Twenty-three
Pages 839–864

Theme: Idea, Motif, and Meaning in Poetry

This chapter takes up in detail a topic that runs throughout all the poetry chapters—the theme or meaning of a poem (see also Chapter 10). In the introductory material, we attempt to describe the terms *theme, idea, motif,* and *meaning*. These are elusive, but *idea* refers to a thought or concept in the abstract; *theme* and *motif* are nearly identical terms referring to the operation of an idea in a work; and *meaning* is the product of idea, theme, and motif taken as a totality in relationship to the work. Once you make these initial distinctions, you can allow the concepts to flow back together, for they invariably do whenever people speak about literature.

Students sometimes present a simplification of the view in MacLeish's poem (page 851) that poetry should simply "be," and therefore they raise the question of whether poems must have themes at all. *Mutatis mutandis,* students sometimes believe that there is a "message" in every poem, and spend their time seeking one out, even inventing messages if they find that nothing comes immediately to mind.

The best teaching strategy is therefore to steer a middle course between too much and too little emphasis on theme. The discussion of *Strategies for Dealing with Meaning* (pages 842–844) pulls together all the ways of looking at poetry that we present in the text. The key idea to communicate in teaching is that every element of a poem *can* contribute to its theme and meaning. In any given poem, however, not all the elements will be equally important or effective. One of your goals in teaching poetry (and this chapter) might be to develop your students' ability to focus quickly on the poetic elements that are most prominent in creating meaning.

Donald Hall, *Whip-poor-will, page 845*

"Whip-poor-will" is firmly established in the countryside of farms and work. In this respect it is like many of the poems of Frost (see Chapter 25) and Kumin (pages 618, 959).

Answers to the Study Questions, page 845

(1, 2) The whippoorwill is an evening bird with a distinctive song that resembles the words "whip-poor-will." The song is vital in affecting the speaker's imagination when he is asleep. Rather than "whip-poor-will," the sound seems more like "Wes-ley-Wells," the name of the poet's grandfather, who inhabited and worked the property for fifty years. The connection between speaker and Wells is the property, the bird, the bed, the experience on the property, and the active life of keeping things going and keeping life together. The poem establishes all these links, thus showing how life and work continue from one generation of people to the next.

(3) The attention to the bird is an important means by which Hall establishes the reality of the situation. Logically, if such details are true and real, then the poet's conclusions will be sound and incontrovertible.

(4) The two poems both link the speaker with the sounds of birds, and both use the sounds to draw conclusions about the nature of life. In "Whip-poor-will," Hall's conclusion is that the bird and his grandfather symbolize the continuity of life and work (especially lines 20–26), while Keats's idea is that the bird's song symbolizes the mystery of the universe and the eternal nature of artistic beauty.

WRITING TOPICS. The bird as a symbol. The idea of continuity. The meaning of the concluding seven lines.

WORKS FOR COMPARISON WITH "WHIP-POOR-WILL"

Eliot, *Sweeney Among the Nightingales*, 799
Finch, *To the Nightingale*, 690
Smith, *Bluejays*, 989
Tate, *The Blue Booby*, 997

ROBERT HERRICK, *To the Virgins, to Make Much of Time, page 846*

Herrick's lyric, one of the carpe diem poems in the "Poems for Study" section of this chapter, is the most moral and least personal; the title indicates that it is addressed to a group rather than an individual.

Answers to the Study Questions, page 846

(1) The title clearly suggests that the listeners, who are "virgins," lose their virginity. The poem, however, suggests a moral avenue of sexuality ("go marry"). The speaker is not directly involved as a seducing participant, and is simply offering advice about how to live.

(2) Time, life, love, youth—all pass. They are given to us for use, and if we do not use them while we can, we will "forever tarry" (i.e., lose out totally on an aspect of life that was made for happiness and fulfillment).

(3) In stanza 1, the *rosebuds* symbolize life—here today and gone tomorrow. The *sun* (stanza 2) serves a parallel function; one day becomes a lifetime. The *carpe diem* theme is stated explicitly in stanzas 3 and 4.

(4) The pattern of rhyme in the stanzas alternates between rising rhymes in the first and third lines and trochaic rhymes in the second and fourth. The effect is both colloquial and natural; this is the way it is, in everyday, common speech. The tone of the poem is public, advisory, paternal, and hortatory; the speaker is concerned and moralistic.

(5) The speaker's advice that the virgins should *marry* emphasizes the distinctions between this poem and the two previous ones.

Writing topics. (For all the *carpe diem* poems included in the chapter.) Analyze speaker, tone, or theme. Comparison-contrast assignments might also be effective in dealing with these poems (see Appendix B). Marvell's poem also lends itself well to an analysis of imagery, and Herrick's to an analysis of rhyme.

Poems in the *Carpe Diem Tradition* for Comparison

Jonson, *To Celia*, 846
Marvell, *To His Coy Mistress*, 852

Ben Jonson, *To Celia, pages 846–847*

This is one of the three *carpe diem* poems in the chapter. In teaching it, you can show your students that meaning is a function of ideas, speaker, tone, and diction. The cynicism of Jonson's speaker is clear. In support of his quest for seduction, he argues that reputation is unimportant, and that Celia's husband can easily be deceived. His theme is that immediate action will satisfy desire; in short, that the ends justify the means. The total meaning combines these ideas with our emotional and intellectual rejection of the speaker's cynical position.

Answers to the Study Questions, page 847

(1) The speaker is presented as eager, cynical, and greedy, ready to prey upon those who are gullible and weak. In this respect he is a satiric figure who, in himself, illustrates the qualities being satirized. He wants to possess a woman who is not willing or available. He sees time as an enemy, love as a commodity, and Celia as an attractive object to be used.

(2) In lines 3–5, time is personified as an enemy who severs lives.

(3) The first eight lines contain the traditional *carpe diem* argument. The speaker asserts that he and Celia should act before *perpetual night* (death) overtakes them.

(4) The speaker shifts his ground at line 9; he is no longer concerned with time, but rather with reputation and the ease with which he and Celia may get away with their *theft*.

(5) The central idea emphasizes the speaker's cynical amorality; he asserts that an act is a crime only if one is caught at it (lines 15–18). The diction also emphasizes the speaker's demeaning and cynical tone; phrases like *sports of love* and *sweet theft* trivialize love (sex) and demean Celia. The argument is thus undercut by the cynical tone and amoral attitude.

Writing topics. The character of the speaker. The situation of the poem and the structure of the speaker's argument. The meaning of "carpe diem" as presented in the poem. The flaws in the speaker's argument.

Poems in the *Carpe Diem Tradition* for Comparison

Herrick, *To the Virgins, to Make Much of Time,* 846
Marvell, *To His Coy Mistress,* 852

Donald Justice, *On the Death of Friends in Childhood, page 847*

This short poem recalls Dryden's "To the Memory of Mr. Oldham" (page 763) in its brevity and poignancy, and also in its conclusion; Justice's friends are in the "shadows," while Oldham is encompassed by "fate and gloomy night." "On the Death of Friends" is extremely sad, even though it mentions no specific friends. The concern of the poem is more about the living, and the dimming of our intellectual lights, than about the dead themselves.

Answers to the Study Questions, page 847

(1) While the subject of the poem may be friends who died in childhood, the theme concerns the difficulty or even impossibility of recovering the past through memory.

(2) Time stops for the dead children; they will not grow beards or become bald in heaven or hell. For the speaker and reader, however, time produces change; we no longer remember the names of the games we played.

(3) The first two lines present images of heaven and hell, and the speaker rejects these locations as being real. "If anywhere," then, memories of the dead might be revived in real locations where we knew them

and played with them, even though we have forgotten the exact circumstances of our experiences. The tone suggested by "bearded" and "sunning themselves" is mildly comic and somewhat regretful (can we believe that dead souls in hell sun themselves by the fires there?). The rhetorical strategy of the poem is the exploration of the "decaying sense" of our memory of the past: We lose everything—our memory of others, our youthful beliefs, and our memories even of our own past. The concluding personification of memory as a guide to help us search for images of the lost friends in the "shadows" (a pun on the darkness of twilight and also the shades or ghosts of the dead) is a fitting climax for this sad and wistful poem.

Writing topics. The tone of the poem. The topic: death of friends or the death of memory? Also, questions 2 and 3.

Works for Comparison with "On the Death of Friends in Childhood"

Field, *Icarus,* 833
Heyen, *Mantle*, 768

John Keats, *Ode on a Grecian Urn, pages 848–849*

A major idea of Keats is explored extensively in "Ode on a Grecian Urn." This is the contrast between the inability of human beings to comprehend the mysteries of art and the universe. Even the song of a bird in a tree represents more than human beings, with their "dull brain(s)," can encompass ("Ode to a Nightingale," page 770). We know, or think we know, what we see and hear, but we have no understanding, words, or ability to describe the ultimate realities which underlie our earthly experiences. We create and see fine things and attribute beauty to them, and these give us our only hints at the immense and vast but still unseen universe of truth that remains beyond our small abilities to understand. It is in this sense that beauty is truth and truth is beauty.

Students might want to compare the poem with the photo of the Grecian vase (page 849). Keats could have seen many such vases in the British Museum. Most probably he was imagining a composite vase, for there is not enough space on ancient vases for all the details he describes.

Answers to the Study Questions, page 850

(1) The ode suggests a dramatic situation; the speaker is contemplating the urn and the reader overhears the resulting meditation.

(2) The paradoxical nature of the urn is established immediately through phrases like *unravished bride* and *foster child of silence and slow time;* the urn exists in real time but is little touched by it. Paradox continues in the description of the figures on the urn (gods or men, eternal or mortal) and in the contrast between the energy (passion) figured on the urn and the calm silence of the urn itself. The urn is a *sylvan historian* that can sing a better song than the poet (*our rhyme*) because it has already transcended time. The images are eternal; the poet's words are temporal.

(3) *Unheard* melodies and "ditties of no tone" are heard in the mind (imagination) rather than through the *sensual ear.* In other words, the idea (Platonic ideal) of the song (poetry, art, beauty) is more permanent than the actual song itself.

(4) Three sets of images are developed in stanzas 1–3 to show this concept of the ideal: nature (leaf-fringed border, tree that will never lose its leaves), love (pursuit, lovers who will never kiss), and music (pipes and timbrels, the youth who will never leave his song). All these images are frozen in time on the urn, unchanging and eternal. These are contrasted (in stanza 3) to *human passion* that leaves only sickness and sorrow.

To this point, Keats has developed paradoxes that oppose real and ideal; these reach a climax in stanza 5. The urn is a silent form and a Cold Pastoral (both contradictory). It is also a "friend to man" because it tells us that "Beauty is truth, truth beauty" (line 49). Keats sustains the *oxymora* of the urn and the poem throughout. Both poem and urn ask us to balance in our minds the real (time, change) and the ideal (permanence, eternity) simultaneously. Ultimately, of course, human beings cannot understand, and thus both urn and poem, like eternity, "tease us out of thought."

WRITING TOPICS. The distinction between heard and unheard melodies. The importance of art and the inadequacy of human beings to understand both human and universal creation. The nature of Keats's speaker.

WORKS FOR COMPARISON WITH "ODE ON A GRECIAN URN"

Shakespeare, *Not Marble, Nor the Gilded Monuments,* 560
Shelley, *Ode to the West Wind,* 776

PHILIP LARKIN, *Next, Please, page 850*

(Questions 1–4) This poem, discussed in the sample essay (pages 861–862), can be taught with the *carpe diem* group at the beginning of the chapter. Any of the questions can be adapted as topics for writing.

WRITING TOPICS. The meaning of the metaphor of the "armada of promises." The nature of the speaker. The mood of the poem's conclusion.

WORKS FOR COMPARISON WITH "NEXT, PLEASE"

Dickinson, *Because I Could Not Stop for Death*, 555
Frost, *The Road Not Taken*, 898
Gray, *Elegy Written in a Country Churchyard*, 579

ARCHIBALD MACLEISH, *Ars Poetica, page 851*

The poem explores the question of meaning versus being. In a real sense, "Ars Poetica" asserts that poems and poets can have it both ways—that a poem can mean and be at the same time.

Answers to the Study Questions, pages 851–852

(1, 2) The first section tells us that a poem should be mute, dumb, silent, and wordless—an apparent paradox, for poems are made of words. But MacLeish explains through similes that the meaning of poems is communicated not mentally but through the feelings, much as people experience fruit, metalwork, statuary, and the flight of birds.

(3) The second section of the poem explains how paradoxes about poetry, such as being motionless and yet climbing at the same time, may be resolved. The moon appears to be stationary, yet over an entire night it moves, rising in the east, crossing the sky, and setting in the west. "Motionless," like "wordless," has more to do with the way we perceive things than it does with apparent actuality. Just as the moonlight releases shadows of trees "twig by twig," so a poem should penetrate the mind "memory by memory," in this way timelessly altering the consciousness of the reader. The lines opening the section also close it. This repetition, as it were, emphasizes the constancy and generality of the poetic experience.

(4) The third section treats the poem as an aspect of life itself. Poetry has nothing to do with "truth" (line 18), for it is not scientific; instead, it is the same as experience, in this way taking on reality without any need for analysis or proof. Whether for grief or love, poetry creates images that touch the human spirit, such as the sadness of "an empty doorway and a maple leaf" or the commonness of the "leaning grasses" or the rareness of "two lights above the sea."

(5) "Ars Poetica" asserts that poems should create a "palpable" set of perceptions that parallel all of life's experiences. The methods of poetry are imagery, metaphor, and symbolism. MacLeish also makes clear that

the experience of poetry is more important than either the words that create it or the intellectual judgments of readers. In that sense, a poem is "mute" and "wordless," and in that sense the poem takes on life, the being and existence of great art. The concluding line is a famous climax of all these ideas.

Writing topics. The poem's paradoxes about poetry. The relationship of art to experience. How poetry is unlike other intellectual forms of expression.

Works for Comparison with "Ars Poetica"

Moore, *Poetry*, 853
Shakespeare, *Not Marble, Nor the Gilded Monuments*, 560
Shelley, *Ode to the West Wind*, 776
Spenser, *One Day I Wrote Her Name upon the Strand*, 856

Andrew Marvell, *To His Coy Mistress, pages 852–853*

This is one of the most famous *carpe diem* poems. Your students may know it, but it will always yield new surprises in class discussion. In teaching, you might focus on the connotation of *coy*, and then consider the logic of the poem, the hyperbole of the first section, and the shifting imagery throughout. The poem is in iambic tetrameter rhymed couplets, and it contains some effective rhyming pairs (e.g., *dust/lust*). The title identifies the characters; the speaker, a would-be lover, addresses his coy (reluctant, playing hard-to-get) lady. *Coy* is a loaded word here; it certainly does not suggest virtue.

Answers to the Study Questions, page 853

(1) In lines 1–20, the speaker sets up a hypothetical situation (*Had we*) in which there would be large amounts of space and time in which to engage slowly in preliminaries to making love. The argument will be, of course, that the world does not furnish these amounts.

(2) Geographical references to the *Ganges* and *Humber* Rivers place the lovers on opposite sides of the earth (use a map or get your students to imagine one). The allusions to Noah's flood and the conversion of the Jews evoke a huge span of time (from Genesis to the Last Judgment). The amatory arithmetic associated with the speaker's admiration of each part of his mistress is extravagantly exaggerated—an ideal example of hyperbole.

(3) The hypothetical *world enough and time* are negated in lines 21–32; the word *But* identifies and begins the refutation. Time is personified

as an ever-pursuing enemy (line 22). The lines are full of images of death and the grave, all suggesting sterility, dryness, dust, and isolation (*quaint virtue* in line 29 is a sexual *double entendre*).

(4) The third stage of the argument (lines 33–46) offers the speaker's logical conclusion: *Now therefore* we should act with urgency and immediacy to "tear our pleasures with rough strife / Thorough the iron gates of life." The imagery suggests moist heat (*dew, fires*) and violence, all pointing toward urgency. The image of *amorous birds of prey* is both playful and daring. By looking at diction and tone in class, students can see the differences between this poem and Jonson's "To Celia" (page 846). The speaker here is much more playful and witty, without any of the demeaning cynicism of Jonson's speaker. The effect of Marvell's poem, however, is one of philosophical sobriety, far removed from immediate action.

Writing topics. The logical development of the poem. The tone: cynical or serious? The character of the speaker. The meaning. The use of exaggeration. The meaning of "carpe diem" as shown in the poem.

Poems in the *Carpe Diem Tradition* for Comparison

Herrick, *To the Virgins, to Make Much of Time,* 846
Jonson, *To Celia,* 846

Marianne Moore, *Poetry, pages 853–854*

This poem may be considered with the "poetry" group contained in this chapter. Once the title announces the subject, the poem argues that there is a place and a purpose for *genuine* poetry that deals with real experience in imaginative ways. Like "Ars Poetica" (page 851), Moore's poem defines poetry by demonstration as well as explanation. It is full of the raw materials of life, and real poetry must be organized to create an emotional and intellectual response.

Answers to the Study Questions, page 854

(1) The diction and stance here suggest that the tone initially is tongue-in-cheek. The speaker is presumably an ordinary person who treats literature, specifically poetry, as something that should be alive and important, and not "fiddle." She is addressing someone who has just said that he, or she, dislikes poetry, and the speaker begins the argument on the listener's side. This preemptive stance is reversed by the *however* in line 2, for her intent is to explain the good qualities of poetry. In lines 5–8, the speaker claims that poetry can be useful because of the emotional responses it evokes.

(2) The subject is that people often consider poetry as distant and remote, a claim that the speaker rebuts. The theme is that, to the degree that poetry is genuine, it deserves admiration and interest.

(3) The speaker in effect denies the original claim, for in demonstrating that poetry is not "fiddle" written by "half poets," but rather is the raw and genuine, she points out that she is really "interested" in poetry.

(4) The speaker considers a series of things (animal and human) that we cannot understand and therefore do not admire: "critic," "baseball fan," and "statistician." All these things are important, but must be distinguished from genuine poetry. Such poetry can develop only if poets become literalists of the imagination and convey real emotion and experience. This idea is stressed in the poem's last five lines, where the speaker suggests that poetry is valuable and interesting if it embodies the real and *raw* aspects of life.

Writing topics. The poem's ideas about poetry. An analysis of the speaker.

Works for Comparison with "Poetry"

MacLeish, *Ars Poetica,* 851
Shakespeare, *Not Marble, Nor the Gilded Monuments,* 560
Shelley, *Ode to the West Wind,* 776
Spenser, *One Day I Wrote Her Name upon the Strand,* 856

Sharon Olds, *35/10, pages 854–855*

Olds uses a domestic context to explore the idea that life is cyclical and that children replace adults. The first sixteen lines make these points metaphorically through imagery and language; the last two lines state them directly. The total meaning grows out of the situation and setting, action, language, and the emotions the poem evokes.

Answers to the Study Questions, page 855

(1) The speaker is a 35-year-old mother who is brushing her ten-year-old daughter's hair at bedtime.

(2) The idea of youth's displacing and replacing age is conveyed in three sets of images related to hair (*dark, gray),* skin (*fine, dry*), and sexuality (images of ovaries as an empty or bursting purse).

(3) As with Pastan's "Ethics" (pages 855–856), emotional engagement with the poem may depend on the reader's ability to experience (or imagine) age.

Writing topics. The comparison of youth and age. The meaning of replacement.

Works for Comparison with "35/10"

Hall, *Whip-poor-will*, 845
Millay, *What Lips My Lips Have Kissed*, 967
Olsen, *I Stand Here Ironing*, 526
Justice, *On the Death of Friends in Childhood*, 847

Linda Pastan, *Ethics, pages 855–856*

This poem concerns an imponderable question, and it does not give a hard-and-fast answer. Perhaps the concern itself is as far as people can go, for their actions may not have influence beyond the specific things they do.

Answers to the Study Questions, page 856

(1) The speaker is a thoughtful person who has benefited from the ethical question raised in her ethics class "so many years ago." However, she is not nearer an exact answer than she was when young, except that her adult thought is that all things are valuable, but that their existence does not depend upon the power of individuals.

(2) In the poem there are two distinct situations (school, museum), and a shift of time and place at line 17. The speaker's response to the ethical question clearly changes, and the poem thus explores the shallowness of youth and the mature consciousness about the impermanence of both art and life.

(3) In lines 1–16, the speaker recalls the ethics classes of her youth and the recurring question about the burning museum. The problem was irrelevant to the young people; they were caring little and chose one answer or the other "half-heartedly." Even when the speaker attempted to personalize the issue by imagining that the old woman was her grandmother (lines 9–16), the matter was of little consequence.

(4) One may claim that the subject of the poem is that growth does not produce absolute knowledge. The theme is that ethical judgments are eternally difficult, for art, life, time and values are almost the same, and all are beyond saving by children (line 25).

Writing topics. The meaning as conveyed though speaker, setting and situation, imagery, or diction.

Works for Comparison with "Ethics"

Dickinson, *After Great Pain*, 884
Frost, *A Considerable Speck*, 902
Jacobsen, *Tears*, 803
Jeffers, *The Answer*, 956

Edmund Spenser, *Amoretti 75: One Day I Wrote Her Name Upon the Strand, page 856*

This poem demonstrates the traditional concern about perpetuating life. Even if we die, the argument goes, our immortality is conferred by the power of verse—an idea that people of the Renaissance borrowed from ancient classical writers.

Answers to the Study Questions, page 856

(1) In lines 1–4, the speaker explains that he and his mistress were on the beach; he wrote her name in the sand twice and each time the waves washed it away. In lines 5–8 the lady draws the obvious moral from these events; she sees the speaker's efforts to *immortalize* here as *vain* (arrogant, proud) and *in vain* (useless). She asserts that she will die and her *name* (memory) will be *wiped out* just as the writing is washed away.

(2) In lines 9–12, the speaker says that the lady will live forever in his verse. The couplet asserts that their "love shall live" beyond the end of the world. While the subject of the poem is therefore the brevity of mortal life and love, the theme is that poetry can immortalize emotions and relationships.

(3) Spenser employs a modified English sonnet form (Spenserian sonnet; iambic pentameter: *abab bcbc cdcd ee*) to organize action and ideas. Each quatrain presents a distinct step in the poet's development of the idea, yet each is linked to the next through rhyme.

Writing topics. The ideas of the speaker or the lady. Setting, situation, and meaning. The idea of immortality through art.

Works for Comparison with "One Day I Wrote Her Name"

MacLeish, *Ars Poetica*, 851
Moore, *Poetry*, 853
Shakespeare, *Not Marble, Nor the Gilded Monuments*, 560
Shelley, *Ode to the West Wind*, 776

JUDITH VIORST, *True Love, page 857*

The ideas about love in this comic and honest poem are valuable for people at any age.

Answers to the Study Questions, page 858

(1) Although the poem is an amusing review of married life, its concluding statement is serious: "We still feel something / We can call / True love." There are no romantic pretensions about this "True love," but in light of the previous material in the poem, the poem asserts that love can last—must last—through many trials.

(2) Most of the poem is devoted to anti-romantic details about daily aspects of married life, such as contrasting views about watching football, wishing death on the husband in preference to his having an affair, "acid indigestion," and so on. They are important in the wife-husband relationship because they are an inevitable and necessary aspect of real life as it is actually lived, not as it is dreamed.

(3) There are many comic situations and statements in the poem, such as lines 9, 17–18, 20–21, and so on. Because of the reality of such situations in life, and because marriage is the part of life the poet is discussing, these situations draw assent about the day-by-day difficulties that life brings. Because the poem's comic view of life makes no claim that elements of daily living are disasters or causes for divisiveness in marriage, they undergird the idea that "true love" must be positive enough to persist even under negative circumstances.

(4) These lines resemble the kinds of things people save up for inclusion during a family argument. They are minor climaxes of the development of the poem, and focus the poem's negative but nevertheless comic details. The other lines of the poem either lead up to these passages or represent conclusions drawn from them.

WRITING TOPICS. Is the idea of "true love" in the poem romantic or anti-romantic? Can "true love" sustain the "hate" situations like those described in lines 21 and 24?

WORKS FOR COMPARISON WITH "TRUE LOVE"

Atwood, *Variation on the Word Sleep*, 915
Donne, *The Canonization*, 871
Heaney, *Valediction*, 950
Lawrence, *The Horse Dealer's Daughter*, 393
Wakoski, *The Ring*, 1004

William Wordsworth, *Daffodils (I Wandered Lonely as a Cloud), page 858*

This poem demonstrates a characteristic aspect of Wordsworth's thought. He is a Romantic poet, and includes Nature as one of his major topics. He is not, however, a poet who provides botanical details about flowers and trees (though in an early draft of one poem he measures the dimensions of a puddle: "I've measured it from side to side. / 'Tis three feet long and two feet wide." Instead, what Wordsworth wants from Nature is evidence of divine or universal power. To him, the invisible strength of the universe, together with the consequent shaping of human character, come mystically through the interactions of human beings and natural phenomena. To Wordsworth, this same mystic power constitutes the subject of poetry and causes the development of the poetic mind.

Answers to the Study Questions, page 859

(1) The occasion is that the speaker is alone, and observes a vast array of springtime daffodils blooming beside a lake. The solitude is important because it permits the direct connection, without interference, of the speaker and the scene.

(2) The participles *fluttering, dancing,* and *tossing,* together with the verbs *stretched, out-did,* and *had brought*—all suggest the living vitality of the flowers. The idea about Nature is that the vegetative world, like the Natural world generally, is not dead, but living, and is a direct manifestation of the universal power of life.

(3) The key to the poem is the fourth stanza, in which the speaker describes the effect that the scene has upon him. He keeps the memory, and in later times, when he is alone "In vacant or in pensive mood," the scene floods his consciousness, and the pleasure fills his heart. This process is not only one of happiness, but is also a creative, constructive, re-creative one which provides the speaker with strength and renewal.

Writing topics. The use of verbs and verbals. The meaning of the experience with the daffodils. The relationship of the Natural world to the human.

Works for Comparison with Wordsworth's "Daffodils"

Arnold, *Dover Beach,* 576
Hopkins, *God's Grandeur,* 722
MacNeice, *Snow,* 558

Writing About Theme and Meaning in Poetry, *pages 859–863*

Prewriting and organization here are important because theme and meaning can be approached from so many different directions (reviewed on pages 859–861). It is often necessary to warn students that in a single essay they cannot consider every element that contributes to meaning—indeed, they probably should not—and therefore it is necessary that they consider only those elements that are most significant and striking. The sample essay on Larkin's "Next, Please" (pages 861–862) illustrates the way meaning can be explored through the device of metaphor. Your students should be encouraged to read this essay and the commentary before they plan their own essays.

Writing Topics for Theme and Meaning in Poetry, *pages 863–864*

(1) Some materials for this essay may be found on page 844. An extended comparison-contrast essay might be augmented with library sources, and if it reaches this scope it might serve as the final essay in your course. Please ask your students to consult Appendix B, on Comparison-Contrast, for guidance in writing. If research materials are to be used, please ask them to use Appendix C, on Research.

(2) The subject matter of the four poems is divergent, but they all share the topics of aging and death. Wordsworth concentrates on how present experience influences and therefore changes the individual through time. Pastan is concerned with the ethical question of choice in both youth and age. Olds wonders about the "replacement" of age by youth. Justice explains the loss not only of childhood friends but also of adult memory. A comparison-contrast of the four works should emphasize the common thread of growth, aging, continuity, replacement, and change, together with the diverging ways in which the poets treat the topic.

(3) This question concerns what is perhaps Keats's most famous sentence. People quote it freely without adequate explanation, and sometimes do so inappropriately. To assign the topic for an essay, therefore, requires a good deal of thought for your students. The study questions for the Grecian Urn Ode (page 850) should be carefully considered in the preliminary and prewriting stages of the essay. Students might also need to discuss the topic of universals and particulars as it is applicable to Keats's poem. For this they will need your guidance.

(4) The creative-writing topic might at first seem to require a discursive poem, which might in some respects become an essay in brief. But if students are reminded that literature communicates ideas through metaphors and symbols, together with word choices, etc., they will see that a narrative or descriptive framework for their poems will be satisfactory as long as the events and details are carefully included. Their brief essays explaining their practices and procedures as poets will also enable them to show how they have applied the principles of Chapter 23.

Chapter Twenty-Four
Pages 865–909

Poetic Careers: The Work of Three Poets

◆ John Donne – pages 865–877

The Good Morrow, page 869

1 • What can you deduce about the speaker? Listener? Setting and situation?

2 • What powers are attributed to love in the second and third stanzas?

3 • How do the images of worlds (globes, spheres) emphasize the power of love?

4 • What ideas about love and passion does the poem explore?

The speaker (a lover) praises his beloved and their passion by comparing them favorably to all his previous romances; he sees their previous lives as a sleep or infancy. The *good morrow* refers to the awakening of their love and the actual events—two lovers awakening in bed. The second stanza takes up the power of love—it controls emotion and perception—and begins an extended conceit on the image of *worlds.* The speaker creates a clear distinction between the public world (*sea-discoverers, new worlds, maps),* and the private world of the lovers that becomes an *everywhere* (see the sample essay, pages 906–908, for a discussion of this imagery). The one world of the lovers becomes two (line 14) and then the two *hemispheres* of eyeballs reflecting faces (lines 15–16), finally resolving back into a single world *Without sharp North, without declining West* (line 18). The tone is exaggerated and affirmative; love and passion are presented as valuable and powerful.

Song: Go and Catch a Falling Star, pages 870–871

1 • What closed form is employed? What building blocks com-

bine to form each stanza? How do rhyme and meter affect meaning and impact?

2 • What does the speaker want the listener to do? What do all the actions in stanza 1 have in common?

3 • What idea about women does this poem explore? What is the speaker's tone? How does the tone contribute to meaning?

The theme here is that no woman can be *fair* (beautiful) and *true* (loyal, honest) at the same time. The speaker lists a series of impossible tasks in stanza 1 to establish an aura of cynicism and difficulty; some of these (envy, the lack of advancement for honest minds) evoke social ills. The second stanza introduces the impossibility of the woman who is both true and fair. The third reinforces this cynical view by claiming that such a woman would become *false* before the speaker could meet her. The lyric is composed of three stanzas, each of which combines a quatrain, couplet, and triplet into a single sentence (iambic, *4a 4b 4a 4b 4c 4c 1d 4d*); the pattern of stanza 1 is repeated in 2 and 3. Rhyme (e.g., *singing/stinging*) and the short seventh and eighth lines of each stanza are especially effective in clinching meaning.

The Sun Rising, page 871

1 • What can you deduce about the speaker? His companion? The setting and situation? To whom is the poem addressed?

2 • What does the speaker tell the sun to do in stanza 1? What distinction is created between worlds? What is the connection of time to love?

3 • What conceit is developed in stanzas 2 and 3?

4 • What does the poem suggest about the power of love?

This lyric (*abbacdcdee*) is similar to "The Good Morrow"; it asserts that love is all-powerful and consuming. The speaker and his beloved (in bed) have been wakened by the sun (*busy old fool*). The speaker tells the sun to deal with the public world (*school boys, apprentices, huntsmen, farmers*) since love creates a private world detached from time. The conceit of spatial manipulation in stanzas 2 and 3 suggests that love can control space, making the lovers and their bed into an entire world. Donne pulls more and more of the cosmos into bed with the lovers; the Indies, *all states, all princes,* and the solar system.

The Canonization, pages 871–873

1 • What does *canonization* mean? Who is canonized in the poem? Why?

2 • How does the speaker defend his love in the first two stanzas?

3 • What mythic and religious mysteries are linked with love/sex in stanza 3?

4 • What canonizes and immortalizes the lovers? What will future lovers ask of these *saints* of love? What does the poem finally imply about love?

This lyric is a defense of love and passion in which both are linked with mysteries of myth and religion. The poem explores the idea that love transforms lovers into *saints* who may become exemplars for future lovers. In stanzas 1–2, the speaker defends his love affair against the objections of an unnamed critic; he tells the critic to mind his/her own business, and suggests that this critic might more profitably go out into the public world, for he, the speaker, and his sweetheart have not *injured* anyone or anything. In stanza 3, Donne employs symbols (*eagle* and *dove),* allusion (the *phoenix*) and sexual puns (*die* = to achieve orgasm) to emphasize the mysterious, overwhelming power of love. The reference to the phoenix and the phrase *die and rise* point toward both resurrection and the reawakening of sexual desire after orgasm. In the fourth stanza, the speaker claims that his and his lady's love will be chronicled in verse (this very poem) and the lovers will thus be canonized and immortalized—they will become saints of love. Future lovers (quoted in lines 37–45) will pray to these saints for a *pattern* of love. The poem thus explores both the power of love and the immortality of verse.

A Fever, page 873

1 • To whom is the poem addressed? What is the relationship between speaker and listener? What's wrong with the listener?

2 • What does the speaker claim that his lover's death would do to the world?

3 • What is the tone of the poem? What point does the speaker finally make about his love? Does the tone emphasize or undercut this point?

The speaker addresses this lyric (*abab, cdcd,* etc.) to a person, presumably his wife or sweetheart, who is sick with a fever. To show the power of the speaker's love, and also the strength of his wit, Donne uses overstatement in equating the fever with the apocalyptic fire that, according to tradition, will end the world and bring on the Day of Judgment. Stanza 1 introduces the paradox of hating all women if the mistress dies. Stanzas 2–4 develop the idea of the lady's fever as the fire that will destroy the world. Stanzas 5 and 6 are based on the idea that fevers are fueled by impurities; since the lady is made of *unchangeable firmament,* the fever cannot last long. The situation would suggest the need for the speaker to be uplifting and amusing; a sick person, after all, needs support and assurance. The conclusion, however, reveals the deep concern and the deep love of the speaker, who speaks of "all else ever," which might be construed as overstatement but which may be taken as absolutely sincere.

The Flea, page 874

1 • Consider the poem as a play. Who are the characters? What action occurs?

2 • What does the speaker want? How does he use the flea's bite and the flea metaphorically? What does the lady do to the flea before stanza 3? How does the speaker adjust his argument to reflect this event?

3 • What is the poem's tone? How does form echo meaning? To what extent does rhyme unify the poem?

"The Flea" is a witty and ingenious song of seduction in which a young man (the speaker) attempts to convince a young lady (the listener) to make love. The poem is dramatic; the tone is tongue-in-cheek; and the argument is both logical and bizarre. Before the first stanza, the flea has bitten the speaker and then jumped to the lady. The speaker claims that this mingling of blood (a metaphor here for sexual relations) is not a sin or loss. The flea *enjoys* before marriage, but the lady denies such joy to herself and the speaker. The phrase *pampered swells* (line 8) is an oblique reference to pregnancy. Before the second stanza, the lady threatens to swat the flea. Now, the speaker's logic and imagery become more bizarre. He claims that the flea has become three individuals (the lover, the lady, the flea), and he expands the image (flea) until the lovers are *cloistered* within the flea's black sides even though the lady and her parents reject (*grudge*) sex. Between stanzas 2 and 3 the lady kills the flea. The speaker readjusts his argument and equates the flea's death with sex, claiming that giving in to his demands will be just as painless and insignificant as the flea's death. The tone is witty and ingenious. We sense no urgency or sincerity in this display.

Holy Sonnet 6: This Is My Play's Last Scene, pages 874–875

1 • List the metaphors for life and death that occur in the first six lines.

2 • What distinction is made between the body and the soul?

3 • What is the subject of this meditation? What does the speaker want?

This Petrarchan sonnet (*abba abba cdcd ee*) is a meditation on death and salvation. The first two quatrains focus on the moment of death, which is evoked by seven metaphors that imply an ending. The body will become earth, but the soul will see God's face. The last six lines focus on salvation and the purgation of sin. The form of the sonnet organizes the meditation and the ideas; the rhymes (e.g., *evil/devil*) emphasize the meaning.

Holy Sonnet 7: At The Round Earth's Imagined Corners, page 875

1 • How does the sonnet form organize the poem's movement and meaning?

2 • What moment is imagined in lines 1–8? What is listed in the second quatrain?

3 • What does the speaker reveal about his own spiritual state in lines 9–14?

Like most of Donne's Holy Sonnets, this one begins as a meditation on a specific moment—the apocalypse and Judgment Day. Lines 1–8 (*abba abba*) create a vivid and immediate image of bodies rising from their graves for judgment; lines 5–8 contain a catalogues of those who will rise from the dead or more directly to judgment from life. In lines 9–14 (*cdcd ee*), the speaker reflects on his own spiritual corruption; he prays for more time to repent his sins and to seek God's grace.

Holy Sonnet 10: Death Be Not Proud, page 875

1 • What human characteristics does the speaker attribute to death? What does the speaker tell death about those whom death thinks it has overthrown?

2 • To what is death compared in lines 5–6? What men die "soonest"? What powers control death? What do all these facts suggest about death?

3 • Explain and resolve the paradox in line 14. Is the sonnet finally about death or about salvation? Explain.

4 • Formulate the rhyme scheme of this sonnet. What type of rhyme predominates? How does rhyme divide the poem into coherent units of thought? To what extent does it echo and emphasize meaning?

This is Donne's best-known sonnet. A meditation on death and salvation, its apparent paradoxes are all resolved by the idea of death as the beginning of eternal life. In this respect, it might be compared with Shakespeare's Sonnet 146, "Poor Soul" (page 986).

The rhyme scheme here organizes the poem into three quatrains and a couplet. The first two quatrains are linked by repeated rhymes (iambic pentameter: *abba, abba, cddc, ee*). In the first quatrain, the speaker characterizes death as needlessly proud, for death really does not have the power to "overthrow" or "kill" anyone. The second quatrain presents two interesting put-downs of death. The speaker claims that death is only another version of "rest and sleep," which are both sources of pleasure. Then, he argues that the "best men" go to death "soonest," implying that death creates a state that people should not fear but envy. The speaker continues to belittle death in the third quatrain, observing that it is controlled by ("slave to") "fate, chance, kings, and desperate men" and resides with "poison, war, and sickness." The paradox in the couplet resolves in the realization that death is the way to eternal life. Donne's sonnet thus explores the idea that death is powerless and insignificant compared to salvation and Divine Grace.

Donne's rhymes are mostly exact and rising, thus helping to make the poem both powerful and memorable. Interesting (and often antithetical) rhyming pairs include "thee-me-be-delivery," "dwell-well," and "eternally-die." The last rhyme, occurring in the couplet, sums up the basic opposition that runs through the poem as a theme. One might recall that the rhyme might still have been exact in Donne's time, for the "Great Vowel Shift" had not fully effected the diphthong sound of / *ay* / that we pronounce today.

A Hymn to God the Father, page 876

1 • To whom is the poem spoken? What does the speaker think about his own spiritual state? What are his sins? What does he want?

2 • What puns do you find? How do they affect tone and meaning?

This poem, a prayer spoken to God, is a confession of sins in which the speaker catalogues his own corruption and seeks divine grace. An important pun is the traditional one on sun-son (*Thy sun* = Son). The speaker's sins are listed in lines 1–14; the request for grace is voiced in lines 15–18. The central pun is on *done* (Donne). In stanzas 1–2, God's work is not *done* and God has not redeemed Donne because the speaker has *more* (sins). Some scholars suggest that *more* is also a pun on the name of Donne's wife (Anne More).

Hymn to God My God, in My Sickness, pages 876–877

1 • What is the situation described by the speaker in the poem? What is about to happen to the speaker?

2 • How does the speaker use a world map as a symbol? What does the map symbolize? What other geographical references are contained in the poem? What do these signify?

3 • Describe the use of the "first Adam" and "last Adam" references? What do they signify? With what paradox does the poem conclude?

"Hymn to God My God, in My Sickness" is reputedly the last poem that Donne wrote, apparently on his death bed (pages 867, 868). One may conclude that even if he was deathly ill, his mind was still powerful. His speaker begins the poem by referring to his impending death, describing the death as "coming to that Holy Room" where he shall become one with the holy music of God.

In the second stanza Donne shifts to one of the poem's major metaphors, namely that the speaker's attending physicians become "cosmographers." Interestingly, this is a metaphor of the person as the world that Donne uses throughout much of his other poetry, as, for example, in "The Sun Rising" (page 871), in which the world becomes "contracted" into the lovers, so that "She is all states, and all princes, I." Here, in this religious context, the image of the world/person indicates that the speaker, like the world, contains a point where "West and East"—that is, death and life—touch and become one. The metaphor thus claims that the transition made by death is not great, because "death doth touch the Resurrection" (line 15). The other geographical references, such as those of Magellan and Gibraltar, are introduced as reinforcement of the map image. All the locations are entrances to richness; by metaphorical transfer, therefore, death marks an entrance to the richness of eternal life.

Closely related to this metaphor is Donne's movement of the poem into the "first Adam" and "last Adam" references, all of which are derived from Paul's First Epistle to the Corinthians (see especially I Cor. 15:22). The speaker's claim of identity with the sweat of Adam (i.e., humanity) and the "last Adam's blood" (divinity) continues the poem's treatment of the living-through-dying metaphor. Donne's stress of the blood of Christ wrapping the speaker "in purple" (line 26) is similar to the imagery evoked by Crashaw in "On Our Crucified Lord, Naked and Bloody" (page 639).

◆ Emily Dickinson, pages 877–891

I Never Lost as Much But Twice, page 881

1 • To what degree is it necessary to know the specific occasions to which the speaker is referring in this poem?

2 • What situation does the speaker propose for herself as a petitioner before God?

3 • What is the religious basis of the image of the beggar at the door?

4 • What is the effect in this poem of Dickinson's use of internal rhyme?

1. Biographers of Dickinson cite the deaths of two men and a woman as having had a profound effect on her. The departure of Charles Wadsworth to live in San Francisco also disturbed her with a sense of deep loss and may indeed be the third loss which she mentions (see page 878). It is not clear from the poem, however, just exactly whose loss the speaker is mourning. Regardless of the specific causes, the poem itself stands alone as an expression not of the speaker's grief but rather as an expression of her need or consolation, for this topic is the major substance.

2. The speaker envisages an idea of wealth and loss. Twice she has lost her substance and twice she has been a beggar asking God for help. She received help twice, but now a new loss has occurred and she is again

poor. The imagery intimating that God is a "Burglar" complicates the speaker's attitudes, however, for this word calls into question the assumption that God is always and eternally good. Dickinson may be asking readers to recall the saying that "The Lord giveth, and the Lord taketh away," except that she is not asking us to add the usual "Blessed be the name of the Lord."

3. The beggar as a person whom God raises from the dust is contained in I Samuel 2:8. Bartimaeus, a blind beggar, sat at the side of the road in Mark 10:48, and Jesus, on the way to Jerusalem, restored his sight. The "door" of God may refer to John 10:9, "I am the door." Lazarus the beggar of course was given the heavenly reward of sitting in Abraham's bosom (Luke 16:23). The image of human beings as beggars-petitioners, and of God as the giver of alms, is therefore well established scripturally.

4. The *-ore* sound occurs five times in *Before, door, store, poor,* and *more,* even though it is a concluding rhyme only in lines 6 and 8. Because the poem is so short, the sound itself becomes a prominent internal rhyme, stressing the idea of the emotional impoverishment of the speaker and therefore of her need for divine restoration.

Success is Counted Sweetest, page 882

1 • Describe the main idea of this poem.

2 • What example is developed in lines 5–12? How does this example develop the idea of the first stanza?

3 • Describe Dickinson's use of metrical form in this poem. How does the form operate in the first stanza? In the second and third?

4 • Consider the nature of Dickinson's diction in this poem. Would you classify it as specific, general, concrete, abstract?

1. The main idea, stated in lines 1–2, is that those who do not achieve success would best be able to appreciate it, likely because people are always dissatisfied with what they have and always seem to want more. The topic is broadened not only to include success, but also victory and triumph.

2. The example is drawn from the victor and vanquished on a battlefield. The image is that the person who has lost and is dying can define victory far more accurately than those who have taken "the Flag today." By extending the subject to the extremes of losing and dying, Dickinson emphasizes the regret, loss, envy, and disappointment that makes the loser

benefit from the loss by gaining vision and understanding even in defeat. For comparison, see "My Triumph Lasted Till the Drums" (page 888).

3. The pattern is a modified ballad measure, which should be *4x, 3b, 4x, 3b,* in quatrains. Only in line 5, however, does Dickinson provide a four-stress line. In all the other lines normally requiring four stresses she substitutes three. The measure operates normally in stanza one, where line two modifies the verb of line 1, and line 4 is the predicate of the subject in line 3. The last eight lines form a single sentence. Thus the measure of stanzas 2 and 3 is almost incidental to the formal pattern. It is as though Dickinson, to stress the idea of the defeated warrior, stretches the grammar along with the anguish.

4. The diction is a combination of general and abstract, though the poem itself is concrete because of the situations. Thus *success* is abstract, and *those who ne'er succeed* is general. *Nectar* is specific, but here it is used as a symbol of the sweet drink of the gods, to be shared by mortals who achieve triumphs. The phrase *sorest need* is applicable to anyone who is trying to find success, and therefore it is abstract. The flag is of course specific, and here it is a metonym for those who have won and accepted the flag of the vanquished as a token to their victory. In short, Dickinson's language is broadly meaningful; the success of the poem is created by the truth and the inclusiveness—the accuracy—of her observations.

"Faith" Is a Fine Invention, page 882

1 • Why is "Faith" included within quotation marks? What do the quotation marks add to the meaning that the absence of quotation marks would indicate?

2 • What does *microscopes* suggest or symbolize in line 3? What "Emergency" might make microscopes better than faith?

3 • Explain the idea of the second line reference to "Gentlemen can *see*—."

1. The quotation marks suggest that Dickinson is referring to a generally or popularly understood definition of the word. Here, it seems clear from the "can see" in the second line, Dickinson is alluding to the famous definition of faith in Hebrews 11:1, "Now faith is the substance of things hoped for, the evidence of things not seen." The entire eleventh chapter of Hebrews, in fact, is testimony to the power of faith. Without the quotation marks the usage might not necessarily be construed as an allusion.

2, 3. *Microscopes* suggests here the analysis and questioning of events of life. The microscope is an instrument that gets beyond the obvious, and therefore it symbolizes a questioning attitude, not the accepting one suggested by faith alone. Thus the microscope marks a rejection of quiescence, and an acceptance of inquiry. The "Emergency" could be a significant event, such as a departure or death, that creates an individual crisis. The phrase is paradoxical. It suggests that "Gentlemen can *see*," or understand, the usual religious explanations for misfortune, but that they are in fact insensible as human beings to the real sufferings of others. In addition, *Gentlemen* suggests exclusion, likely based on hierarchy. The gentlemen form the group who interpret faith and provide comforting platitudes for those experiencing pain, but their answers do not deal with the pain itself.

I Taste a Liquor Never Brewed, *page 882*

1 • What is the topic of this poem? Why is a prose restatement of the ideas inferior to the poem itself?

2 • In minimizing Dickinson's verse, Thomas Bailey Aldrich in 1903 offered a rewritten first stanza by, as he said, "tossing a rhyme into it," as follows:

> I taste a liquor never brewed
> In vats upon the Rhine;
> No tankard ever held a draught
> Of alcohol like mine.

What is the principle on which Aldrich made his revision, and in what way is it relevant to an evaluation of Dickinson's stanza?

3 • For the last line, Emily Dickinson herself composed an alternative, which she wrote in the manuscript of this poem:

> Leaning against the—Sun—

Because she did not publish the poem, we do not know her final intention. However, what improvement, if any, does the alternative line offer the poem?

1. The topic is the speaker's statement about the ecstasy and exhilaration she feels with life, both now and in the future. She bases the poem on the analogy of being "drunk with the wine of life." She uses the phrase "liquor never brewed" to explain the expansive mood, in line with ideas

like those expressed by Keats ("Grecian Urn"), "ditties of no tone," and Emerson ("Bacchus") "wine which never grew/In the belly of the grape." Any prose restatement is dull by comparison with the poem because the paraphrase kills the imaginativeness and daring of Dickinson's word choices.

2. Aldrich's principle is that the ballad stanza should be regular, with four stresses in lines 1 and 3, and rhyming words ending lines 2 and 4. Aldrich obviously concluded that Dickinson had violated this principle because she made line 3 have seven rather that eight syllables, and used *Alcohol* in line 4 as a very slant rhyme with *Pearl* in line 2. Modern readers are likely to find such insistence on mechanical regularity totally irrelevant to the joyful state of mind Dickinson presents in the poem.

3. The image in the alternative suggests that its speaker would be leaning drunkenly against the sun as though it were a lamppost. The image is clever, joyful, ridiculous, far-fetched, and daring, and for this reason it would be a definite improvement over the image in the text, which suggests simply that the speaker (the "tippler") has come from "Manzanilla" (i.e. drinking wine). Moreover, the last word of the alternative—*sun*—creates a perfect rhyme on which to end the poem. Although perfect rhymes were not one of Dickinson's objectives, here the word that makes the good rhyme is an improvement.

Safe in Their Alabaster Chambers, page 883

1 • Who are the "members of the Resurrection?" Why are they *meek*? In what way are they safe?

2 • Contrast the subject matter of the second stanza with that of the first.

3 • Consider the words *Crescent, Arcs, Firmaments, Diadems,* and *Doges.* How do the associations of these words broaden the meaning of the poem?

4 • In the last line, why is everything *soundless*? What idea does Dickinson suggest with this word?

1. The "members of the Resurrection" are the dead, so named here because often on tombstones inscriptions read that the dead person lies below, awaiting and anticipating a joyful resurrection. The word *meek* refers to Matthew 5:5, "Blessed are the meek, for they shall inherit the earth." The dead in the grave are safe from any more worldly pain.

2. The second stanza refers generally to the passage of time, to the

eternal movement of heavenly bodies, and to the constant change in governments and therefore in human society. This stanza is designed to suggest how long the dead must wait for their eventual resurrection.

3. *Crescent,* in addition to its probable reference here to the earth's curved surface, suggest the location in the mid east—the fertile crescent—where the mythical garden of Eden was located. *Arcs* suggests the Ark of the Covenant—the pact God made with the ancient Hebrews (Exodus 25:16–21; Numbers 10:33 and elsewhere). *Firmament* is also a Biblical word, signifying the heavens, in the shape of an arch. The word is also prominent in Joseph Addison's hymn "The Spacious Firmament on High," for which Haydn set his well-known music. *Diadems* is Biblical (see Isaiah 62:3) and is also an important and repeated word in the common hymn by Edward Perronet (1726–1792), "All Hail the Power of Jesus' Name," with music by Oliver Holden (1765–1844). *Doges,* or *dukes,* suggests the Venetian Republic, which had lost its eminence early in the nineteenth century. All these words suggest the broad historical and religious milieu of Dickinson's ideas.

4. *Soundless* suggests the insignificance of human activities in the context of eternity. Worldly power and the worlds which contain it shall pass, and they will be unimportant compared with God's resurrective power.

Wild Nights—Wild Nights, page 883

1 • How specifically should the title, "Wild Nights," be taken?

2 • What is the reading and interpretation of "done" in lines 7 and 8?

3 • What is the metaphor of stanzas 2 and 3? How extensive is it?

4 • In stanza 2 there are no complete sentences, and in stanza 3 the last two lines comprise a sentence in the subjunctive mode. Relate this relative incompleteness to the theme of the poem.

1. The title cannot be interpreted literally because it is general. However, *nights* in this context clearly signifies a time of love. Therefore the speaker is suggesting emotional, and also physical, abandon and release.

2. The reading should probably be that once a person knows the satisfaction of unity with a loved one, there is no further need for the controls (the "chart" and "compass") that keep a person seeking for love and tentatively establishing and then relinquishing unsatisfactory relationships. Hence, chart and compass may be "done" away with.

3. The metaphor is that of a ship going to port (line 6) and reaching a state of paradise (line 9). The metaphor is coextensive with lines 5–12,

comparing the emotional identity (the "Heart" synecdoche in line 6) of an individual to a ship sailing to a safe and secure port. In this poem, the port is the *thee* of lines 2 and 12.

4. The poem is about the speaker's yearning for the "thee" listener. Because the relationship does not exist, the poignancy of the unfulfilled desire is underscored by the absence of declarative sentences.

There's a Certain Slant of Light, pages 883–884

1 • Explain the premise of this poem. That is, how does the poem relate a condition of light to human mood and character?

2 • Describe the tone of the first stanza.

3 • Explain the line "Where the Meanings are" (line 8).

4 • What is the relationship of the last stanza's metaphors and simile to the principal idea of the poem?

1. The premise is that mood and character are not fixed but rather are continuously shaped by changing conditions. In this poem, the condition is a "certain slant of light" that is disturbing, unsettling, and depressing. The hurt is not temporary, like the slant of light, but is a permanent "internal difference" that remains as a part of life's conditions, literally an "imperial affliction" from the universe.

2. The tone is built up out of the swift movement from the reference to the slant of light to the weight, or "Heft," of "Cathedral Tunes." The shift from one sense—sight—to two others—the perception of weight and also the sound of music—creates surprise and also humor. Cathedral music is usually considered as dignified, but the choice of the word "Tunes" minimizes the sound, creating an anti-climax from the idea of "Heft." In addition, the reference to "Cathedral" is irreverent. These combinations create the complex tone that is both serious and comic.

3. The meanings of life, as suggested in line 7, are all internalized, whether through the conscious process characteristic of much of our learning, or through the unconscious process suggested in this poem. The poem indicates that such meaning may not be perceived consciously; the effect of the certain slant of light is nevertheless real.

4. In lines 13 and 14 there are two personifications: landscapes listen and shadows momentarily stop breathing. In lines 15 and 16 the simile is to the appearance of a dying person (the "Distance / On the look of Death"). These figures, joining landscape and death to the slant of light,

are a climax to the main idea, suggesting both the universality and finality of the mood and feelings created on "Winter Afternoons."

The Soul Selects Her Own Society, page 884

1 • What condition of the soul or personality does Dickinson describe in this poem?

2 • What metaphor does Dickinson use in reference to the soul? What meaning does the metaphor lend to the concept of soul as developed in the poem?

3 • How does Dickinson use the lengths of the second and fourth lines of the stanzas to complement the shutting down of communication she describes in the poem?

1. The soul as imagined in this poem is independent of the will of a person because it ("she" in the poem) dictates the friendships and associations that the person might have. Thus the soul, after determining the associates, closes the door to others (line 2) and remains unmoved even by those with great power and prestige (stanza 2). So firm is the soul that it literally closes the person off from others, as though a stone (gravestone?) has been put into place between the person and the world.

2. The metaphor is that the soul is a queen or even a goddess, living within a holy of holies which may be closed to prevent future communication with subjects ("her divine Majority," line 3), with busy people of the world pausing in chariots to seek admittance (lines 5 and 6), and even with "an Emperor" (line 7). The soul thus has great worth and value, being empowered to make one selection from everyone within the sphere of acquaintance (lines 9, 10). At the end, the metaphor of "valves of her attention" suggests that the soul is like a great organ playing all pipes from high to low. Once these valves are closed, however, the instrument becomes as silent as stone.

3. In stanzas one and two these lines contain, respectively, four and then three words. In the last stanza, however, the lines are reduced to two words each, being, metrically, a spondee ("Choose One," line 10) and a single iamb ("Like Stone," line 12). Rhythmically, this reduction creates emphasis upon the abruptness of the action and the simile with which the poem closes.

Some Keep the Sabbath Going to Church, page 884

1 • What concept of worship is presented in this poem?

2 • Consider the lines in which the speaker refers to "I" (lines 2, 6, 12). What is the tone of these lines?

3 • In what way does God, the "noted Clergyman," preach in the orchard of worship in which the speaker observes the Sabbath?

1. The poem contrasts a formal church service and the spontaneous experience of being with Nature in the home orchard. The idea is that in the natural world a person is closer to God than in a worship service where the service itself, because it is the focus of attention, interferes with his or her relationship to God.

2. The tone is one of cleverness and challenge—playful pride and mockery. In line 2 the speaker admits to keeping the Sabbath by staying away from church. (Remember that Exodus 20:8–11 commands the keeping of the Sabbath; also remember that this commandment was usually heeded in the nineteenth century.) In line 6 the speaker endows herself with wings, and in the last line she indicates a belief that her way of keeping the Sabbath makes her life a constant process of going to Heaven. Certainly these statements were intended to shock the more conventional readers of 1864, the date of first publication. This poem was one of the few poems of Dickinson published during her lifetime.

3. The exact means are not disclosed, unless one assumes that Dickinson is alluding to statements like that in Psalms 24:1, "The earth is the Lord's, and the fullness thereof, the world and those that dwell therein." If the allusion is admitted, then all the elements of nature—the bobolink, the orchard, the singing sexton (presumably a bird)—become the means through which "God preaches." By the natural, pantheistic-like idea of the poem, any title attributed to God is an understatement. Therefore the appellation "noble Clergyman" is designed as a rhetorical reminder of the intensity of God's power. There is also a strong note of defiance and unconventionality in the choice of phrase.

After Great Pain, a Formal Feeling Comes, pages 884–885

1 • What is meant by *formal* in the first line?

2 • What do the images of the poem have in common?

3 • What is the connection of the poem's subject with the *He* of line 3?

1. Ordinarily *formal* refers to appropriate and ritualized manners. That is partly its meaning here, but also the word suggests the images that follow. The feelings after great pain, in other words, are molded into rigid patterns beyond the conscious control of the individual—almost into a set of analogous physical shapes.

2. The images have a common thread of stiffness, numbness, heaviness, and rigidity, as though the feelings with which they are compared are being held in suspended animation and emotional isolation. Thus *Tombs* (line 2) force people into appropriate ceremoniousness, literally forbidding anything but solemnity. The *Wooden* way (line 7) suggests a lack of spring and spontaneity, a total heaviness of foot and of spirit. The *Quartz contentment* is hard and shiny, crystallizing and encapsulating the individual in passivity and incapacitating him or her to have further emotional interchanges. The *Freezing* image of lines 12 and 13 (is the total number of lines in the poem—thirteen—significant?) connects the ending of the poem with *Tombs* at the beginning: The response to great pain is a kind of death, even though the individual goes on living, because the emotional connections he or she once had are now gone, and thus a link with life has been frozen or killed. For comparison, see "My Life Closed Twice," page 889.

3. The *He that bore* of line 3 is a reference to Christ's carrying of the cross (see John 19:17). The connection with the poem is made at the end of the second line with *Tombs*, presumably an association with the tomb in which Jesus was laid (see Matthew 27:60 and elsewhere) and therefore also prompting the third-line outcry about the passion.

The reference underlies the intensity of the *great pain* of line 1, for it makes the passion seem both comparable and immediate. Even though line 4 does not cohere grammatically with line 3, it nevertheless preserves the topical and thematic connection because it is a virtual reenactment of the disorientation about time that a person in great grief might experience. Though the line is fragmentary, therefore, it is especially dramatic.

Much Madness Is Divinest Sense, page 885

1 • How may the first three lines be resolved grammatically? How does this resolution assist comprehension of these lines?

2 • How does the speaker suggest that the opening paradox is applicable to politics?

3 • Why does the speaker refer to "you" in line 6 and "you're" in line 7?

1. In the first three lines, Dickinson's use of the dash creates an immediate difficulty of understanding. This problem may be resolved, however, if the lines are understood thus:

> To a discerning eye, much madness is divinest sense
> [and] much sense [is] the starkest madness.

This resolution enables the lines to be seen as a description of a topsy-turvy world, in which things are seldom what they seem. The rhetorical arrangement of lines 1 and 3, a chiasmus or antimetabole on *madness-sense,* and *sense-madness,* also suggests that the lines are to be read as a unit, with *To a discerning Eye* as the modifying phrase grammatically.

2. The use of the words *Majority ... prevail* in lines 4 and 5 indicates that the speaker is criticizing the political decision making process of democracy. The idea is a play on the idea of the proverb "vox populi, vox dei" ("the voice of the people is the voice of God"). If the people embody collective madness in their voting patterns, therefore, that madness is the "divinest sense" that will prevail. By the same token, the sensible person who dissents on reasonable grounds will be branded the mad one. Also, the concluding image of being "handled with a Chain" suggests the political associations of the poem.

3. When speaking of personal, inner feelings, Dickinson does not have her speakers include references to the second person. In this poem, however, the use of the second person may be suggested by the "majority" of line 4 and the political associations considered in question 2. The *you* is introduced as a means of extending the context and general application of the poem as statement. In other words, the "discerning" reader is being drawn into this poem to verify the ideas there, whereas in Dickinson's purely personal poetry the speaker is the sole voice verifying personal experiences that the reader has not necessarily shared.

I Heard a Fly Buzz—When I Died, page 885

1 • What is the imaginary situation being narrated in the poem?

2 • What is the effect of the fly upon the tone of the poem?

3 • What is the meaning of the last two lines? What is their effect?

1. The situation here is a deathbed scene. In the nineteenth century people who were gravely ill did not die in hospitals, but rather at home, often directly in front of family and friends, who maintained a bedside vigil. The witnesses of course would be tearful (line 5) and would prepare

themselves for the moment of death (line 7). The dying person would give personal effects and properties to the persons present, who were also witnesses of the gifts and final wishes and even wills (lines 9–11). The giving of testimony and acknowledgment of the presence of God ("the King," lines 7, 8) would also take place. Amid the scene, the speaker notes the appearance of a buzzing fly, which is her last connection with the living world. The personalized imagining of death or deathbed scenes is not unusual even today, and it was even less unusual at Dickinson's time, when death was more common among the young than it is now. Swift, for example, wrote "Verses on the Death of Dr. Swift, D.S.P.C.D.," a poem about how people would respond to his own death. Death is also a frequent topic of Donne's poetry, and Gray's "Elegy Written in a Country Churchyard" contains an "Epitaph" demonstrating the poet's concern with Death. Mark Twain satirized such preoccupations in *Huckleberry Finn,* with the dead Emmeline Grangerford's poem about the death of "Stephen Dowling Botts Dec'd" (Chapter 17).

2. The fly is an intrusion upon what should be a serious occasion; it is "uncertain, stumbling," and therefore it is mildly comic. With respect to the tone, the fly saves the imaginary situation from becoming sentimentalized because it represents reality and everyday life. As it were, the fly enables Dickinson to focus on the seriousness of the last lines, and to deepen their humanness because they describe real life more adequately than tearful farewells by vigil-keepers would do.

3. The last two lines constitute a powerful ending for the poem. They are connected to the sound and light represented by the fly because the fly interposes itself between the light and the speaker. Thus the phrase "the Windows failed" is logical in the narrative because the speaker has been conscious of the fly outlined against the light. The use of *Windows* is a metonym—the substitution of one thing (*Windows*) for another with which it is closely associated (light), and here it emphasizes the idea that death is a termination of the world externally as well as internally. In the last line, *see to see* is a way of describing death as a loss of capacity. The first *see* is thus the power to perceive, and the second *see* is the visual function of this power.

I Like to See It Lap the Miles, pages 885–886

1 • How does Dickinson succeed in describing a sense of motion about a train, even though there is only one complete sentence in the poem?

2 • What is the dominant metaphor in the poem? How does Dickinson keep the metaphor from seeming ordinary?

3 • How does Dickinson preserve a comic, playful, light tone throughout the poem?

1. She begins the poem with the construction "I like to see it ..." and then she includes ten one-syllable infinitives in this complementary position, of which *it* is the recurrent subject. Thus the speaker likes to see it *lap, lick, stop, step, peer, pare, crawl, chase, neigh,* and *stop,* with the present participle *complaining* in line 11. All the infinitive complements and the participle stress the movement of the train.

2. The major metaphor is common: The train is like an iron horse. (Dickinson may be speaking of the Amherst-Belchertown railroad, which had opened in 1853.) She keeps the metaphor fresh, first, by not mentioning ever that she is describing a train, second, by stressing the train's movement, and, third, by withholding the verb most appropriate to a horse, *neigh,* until line 15. The metaphor thus is not completely fixed in the reader's mind until the poem is almost ended, and therefore the poet has given the topic the descriptive freshness of the first fourteen lines. The metaphor, in fact, is rather surprising when it becomes apparent, and it is certainly fun.

3. She uses a number of overstatements which by being overblown create amusement. There are *prodigious* (line 4), *supercilious* (line 6), *Boanerges* (line 14), and *omnipotent* (line 16). In addition, the complaining in a horrid, hooting stanza (lines 11, 12), the chasing (line 12), and the neighing (line 14) are also comic. Another playful idea is that after all the hooting, the creature-train becomes *docile* once it stops (line 15). The metaphor *stable* for a railway roundhouse is also comic. These are only the major ways in which Dickinson exhibits good humor and geniality in the poem.

I Cannot Live with You, pages 886–887

1 • What is the dramatic situation imagined in the poem? Who is the "you" being addressed?

2 • What reasons does the speaker cite in support of the opening denial? How is the poem structured to embody these responses?

3 • How do the thought and the sentences cohere from lines 5–10? What purpose is served by the difficulty of these lines?

1. The situation is that the speaker responds to a question of the "you" listener that the two should live together, presumably in marriage.

The speaker answers negatively, and then explains her refusal. Her reasons, together with the concluding summary, form the poem, which is more a personal, written letter than an intimate, spoken speech. Once the poem is completed, there is no opportunity for response, and the concluding word, "Despair," indicates the finality of the statement and the speaker's deep grief. There is no way to identify the "you" as a specific person, although biographers indicate that the circumstances of the poem fit Charles Wadsworth (see page 878). The best we can do as modern readers is to consider the speaker and the "you" as two dramatic characters who must part permanently, and the poem as an expression of both denial and anguish.

2. Lines 1–12 form a negative denying the possibility of living together, citing a religious barrier (the Key kept by the Sexton, line 5). Lines 13–20 further deny living together because of the impossibility of the two dying together; neither could predecease the other. A third section is lines 21–44, in which the denial extends to the impossibility of the two being resurrected together: a– the speaker could not admire Jesus more than the "you" in Heaven because she admires "you" for shining nearer. b– She would be ill judged for crowding out her vision of Paradise by filling her sight with "you." c– She could never bear to be anywhere in Heaven without the "you," because being apart, even in Heaven, would be "Hell" to her. The conclusion, lines 45–50, summarizes the vastness between the two, who have only prayer for consolation and despair as a permanent condition.

3. The passage is difficult, even after repeated readings. If one includes the fourth line, however, a continuous grammatical connection may be formed:

> Behind the Shelf [which] the Sexton keeps the key to,
> Putting up [on the shelf] our Life—His Porcelain—Like
> a Housewife's discarded cup [that is] quaint or broke[n].

The fragmentary, difficult lines complement the elliptical thought of a person trying to speak while in extreme emotional pain. Hence the style here is appropriate for the subject and for the grief of the speaker. Beyond the religious barrier mentioned in lines 5–10, the speaker suggests that the "you" may have gone on to a new relationship (the "newer Sevres" china that "pleases") to replace the cracked and now dead relationship.

One Need Not Be a Chamber—To Be Haunted, PAGES 887–888

1 • How is the metaphor comparing a house to the mind developed in the poem to demonstrate the frightening nature of identity?

2 • To what degree is "One Need Not" successful?

1. In the first stanza the poem asserts that our brains have their own corridors, or hallways, where we may meet horrid fantasies. At the end the image is a single room where a "superior spectre / Or More" is waiting within the room of the mind, more deadly than a real-life assassin (who can, after all, be shot if a person borrows a revolver for self-protection). In between, the mind is compared to a "cooler Host" (line 8), ready to give a terrorizing party for the individual. In line 12 the metaphor of the house is briefly abandoned for a "lonesome Place," which could be anywhere, most likely outdoors. Here, the image is that the mind—"one's self"—is like a lurking bandit. Even here, however, the room image is the Abbey (lines 9, 10), where the stones themselves might chase the terror-stricken victim. The poem suggests that such fright is less harmful than the horrors within the mind. These many separate representations of the mind as a haunted house, five in all within the five stanzas, create consistency and unity.

2. "One Need Not" deals abstractly but successfully with a difficult topic. With its many comparisons, it does not reflect a single experience—difficult as it is anyway to determine the exact incidents which may have given rise to Dickinson's other very personal poems. The success of the poem depends on the reader's willingness to concede, at least for poetic purposes, that the mind's inner recesses are like a vast mansion that may be haunted by invasive and frightening ghosts. For comparison, see "The Heart is the Capital of the Mind" (page 888), and also Frost's "Desert Places" (page 764).

The Bustle in a House, PAGE 888

1 • How does the first line of the poem promise a certain kind of setting? How does the second stanza indicate that the setting is metaphorical?

2 • A student once suggested that line 6 of this poem, "And putting love away," is cold and unfeeling. What argument might be made to support this assertion? How do the remaining two lines suggest that the student may have been wrong?

3 • In what way does this poem depart from the ballad measure Dickinson often uses?

1. The opening line suggests a household where a family member has died the day before. The "Bustle" refers to the hushed solemn preparations that need to be made before the funeral—cleaning, preparing invitations, writing notices to friends, and so on. In the second stanza the "Sweeping of the Heart" (line 5) indicates an entirely different setting—the interior one of adjusting to life in view of the reality and permanence of death. The appearance of the word *Heart* indicates the beginning of the metaphor.

2. The thought of "putting Love away," if taken out of context, might seem cold and unfeeling if it is taken to mean that the living can forget the dead. In the poem however, the metaphor of housework applies. Hence the love being put away is like storing something in a closet, or on a shelf until a change of season makes it necessary again. This analogy, together with the concluding reference to the reuniting of the dead in Eternity, lends a strong note of poignancy and yearning to the poem. The second stanza hence expresses deep feeling, though it also expresses resignation and acceptance.

3. In this poem Dickinson modifies the first lines of the two stanzas. Each line (1 and 5) has six syllables, and therefore three rather than four iambic feet. The effect is that the syllables *Bus, House,* and *Sweep, Heart,* are stressed rhythmically. Both the lines, in fact, are almost metrical twins. For this reason, the rhythmical echo that line 5 makes of line 1 creates an element of surprise once the word *Heart* is found in the same position as *House.* This type of control enables Dickinson to achieve a powerful effect within a very brief compass.

My Triumph Lasted Till the Drums, page 888

1 • Who is the speaker of this poem? What kind of dramatic situation has prompted the speaker to begin the poem?

2 • In what way are lines 9–16 a contrast to the first eight lines, and in what way are they a reflection upon them?

3 • What kind of image of the dead in warfare is developed here? Does Dickinson stress the horror or the anguish of war?

1. There is no clear identification, but from the situation the speaker is a member of a victorious army, perhaps even a commanding officer. The victory has been celebrated by drum rolls, and the speaker is elated. After the noise, however, the speaker inspects the dead, and upon seeing

their "finished Faces" (line 5), he, or she, loses all elation, and in fact feels so "chastened" (line 4) that the speaker wishes to become one of the dead.

2. The last eight lines, the second half of the poem, are a reflection upon warfare and upon what people might learn from it if only they could be sensible and caring. The speaker of this second half is the same as in the first, except that here the topic is contrasted because it is abstracted from the specific situation of the first half. In this second part the question of how we know the future is treated, specifically how we could use the memory of past warfare to predict that future warfare would produce the same regret and guilt in the victors as that described in the first part. Thus, if the future could contain something of this retrospective guilt, people would avoid warfare. The concluding reference to the bayonets (a metonym for those who have killed) becoming contrite only after the act of killing is an effective coda to this thoughtful and sensitive meditation.

3. The image of the dead is not immediate or visual. We read only that the dead have "finished Faces" and that they have "turned" their "Conclusion" on the speaker (lines 5, 6). There is hence nothing graphic, but rather Dickinson directs the topic inward to the responses of the speaker. The subject is therefore more the anguish of war than physical horror and agony. For comparison, see Wilfred Owen's "Dulce et Decorum Est" (page 681), Randall Jarrell's "The Death of the Ball Turret Gunner" (page 550), lines 33–36 of Thomas Gray's "Elegy Written in a Country Churchyard" (page 580), and Whitman's "Reconciliation" (page 759).

The Heart is the Capital of the Mind, pages 888–889

1 • What is the metaphor on which the poem is based? What is the effect of this metaphor?

2 • The second stanza seems difficult grammatically. How can the language be read?

3 • How may this poem be compared with "One Need Not Be a Chamber" (page 887)?

1. The metaphor is that the individual is like a country, a continent, with the mind as a single political unit coincidental with this country. The capital is the heart; that is, the emotions are the primary source of strength and control, and the recipient of the individual's mental and physical resources. The population is one. The argument might seem solipsistic, but the poem is more about knowing oneself than about mak-

ing the world over in one's self-image. The effect is surely, however, to indicate Dickinson's stress on individual consciousness and identity.

2. The stanza is ambiguous primarily because of the punctuation and also because of the elliptical constructions. There are two possible ways to read the lines, with each being acceptable because both stress the need for learning about oneself:

[a] The population [of this Continent] is One—numerous enough. Seek this ecstatic Nation: It is Yourself.

[b] The population [of this Continent] is One. This ecstatic Nation [is] Numerous enough. Seek [it]; it is Yourself.

3. The poems are comparable because both metaphorically equate an individual with houses and nations. There the similarity stops, for "The Heart" is optimistic while "One Need" is pessimistic. "One Need" asserts the potential horror of the mind, and it compares this horror to a haunting ghost that frightens the individual in both familiar and lonely settings. By contrast, "The Heart" is more expansive just as it is more in accord with the need for adjustment and self-knowledge. Ironically, "The Heart" by its comprehensiveness includes the view of "One Need," because one of the things a person might face in seeking self-knowledge is the potential for horror described in "One Need."

My Life Closed Twice Before Its Close, page 889

1 • In what way does the structure of this poem not conform to the strict confines of the two-stanza ballad measure?

2 • In lines 2–6, the speaker raises questions about the nature of a possible "third event" that might occur to her. Does the speaker therefore anticipate that this third event will be disastrous?

3 • How are the last two lines connected to the topic matter of the poem?

1. The sentences do not fall regularly within the pattern of the stanzas. Line 1 is a complete sentence that features the use of *close* in both a figurative and literal sense of dying. Lines 2–6 form an extensive sentence that continues for five lines; these lines do not strictly fall within the line and stanza patterns. The last two lines, like the first line, form a separate unit of statement. Thus the two stanzas, though the rhythms and rhymes are fairly regular, are stretched by the content of the poem.

2. Because the first two events were figurative endings of the speaker's

life, the implication of lines 2–6 is that "Immortality" might have a third event equally bad in store. But the language is ambiguous, for the description "So huge, so hopeless to conceive" may equally describe a favorable as well as unfavorable event. The question of what Immortality might "unveil" is therefore still open, even though the previous experiences have been bad. In the light of the last two lines, the "third event" is clearly about the nature of heaven and hell in an afterlife. Dickinson considers similar subject material in "I Never Lost As Much But Twice" (page 881).

3. These lines are perhaps the best known of any that Emily Dickinson wrote. Though they are often excerpted they belong within the poem, and are essential to the poem's ideas. In effect they constitute a denial of the speculation about the magnitude of anything that immortality might offer to the speaker. We commonly regard going either to heaven or hell as the two big events that death has in store for human beings. But, says the speaker, because her life has already been "closed" twice before her actual death, she has already experienced both heaven and hell. The poem therefore ends on a skeptical as well as a memorable note: Nothing that Immortality can provide—not heaven, and not hell—could be either better or worse than what she has known in life because of the partings she has experienced.

A Word Made Flesh Is Seldom, page 889

1 • What is meant by the dichotomy in the poem between the Word (concept, idea) and the Flesh (the Incarnation, the physical identity). Does the poem seem to limit the application only to the divinity and Incarnation of Christ?

2 • Explain the idea explored in the second stanza.

1. The poem depends for its context on the first verses of John, beginning "In the beginning was the Word. . . . " The speaker indicates that the knowledge of the Incarnation has been "very food" for "each one of us." That is, the knowledge that Jesus took on an earthly presence has given spiritual strength to generations of believers. There is some ambiguity about the transference from the ideal to the actual. The obvious meaning is the one proposed in the Gospel of John. But the poet may also be stating that all those living are physical manifestations of the divine concept ("Word") of life. Such ambiguity would be in line with Dickinson's ideas as proposed, for example, in "Some Keep the Sabbath Going to Church" (page 884).

2. The second stanza seems to be a straightforward enunciation that

the "Word" of God, "Made Flesh and dwelt among us" (line 13), "has not the power to die" (line 10). This idea seems to be in line both with the Platonic concept of universals having eternal truth, and also with the Biblical assertion that the word of the Lord "endureth forever" (I Peter 1:25). With the Word having such a distinct breath, the "Spirit" can indeed become "cohesive." The Biblical context makes this aspect of Dickinson's idea plain. There also seems to be a slight element of uncertainty in this second stanza, for the idea of "loved Philology" indicates that the whole concept and system of the "Word made Flesh" may be dependent more on human than divine perceptions. The ideas here are difficult and somewhat tortuous, but the presence of the negative ideas implicit in "It may expire," "condescension," and "consent," the second stanza suggests Christ's Incarnation is accepted by the speaker, but with reservations.

I Never Felt at Home—Below, pages 889–890

1 • What ideas does the speaker explore in this poem? What restraint does the speaker recognize upon her somewhat rebellious attitudes?

2 • What is suggested by the use of quotation marks around the final words, "Judgment Day"?

3 • Describe the relationship between the form and rhyme, on the one hand, and the content, on the other.

1. The poem begins with the speaker's description of her sense of general alienation from the world, both "Below" and in the "Handsome Skies." This is a broad, sweeping claim, and when she applies it to "Paradise" she makes the analogy that an afterlife will be no more congenial to her than this life has been. She continues in this vein for the next eleven lines, citing comic instances to assert that the afterlife will be a bore. One will always have to wear Sunday best; there never will be any chance to play; Wednesday afternoon will be lonesome; and, above all, God will be like a telescope that provides a continual supervision of Edenic residents who want to be wayward. The restraint is of course explained as the "Judgment Day" in the final line. This structure, from rebelliousness to acceptance, may also be traced in George Herbert's "The Collar" (page 802).

2. The last line represents the major heavenly restraint upon the speaker's rebellious feelings; it is the "Judgment Day." Interestingly, the inclusion of "Judgment Day" within quotation marks suggests that the

speaker is introducing an idea that she has not felt at home with, but about which she has been told. Even at the end, in other words, the speaker still expresses a degree of rebelliousness.

(3) The first stanza is a normal hymnal stanza, with a regular 4a, 3b, 4a, 3b pattern and with rhymes on lines 1–3 and 2–4. This regularity seems consistent with the speaker's positive expression of her sense of never feeling at home. As the poem develops, the rhythm becomes more varied and the poet uses inexact rhymes, such as "time" with "lonesome," and "Nap" with "Telescope." One might claim that this employment of irregularity is appropriate to the topic of the speaker's general malaise with a rigid concept of an eternally regularized paradise. Interestingly, with line 11 the rhyming word "say" is introduced, and this rhymes with "away" and the final word "Day." This return to regularity is consistent with the idea of "Judgment Day" closing the poem. There is a judgment, and it does keep her thoughts—and rhymes—in line.

I Died for Beauty—but Was Scarce, page 890

1 • Who is the speaker and what has happened to her?
What has happened to the man in the "adjoining Room"?
What dramatic situation is described in the poem?

2 • Why does the man who died for Truth ask the speaker why she "failed" (line 5)?

3 • Explain the final stanza. What idea do you think it represents on the part of the speaker? The poet?

1. The speaker of this poem, like the speakers of "I Heard a Fly Buzz" (page 885) and "Because I Could Not Stop for Death (page 555), is speaking after the fact of death. She states that she has died "for Beauty" and has been "adjusted in the tomb." The man in the adjoining grave claims a kinship with the speaker because, as he says, he died "for Truth." The identification of beauty and truth ("Themself are One") makes a bond between the two, and so they meet "a Night" and talk to each other "between the Rooms." They speak for an indefinite period of time until the Moss reaches their lips and covers up their names.

2. "Failed" is a synonym for dying, but it also implies that the speaker's goals may not have been fully visualized or realized. The use of this word hence suggests that the concepts of beauty (and truth) may not be fully understood or understandable.

3. The final stanza represents the view that death and time make human concerns meaningless. If there is a reality of universals existing in an eternal world of ideas, human beings cannot know about them because of the finiteness of life and the overwhelming power of the grave. For this reason this poem may be contrasted with poems such as "This World Is Not Conclusion" (page 890), in which Dickinson expresses a more optimistic understanding of an afterlife. "I Died for Beauty" is an expression of sorrowful, extreme pessimism.

The connection between beauty and truth is made in the conclusion of Keats's "Ode on a Grecian Urn" (page 849). In terms of the finality of death as a cessation of human dreams and potential, "I Died for Beauty" may be compared with Gray's "Sonnet on the Death of Richard West" (page 617) and Ransom's "Bells for John Whiteside's Daughter" (page 979).

I'm Nobody! Who Are You?, page 890

1 • What does the designation "Nobody" mean in the poem? What advantages are educed for being nobody?

2 • What is meant by the poem's distinction between "Nobody" and "Somebody"?

3 • What attitude toward the public does the speaker express? How consistent is this attitude with the claim the speaker makes to be "Nobody"?

1. "Nobody" likely refers to a status of privacy or anonymity. The speaker expressly denies any kind of public admission of her need for privacy. The cleverness of the first stanza results from the fact that the listener, who is also "Nobody," should not tell anybody about this detail. The existence of anyone admitting to be "Nobody," in other words, would probably then become "Somebody." This detail would then focus such attention on the new Somebodies that they would lose their preferred seclusion.

2. The play on the words *nobody* and *somebody* is probably as old as the language. The common interchange is the following:

> "Who did this?"
> "Nobody."
> "Nobody didn't do it. It must have been Somebody."

Somebody, in other words, is always responsible, and is therefore the public one. Ironically, both Nobody and Somebody are always doing something, and thus both are equally responsible for what happens.

3. The attitude of the speaker toward the public is contained in the phrase "admiring Bog" in the last line. It is difficult to define exactly the reasons for the negative attitude, but clearly the speaker considers being a Somebody in the public spotlight as being like a frog, croaking out unpleasant noises for the bog to hear. Certainly the speaker's attitude is negative and censorious.

This World Is Not Conclusion, pages 890–891

1 • What does the speaker mean by saying "This World is not Conclusion"?

2 • What does the speaker mean by the phrase "through a Riddle" in line 7?

3 • Explain the conclusion about the Tooth nibbling at the soul.

1. The statement "This World Is not Conclusion" seems to be an outright claim of belief in life after death. There is no claim for a resurrection of the body, as would be consistent with some orthodox Christian views of Heaven, but the speaker does not that the world after death is "invisible, as Music— / But positive, as Sound." These statements are made without qualification or ambiguity, unlike the ideas about Paradise in "I never Felt at Home—Below" (page 889).

2. The phrase "through a Riddle, at the last" is stated in the context of Philosophy that does not know, Sagacity that must go, and scholars who are puzzled as they try to make guesses. Consistent with these situations of uncertainty, the riddle likely refers to some of the paradoxes that are expressed in the New Testament, such as the last being first (Mark 10:31 and elsewhere) and the need for losing one's life in order to find it (Matthew 16:25 and elsewhere). Dickinson does not explain the phrase any further, however, and readers must therefore infer her meaning.

3. The final two lines state that narcotics or painkillers cannot "still the Tooth / That nibbles at the soul." These lines are best understood in the context of the previous six lines. The narcotics seem to be a– the tenuous grasp at truth by Faith, b– the gesturing of preachers from their pulpits, and c– the strong Hallelujahs sung by congregations. These, the speaker implies, tend to deter understanding of eternal life. The yearning for an afterlife, however, is never quite stilled in the individual, for it is constant and unremitting, like a toothache. In short, when all the claims of philosophy and theology fall short in persuading the individual that the world is not conclusion, the still small voice within is silently asserting this truth.

◆ Robert Frost, pages 891–903

The Tuft of Flowers, pages 894–895

1 • What is the setting and situation? What feelings about the human condition are expressed in lines 1–10?

2 • What does the butterfly symbolize? To what does it lead the speaker?

3 • What does the tuft of flowers represent for the speaker? How does it change his perspective on the human condition?

The poem (in iambic pentameter rhymed couplets) presents a process of discovery in which the speaker realizes that human beings are bound together in a spiritual unity with nature, beauty, and each other. The poem creates this meaning by narrating the process of discovery. In lines 1–10 the speaker feels isolated and *alone;* he cannot find the mower and he thinks that it is human destiny for *all* to be alone. In lines 11–20 a *bewildered butterfly* leads the speaker to a tuft of flowers spared by the mower; the butterfly represents both the speaker's questioning spirit (*tremulous wing*) and the tenuous bond between speaker, mower, and nature. Lines 21–30 describe the beauty and love embodied in the tuft of flowers. This single object awakens the speaker to all of nature and the kinship among all humanity. He concludes that "men work together… whether they work together or apart."

A Line-Storm Song, pages 895–896

1 • Describe the relationship between the form of the poem and its subject matter.

2 • Describe Frost's use of natural references, amid which the speaker asks his loved one to join him in love.

This love song uses conventional rhyme and a varying pattern of rhythm, building what is essentially a hymnal stanza into eight-line units, and repeating its refrain at the ends of the first and last stanzas ("And be my love in the rain"). For a love poem, the language is unique. There is no mention of moonlight and roses, but rather the flowers are "wet," clouds are "tattered and swift," waters are "aflutter," feet are "dry-shod," and the east wind is "whelming." Like a typical ballad, this poem tells the story of love that has persisted in all ages and times of human history. To the speaker, love is as old as the "ancient lands where" the sea has ebbed and flowed again and again ever since the early days of the world. The experience of love is like the sea's recovering the land, a constantly repeating event that takes place "in the rain." Through this and other images of nature and natural forces (a storm-tossed world of silent birds and a wood-world filled with "torn despair"), the speaker allies the reemergence of love to the natural history of the world itself. The bold sweetness of the poem's sentiments is underlined by the power of the language describing the natural world in which love must emerge from storm and shower.

Mending Wall, pages 896–897

1 • What is the setting and situation? Who are the characters?

2 • What is the neighbor's attitude toward walls? How did he get this attitude? What is he like?

3 • What is the speaker's attitude toward walls? How does Frost show that the speaker is ambivalent? How is the speaker different from the neighbor?

The poem (in blank verse) isn't really about walls. Instead, it employs a specific action and situation to explore the differences between two types of personalities. The two characters—speaker and neighbor—are repairing the wall between their farms. The neighbor believes that "Good fences make good neighbors" (line 27, 45); his views are conservative and traditional, inherited from his father (line 43). He is neither introspective nor philosophical; he does not question inherited wisdom. The speaker is much more philosophical, ironic, introspective, skeptical, and amused. He knows that walls can be silly or worse—"Something there is that doesn't love a wall"—but he is ambivalent about them; he calls the neighbor to start work (line 12) and helps rebuild the wall. The speaker's tone and attitude combine questioning with ironic humor and whimsy. These are reflected in the speaker's assertions that *a spell* must be used to make some stones balance, that wall-building is "just another kind of outdoor game," that his apple trees will never invade his neighbor's pines, and that the *Elves* knock walls down. The speaker is thus uneasy and unsure about walls; he makes quiet fun of his neighbor's attitude, but he recognizes the need for some walls and he helps rebuild this one year after year.

One might note that the line "Good fences make good neighbors," is often misquoted by people who attribute the idea to Frost, without realizing that it is really the benighted fence-mender who says it. Unfortunately, many writers are subject to similar misquoting—a hazard, probably, of having the ability to present an opposing view dramatically.

Birches, pages 897–898

1 • What two ways of bending birches does the speaker describe? Which way damages the trees? What does each way symbolize?

2 • What kind of escape from earthly care does the speaker want? Why is the word *toward* (line 56) in italic?

Bowed birches remind the speaker of two ways that trees can be bent: ice storms and swinging boys. The ice-storms (lines 5–20) damage the trees permanently; the birches "never right themselves." Such bending is harmful, destructive, symbolic of death. A child swinging on the birches (lines 21–40) does not do such damage; instead, such swinging, according to the speaker, takes "the stiffness out of them" (line 30). The speaker was once a "swinger of birches," and he dreams of returning to this pastime as a regenerative process, to escape from the earth (drudgery) for a while and then to "begin over" (line 50). Birch swinging symbolizes a temporary escape that will not break or damage the speaker permanently; he seeks escape and then return. The italic t*oward* indicates the denial of permanent removal.

The Road Not Taken, pages 898–899

1 • What do the two roads symbolize? What is the speaker's attitude toward them? What must he decide?

2 • How are the roads different? Which does the speaker choose? Why?

3 • What does the speaker know about the unchosen road? What will be the effect of his choice?

This poem explores the idea that every choice we make determines what we are and what we will be. The two roads symbolize choices of direction—career, personal involvements, activities, development of character. Stanza 1 sets up the circumstances of the choice; the roads *diverged* and the speaker was *sorry* he could not choose both. Stanza 2 suggests that the two roads (choices) were almost equal, but there is a difference. The speaker picked the one that *wanted wear* and was *less traveled* (less conformist, traditional, normal, and popular). Stanza 3 takes up the inevitable closure produced by choice; the speaker saved the unchosen road "for another day," but he knew that he would never "come back" (face the same choice again) because "way leads on to way" (each choice leads on to subsequent choices predicated upon the first). All this is in the past; there is no present in the poem. In the last stanza, the speaker considers the impact of such choices on the future; although one choice may seem insignificant, it will have made "all the difference."

'Out, Out—', pages 899–900

1 • To what does the title allude? How does the allusion help shape meaning?

2 • What is the setting and situation? What types of imagery are employed here? What is the boy doing? What happens?

3 • Trace the poem's movement from accident to injury to death. How does the speaker make each seem accidental, surprising, and relatively insignificant?

The title is an allusion to Shakespeare's *Macbeth;* it is quoted from Macbeth's speech about the emptiness of life:

> Out, out, brief candle!
> Life's but a walking shadow, a poor player
> That struts and frets his hour upon the stage
> And then is heard no more. It is a tale
> Told by an idiot, full of sound and fury,
> Signifying nothing. (5.5.23–28)

The title thus suggests that the poem will explore the uncertainty and emptiness of life. Even without the allusion, this sense of unpredictability and uncertainty comes across. The setting and situation are set up in lines 1–8 with images of sound (onomatopoetic *snarled and rattled),* smell (*sweet-scented stuff),* and sight (dust, sticks, mountains). Our sense of the instant is expanded in lines 9–14; we learn that the day has been uneventful, work is over, and it's supper time. The boy's hand is severed by accident in one moment of inattention. The poem moves by easy steps to death; each one is unanticipated. The *rueful laugh* and the *spoiled* life are followed by fading pulse (*No one believed*) and then death. No one understands what is happening; the death, like the cut, is a product of chance. Those (we don't know who *they* are) who *turned to their affairs* underscore the insignificance and randomness of chance events.

The Oven Bird, page 900

1 • What is the oven bird? What is the significance of the time of the bird's appearance? Why does the bird stop singing.

2 • What is the meaning of the final lines? How may they be interpreted as symbols?

The oven bird is apparently native to New England. Not all students have heard it, but they do know birdsongs in general. The speaker introduces the bird as a creature of mid-summer and autumn ("the other fall we name the fall"). The call of the bird therefore signifies the changing of the season, from summer growth and fall harvest to the diminution of activity and the stasis of winter. After most birds have made their calls and created their nesting broods, they stop singing, but this one is different, and apparently continues singing (line 12). The concluding final lines are typical of Frost's carefully controlled symbolism. The "diminished thing" refers specifically to the loss of the harvest available to birds, but it also, symbolically, refers to reductions in the quality of human life, through age, changes in customs, reductions in the allocation of resources, and so on. The final lines are among Frost's most memorable.

Fire and Ice, page 900

1 • What two types of cosmic destruction does the poem describe?

2 • With what emotions are fire and ice associated?

The poem investigates the destructive power of human passion (desire and hate) through the symbolism of cosmic destruction by fire or ice. The title and lines 1–2 refer to two modes of ending the world; fire (war, apocalypse, being swallowed up by a gigantic explosion of the sun into a supernova) and ice (ice age, cooling, dying of the sun and the consequent extinction of all life). Fire is linked with desire; ice with hatred. The speaker knows both, and knows that both are strong enough to end the world.

Nothing Gold Can Stay, PAGE 900

1 • What do the leaf, human history, and a single day have in common? In what sense do all begin in gold?

2 • What does "gold" symbolize? What happens to everything that is gold?

The poem explores the idea that happiness, perfection, bliss (all symbolized by gold) cannot and will not endure. The apparent paradox of line 1 is based on the fact that buds appear to be gold rather than green. The speaker looks at the falling away from gold in nature, human history, and time. The leaf, humanity, and the day all begin in gold (bud, Eden, dawn) and decay quickly; perfection in any form lasts only for *an hour.*

Misgiving, page 901

1 • What do the leaves promise in spring? How are they changed by the fall?

2 • What do the leaves symbolize? The spring and fall? The wind?

3 • In what ways does the speaker hope to be different from the leaves?

The poem investigates the human fear of the unknown (adventure, death) through the metaphor of leaves driven by the wind. Stanzas 1–3 develop the metaphor and the leaves as a symbol for aging humanity. In spring (youth), the leaves promise to travel with the wind. In fall (age), however, the leaves become *oppressed* by sleep (fear, reluctance) and they ask the wind to *stay with them.* Early promises of flight give way to a *vaguer and vaguer stir* or a *reluctant whir* that does not change or move the leaves. In the last stanza, which is a plaintive expression of hope, the speaker expresses the wish to be different and to have the courage to move *beyond the bounds of life* in question of knowledge when he is *free.*

Acquainted with the Night, page 901

1 • What is the speaker like? What does he know? What has he done?

2 • What are the central symbols in the poem? How do they create meaning?

3 • What aspects of human existence does the poem reveal?

The poem, in iambic pentameter terza rima (*aba, bcb, cdc, dad, aa*), investigates the human dilemma of loneliness and isolation. Night is the central symbol for sadness, loneliness, and all the negative aspects of life. The speaker's acquaintance *with the night* suggests that he has experienced life's bitterness; *acquaintance* also implies cold knowledge rather than warm familiarity. Subsequent images (rain, furthest city light, saddest city lane) reinforce the initial symbol of night as sadness, misery, isolation. The watchman that the speaker passes suggests a denial of human contact and perhaps suspicion and guilt; the silence and *interrupted cry* (stanza 3) hint at isolation and violence. The *luminary clock* (a lighted clock on a post or perhaps the moon) is detached and non-judgmental; it indicates that time is *neither wrong nor right*. The repetition of *I have* seven times, the repeated end rhyme, and the interlocking terza rima all pull the poem together. The rhymes (e.g., *beat/feet/street*) clinch ideas. The high number of end-stopped lines combined with the repetition suggests compression and sparseness.

Design, page 901–902

1 • What three white objects are described in lines 1–8? what do they symbolize? What *design* do they suggest?

2 • What question does the speaker consider in lines 9–12? What answer does the closing couplet suggest? What does the answer imply about the cosmos?

The speaker uses the coincidence of three white things coming together in nature to imply that the universe is controlled by evil designs or by no intelligent plan at all. Frost uses a modified sonnet form (*abba, abba, acaa, cc*) to organize these ideas and to create a tight network of rhyme sounds that clinch ideas throughout. In lines 1–8, the speaker observes the deadly convergence of white flower, spider, and moth; all three ironically (because white) symbolize *death and blight* and evil (*witches' broth*). The third quatrain asks what brought these three things together; the idea of design is emphasized in the unnatural whiteness of a normal blue flower. The couplet answers the question: either malevolent intelligence (*design of darkness to appall*) or pure chaotic chance (*if design govern*).

The Strong Are Saying Nothing, page 902

1 • What situation is described in the first fourteen lines? What is the virtue of the references to the spring plowing and planting?

2 • A reader has asserted that the final two lines are abrupt and that they change the context of the poem so significantly that they are obscure. How justifiable is this criticism?

The poem is a well visualized picture of the activities of an agricultural spring. The "rumpling" of the soil is of course spring plowing; the hoe is used for certain "selected" seeds that are planted in the hopes of a summer harvest of table vegetables. The second stanza is particularly noteworthy in its presentation of an almost painterly vision of people in the fields working at their springtime tasks. Incidentally, Frost alludes to his own "The Tuft of Flowers" in line 6, which concerns men working alone in "lots plowed far apart."

We should notice that the details of planting all refer to the earliest work that is done in the earliest spring, in the hopes that there will be no killing frosts to destroy the work. It may be too cold, for example, for the bees to arrive to carry on their springtime and summer tasks of pollinating blossoms for the summer fruiting of blooming vegetables and fruits. In short, all the tasks that Frost describes involve hope and anticipation; the world still looks barren, with "no cry of what is hoped to be."

Therefore there is a connection between the first fourteen lines and the concluding two, even though the shift from agriculture to "little or much beyond the grave" may at first seem abrupt. The connection is that the seeds of faith must be sown even when there is no absolute certainty that they will ever reach the stage of harvest. The implication for assuming the existence of an afterlife is that it does not just happen. It must be cultivated during the life we have, just as the earliest spring preparation is needed if a good fall harvest is to be obtained. Although the final two lines still may seem abrupt, they are nevertheless connected in this symbolic way.

Frost's final sentence preserves the symbolism of the early preparation of the earth. Just as springtime and summer growth, along with fall harvest, may occur, it is too early to judge what will happen until the conditions for harvest are actually seen. Thus, "the strong" will say nothing positive until they see more and learn more. This conclusion is negative in comparison with the final stanza in "Misgiving" (page 901).

A Considerable Speck (Microscopic), pages 902–903

1 • What is the setting and situation? What does the speaker find on his paper? How does he deal with it? Why?

2 • To what extent do rhyme, meter, and diction contribute to tone and theme?

3 • How is "on any sheet the least display of mind" used with a double meaning?

Frost's tone here is playful, ironic, and wry. He uses an insignificant insect and event to make the assertion that there is a general dearth of intelligence in the world. Tone is established in part by the iambic meter, the rhymes (e.g., "ink-think," "feet-complete"), and the colloquial diction. The speaker finds a microscopic insect on his blank paper and eventually recognizes it as "an intelligence" (line 15). He spares the mite partly because it is innocent and partly because he is glad to find "On any sheet the least display of mind." The implication is that many written and printed things are mindless. This conclusion makes the poem amusing and memorable.

Writing About a Poet's Work, *pages 903–909*

This section discusses biographical, developmental, and comparative approaches to a number of poems by a single author. The most accessible type of essay for students is the comparative one in which students can write about a common element or technique in a number of poems. The sample essay illustrates such an approach to Donne's love poetry (pages 906–908).

Writing Topics for Donne, Dickinson, and Frost, *page 909*

The following topics are designed to give students the opportunity to concentrate on the works of the poets and not on secondary sources. Any of the topics, however, may be assigned as a research paper. In such an event, students will wish to consult Appendix C, on research, for guidance in using library resources and in collecting notes and transforming them, along with their first-hand observations, into their finished research essays.

Donne

(1—6) Any of these topics should bring in a number of separate poems, including those to be found elsewhere in the text.

1, 2. These two topics are of course interrelated. The topic of becoming a saint of love in "The Canonization" is typical of the use of religious imagery in the love poems, just as the idea of being ravished in "Batter My Heart" shows the use of sexually related images in the religious poems. Granted the comparative difficulty of Donne's poems, an essay on about him could be made in reference to no more than two of the poems. Of course it would also be workable to show how the relationships work within a larger number of the poems.

3. Donne's use of metaphor and conceit is one of the topics that Donne's poetry invites. Again, it would not be inappropriate to use both

romantic and religious poems, such as "The Good Morrow" and "A Hymn to God My God." The goal would be to determine the degree to which metaphors and similes permeate the thought of the poems. Because just about everyone who writes about Donne takes into account his use of the metaphysical conceit, this topic would provide a good opportunity to create a research assignment.

4. As any reference to the need for annotation in Donne would indicate, Donne's poetic diction is intelligent and elaborate. Certainly a discussion of diction would benefit from the close textual analysis of a number of poems, attempting to show the proportions and relationships of specific and general words, together with any other aspects of diction that students could uncover.

5. This topic would best be undertaken with just a few of the love poems. The goal might be to compare Donne's poems with some other, more traditional, love poems in the text, such as Shakespeare's "Let Me Not" (page 757) or "Green Grow" and "A Red, Red Rose" by Burns (613, 652). Obviously, if poems of later periods are introduced, the idea would be to make comparisons of sensibilities. The goal would be to determine the degree to which Donne brings philosophical and scientific material to bear in his love poetry. Also, the objection should be considered that Donne's love poetry is deficient because he designs his poems to make his lady think, not to flatter her.

6. The problem in undertaking to analyze the prosodic and formal aspects of Donne's poetry is to keep the essay unified. Too often a study of rhythm and rhyme encourages a breaking off of material, so that separate essays rather than unified essays are produced. If students could unify their essays by indicating that Donne uses, say, "intricate rhyme schemes," or "varying stanzaic patterns," then their essays could be unified through the constant comparison of the various examples from the poems.

Dickinson

(1—6) The selection of poems to study for any of the topics on Dickinson would of course vary depending on the topic.

1. Any of the poems would demonstrate her brevity. Poems like "Some Keep the Sabbath Going to Church" and "Wild Nights" might be used as the base for personal subject matter and ideas.

2. Dickinson of course was one of the most highly personal but also private poets. Poems such as "I Never Felt at Home," "My Life Closed Twice," "I Cannot Live with You," and "I Never Lost as Much but Twice"

would furnish the basis for an analysis in depth of her expression, although the causes for what she says must forever remain obscure.

3. Images, of course, can be supplied from any of the poems, such as the "pile" of mountains in "I Like to See It Lap the Miles" or the soul shutting the door in "The Soul Selects Her Own Society."

4. The subject of death might be treated in "I Heard a Fly Buzz" and "Safe in Their Alabaster Chambers," together with others. Religious topics are dealt with in poems like "'Faith' Is a Fine Invention," "A Word Made Flesh Is Seldom," and "Some Keep the Sabbath." A great number of the poems deal with personal pain, such as "I Cannot Live with You," "I Died for Beauty," and "My Life Closed Twice Before Its Close."

5. Dickinson's humor and irony may be found in "'Faith' Is a Fine Invention" and "I Keep the Sabbath," and may also be traced in some of the more serious poems, such as "I Never Lost as Much but Twice," and "There's a Certain Slant of Light."

6. All the poems the anthology (there are twenty-six in all) would furnish ample material for an analysis of the appearance of Dickinson's poems on the page. If you wish a more extensive paper on a greater number of poems, it may become necessary to send your students to the library for a fuller collection of Dickinson's verse.

Frost

1. Frost's ideas generally emerge through his accumulation of detail, so that attention to the conclusions of many of his poems will enable students to develop ideas about his thought. "Mending Wall," for example, provides material for considerable analysis, as does "Birches," along with just about all the poems.

2. A consideration of Frost's topics and images of course is a natural way to approach him. Questions might concern the issue of why Frost chooses the topic matter of everyday rural life. How does he make it relevant for readers whose lives do not involve them in such life? (Example: In "The Road Not Taken," the topic is apparently a country road, but the meaning concerns paths of existence and choices of life that everyone makes.)

3. Students undertaking to write about Frost's poetic persona might note the brief discussion on page 893. Most of the poems included here involve the observer of the country scene, but "A Line-Storm Song," "Fire and Ice," "Acquainted with the Night," and "Misgiving" provide mate-

rial for the assertion that the poet creates a greater variety of voices than he is sometimes given credit for.

4. For a treatment of the structuring in Frost's poems, it might be good to zero in on a group of poems, such as "Birches," "Mending Wall," and "The Tuft of Flowers," and attempt to bring together common patterns of structure. It might prove interesting to compare such poems with, say, "Misgiving" and "Acquainted with the Night" to determine how rigidly Frost adheres to the specific/general pattern of movement within his poems.

5. Many of the poems included here could serve as the basis for studying Frost's diction. Probably the best plan would be to work on poems like "'Out, Out—'" and "The Strong Are Saying Nothing," and then to contrast these with a poem like "Nothing Gold Can Stay." Such a comparison would provide material for determining the degree to which Frost's word choices vary with his subject matter.

6. The poems selected for this anthology provide a wide variety of Frost's poetic forms, from the heroic couplets in "The Tuft of Flowers," to the blank verse of "Mending Wall," to the unique rhythmical lines of "A Line-Storm Song" to the use of tercets concluded with a couplet to make up the sonnet "Acquainted with the Night," to the interestingly varied rhythms in "The Strong Are Saying Nothing." Students should be able to arrive at fascinating conclusions about the many forms that Frost uses.

Chapter Twenty-five
Pages 910–1012

Additional Poems

Leonard Adamé, *My Grandmother Would Rock Quietly and Hum, page 910*

The speaker evokes memories of his grandmother, his Hispanic background, and his happy childhood. The Grandmother represents a period of peace and joy, calm acceptance, and the speaker's Mexican heritage. Lines 1–45 focus on memory and past; the speaker's childhood is contrasted with the poverty and turmoil of the Grandmother's girlhood in Mexico (lines 34–45). Specific images (*braids, papas, café*) make the speaker's childhood vivid and immediate. For the speaker (lines 46–56), the Grandmother's empty house can still create nostalgia for Mexico and a vanished childhood.

A. R. Ammons, *80-Proof, pages 911–912*

This is a poem that combines humor and seriousness. The poet is writing in a comic mode. Ammons's speaker determines the composition of his body based on a weight of 175 pounds, and concludes that he himself is only a fifth of that—35 pounds. All the rest consists of matter such as "steaks & chops & / chicken fat." Inasmuch as poets often employ poetry to determine their own identities and their place in the universe, the speaker's self-analysis creates laughter and surprise. The stress on the word "fifth" (lines 1, 19) refers not only to the fraction of the speaker's body that is himself, but also to a bottle of whiskey. The concluding ambiguity on "100 % spiritual" therefore refers both to the mind or soul and also to spirituous liquor.

Maya Angelou, *My Arkansas, page 912*

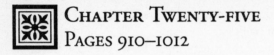

Angelou explores her own reactions ("My Arkansas" rather than simply "Arkansas") to a state deeply scarred by racial strife. Arkansas' history of violence against African Americans disturbs the speaker's perceptions of the land and nature. The "old crimes" that "pend from poplar trees" imply lynchings. The "sullen earth" (see Shakespeare's "When in Disgrace," page 985) is "red" with clay and blood. In stanza 2, the speaker observes that the history of racism has eroded even the light shining on the land, and, if light may be construed as a symbol of tolerance and intelligence, the land is yet to be illumined. In stanza 3, she states that racial hatred and attitudes ("ante-bellum lace") of the past are still very much alive. Indeed, the past is still the present, and the present is "yet to come."

ANONYMOUS, *Barbara Allan,* PAGES 912–913
ANONYMOUS, *Lord Randal,* PAGES 913–914
ANONYMOUS, *The Three Ravens,* PAGES 914–915

These popular ballads tell of both horrible and touching events. Barbara Allan, by slighting a young swain, has caused his death, and his death is causing hers. Lord Randal is poisoned by his true love. The sweetheart of the dead warrior in "The Three Ravens" quickly joins him in death. All the narratives present only the high points and concluding scenes. Commonly, there is much dialogue to make the poems dramatic. In "Lord Randal" the mother asks questions and the son answers. In "Barbara Allan" the sick swain and Barbara Allan engage in dialogue, and the last stanza is Barbara's farewell to life. In "The Three Ravens," the three birds observe and describe the sad drama unfolding below them.

An important technique of the ballad, in light of the fact that there are many stanzas and that interest must be preserved, is the dramatic delay in the disclosure of what has happened. Thus, the guilt must build in Barbara Allan before she, like her slighted lover, succumbs to death. The will of Lord Randal, the mention of which is delayed until the final stanza, indicates that his death has been caused by his sweetheart. The drama of the "lemman" and the knight unfolds as one of the birds describes the place of death as a potential spot where they may obtain food, and where they will be opposed by the hawk, the hounds, and the sweetheart as long as she lives.

The ballads commonly have a refrain, which may be like the *With a down, derry, derry, derry, down, down* of "The Three Ravens" or the varying repetitions in "Barbara Allan." These refrains may be integrated with the action of the narrative, or they may serve as brief interludes separating the stanzas of narrative and dialogue.

Margaret Atwood, *Variation on the Word "Sleep," pages 915–916*

This is a love poem of intense longing. Using the phrase "I would like to" over and over, like an incantation, the speaker conveys deep emotion, creating thereby a kind of continuous motif of desire. Wanting to enter into the loved one's sleep—one of the most personal and intimate of experiences—shows the intensity of the speaker's wish. There is genuine tenderness in the way going to sleep is presented—like entering a waterworld of beauty in motion—emphasized by the speaker's desire to protect the loved one against whatever might be fearful in the dream. Finally, the speaker's wish to be as necessary and as natural to the loved one as the very air he/she breathes tells us that the speaker wants to be essential to life of the loved one. A major achievement of the poem is that it conveys so passionate a desire with such simplicity and calm.

W. H. Auden, *The Unknown Citizen, pages 916–917*

Auden employs an ironic tone and sociological jargon to satirize the loss of identity and individuality in modern society. The epitaph and the poem are spoken by a representative of the state, who identifies the citizen by number rather than name. The speaker knows the citizen's statistics thoroughly, and he praises the citizen's tendency to conform in all matters. The citizen's work habits, social behavior, consumption, and ideology were all known and normal. He had the right appliances ("everything necessary to the Modern Man"), opinions, and number of children. In most respects, the citizen is certainly not "unknown" in the sense of "unknown soldier." But the state cares nothing about the inner man ("Was he free?" "Was he happy?"). In this sense, the citizen is *unknown*. While the speaker's tone is smug and admiring, the tone of the poem is ironic and contemptuous. The poet deplores modern dehumanization and conformity. Auden also uses the rhyme to create the tone and clinch ideas; note that even the epitaph rhymes (*78/State*). For comparison, see Howard Nemerov's "Life Cycle of Common Man" (page 970).

Imamu Amiri Baraka (LeRoi Jones), *Ka 'Ba, page 917*

The poem contrasts the beauty of black lives and the glory of the African-American heritage with the enslavement and degradation encountered by blacks in the society of the United States. African Americans defy the chains and limitations of their world ("dirty courtyards," "physics," "grey chains in a place full of winters") through "the stream of their will." Although they suffer, kill, and fail, their world is vital and lovely. Their heritage is freedom, sunlight, and Africa. At the close, the speaker wonders what "magic spells" or "sacred words" will restore African Americans to themselves and their "ancient image." Compare this poem to Gwendolyn Brooks's "Primer for Blacks" (page 922), which also deals with the problem of black self-images.

Marvin Bell, *Things We Dreamt We Died For, pages 917–918*

Bell uses metaphors for patriotism ("Flags of all sorts") and scholarship to imply that the academic opposition to war and the defense of learning is fraudulent. The "causes" put away in "closets full of bones" may imply earlier or youthful periods of radicalism. These "plunderers" have gained fame and fortune through such activity. The term "dreamt" suggests that the whole process has been a sham and an illusion for those "saviours" of literature and the young.

Earle Birney, *Can. Lit., page 918*

The speaker blames Canadian history and habits for the dearth of great Canadian literature. The first stanza establishes a metaphor based on birds that fly away. The vast spaces of Canada and the ongoing *civil war* between the French and the English subverted the impulse to develop great national poets such as Dickinson or Whitman (both of whom are named in the poem). Energy has gone into conflict and control instead of literature.

William Blake, *The Sick Rose, page 919*

William Blake, *Ah Sun-flower, page 919*

Both poems are a part of Blake's critical and revolutionary views of the life and society of his time. His idea is that the potential flourishing of human life is lopped off because of the defective social and political structure. The "Rose" may be taken to symbolize beauty, perfection, innocence, and the capacity to develop. But it is destroyed by the "invisible worm," which Blake probably intended as a symbol of the cultural perversions that divert and truncate growth, and that thus reinforce injustice in society. The "worm" is also associated with the form of a "snake" or "serpent" that Satan assumed when he tempted and subverted Adam and Eve. Thus evil, as human beings are now constituted, begins inwardly and spreads corruption outwardly.

The "Sun-flower" may be taken as a symbol of youth, yearning, innocence, or repressed sexuality. It is made weary by tracing the movement of the sun across the heavens ("steps of the sun") and seeks that "sweet golden clime" where the "journey is done" (this certainly represents an ending of suppression, but it may also represent fruition and fulfillment). Stanza 2 offers two parallel symbols of repression: the "youth" who has "pined away with desire" and the "pale Virgin shrouded in snow." These figures, like the Sun-flower, seek to be free of restraint. Interestingly, "Ah Sun-flower," in keeping with its subject of yearning and lack of fulfillment, is a long sentence fragment.

Louise Bogan, *Women, pages 919–920*

"Women" explores the idea that women, placed into a largely dependent position, have assumed a character that is self-limiting and self-demeaning. In a world where they have no responsibility, and where men make decisions, women withdraw into the "tight hot cell" of themselves (like an oven) and do not experience life fully. They are passive ("wait") and lack flexibility or moderation ("stiffen," "Too tense, or too lax"). The concluding stanza is reminiscent of the "Alice Ben-Bolt" type of woman ("She shook with delight when you gave her a smile, / But trembled with fear at your frown."), but the speaker implies in the last two lines—but only implies, for this is not a revolutionary poem—that women would be better off if they would let this sort of life "go by"; i.e., stop giving in to the circumstances of exclusive domesticity and self-effacement that are suppressing them.

Arna Bontemps, *A Black Man Talks of Reaping, page 920*

This lyric is a truncated sonnet (*abab, cdcd, efef*). The quatrains organize the speaker's thoughts and feelings. The poem expresses the sorrow and bitterness of black existence. The central metaphors are sowing (i.e., labor of any sort, but usually "stoop labor") and reaping (wealth, happiness, reward, advancement). The speaker observes the vast extent of his own sowing (lines 1–6), the meagerness of his harvest (7–8), and the fact that his "brother's sons" (i.e., white brother's sons) benefit from his labor (9–10) while his own children (people, blacks) collect the leavings in fields "they have not sown, and feed on bitter fruit." The poem thus implies that African Americans labor in vain, since they are excluded from reward or advancement of any kind. Perhaps this point is underscored by the absence of the last two lines, indicating graphically the lack of reward about which the poem speaks.

Anne Bradstreet, ***To My Dear and Loving Husband, page 920***

The poem is unusual because it is about the fulfillment the speaker finds in married love, for usually love poems are about the love, yearning, and dedication of unmarried lovers who speak more about their own feelings than about their objective assessments of their loved ones. The poem is also unusual because the speaker is a woman praising her husband. She speaks of the closeness, passion, and value of their love, which seems so strong that she intimates that her concept of immortality is to continue loving her husband "when we live no more" (line 12). For comparison, see Elizabeth Barrett Browning's "Sonnet 43: How Do I Love Thee" (page 923), the conclusion of which is similar to that of Bradstreet's poem. A poem in which a loving husband praises his wife is O'Shaughnessey's "A Love Symphony" (page 693).

Robert Bridges, ***Nightingales, page 921***

Bridges's poem contrasts expectation with reality (or the ideal with the real) by evoking and then reversing the traditional view that the songs of nightingales exhibit a link between ordinary life and the magical, mystical world of pure beauty. In lines 1–6 the speaker addresses the nightingales, calling forth the beauty and immortality of their songs (compare Keats's "Ode to a Nightingale," page 770). The nightingales reply in lines 7–18. Their world is neither beautiful nor ideal, and their songs embody "the voice of desire" and a "dark nocturnal secret." Their "art" cannot communicate the "forbidden hopes profound." They are, in short, creatures of Nature, whose role is to make the night beautiful, but also to retire during the day when "the innumerable choir of day / Welcome the dawn."

Joseph Brodsky, ***In Memory of My Father: Australia, page 921***

The poem wrestles with the complex emotions and memories which accompany a parent's death, but conveys loss and longing in part by the need to use humor to cover grief. The speaker has dreamed that his dead father is not dead but is in Australia (virtually the other side of the world, and therefore a humorous approximation of the "Other World" of death). Surprisingly, the dead father is not transformed by death into a gentle, wise patriarch, but is instead a complainer from the word go—just, one would imagine, as he was in life. Still, the speaker finds this noisy reminder of the father's flaws better than the reality, which is a can of ashes given the survivor with a voucher as the summation of a human life.

With another touch of humor, the speaker calls the father's cremation his attempt to "play genie" by emerging as a cloud over the chimney of the crematorium. For many readers, it is impossible to read this poem, despite the humor, without thinking of the crematoria of the Holocaust.

Gwendolyn Brooks, *Primer for Blacks, pages 922–923*

Brooks is a black whose first audiences were mostly white. In 1967 she began directing her work toward black readers. This poem reflects that shift; it attacks African Americans for self-denigration and low self-esteem ("self-shriveled"), and asserts that blackness is power and glory. The speaker castigates the "slack in Black" who believe that "It's great to be White." The speaker argues that African Americans have geographic power, and she concludes that all blacks must learn to find value and strength in their blackness.

Elizabeth Barrett Browning, *How Do I Love Thee, page 923*

This is the most famous of all Elizabeth Browning's poems. Her speaker describes the abundance of her love with reference to infinite spaces and abstract ideas ("the ends of Being"). In the second quatrain, the love is measured against daily necessities ("quiet need") and ideals of freedom and purity. In lines 9–12, the speaker asserts that her entire life expresses her love; she loves with a child's faith and with all her "breath." Lines 13–14 suggest that the love will continue after death. Note that the speaker describes her own attitudes and dedication, and says nothing at all about specific qualities of the husband. Compare this poem with Bradstreet's "To My Dear and Loving Husband" (page 920).

Robert Browning, *Soliloquy of the Spanish Cloister, pages 924–925*

This poem is a masterpiece in the mode of the dramatic monologue. As the speaker, a cloistered priest or monk, talks himself alive, he also reveals that he is a fish out of water, a man filled with anger and contradictions. The poem is simultaneously comic and frightening; the speaker is a monster of envy, but he does not know it. He is in the same order with "Brother Lawrence," bur he believes that Lawrence's apparent indifference to lovely women is a cover for lechery. In fact, however, the speaker is projecting his own desires onto Lawrence, for it is he, the speaker, who speaks longingly of "Dolores" and "Sanchicha" as they wash their hair in the tank outside the "Convent bank." To gain revenge on Lawrence, he states that he intends to hide his pornographic novel, open to a particularly juicy part, amid Lawrence's harvest, to get him damned by seeing the profane text (whose book is it, and who will be damned by looking at it?). The speaker has other schemes, all of which contrast sharply with his ordained role of monk. Of course, Lawrence is a virtual saint, while the speaker shows himself to be in a state of anger, envy, hatred, suppressed lust, and hypocrisy. A similar poem by Browning is "The Bishop Orders His Tomb at St. Praxed's Church."

George Gordon, Lord Byron, *The Destruction of Sennacherib, page 926*

This poem is the best known of the poems in Byron's *Hebrew Melodies* (1815), the last major work he published before he left England, to remain in virtual exile until his death. The poem demonstrates Byron's virtuosic metrical skill, being almost entirely in anapæsts, with occasional amphibrachs and iambs as substitute feet. Byron's opening simile, comparing a wolf attacking a sheepfold to the Assyrian army attacking the Hebrews, is striking, filled as it is with the implication of the innocent and helpless sheep and the vicious attacker. The power of human warriors, however, is nothing before Divine power, for it is the "Angel of Death" which lays the Assyrian host low. In the final stanza, Byron mentions the "widows of Ashur" who lament their dead. But by returning quickly to the supposed falsity of the Assyrian religion ("the temple of Baal"), Byron avoids concentrating on the fact that the Assyrians were people too, with homes, wives, and responsibilities, and that their deaths might be cause for pity and sorrow. Instead, he concludes on the note that God will protect the Chosen People against war and injustice. Ogden Nash, in "Very Like a Whale" (page 969), parodies Byron's metaphor of the wolf on the fold.

Thomas Campion, *Cherry Ripe,* pages 926–927

Campion himself set many of his poems to music, this among them. Those listening to a musical rendition, however, would need to pay close attention upon first hearing, for the text is complex. The basic metaphor of the poem is the garden, which stands for the lady's beauty—a conventional comparison. The roses are her cheeks, the lilies her skin, along with other metaphors to suggest her beauty and desirability. The cry "cherry ripe" was apparently commonly used during the Renaissance by fruit sellers to advertise their wares. In the poem, it suggests that no one may have the fruit (i.e., kiss the lady's lips) unless she herself declares her willingness, perhaps when she is mature, perhaps when in love. At first, the poem therefore seems to suggest that the lady's beauty might be for sale. But by the last stanza we have seen that her beauty brings the need for wise decisions about where she will give her love. The poem is thus a morality lesson, one which shows surprising respect for a woman's freedom of choice and destiny.

Lucille Clifton, *this morning, page 927*

Prosodically, this poem is an exercise in rhythm and emphasis. The topic is self-recognition and pride in oneself. Whereas at an earlier time a black might be ashamed of the African background, now this heritage is one of which the speaker is proud ("i met myself / coming in / a bright / jungle girl"). The speaker goes on to compare herself metaphorically with a "black bell" that rings out her vitality for all to hear and see. "Bell" may also be a pun on "belle," for the speaker's sense of identity encompasses and comprises all images of beauty and joy.

Lucille Clifton, *the poet, page 928*

In this brief poem of six lines the speaker cites a number of reasons for which she creates poetry. She would like to be restrained, but poetry is in her bones, in her very being, and her need for expression is spinning and churning at the center of her existence. Though she has fears of seeming foolish, her poetry is like a dance that she must perform. Indeed, she cannot separate her art from her life, despite whatever obstacles she might encounter.

Stephen Crane, *Do Not Weep, Maiden, for War Is Kind, page 928*

The poem is a strong and ironic anti-war statement. Stanzas 1, 3, and 5 focus on the losses and deaths produced through war: A maiden loses her lover (lines 1–5), a baby loses her father (12–16), and a mother loses her son (23–26). There is nothing "kind" about the losses or about war. Stanzas 2 and 4 mock the symbols of passion that encourage war: booming drums, unexplained glory, the blazing flag of the regiment, the eagle on the flag. Both stanzas close with the same image of war's reality: "A field where a thousand corpses lie." The realities of carnage and loss are thus contrasted with the illusions of ideals. Compare Owen's "Dulce et Decorum Est" (page 681) and Cummings's "next to of course god america i" (page 929).

Countee Cullen, *Yet Do I Marvel, page 929*

Cullen, a poet of the Harlem Renaissance, was a pioneer in dealing with topics concerning the conditions and aspirations of African Americans. In this poem, which is a Shakespearean sonnet, Cullen's speaker uses each of the quatrains to take up a different aspect of the mysteries of God's ways. In the first, the speaker questions the necessity of death. "Good" and "kind" are ironic, and "well-meaning" suggests less than ideal results. The allusions to the myths of Tantalus and Sisyphus (lines 5–8) emphasize the futility of existence; these men are fated never to complete their assigned tasks. The third quatrain explores humanity's inability to understand any of God's purposes. The couplet offers the most mysterious and paradoxical problem—a black poet asked to "sing" (write poetry) out of the bleak wretchedness of black existence; this is the mystery of God's demands that the speaker finds most remarkable.

E. E. Cummings, *next to of course god america i, page 929*

The poem satirizes the clichés and banalities of super-patriotism. The quoted material (lines 12–13) is spoken by an impassioned yet ignorant traditionalist who sees death in war as heroic and admirable (compare Owen's "Dulce et Decorum Est," page 681, and Crane's "Do Not Weep, Maiden," page 928). His monologue is full of half-witted, half-digested, and fragmented phrases from patriotic songs. The alliteration and repetition (especially in lines 7–8) underscore the speaker's fatuousness. Line 14, spoken by a detached observer, puts the preceding diatribe into perspective and also indicates that this particular "voice of liberty," now mute, is really a voice that tries to suppress, not liberate, the human spirit.

E. E. Cummings, *if there are any heavens, page 930*

This is a successful poem about a topic—love for one's mother—that frequently goes off the deep end into sentimentality. Without claiming that he/she loves dear old Mom, the speaker conveys a deeper affection. The setting is a heaven that the speaker's mother will have "all by herself." (Although the poem does not explain why the mother might be deserving of her own heaven, we might assume that it is a reward for hardships tolerated in life.) This heaven will not be strewn with pansies or fragile lilies of the valley, but rather will be filled with "blackred roses" (line 4). The scene visualized is one in which the mother will almost be holding court, as if she were a queen, with the speaker's father standing by, "swaying over her / silent." The final three lines capture a sudden scene of respect and adoration, and the poem ends strongly. Because Cummings is often ironic, some critics have claimed irony here, but this poem seems straightforward, without ironic complications. It is a masterly personal tribute.

JAMES DICKEY, *The Performance, pages 930–931*

This poem is a product of the Pacific theater of World War II between the United States and Japan from 1941 to 1945. Early in the war the Japanese invaded and occupied the Philippine Islands, and many Americans were captured and were subject to atrocities. Dickey's speaker tells the story about one of the captive pilots, whom he names Donald Armstrong. In relaxed moments before his capture, the speaker says, Armstrong had performed physical feats like standing on his head. When captured by the Japanese he continued to do this exercise, even though he was about to be beheaded. Ironically, the speaker points out that the executioner would just as soon have cut off Armstrong's feet as his head, except that Armstrong, after having dug his own grave, knelt before it with dignity to receive the blow.

"The Performance" hence demonstrates, on the one hand, the sort of violence that characterizes Dickey's well-received novel *Deliverance* (1970), and on the other, the courageousness of a human being, insisting on his individuality and rights even against the greatest odds. Readers may note that the name "Armstrong" is the name of the radio hero "Jack Armstrong" of the 1930s and 1940s. To the highest degree, this name embodied the idea of the "All-America Boy," who excelled in all athletic competition and carried this excellence into all avenues of life.

JAMES DICKEY, *Kudzu, pages 931–933*

Kudzu is a plant used for animal food and forage in its native countries of China and Japan. It was imported into this country for experimental purposes, and, naturally, got out of hand, just as creatures like the Starling and the Gypsy Moth did. In the United States kudzu is invasive, covering native shrubs, bushes, and trees, and starving out its host plants. In much of "Kudzu," Dickey describes the habits of this plant, telling the story that in Georgia, "the legend says / That you must close your windows / At night to keep it out of the house" (lines 9–11). Dickey's speaker notes that kudzu covers telephone poles, houses, cows, and pigs, and that its confines offer a perfect hiding place for poisonous snakes. Dickey observes how an organized group of men uses sticks to destroy the hiding snakes. As a final insult of the plant, the speaker notes, kudzu becomes ugly and black when it freezes. The kudzu may be taken as a symbol for the invasiveness of foreign plants upon native American *flora,* but it may also be read as a symbol of similarly invasive foreign—specifically Japanese—industrial products. The conclusion is a general one: There are terrors within and without, and kudzu is one of the most prominent of external terrors. The poem is characteristic of Dickey's poetic craft, for it exhibits a good deal of description, with an accent on the violent, dangerous, and threatening.

JAMES DICKEY, *The Lifeguard, pages 933–934*

In this poem about death, guilt, and resurrection, the speaker-lifeguard becomes a Christ figure in his own dream vision. Stanza 1 establishes setting and situation. The children (probably at summer camp) are asleep at night; the lifeguard is alone, lying in a boat tied up in a boathouse. In stanza 2, he walks on the water in quest of the miracle of resurrection. Stanzas 3–6 flash back to an earlier failure at salvation (saving a drowning child that afternoon). Although the children had faith, the speaker failed to save the "one who had sunk from my sight" despite many attempts to see and recover the dead child. Stanza 4 is full of images of cold, water, dark, and death, while stanza 5 conveys the speaker's "defeat" and the children's disappointment. In stanza 6, the speaker hides in the boathouse awaiting night and the moon reflected on the water. Stanzas 7–10 embody the present dream (or reality) of resurrection; the lifeguard walks to the center of the lake to be the "savior of one who has already died in my care." He calls out; the child answers and rises from the depths. The child of "water" can represent either rebirth (and baptism) or illusion (and death).

H. D. (HILDA DOOLITTLE), *Pear Tree, page 935*

The images are all important here. The speaker sees the fertile and beautiful pear tree in linked images of silver and strength. In lines 1–7, the tree is imagined as "silver dust." The strength is conveyed in verbs ("lift," "mount," "reach," "front") and in images of height and mass. The flower and leaf also combine images of silver and strength. The "thick" flowers will bring "summer and ripe fruits" in their "purple hearts."

RITA DOVE, *Ö,* PAGES 935–936

This is an unusual speculative poem developing out of the speaker's thoughts about the Swedish word for "island," which is the "Ö" of the title. The word is just right, conveying onomatopoeically, by the pursing of the mouth (the speaker tells us how to say it in lines 1 and 2), the image of the thing being symbolized. The contemplation of the rightness of the word leads to a series of fanciful symbolic possibilities, all of which are related to the power of language. It would of course be literally impossible for the house on the corner to take off over the marshland (lines 14–17), but if the words are right, they may effect even greater changes. The concluding stanza is a powerful tribute to the capacity of words to alter the direction of our lives, for once human beings begin to learn, "nothing's/ like it used to be, not even the future." As a tribute to the strength of language and ideas, this poem may be compared with Shelley's "Ode to the West Wind" (page 776).

Michael Drayton, *Since There's No Help, page 936*

This English or Shakespearean sonnet, spoken by a male lover to his mistress, captures the moment in which their relationship is about to fall apart. While the poem may be somewhat difficult for students, it deals with easily understandable feelings. In the first quatrain, the relationship seems doomed and the speaker seems resigned (and even "glad") about it. The second quatrain continues in the same vein. Here, however, a claim might be made that the speaker is protesting too much. His hyperbole is shown in words like "forever," "all our vows," and "not one jot." We get a clearer view of the speaker's feelings in lines 9–14, where he claims that his mistress could save the relationship. He is willing, and needs her words to save their love, which like a dying person ("bed of death") will expire without her saving intervention. The tone of the sonnet thus shifts from the apparently cavalier "you get no more of me" of line 2, to the hopeful "From death to life thou mightst him yet recover" of line 14.

Paul Laurence Dunbar, *Sympathy, page 936–937*

This lyric voices the emotions and desires of African Americans in general and of a black poet in particular. The caged bird symbolizes blacks and the black poet. The bird's imprisonment metaphorically captures the essence of black status. Stanza 1 contrasts the bird's cage (imposed limitations) with natural freedom and beauty. Stanza 2 expresses the bird's driving desire to be free. Stanza 3 identifies the bird's song (a traditional symbol of poetry) as a plea for freedom. Compare Cullen's "Yet Do I Marvel" (page 929).

Richard Eberhart, *The Groundhog, pages 937–938*

The poem embodies an intellectual and emotional process of discovery and renewal based on four separate observations of the decay of a dead groundhog. The animal itself symbolizes natural processes and rebirth (consider February 2, Groundhog Day). At the first observation in June (lines 1–25), the speaker is shocked by the "ferocious" vitality and "Vigor" of Nature. He reacts with "love" and "loathing," passion and prayer. In the second stage ("Autumn," lines 25–32), the ferocious activity of Nature in decay yields a "bony sodden hulk," and the speaker's initial emotions modulate to consideration and wisdom. On a third viewing ("Another Summer," lines 33–40), the vitality of nature and the decay of the groundhog (now only hair and "bones bleaching") is further humanized and intellectualized through images of architecture and geometry. In the final scene ("three years, now," lines 41–48), the lesson of the groundhog—the ferocious vitality of Nature—is applied directly to humanity. The speaker understands and accepts Nature red in tooth and claw in the human spirit, and he recognizes the inevitable cycle of life and death. The three figures cited in lines 46–48 thus represent this vitality, intellect, and cycle from life to death through various endeavors in different times of history.

T. S. Eliot, *The Love Song of J. Alfred Prufrock, pages 938–941*

This poem is difficult but rewarding. It offers a splendid opportunity to examine speaker, setting and situation, imagery, metaphor, allusion, and theme. The dramatic monologue is spoken by Prufrock (the name is both a pun [on "prudish"] and a parody [of elegant names]), a man who feels trapped in the hell of his own inadequacies (hence the epigraph from Dante's *Inferno).*

The dramatic situation is that Prufrock, a cultured man going to an afternoon tea, is consumed with an "overwhelming question" of whether or not to make a proposition to one of the cultured women taking "toast and tea" (hence the ironic title "Love Song"). His reluctance, indecision, and fear of rejection dominate lines 1–83. The "you and I" in line 1 have been variously identified as Prufrock and a friend, Prufrock and the reader, or Prufrock and himself (perhaps even Prufrock's ego and superego or desires and self-consciousness). The metaphor of evening as an etherized patient (lines 2–3) suggests Prufrock's difficulty in dealing with his feelings. This is contrasted throughout the poem with the sexual life of the lower classes ("cheap hotels"), almost always linked with water images ("oyster shells") that suggest sexual activity.

The impending visit and the "overwhelming question," combined with Prufrock's ongoing impulse to revise, rethink, and retreat, recur as the central *motif* of the first section of the poem in lines 10–14, 25–31, 46–49, and 79–83. Failure, reticence, and withdrawal, the crisis of the poem, occurs in lines 84–86: Prufrock has been "afraid." He rationalizes and justifies his failure in lines 87–111, assuming that his approach would have been out of place, badly done, misunderstood, and rejected. He imagines that the woman to whom he spoke would have told him that "That is not what I meant at all."

In the last twenty lines, Prufrock offers an accurate assessment of his own present and future. The *Hamlet* metaphor (lines 111–119) identifies him as an insignificant and foolish character, far removed from the vital centers of life. He realizes that life and time have passed him by. The mermaids (sea imagery, sexuality) represent a fulfillment that Prufrock will never have ("I do not think that they will sing to me"—one of the most sorrowful lines in modern poetry). He can experience such vision in his dreams (lines 125–130), but *human voices* (reality, society, responsibility) remind him of his failures and inadequacies.

John Engels, *Naming the Animals, page 942*

The title, which is ironic, alludes to Adam's "naming the animals" in Eden (in Genesis). The dead deer and the captured one (lines 1–10) represent the speaker's desire for control, as though in a perverted way he can count only those things over which he has "dominion" (the word is Biblical). In a real sense, the poem represents an attack upon our civilization, as represented by the speaker, which has sought to control Nature, and to use the things of the earth exclusively for human benefit. Once we subdue and kill things, so that they do "not watch back" (line 17) we have controlled them and have therefore "named" them. The three does (line 11) do not count because they are still alive and wild, still a part of Nature, and not a part of human history until they are captured or killed.

Mari Evans, *I Am a Black Woman,* pages 942–943

Evans's open-form poem celebrates the power and strength of the black woman in the context of centuries of racial hatred, suppression, and war. The bitterness caused by this life is implied in the image of a song "written in a minor key." The long history of poverty and destruction is evoked by the images of death and birth (lines 10–12) and the four allusions to lynching and war (13–20). The last fourteen lines express the constructive power of the black woman; key terms are *strong, tall, defying, impervious,* and *indestructible.*

CAROLYN FORCHÉ, *Because One Is Always Forgotten, page 943*

This poem is a product of two years that Forché spent in El Salvador in the late 1970s. The atrocity described calmly in lines 7–10 refers to a custom of hanging trash on the boughs of fruit trees that were not producing. The Salvadoran army mocked this custom by murdering rebellious peasants, peeling their facial skin, and hanging it on trees. The speaker of the poem contrasts this barbarism with the need for strength like that possessed by Viera and others. Thus, the concluding paradox that "the heart is the toughest part of the body" (line 12) is that great skill is needed to commit the horror being committed by the "boy soldier." If this skill and care were turned to a good end, the poem implies, there would be no need for the toughness and callousness that must be developed to stand up to the brutalities of warfare and the suppression of civilian populations.

DAN GEORGAKAS, *Hiroshima Crewman, page 944*

The first atomic bomb was dropped over Hiroshima, Japan, in August of 1945. The American plane that carried the bomb bore the name "Enola Gay," and the men in the crew did not understand until later the true dimensions of the destruction that they had unleashed. Afterward, the former crewmen experienced great psychological disturbance. In "Hiroshima Crewman," Georgakas centers on one crew member who in dealing with his feelings entered holy orders and took vows of silence. The concluding lines focus on atrocities committed by the Germans (Auschwitz, Dachau), but the speaker implies that no one side was guilty of all the atrocities, for "war produces many brands" of horror. It is war itself, in other words, that is guilty.

NIKKI GIOVANNI, *Woman, page 944*

The speaker asserts that men have not supported the aspirations (needs, dreams, desires) of women—an argument couched in five metaphors ("blade," "robin," "web," "book," and "bulb"). Each metaphor suggests growth, creation, and order. In each, "he" refused to cooperate in the process of fulfillment. The final stanza suggests that women must seek such fulfillment, definition, and value within themselves, without recourse to the support of men.

Marilyn Hacker, *Sonnet Ending with a Film Subtitle, page 945*

This is a traditional Shakespearean sonnet, with only a slight variation in the last two lines (*abab, cdcd, efef, ef*). Though the form is traditional, however, the content is not. It is a personal expression by a rebellious speaker who is furious against a "bastard" who was apparently a departed husband or lover, who may perhaps have given her a "Venereal Disease" (line 3). The rebellion takes the possible directions of recommending that women "break our fetters / And raise our daughters to be Lesbians," or that the speaker could fortify her "rhetoric with guns" (line 10). Despite the rage smoldering in the poem, however, one might note the humor of the concluding line. The line might be construed as an admission of helplessness, or else as a modification of the French saying, "Je ris pour ne pas pleurer" (I laugh in order not to cry).

John Haines, *Little Cosmic Dust Poem, pages 945–946*

This poem contrasts the immensity of the universe with the miracle of life and love. Astronomers have concluded that our solar system, including the earth, was created out of the "debris of dying stars." In its death throes, an exploding star underwent catastrophic expansion, and created the many elements, such as oxygen, carbon, silicon, iron, silver, and gold, that have made life on earth possible. Astronomers have further speculated that the solar system will one day (in perhaps five billion years) be enveloped by the sun as it expands and dies, thus returning everything on earth to the status of "cosmic dust." In the light of these cosmic mind-boggling details, of this "silence and waste to come," life of any sort is miraculous, and love is one of the greatest and most precious of miracles.

Donald Hall, *Scenic View, page 946*

This poem demonstrates how poetic imagination and playfulness may combine with ironic seriousness. On the surface, "Scenic View" is based on the comic hypothesis that cameras taking pictures of a mountainous landscape drain the mountain scene of color. Eventually there will be so many photographs—so popular is the scene among amateur photographers—that all the color from the green and white mountains will have been transferred, bit by bit, into photograph albums, and the mountains will be "unseeable." The "intractable granite" peaks will still be there, however, but because of their invisibility, passing airplanes may crash into them. The serious undercurrent of the poem, never mentioned by the poet, is that increasing pollution, smog, acid rain, and haze may be the influence causing the fading-out of the scene. Thus the point may eventually be reached when the air will indeed make the mountains "unseeable," but the cause may be horribly real, not fanciful.

Daniel Halpern, *Snapshot of Hué, page 946–947*

Hué, a major Vietnamese city, was the scene of particular heavy attack and counterattack, bombing and shelling, and bitter streetfighting during the Tet Offensive of the War in Vietnam. The poem supposes that the speaker visits the city after the war is over and after the wreckage has been cleared away. The bridges are apparently restored, and there is much traffic on the streets, and the sun is "posted above"; in short, things are back to normal. The implication of the poem is that if things can now be normal, why should they ever have been otherwise? What was the purpose of the war, the "telling piles on corners" (line 5), the "debris that contained a little of everything" (line 6) and the "impenetrable" sky, presumably blackened by smoke by burning buildings (line 8)?

Daniel Halpern, *Summer in the Middle Class, pages 947–948*

Beneath what seems a cheerful description of America in a holiday mood there emerges a picture of lives undifferentiated by individuality, moving inexorably from banality to extinction. The tone is complex: There is humor in the picture of overweight fathers playing ball with their sons and of cooks preparing food and setting the tables for the mosquitoes to have their "evening meal." But the picture of a world "in unison" as being quintessentially American is chilling, and the final "total darkness" once the TV goes off constitutes a seriously negative judgment on American life.

H. S. (Sam) Hamod, *Leaves (for Sally), page 947*

In this poem the speaker tells of his Arabic father, who constantly sent grape leaves to him and his wife when he was alive, and whose leaves are still to be found in their home freezer, as though the father were still alive. This concrete evidence of the tradition of the old country causes the speaker to think of his heritage, and to trace his own development as a poet to the poetic impulses of his father. Although he did not understand his father's songs because they were in Arabic, the songs were poetry nevertheless. The idea of "Leaves" is that the human spirit is influenced not only consciously, but subliminally. The memory and creativity of the speaker's father will continue to exist, like the symbol of the grape leaves, within the speaker's mind, and they will influence his ideas and words as long as he lives. It is in this way that a national tradition is passed down from generation to generation.

Frances E. W. Harper, *She's Free, page 949*

The poem, with four-stress lines mainly in anapaests with commencing iambs, and with rhyming couplets (*aa, bb, cc, dd; ee, dd, cc*), is a modified sonnet, with the octave describing the flight of a black slave woman going north to flee slavery in the South. She braves great danger to leave "the hand of oppression," even though her only "crime is the hue of her face." The concluding sestet describes her success at evading bloodhounds, hunter, and posse; her life of difficulty is not over, for she will still "brave" the troubles of "poverty, danger, and death." But the glory of her flight is that she "is no longer a slave."

Michael S. Harper, *Called, pages 949–950*

The poem, describing the burial of a dog which had formerly been chained but which has broken loose and been killed, offers a series of images that contrast life and death, heat and coolness, light and dark, movement and stillness. The grave, black dirt, the animal's body, and the image of "the bed" and "earth and rock / which will hold her," the sunset, and the past tense of "called" all embody half of this contrast. The opposition is established in the "heat" (apparently the heat of oestrus, which caused the dog to break free) the "brother," the three questions that end the poem, and the present tense of "calls." The act of burial brings the speaker and his companion into direct contact with these two opposite aspects of a natural cycle. Compare Engels's "Naming the Animals" (page 942) and Stafford's "Traveling Through the Dark" (page 994).

Robert Hayden, *Those Winter Sundays, page 950*

Hayden's speaker tells of his father's love, expressed through mundane acts, and of his childhood inability to understand or appreciate that love. The speaker focuses on his father's habitual Sunday morning efforts to warm the house for the family, for which "No one ever thanked him" (line 5). The poor and hard life is vividly expressed in images like "blueblack cold" and "cracked hands." Life was bitter for both father and son; the father always "got up early," but the son was reticent because he feared the "chronic angers of that house." The adult speaker understands, in retrospect, that driving "out the cold" and polishing "my good shoes" were acts of love. He calls them "love's austere and lonely offices." But the child never realized this; he spoke "indifferently" to his father, and now, even though he understands his past, he thinks about his childhood with regret.

In this age of automatic thermostats and easy heating, students might benefit from learning that during the days when houses were heated by coal-burning furnaces, coal fires had to be "banked" each night, so that they would not burn out and leave the house freezing. In the mornings, however, the house was cold, and someone would need to go downstairs to the furnace, shake out the ashes, and put on fresh coal to get a roaring fire going so that the house could be warmed up. In "Those Winter Sundays," this task is the regular responsibility of the speaker's father.

Seamus Heaney, *Valediction, pages 950–951*

This poem is from Heaney's *Death of a Naturalist* (1966). The topic is the breakup of a relationship, and the poem describes the solitude, regret, uneasiness, and sorrow that the speaker feels after the rupture. Most notable is the expanded metaphor of a ship at sea in lines 5–16: Time rides "easy" at anchor; absence creates a stormy sea with the ship of love being cast adrift without anchor. Thus the speaker suggests that he is being tossed about emotionally, and the emotions that are controlling him are powerful, unpredictable, and dangerous. The title of the poem, "Valediction," suggests a comparison with Donne's "A Valediction: Forbidding Mourning" (page 658) and Burns's "A Red, Red Rose" (page 652).

George Herbert, *Love (III), page 951*

This three-stanza lyric is a combined meditation and brief drama about the relationship between God (Love) and the soul ("me," the speaker), expressed in an extended metaphor in which Love is an Innkeeper and the speaker is a Guest at the Inn. The primary speaker is the "I" of the poem, the soul of the speaker, who tells the story of the encounter with God and who quotes his dialogue with God. The speaker feels that he is an unworthy guest because he is guilty of "dust and sin" (i.e., being mortal and being therefore sinful). Despite the soul's self-deprecation, however, Love welcomes the soul as a guest "worthy to be here," and gives two explanations of why the soul is worthy: In the second stanza, Love smiles while asking the rhetorical question, "Who made the eyes but I?" In other words, the soul was created and formed entirely by God. In stanza 3, Love points out that He "bore the blame" for the soul's imperfections. Thus Love alludes to the divine roles of creator and redeemer. Love's "meat," the body and blood of Christ, is the sacrament of communion—the conduit of divine Grace.

Robert Herrick, *Corinna's Going A-Maying, pages 952–953*

This *carpe diem* lyric is built on the pastoral tradition of equating the spring season with growing passion. In it, Herrick combines religious and natural imagery to suggest that a lifetime passes as if it were a single day and that living must be seized with energy and reverence. May Day, them, becomes a lifetime: Corinna is encouraged to rise and gather the flowers of love and marriage. Words like *matins, hymns*, and *profanation* link Nature and love with religion. The speaker wants Corinna to dress and pray quickly since their rituals of love will provide both sanctity and "gems in abundance." Stanza 3 the fuses the worlds of Nature, religion, and society. In stanza 4, many boys and girls have already *kissed* and many *locks* have been *picked*; many have returned home, eaten *cakes and cream*, plighted *troth*, rolled in the grass to create a *green gown*, and *chose[n] their priest*. Stanza 5 advances the traditional *carpe diem* argument with Herrick's moral focus on marriage, encouraging Corinna to "take the harmless folly of the time."

William Heyen, *The Hair: Jacob Korman's Story, page 953*

Heyen's poem responds to images deep in the memory of twentieth century life: the roundups of Jews to be taken to the death camps and the huge mounds of hair taken from Jews, especially Jewish women to be used in Germany for household items such as pillows or rugs. Conventional wisdom for many years had it that the Jews went passively to their death, but Heyen corrects that misapprehension by describing a scene of wild though unsuccessful resistance. The image in line four, of a wheel turning, recalls the old concept of the Goddess Fortune who, with her wheel, spun out the fate of individuals with total indifference to whether lives were up or down, or to how long they would stay up or down. The concluding image of the field of hair demonstrates the ferocity with which the women who died tried to defend themselves against the inhuman actions of the German SS guards.

Roberta Hill, *Dream of Rebirth, page 954*

Hill, a member of the Oneida Indian nation, presents a vision of despair and starvation (lines 1–7) based on historical oppression (8–11). This vision is modified by dreams of rebirth and revitalization (lines 12–16).

Gerard Manley Hopkins, *The Windhover, page 954*

This song of praise to Christ gains much of its impact from Hopkins's "sprung" rhythms and vibrant alliteration. The rhymes are also powerful; the scheme is that of an Italian sonnet (*abba abba cdc dcd*). Lines 1–8, the octave, describe the glorious energy and valor of the falcon (Windhover) that the speaker "caught" sight of "this morning." This glory is conveyed in the image of the noble ("dauphin") bird "riding" the wind. The first triplet (lines 9–11) produces the transition from falcon to Christ. The bird combines beauty, valor, pride, strength, and action, but the "fire" of Christ ("thee, O my chevalier") is a trillion (in British English "billion" means "trillion") times more lovely and dangerous. Christ's glory (lines 12–14) transfigures the earth and makes "embers" "gash gold-vermilion."

Gerard Manley Hopkins, *Pied Beauty, page 955*

The lyric praises God by enumerating an assortment of "pied" (dappled, varied, dazzling, freckled) aspects of creation. The "skies," "cow," "trout," "chestnut-falls," "finches' wings," and "Landscapes" are all streaked, spotted, or multicolored. The tools ("gear," "tackle," "trim") of trades are "pied" in their overwhelming variety. In lines 7–9, the speaker moves to images of variety in movement, behavior, and taste. Lines 10–11 gather all the images to their focus. God "fathers-forth" all the infinite variety of creation. All this variety justifies praise of God, and the speaker encourages readers to praise God also.

Julia Ward Howe, *Battle Hymn of the Republic, pages 955–956*

Howe was a well-known nineteenth-century activist in causes for women's liberation and the emancipation of the slaves. The "Battle Hymn of the Republic" became immediately popular among Union soldiers during the Civil War, and has remained her most popular poem and one of America's major patriotic songs (sung to the music of "John Brown's Body"). The poem is noteworthy because it unites Christian faith with the cause of freedom. It is based on the idea that religion should bring about social action ("let us die to make men free," line 27), and therefore it shares with the well-known hymn "Onward, Christian Soldiers" (by Sabine Baring-Gould and Sir Arthur Sullivan) the idea that religious faith recruits its believers into a battle on the side of righteousness and reform.

LANGSTON HUGHES, *Negro, page 956*

Hughes looks at the plight of African Americans through a series of images that encompass wide expanses of time and space. The identical first and sixth stanzas frame and unify the poem, defining the speaker as a symbol for all African Americans and linking him with "night" and Africa. The repetition of *I* as the first word of ten of the lines maintains this clear focus on speaker and symbol. The speaker identifies himself as a "slave," "worker," "singer," and "victim." In each case the subsequent lines create a historical or geographical context suggesting that the suffering of bondage and enforced labor has continued throughout time (Caesar to Washington, the pyramids to the Woolworth Building) and all over the world (Africa to Georgia, the Congo to the Mississippi).

ROBINSON JEFFERS, *The Answer, pages 956–957*

This poem, like "The Purse-Seine" (page 805), reflects Jeffers's conviction that humanity is much less than admirable. The question, unstated here, is how to preserve life on earth, inasmuch as human beings have now developed the power, if misused, to destroy it. The speaker offers a series of answers, each of which catalogues aspects of suffering. He suggests that we not be "deluded" by false dreams of "universal justice or happiness" and that we look to history for a pattern of survival. He also suggests that we avoid violence, keep our integrity, and "not wish for evil." Integrity and wholeness represent the best solution. This unified perceptiveness requires seeing human life in the context of the "wholeness of life and things" and "the divine beauty of the universe" (line 9). Only if we "love" the whole cosmos, and not just "man / Apart from" it, can we avoid despair and the continued deterioration of the environment. The idea is that all future decisions must be made not only in the light of economic, social, and political expediency, but also in the light of environmental consequences.

MARY NOËL KERNAN, *Majdanek, page 957*

Sister Noël's poem is remarkable in that the speaker's reactions appear to be totally effaced. The poem is almost all description—and largely a description of living things in the vast green areas of Majdanek, the German death camp near Lublin in Poland. The speaker includes references to the naturally lovely scene including dandelions, grass, birds, sundrenched air, and lilacs. Yet counter to the beauty of the scene run some early warnings: the birds crying out, the very word "Majdanek," the watchtowers appearing like "windmills gone awry." Soon we learn that the green areas were "meadows marked for massacre"—the alliteration of the *m* sounds ironically emphasizing the lyric-sounding phrase. It is a Jewish custom to honor the dead by bringing a pebble to place on their grave stone, and the pebble taken in the first stanza is thus more than a souvenir. The final words, like the last line in Shelley's "Ozymandias" (page 778), serve as a caveat to all who believe themselves safe from twentieth-century history.

Carolyn Kizer, *Night Sounds, page 958*

To portray the loneliness of failed love, the poem fuses images of the nightscape with the speaker's feelings. The central images are visual and auditory. The moonlight is cold, disturbing, and a "map of personal desolation." The night sounds (lines 2–6: "voices," "weeping," "love-cries") stress the speaker's isolation. She alters the "history" of the relationship (lines 10–17), seeking comfort in the lover's restlessness and abstraction, but the attempt fails in the memory of joyous sexuality (lines 18–19). The speaker is left with the sounds of other "distant voices" and "a dog's hollow cadence."

Etheridge Knight, *Haiku, pages 958–959*

These haiku from Knight's first book, *Poems from Prison,* reflect the black poet's experiences when he spent six years in prison for robbery (1960–1966). The sequence begins by presenting three images of prison life, and then deals with black existence, nature, and poetry. Images are central here; they define the world and evoke overtones. Convicts being "like lizards," for example, suggests both cautious movement and wary intelligence. Stanzas 4 and 9 focus on the discipline and the power of art. The "blues song" and "jazz" are both ways for Knight to talk about his own poetry. Indeed, the concluding haiku focus on his poetic skill; he identifies his craft as "jazz" and claims that there is nothing "square" about it.

Maxine Kumin, *Woodchucks, pages 959–960*

The speaker comes to painful realizations about herself (and human beings) while destroying the woodchucks that are gobbling up her garden. Her "case" against the critters is "airtight," like the gas chambers alluded to in the last two lines, and she plans to use a "knockout bomb." The gas fails (stanza 2), and the woodchucks continue to feast. The speaker's "Darwinian pieties" lead her to a more effective means of destruction. The poem expresses the beginnings of pity and regret in the image of the "littlest woodchuck's face" and the body in the "everbearing roses." At the same time, the speaker experiences the rise of the "murderer" and the "hawkeye killer" lurking inside her. Killing the last woodchuck becomes a contest of extermination, and the last two lines suggest a link between the speaker and Nazi Germany. The poem finally suggests that all killing is dehumanizing and destructive for both killer and victim. The speaker is horrified and fascinated at the same time. She moves from a state of innocence to experience, and thus learns unpleasant things about herself. Kumin, a Pulitzer-Prize winning poet, combines a closed form (*abcacb; defdfe; ghigih; jkljlk; mnomon*) with slant rhymes and some run-on lines, to create a narrative in which rhyme works almost subconsciously to reinforce meaning.

Joanne Kyger, *Destruction, pages 960–961*

"Destruction" may be read as a companion poem to Kumin's "Woodchucks." Kyger's description of the havoc created in an empty house by a marauding bear is both awe-inspiring and comic, particularly if the house belongs to someone else and not to us. The idea of both "Woodchucks" and "Destruction" is that the spheres of human beings and animals are separate, and when they intersect, destruction of one or the other may be the result. In "Woodchucks," it is the creature kind. In "Destruction," it is the human structure. Particularly amusing is the bear's consumption of the "35 pounds of granola" and his choosing to go "out the back wall" on his way back to his cave. Of significance is that the speaker in "Destruction" attributes no malevolent motivation to the bear, to whom food is food, to be eaten whenever and wherever it is found.

Irving Layton, *Rhine Boat Trip, page 961*

Layton, a major Canadian poet, draws together two strands of imagery related to German history and myth to suggest that modern atrocities of death have blotted out all that went before. Each image of the mythic past ("castles," "grapes," "Lorelei," sweet singing) is canceled and displaced by an image of carnage and death (*ghosts, blinded eyes, crimson beards of murdered rabbis, wailing of cattle-cars*).

Alan P. Lightman, *In Computers, pages 961–962*

Lightman teaches at the Massachusetts Institute of Technology, and has come to poetry through science. This poem is a product of our computer age, in which more and more miraculous functions and achievements are being claimed for computers. At the same time, increased industrialization is increasing pollution, and is therefore making it less likely that the earth can continue to support life. At some point, scientists have speculated, waves of human emigrants might be forced to leave the dying earth to take up residence on the moon, or on Mars, where they will have to live in artificially created and controlled environments. At that point, all they will have from earth will be recorded on computers—things such as sunsets, the movements of gazelle, the winds, and snowfalls. The final two lines are a grimly ironic response to this prospect.

Audre Lorde, *Every Traveler Has One Vermont Poem, page 962*

"Every Traveler Has One Vermont Poem" depends upon the shock of the next-to-last line, when into the natural beauty of the countryside there intrudes the reality of human ugliness in the form of racism. The pastoral then becomes social commentary, and one is led to wonder about these "tanned boys" and the unreflective and self-centered world in which they live. The title is at first amusing because of its assertion that a "Vermont poem" (probably a poem on the beauties of the state, as this one starts out to be), is almost obligatory for a traveling poet. But the title becomes bitterly ironic, almost tragic, when one realizes the content of such a poem for a poet of color, because even the beauty of the landscape cannot compensate for the violation the poem describes.

Richard Lovelace, *To Lucasta, Going to the Wars, pages 962–963*

This lyric asserts that love cannot exist without honor. Although the tone is light and witty, the poem is serious. The speaker is leaving Lucasta because his honor demands that he go to war to serve King and Country. Lucasta is "chaste" and "quiet." War is personified as a "new mistress" with great vitality, and the speaker comically calls his departure, therefore, a type of "inconstancy." Finally, the speaker asserts that his love for Lucasta is based on a greater love for honor, a driving force in his life.

Amy Lowell, *Patterns, pages 963–965*

Lowell's anti-war poem protests against rigid "patterns" of thinking and behavior that constrict life and lead to war. The speaker, an aristocratic woman walking in her garden and mourning the death of her fiancé in battle, grounds her protest in images that evoke four distinct patterns: formal gardens, stiff clothing, social and sexual decorum, and warfare. Stanzas 1 and 2 combine the patterns of garden and clothing; the speaker's "whalebone and brocade" (clothing of the eighteenth century) make her "a rare pattern" like the formal garden. Her "passion" fights against both patterns. Stanzas 3–4 add the pattern of social and sexual restraint. Again the speaker notes that her "stiffened gown" conflicts with the "softness of a woman." The stanzas present an erotic dream (and an escape from patterns) in which the speaker discards her rigid dress, bathes in a fountain, and is discovered and embraced by her lover, but the dream conflicts with the reality of patterns. Stanzas 5–6 introduce two further aspects of pattern—war and the proper behavior for grief. The letters on the paper informing her of her lover's death "squirmed like snakes," but the speaker stiffly "stood upright" and returned "no answer"; i.e., her desire to mourn is held in check by patterns of social restraint. In stanza 7, the speaker has a vision of what might have been—an escape from patterns through love with her dead fiancé. This is canceled in stanza 8, which reveals the speaker's future. She is condemned to rigid and unchanging patterns of dress, behavior, chastity, and loneliness. In the last lines the speaker breaks decorum—the pattern of appropriate language—and rages against all these patterns. See also the first sample essay in Appendix B.

Cynthia MacDonald, *A Critical Age, pages 965–966*

The poem is a series of similes, intended to guide the reader to a particular set of emotions rather than to any intellectual certainty. Through the similes repeated in the "So that's what it's like" pattern, the poet demonstrates frustration and ignorance—the sense that one can never truly understand or communicate with others, never be certain about truth. Filled with that awareness, the poet holds up Moses as an example, who, "within himself, . . . seized on what he could," and found at least for a time enough "conviction. . .to part the sea." But certainty held too long becomes "convict labor," something provided only under duress. Ultimately, in a critical age, one has no real certainty, only oneself as a guide, and the realization that truth and reality, for all one's efforts, can never really be captured or communicated.

Heather McHugh, *Lines, page 966*

The poem addresses the disparity between what we want in life and the things for which we will settle. Through a series of images—one very appealing, that of the subway as a wind instrument with many stops—the poet brings us to a sense that everything comes to an end. Even the man who is deeply in love has just heard the word "goodbye." But by contrast, an old man, rejoices "just to be alive." Thus at different points in our lives we are all happy with different things, and truth is always contingent upon the individual and the circumstances involved.

Claude McKay, *The White City, page 967*

This sonnet utilizes elements of the Petrarchan sonnet in its paradoxes, irony, and capitalized personification. McKay uses this tradition to express his simultaneous acknowledgment of the material grandeur and appeal of white society, and of the rage and resentment it can elicit from a black who both is and is not a part of it. The speaker is obviously highly educated in the traditions of White European culture. But he does not belong, and uses one of that culture's most complex literary achievements to declare both his mastery and his rejection of the white world and the city which is its symbol.

Edna St. Vincent Millay, *What Lips My Lips Have Kissed, page 967*

This poem is a sonnet, using the traditional subject matter of love. But there are several surprises: The speaker is female; the love is remembered, not actual, and thus the tone is nostalgic; finally, the female speaker is apparently reflecting upon a past series of lovers—so many that she has forgotten them as individuals. Such a confession has traditionally been unusual for a woman, since it opens her to charges of promiscuity. The speaker keeps that judgment in abeyance, however, by turning the subject, in the sestet, fully to her present state. Now, she asserts, she is old and alone, and her summer has gone.

Vassar Miller, *Loneliness, pages 967–968*

The poem's structure is unusual: six-line stanzas unified by rhythm and verbal repetitions rather than rhyme. The subject matter is a description of an apparently self-imposed discipline of silence and meditation. But the speaker, aware of the dangers of deliberate alienation from human contact, cries out to God for help. The danger is that the speaker will become so satisfied with this state of sensory deprivation that he or she may be unable or unwilling to return to life. Thus loneliness, which is a dreadful state to many people, is here asserted to be satisfying and alluring. By crying out to God for rescue, however, the speaker shows that he or she is not totally alone.

John Milton, *O Nightingale!, page 968*

In this love sonnet, addressed to the nightingale, the speaker asks for success in love. For years the bird (the traditional aid to lovers) has not assisted him, for no reason that he can tell (line 12). Now he asks, on the condition that "Jove's" will is linked to the bird's song (lines 7–8), that the nightingale aid him because he is a servant of both poetry and love. The poem is noteworthy, partly because it gives a seldom seen aspect of Milton's work, and partly because of the sense it gives of humankind as part of the created world, living with and subject to the powers of Nature, shown as birds, flowers, woods and groves, and even the seasons in their passing.

Thomas Moore, *Believe Me, If All Those Endearing Young Charms, pages 968–969*

The Irish poet Thomas Moore was phenomenally popular in the nineteenth century, and this poem is still widely recognized and sung. It is a song that celebrates love in the present and in the future. Although age will change the loved one, the love depends not on the physical state but on the continuity of the speaker's fondness. In the second stanza, the governing simile is that of the sunflower, which constantly turns to the sun, just as the lovers constantly turn to each other. In class, the poem serves as the springboard for vigorous discussions. It may be contrasted with some of the anthologized poems that stem out of the *carpe diem* tradition. See also Blake's "Ah, Sun-flower" (page 919).

Ogden Nash, *Very Like a Whale, pages 969–970*

This poem is an amusing disclaimer against the poetic use of metaphors and similes. It should be read jointly with Byron's "The Destruction of Sennacherib" (page 926). It is also instructional, however, for it invites readers to consider the justness and appropriateness of metaphorical language along with the meaning of metaphor. Nash's humor is based on the logical fallacy of *reductio ad absurdum*. Virtually any simile or metaphor, if pushed far enough, can seem inappropriate or even silly, and some, like the mice, the snow, and the petticoat, are silly from the start.

In lines 1–4, Nash's speaker lays out possible objections to metaphors and similes. Lines 5–22 illustrate the objections, using Byron's poem as the example. Lines 23–26 describe what the speaker thinks should have been said—without simile or metaphor, had Byron dispensed with them. Lines 27–30 state the need for reality as opposed to metaphor.

HOWARD NEMEROV, *Life Cycle of Common Man, pages 970–971*

Nemerov, who died in July, 1991, was honored by the Library of Congress from 1986–1988 as Poet Laureate. His output of poems and novels was considerable and distinguished. "Life Cycle of Common Man" is an unusual poem because it relentlessly considers what human life has become in our age of consumerism. To verify Nemerov's statistics, his common man must have consumed a fifth of gin in an average of about six days, and daily must have smoked cigarettes at an alarming rate of combustion. On a sobering note is the vast number of "beasts" (beef cattle, chickens, hogs, lambs, fish, crustaceans) who had to die "to provide" the common man "with meat, belt and shoes." The irony at the poem's end is particularly powerful, for the common man is there considered as a comic-strip figure, speaking not in the real world of communication but rather in speech balloons. While human beings generally may profess to claim nobility and dignity, the commercial and advertising emphasis on making the common man a consuming unit rather than a complete human being has vitiated this claim. "Life Cycle" may be compared with Auden's "The Unknown Citizen" (page 916).

JIM NORTHRUP, *wahbegan, pages 971–972*

Although the title is an Ojibway name, its sound is close enough to the English word "woebegone" to convey the feeling of the poem. From the first word of the poem—"Didja," used twice—it is clear that the speaker wants to address the reader intimately and directly. His description of his brother who "died in the war but didn't fall down for fifteen tortured years" reminds us of the terrible scars left on America by the war in Vietnam. We are left to reflect on the real price of wars, and to wonder how we determine whether our course in turning so often to warfare has been justified by the cost in mental anguish and suffering.

NAOMI SHIHAB NYE, *Where Children Live,* PAGE 972

"Where Children Live" is a poem about children as children themselves create their own identities. Adults may try to impose their visions, and give children "swings, leafy plants, slow-motion back and forth" (line 10), but children do their own things and make their own messes, so that they imprint their characteristics on the locations where they have been playing. The poem is unique in creating sentiment, without being sentimental, about a subject that very easily may go over the edge.

Frank O'Hara, *Poem (The Eager Note), pages 972–973*

"Poem" is built on a bizarre reversal of expectations and their tragic and ironic outcome. There seem to be two time schemes in simultaneous operation: The speaker's receipt of the eager and apparently happy note, prompting him to pack quickly and head "straight for the door," is played against the mystery of the statement "It was autumn / by the time I got around the corner" (lines 5–6) and the concluding statement that the invitation had been issued "several months ago" (line 16). The speaker's understated words "I did appreciate it" (i.e., the death), and his effort to pretend that the death is part of a host's careful preparation for a guest, all suggest a considerable depth of emotion beneath this deliberately commonplace description of a nightmarish, macabre experience.

Simon Ortiz, *A Story of How a Wall Stands, pages 973–974*

Ortiz, like Leslie Marmon Silko, is a poet of New Mexico, and writes of Indian and family traditions about the connections of people with sand, canyons, and mountains. He has published four volumes of poetry. "A Story of How a Wall Stands" is a graphic illustration of how metaphor operates. The story is that of how a wall at Aacqu (Acoma) is put together, with much showing but much more not showing. It is the foundation, the patience, and the workmanship that make the wall last. Metaphorically, the same method nurtures the young, gives them a place in their society, and creates the strength which makes them endure "a long, long time."

Dorothy Parker, *Résumé, page 974*

This ironic and funny poem is based on the startling idea that one "might as well live" simply because all the ways of committing suicide are either uncomfortable or unreliable. Each statement is understated in some way: For example, razors don't just "pain you," and rivers are far deeper and wetter than "damp." The speaker's tone of sophisticated ennui suggests that one lives because doing otherwise is just too much trouble. The title "Résumé" (suggesting both a summary and also the vita that one presents as part of a job application) is an understated, whimsical, offhand defense of life, with the implication that there are many strong reasons for living—including enjoying the laughter from a poem like this one.

Linda Pastan, *Marks, page 974*

Students take great delight in the metaphor of this poem. Some may want to take the conclusion seriously, and it is therefore important to stress that this part can be read in context as a joke or quip. Even so, however, the poem contains an underlying note of annoyance. The extended metaphor is that of school and grades. Housework is like taking a course: The speaker receives a varying report card, including an *A* for cooking and an *Incomplete* for ironing. The son and daughter give grades based on a superior-average and a pass/fail system. The conclusion, "Wait 'til they learn," is an implied threat, but granted the poem's tone of affectionate banter, the threat is to be seen as a joke. The poem thus explores the speaker's sense that she, like most people, is constantly being rated, and that even those who love her find her not fully adequate. The playful metaphor, which puts this situation in an original light, is accurate, vivid, and refreshing.

Marge Piercy, *The Secretary Chant, pages 974–975*

The subject of this poem is the dehumanization of women secretaries, since this is *The Secretary Chant*, not ***a** secretary's chant*. The first-person speaker describes how her character is submerged by the functions and sounds of her work, for in the business world she is little better than the machines she uses. The parts of her body described and many of the activities in which she engages are quintessentially female (such as hips, breasts, navel, delivery of a baby), but here they perform mechanical rather than human functions.

Marge Piercy, *Will We Work Together?, pages 975–976*

This poem is a powerful dramatic monologue, spoken by a woman speaker (let us assume a woman) to her lover. It is an expression of intense love, as its metaphors demonstrate. The speaker is like a lantern, for she lights up "the corners" when the two are together. She also becomes a source of warmth, "bright / as a fireplace roaring / with love." A movingly observed part of the speaker's words are the lines "My body wears / sore before I can express / on yours the smallest part / of what moves me.

Words / shred and splinter." Granted the intensity of the speaker's monologue, the conclusion is not an anti-climax, but rather a continuation of her desire to find and create meaning and usefulness "from this fierce sturdy / rampant love." An interesting issue for classroom discussion is the reason for which the poem's title is phrased as a question.

Sylvia Plath, *Last Words, page 976*

The poem juxtaposes images from ancient Egyptian practices of mummification and from daily life in the modern kitchen. The speaker sees herself losing life slowly, to the point where a mirror held against her lips (like that used in Shakespeare's *King Lear* to see if Cordelia still breathes) will soon show nothing. Yet oddly enough, the speaker demonstrates a macabre rejoicing in the household things which are part of her burial, because they are lustrous and "warmed by much handling" (line 18), and might be a comfort in the grave. Indeed, line 23 describes an almost ecstatic joy at the virtual loss of personality ("I shall hardly know myself") in the dark sarcophagus. It is as though, finding motherhood and housekeeping to be destructive, this speaker determines to love the things killing her rather than to escape them.

Sylvia Plath, *Mirror, pages 976–977*

The personified mirror speaks of its life, in which it reflects and has come to love the wall opposite itself. Yet it also reflects the woman who sees herself aging daily, changing from a young girl into an old woman resembling a "terrible fish" (lines 17, 18). The fish is clearly a symbol of a horrible and inevitable transformation from loveliness to ugliness. The "truthful" mirror (line 4) reminds its owner that her days are running out, and that when her beauty is gone she will be considered less than human.

Katha Pollitt, *Archæology, pages 977–978*

Using the activities of an archaeologist as a metaphor, the author raises questions about the choices we make in life. The speaker suggests that any choice might turn out to be a disappointment, like the "ancient grocery lists" an archaeologist uncovers rather than some wonderful, history changing document. In light of such possibilities, one may regret the time and effort spent on foolish dreams. But then comes the speaker's advice: "Pack up your fragments," and continue the effort; try to make something meaningful and beautiful out of the work that has been done.

The poem is a call to dreams and to commitment to them. While admitting the doubts that may come, Pollitt asserts that human inventiveness can create meaning out of disorder as it summons up the life of the past.

Ezra Pound, *The River-Merchant's Wife: A Letter, page 978*

The poem tenderly reflects a happy marriage, albeit one very different from modern assumptions about marriages of choice. The speaker is the young wife, who is subservient by our standards (see her reference to her husband as "My Lord you" [line 7]). Clearly, however, their love is deep and fulfilling. The details of Chinese village life in the eighth century (the children's occupations, the monkeys overhead, and the young wife's description of her decorous bashfulness) are vivid and compelling. The speaker's unexpected declaration of transcendent love (lines 12–13), her sorrow at their separation (line 18), and her eagerness to rejoin her young husband (lines 26–29) are poignantly rendered, and in this way the poem transforms an alien time and place through the moving recognition of shared experiences.

John Crowe Ransom, *Bells for John Whiteside's Daughter, page 979*

This poem avoids sentimentality, despite its painful subject matter, by describing the child's death as a "brown study" (line 3), as though she could awaken and return to her usual busy life. Similarly, those who knew her are astonished and vexed, but not overwhelmed in tears (line 19). The contrast between the child alive and dead, now "lying so primly propped" (line 20) is sharply drawn, since her life is described in images of sound and joy, color, and motion. The speaker's tribute, that the geese themselves cried "in goose, Alas" (line 12), expresses the poem's mixture of fond memory and deep sorrow. For comparison, see Wagner's "The Boxes" (page 1003).

Theodore Roethke, *The Waking, page 979–980*

The *terza rima* form used here is immensely demanding in English poetry, and it creates a complex and incantational concentration of rhyme and verbal repetition. The poem deals with the closeness of death (sleep), and the truth that life (wakefulness) leads us inevitably toward death; therefore, wisdom suggests that we take that "waking slow," savoring life while we have it. Here the *carpe diem* occasion of the poem comes through fully, but it is clear that the speaker is not just writing a seduction poem, but is fully aware that all things are subject to "what falls away" (line 17).

Luis Omar Salinas, ***In a Farmhouse, page 980***

The speaker of "In a Farmhouse" is an eight-year old migrant worker child, forced to work in the fields with the other family members so that they can live through the year. The ironic last stanza points out the disparity between Christian promise of happiness in a life to come and the reality of the child's earthly life. The irony is signaled by words that are oddly incompatible with the expected vocabulary of the speaker: "profoundly, / animated by the day's work / in the cottonfields" (lines 5–8). The poem thus questions the moral basis of our national economic well-being, and about our society's professed concern for children.

Sonia Sanchez, ***right on; white america, pages 980–981***

A striking thing about this poem initially is its disjointed presentation on the printed page, a graphic reminder that the world is disordered. The speaker refers to two major moments in American history: Custer's last stand, and the daily shootouts which popular history tells us were real parts of our past. Although native Americans lost most of their land and their culture, they literally blew "custer's mind / with a different / image of amer-ica" (lines 8–10), a point made with savage humor. The prophetic assertion is that the past persecution of minorities has not stopped, but is an ongoing condition in white America.

Carl Sandburg, ***Chicago, pages 981–982***

The speaker's recitation of the attributes of this raucous city, repeated with pride in the last section, gives the poem a far tighter organization than at first appears. The images are pictorial, a series of action vignettes out of which the young, strong, vitally male city emerges with brashness. The speaker's descriptions of the city in its vital processes of "Building, breaking, rebuilding," parallel the attributes for which poets have praised the earth: fecundity and the capacity to live and grow.

Siegfried Sassoon, ***Dreamers, page 982***

That the poem is a sonnet reminds us of the customary content of that form. Here, the speaker contrasts the ugliness, pain, and suffering of the soldier and the ordinary pleasures of civilized life. Even the daily grind of "going to the office in the train" (line 14) is part of the "hopeless longing" (line 12) of these "citizens of death's gray land" (line 1). The trench warfare of the first World War may be far different from future wars, but the suffering and waste of war will never change.

Alan Seeger, *I Have a Rendezvous with Death, pages 982–983*

The poem turns on the paradox of a–springtime as a time of death, not life, and b–the acceptance of this fact as a "rendezvous," i.e., a love meeting to which he is "pledged" (line 23). It is the ironic situation, in which soldiers are nothing but helpless pawns, that creates the argument of the poem. Implicitly, Seeger ironically deplores the institution of warfare in light of the earth's fecundity and the attractions of human love.

Brenda Serotte, *My Mother's Face, page 983*

This poem begins with an ordinary situation: The speaker looks in a mirror while getting ready for work. But she observes there not herself but rather her mother. The poem leads the reader into a magical transformation of appearance and reality: Not only is the facial appearance real, but so is the entire image, including the mother's movements reflected in the mirror ("like I do," line 10). The speaker's observations are deeply moving, and the poem's muted but powerful conclusion cannot be forgotten. For comparison, see Cummings's "if there are any heavens" (page 930) and Roethke's "My Papa's Waltz" (page 697).

Anne Sexton, *Three Green Windows, pages 983–984*

The windows are metaphorically green because they look out onto the leafy trees beyond them, blocking out all else. Looking at them, the speaker is stirred by childhood memories and present fantasies. In this sensuous and half-humorous moment, she muses about losing all physical and social concerns, and she regresses to restful comfort amid images of natural beauty.

William Shakespeare, *Fear No More the Heat o' the Sun, pages 984–985*

This song from Act IV of *Cymbeline* blends two themes: The first is that death is the great leveler, the end to which all persons, however powerful or powerless, must come. The second is that death is a restful and safe haven, where one is free from injustice, discomfort (like the sun's heat), slander, and censure. The final stanza is a blessing, a kind of magic spell over the grave, to keep it safe from predators or spirits, so that the lost one may rest in peace.

William Shakespeare, *Sonnet 29: When in Disgrace, page 985*

This is one of the better-known sonnets, and it is noteworthy because it departs from the usual Shakespearean sonnet structure: Lines 9–14 form a unit, a sestet. In lines 1–8 the speaker cites circumstances in which his self-doubts overwhelm him. In lines 9–12 the speaker notes that the remembrance of the *thee* who is the listener of the poem, a memory occurring almost at random, lifts his spirits. The analogy of these lines is that of the soul departing from earth and singing as it passes into heaven. The simile also indicates that the speaker's joy is like the return of the lark's song at day's beginning.

William Shakespeare, *Sonnet 146: Poor Soul, page 986*

This sonnet attempts to put into perspective the things that are important and valuable in life. The speaker laments the over-attention that he or she has paid to physical needs, the metaphorical "outward walls" (line 4) of the "fading mansion" (line 6) of the body, which, we are reminded, is made up of nothing more than "sinful earth" (line 1). Concluding that the metaphorical "lease" on life is short (line 5), and that flesh will decay, the speaker exhorts his or her soul to focus on things divine, to cultivate the spiritual rather than the physical, so that eternal life will overcome death.

If you have time, you might indicate that this poem brings up the interesting question of conjectural emendation in the text of Shakespeare's work. In the 1609 edition of the sonnets, the second line begins "My sinful earth," thus repeating the last three words of the first line ("My sinful earth these rebel powers that thee array." Editors have made a number of suggestions about what should be there to replace the obvious compositorial error. "Thrall to" is only one of the conjectures, but no one can ever know what Shakespeare actually wrote.

Karl Shapiro, *Auto Wreck, pages 986–987*

This poem could not have been written except in our age of cars. As witness to a terrible automobile accident, the speaker confronts the horror of accidental mutilation and death, pointing out that, while many deaths are explicable or at least understandable, the carnage of collision is especially terrible because it is also especially illogical. The vivid description, and the uses of color, sound, light, and darkness, all contribute to the poem's impact. The survivors, in a state of shock (line 14), confront unanswerable questions which in their mystery can only be dealt with by "the occult mind" (line 36), for accidental death makes logic and reason irrelevant.

Sir Philip Sidney, ***Astrophil and Stella, Number 71, page 987***

In Sidney's sonnet sequence, Astrophil means a "star lover" and Stella means "a star." The speaker, after paying his lady a series of compliments (such as that she is all goodness, all virtue, the possessor of an inward sun, and so on), ends with a sudden and dramatic shift of tone. Despite the catalogue of spiritual virtues, we find that his desire breaks into his thought, demanding to be fed. Thus the poem asserts that spiritual love is not enough to satisfy the body's powerful needs.

Jon Silkin, ***Worm, pages 987–988***

Concentrating on a lowly and unattractive subject, the speaker describes in lines more like prose than poetry the life of a worm. Unlike self-centered human beings (line 1), this little fellow makes the rich soil needed for human food, and yet to most of us it is at best insignificant and at worst repulsive. The disparity between these responses and the reality of the worm ("useful," "virtuous" [lines 15, 20]) leads us to reassess our easy assumptions about what makes the world a viable pace for human beings.

Leslie Marmon Silko, ***Where Mountain Lion Lay Down with Deer, pages 988–989***

The poem is cast visually in the form of a physical journey up a mountain to a high point, which is paralleled by a journey through time, back almost into a racial memory to the beginning of creation. In a sense the speaker (if he or she is meant to be a literal person) is telling a Creation myth and at the same time lamenting the changes that have occurred in recent history. The tragedy is that the Navajo people, tribes, cultures, and past ways of life, are now forgotten, along with the "old songs" that told the stories (line 17). By implication, no one now cares, except those who are affected by the poem.

Dave Smith, ***Bluejays, page 989***

The situation is the interplay between a girl and a flock of bluejays. These birds are noisy and raucous, responding only with more noise to the girl's efforts to get them to come to her. But they do not fly away, and thus the speaker compares them to boys, afraid of beauty but fascinated by it. In that sense the poem is a paradigm of a pre-adult sexuality, in which the female attracts males, and they hover about her, unable to leave but also unable to approach her except in groups, and even then at a distance.

Stevie Smith, ***Not Waving But Drowning,*** **page 989–990**

The poem uses the image of a drowning man waving frantically to those ashore, who mistake his gestures for greetings. The symbolic parallel is the frequency of human misunderstandings in communication, sometimes with tragic results. The situation becomes poignantly moving when we realize that this failure to be understood has been typical of the dying man's entire life.

W. D. Snodgrass, ***These Trees Stand . . . , page 990***

The poem reflects a modern poet's wry realization that his is a very limited art; yet clearly it gives him joy. In the midst of grandiose words and concepts like the "heavens," the "steep celestial gulf," and "civilizations," (even though they are coming down with "the curse,"), here is the poet, "walking through the universe"—and attention must be paid. The poem is full of echoes: Lucinda, the kind of name that poets for hundreds of years after Elizabeth I gave their lady loves, the allusion in "Lucinda's skirts" of Herrick's "Whenas in silks my Julia goes," of Eliot's "Wipe your hand across your mouth" (page 940). Snodgrass puts them all together in a moment of high good spirits, and announces that even if the world were to end right now, he's walking through the universe, and having a great time, and (by implication) everyone should do the same.

Cathy Song, ***Lost Sister, pages 990–992***

The poem details the repressed and restrained life of a Chinese woman, with her feet traditionally bound (line 16), and contrasts her life with the physically freer life of a woman who emigrated to the United States. But the speaker finds a good deal to admire in those women who remained in China (line 22). By contrast the expatriate finds the loneliness of unfamiliar and threatening surroundings. None of the women leaves any "footprints" (line 61), i.e., no special marks of identity, whether in the homeland or in the new land, but the traditional woman at least has the identity of being part of a long line of women upheld by well-understood and honored traditions.

Gary Soto, ***Oranges, pages 992–993***

"Oranges" is a short narrative poem about the tentative but inexorable process of growth. The speaker recalls an incident of his boyhood (he was twelve) and his first date with a girl. Trying to impress the girl, he takes her to a drugstore and offers to buy her candy. The chocolate the girl asks for costs a dime, but the speaker has only an orange and a nickel, which he offers to the "saleslady" as payment. We presume after line 43 that the saleslady has understood the speaker's need to impress the girl, and that she has accepted the nickel and given him the chocolate. At the poem's end, the girl is opening the chocolate while the speaker is peeling his orange. The concluding image of seeming to make "a fire in my hands" symbolically suggests the emergence of adolescent sexuality.

Gary Soto, *Kearney Park, pages 993–994*

"Kearney Park" is a short narrative. The speaker describes his memory of dancing and happiness, and, by implication, he describes one of the experiences that make up his mind and poetic spirit. At sunset in a park, the speaker throws himself into a dance to the throbbing music of the accordion and the drums. His grandmother is there urging him on in Spanish, and with the noise and the shouting and the clapping, he and his partner, "who is a brilliant arc of smiles, / An armful of falling water," spin, dip, and laugh until they seem merged with the intensity of the dance.

Edmund Spenser, *Amoretti 54: Of This World's Theater, page 994*

This sonnet is in the tradition of the lover's complaint. The speaker laments his being able to do nothing to induce his beloved to respond to him with kindness, and he concludes that her insensitivity and unkindness to him renders her something less than human (line 14). The tone is both angry and frustrated, and in such a mood the speaker thinks of life as a theater, in which he acts out his emotions, in tragic or comic mode, with great earnestness and depth, even though to no avail.

William Stafford, *Traveling Through the Dark, pages 994–995*

The subject of this poem is the loss and possible extinction of the natural world that result from the encroachment of people upon the environment. Specifically, the topic is an incident in which a pregnant doe has been run over and killed on a highway. The speaker, coming upon it in the dark, describes his thoughts about saving the living but unborn fawn. The pathos is intensified by the fawn's being pictured as "alive, still, never to be born" (line 11). As the speaker decides what to do, it is as if the whole landscape listens. But his decision is virtually fixed by his participation in mechanized society; the lights of his car are focused forward, and he examines the doe "by the glow of the tail light" (line 5), as if Nature has been forgotten and deserted by human civilization.

Gerald Stern, *Burying an Animal on the Way to New York, page 995*

As with Stafford's poem, the subject is the killing of animals on highways. Here the speaker addresses a generalized listener-driver who feels regret at the sight of a dead animal being powdered and vaporized by the many passing cars. The speaker suggests that the cars passing over the body, and carrying traces of it along the highway, are in fact burying it. Consequently, not only the body but the animal's ghost is being spread along, and the driver is asked both to imagine the death and be alert to the "twittering" of the passing spirit. The situation is indescribably sad.

Wallace Stevens, *The Emperor of Ice-Cream, pages 995–996*

This poem is in the *carpe diem* tradition, dressed in modern garb. It proceeds in images, which initially suggest sensual enjoyment: big cigars, muscularity, girl/boy flirtation, ice-cream, and concoctions made of "concupiscent curds" (lines 1–8). The contrast beginning with line 9 focuses on the impoverished life and death of a woman and the grotesque reality of her corpse. Thus, if be is the "finale of seem" (i.e., an honest attempt to understand life's realities as opposed to illusion), we recognize that death is the reality that none can avoid. In this circumstance, what can human beings do? The speaker's answer is perhaps an avoidance: Live for the moment, even though we know that the moment is fleeting and brief; follow the pleasure and sweetness of the "emperor of ice-cream." This leader's empire may melt away, but it gives pleasure while it exists.

Mark Strand, *The Remains, page 996*

Strand, honored by the Library of Congress in 1990 as American Poet Laureate, was born in Canada. One of his themes, evident in "The Remains," is the paradoxical nature of existence. The paradox is that the speaker tries to forget the past and move into the future, but discovers that the past still exists within him. The major idea is that the road to self-fulfillment, necessarily requiring internal growth, forces a person to become distant from everything and everyone in the past. Thus change requires a constant saying of goodbye. Time tells the speaker what he or she is, because individuals change or develop only within their histories. Past experience, part of memory, is also part of the present, though it has vanished in all other ways. It is therefore still within the speaker (*my life remains,* line 12) despite all changes (line 11).

May Swenson, ***Question, pages 996–997***

The speaker suggests that the body provides a horse (i.e., a means of movement) and a hound (something to find things for us), and wonders what she/he will do when they are gone, i.e., when they are dead. What will it be like to be without a body, and to "lie in the sky"? Even worse, with only clouds for clothes, how will the speaker hide? Amid questions about what death is like, the speaker also suggests that in life we can hide who we are, but once dead there is nothing left but truth.

Jonathan Swift, ***A Riddle (The Vowels), page 997***

The poem is a short virtuoso piece which illustrates the vowels (*a* in *glass*, *e* in *jet*, *i* in *tin*, *o* in *box*, and *u* in *pursue*). The idea here is to demonstrate the immense range of topics to be found in poetry. The content of Strand's "The Remains," for example, is exceedingly paradoxical, difficult, and problematical. By contrast, Swift's intention here is to be as simple and unambiguous as possible—to offer the reader an easy puzzle, and to use his poem as a mnemonic guide by which children might learn one of the most basic details of civilization. For another poem-puzzle for comparison, see Sylvia Plath's "Metaphors" (page 666).

James Tate, ***The Blue Booby, pages 997–998***

On one level, the poem describes the mating ritual of the booby, whose silly name makes it easy for the reader to become relaxed and positive. The male booby, a simple, undemanding fellow, has found the courting behavior which has the perfect "magical effect" (line 31) on his mate. Thus the reader is prepared, at line 37, to understand their mating not as copulation but as lovemaking, and to perceive how distant stars are reflected in the foil lining their nest "like the eyes of a mild savior" (line 41). Their behavior becomes part of the scheme of things in the universe, which for this reason seems gentle, benevolent, and loving. The poem thus is an idyll, an Edenic vision of a desirable and enviably unfallen world.

Alfred, Lord Tennyson, ***Tithonus, pages 998–1000***

In the myth, Tithonus, a mortal, is loved by Eos or Aurora, the Goddess of the Dawn. She gains from Zeus the gift of immortality for her lover, but she forgets to ask for eternal youth (Gods and Goddesses have great power, but they do not necessarily have great intelligence). Thus, Tithonus grows old and infirm, but cannot die, while Eos stays forever young and beautiful. "Tithonus" is a dramatic monologue: The speaker is Tithonus, and the listener is Eos. In lines 1–4, he portrays the cyclical nature of the world, and in line 5 he separates himself from it. "Only" he is consumed by immortality, being isolated from both youth and death. Eos's tears indicate that she is helpless, for "The Gods themselves cannot recall their gifts." It seems clear that the wish of Tithonus is to return to the natural cycle of life and death.

DYLAN THOMAS, *A Refusal to Mourn the Death, page 1000*

The language here calls upon Biblical and theological tradition: "mankind making" (line 1), "Fathering" (line 3), "Zion" (line 8), and "synagogue" (line 9) all elevate the event of a dying child to a dignified and serious level. The initial statement about the refusal to mourn is perplexing and startling: How could a person not mourn so terrible a death, especially that of a child? But the speaker widens this individual case into a universal one, and determines that it is all death, any death, which is the issue, in all its stark tragedy. As is typical of Thomas, the music of the poem is stressed, with complex rhythms and rhymes. The announced refusal to mourn becomes a stately elegy, itself a form of mourning.

CHASE TWICHELL, *Blurry Cow, page 1001*

This poem is like James Wright's "A Blessing" (page 594) inasmuch as it too considers a rural scene. Twichell's vista contains two cows and also a woman carrying laundry. Her language ranges from plain and direct ("two cows stand," "the hot sting of a deerfly") to metaphorical ("sudden slur," "mirage of laundry"). The "blurry cow" refers to how the animal appears to the observer in the moving train, not to the objective cow itself. The last two lines stand as a summary of the meaning of the rural images; one's life is built from such afterimages of many days on earth. The poet captures the connections between experience and character, on the one hand, and the sights that seem temporary but which register permanently on the mind, on the other.

MONA VAN DUYN, *Advice to a God, pages 1001–1002*

The Greek God Zeus, who wooed many a mortal woman, could not appear to mortals in godly form, since his awesome power would kill them, so he came in other guises. Thus his sexual union with Danae, the situation which presumably has just happened as the occasion of this poem, is presented in myth as a shower of gold which fell upon her. In the poem, the speaker calls upon Zeus to explain his departure, and asks him to warn her against love, which ultimately brings helplessness. At line 26, the speaker asks Zeus to reveal the weakness in his strength: Were he to allow himself to be compassionate, he would be unable to bear the pain of humanity. His indifference is thus his protection. Underlining the poem's irony is the detail that the legendary shower of gold consists of golden coins, together with other images suggesting the coldness of money and commerce.

Tino Villanueva, *Day-Long Day, pages 1002–1003*

"Day-Long Day" is a poem of social protest. It describes the long, hot, arduous labor of picking cotton for migrant workers, and the "unbending dreams" (line 14) of a mother who wants her child freed from this misery. The mingling of Spanish and English presents the mixture of two cultures and two peoples. The demands of the harvest turn the family into "sinews and backs" (line 8), and their exhaustion at day's end and their powerlessness combine to damn the child to become part of the world they cannot escape. For comparison, see "In a Farmhouse," by Luis Omar Salinas (page 980).

Shelly Wagner, *The Boxes, pages 1003–1004*

The poem describes an unbearable human tragedy—the accidental loss of a child and the unending grief it brings. Focusing on the police search through every sort of box or place of concealment in which the child could have been caught or imprisoned, the poem leaves us with the one box, both coffin and earth, in which his body is now held. The mother's agony is expressed indirectly, as she imagines going to the graveside and urging the boy, with the sternness a mother might use to a naughty child, to come home to bed where he belongs. The description of the police search, now familiar because of on-the-spot TV news coverage, is chilling. Wagner renders the drowning and the mother's grief indirectly, presenting a kind of denial on the mother's part as shown in her desire to sit by the bedside of her "sleeping boys." The powerful concluding lines make her grief both immediate and crushingly poignant.

Diane Wakoski, *The Ring, pages 1004–1005*

The ring is a remnant of the speaker's ended marriage. Worn on her key chain, it symbolizes for her not love but "possession, power" (line 12).

It also reminds her of the past, of her now lost beauty, and of the failure of her search for love (line 16). The divorced husband's search for love has also been unsuccessful, since the speaker observes that he has gone to "other wives" (line 10). But the poem's concentration is on the speaker, and the final stanza introduces powerful images of fragile illusion, brokenness, pain, and loneliness. For comparison, see Carolyn Kizer's "Night Sounds" (page 957).

ALICE WALKER, *Revolutionary Petunias, page 1005*

The poem presents a vivid picture of the black underclass in American society. Touched with a smattering of traditional culture (note the names of the woman's five children (lines 18–20), and probably unable to get justice from the white legal system, "Sammy Lou of Rue" revenges her husband's death with the tool at hand, a farmer's hoe. White society, by contrast, has more efficient machinery, and will dispatch her by the "electric chair" (line 23). Her final words give the dimensions of her world—the word of God and the demands of her garden (lines 21–26).

EDMUND WALLER, *Go, Lovely Rose, page 1006*

This is a lovely and haunting poem. It establishes the image of the rose, a conventional comparison used by many poets of love lyrics, but it uses the flower as a metaphor of the beauty, fragility, and impermanence of life. It is a perennial favorite of readers, and has often been set to music. The situation of the poem is a dramatic one, in which the speaker addresses a rose which he is about to send to a lady. The brevity of life that is the common lot of both rose and woman suggests that the poem is more a philosophical reflection than the invitation to sensual experience which is the basis of *carpe diem* poetry.

ROBERT PENN WARREN, *Heart of Autumn, page 1006–1007*

"Heart of Autumn," by the first of America's poet laureates, is in the tradition of pastoral poetry, in which the autumnal season has conventionally signaled the winding down of life. It is also a nature poem, and its details of hunting and shooting wild geese demonstrate strongly the device of onomatopoeia ("Some crumple," "Some stagger," "last glide," "far glint," "great wing-beat"). The basic metaphor of the poem is that the destiny of the geese is like that of the speaker (and all persons), for all living things know "time and distance." The geese are in one respect more fortunate than human beings, for they "know / The path of pathlessness, with all the joy / Of destiny fulfilling its own name," while the speaker does not know why he "is here." Nevertheless, the poem's concluding lines, with their strong yearning, are uplifting and exalting.

BRUCE WEIGL, *Song of Napalm, pages 1007–1008*

Students may need reminding that napalm is an incendiary substance, gelled gasoline, used in anti-personnel weapons. When it is exploded and when it burns, it sticks to the person it splashes on, creating horrible and painful burns, which are usually fatal. The narrator of "Song of Napalm" is apparently a Vietnam veteran who has returned home and is resuming a normal, peaceful life, but even though he is safe and is in love, he cannot forget the image of a child he saw who was killed by burning napalm, "Stuck to her dress like jelly." The vision is indelible, and no present or future happiness "can deny" the reality of the horror the speaker has experienced. For comparison, see Owen's "Dulce et Decorum Est" (page 681) and Dan Georgakas's "Hiroshima Crewman" (page 944).

PHYLLIS WHEATLEY, *On Being Brought from Africa to America, page 1008*

The speaker, who is visualized as a person displaced from his or her native Africa in the eighteenth century, accepts the supremacy of Colonial America and the Christian religion. In the speaker's white/black imagery, white equals the angelic and the saved, black the "sable race" (line 5), the benighted soul (because non-Christian), and God's judgment on Cain (line 7). Although the concluding lines exhort Christians not to condemn blacks, they do so only in the belief that blacks, once converted, become equal to whites. There are many poems in the anthology with which this poem may be contrasted.

RICHARD WILBUR, *The Sirens, page 1008–1009*

One of America's Poets Laureate, Wilbur has established himself as a major poet and translator. The poem uses the mythical sirens of Homeric poetry as its title, but the "sirens" calling the speaker are not personified, but are viewed as lands the speaker has "never seen / And shall not see, loves … [he] will not forget, / All … [he has] missed, or slighted, or foregone." The theme is that of yearning. Obvious comparison may be made with Tennyson's "Ulysses" (page 828) and Merwin's "Odysseus" (page

825). "Siren Song" by Margaret Atwood (page 823) invites comparison because of the title, but the poems are vastly different in subject and tone. The last lines of "The Sirens" are particularly striking and resonant.

WILLIAM CARLOS WILLIAMS, *The Red Wheelbarrow, page 1009*

The red/white contrast of the mentioned objects bears the weight of the poem's only assertion, "so much depends ..." The wheelbarrow, the rain, and the white chickens are simple but essential to the life of the farmer and therefore to all life.

WILLIAM WORDSWORTH, *Lines Written in Early Spring, pages 1009–1010*

The poem contrasts the beauty of the natural world with the horrors of injustice and persecution that human beings (Wordsworth uses the word "man") have committed on themselves. Wordsworth's speaker, observing the loveliness of a natural scene in spring, finds there the basis for the conclusion that living things enjoy the beauty in which they live. The speaker then posits the argument that if this belief is correct and is both God-given and God-intended, then there is ample "reason to lament / What man has made of man" (line 24). The simple stanzaic form of the poem underlines its elementary but also emphatic assertion. The speaker sees nature not just as a pleasant respite for human beings but also as the source of divine truth and philosophical reflection.

WILLIAM WORDSWORTH, *The Solitary Reaper, pages 1010–1011*

The initial situation visualized in the poem is simple and compelling. The speaker, walking in the Scottish Highlands, comes upon a young woman who is cutting and binding grain, and who is singing as she works. Because he cannot understand her language, he speculates upon the meaning of her song. In doing so, his thoughts take the experience far beyond the specific time and place, making of it a universal moment, one which remains in memory long afterwards. The solitary singer is emblematic of the mystery of the sources of art; her song is the symbol of the wide ranges of human experience and deep feelings.

William Butler Yeats, ***Sailing to Byzantium, pages 1011–1012***

From the vantage point of age, the speaker reflects upon life. In youth we are caught up in "sensual music" (line 7) and ignore the more permanent things of the intellect. In stanza 2 the speaker compares the aged man to a scarecrow, "paltry" (line 9) unless his soul sings a song of intellectual and spiritual achievement. Then swiftly, the speaker calls upon the memory of Byzantium, to Yeats the primary symbol of civilized achievement, in order to learn from its sages how to become part of "the artifice of eternity" (line 24). Dreaming in stanza 4 of this post-physical state, the speaker sees himself as an intricate and beautiful work of art embodying creative wisdom. Thus in this poem Yeats stresses the importance of art (which is as intellectual as science or philosophy), which is the only means by which time-bound human beings can gain the eternity which many religions have promised.

Paul Zimmer, ***The Day Zimmer Lost Religion,*** **page 1012**

The title is ironic. It should be "Zimmer's Coming of Age," for the poem describes the thoughts of a young speaker who, raised as an observant Catholic, chooses to miss Sunday mass. As a result, he speculates that a pugnacious and aggressive Jesus will "wade into" his "blasphemous gut" and knock him out, as though he is in a boxing match cheered on by the devil in a "reserved" seat roaring "until he got the hiccups" (line 7). The imagery of the poem abounds with the holy objects of Catholic worship together with the symbolism of the boxing ring, such as facial "cuts and mice" (line 17), "drop me" (line 5), and "I was grown up and ready for Him now" (line 21). The principal mode of description is overstatement, producing the poem's irony and also its comedy (the similes are fresh, clever, and funny). The poem offers a comic parallel and contrast to St. Paul's famous assertion that when he was a child he thought like a child, but when he became a man he put away childish things (I Corinthians, 13:11).

Resources for Poetry (Chapters 13–25)

Audiotape Recordings of Poetry

Readings Mainly by the Poets Themselves, and also by Skilled Actors

For countless decades, poets have been reading their poems to eager and curious audiences at colleges, universities, and poetry workshops. Often they introduce their poems briefly, and then provide a reading. They often discuss poetry in general and their own poems in particular. Only rarely do they just read their poems without comment. Prior to the invention of the tape recorder, these readings were totally lost. In the last fifty years, however, many of poetry readings have been taped, and it is now unusual if someone does not make a taping of the reading. Usually these tapings are privately maintained in the English department or the College library, and they are not available to the larger public.

A great service for lovers of poetry is being accomplished by commercial recording companies, usually quite small and dedicated, who have arranged with many individual poets and actors to make studio recordings for wide distribution. In this way, the voices of many contemporary poets have been preserved, along with the voices of many other major older poets such as Robert Frost, Dylan Thomas, T. S. Eliot, Ezra Pound, Wallace Stevens, and William Butler Yeats. The most significant commercial sources of such recordings are these:

- Caedmon Records (the pioneer in poetry recordings)
  1995 Broadway
  New York City, New York 10023

- Spoken Arts
  510 North Avenue
  New Rochelle, New York 10801

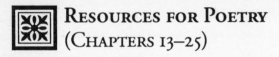

- Watershed Tapes
  P. O. Box 120216
  East Haven, Connecticut 06512

Recordings of many of the poets in the fourth edition of **Literature: An Introduction to Reading and Writing** are available for purchase from these sources. Many of the older tapings have been remastered, and their quality has been improved through this process. The list below refers to these companies whenever it is known that a commercial audio cassette is available.

Many recordings exist, however, that are not available commercially. The Poets House in New York City contains an archival treasure—The Axe-Houghton Poetry Tape Archive—of recordings of many poets who have given readings at the Academy of American Poets (584 Broadway, Suite 1208, New York City 10012), the Poets House itself (72 Spring Street, New York City 10012), and other nearby important poetry workshops and projects such as the Poetry Project at St Mark's Church in New York and the 92nd Street YMCA. These audiotapes, deposited in the Axe-Houghton Archive, are noted below with the designation "Poets House."

Following, then, is a listing of 73 poets included in the anthology for whom tapes are A–available commercially, as indicated by the publishing company that has issued them, or B–on deposit in the Axe-Houghton Archive at Poets House.

A. R. Ammons

1. Poetry reading, Academy of American Poets, March, 1965. Poets House.
2. Interview, June, 1980. Poets House.
3. Conversations with A. R. Ammons, February, 1980, in the Academy of American Poets Conversations series. Poets House.

Margaret Atwood

- Readings in the Caedmon *Voices in Time* series, 1977. Caedmon.

W. H. Auden

1. Readings in the Caedmon *Voices in Time* series, 1955.
2. Readings in the Spoken Arts Series, *Modern American Poets Reading Their Poems*. Spoken Arts.
3. Readings at the Academy of American Poets, January and March, 1966. Poets House.

Imamu Amiri Baraka

1. Reading, St. Marks Poetry Project, general series. Poets House.
2. Symposium at the St. Marks Poetry Project, May, 1985. Poets House.
3. Discussion of African American Oral Traditions, Poets House, March, 1990. Poets House.

Marvin Bell

1. Reading, Academy of American Poets, January, 1970 (with Diane Wakoski). Poets House.
2. Reading, Academy of American Poets, May, 1977. Poets House.

Elizabeth Bishop

1. Readings in the Spoken Arts Series, *Modern American Poets Reading Their Poems*, 1985. Spoken Arts.
2. Private recording of a poetry reading, 1982. Poets House.
3. Reading at the Academy of American Poets, May, 1969. Poets House.
4. Conversations with Elizabeth Bishop. Academy of American Poets, November, 1977. Poets House.
5. Reading of Bishop's poems by Randall Jarrell. Academy of American Poets, 1964. Poets House.

Louise Bogan

1. Readings in the Spoken Arts Series, *Modern American Poets Reading Their Poems*, 1985. Spoken Arts.
2. Reading at the Academy of American Poets, November, 1968. Poets House.

Joseph Brodsky

1. Reading at the Great Neck Library, October, 1973. Privately recorded tape. Poets House.
2. Reading at the Academy of American Poets, December, 1980. Poets House.

Gwendolyn Brooks

1. Reading at the Academy of American Poets, May, 1983. Poets House.
2. Readings in the Spoken Arts Series, *Modern American Poets Reading Their Poems*. Spoken Arts.

Olga Broumas

1. Commercial recording, 1981, *If I Yes*, Watershed.
2. Reading at the St. Marks Poetry Project, October, 1986. Poets House.

Lucille Clifton

1. Reading at the Academy of American Poets, May, 1983. Poets House.
2. Reading in the Family Stories Series, Snug Harbor Cultural Center, June, 1990. Poets House.

Countee Cullen

- Readings in the Spoken Arts Series (with Richard Eberhart), *Modern American Poets Reading Their Poems*. Issued by Spoken Arts in 1985.

E. E. Cummings

1. Readings in the Spoken Arts Series, *Modern American Poets Reading Their Poems*. Issued by Spoken Arts in 1985.
2. *E. E. Cummings Reads*. A selection of poems recorded in 1953. Issued in 1993 by Caedmon.

James Dickey

- Readings in the Spoken Arts Series, *Modern American Poets Reading Their Poems*, 1985. Spoken Arts.

Emily Dickinson

1. A discussion of Emily Dickinson's poetry by May Swenson at the Academy of American Poets, April, 1984. Poets House.
2. A discussion of Emily Dickinson's poetry by Susan Howe in the "Passwords" Series, May, 1990. Poets House.
3. *Poems and Letters of Emily Dickinson,* read by Julie Harris, 1991. Caedmon.

H. D. (Hilda Doolittle)

1. Readings in the Spoken Arts Series, *Modern American Poets Reading Their Poems.* Issued by Spoken Arts in 1985.
2. Reading, "Helen in Egypt," issued by Watershed in 1981.

John Donne

- *A Treasury of John Donne,* read by Robert Speaight. Spoken Arts.

Rita Dove

- A reading of Selected Poems, issued by Random House Audio Books, 1993.

Richard Eberhart

1. Reading at the Academy of American Poets, December, 1969. Poets House.
2. Reading in the Spoken Arts Series (with Countee Cullen), *Modern American Poets Reading Their Poems,* 1985. Spoken Arts.

T. S. Eliot

1. Reading in the Spoken Arts Series, *Modern American Poets Reading Their Poems.* Issued in 1985 by Spoken Arts.
2. Reading of Selected Poems, including "Macavity" and "Sweeney Among the Nightingales." Issued by Caedmon in 1991.

Carolyn Forché

- Reading at the Academy of American Poets, December, 1978. Poets House.

Robert Frost

1. A private recording of a public reading, 1950. Poets House.
2. A private recording of a public reading, 1952. Poets House.
3. Reading in the Spoken Arts Series, *Modern American Poets Reading Their Poems*. Issued in 1985 by Spoken Arts.
4. *Robert Frost in Recital.* Recordings made during readings in 1951, 1952, and 1953. Issued by Caedmon, 1992.

Allen Ginsberg

1. Reading in the Spoken Arts Series, *American Poets Reading Their Poems*, 1985. Spoken Arts.
2. Reading, *The Lion for Real*, 1989, for Great Jones. Poets House.

Robert Graves

- *Robert Graves Reads*, a selection of poems recorded in 1957. Caedmon, 1993.

John Haines

1. Reading and discussion with Sonia Sanchez at the NY/NJ Teachers Conference, April 1992. Poets House
2. Reading at the Academy of American Poets, March, 1980. Poets House

Donald Hall

1. "Names of Horses," 1985. Watershed.
2. Reading in the Spoken Arts Series, *Modern American Poets Reading Their Poems*, 1985. Spoken Arts.

Seamus Heaney

- Reading at the Academy of American Poets, the "Education of the Poet" Series, March, 1987. Poets House.

Anthony Hecht

- Reading in the Spoken Arts Series, *Modern American Poets Reading Their Poems*, 1985. Spoken Arts.

William Heyen

1. Three readings in 1991 issued by Time Being Books
2. Reading of poems from *Erika* and *Pterodactyl Rose.* Poets House

John Hollander

- Reading in the Spoken Arts Series, *Modern American Poets Reading Their Poems*, 1985. Spoken Arts.

Langston Hughes

1. *Langston Hughes Reads and Talks About His Poems.* Issued by Spoken Arts in 1985.
2. *Langston Hughes Reads,* poems recorded for the BBC in 1962 and 1964. Issued by Caedmon in 1992.

Richard Hugo

- Reading at the Great Neck Library, privately recorded. Poets House.

Randall Jarrell

1. Reading at the Academy of American Poets (also including the reading of poems by Elizabeth Bishop), 1964. Poets House.
2. Reading in the Spoken Arts Series, *Modern American Poets Reading Their Poems.* Issued in 1985 by Spoken Arts.

Robinson Jeffers

- Reading in the Spoken Arts Series, *Modern American Poets Reading Their Poems.* Issued in 1985 by Spoken Arts.

Donald Justice

- Reading at the Academy of American Poets, March 1975. Poets House.

Carolyn Kizer

- Reading at the Academy of American Poets, March, 1986. Poets House.

Joanne Kyger

- Reading at the St. Marks Poetry Project, March, 1982. Poets House.

Audre Lorde

1. Reading at the Academy of American Poets, March, 1977. Poets House.
2. Reading at the St. Marks Poetry Project, April, 1976. Poets House.

Cynthia MacDonald

- Reading at the Great Neck Library, March, 1978. Privately recorded. Poets House.

Archibald MacLeish

- Reading in the Spoken Arts Series, *Modern American Poets Reading Their Poems.* Issued in 1985 by Spoken Arts.

Heather McHugh

- Reading at the Great Neck Library, 1979. Privately recorded. Poets House.

James Merrill

- Reading in the Spoken Arts Series, *Modern American Poets Reading Their Poems*, 1985. Spoken Arts.

Marianne Moore

- Reading in the Spoken Arts Series, *Modern American Poets Reading Their Poems.* Issued in 1985 by Spoken Arts.

Carol Muske

- Reading at the Academy of American Poets, October, 1980. Poets House.

OGDEN NASH

- Reading in the Spoken Arts Series, *Modern American Poets Reading Their Poems*. Issued in 1985 by Spoken Arts.

NAOMI SHIHAB NYE

- Reading in the Poets House Festival Series. "Southwest Poetry," a joint appearance with Joy Harjo, March, 1991. Poets House.

SHARON OLDS

- Reading and discussion at the NY/NJ Teachers Conference, 1987. Poets House Education Series. Poets House.

LINDA PASTAN

1. Reading at the Great Neck Library, 1975. Privately recorded. Poets House.
2. Reading in the "Family Stories" Series at the Snug Harbor Cultural Center, May, 1990. Poets House.

SYLVIA PLATH

- Reading in the Spoken Arts Series, *Modern American Poets Reading Their Poems*. Issued in 1985 by Spoken Arts.

EZRA POUND

1. Reading in the Spoken Arts Series, *Modern American Poets Reading Their Poems*. Issued in 1985 by Spoken Arts.
2. *Ezra Pound Reads*, a selection of poems recorded in 1960. Issued by Caedmon in 1993.

JOHN CROWE RANSOM

- Reading in the Spoken Arts Series, *Modern American Poets Reading Their Poems*. Issued in 1985 by Spoken Arts.

THEODORE ROETHKE

- Reading in the Spoken Arts Series, *Modern American Poets Reading Their Poems*. Issued in 1985 by Spoken Arts.

Muriel Rukuyser

1. Reading at the Academy of American Poets, December, 1976. Poets House.
2. Reading at the Great Neck Library, 1975, privately recorded. Poets House.

Sonia Sanchez

- Reading and Discussion at the NY/NJ Teachers Conference, Education Series, April, 1992, with John Haines. Poets House.

Carl Sandberg

1. Reading in the Spoken Arts Series, *Modern American Poets Reading Their Poems*. Issued in 1985 by Spoken Arts.
2. *Carl Sandberg Reads*, a selection of poems recorded in 1951 and 1952. Issued by Caedmon in 1992.

Anne Sexton

1. Reading in the Spoken Arts Series, *Modern American Poets Reading Their Poems*. Issued in 1985 by Spoken Arts.
2. Readings in the "Voices in Time" Series, 1974. Caedmon.

William Shakespeare

- A Selection of Shakespeare's Sonnets read by Sir John Gielgud, recorded in 1963 and 1988. Two cassettes, issued by Caedmon.

Leslie Marmon Silko

- Reading at the Academy of American Poets, April, 1987 (Writers/Readers Series). Poets House.

W. D. Snodgrass

- Reading in the Spoken Arts Series, *Modern American Poets Reading Their Poems*, 1985. Spoken Arts.

William E. Stafford

- Lecture, "Where the Words Come From," at the Academy of American Poets, March, 1967. Poets House.

Wallace Stevens

1. Reading in the Spoken Arts Series, *Modern American Poets Reading Their Poems*. Issued in 1985 by Spoken Arts.
2. *Wallace Stevens Reads*, a selection of poems recorded in 1956. Issued in 1993 by Caedmon.

Mark Strand

- Reading in the Spoken Arts Series, *Modern American Poets Reading Their Poems*, 1985. Spoken Arts.

May Swenson

- Reading in the Education/Poet Series at the Academy of American Poets, November, 1978. Poets House.

Dylan Thomas

1. Reading of May, 1952, private recording. Poets House.
2. *Dylan Thomas Reads*, a selection of works recorded in the early 1950s. Issued by Caedmon in 1993.

David Wagoner

- Reading in the Spoken Arts Series, *Modern American Poets Reading Their Poems*, 1985. Spoken Arts.

Diane Wakoski

- Reading at the Academy of American Poets, January, 1970. Poets House.

Robert Penn Warren

- Reading in the Spoken Arts Series, *Modern American Poets Reading Their Poems*. Issued in 1985 by Spoken Arts.

Richard Wilbur

- Reading at the Academy of American Poets, April, 1969. Poets House.

William Carlos Williams

- *William Carlos Williams Reads*, a selection of poems recorded in 1958. Issued by Caedmon, 1993.

William Wordsworth

- *A Treasury of William Wordsworth*, a selection of poems read by Robert Speaight. Spoken Arts.

James Wright

1. Reading in the Spoken Arts Series, *Modern American Poets Reading Their Poems.* Issued in 1985 by Spoken Arts.
2. Reading in the Academy of American Poets Poetry Series, "The Music of Poetry," March 1967. Poets House.
3. Conversations with James Wright at the Academy of American Poets, March, 1977. Poets House.

William Butler Yeats

- *The Poems of W. B. Yeats*, readings by various readers, including some poems read by Yeats himself. Spoken Arts.

Part III
Pages 1015–1598

Drama

Coverage of the Manual

The plays included in the text feature introductions, explanatory glosses and notes, study questions, and writing topics. Because this material is relatively extensive, we have limited coverage in the manual to discussions of some of the more vexing study questions and suggestions about teaching. We also direct you, where possible, to filmed or videotaped versions of the plays that you might use to supplement the texts.

Organization of the Drama Section

Unlike the other major sections of the text, the drama section is not organized according to discrete elements. Rather, the elements of drama are introduced and discussed in the first part of Chapter 26. This material is followed by four short plays, any one of which can be used for classroom illustration. Chapters that focus on tragedy, comedy, and realism in drama follow this introductory chapter, together with a brief chapter on film, which was new in the third edition. While the elements of drama remain important considerations throughout the drama section, these later chapters focus on the distinctive qualities of the mode (i.e., tragedy, comedy, realism, nonrealism, film).

Organization of Each Drama Chapter

Each chapter follows the general plan pursued throughout the book: introductory material followed by a selection of plays. The plays are accompanied by extensive apparatus, including introductions, notes, glosses, questions for study and classroom use, and "General Questions" for writing and further discussion. Each chapter concludes with a section on writing, which comprises discussions of strategies for writing about specific aspects of drama, sample essays, commentary, and additional writing topics. The sample essays take up elements or aspects of one of the plays included in the chapter; they can be used for your own writing assignments or for supplementary reading.

Suggestions for Teaching Drama

We do not expect that you will use all the plays during an introductory course (unless the course is focused on drama). The broad scope of the selections provides for variation and flexibility. We do recommend, however, that you begin with the elements of drama in Chapter 26. Any one of the plays in the chapter will illustrate various aspects of the elements, and some plays will highlight specifics. *The Bear* illustrates the nature of dramatic involvement and also the qualities of comedy and farce. *Trifles* is ideal for demonstrating dramatic responses between characters on stage together, and also showing the changes and developments of their characters. *Tea Party* is brief enough to be read and discussed in one meeting of class, and it may be used to show the power and compactness of dramatic dialogue. *Before Breakfast* is a virtuoso piece illustrating how dramatic interest may be centered upon just one major character on stage. Though the plays show great variety of topic and treatment, any or all of them may be used as examples for most of the elements of drama.

For the remainder of your course, you may pick and choose as your interests dictate. You might concentrate on a specific mode of drama, or offer your students a wide variety, combining, for example, tragedy with comedy. You might also explore the possibility of a thematic orientation here, focusing on plays that deal with topics such as love, marriage, the family, and society.

In teaching drama to students with little or no background, you will need to be sure that they understand how plays work on the stage so that they can build imaginative theaters in their minds. To this end, we have discussed aspects of production at some length. We recommend that you encourage students to go to whatever live theater may be easily available. We also suggest that you screen a film or videotape of at least one play or film you are teaching, if time permits. Some instructors find that using class time for complete viewings may preempt valuable instruction time. One solution to the problem is to show only selected parts of the videotape in class; another is to set aside larger blocks of time outside of class for complete viewing.

Many other strategies can be used in the classroom to make plays come alive. One of these is an open-book reading of an entire short play, as we have suggested for *Tea Party.* The time taken for readings will of course vary, but plays like *Trifles* and *The Bear* should take no more than thirty-five to forty minutes. While you cannot expect your students to give polished readings, the spoken words will often carry more impact than just the words on the page. Another approach, particularly for longer plays, is to have students enact specific and crucial scenes, such as the play-within-the-play in *A Midsummer Night's Dream,* some of the soliloquies of Hamlet, or the confrontation of Biff and Willy Loman in *Death of a Salesman.* The scenes from *Citizen Kane* and *The Turning Point* are of course made to order for brief classroom enactment. This sort of pointed work might involve out-of-class preparation, but the results can be quite impressive, particularly if student-actors and the class at large can discuss why individual readings were made, why vocal inflections were done, how another reading might have created a different effect, and so on.

Also, to bring theater alive for your students, you might look into the possibility of using some of the expertise available in your college's theater department. Given this possibility, another broad range of options is available. You might, for example, arrange for a group of theater students to stage one of the text's short plays for your class (either a memorized or an open-book reading). At some larger schools, a significant number of literature classes might study the same play at the same time. In this situation, a drama department, given enough lead time, might be willing to plan a full-scale production of one of the plays in the text. Keep in mind that theater students are eagerly looking for audiences; such projects can be mutually constructive.

In teaching an individual play, your approach will be determined by the available time and the level of preparation. If there is little time, you can deal only with the play's major features: what happens, why it happens, the major characters, the subjects, and major themes. Even this sort of overview can teach students much. If you have more time, you can have your students examine conflicts, structure, irony, and language, for a close look at these aspects will help them to become more disciplined readers of drama. In any event, your approach should always be geared to the needs and abilities of students. A close analysis of the "flower imagery" in *Hamlet* or the Ovidian elements in *A Midsummer Night's Dream,* for example, is rarely as useful as a study of Hamlet's character or the structural importance of Bottom and his crew of "hempen homespuns."

Chapter Twenty-six
PAGES 1015–1068

Drama: An Overview

The introductory material provides a definition and description of the major aspects of drama and theater (pages 1015–1017), a survey and brief history of types of drama (pages 1017–1019), and a discussion of the elements of drama (pages 1020–1026.) Most of this can be assigned as outside reading; only the discussion of the elements should require classroom review, and this can be combined with study of specific plays. The section on "How to Read a Play" (pages 1026–1027) may help students come to grips with this experience.

Anton Chekhov, *The Bear, pages 1027–1037*

Most notable in this play is the swiftness with which antagonism changes to love. Students may deny the realism of the play because of this speed. However, while there is no need to claim fidelity to real life for *The Bear,* it is true that Chekhov points out that the self-dramatizing major characters are both romantic and impulsive, and that their love is credible enough even if the circumstances in which they fall in love are not.

Though the play is short, it contains a number of major and minor conflicts. The major one is between Smirnov and Mrs. Popov. Also, it is clear that both major characters bear their own inner conflicts, such as the rage that Mrs. Popov exhibits at the cruelty and infidelity of her dead husband, and the anger that Smirnov bears toward women as a result of his misfortunes in love. There is a servant-master conflict between Mrs. Popov and Luka, and also between Smirnov and his offstage groom Semyon (speech 45). There is also a conflict over the extent of the loyalty that the living owe to the dead, not to mention the general battle between the sexes out of which Mrs. Popov and Smirnov find love.

Answers to the Study Questions, page 1037

(1) At the opening Mrs. Popov is in mourning for her husband, who has been dead for seven months. She indicates, however, that her life had

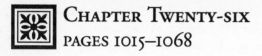

been difficult with her husband inasmuch as he had been unfaithful and had also been mean and cruel (speeches 4, 72). Even though she is trying to be a model of faithfulness to his memory, she is obviously also angry at him. At the play's opening, Luka's practical advice and his directness show that her behavior is overdrawn, sentimental, and just plain silly (particularly because of her deep feelings).

(2) Smirnov has come to collect a debt owed by the dead husband (speech 21). He is gruff, loud, and outspoken. He tells Mrs. Popov that he has had his fill of love, having been jilted nine times and having jilted women twelve times (speech 69).

(3) Luka is important because he is the first one to speak with Mrs. Popov, and on occasion he is also alone with Smirnov. There could be no dialogue without him. As a character, he is outspoken but not very brave or strong. His reactions (exclamations, handwringing, signs of developing anguish, rushing offstage to get help, etc.) to the actions and emotions of Smirnov and Mrs. Popov underscore their anger and make their eventual embraces seem especially unlikely and therefore funny.

(4) Smirnov's repeated and angry requests for money occasion Mrs. Popov's asking him to leave. When he refuses and becomes more angry, she calls him a bear, a brute, a monster (speeches 101, 103, 111). As the anger and insults mount, Smirnov challenges her to a duel (speech 112).

(5) Toby is the horse who had been the favorite of Mrs. Popov's husband. He symbolizes the shifting of her emotions, because at the start she orders an extra bag of oats for him, but at the end, when she has fallen for Popov, she withdraws the request, indicating that her vigil for the dead husband is over (speeches 8, 154).

General Questions

(1) Laughter is of course unpredictable. Some likely spots at the start are Luka's observations about his dead wife, about living like spiders, and about the waving of the fanny. The play takes off from there. Certainly Smirnov is quite funny, for he says outrageous things, imitates his offstage groom, criticizes his handling of the horse, spits out water (probably), breaks chairs, and clearly indicates his increasing desire for Mrs. Popov. Students will, let us hope, find other spots that they think are funny.

(2) All of the things cited in the question point out the extravagance in language and action characteristic of farce. Normal feelings and responses are inflated, stage business (such as the breaking of chairs, etc.) is exaggerated, and speeches are loud and out of proportion. The novelist

Henry Fielding, in an early play (*The Author's Farce*), said that the aim of farce is "to make you laugh." The primary goal is laughter, and in farce, everything is directed toward that end.

(3) From the shortness of their acquaintance and the increasing hostility of their speeches to each other, one could never predict that Smirnov and Mrs. Popov would be falling in love at the play's end. But because both are portrayed as being committed to love (Mrs. Popov's dedication to mourning for her dead husband, Smirnov's many affairs), their falling in love is sudden but not surprising, granted that their relationship takes place in such a heightened emotional atmosphere.

(4) Each of the ideas listed here could result in extensive discussion, or else in an essay-length treatment. "The Difficulty of Keeping Resolutions," for example, might involve introducing the declarations about life of both Mrs. Popov and Smirnov, and then considering the circumstances of their lives that make the resolutions unlikely. A discussion of this topic need not consider their meeting and falling suddenly in love, but rather might treat the general directions in which their characters and circumstances would point them, the idea being that decisions made at one time may not necessarily apply later.

Susan Glaspell, *Trifles, pages 1038–1049*

This play examines the agony and desperation that often occur in life (good pieces for comparison are *Before Breakfast* and *Tea Party*). It also explores traditional male attitudes toward women, together with the expression of female responses to these attitudes. The key irony in the play, of course, is that the two women characters do what the men cannot do; they solve the problem of motive based on the evidence of "trifles," and they pass judgment on the murderer based on both the crime and the context.

Although the play is set on a farm and concerns a family murder, it is really about marriage, society, and the relationship between men and women. These thematic concerns are repeated on three levels: the history of the Wrights' marriage, the traditional repression of women, and the conflict between the men and women in the Wrights' kitchen. In each case (and in general), woman is protagonist and man antagonist. In the context of the play, we find resolution in the women's decision to suppress the evidence against Minnie Wright. In a our larger society, however, the conflict remains unresolved.

Answers to the Study Questions, pages 1048–1049

(1) The men enter first in a group and move directly across the stage to the stove. The two women follow; they move "slowly," "look fearfully about," and remain "near the door." The two groupings and the differences in movement establish traditional hierarchies and suggest very different attitudes toward the murder investigation. The preserves have frozen and almost all the jars have broken. The men are not concerned about this fact, but all the women are concerned (including Mrs. Wright, in jail). This difference is further evidence of the restrictions blinding the men and the freedom of the women to see things as they are and to draw conclusions accordingly.

(2) Hale reports that he found Mrs. Wright in the kitchen, rocking back and forth and pleating her apron, and also finding Mr. Wright upstairs, strangled in his bed. Hale is observant, and his testimony is accurate as far as it goes. He doesn't notice signs of disturbance in the kitchen, and he doesn't make much of Mrs. Wright's "laugh" or her "scared look."

(3) The authorities need a motive. The sheriff is convinced there is "nothing" in the kitchen that will establish motive. Because the women deduce the motive from looking at "kitchen things," we may conclude that the men are restricted by traditional thinking about men and women.

(4) The badly stitched square suggests to the women that Mrs. Wright was upset ("didn't know what she was about"). Mrs. Hale resews the square. She may suspect Mrs. Wright at this point, but her action is presented as instinctive rather than as a conscious suppression of evidence.

(5) Mrs. Hale reveals that Minnie Foster had been a pretty but frail young woman who liked to sing. Her childless marriage removed her from social contact, and also isolated her on the farm with Wright, a dour and hard man who was "like a raw wind that gets to the bone" (speech 103). This background, scattered throughout, lays the groundwork for motive, but it also begins the justification of Mrs. Wright's actions.

(6, 7) The broken cage and the strangled bird provide evidence of the motive for the murder. The women look at each other with "growing comprehension" and "horror" at this point. This is the crisis; the women have proof of motive and must decide what to do with it. The cage symbolizes the Wrights' marriage or Minnie's status in it (it also parallels the jail, visually). The fact that the cage is broken reflects the current status of the marriage and Minnie's desperate act to escape. The bird with its "neck wrung" is a visual parallel to the strangulation of Mr. Wright, but symbolizes the cruelty that Wright had inflicted on his wife (she had been "like a bird herself" in her youth [speech 107]). It seems clear, from this point on, that the knot used to strangle Wright was one of Minnie's quilting knots.

(8) At first, the women have different reactions to the evidence and their developing interpretation of it. Mrs. Peters is torn; she understands the situation, but she is conventionally fixed on the idea that "the law has got to punish crime." Mrs. Hale blames herself for not helping Minnie, and feels that the murder was justified. Finally, however, they tacitly agree to cover up the crime; both try to hide the box containing the dead bird. Mrs. Peters cannot do it, so Mrs. Hale puts it in the pocket of her coat (page 1048, speech 147.1, S.D.).

(9) Mrs. Hale feels partly responsible because she did not provide human contact and support for Minnie: "Oh, I wish I'd come over here once in a while! That was a crime!" (speech 134). She knew how wretched Minnie was, but she didn't visit. Her guilt is justified only insofar as society as a whole is responsible for the conditions and conventions that led to Minnie's desperation and isolation. Nevertheless, Mrs. Hale feels personally at fault, and this contributes to her final decision.

General Questions

(1) The title and the word "trifles" refer to domestic matters or concerns that the men consider insignificant and funny. Ironically, these trifles have a profound impact on life, death, and judgment in the play. They reveal the shape of the pathetic life of the Wrights, and also the events leading up to the murder. The men's mocking attitude and the women's sensitivity to trifles underscore the basic distinctions in the play.

(2) It is important to the play that the male characters be flat, static, and representative. The result is that they and their attitudes are universalized. Puffed up as they are with their own importance and sense of superiority and competence, their minds work in narrow and conventional patterns, and they are thus condescending toward the women who worry about "kitchen things." They therefore miss the significance of the trifles of the kitchen, and also miss the women's agitation.

(3) By contrast with the men, Mrs. Hale is strong, assertive, and sympathetic. From her role as a subservient wife, she grows during the play, and is therefore round. She quietly makes light of the men and their work, wishing they would be quick about getting evidence. She picks up on the significance of the trifles, and understands the crime without difficulty. She feels a sisterly responsibility for Minnie, and thus blames her-

self for Minnie's solitude and isolation. The high point of her growth is the decision she makes, along with Mrs. Peters, to hide the evidence.

(4) Students may agree or disagree, so long as they present a good argument. Glaspell keeps Minnie offstage so as not to prejudice the judgment of readers: We must decide about justice without seeing the criminal/victim. In addition, keeping Minnie offstage helps to universalize her as an everywoman figure.

(5) The symbolism of the cage and bird suggest, first, the status of Minnie Wright on the Wright farm. Her nature and her freedom have been lost because she has been almost literally caged. Beyond that, there is a general value in the symbol, suggesting that traditional marriage (women used to vow that they would obey their husbands) is a cage. The word "knot" links the quilting (a "womanly" occupation and thus an amusing trifle to the men) to the rope which was knotted about Mr. Wright's neck.

BETTY KELLER, *Tea Party, pages 1049–1053*

This brief play was originally designed as a teaching instrument for students actors. Its brevity therefore makes it perfect for an introduction to dramatic character, situation, setting, and meaning. The story is that two aged and desperately lonely sisters plan to entertain their paper boy on his collection day, but the boy snubs them and thus baffles their plan, leaving them as lonely and bereft as before. One's first response to the paperboy's snub is to claim that he is unkind, knowing that the sisters wish to take up his time and not wanting to have anything to do with them. On the other hand, the play makes it clear that he has spent such time with the ladies before, and now does not wish to get caught with them again. He does, in fact, have other papers to deliver and other customers from whom to collect. Thus, while life goes on busily outside the window of Alma and Hester's home, it remains stopped inside, and all the ladies have left is their silence and loneliness.

Answers to the Study Questions, page 1053

(1) The major conflict in the play is the advancement of age, senility, illness, and death upon Alma and Hester. The minor conflict is their loneliness, their attempts to encourage visits, and the refusal of others, as represented by the paperboy, to tolerate the two ladies, thus highlighting their solitude. The two also have minor conflicts, as shown by their discussion about circumstances and dates of past events.

(2) The two sisters discuss their seating arrangements so that they might center the visiting boy between them and hold him, therefore, for a more extended conversation. We learn that they have made these arrangements before because they mention a previous visit by "Charlie" (speeches 14–17).

(3) Alma's use of the twenty-dollar bill (speech 45) shows that she is capable of manipulation, for she expects that the paperboy will not have change and will therefore need to return another time for his money. Obviously, the discussion about the $20.00 and the previous paperboy shows that the women know that they can work this subterfuge only a limited number of times.

(4) Alma is four years younger than Hester, who states that Alma was too young to have known whether the correct name of the ship was the *Bainbridge* or the *Heddingham*. We may conclude that Alma is remembering what others told her, whose memories may have grown dim, while Hester is remembering what she actually saw. Therefore both sisters are still in sound mind, even though they may be differing on a factual matter.

General Questions

(1) The setting is described precisely. If students make a scheme of the furniture arrangements, they will see that the plans for serving, sitting, and so on, are exact. Generally, the changes and developments of characters in a play are related directly to place, time, and circumstances on stage. In *Tea Party*, for example, the discussions about how to serve the paperboy indicate that the ladies have been engaged in their pathetic arrangements as hosts for relatively unwilling people for a long time, and that the only interludes from their loneliness will be to continue these arrangements. The setting in this short play therefore highlights the plight and the pathos of the major characters.

(2) The women are at the end of the so-called "golden years" of old age, and the future will present even more difficulty and disability. *Tea Party* dramatizes these difficulties in detail. One might cite the play in strengthening a sociological/political argument because it vividly illustrates, better than an extensive treatise with generalized commentary, the physical inabilities and the isolation of the aged.

EUGENE O'NEILL, *Before Breakfast, pages 1053–1060*

O'Neill's play is a study in character and perspective, and it also provides a good actress with a virtuoso acting piece. Because Mrs. Rowland is on stage throughout, we focus on her, and might conclude that she is the sole cause of difficulties in her marriage. From what we may learn of Alfred through her speeches, however, we may conclude that he has not been without fault in the troubles the couple has experienced.

Answers to the Study Questions, pages 1059–1060

(1) The setting implies that the Rowlands are poor, bohemian, and careless. The plants "dying of neglect" symbolize the decaying relationship between man and wife.

(2) O'Neill uses negative adjectives to convey the impression that Mrs. Rowland is careless and coarse. These are "slovenly," "drab," "formless," "shapeless," "shabby," "worn," "characterless," "nondescript," "pinched," "weak," and "spiteful." Her initial actions—putting on the apron, getting a drink—are equally negative. She moves "slowly," "wearily," and acts with "clumsy fingers." There is also a vindictive aspect to her; she "hastily" sneaks a drink, and then "stealthily" finds and reads Alfred's letter from Helen. These initial impressions are expanded in her speeches to Alfred throughout the play. See also the sample essay, page 1064.

(3) Throughout the play, Mrs. Rowland treats Alfred with condescension and derision. She accuses him of being "lazy," "good-for-nothing," "silly," and of being a coward. Her taunts become especially sharp and vindictive when she speaks about Helen, just before Alfred cuts his own throat.

(4) It seems clear that Mrs. Rowland became pregnant during the premarital affair. She did not wish to be bought off because she assumed that Alfred, being an heir, would eventually come into a huge amount of money, a much larger amount than she would have been given for going away. This situation does not reflect favorably upon either Alfred or Mrs. Rowland.

(5) The crisis occurs after Alfred nicks himself when shaving and then begins to stare at himself and Mrs. Rowland. It is at this point that he probably thinks of suicide. Other signs of crisis include Alfred's growing "pale" and shaking "dreadfully." Mrs. Rowland's unsympathetic mockery of his relationship with the pregnant Helen pushes Alfred to suicide and the play to its sudden catastrophe. The catastrophe is Alfred's slitting his throat and Mrs. Rowland's discovery and genuinely terrified response.

(6) Mrs. Rowland is defensive in her attitude toward Alfred's affair with Helen. She is unsympathetic to Helen's pregnancy, and claims that Helen is old enough to have known better. She also threatens Alfred's relationship with Helen by stating that she will refuse the divorce he needs so

that he may remarry. She insults Helen, saying that she thinks of the other woman as being "no better than a common street-walker" (paragraph 29).

General Questions

(1) The setting shows the characters to be poor, careless, and negligent of themselves and their surroundings, suggesting the deterioration of character that results in neglect. Significant details are the size and location of the apartment, the dying plants, the clothing hung on pegs (no closets), and the clothesline. This tacky setting suggests the darker side of realism and verisimilitude.

(2) Mrs. Rowland is flat, static, and stereotyped. These choices, and the missing first name, suggest that she represents a type. She is not, however, without a certain depth of character, as is indicated by the fact that she goes out to work, thus shouldering financial responsibility, and also that she has thought about the implications of Alfred's affair.

(3, 4) By keeping Alfred offstage (except for his hand), O'Neill presents the conflict completely from Mrs. Rowland's perspective. For this reason, the play is much like Browning's "My Last Duchess" (page 578). O'Neill gives Mrs. Rowland exclusive control of the stage, to show, through her speeches and attitudes, her anger and resentment at her situation. Had Alfred been brought on stage to speak with her, the focus and impact of her personality might have been diffused. In addition, we would have had to consider the real problems of Alfred's irresponsibility, drinking, and guilt. Mrs. Rowland's view of Alfred is distorted by her anger, limited mentality, and feelings of grievance. She does not value the things valued by Alfred, such as art, education, and poetry. Indeed, she terms poetry "silly." Her views about Alfred are not without some justification, but her personality renders it impossible to grant her more understanding and sympathy than that.

(5) By presenting the background out of order and in fragments, O'Neill creates tension and prolongs the revelation of Mrs. Rowland's character. Chronologically, Alfred graduated from Harvard (why Harvard?), began writing poetry (why poetry?), and became involved with his future wife, who became pregnant (why does O'Neill make her father a grocer?). Alfred's father tried to buy Mrs. Rowland off; she refused; they married; and the father died with his fortune being claimed by creditors. Once this information is put back in order, Mrs. Rowland's interest in the Rowland money seems clear.

Writing About the Elements of Drama, *pages 1060–1067*

This section aims to help students formulate ideas for essays about how significant elements work toward dramatic meaning and impact. The section may be assigned in conjunction with any play in the text; it is as relevant to tragedy or comedy as it is to the four plays in the chapter. Students can be directed to this discussion and the relevant cross references whenever they write about a particular element.

The topics for discovering ideas (pages 1060–1063) suggests the development of central ideas about specific aspects of a play, and also refers students to earlier relevant sections. The section also treats organization and provides a sample essay on O'Neill's stage directions in *Before Breakfast* (pages 1064–1066).

Perhaps the most important point in teaching this material is selectivity. In an effort to fill pages as easily as possible, students often summarize dramatic events or else present random but disconnected observations. The solution is selectivity and focus; press the students to think about and deal with only one or two topics for any given play.

The boxed section on page 1063, "Referring to Plays and Parts of Plays," contains answers to questions that many students have asked about how to refer to acts, scenes, lines, and speeches in plays. Be sure that your students know about the suggestions contained there.

Writing Topics for *Drama: An Overview, pages 1067–1068*

(1) The point about sentimentality is key to *Tea Party*. The most important consideration is that the sisters, despite their pathetic attempt to overcome their isolation and loneliness, and despite their vulnerability, exhibit individuality, determination, understanding, and a certain combativeness. These strengths keep the play away from the edge.

(2) This topic requires the reading of an additional Chekhov play, and enough alertness to see points of similarity and difference. All the mentioned plays are popular, but none of them has the boisterous good humor which has made *The Bear* an enduring favorite.

(3) This question is discussed in this manual in response to both the first specific and general questions for *Before Breakfast* (please use the text page guide in this manual, pages 1059–1060, for the locations of these discussions).

(4) A good case may be made that *Trifles* is about all the points except crime; Mrs. Wright is not a criminal. A good topic might also be bottled-up anger. It would of course be unthinkable today for anyone like Mrs. Hale and Mrs. Peters to poke around at the scene of a murder. The play as we have it could only have been set in a rural area during a past day, when law officers were comparatively unskilled in systematic and controlled investigations.

(5) This topic is potentially one of the most rewarding of the group of questions. Glaspell uses many of the same speeches and situations in both play and story, but it is clear that within the short-story framework she is free to clarify the focus on Martha Hale and also to explain more of the thoughts and considerations of the characters. In the dramatic form, she is constrained to present only dialogue and action, whereas in the story form she fleshes out the dramatic materials. The story is hence more visual than it otherwise might have been, inasmuch as fiction often contains greater discussion and abstract explanations than drama. (Story: page 155. Play: page 1038)

(6) The list of topics might create an extensive essay. If students settle on a single aspect, however, and pinpoint specific actions and character traits in just a few plays, the essays might be kept within manageable limits. If you use question 6 for a term paper, many more of the topics might be developed.

(7) The problem students will encounter in this essay, as in any essay entailing the consideration of a number of separate works, is to preserve thematic unity. The key to keeping things together is to utilize the topics as the basis of the discussion. Thus the topic of dialogue may be kept foremost while various plays are described and compared as they relate to this topic. The same applies to action, use of soliloquies and asides, stage directions, and so on.

Chapter Twenty-seven
Pages 1069–1315

Tragedy: Affirmation Through Loss

The goal of this chapter—by far the longest in the book—is to introduce students to the concept of tragedy and the special considerations that come into play in dealing with tragic drama. The material on tragedy has been extensively revised for the fourth edition (pages 1069–1081). It is focused largely on ancient Athenian tragedy, but it also deals with general aspects of tragedy that are relevant for the later plays (see pages 1076–1077). The chapter also includes extensive introductory material on each of the three tragedies included here. The opening discussion takes up the origin and nature of tragedy in ancient Greece (pages 1069–1073).

If you assign one or all of the tragedies for your students, you can begin with a general discussion of the mode (i.e., tragedy) or you can develop a working definition based on the introductory material in conjunction with the play under consideration. In any event, some class discussion of the mode will be helpful for students, especially since in modern usage the term *tragedy* is loosely applied to any unhappy or unfortunate event. (The development of the word and the genre is considered on pages 1069–1070).

Sophocles, *Oedipus the King, pages 1081–1122*

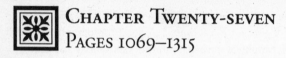

If you assign *Oedipus the King*, you should have the students read the introduction to Greek theater (pages 1069–1081) and the introduction to the play (pages 1081–1082). Both explain many of the conventions of Greek drama that students may find odd or intrusive. In teaching the play, you may need to prepare arguments against the propositions that, realistically, Oedipus is a fool (why couldn't he see what we saw?) or, symbolically, as nothing much more than a representative figure illustrating that human beings are the pawns of fate and destiny, without any capacity to control their lives. Neither is an accurate assessment of Oedipus. His circumstances are quite singular, and he is not fool—at the beginning of his career he solved the riddle of the sphinx, and for twenty years he has ruled Thebes successfully.

Oedipus is like a murder mystery in which the reader (or viewer) already knows "who did it"; the pleasure and agony are produced as we follow the slow process of discovery. But *Oedipus* offers a twist; the detective discovers finally that he himself is the murderer. One of the play's central problems is whether Oedipus's tragic fall is a result of fate or character. Is he controlled by forces beyond his control, or by aspects of his character that led to errors in judgment and action? A good teaching approach is to balance these two alternatives and present each side of the argument with equal force.

At least two productions of *Oedipus* are available for classroom use. A 45-minute film or videotape of a production done in masks in an ancient Greek theater is available from Films for the Humanities (Box 2053, Princeton, NJ 08540). A 1957 color film of Tyrone Guthrie's Stratford (Canada) production of Yeats's version of the play is available from Contemporary/McGraw-Hill Films (1221 Avenue of the Americas, New York, NY 10020). This version is done in papier-mâché masques and fine costuming; it thus gives a remarkably authentic sense of at least this aspect of ancient Greek productions of the play.

The following questions, answers, and comment can serve as a programmatic teaching guide to *Oedipus;* the material may be used to organize either class discussion or lecture.

I. PROLOGUE (lines 1–150).

1. **The first stage direction (S.D.) and Oedipus's opening speech (lines 1–13) provide exposition about the state.**

What does the first S.D. tell you about the city? About Oedipus?

Since the people are supplicants—praying to Oedipus for help—we know that something is seriously wrong. Since the prayers are addressed directly to Oedipus, he is identified as a significant power.

What do we learn about Thebes in Oedipus's first speech?

Prayers to Apollo and the cries of mourners weigh the city down; there is death and mourning.

What is Oedipus's attitude toward the people? Toward himself?

He calls the people *My Children,* suggesting dominance. He refers to himself as "I, Oedipus, a name that all men know." His greatness is based on defeating the Sphinx and on his own success as ruler for twenty years.

2. **The priest's answer (lines 14–57) is expositional.**

What does the priest tell us about the city's current problem? About Oedipus?

Thebes is facing plague, sterility, famine, divine fire, and death. Oedipus once saved the city from the Sphinx; he holds the power here.

What attitude toward Oedipus is reflected in the priest's speech?

Respect, awe, the expectation that he will make everything right.

How do the people (chorus) put pressure on Oedipus throughout the play?

Their expectations; they assume he can fix whatever is wrong.

How are these expectations ironically right?

They are ironic because Oedipus unwittingly caused the problem in the first place. They are also ironic because making things better will require self-banishment.

3. **In answering the priest and supplicants (lines 58–78), Oedipus claims to be well aware of the suffering; he says that "not one of you [is] so sick as I" (line 61). How is this claim an instance of foreshadowing and irony?**

It is ironic because he will turn out to be sickened by his own life and he is the source of the plague that is destroying Thebes; in addition, Oedipus's assertion ironically foreshadows the catastrophe and resolution.

What steps as Oedipus already taken to correct the situation?

He has previously sent Creon, his brother-in-law, to the Oracle at Delphi to find out what must be done. Note: At this point you might want to describe and explain the Oracle at Delphi. You might also discuss the symbolic value of the oracle (the voice of Apollo, it represents divine will) and the frequency with which this oracle influences the play's action.

4. **No sooner mentioned, than Creon arrives from Delphi (84 s.d.). This is an example of the compression of time in drama and of the kind of coincidences that often occur in this play. Creon returns and reports Apollo's message; we learn more background about Thebes and Oedipus.**

What happened long ago to Laius, the former king?

He was presumably killed by bandits, but in fact was killed by Oedipus.

Why weren't the "murderers" tracked down at the time?

The Sphinx told the Thebans to turn away from obscure problems and instead try to learn things that "lay" at their "feet." (lines 130–131).

What must be done now?

Thebes must be purged, cleansed, purified. The murderer(s) of Laius must be punished by death or banishment.

What does Oedipus promise to do?

He will begin the search for the murderers again; "make it plain" for all to see.

What personal reason does Oedipus give to finding the killers?

"Whoever murdered him may also wish to punish me" (139). The personal reason is therefore self-preservation.

How is this entire speech ironic, given what we know about events?

His quest for justice and vengeance will lead him to himself. Laius's murderer could only kill Oedipus if he committed suicide.

How is Oedipus's promise to make everything plain consistent with his personality?

It reflects his need to know or discover hidden things.

II. **PARADOS (lines 151–220). This is chanted by the chorus on their first entrance. At the time of Sophocles, it was accompanied by dance movements in which the chorus moved back and forth across the orchestra, or dancing area. The chorus represents the voice of the people, reflecting standard values and attitudes. The entire parados is basically a prayer to the gods interrupted by a vivid description of the plague (lines 173–190). Thus, early in the play, the plague is linked directly to the power of the gods.**

On which gods does the chorus call? What do they want the gods to do? What is the chorus's attitude toward the gods and prophecy?

The gods are Zeus, Apollo, Athena, Artemis, and Bacchus. They want the gods to cure the city and destroy the murderer. Their attitude is respectful, awestruck, believing, reverent; this is the social and ethical standard—the public and traditional position.

III. EPISODE 1 (lines 221–467). Initially, Oedipus responds to the prayers of the chorus and claims that they will have relief if they obey him. He demands any information about the murderer of Laius that the chorus might have (lines 221–228). Oedipus places a curse on both the murderer and anyone who knows about the murder and does not reveal the information.

What kind of curse is placed on the murderer and those who have knowledge of him?

Ostracism and a prohibition from religious rites.

How does Oedipus ironically turn this curse on himself?

He curses himself if he has knowledge of the murderer (lines 254–256).

Why is Oedipus's claim that he will fight for Laius "as if for my own father" (line 269) ironic?

Laius is his father; we know it and he does not.

What second way of getting information about the murder does the Choragos suggest?

The prophet and seer, Tiresias.

What is the significance of Tiresias's blindness?

The importance is to accent the ironic reversal: Tiresias is blind but can see the truth; Oedipus has sight but is blind. The blindness also foreshadows Oedipus's self-blinding at the catastrophe.

2. **Tiresias arrives on stage at line 301 S.D. Oedipus explains the whole problem—the plague and the defilement—and asks for help (lines 305–20). This is, of course, a method of review for the audience.**

What is Tiresias's first response? Why does he react this way?

He does not want to say anything; he wants to leave: "Let me go home" (line 325). He reacts this way because he knows the truth and he anticipates the agony that revelation will produce.

How does Oedipus respond to Tiresias's refusal to speak? What does this show us about Oedipus?

He flies into a rage, becomes abusive, and accuses Tiresias of traitorousness. Oedipus is a king, and is accustomed to being obeyed immediately. He wants answers quickly and suspects those who seem evasive. When his will seems thwarted, he intimidates those who are crossing him.

What other instances of rage are significant in Oedipus's life?

He rages at the feast in Corinth, at Delphi, at the place where three roads meet, in conversation with Creon, and at the catastrophe.

3. **Tiresias tells Oedipus the whole truth: "you are the vile polluter" (358); "You are the murderer" (367); "You live ... in the greatest shame" (372). Because we know this is true, our interest is not in the revelation, but rather in Oedipus's reaction to it. Again we see blind rage.**

How does Oedipus respond?

He calls Tiresias blind and a liar, accusing him of plotting usurpation with Creon; he belittles seers and prophecy.

How does the Choragos react?

The Choragos suggests that both men have spoken in anger (line 410). The chorus embodies moderation and calmness.

What does Oedipus's rage and accusation drive Tiresias to do?

Deliver a prophecy (lines 417–433) and tell truth in an indirect riddle (454–467).

What does Tiresias prophecy for Oedipus?

Blindness and wretchedness.

What does Tiresias imply will be revealed?

Truth about Oedipus's birth.

On what aspects of Oedipus's life does the riddle touch?

His birth in Thebes, future blindness, incestuous marriage, and parricide.

Why doesn't Oedipus recognize the truth here?

(1) His thinking is clouded with rage. (2) He thinks that Polybus and Merope are his parents. (3) He sees no connection between himself and the bandits who murdered Laius.

IV. **STASIMON 1 (lines 468–517). This embodies the choral reaction; each stanza takes up a different aspect of the chorus's feelings and responses to what has just happened between Oedipus and Tiresias.**

What is discussed in each stanza?

Strophe 1 considers the power of Apollo over the murderer.

Antistrophe 1 discusses the killer and his doom. Strophe 2 expresses fear and confusion. The chorus also reaffirms its faith in Oedipus and in his power to solve the problem.

V. EPISODE 2 (lines 518–867).

1. The debate between Oedipus and Creon.

About what is Creon upset?

Creon is upset by Oedipus's charge of treason and usurpation.

How does the Choragos explain Oedipus's words?

The Choragos states that Oedipus spoke in anger.

Of what crimes does Oedipus accuse Creon? What proof does he have?

Oedipus accuses Creon of murdering Laius, stealing the throne, and plotting treason with Tiresias. He has no proof at all; Creon calls it unsupported thought (line 613).

What emotion(s) dominate Oedipus during this debate? Does he ever really hear Creon?

Rage or mindless willfulness prevents Oedipus from hearing. This rage is an extremely important factor in Oedipus's personality.

How does Creon defend himself and refute the charges?

Creon bases his defense on reason and religion. He correctly points out that he has all the power and influence of kingship without the anxieties (lines 588–607). Also he tells Oedipus to check with the Oracle(line 608); he condemns (curses) himself to death if he has lied (line 612).

Characterize Creon. How is he different from Oedipus?

Creon is rational, calm, careful, prudent, not hasty. Some of his representative statements are these: "I never talk when I am ignorant" (line 574); "think about this rationally, as I do" (line 588); "a prudent man is never traitorous" (line 605).

2. Jocasta appears for the first time at line 638 s.d.; she is upset with Oedipus and Creon for stirring up private troubles during Thebes's sickness.

What does Jocasta want the men to do?

She wants them to stop arguing and go inside.

How does the chorus echo Jocasta?

They want Oedipus to defer to Creon.

Why does Oedipus view this as a him or me situation?

Absolving Creon implies that Tiresias was right; Oedipus will face exile or death.

What is Creon's view of Oedipus's character?

Creon sees Oedipus as sullen, angry, and unreasonable. Creon states that "Natures like yours are hardest on themselves" (line 679).

3. **The conversation between Jocasta and Oedipus (lines 682–867). Jocasta's questions about the argument provide an opportunity for more background. Oedipus explains Tiresias's accusations and discusses his own history.**

What is Jocasta's attitude toward prophesies? What accounts for this attitude? What proof does she offer?

Jocasta rejects the prophesies: "no mortal is ever given skill in prophecy" (lines 713–4). Her proof is that a major prophecy has not come true, for she believes her child dead and also that Laius was killed by foreign robbers.

How is this proof ironic?

Oedipus is the child; neither knows it.

Why does Oedipus begin to suspect that he may have killed Laius?

He remembers killing some men at Phocis—a place where three roads meet.

How does Oedipus push for additional information at this point? Why?

He asks about Laius's appearance and the size of the traveling party. He wants the one survivor called so that he can be questioned. Oedipus's drive toward truth is a function of his character and also a result of his initial vow. It parallels his quest for information about his parents.

What occurred at the feast?

"A man denied I was my father's son."

How did Oedipus react?

He could barely control his depression, and he was driven to find out the truth: "It kept grinding into me" (line 790).

Where did Oedipus go to discover the truth about his parents?

To discover the truth about his parents, he went to Delphi consult the oracle in the temple there.

What prophecy was delivered?

The oracle declared that Oedipus would murder his father, marry his mother, and be the father of children by his incestuous relationship (lines 796–798).

What was Oedipus's response? How is his reaction characteristic?

He fled; his reaction is characteristically hasty and irrational because he gained no real information about his parents.

What happened at the place where three roads meet?

Oedipus killed a group of men, including his [unknown] father, who tried to push him off the road: "I killed them all" (lines 805–818).

What was the psychic trigger of Laius's death?

Oedipus's rage at being struck (his father struck out at him). The past is parallel to the present; Oedipus has not changed.

What is Oedipus on the verge of knowing?

That he killed Laius, not that he killed his father; he does not yet suspect that Laius was his father.

Why does Oedipus want to interview the lone survivor; what is his last shred of hope?

He wants to know if it was robbers or one man (line 849).

What conflicts have emerged up to this point in the play? Which are emerging as central?

The conflicts are these: Oedipus-Tiresias; Oedipus-Creon; Oedipus-plague; Oedipus-gods/fate; Oedipus-himself (his rage, depression, haste, drive, demand to know the truth). The last two emerge as central; the others reflect these.

VI. STASIMON 2 (lines 868–915). This is a significant point in the play because the chorus separates itself from Oedipus for the first time.

What point does the chorus make about itself in Strophe 1?

It claims reverence, orthodoxy, and obedience to the laws of the gods.

What point is made about tyrants in Antistrophe 1?

Tyrants are ruled by pride (hubris) and often fall through impiety.

What sins are discussed in Strophe 2?

Haughtiness, pride, sacrilege, unholiness, and injustice. These are implicitly linked to Oedipus.

What does the chorus say about the state of religion in Antistrophe 2?

Prophecy is ignored, Apollo is abandoned, and religion slips away (line 915).

VII. **EPISODE 3 (lines 916–1090). The information of the first messenger (shepherd). We see Jocasta going to pray; she speaks to the chorus.**

How does Jocasta describe Oedipus's state of mind?

Jocasta states that Oedipus is excited and irrational.

What news does the messenger from Corinth bring? Why is it good news?

Polybus is dead and Oedipus will be made king of Corinth. The news apparently frees Oedipus from the horror of the oracle delivered at Delphi.

What attitude toward prophecy and oracles do Oedipus and Jocasta express?

Both Oedipus and Jocasta reject oracles completely. Jocasta asks, "Oracles of the gods! / Where are you now?" (lines 951–952). Oedipus asks "why should we look to Pytho's vapors?" (line 969).

How is this good news about Polybus ironically reversed?

Polybus was not Oedipus's father; the baby was given to Polybus by the Messenger, who got the baby from another shepherd, who worked for Laius.

What does Jocasta know at this point that Oedipus does not know?

She has put all the clues together and discovered the full horror of the truth; she knows that Oedipus, her son, murdered his father and married his mother.

Contrast the attitudes of Jocasta and Oedipus toward pursuing the investigation to its end.

Jocasta wants Oedipus to stop: "Pay no attention ... give up this search ... please don't do this thing." Oedipus is driven; he cannot give up with "clues like this within my grasp." See lines 1061–1077.

What does Jocasta intend when she enters the palace? How do you know?

Suicide is indicated by her promise never to address Oedipus by any name other than man of misery and by the Choragos's reference to savage grief.

VII. STASIMON 3 (lines 1091–1114). This represents a momentary sense of anticipation and possible joy that Oedipus's origins may be explained to his credit.

What is the chorus anticipating about Mount Cithaeron?

That Cithaeron, "at tomorrow's full moon," will be shown to have been the home country of Oedipus.

Why does the chorus ask "who was your mother, son?"

The ask, anticipating that the answer will provide a satisfactory outcome of this question that is so vital in the play.

VIII. EPISODE 4 (lines 1115–1190). Catastrophe, peripeteia, anagnorisis. The interview with the shepherd who gave the baby to the Corinthian and who survived the murder of Laius leads to the revelation of truth.

Why won't the old herdsman look at Oedipus; what does he know about him?

He recognizes Oedipus as the murderer of Laius; he does not realize the full truth, however, because he does not link the man with the child.

Discuss the coincidence that this shepherd (a) saved the infant Oedipus, (b) was with Laius at the crossroads and was the lone survivor, and (c) will now be the agent of revelation.

Such coincidence suggests divine will; it also implies that a person cannot escape his or her fate.

How is Oedipus's behavior with the herdsman (threatening torture) consistent with his character?

He knows that he is about to hear the dreaded thing, but he is driven on by his compulsion for full disclosure.

What does Oedipus discover about himself?

See lines 1187–1190. Oedipus realizes the full truth of his monstrousness in birth, marriage, and murder. This is the moment of anagnorisis; it is also the catastrophe.

X. STASIMON 4 (lines 1191–1232). Here, and later, the chorus draws a moral about Oedipus's life and provides a final reaction to him.

What moral does the chorus see in Oedipus's life?

They feel that human beings must appraise their lives as worthless and that no mortal can be judged fortunate (lines 1191–1201). In the last lines, they assert that no man can be considered happy until "he has crossed the border of his life without pain" (line 1543). In other words, they assert that no one can be judged fortunate until he or she is dead.

How are Antistrophe 1 and Strophe 2 a summary of Oedipus's life?

The first reviews Oedipus's rise; the second reviews his wretched fall.

What are the chorus's feelings toward Oedipus now?

Pity and fear; they wish that they had never seen him.

XI. EXODOS (lines 1233–end). Resolution, dénouement, tying up loose ends.

What does the second messenger report about Jocasta? About Oedipus?

Jocasta has committed suicide by hanging. Oedipus has blinded himself in a frenzy by stabbing his eyes with the gold pins from her dress. The pins may be taken to symbolize both (a) the goad with which Laius tried to kill Oedipus, and (b) Oedipus's crime of incest. Again, symbolically, Oedipus blinds himself because he recognizes his guilt and also because he cannot bear to look on his sins any longer.

What does the messenger say that Oedipus wants now? What does Oedipus want from the Chorus?

He wants to be exposed to the people as Thebes's pollution and then banished (line 1300). He wants the chorus to lead him out of Thebes.

Whom does Oedipus blame for his tragic life and fall?

He blames the god Apollo (lines 1339–41).

What is Creon like as the new king? What acts indicate his carefulness, reverence, political wisdom, and kindness?

Creon treats Oedipus with cool compassion and calculation; he wants to consult the gods and have sure knowledge before he acts. He displays kindness in having Oedipus's daughters, Ismene and Antigone, brought to him and in grasping Oedipus's hand. His political acumen and careful statesmanship are evident in his assertion that "I never promise when … I'm ignorant."

Discussion of the "General Questions," page 1121–1122

(1) The play follows a traditional five-step pattern, but exposition is distributed throughout because so much of the story has already occurred when the play begins. Exposition occurs in the opening dialogue, where we learn of the plague afflicting Thebes because of the hidden murderer.

Complication builds as Tiresias accuses Oedipus of the crimes and Creon delivers the message of the Oracle at Delphi. The crisis occurs when Oedipus vows to find the murderer, no matter what the search entails. The keys to the crisis are haste and anger; these lead Oedipus down a one-way path into tragedy. The *peripeteia*, *catastrophe*, and *anagnorisis* all occur at the same instant when Oedipus discovers the truth of his parentage. These revelations affect Jocasta and Oedipus most immediately; she commits suicide and he blinds himself. The resolution involves the passing of power to Creon and the consideration of Oedipus's future (he will be banished).

(2) Oedipus was the only son of Laius, king of Thebes, who was warned that his son would kill him and marry Jocasta. The baby's feet were pierced and he was given to a shepherd to expose on Mount Cithaeron. The shepherd relented and gave the baby to another, who gave the child to Polybus and Merope, the childless king and queen of Corinth. They named him Oedipus because of his injured feet and raised him as theirs. (See text page 1082 for additional details about the legend of Oedipus.)

Years later, Oedipus was told that Polybus and Merope were not his parents. Deeply troubled, he asked Polybus and Merope, who insisted that he was theirs. But Oedipus could not rest; he consulted the Oracle at Delphi. The Oracle refused to answer his question, but told him that he would murder his father and have children by his mother. Horrified, Oedipus fled Corinth, vowing not to return until Polybus and Merope were dead.

While traveling toward Thebes, Oedipus came to the junction of three roads. There, he met a nobleman (Laius) who ordered him off the road. The man struck Oedipus with a goad; Oedipus became enraged and killed the noble and all but one of the servants accompanying him.

When Oedipus arrived at Thebes, he found the city terrorized by the Sphinx; she ate Thebans who couldn't answer her riddle. At the same time, Laius's body was discovered. Creon offered the crown and hand of Jocasta to anyone who could free the city. Oedipus solved the riddle (the Sphinx committed suicide), was crowned, and married Jocasta. The lone survivor of Laius's retinue returned, found Oedipus king, and asked to become a shepherd in a distant region.

Oedipus ruled for twenty years, and he and Jocasta had two sons and two daughters. At the end of these twenty years, Thebes is afflicted by a plague (the play begins at this point); Oedipus sends Creon to Delphi to discover the cause. Creon learns that the murderer of Laius defiles the city by living unpunished.

Oedipus begins the investigation; he swears to find and banish the murderer. Tiresias is consulted; he accuses Oedipus, who flies into a rage. The shepherd who gave the baby to Polybus is consulted. The survivor of Laius's group is consulted; he is the man who was ordered to kill the baby. Finally, the truth is revealed. Horror abounds; Jocasta commits suicide and Oedipus blinds himself (he will be exiled from Thebes).

Sophocles's arrangement of the elements of the story produces a highly focused and effective theatrical moment. Pieces of the past are revealed only as they are needed to tighten the web around Oedipus. Keeping the play in the present maintains pressure on Oedipus throughout. Such an arrangement also raises the level of dramatic irony considerably. The audience knows the whole story, while the staging begins at the very end, on the very last day of Oedipus's reign.

(3) The central conflict is either Oedipus against the gods (fate) or against himself (anger, haste, irrationality). There is no right answer; a decision depends on one's view of the genesis of tragic fall in the play.

(4) Reporting (rather than staging) violence is a convention of Greek and Roman drama. The result of reporting is the absence of violent action. Incidentally, reporting became a characteristic of French drama, while action and spectacle became prominent in English and (later) American drama. There are advantages to reporting rather than action: The playwright can focus on character and on the reaction to violence, rather than the violent act itself. Moreover, the spectators can (and readers can) imagine violence in more horrid detail than staging can present (such, of course, is not the case with contemporary film and the full range of special effects available to directors).

(5) Coincidence is best embodied in the single character who reappears at every crucial moment on Oedipus's life. This is the herdsman who took the infant to Mount Cithaeron, accompanied Laius on his fatal journey, survived Oedipus's attack, and reveals all at the close of the play. Although coincidence is common in drama, this much suggests the operation of fate or the gods. Coincidence is a prime factor in arguing for a tragedy based on fate.

(6) Virtually everything Oedipus says and does in the play is ironic because we know so much more than he does. His vow to hunt down the murderer, his claim that the murderer may try to kill him, his treatment of Tiresias and Creon, and his joy at Polybus's death, are all stunningly ironic.

(7) *Oedipus,* like *Hamlet,* is a tragedy in which individual fortunes rebound on the state. Initially, Oedipus's secret guilt leads to plague and famine in Thebes. In the end, his fall leads to a shift in the kingship and

possible questions about succession (where do Oedipus's two sons fit into the future of the crown?). These imply an unstable future for Thebes.

(8) The Chorus and Choragos (*Koryphaios*) represent the Theban public; they embody moderation, reason, and reverence for the gods. They also communicate the choral reaction to the events and conflicts in the play. Stasimon 1, for example, expresses the chorus's reaction to the news about the murderer and the accusations of Tiresias. Similarly, the Choragos is a voice of reason and a mediator. He reminds Creon, for instance, that Oedipus often speaks in anger, without thinking. At the close of the play, the chorus draws its own moral from the fall of Oedipus; their conviction that no person can be considered happy until dead underscores the instability of power and glory.

(9) Oedipus's quest for the murderer quickly becomes a quest for the truth of his own past. The nature of the quest changes when Oedipus realizes that he may have murdered Laius. From that point on, he is driven toward a discovery of his own past and recognition of the present horror.

The Rebirth and Development of Drama in the Centuries Before Shakespeare, *pages 1122–1127*

This section has been revised to show the connection between ancient drama and drama at the time of Shakespeare. Accordingly, greater attention is paid than in previous editions to the Corpus Christi Plays and other religious plays (pages 1122–1124). The section on "Renaissance Drama and Shakespeare's Theater," which reflects recent archaeological discoveries in the theater district of Shakespeare's day, provides a detailed introduction to the physical conditions and stage conventions of the Elizabethan public theater, particularly the Globe. Also included is an artist's sketch of the new Globe stage now under construction in accordance with best judgments of what Shakespeare's actual Globe was like. It is important for students to develop a knowledge of theater conditions during Shakespeare's day because many aspects of his plays were determined by the conditions and conventions of his stage and the expectations of his audiences. Material on the Globe beginning on page 1125 can be assigned in conjunction with *Hamlet* and/or *A Midsummer Night's Dream* (beginning on page 1325). The material will help clarify the less realistic aspects of either play.

William Shakespeare, *Hamlet,* pages 1098–1202

Hamlet is a touchstone of Western civilization. Your students will be enriched by studying and understanding it, although comprehension at any level will require great care and attentiveness. Shakespeare's language, although different in many respects from Modern English, is comprehensible. At times, however, the syntax may need unraveling, and also the issues and interests of Shakespeare's characters may need explaining. The glosses, notes, and questions should help. As much classroom instruction and discussion as you can provide should help more.

When you begin the play with your students, you should estimate what they can reasonably hope to get out of the work, and gear your presentation to that level. You will need to establish priorities about what to stress. We suggest the following: (1) What's happening—the story, the plot, the pattern of the plot. (2) Who are these people—the protagonist, his personality, his dilemma, his motives, his growth; the antagonist, his situation and motives. (3) Why should we read about a dead Danish prince, anyway—the universal ideas about human responsibility, choices between responsibility and desire, justice, and revenge that the play explores.

Students' appreciation and comprehension of *Hamlet* can be significantly enhanced by watching a production after they have read the text. In 1990, a new film production, featuring Mel Gibson and Glenn Close, received wide circulation. Many of your students may have seen that. Including the Mel Gibson production, the following videotapes and audiotapes are available:

- Videotape (1948), 153 minutes, directed by Laurence Olivier. Starring Laurence Olivier, Basil Sydney, and Jean Simmons. Audio-Brandon Films, 34 MacQuesten Parkway South, Mount Vernon, NY 10550.
- Videotape (1969), 114 minutes, directed by Tony Richardson. Starring Nicol Williamson, Sir Anthony Hopkins, and Judy Parfitt. Audio-Brandon.
- Videotape (1980), 222 minutes, starring Derek Jacoby. Time-Life Video, Box 644, Paramus, NY 07652.
- Videotape (1990), 135 minutes, directed by Franco Zeffirelli. Starring Mel Gibson, Alan Bates, Glenn Close, and Helena Bonham Carter. Available in most video outlets.
- Videotape (1990), 175 minutes, directed by Kevin Kline and Kirk Browning. A Joseph Papp/Great Performances Production in modern dress (Thirteen/WNBT). Starring Kevin Kline and Diane Venora.

- Audiotape (1979), directed by Howard Sackler. Starring Paul Scofield. Issued by Caedmon (CP232), 1995 Broadway, New York City, NY 10023.
- Audiotape (1992), 210 minutes, four cassettes. Starring Kenneth Branagh. A BBC Radio Production, issued by Bantam Doubleday Dell.

Please note that any specific production available on film is likely also to be available on videotape in the near future. These films or tapes, and numerous other productions of *Hamlet*, are available from many other film distribution companies as well. The BBC/Time-Life production (1980) has obviously cut the least from the text.

The following programmatic guide to *Hamlet* is mostly a series of questions that can be used to shape class discussion or lectures. A significant number of answers, lecture points, and points for review are also included. The guide is organized in a scene-by-scene approach to the play. Questions are printed in italic, and answers follow immediately, indented, in regular type. To conserve space, at times we provide only a line reference as an answer, thus pointing our question directly into the text of the play. Rosencrantz and Guildenstern are abbreviated as "R&G" throughout. The guide includes all the study questions listed at the end of the play.

Act I. Exposition: The establishment of character, situation, conflict.

1.1: The watch on the battlements, Horatio, the Ghost.

This scene establishes that there is something wrong (rotten) in Denmark; what aspects of the scene tell us that things are not right?

(1) The nervousness of the watch; the first words are "Who's there," establishing a tense and questioning tone. (2) The appearance of the Ghost. (3) The preparations for war (lines 70–79). (4) The problem with young Fortinbras (lines 95–107). Shakespeare thus uses minor characters here to introduce us to deeply troubled and chaotic circumstances.

Whom is Horatio going to tell about the Ghost? Why?

Horatio recognizes that it is his duty to tell Hamlet, on the grounds that the spirit, dumb to them, "will speak to him" (lines 169–173).

The most important character we meet in 1.1. is Horatio; what is he like? How is he different from Bernardo and Marcellus?

Horatio is educated and a rationalist; at first, he thinks the watch have imagined the Ghost. He understands the grave significance of the Ghost and recognizes his duty to inform Hamlet about the appearance.

Note: A broader approach to the scene can be achieved with three questions: (1) What is the function of the scene? (2) What mood is established in the scene? (3) What do we discover about Denmark in the scene?

1.2 The Court: Claudius, Gertrude, Hamlet, Laertes, Polonius, etc.

This scene establishes initial images of Claudius, Hamlet, etc. It also contrasts with the first scene because it shows normal court life. The king is speaking to his subjects and hearing their concerns. The scene illustrates the way in which a Renaissance court would actually have operated, with the king at the center and with the courtiers in attendance. The King's job is to make declarations, listen to petitions and either grant them or not, and give advice.

What is the first impression of Claudius as king and speaker?

Claudius seems in control of things. He controls the attention of the courtiers, and the first scene is structured so that he is seen dealing well with business and with the petitions of his subjects.

What problem concerns young Fortinbras? How does Claudius deal with it?

Fortinbras is planning to invade Denmark with a Norwegian army. Claudius resolves to send Cornelius and Voltimand to the uncle of Fortinbras, so that the uncle may quash the invasion plans (lines 17–42).

What business does Laertes raise? How does Claudius deal with it?

Laertes wants to return to Paris; Claudius asks Polonius, Laertes's father, if the matter has been settled within the family. When Polonius indicates his blessing, Claudius approves (lines 43–63).

The next piece of business is Hamlet and his behavior. What is the problem with Hamlet?

Hamlet is still mourning the death of his father; the clouds still hang upon him.

What sets Hamlet apart? How is his clothing different?

He is the only one dressed in black mourning clothes; in blocking the scene, most directors keep him well away from all other characters, ignoring the activities of the court. He is obviously depressed and unsettled.

What thematic point is introduced in Hamlet's "Seems, madam" speech (lines 76–86)?

Appearance vs. reality (see the second sample essay, pages 1312–1313).

How do Claudius and Gertrude try to deal with Hamlet's sadness?

Both assert that death is natural and inevitable, and that now that the mourning period is over, Hamlet should cheer up and take up normal life as he had been living it before King Hamlet's death (lines 87–117). The argument is especially ironic in light of old Hamlet's unnatural death.

What does Hamlet's first soliloquy (129–159) tell us about him?

He is depressed, suicidal, and bitter; he is bothered by his father's death, his mother's remarriage, and the fact that he is not king.

What do we find out about Horatio in his conversation with Hamlet (lines 160–258)?

He is Hamlet's friend and fellow student. Hamlet wants them to be equals (friend instead of servant); he likes and trusts Horatio.

What does Horatio tell Hamlet? What does Hamlet decide to do? Why?

Horatio tells Hamlet about the Ghost. Hamlet decides to see for himself, and arranges to meet the guard upon the platform between eleven and twelve o'clock in the evening. He is uneasy about the spirit, believing that there may be "some foul play" (line 257) that it is his duty to uncover.

1.3: Exposition of subplot. We meet Laertes, Ophelia, Polonius.

The scene occurs in three conversations: Laertes-Ophelia (lines 1–51); Polonius-Laertes (lines 51–88); Polonius-Ophelia (lines 88–136).

What do we find out about the relationship between Hamlet and Ophelia? What is Laertes's attitude toward the two?

Hamlet is courting Ophelia. Laertes thinks Hamlet is trifling and advises Ophelia to stay away from the prince. He is worried about her chastity and the family's (especially his own) reputation. Ophelia's last remark suggests that Laertes is better at giving advice than following it.

What advice does Polonius give Laertes? Is the advice good? Original? What does it show about the character of Polonius?

Polonius gives Laertes the advice that most fathers might like to give sons who are leaving home and going out on their own (e.g., be careful, don't let money interfere with friendship, listen to advice, don't be overly conspicuous in dress, be true to your character). It is often claimed that the advice is trite and hackneyed, and some stagings of the play have both Laertes and Ophelia laugh at Polonius behind his back as he speaks. Polonius, however, has been a trusted royal adviser and, though he is getting old, his advice is well meant, and he speaks with great concern and affection. Without doubt he has said many of the same things before, but most parents give advice to their children as long as the children are at home. One must emphasize that Polonius is an upper-class father, and that in Shakespeare's time the father had absolute family authority. Polonius is thus using his position to give advice, and in the remainder of the play, until his death, his primary concern is to advance his family. Thus, by showing concern for Laertes, he is concerned about family honor. By controlling Ophelia, he is trying to preserve her for an advantageous marriage. This would be the highest honor and prestige he could bring to his family.

What is Polonius's attitude toward Ophelia's relationship with Hamlet? What reasons does he give for this attitude? Is he more concerned with Ophelia or himself? What does he tell Ophelia to do regarding Hamlet?

He holds the same (but stronger) opinion as Laertes. He is afraid that Hamlet is out only for sex, and he warns Ophelia to stay away, because if Ophelia falls, her fall will hurt his reputation and that of the family, and it would ruin her chances for an advantageous marriage. Hamlet would, of course, make the perfect husband for Ophelia, but Ophelia and the family would benefit by marriage only, not by a sexual liaison. In any event, it is unlikely that Polonius understands the depths of Ophelia's feelings.

What is Ophelia like? How does she respond to Laertes and Polonius? To what extent does she or does she not behave according to her own will?

Although much of this depends on how Ophelia is played, the text suggests that she is compliant, obedient, perhaps too dutiful, and easily controlled. These qualities, together with her apparent love for Hamlet, will prove to be her emotional undoing as she goes mad later in the play.

1.4: Hamlet, Horatio, and the Watch meet the Ghost.

A key question for Hamlet is what kind of ghost he faces. What are the two possibilities? Why is the question important? How does the problem affect Hamlet's subsequent action?

The two possibilities are that the ghost may be real, or a manifestation of the devil (Spirit of health or goblin damned [lines 40–42]). The possibility of the latter produces doubt and causes Hamlet to seek proof.

1.5: Hamlet and the Ghost

What does the Ghost tell Hamlet about who caused his death? What does the Ghost want Hamlet to do? What special instructions does the Ghost give Hamlet about Gertrude?

He explains that his brother Claudius, now king, killed him by pouring poison into his ear when he was sleeping. The Ghost wants Hamlet to revenge "his foul and most unnatural murder" (line 25. In other words, the ghost wants Hamlet to kill Claudius, but to leave Gertrude's punishment "to heaven" (lines 84–88).

Why does Hamlet swear the watch to secrecy?

He wants to watch Claudius secretly.

Why does Hamlet decide to pretend insanity—put on an "antic disposition"? Why can't Hamlet act against Claudius at this point?

Feigned madness will protect him (i.e., people will explain strange behavior as a result of his mental disturbance, without seeking other motives) while he is trying to get the necessary proof of the Ghost's honesty.

What is Hamlet's reaction to the Ghost's demands?

At first, he swears immediate action (lines 93–112), but at the end of the scene he expresses reluctance and unwillingness about his new role, and he indicates that the "spite" of murder is "cursed" (lines 188–189).

Act I Review: Act 1 establishes the character, conflicts, and situations. It reveals that much is wrong. The Ghost tells Hamlet about murder and usurpation. By the end of Act 1, Hamlet believes that he knows what he must do: He must confirm the Ghost's accusations, and must defend himself from Claudius while doing so. Act 1 also establishes the major characters. Hamlet is melancholic, upset about his mother, introspective, and traumatized by the Ghost. Claudius is smooth, politic, efficient, murderous, lustful, and evil (if we believe the Ghost). Polonius is past his prime, and is unable to wield a great deal of power. Ophelia is obedient and dutiful, but there are strong forces in her that may cause her trouble. Laertes is a concerned brother, and Horatio is a scholar and rationalist who is trusted by Hamlet.

The central problem here and throughout is delay. Why doesn't Hamlet kill Claudius immediately? This is not really a problem (see the sample essay, pages 1308–1310). The problem is rather that of how Shakespeare justifies Hamlet's delay and makes it credible. One answer is the problem of confirming the Ghost's words. The Ghost might be a devil; Hamlet needs more evidence. Once he thinks he has it, he kills—and kills the wrong man (Polonius). This causes more delay. A second answer: the problem of character. Hamlet is introspective and contemplative. His introspective nature accounts for the soliloquies in which he accuses himself of delay despite the reasonableness of delaying. If this delay could not be justified, according to the codes of revenge, then it would be a character flaw. If it is not justified, then it is not a flaw.

Act II. Complication: Three Main Lines of Development

1. Hamlet's quest for proof; 2. Hamlet's introspection and self-accusation in soliloquies; 3. Claudius's defensive actions through Rosencrantz, Guildenstern, and Polonius.

2.1: Focus on Polonius and Reynaldo, then Ophelia

What does Polonius want Reynaldo to do in Paris? What does this show us about Polonius?

Polonius wants to keep track of what Laertes is doing in Paris, and asks Reynaldo to learn whatever he can, even if doing so means dropping hints that Laertes is carousing and misbehaving (a "bait of falsehood" [line 60]), so that such action may be confirmed or denied. The action shows the extreme to which Polonius will go in insuring the reputation of his family. He fears that Laertes might do something that might cause embarrassment or disgrace, and he is willing to use people in the service of his suspicions. It would seem that his interest is in maintaining the level of family respectability so that a potential match of Ophelia and Hamlet would not be compromised.

What does Ophelia report about Hamlet?

She reports that Hamlet came to her greatly disordered and disturbed, seemingly out of his senses (lines 74–81, 85–97).

What conclusions about Hamlet does Polonius draw?

He concludes that Hamlet is mad for love: "The very ecstasy of love" (line 99).

What will Polonius do with this information? What does this tell us?

"I will go seek the king" (line 98). Polonius has earlier suspected Hamlet of just toying with Ophelia. This new information makes him believe he was wrong. His action and behavior show his belief and hope that Hamlet might be brought to marry Ophelia (and overcome the "madness"), and thus to elevate the family beyond his greatest expectations. By reporting to the King, he probably hopes to bring the King about to his way of thinking, and to see that Hamlet should marry Ophelia.

2.2.A (lines 1–40): Claudius and Gertrude greet R&G

Why are R&G in Denmark? How does Claudius plan to use them?

Claudius wants R&G to watch Hamlet, and find out what is troubling him ("aught to us unknown" [line 17]).

To what extent do R&G cooperate with Claudius? To what extent does their cooperation justify their deaths later in the play?

Hamlet claims that they courted power and paid the price; they clearly agree to be used for profit. It seems clear, at the start, however, that R&G believe that they really might be helping Hamlet.

2.2.B (lines 40–85): Resolution of the Fortinbras problem

How has the threat to Denmark posed by young Fortinbras been resolved? What does he plan to do with his army?

The king of Norway dissuaded him; Fortinbras plans to attack Poland instead, and seeks permission to cross Denmark.

2.2.C (lines 85–170): Polonius's explanation of Hamlet's madness

Describe Polonius's language. What does it show us about him?

It is extremely wordy. It shows that he is nervous, for he is trying to lead the King and Queen to the conclusion that there might be a marriage between Hamlet and Ophelia. He cannot openly suggest such a marriage because a proposal must come from the royal family. His confusion, and his false starts, are thus amusing.

What does he report about Hamlet? How does he prove it?

He claims that Hamlet is mad for love, and cites Hamlet's letter and behavior.

How does Claudius react?

He is interested but doubtful, and asks, "How may we try it further?" (line 159).

What plan does Polonius come up with?

To use Ophelia and to spy on the meeting: "I'll loose my daughter to him. Be you and I behind an arras" (lines 162–163). This plan shows his assumption that his will as a father takes precedence over Ophelia's own feelings and involvement in promoting the business with Hamlet.

2.2.D (lines 170–220): The confrontation of Hamlet and Polonius

How does Hamlet act? On what things does Hamlet focus in his pretended insanity? How is there method in his madness?

Hamlet pretends to be mad; he focuses on Polonius as whoremaster, daughters, death, graves, and the emptiness of language. All these are relevant to Hamlet's situation.

2.2.E (lines 221–430): Hamlet meets R&G.

What do R&G try to find out from Hamlet? How successful are they?

They want to learn the cause of his behavior. They do not.

What does Hamlet want to know from R&G? Why is this important? How does R&G's confession that they were sent for affect the way Hamlet deals with them?

Hamlet wants to know if they were sent for (lines 265, 269, 275, 281, 284). When they admit it, he recognizes them as Claudius's tools, but confesses that he is "but mad north-north-west; when the wind is southerly, / I know a hawk from a handsaw" (lines 361–362). The scene is ironic. Hamlet thinks he knows the reasons for R&G's inquiries; R&G do not.

What news do R&G bring Hamlet? Who is on the way to the court?

They report the approach of a traveling company of actors. Polonius brings the same news almost immediately. When with Polonius, Hamlet resumes his feigned madness.

2.2.F (lines 430–end): Hamlet and the actors, the closing soliloquy

Hamlet wants to hear the speech about Hecuba and the Fall of Troy. How is this relevant to the problems of Hamlet?

Hecuba was a loyal queen; Priam was killed through treachery. There are oblique parallels to Denmark's situation and to Hamlet's concerns.

What play does Hamlet arrange for? Why? When will it be acted?

Hamlet arranges for the actors to present "The Murder of Gonzago." The action of the play closely parallels the crimes that the Ghost has accused Claudius of committing. Hamlet will use the play "to catch the conscience of the king" (line 580).

Of what does Hamlet accuse himself in the soliloquy (lines 523–62)? Are the accusations accurate?

He calls himself a dull rogue, coward, and villain for not feeling or taking action. He is, of course, taking action, so his accusations are not literally true.

What point does Hamlet make again about the Ghost in his soliloquy?

The Ghost may be a devil trying to damn Hamlet (lines 574–79).

Act II Review: Act 2 advances the conflicts of the play and focuses the action; it can be reviewed with six questions: 1. How is the characterization of Hamlet advanced? 2. What do his soliloquies show us? 3. How has Hamlet moved closer to the confirmation of the Ghost's accusations? 4. What defensive or protective actions has Claudius initiated? 5. What role does Polonius play in Act 2? 6. How does our opinion of Polonius change?

Act III. Crisis and Confrontation: Hamlet's Act

3.1.A (lines 1–28): Claudius and R&G

What do R&G report to Claudius? How successful are they as spies?

They have been unable to discover anything; Hamlet will not answer them.

3.1.B (lines 29–55): Claudius, Polonius, and Ophelia: the Test of Love

What do Claudius and Polonius set up for Hamlet using Ophelia?

They set up the chance encounter that will test whether Hamlet's madness is derived from love. The scene is ironic. Claudius wants to know if Hamlet's behavior really results from love or from suspicion, while Polonius believes that if the behavior is from love he may become the father-in-law of the Prince of Denmark.

How is this confrontation like the play-within-the-play that Hamlet uses later in Act 3 to test Claudius's guilt?

Both are staged actions; both involve audiences; both are designed to test information through reactions.

To what extent does Ophelia's role in this test change or confirm our opinion of her?

Ever pliant and obedient, Ophelia allows herself to be the tool of Polonius and Claudius. To the extent that she is playing out their instructions, she is an actress, even though she does not fully understand the role she is playing. Hamlet, who knows that Claudius and Polonius are trying to manipulate him, and may also believe that Ophelia is in on the plan, therefore takes out all his anger and suspicion on her; he therefore brutally associates her with face painting, fraud, and deceit later in the scene.

3.1.C (lines 56–88): Hamlet's "To Be or Not to Be" soliloquy

What is Hamlet contemplating? Is he actually suicidal? Is his contemplation personal or abstract?

Hamlet's depression leads him to contemplate death ("not to be") and suicide in an abstract and impersonal manner ("cowards of us all," 83); this is really an abstract exercise.

3.1.D (lines 89–149): Hamlet and Ophelia in the Lobby

What does Ophelia try to give to Hamlet? Why? What does Hamlet say about his feelings toward Ophelia?

She tries to return favors as part of the test; he refuses them. At this point, Hamlet is playing with Ophelia; he claims that he loved her once and then denies it (lines 115, 118).

How does Hamlet treat Ophelia? Does his treatment (and attitude) change? If so, how and when? Why does he ask Ophelia about Polonius (line 130)? Does he know (or discover) that he is being watched?

Hamlet begins by toying with Ophelia and ends up in a rage. The change seems to occur at line 130 when he asks about Polonius. Since the text does not account for the shift, many directors stage the scene so that Hamlet spots movement behind the arras at this point. If staged this way, the subsequent tirade reflects Hamlet's return to feigned madness and his real disappointment with Ophelia.

What does Hamlet stress in his tirade against Ophelia? How is this relevant?

Hamlet stresses honesty in women, the falsity of using makeup, and the manipulative roles that he believe women take against men. He may be speaking in anger against her; he may also be inveighing against the King and the Queen and Polonius; and he may be reflecting on his own needs for playing a role to acquire more information about the truth of the Ghost's information. Hamlet is a complex character, and the situation is clearly causing him to become distrustful and easily angered.

3.1.E (lines 150–188): Reactions to Hamlet's behavior

What is Ophelia's reaction to Hamlet? What is Claudius's?

She thinks he is mad. He is suspicious; he concludes that the source of Hamlet's behavior is not love, but something more sinister and threatening to him (lines 162–166).

How does Claudius plan to deal with Hamlet?

Claudius proposes to send him "with speed to England," ostensibly to serve as an ambassador to secure tribute from the English, to take his mind off his melancholy and therefore to get him back to normal.

What is Polonius's reaction to the confrontation?

He still thinks love caused the madness; he cannot give up his hope that Hamlet might yet marry Ophelia and thus benefit him.

What new plan to find Hamlet out does Polonius offer?

He proposes that Gertrude speak to Hamlet and that he eavesdrop (lines 181–187).

3.2: **The Crisis of the Play.** Before a close reading, ask your students what and where the crisis is. The crisis is Claudius's reaction to the play-within-the-play. It sets Hamlet and Claudius on a collision course; each knows the truth about the other at this point.

3.2.A (lines 1–126): Hamlet's instructions and preparations

What does Hamlet tell the actors about acting and drama?

He does not want the actors to over-act or ad-lib. Drama (playing) is defined as holding "the mirror up to nature" (line 20).

How does Hamlet explain his relationship to Horatio? What does Hamlet want Horatio to do during "Gonzago"?

Hamlet likes and trusts Horatio because the latter is well-balanced, honest, and controlled. The "pipe" (recorder, oboe, or flute) metaphor here (lines 65–66) indicates that Horatio cannot be manipulated and is a true friend. Hamlet trusts Horatio, and wants him to observe Claudius during the murder scene in "Gonzago" to see if his guilt will show itself.

Hamlet (line 85) says "I must be idle." What course of action does this involve? How does Hamlet sustain his antic disposition?

Idle here means foolish or insane. Hamlet sustains the illusion of madness by speaking pointed nonsense and punning suggestively.

3.2.B (lines 126–246): The Dumb Show and "The Murder of Gonzago"

What is a dumb show? What happens in this dumb show? How is it relevant? Why doesn't Claudius react to it?

It is a pantomime enactment of the entire play, including the murder. Claudius's failure to react is inexplicable, unless we assume he isn't watching the actors. The text does not provide an answer here. In performance, however, many directors choose to have Claudius busy chatting with others and with Gertrude at this point.

Summarize the plot of "Gonzago." How is it relevant to Hamlet? What are the parallels between the characters in Hamlet and "Gonzago"? Why is "Gonzago" an effective test of the Ghost's accusations?

"Gonzago" includes all Claudius's major sins: murder, lust, usurpation, and an unsavory marriage. The player King represents Old Hamlet, the Player Queen Gertrude, and Lucianus Claudius. The parallels make the play an ideal test of Claudius's guilt.

How does Claudius react to the staged murder?

He is deeply disturbed; he orders the play to stop, asks for light, and rushes out (lines 252–255).

Why is this the crisis of the play? What does Hamlet learn about Claudius at this point? What does Claudius learn about Hamlet?

To this point, both Hamlet and Claudius have avoided confrontation and direct action. Now, both will attempt to act: Hamlet to kill the eavesdropper in 3.4. and Claudius to sent Hamlet off to execution in England. Both initial attempts at action are unsuccessful.

3.2.c (lines 246–364): Reactions to the play and events

How has Hamlet's position changed?

"I'll take the ghost's word for a thousand pound" (lines 271–2); he is convinced of Claudius's guilt.

What do R&G report to Hamlet? Whose interests do they represent? How does Hamlet treat them? Explain the metaphor of the recorder.

They represent Claudius's interests and report his rage as well as Gertrude's desire to speak with Hamlet. Hamlet treats them with scorn and anger; he accuses them of trying to play him as they would a recorder.

3.2.d (lines 365–407): Hamlet's soliloquy

What is Hamlet's frame of mind? What is he ready to do? How does his language and imagery reflect his attitude?

He is ready to revenge (drink hot blood); images like "witching time of night" and "Hell itself breathes out contagion" suggest his commitment to bloody (and evil) deeds.

What is Hamlet's attitude toward his mother here?

He is going to her room to speak with her, and is angry with her because of her closeness to Claudius. Does he suspect her of conspiracy with Claudius against his father? He resolves not to kill her, but to speak daggers to her (to get her to part from Claudius).

3.3: Claudius at prayer and Hamlet's avoidance of revenge

What does Claudius have planned for Hamlet?

Claudius goes through with his plan to send Hamlet to England (to be killed), and asks R&G to accompany the Prince (lines 1–7).

What is Rosencrantz's vision of the state and the death of a king? Why is this vision ironic in connection with Claudius?

A king's death produces universal sadness and chaos because of the disorder in the cosmos. This is ironic because Claudius as a usurper has already produced cosmic disorder.

What does Claudius reveal in his soliloquy? How does his speech affect your evaluation?

The soliloquy reveals that Claudius is guilty and that he feels guilt; it humanizes him by showing that he is not pure evil.

What reasons does Hamlet give for not killing Claudius at his prayers? Are they convincing? In character? What else is on his mind at this point? Why is Hamlet's decision here ironic? To what extent does this scene support either Hamlet's own sense that he is guilty of delay or the nineteenth-century argument that Hamlet's tragic flaw is his inability to act?

This moment is hotly debated by critics. Hamlet says that he avoids acting because he would send Claudius's soul to heaven, and sending him to heaven would certainly not be revenge. Instead, Hamlet states that he wants to kill him when he will be damned, just as Hamlet's father was killed with his sins on his head, without the ministrations of a priest. Some critics are struck by the uncharacteristic bloodthirstiness and bad theology here. Ironically, Claudius cannot pray (see lines 97–98). In any event, Hamlet clearly has his mother, whom he is going to meet, on his mind (line 95). Since Hamlet acts with speed in 3.4, this moment of delay should not carry too much weight.

3.4.A (lines 1–24): The death of Polonius

What is Polonius doing in Gertrude's chamber?

Polonius, who is still trying to test Hamlet's behavior and who therefore hides during the confrontation, advises Gertrude to tell Hamlet that she has been protecting him and that he should straighten out (lines 1–7).

How does Hamlet treat Gertrude? What frightens Polonius? How is Polonius killed? Why is he killed? Whom did Hamlet hope he was killing? Hamlet calls Polonius a "wretched, rash, intruding fool" (line 31); is this accurate? To what extent is Polonius responsible for his own death? What does this act show us about Hamlet?

Hamlet verbally attacks Gertrude; she becomes afraid and calls for help (lines 20–21). Polonius also calls out from behind the arras, and Hamlet runs him through, believing that the person in hiding might be

Claudius (line 26). In any event, the killing shows that Hamlet can act impetuously and with speed when the occasion demands it. Polonius has been intervening in royal affairs since the play's opening, even though his motivations have been for his own advancement and that of the family. He has not understood what is going on, and thus he has been an "intruding fool." Because he is hiding, and could be a threat as far as Hamlet is concerned, Polonius brings about his own death, even though he intends Hamlet no harm.

3.4.B (lines 35–217): Hamlet's lecture and the Ghost's return

What two men does Hamlet compare? What points does he make about Claudius? About Gertrude's behavior? What seems to disturb Hamlet most here? What effect does this lecture have on Gertrude?

Hamlet compares old Hamlet to Claudius (in production, he often holds miniature portraits of both men up to Gertrude. He is wearing the miniature of old Hamlet; she wears the miniature of Claudius). He accuses Gertrude of shifting from godlike grace to a murderer, villain, and usurper because of lust. He seems far more upset by Gertrude's remarriage than by his father's murder. Later, he tells Gertrude to avoid Claudius's bed.

Why does the Ghost return?

Hamlet assumes the Ghost returns to criticize his delay (tardy son). The Ghost says that he has come "to whet thy almost blunted purpose" (line 111). Thematically, the return of the Ghost brings to mind the details of Act 1 and the accusations of murder against Claudius. In addition, the Ghost is scary and mysterious, and his presence deepens the mood of anger, depression, and death.

What is Gertrude's opinion of Hamlet's mental state? What does he tell her? What does she promise?

She thinks him mad. He explains that he is mad in craft and warns her not to tell Claudius. She promises to keep silent.

What does Hamlet know about R&G and the impending trip to England? What does he plan to do about the problem?

He knows they cannot be trusted and are leading him to knavery. He plans to destroy them through their own devices (see lines 200–210).

ACT III REVIEW AND INTRODUCTION TO ACT IV: Act 3 has focused on Hamlet: (1) His efforts to confirm the Ghost's accusations; (2) his avoidance of revenge during the praying scene; (3) his accidental killing of Polonius; (4) his interview with his mother. Throughout Act 3, Hamlet is active. The death of Polonius, however, puts Hamlet into a defensive position and gives Claudius the upper hand. Thus, in Act 4, the focus shifts away from Hamlet (who goes to England) to Claudius. While Act 3 focuses on Hamlet's attempts to gain vengeance, Act 4 focuses on Claudius's attempts to eliminate Hamlet. Act 4 begins with Claudius's first plan of attack—to have Hamlet murdered in England. It ends with his second plan: the rigged fencing match.

Act IV. The Tightening Web: Claudius's counter-moves

4.1: Claudius and Gertrude

What does Gertrude report to Claudius? What does Claudius realize about Hamlet's killing of Polonius? What does he plan to do with Hamlet?

She reports Hamlet's madness and murder of Polonius. Claudius realizes it was meant for him (line 13); he plans to send Hamlet to England at dawn, now as a way of ostensibly getting Hamlet out of court so that the crime may be forgotten. (lines 40–45).

4.2: Hamlet and R&G

What is Hamlet's attitude toward R&G?

He scorns them as sponges who soak up Claudius's orders, rewards, and authority. They have become mere extensions.

4.3: Claudius and Hamlet

How does Hamlet act with Claudius when questioned about Polonius?

He maintains the appearance of madness but drops hints to trouble Claudius.

What has Claudius planned for Hamlet in England?

Claudius plans to have Hamlet killed in England. He has now let R&G into his confidence, and hints at rewards for them if they will accompany Hamlet and see to it that the orders are carried out (lines 51–65).

Why does Claudius plan to have Hamlet killed?

There are two reasons: Hamlet's popularity with the people and Gertrude's love. Claudius wants Hamlet dead, but he wants his own hands to appear to be completely clean. This plan is consistent with Claudius's willingness and ability to use people to his own ends throughout the play. He uses Polonius, Ophelia, R&G, Laertes, &c, and most of these people willingly allow themselves to be used out of duty or the hope of advancement.

4.4: Hamlet on the way to the seacoast and England

Where are Fortinbras and his army going? What does Hamlet learn about the land that will be fought over? How does this meeting influence Hamlet's thinking (soliloquy, lines 32–66)? Of what does Hamlet accuse himself?

They are going to fight over a barren plot of land in Poland worth nothing but honor. Hamlet sees this instance as a rebuke of his own tardiness and lack of passion. He argues that he has far greater cause to act than Fortinbras and yet lets all sleep. The charges are not an accurate reflection of the situation; at this moment, Hamlet is powerless to act.

4.5.A (lines 1–70): Ophelia's insanity

What is Ophelia's condition? How does her language convey her madness? How is her madness different from Hamlet's?

Ophelia's madness—the real thing—is conveyed in fragmented grammar, nonsense, bawdy songs, and oblique allusions to Polonius's death. There is no apparent method in her madness, but her speeches show what has unhinged her. They also show her kindness and vulnerability.

Why is Ophelia mad? How is madness consistent with her character?

Her madness evolves from her father's death, Hamlet's treatment of her, and a sense of betrayal of her affections for Hamlet. Throughout the play, she has been guided by Polonius or her brother; now she has no one. The madness is consistent with her obedience, sense of duty, and selflessness. In a structural sense, her madness symbolizes the effects of the original murder of King Hamlet by Claudius. Evil, in short, begins with one action, which spreads out to destroy everyone in its path.

4.5.B (lines 71–151): The return of Laertes

What is Laertes's attitude on returning to Denmark? What does he want? How is he comparable to Hamlet? Is he more or less justified than Hamlet?

Laertes is enraged over Polonius's death and secret burial; he blames Claudius and wants revenge (lines 133–134). As a son whose father has been murdered, Laertes is an exact parallel to Hamlet; his desires are equally motivated. This twist of the plot ironically makes Hamlet parallel to Claudius and reveals the moral corruption inherent in vengeance.

4.5.C (lines 152–214): Laertes and Ophelia, Laertes and Claudius

How does Ophelia behave with Laertes? What is the focus of her madness? What is Laertes's reaction?

Ophelia's madness continues; she dwells on images that suggest Polonius's death. Laertes's desire for revenge grows.

What does Claudius offer Laertes?

Claudius offers "satisfaction" (line 204); that is, that Hamlet will be eliminated. Laertes asks that no honors be given to Hamlet after death (lines 197–214).

4.6: Horatio and the Sailors

What does Hamlet's letter reveal?

The letter reveals that Hamlet will return to Denmark while R&G go on to England.

4.7: Claudius and Laertes hatch a plot

What had Claudius proven to Laertes about Polonius's death? What news does he expect from England? What news does he get?

He convinces Laertes that Hamlet killed Polonius while trying to kill him. He expects to hear that Hamlet has been executed; instead, he hears of Hamlet's safe return.

How do Claudius and Laertes plan to murder Hamlet? To what extent is Laertes manipulated by Claudius? To what extent is Laertes the author of this plan? How is Laertes's commitment to revenge different from Hamlet's?

They plan to murder Hamlet by trickery during a fencing match. Claudius invents the plan, but Laertes adds the detail of the poison (lines 139–147). He manipulates Laertes into doing his dirty work, but Laertes is willing to go along. Laertes's commitment is absolute; he is willing to cut Hamlet's throat *i'th'church.*

What do we find out about Ophelia in this scene?

Ophelia has drowned herself in a nearby stream. Gertrude explains the death as an accident (she fell off a bough, and the weight of her clothing dragged her under the water; lines 164–183).

Act IV Review and Introduction to Act V. Just as Act 3 was mostly Hamlet's act, so Act 4 is mostly Claudius's. Having killed Polonius in Act 3, Hamlet is on the defensive in Act 4; Claudius is on the offensive. The Act contains Claudius's two plans for getting rid of Hamlet: the English execution and the rigged fencing match. The re-introduction of Laertes as a secondary revenger (and a parallel to Hamlet) complicates the neatly unfolding structure of the play, but Laertes is quickly co-opted and absorbed by Claudius; Laertes becomes a willing tool for Claudius. By the end of Act 4, then, the two central thrusts of motive-action are clearly established: Hamlet's desire to eliminate Claudius and Claudius's desire to eliminate Hamlet. These two forces meet head on in Act 5, where the resolution is death.

Act V: Vengeance, Catastrophe, and Resolution

5.1.A (lines 1–55): The Clowns (Gravediggers)

What is the subject of the clowns' conversation? How is this subject relevant to the play? To what extent is the conversation amusing?

The general topic is death and decay. Death permeates *Hamlet*, and this scene provides another focus on this central fact, but does so comically. Death is of course heavy material for comic relief, but the treatment is successful. The idea of comic relief is that it siphons off the emotional pressure building up as a result of the various conflicts and tensions. Rather than have the audience laugh at the wrong point in the action, Shakespeare provides a legitimate outlet for laughter. The result is that when the concluding dueling, poisoning, and dying are over at the end of the play, an inappropriate response of laughter has been left behind, and the audience is left free to focus on the deaths and to respond sympathetically.

5.1.B (lines 56–201): Hamlet and the Clown

To what extent is this conversation also comic relief? About what do the skulls make Hamlet think? What subject is the overall focus of this conversation? How is this subject relevant to Hamlet's earlier considerations? How does Shakespeare make his comic relief work thematically?

Again, the focus is on death. Hamlet has spent most of the play considering death, salvation, damnation, and suicide. His abstraction in this scene suggests his readiness to face death. The comic relief is not wasted; it reflects one of the play's central concerns. Yorick's skull makes the idea of death immediate to Hamlet. References to Alexander the Great and Caesar suggest death's universal and leveling power.

5.1.C (lines 201–282): Ophelia's funeral

How does Laertes act? What point does Hamlet make about his own feelings for Ophelia? About Laertes?

Laertes acts with conventional grief. Jumping into a grave may seem overly demonstrative, but it is not unusual in some cultures. To most audiences today, however, Laertes seems to be carrying things too far. Hamlet claims that he can overmatch Laertes since his feelings are greater.

5.2.A (lines 1–80): The fate of R&G

What orders were R&G carrying? What did Hamlet do to R&G? To what extent is their fate just? What is Hamlet's attitude toward their fate?

R&G had orders from Claudius for Hamlet's immediate execution (lines 18–25); Hamlet altered the orders so that R&G would be killed upon arrival in England (lines 38–47). Hamlet thinks they deserved to die (lines 57–62) because he assumes that they were in league with Claudius.

5.2.B (lines 81–179): Hamlet and Osric

What is Osric like? Why does Hamlet call him a "water-fly"? What is his language like? How is he like Polonius? How does Hamlet mock Osric? What is Osric's business with Hamlet?

Osric is an overdressed dandy who is a cause of humor. Hamlet's reference to him as a "water-fly" reflects his pretentious clothing and manners. Osric has the courtier's manner of speaking in indirection and circumlocution. Hamlet mocks his manners with the bonnet business, and mocks his overly courtly doubletalk by feeding it back to him (lines 109–119). Osric's task is to deliver Laertes's challenge; his effect is to create another scene of comic relief before the final resolution in death.

5.2.C (lines 179–206): Hamlet and Horatio

What is Hamlet's attitude toward the fencing match?

He thinks he will win (line 194), but is suspicious (lines 194–201).

What has Hamlet learned by this point in the play?

Hamlet has learned the virtues of patience, acceptance, and readiness (see lines 202–6). He accepts the providence of all things and believes that the readiness is all. Ironically, these lessons will neither help nor save him, because he will be forced to act suddenly when he finally acts.

5.2.D (lines 207–344): The fencing match; the catastrophe

How do Hamlet and Laertes act toward each other before the match? Which is sincere?

The men exchange pardons and love; only Hamlet is sincere.

Who wins the first two bouts? What is Laertes's problem? How does he solve it?

Hamlet wins both; Laertes cannot get a legitimate hit with the poisoned foil, so he stabs Hamlet between bouts. This violation of the rules of fair play underscores Laertes's corruption and his commitment to vengeance.

How is Gertrude killed? Laertes? Claudius? In what way are all three deaths ironic?

Gertrude is killed with the poisoned wine that Claudius prepares for Hamlet. Laertes dies from his own unbaited and poisoned foil, and confesses that "I am justly killed with mine own treachery" (line 290) while naming Claudius as the guilty one. Hamlet, learning this fact and having almost no time left to live, kills Claudius with both the poisoned sword and the poisoned wine. Ironically, he therefore revenges himself not so much for his father's death but for his mother's and his own. The deaths of both Claudius and Laertes are ironic because they are killed with their own weapons. Gertrude's death is ironic because the poisoned wine was not for her.

Why does Hamlet want Horatio to stay alive? What is Hamlet's final concern?

He wants Horatio alive to tell his story (lines 326–332); he is concerned about his reputation (wounded name).

5.2.E (lines 345–386): Resolution; tying up of loose ends

Who will be the next king of Denmark?

Fortinbras will probably be the next ruler (line 339).

What does Horatio plan to explain to the unknowing world?

He will tell the story of "how these things came about"; i.e., murders, arbitrary judgments, unpremeditated slaughter, treachery, and self-ruin (lines 362–369).

What is Fortinbras's attitude toward Hamlet?

Fortinbras treats Hamlet with honor and respect; he calls him most royal and has the body like a soldier. Thus, Fortinbras implicitly accepts the justice of Hamlet's cause and Claudius's (as yet undisclosed) villainy.

Discussion of the "General Questions," pages 1231–1232

(1–4) All these topics focus on character. Claudius, Horatio, R&G, and Polonius are discussed at length above. Of the women, Ophelia is the more fully developed. We see Gertrude mostly from Hamlet's perspective, and he considers her morally weak. We learn that she is a loving person and that she thinks well of her son. That she married with undue haste after the funeral is a fact, but she may have been thinking more of the continuity of the state and her role in the succession than about her own feelings. She seems totally committed to Claudius and to helping him in his rule. There is never any suspicion that Gertrude knew that

Claudius killed King Hamlet or that she learns about the killing as the play progresses. Hence, her second marriage is more an indication that she appreciates her role as queen, with all its powers and privileges, than an indication of evil or even weakness.

Ophelia, as noted above in discussions of 1.3 and 4.5, is controlled by the men in her life: Polonius, Laertes, and Hamlet. In her dutiful cooperation with Claudius and Polonius, she is used in a situation she does not understand, and the treatment she receives from Hamlet, indicating to her that she is scorned rather than loved, is one of the situations bringing her down. We may conclude that the murder of her father causes her deep grief, and also that her death is a suicide brought about by all the evil circumstances of the court.

Revenge is a major influence on character in the play: Hamlet, Laertes, and Fortinbras are all parallel revengers. Fortinbras wants to avenge his father's defeat and death at the hands of old Hamlet. He seeks to do so through military action against Denmark. Although deflected from Denmark to Poland by his uncle, he ultimately claims the Danish throne and gains the dying Hamlet's approval.

Hamlet's quest for vengeance is complicated by his need to prove the Ghost's accusations, his fixation on his mother's incestuous relationship with Claudius, and his own guilt about what he sees as delay. These combine to postpone his killing of Claudius until it is too late to escape death. Hamlet's is perhaps the most thoughtful but least effective quest.

Laertes commits himself more directly to vengeance, but also allies himself with evil. He is not interested in corroborating evidence or finding truth; his is thus the most corrupt quest for revenge.

(5) There are at least two ways of looking at conflicts in *Hamlet.* If one views Hamlet as a man incapacitated by his own character and responsibilities, the conflict is internal. If one considers the play in terms of action and political dynamics, the central conflict is between Hamlet as protagonist and Claudius as antagonist. From this perspective, Hamlet's conflicts with R&G, Polonius, and Laertes are all secondary, because all these characters serve as (witting or unwitting) extensions of Claudius. In either event, resolution occurs in the catastrophe.

(6) The crisis occurs in Act III. scene 2 (see above), during the play-within-the-play. Claudius's guilty reaction fixes Hamlet's subsequent course of action, as it does those of Claudius, and the outcome is then inevitable.

(7) In terms of immediate action, Claudius murders only one person (Old Hamlet), cooperates in the murder of another (Hamlet), and acci-

dentally kills a third (Gertrude). The rest are killed by Hamlet (directly or indirectly). From a broader perspective, however, Claudius is responsible for all the carnage. His original murder of an anointed king, combined with his taking over the throne along with the queen, upsets cosmic order (the Great Chain of Being) and introduces destructive chaos into the world of the play. The first destructive act thus causes a chain reaction of suspicion, accusation, plotting, counter-plotting, plans for elimination, depression, suicidal thoughts, and uncontrollable anger that finally result in all the deaths.

(8) When *Hamlet* begins, the state is already diseased and disordered; the first scene suggests unnatural and chaotic events. The close of the play holds the promise of order and control; Fortinbras makes a valid claim to the throne, and Horatio suggests it will be upheld. Nevertheless, Denmark has lost both a good old king and a prince with great potential. Order returns with the death of Claudius and the emergence of Fortinbras as a strong leader, but the price is monumental.

The Theater of Arthur Miller, *pages 1232–1233*

This discussion provides an introduction to the modern theater and many aspects of contemporary drama and staging. It could also be usefully assigned in conjunction with Tennessee Williams's *The Glass Menagerie* (beginning on page 1519).

Arthur Miller, *Death of a Salesman, pages 1233–1302*

Miller's American masterpiece illustrates the evolution of modern tragedy. The introduction to the play (pages 1233–1236) briefly surveys the stage history, the concept of the common man as tragic hero, and the critique of the American Dream that parallels the fall of Willy Loman.

The play, like Williams's *The Glass Menagerie,* represents a midpoint between the total realism of Henrik Ibsen and the nonrealism of Edward Albee. And like *Oedipus* or *An Enemy of the People,* it embodies the end of a much longer story. Here, however, this longer story is brought into the present through dramatized fragments of memory. These scenes of past action come out of Willy's head; they are consequently subjective and distorted visions of the past rather than accurate recreations. Psychologically, they suggest that the past is always in the present, shaping our thoughts, actions, fears, and dreams.

There are two crises in the play. Both occur on stage and within Willy's mind; students will have to decide which is the primary one. The first is Biff's discovery of Willy's adultery (pages 1290–1292); this single moment shapes the future of both Willy and Biff (i.e., the present action of the play). It also accounts for the ongoing alienation between father and son, Biff's self-destructiveness, and Willy's guilt. The second crisis is Willy's decision, while in conversation with Ben, to commit suicide; it shapes the catastrophe, which follows closely when Willy drives off to his death (page 1301, 930.1), and the resolution of the play (the Requiem). Willy and Biff each experience a partial recognition. Willy realizes that he has run out of lies, dreams, and illusions (page 1285, speech 522) and that Biff loves him (page 1299, speeches 889–894) Biff recognizes that he does not want Willy's version of the American Dream (page 1298, speeches 882–888).

In teaching *Death of a Salesman,* you might focus mostly on character and theme. The chief character for discussion is Willy. Students will perceive him as a good deal less heroic that Oedipus or Hamlet, but his problems are equally consuming and fatal. A key question: What makes Willy heroic? Thematically, the play explores ideas about individual dignity, the impact of a single trauma on subsequent life, and the corruption of the American Dream. All these points can lead to effective discussion.

The play was first produced on Broadway in 1949 with Lee J. Cobb as Willy Loman. Cobb was a large man; Miller had to revise parts of his original script to accommodate Cobb's enactment. The present text—the one Miller published in his complete works—reflects these changes. In 1984 the play was revived on Broadway with Dustin Hoffman in the lead. This production was filmed for television, and was broadcast in 1985. Hoffman played Willy as a small and nervous man always on the edge of collapse. In many respects, his performance was closer to Miller's original conception than the 1949 production with Cobb.

Answers to the Study Questions, pages 1302–1303

(1) The first stage direction suggests that Willy's world is fragile and dreamlike. We are presented with a setting that is only partly real (or realistic). Willy himself is described as exhausted; the large sample cases represent his burdens. Every move combines weariness and anxiety. In addition, there are clues early in the play that Willy is losing touch with reality. One is his inability to drive (page 1210, speech 12). The other is his assertion that he "opened the windshield" of the car (page 1238, speech 22). It is clear of course that Willy could not have opened the windshield

of his post-war Studebaker (the windshield did not open), and it is also clear that he is thinking about the car he owned in 1928. Willy's confusion becomes even more evident when he slips completely into memory for the first time (page 1245, 195.1). Here, a number of events that occurred in 1928 merge together into one memory sequence. Willy, in short, is "losing it" in the course of the play.

(2) Stealing is a motif that runs throughout the play. In the past, Willy encouraged (or at least tolerated) the boys' thievery from construction sites (the very apartment houses that now hem him in). Biff has a long and sorry history of stealing: the football, the sporting goods, a suit, Oliver's pen. Much of his post-1928 thievery is clearly self-destructive. Happy steals in another way; he takes women from other men simply to prove to himself that he can do it. Willy himself cheated on his wife when on his selling trips. Willy's toleration of stealing suggests a link between this sort of dishonesty and the emphasis he places on appearances (smiling, being well liked) and selling (one's product, one's self).

(3) Willy's claim never to have told Biff anything but decent things reflects the degree to which Willy deludes himself. At least by example, Willy has shown Biff that dishonesty is acceptable and that appearances matter more than substance. He continues to stress appearances in the present, maintaining the illusion of his pay check and insisting that Biff look and act just so (sell himself) in his interview with Oliver. In effect, this line is directly contradicted by Biff's claim that "we never told the truth for ten minutes in this house" (page 1298, speech 867).

(4) Throughout the play, Willy cannot (or will not) deal effectively with machines. He continually wrecks his car, the refrigerator is always in need of repair, and the wire recorder (a precursor of tape and cassette recorders) in Howard's office terrifies him. These machines represent the (1949) present—the world that Willy can no longer deal with adequately. For Willy, the present time, dominated increasingly by machinery, is contrasted with the past of Dave Singleman, 1928, Uncle Ben, and Willy's childhood memories of his father.

(5) Willy is asking Bernard about the secret to success, achievement, dignity, and recognition—fulfillment of the American Dream. He clearly understands, at least part of the time, that he and his sons have tried to be successful, but that somehow they have failed to reach the heights of success. Charley and Bernard illustrate the truth that there is no secret beyond hard work and a concentration on substance rather than style (early in the play, Willy observes that Charley is liked, but not well liked).

Looked at another way, the secret might be that Willy has lived according to a false system of values, and has imbued his sons with the same values.

(6) This is a complex and disturbing moment in the play—it brings together all of Willy's desperation, confusion, and agony. On the one hand, the garden represents the past: a time before the house was hemmed in by brutal and impersonal apartment houses and before The Woman in Boston—a time when Willy was still idolized as a heroic figure by his sons. Willy's need to plant a garden reflects his desire to return to this state of innocence. On the other hand, having "things in the ground" or growing can be taken to represent success, achievement, and security. Willy's desperation reflects his knowledge that his life is empty and fruitless. In addition, he understands that his sons (who are, of course, other kinds of growing things) are not thriving in the "soil" in which he has planted them.

(7) Biff's line (page 1298, speech 867) indicates his realization that the Loman men have consistently deluded themselves with half-truths and unrealistic dreams. To some extent, this continues to be true to the end of the play. Only Biff comes to a realistic assessment of his own life and abilities; he understands that he will be more content on the land. Willy remains partly self-deluded right to the end; he assumes that his funeral will be well attended and he imagines that the insurance money will make Biff a success. Happy's last lines indicate that he remains trapped in Willy's deluded visions of success.

(8) Linda's final line is open to various interpretations; give students free rein with this one. It might imply that the Lomans are free of hot air and self-delusion. If so, the assertion is not true, at least for Happy. The line might also suggest that the Lomans are free from the false values and standards of Willy's American Dream. Again, this is not true for Happy. It could also mean that, with the house free and clear, the family is free to grow and expand without the constant, nagging worry of making payments and the pressure of living from paycheck to paycheck to keep from being dispossessed. This meaning is true, except that neither Linda nor Willy ever had any idea of what to do with freedom if it came to them. That may be the greatest tragedy of all.

Discussion of the General Questions, page 1303

(1) The degeneration in the setting (the house, the surrounding scrim) reflects the degeneration of Willy over the years. The past (of 1928 and before) is indicated by green light, the shadow of leaves, blocking that moves characters through the wall-lines of the house, and Ben's flute music.

The present is reflected in the angry orange glow of the apartment houses and the realistic blocking in which the wall-lines of the house are observed. The staging of present action is mostly realistic, while the staging of memory sequences reflects the nonrealistic nature of dreaming and memory.

(2) Generally, detailed stage directions are designed to help the reader understand the play and experience it fully. In this case, however, Miller's lengthy stage directions suggest that he wrote with readers (rather than actors or viewers) in mind. Stage directions that cannot be played on the stage clearly indicate the double audience (spectators and readers) that modern playwrights address.

(3) Willy's suicide is foreshadowed at the very beginning of the play when Linda asks if he smashed up the car (page 1237, speech 5). Later in the first Act, Linda tells her sons that "all these accidents in the past year weren't—weren't accidents" (page 1261, speeches 648–663). These comments directly anticipate Willy's vehicular suicide at the close of Act 2. Suicide is also foreshadowed and symbolized in the rubber pipe and "the new little nipple on the gas pipe" that Willy has apparently installed in the basement (page 1261, speeches 667–672).

(4) All the characters in the present are real and realistic (the 1949 version of the Lomans, Charley and Bernard, Howard, Jennie, and the people in the bar). These characters act and speak realistically. The hallucinatory characters that emerge from Willy's memory include the 1928 Lomans, Charley and Bernard, Uncle Ben, and The Woman. These figures are a good deal less developed or realistic; they have been flattened out and stripped of inessential characteristics through the subjective filter of memory and guilt. Their stage movement is often nonrealistic; their language is formulaic and repetitive.

(5) The four central symbolic characters of the play are Willy, Dave Singleman, Uncle Ben, and The Woman (Howard, Charley, and Bernard are secondary symbols). Willy, the low man, embodies failure and false values. Dave Singleman (present only by reference) symbolizes the single (or singular) man; he is Willy's personal symbol of success. Uncle Ben represents another version of the American Dream; he is the self-reliant pioneer/exploiter who opens new territories and carves wealth out of the land. Willy's father is a much less well-developed version of this same symbol. It is this romanticized and sentimentalized dream to which Biff is drawn at the end of the play. The Woman symbolizes guilt and trauma (as well as past pleasure) for Willy and for Biff; the sound of her laugh or a knock on the door catapults Willy back to the horror of that moment of discovery.

(6) Willy is heroic in his struggle for dignity, his willingness to go back on the road; he simply will not accept defeat. He even (mistakenly) sees his death as a heroic victory that will make people appreciate him and give Biff a new start in life. His central failing is self-delusion (lies, dreams, hot air). This blinds him to the realities of his own life and his sons' lack of ability. It can be argued that Willy's failure comes from within, from the lies and illusions he has fostered all his life. Conversely, students might argue that Willy's values reflect those imposed by a corrupt society; he measures himself against an invalid version of the American Dream. From this perspective, Willy's failure is society's failure.

(7) Willy says to Charley, "you never told him [Bernard] what to do ... you never took any interest in him." Charley replies, "My salvation is that I never took any interest in anything" (page 1279, speech 341). The exchange epitomizes the differences between the two father-son relationships. Willy took an interest; he passed on his own values and delusions to his sons. Charley apparently let Bernard shape his own values and life, guiding only by example. To put it another way, Willy invested too much of his own life in his sons. Moreover, he willingly set himself up as a heroic ideal—an ideal that is destroyed for Biff in a single moment of revelation. Charley never fostered illusions of heroism in Bernard; there were no heroic ideals to be exposed as fake.

(8) Linda is completely supportive of Willy; she accepts his lies and exaggerations (even when she knows they are false), and she fights for him against Biff and Happy. Linda is both an admirable and a culpable character (let the students decide which predominates); her support is both essential and destructive. It creates a reasonably strong marriage, but it also allows Willy to sustain his illusions far too long.

(9) Happy is an exaggerated and degenerated version of Willy. He embodies all the faults of Willy's dreams and delusions: the emphasis on externals and on being well liked, lies about achievement. He continues to pursue the same corrupt dream, "to come out number-one man" in the world of selling. His obsessive conquests of other men's women suggests a continual need to compete and prove himself to himself in the only arena in which he can still be successful. Happy is not happy, and probably never can be.

In contrast, it can be argued that his brother Biff changes—that he has the most significant and beneficial *anagnorisis,* or recognition, in the play. Such knowledge suggests the potential for a more fruitful and happy life in the future. If students accept that Biff's return to the land embodies a viable alternative to Willy's dreams, then Biff's recognition implies hope. Looking at the play from this perspective, with Biff as the educated protagonist, creates a radical shift; it changes the focus from Willy's tragic fall to Biff's comedic redemption. One problem with this perspective is that Miller forces readers to be suspicious of Ben's version of the American Dream and of Biff's ability.

(10) Willy's assertions about being "well liked" are symptomatic of his commitment to dreams, illusion, and style rather than substance. He preaches this dogma to his sons, but it has not worked for him and will not work for them. Miller gives the explicit refutation of this philosophy to Charley (page 1280, speeches 366–368). Moreover, Charley and Bernard are living refutations of Willy's belief in style over substance.

(11) For Willy, 1928 was the last really good year, the year of promises, the year of "a hundred and seventy dollars a week in commissions" (page 1272, speeches 144–146). It was the year that Frank Wagner (may have) promised him a position in the home office, Biff played the championship game, and Ben last visited. It was also the year in which Willy's adultery was discovered by Biff—the end of the boy's hero worship of Willy. For the nation, 1928 was the last year of optimism and prosperity, for the great depression began in 1929. These two patterns come together for Willy. For him, 1928 was the end of hope and innocence.

Writing About Tragedy, *pages 1304–1314*

This section discusses and illustrates several ways that students can plan and write essays about tragic drama. While the discussion does not focus specifically on the elements introduced in Chapter 27, you can easily assign such an essay in connection with *Oedipus the King, Hamlet,* or *Death of a Salesman.* All three plays lend themselves to investigations of plot, structure, conflict, setting, character, tone, language, and theme. *Oedipus the King* and *Hamlet* offer excellent opportunities for writing about irony, and *Death of a Salesman* is especially rich in symbolism. Because approaches to these topics are covered in Chapter 26, we introduce two new types of essay in this chapter. The first is an essay about a problem (pages 1304–1307). Here, we discuss ways of formulating and writing about a problem in literature. The sample essay (pages 1308–1310) takes up the problem of delay in *Hamlet.*

The second type is an essay on a close reading of a passage from a play (pages 1310–1312). In this example, the close reading focuses on content (rather than style) and relates the passage to a theme of the play. The sample essay (pages 1312–1313) focuses on a key passage from *Hamlet* and links it to the theme of appearance versus reality. Both of these essay types can be valuable and useful not only for discussing tragedy but also for dealing with the other genres.

Writing Topics for *Tragedy: Affirmation Through Loss, pages 1314–1315*

(1) The first topic suggests an in-depth treatment of the importance of vision and understanding in *Oedipus the King*. Some of the ideas for such a paper are included in this manual in the discussions of the questions for that play. A full treatment, however, should include most of the topics detailed in question 1 here.

(2) The second question, also on *Oedipus,* deals with the issue of free will and control. The topic is quite difficult, and students will not create definitive answers to the problem in their papers, but it is important for them to consider as they study tragedy.

(3) The third topic, on the subject of the women in Hamlet, might seem offensive to some of your students. They may need reminding that it is Hamlet who makes the assertion, and that it is their task to consider the rightness of the remark. Quite important in this consideration is the status of both women, and their niche in the society of the Renaissance as Shakespeare reflects it in the play.

(4) The fourth question, on the topic of the three young men in *Hamlet,* requires the technique of comparison-contrast (see Appendix B). It seems reasonable to request that students use details about Fortinbras and Laertes, who are minor characters, to highlight qualities about Hamlet himself.

(5) The fifth question will require as much knowledge of sociology and other cultures as students possess. Obviously, the play succeeds in various periods and cultures because the characters, conflicts, and themes remain as relevant today as they were more than forty years ago. Willy is a universal figure; the low man instead of every man. His dreams and delusions are universal in type if not in detail. All cultures produce value systems and standards that individuals either follow or reject as they seek success and dignity. The details of Willy's fall are of course peculiarly American, but the pattern of his struggle is transcendent.

(6) The sixth question might be easier for students than the fifth. *Death of a Salesman* attacks a specific version of the American Dream that is based on style, competition, and wealth. This dream and these values are championed by Willy and Happy; Biff realizes that it is no longer valid for him. Howard represents success in this mode, and he comes across as self-absorbed, heartless, and petty. Charley and Bernard represent a different (and more viable) American Dream—success through hard work, realism, and intelligence.

(7) The last question is a searching one; it would be most appropriate as a longer assignment in which extended comparison-contrast is the means of supporting the assertions about tragedy that students will be making. (See Appendix B.)

Chapter Twenty-eight
Pages 1316–1423

Comedy: Restoring the Balance

This chapter is designed to introduce students to the major aspects of comic drama. To that end, it begins with introductory material that discusses the history, nature, and pattern of comedy, as well as comic characters, language, and types of comedy (pages 1316–1323). In reviewing this material in class, you might emphasize the distinction between *comic* and *funny*. Like the terms *tragic* and *tragedy*, the terms *comic* and *comedy* are used colloquially with a far broader application than is useful in understanding drama. In plays, the terms refer not only to a tone or attitude, but also to a reasonably well-defined pattern of action that usually (but not always) leads to a resolution that is affirmative and regenerative. In satiric comedy such as *Love Is the Doctor*, this regenerative impulse can be transferred from the play to the audience, the readers, and the world at large.

Key points in discussing comedy include the distinctions between *high* and *low* as well as *romantic* and *satiric*. The chapter is designed to illustrate these distinctions with reference to three superb examples of comic drama. *A Midsummer Night's Dream* combines high comedy with low comedy. *Love Is the Doctor* contains low comedy and farce throughout, while *Am I Blue* mixes low comedy with some aspects of normal comedy. All the plays have some aspect of romantic comedy. *Am I Blue* presents details about a developing relationship, but *Love Is the Doctor* contains no such details at all, and *A Midsummer Night's Dream* treats the romantic developments and conflicts through a haze of magic. Of the three plays, the strongest satire is to be found in *Love Is the Doctor*.

If you have the time to include videotapes or audiotapes for use in your class, Shakespeare's *A Midsummer Night's Dream* is available in a number of commercial productions, including a ballet version:

- Videotape, 1935, b/w (117 minutes). Directed by Max Reinhardt, starring Olivia de Haviland, Mickey Rooney, Dick Powell, Victor Jory, and James Cagney. United Artists Corporation, 727 7th Avenue, New York, NY 10019.

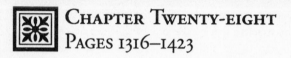

- Videotape, color, undated. Directed by Joseph Papp, New York Shakespeare Festival. Films for the Humanities, Box 2053, Princeton, NJ 08540.
- Videotape ballet, 1966 (93 minutes). A "fantasy" of *A Midsummer Night's Dream* by the New York City Ballet Company. Directed by Dan Eriksen. Starring Suzanne Farrell and Edward Villella.
- Videotape, color, 1968 (124 minutes). Directed by Peter Hall. A Royal Shakespeare Company Production, starring Diana Rigg, David Warner, Ian Richardson, Bill Travers, and Helen Mirren. Audio-Brandon Films, 34 MacQuestern Parkway South, Mount Vernon, NY 10550.
- Videotape, color, 1982 (120 minutes). Starring Helen Mirren and Peter McEnery. Time-Life Video, Box 644, Paramus, NJ 07652.
- Audiotape (49 minutes). Starring Eithne Dunne and Eve Watkinson. Spoken Arts, 510 North Avenue, New Rochelle, NY 10801.

These films and/or tapes are also available from other distributors. It is a good idea to delay showing a film until after the students have read the plays and begun class discussion. Too often, students come to believe that watching a film (or tape) can replace reading the play. In addition, the characterizations and interpretations created by actors and the director may affect the students' own reading of the play.

WILLIAM SHAKESPEARE, *A Midsummer Night's Dream*, *pages 1323–1378*

This is one of Shakespeare's funniest and most accessible comedies. If you teach it without (or before) doing *Hamlet,* it might be helpful to assign the introduction to Shakespeare's theater and life (pages 1122–1129). The first of these will help students understand many of the important conventions of Elizabethan theater. The introduction to *A Midsummer Night's Dream* (pages 1323–1324) provides a survey of plots, characters, and themes.

Teaching this play is a delightful experience. It provides an opportunity to deal with a number of dramatic elements at the same time. The three that can be most successfully emphasized in teaching are plot, character, and theme. Language (especially the different types of poetry) can be explored if time permits. The central plot (the four lovers) illustrates the New Comic pattern of blocked and then triumphant love. This plot is recapitulated (with a pathetic ending) in "Pyramus and Thisby," the play-within-the-play. The characters in the central plot are flat and conventional types that exemplify the dangers of irrational love, infatuation, and uncontrolled doting. In this plot and in the fairy plot, Puck serves as a jester, trouble-maker, and bizarre version of Cupid.

Thematically, the play explores at least two interconnected subjects: love and imagination. The absurdities and dangers of dotage are illustrated in the plight of the four lovers, the conflict produced by Titania's infatuation with her changeling child, her subsequent adoration of Bottom, and the pathetic deaths of Pyramus and Thisby. The power of imagination (and the intersection of imagination, perception, art, love, and dreams) is explored through the rehearsal process, the play-within-the-play, Theseus's commentary, and the device of love-in-idleness (the flower whose juice produces boundless infatuation).

Another approach to teaching structure and theme in this play is to contrast it (and "Pyramus") with Romeo and Juliet (written at about the same time). All three follow similar plots and offer related examination of blind love. *Romeo and Juliet* is often taught in tenth or eleventh grade; if your students are familiar with it, you can use the play as a parallel to both the comedy of *A Midsummer Night's Dream* and the pathos of "Pyramus." In such an approach, Lysander parallels Pyramus and Romeo; Hermia parallels Thisby and Juliet. The blocking agents are similarly parallel: 1–Egeus and the old Athenian law; 2–the wall; 3–the Montague-Capulet feud. In all three cases, the attempt to circumvent the obstructions involves moving outside the normal constraints of law or society (into the night, woods, Ninus's Tomb, a secret marriage, away from Verona).

Answers to the Study Questions, pages 1378–1380

(1) Lines 1–19 supply exposition and characterization. Theseus and Hippolyta are to be married in four days; this provides the general time-frame of the play. In the past, Theseus fought a war against Hippolyta (Queen of the Amazons) and captured her (lines 16–19). Their relationship, once characterized by the irrationality and passion of war, has evolved into a rational and harmonious dynastic alliance. However, they have very different attitudes toward the approaching marriage. Theseus is typically anxious and impatient; for him, time moves slowly, and the moon is a blocking agent delaying the fulfillment of his desires (lines 2–6). For Hippolyta, time is moving quickly and the moon (a silver bow) symbolizes Diana, goddess of chastity and the hunt (7–11). Theseus and Hippolyta (along with Athens

itself) represent absolute order, rationality, law, and authority. Indeed, Theseus will learn in the course of the play that the rigor of the law must be relaxed in acknowledgment of the higher authority of love.

(2) Hermia and Lysander are conventional and typical lovers; their problems are explained in Act I, scene 1, lines 20–127. Egeus wants Hermia to marry Demetrius; she wants to wed Lysander. Egeus accuses Lysander of bewitching Hermia by moonlight (linking love, moonlight, magic, and irrationality). He invokes the ancient law of Athens which requires that Hermia obey Egeus, die, or become a nun at Diana's temple (since comedy is typically concerned with sexual and social regeneration, the third choice is, in comedy, a fate worse than death). Theseus gives Hermia four days (until his own wedding and the new moon) to choose. We also learn that Hermia and Lysander are desperately in love, that Egeus favors Demetrius, that Demetrius and Lysander are identical as far as wealth and status are concerned, and that Demetrius has previously courted Helena. The ensuing conversation (lines 128–79) reveals the depths of young love (perhaps infatuation). Lysander plots an escape from Athens (156–68) by running off to a rich aunt's house (no financial sacrifice here) and Hermia agrees.

(3) Helena is love-sick for Demetrius, jealous of Hermia's power to attract men, and extremely self-deprecating. Her negative self-image and low self-esteem are the result of Demetrius's scorn. Although the world considers her fair, she sees herself through Demetrius's eyes. Hermia and Lysander tell their plans to Helena to make her feel better. She, in turn, will tell Demetrius all to gain a moment of attention. Helena's soliloquy about love (discussed below in the "General Questions") is a central thematic statement that provides a definition of the kind of blind and irrational love examined in the play.

(4) The hempen homespuns meet to assign roles for "The most lamentable comedy, and most cruel death of Pyramus and Thisby." They hope to present the play at court to celebrate Theseus's marriage and thus earn a pension (see IV.2.14–15). The casting of Flute as Thisby comically duplicates Elizabethan stage practices. Bottom's eagerness, energy, and conceit are reflected in his desire to demonstrate his acting skill and to play every role. He shows his limited education through his misuse of words. Here, he misuses *generally* (2), *aggravated* (69), and *obscenely* (91).

(5) The action of Act II, scene 1, lines 1–145 is expository, introducing Puck, Titania, Oberon, and the conflict over the changeling. The fairy's lyric verse (2–13) is a characteristic mode of poetry for the spirits; it contrasts with Theseus's blank verse and the lovers' rhymed couplets. Puck

is identified as Oberon's jester, a roguish trickster, and a trouble-maker (lines 32–58). His love of trickery and confusion becomes important later when he is trying to deal with the four lovers.

(6) The conflict between Oberon and Titania over the changeling is introduced by Puck (II.1.18–31) and explained more fully by Oberon and Titania (60–145). Titania is infatuated with the child; she spends all her time with him and ignores Oberon. Oberon is jealous, but he also has the right of command (as husband and King) over Titania. Her involvement with the child disrupts her normal relationship with Oberon. This conflict is further complicated by Oberon's previous relationship with Hippolyta and Titania's with Theseus (64–80). As the ruling spirits of nature, Oberon and Titania are linked (through the Great Chain of Being) to cycles of time and season. Their discord disrupts these cycles (81–117). Oberon claims that the chaos can be fixed if Titania hands over the child. She refuses, claiming that the boy was given to her by his dying mother.

(7) Oberon plans to humiliate and cure Titania by using love-in-idleness to put her madly in love with something monstrous. This shift of affection will make it possible for him to get the changeling. Oberon explains the source of the flower's magical power (155–72); the flower symbolizes the kind of blind and hasty love that Helena described in the first soliloquy. Oberon enchants Titania (II.2.1–34) by squeezing the juice from love-in-idleness on her eyes and reciting the appropriate lyric incantation; he hopes that she will wake when "some vile thing is near."

(8) When Demetrius and Helena appear in the woods, he is chasing Hermia and Lysander, planning to seize one and kill the other. She is pursuing Demetrius, seeking any attention at all (even abuse, see II.1.202–10). He runs off, threatening Helena with injury if she follows. She pursues, claiming that she will "die upon the hand I love so well." Oberon, who announces that he is invisible, overhears the exchange and decides to correct the situation by using love-in-idleness to change Demetrius's affections. As a being accustomed to command, Oberon orders Puck to take care of things, and Puck does what he is told, only he makes the innocent mistake of squeezing the juice in Lysander's eyes (II.2). When Helena awakens Lysander, he instantly falls madly in love with her (see II.2.103–22). Helena assumes that this adoration is mockery (123–34). With the enchantment of Lysander, the love relationships among the four lovers move to the second stage—a perfect round-robin in which no love is reciprocated.

(9) In III.1, Puck disrupts the rehearsal and transforms Bottom. He gives Bottom an ass-head for at least three reasons: 1–it is a good joke and

consistent with Puck's love of trickery; 2–it is appropriate since Bottom (with a pun on the name) is already an ass; 3–it provides a suitably vile object of affection for Titania. When Bottom awakens Titania with his singing (III.1.115), she falls madly in love with him. Bottom's reaction is significant; he asserts that she has no reason to love him, but that "reason and love keep little company together now-a-days" (III.3.128–32). The speech, a key thematic statement, is ironic because Bottom (the fool) can see what none of the more noble or educated characters can understand.

(10) In III.2., Puck reports to Oberon about the transformation of Bottom, Titania's love, the harassment of the mechanicals, and the anointing of the Athenian's eyes. When Demetrius and Hermia arrive, the fairies realize that an error has occurred. Demetrius is pleading his own love; Hermia is seeking Lysander. Oberon accuses Puck of intentionally anointing the wrong man's eyes to cause trouble; he sends Puck off to get Helena and he puts the flower juice in Demetrius's eyes. While Puck did not intentionally produce this chaos, he enjoys it immensely (see III.2.110–21); he realizes that two men will now woo Helena, and he finds such mortal foolishness highly amusing.

(11) When Demetrius wakes up under the influence of love-in-idleness (137) and spots Helena, he falls madly in love with her. This situation (stage three of the love relationships) exactly reverses the one that began the play; now both men love Helena and loathe Hermia. Because Helena's self-image is so badly damaged, she assumes that both men are mocking her. When Hermia joins in the fray (177), Helena assumes that she is part of this confederacy of mockery.

(12) Once the four lovers are together in the woods (III.2.177), things become progressively more chaotic and dangerous. The men decide to fight a duel over Helena (254–255), and the women begin to fight (at first verbally and then physically). The potential for disaster here is real (although we never believe it because Oberon and Puck remain in attendance). The men could kill each other; the women could be abandoned to wild animals (compare "Pyramus"). Oberon takes control of the situation at line 345, and orders Puck to abort the duel, mislead the lovers through the night, and use the herbal antidote (Dian's bud) on Lysander, thus restoring his love for Hermia. The play begins to reverse direction and return toward order, daylight, and Athens. Puck uses trickery to mislead the young men, prevent the duel, collect the lovers in one place, and put them to sleep. By using Dian's bud on Lysander, he moves the love relationships into the fourth stage (as realized in IV.1.): two reciprocally loving couples.

(13) Resolution begins in IV.1. with the rapprochement between Oberon and Titania. Oberon uses Dian's bud (IV.1.70) to release Titania from her infatuation partly because he has begun to pity her (IV.1.46) and partly because she has surrendered the changeling (IV.1.52–62). Oberon also orders Puck to restore Bottom to his original shape so that he can awaken and return to Athens; the events of the night will become an inexplicable dream for him. When Titania awakens, she is restored to harmony and amity with Oberon. This restoration is visually symbolized on stage by music and dancing (IV.1.82–92), traditional symbols of harmony and order. This rapprochement is significant because it restores cosmic order and it suggests that order will be similarly restored at every other level of action.

(14) The play reverses direction when the fairies exit and the rulers enter (IV.1.101), shifting from night to day, gods to human beings, and nature to society. Theseus and Hippolyta are hunting on the morning of their wedding day. Theseus spots the lovers, has them awakened, and asks for an explanation of their presence together. The explanations reflect the dreamlike confusion that the lovers have experienced. Lysander begins to tell how he and Hermia arrived in the wood (145–152), but Egeus interrupts, demanding legal action. Egeus has not changed; he has not gone through the long night of passion and confusion which has purged the minds and cleared the eyes of the lovers. Demetrius best expresses the changes that have occurred (159–175). He admits that fury and fancy (both irrational passions) drove him and Helena to the wood, but that his infatuation with Hermia now seems childish. Hermia and Helena do not speak. The conflict resolves into two reciprocally loving couples. Given this situation, Theseus overrules Egeus and abrogates the Athenian law. This reversal of Theseus's earlier position, possible because Demetrius no longer wants to marry Hermia, represents a moderation of Theseus's earlier rigidity and an acknowledgment that there are powers above the law.

(15) Comedies often end in marriage, and this one has been headed toward a royal wedding since the opening. Yet this wedding and two others occur offstage and are reported by Snug (IV.2.13–15). Why didn't Shakespeare stage the weddings? One answer is found in the dynamics of the play; one line of action ("Pyramus") remains incomplete. Staging the weddings would provide premature formal closure. This, in turn, opens the question of why "Pyramus" is treated as a co-equally important line of action.

(16) Pyramus and Thisby are young lovers separated by a wall because their families have a long-standing feud. They plan to overcome these obstructions by leaving the city and meeting at night at Ninus's

tomb. The plan leads to disaster because of irrational haste. Thisby arrives at the tomb first, is frightened by a lion, and drops her cape, which the lion bloodies. Pyramus, finding the bloodstained cape by moonlight, assumes that Thisby is dead and kills himself. Thisby returns to the tomb, finds Pyramus's body, and also commits suicide. The parallels between this story and Romeo and Juliet are numerous.

(17, 18) The masque combines a number of traditional symbols of harmony and order to bless the marriages (it thus replaces the wedding as the formal ritual of order and closure that ends the play). It also embodies a fusion of the two worlds of the play; the kingdom of night, the supernatural, magic, and dreaming flows into the world of daylight, order, and rationality. In the epilogue, Puck suggests that we should consider the play a dream that we experienced while slumbering. The statement neatly puts us on a par with Bottom and the lovers. It also links fantasy and imagination with drama and art (illusion) and thus reinforces the connection among poets, lovers, and madmen advanced by Theseus (V.1.4–22).

Discussion of the General Questions, page 1380

(1, 2) Most of the characters are flat, conventional, and representative; some are symbolic. Theseus and Hippolyta represent law, order, and rationality. Theseus changes to the extent that he learns to moderate the rigor of the law. Egeus is the conventional angry and irrational father who obstructs love. He neither learns nor changes. The four lovers are equally conventional and flat, but they are educated and purged of love madness through their long night of chaos and passion in the woods. When they awaken, their relationships and feelings have become regenerative and reciprocal love. Oberon and Titania symbolize the power and cycles of nature. In addition, they represent chaos and passion (at first) just as Theseus and Hippolyta represent order. They change to the extent that their relationship returns to harmony and accord. The mechanicals, also conventional, represent the lower class. Although the play is set in ancient Athens, they are clearly based on Elizabethan rather than Greek or mythological figures.

(3) Each group of characters has a characteristic mode of language. Theseus and Hippolyta speak blank verse, as befits their status and dignity as rulers. The four lovers speak mostly in less dignified and more amusing rhymed couplets. When not playing roles in "Pyramus," the mechanicals speak in prose, consistent with their low status. The fairies speak in both blank verse and in rhymed couplets, but they are also the only characters to speak in lyric poetry (variously rhymed lines of iambic tetrameter and other

variant meters). This kind of verse sets them apart from the rest of the characters and suggests their complete otherness from the human beings.

(4, 5) The two-place structure, its symbolic import, and its relationship to the dramatic structure of the play are discussed in the sample essay (pages 1421–1422). Both the world of the forest and the world of the city change for the better. The woods, initially disordered (as is all of nature, see II.1.81–117), become ordered with the resolution of the conflict between Oberon and Titania. Similarly the city, which initially embodied overly rigid law and order, is modified by Theseus's decision to overrule Egeus and permit the marriage of Hermia and Lysander. Most of the characters who make the round-trip from city to woods to city undergo some sort of learning or altering experience which improves them. The lovers suffer the dream-like chaos of Oberon's manipulation, and emerge more rational and matured. The rulers (especially Theseus) learn that law must be tempered by judgment and higher authority. The mechanicals neither learn nor change; they go to the woods to rehearse, and their round-trip simply heightens the confusion.

(6) Helena's soliloquy is a key thematic statement of the characteristics of irrational love. This kind of love distorts perception and evaluation (I.1.232–233); it is blind, rash, immature, changeable, and lacking in judgment (234–241). Many of the relationships in the play illustrate this type of love. Chief among these is the shift in passion produced among the four lovers by love-in-idleness. The most extreme instance of this type of love is Titania's blind infatuation with Bottom. In some ways, the lovers are educated and transformed during their long night in the woods; they emerge into the daylight world on the day of Theseus's wedding with a stronger and more regenerative love.

(7, 8) *A Midsummer Night's Dream* explores the nature of drama and the links between drama (illusion, art) and imagination (passion, madness, dreaming, and love) in three ways: 1–through the mechanicals' production of "Pyramus"; 2–through the internal audience's reaction to "Pyramus"; and 3–through thematic statements (such as Theseus's in 5.1.4–22). The mechanicals have no understanding of drama as a mimetic art. Their concerns over lion, sword, moonshine, and wall (3.1.) and the solutions they come up with indicate that they make no distinction between illusion (drama, art) and reality. In addition, they assume that their audience will make no distinction; the difference never occurs to them. The internal audience for "Pyramus"—the nobility and the four lovers—are more concerned with their own wittiness than with the play. For the lovers, the play-within-the-play recapitulates lessons that they have just experienced, but the connection never occurs to them. Shakespeare expects us to be a better audience, seeing both the connection between the main plot and the "Pyramus" plot, and judging the lovers on their failure to see it. In opposition to all this failure, the play includes a thematic line that argues for a linkage among passion, imagination, dreaming, illusion, art, and love. This connection is articulated (negatively) by Theseus at the beginning of Act Five and underscored in Puck's epilogue.

(9) Both plays-within-plays parallel the main plots of the plays of which they are a part. In *Hamlet,* the drama is made to be an exact parallel of the murder of King Hamlet by Claudius. Thus, "The Murder of Gonzago," with some parts putatively interpolated by Hamlet himself, is used as an ongoing part of the plot whereby Hamlet tries to secure confirmation of the initial accusations of the Ghost against Claudius. In addition, "The Murder" occurs midway in the play, and it is a crisis and climax in which the future actions of both Hamlet and Claudius are set. "Pyramus and Thisby," by contrast, is a part of the sub-plot concerning the rude mechanicals, but coming at the end as it does, it also serves as an alternative ending and as a commentary on the action. Therefore, it serves two purposes: (a) to show the realistic, true-to-the-world fact that confusions such as those dramatized in the main plot can produce disastrous outcomes, and also (b) to tie together the upper and lower groups of people presented in the play, demonstrating the qualities of each and the comparative understandings of each. "Pyramus," while a commentary, is also a part of the resolution of the plot and a return to the world as it was before the confusions of the play.

The Theater of Molière, *pages 1380–1383*

Molière, *Love Is the Doctor, pages 1385–1400*

This play is one of Molière's typical farcical comedies. He put it together rapidly, within a five-day period, in 1665, and it was well received at the Court of Louis XIV at Versailles. It demonstrates to the highest degree the plot of intrigue, so much so that it would serve as a prototype for many such plays that followed it in the seventeenth century, and also for romantic-intrigue novels in the eighteenth. The major flaw in *Love Is the Doctor* is the introduction of the detail about the traveling druggist or Mountebank who is selling "Orviétan." This allusion is totally lost on a modern audience, and Molière, after the brief scene between Sganarelle and the Mountebank, drops this thread of the plot entirely. For us to read the play successfully, we must take the Mountebank episode, thematically, as an example of the gullibility that will lead Sganarelle to be fleeced of his fortune in the concluding scenes.

Answers to the Study Questions, pages 1401–1402

(1) We learn in the first scene that Sganarelle is wealthy and that he has self-seeking relatives and friends. He is a widower and he has only one daughter, who has symptoms of some sort of illness. He shows a willingness to listen to suggestions, but he also shows shrewdness in exposing the motivations of those who try to use his openness to make money for themselves. He is, in effect, a traditional *satirist* figure; that is, he is the character in a satire who makes satiric commentaries (as at the end of the scene), who serves to bring out the negative qualities of others, and who himself exhibits qualities that the author is satirizing.

(2) The relationship on Sganarelle's part is one of paternal dominance, and on Lucinda's part is one of assumed deference. Sganarelle speaks to Lucinda as though to a tiny girl, not to a young woman. He clearly is concerned about her, but is totally unable to understand her. The relationship is shown to be exaggerated and comic because the play is a comedy, and a disobedient daughter (like, say, Juliet in *Romeo and Juliet*) would set a tone not of comedy but of tragedy.

(3) It is important structurally to learn that a young man has shown interest in Lucinda, and that he has made overtures to her, because it is this young man (Clitander) who intrigues with Lisette to win her in marriage in the last scenes of the play. His later appearance is hence not illogical, for, though the audience has not seen him, both Lisette and Lucinda have.

(4) Lisette is the *soubrette*, the maidservant who is secure in the home and gets the plot moving. She is a figure out of the *Commedia dell'Arte*, essentially flat, exhibiting great independence, and very little sign of humility or deference toward her master. She is an intimate of Lucinda, inasmuch as Lucinda's mother is dead, and a maidservant would have been a greater friend and intimate anyway (cf. the Nurse in *Romeo and Juliet*).

(5) Sganarelle does not want his daughter married (I.5) because he wants to keep all his money for himself, and does not want to give his daughter and her husband a marriage settlement. This strain of selfishness and his clear disapproval of his daughter's hopes of married happiness make him a deserving gull at the end. If he had granted consent, he would not have forced Lucinda and Clitander into the intrigue, and everyone would

have been happy about the relationship, including Sganarelle himself.

(6) In III.1, Dr. Fillpocket speaks extensively of how doctors hoodwink gullible people and thereby fill their pockets. Sganarelle is one of the gullible ones of whom Fillpocket speaks. Furthermore, this quality of gullibility is essential as a trait if Clitander is to be successful when he masquerades as a famous doctor and whisks Lucinda away right under Sganarelle's nose. Lisette's skepticism refutes Sganarelle's exaggerated faith, and it puts Molière's satire into prominence.

(7) Dr. Slicer is positive about his knowledge of medical practice, and his authority is the word of the ancient Hippocrates. Lisette, by contrast, speaks from her knowledge of reality. The person is dead, and no ancient medical authority can contradict that. The contrasting views, with Lisette deflating Dr. Slicer's pomposity, makes the scene comic.

(8) Pantomime action is an important part of the staging of a play. Students might imagine the sorts of responses that people might make when receiving a large sum of money. Some students who have a background in dance or theater might even create movement that would illustrate Molière's point about the greediness of the doctors.

(9) By having the doctors discuss their mules and horses, together with the controversy in which a sensible doctor is censured by a stupid doctor who outranks him, Molière demonstrates the venality and lack of professional integrity of the doctors.

(10) Slicer recommends bleeding; De Pits, purgation through vomiting; Gouger, laxatives and also, apparently, emetics; Golfer recommends both purging and bleeding (probably until the patient dies). The doctors Slicer and De Pits are truthful because they each attack the proposed remedies of the other. The scenes of the prescriptions are comic because the doctors are demonstrating their witlessness and their combativeness.

(11) Sganarelle is alternately amused and befuddled by the jargon of the doctors. His attempt to find medical truth causes him to seek out a charlatan of another sort. By the time Clitander appears in the final act, Sganarelle is a sitting duck for any medical quack who comes along.

(12) Ostensibly, Dr. Fillpocket is telling his colleagues to present a united front of knowledge to the world. In practice, however, his logic is that the reason for unity is to keep up public confidence in doctors, or else the profession will lose its privileges and its wealth. The speech is comic because, presumably, the audience is only overhearing it; the doctor may therefore express truths that otherwise would never be uttered by the medical profession. The questions about seriousness and the degrees

of truth will best be left to students for their discussion and/or writing.

(13) The stratagem is that Clitander will masquerade as a famous doctor who cures patients by unusual means such as "words, sounds, letters, signs, and mystical rings" (III.5.5). That Sganarelle has already shown great faith in doctors is assurance that he will trust a doctor that Lisette recommends (after all, she has shown skepticism, and her enthusiasm must therefore seem to him like the highest recommendation possible).

(14, 15) The irony is that Clitander is speaking directly and honestly to Lucinda, while Sganarelle believes that he, as a "doctor," is deceiving her in order to cure her. Sganarelle's joining in on the deception, and signing away the twenty million, is of course the deception being practiced on him even though he believes that he is the one doing the deceiving. The final scene is kept comic and light by the singing and dancing. A dark production could keep Sganarelle disgruntled, but more likely is that Sganarelle joins the concluding dance. His last words indicate anger, but they could also suggest that he simply gives up and participates in the merriment.

Discussion of the General Questions, page 1402

(1) Because Sganarelle is the figure in constant focus in the play, he is the protagonist. This role is complicated by the fact that the antagonism is the love of Lucinda and Clitander, and by the comic plot that makes them triumphant at the end. Conflicts develop between Sganarelle and a–his friends and relatives, b–his daughter, c–Lisette, and finally d–the scheme of Clitander and Lucinda to marry despite his opposition, and to wheedle him out of twenty million. There are also amusing conflicts between Lisette and the doctors, and among the doctors themselves. The satiric conflict is that of quackery and ignorance within the medical profession.

(2) The "biter bitten" comic twist is a common one in humor. Shakespeare, for example, uses it in *Twelfth Night* (Malvolio), and Jonson uses it in *Volpone*. Sganarelle is the bitten one in *Love Is the Doctor,* for his unwillingness to consent to a marriage for his daughter produces the plot that enables Lucinda and Clitander to win the twenty million away from him. Humor is a complicated topic. Henri Bergson draws attention to the idea that the inability to adjust is the primary cause of humor. Certainly this inability is present in Sganarelle, who is the rigid and unyielding *paterfamilias* in many respects. In addition, Thomas Hobbes holds that laughter develops from superiority over a comic object or butt of humor. Sganarelle, like Malvolio, is such an object. The topic of laughter is interesting, and it makes for both informative and amusing classroom discussion.

(3) To deal with Professor Knutson's assertions, students should focus on the doctor scenes: II.2–5, and especially III.1.

(4) Of the funny physicians, Dr. Slicer stands out by supporting a senior doctor who killed a patient (II.3.8) and by his insistence on medical procedures even though patients are dying. Dr. Gouger is funny in recommending a treatment, reassuring Sganarelle that if Lucinda dies, the death will have happened "in accordance with proper procedures" (II.5.9). Obviously, the most fully developed doctor is Fillpocket, who shows a good deal of self-awareness and also cleverness in his speech to the contending doctors. The "rabbit" and the "turtle" are funny, while not, of course, real. In fact the doctors are all lively and memorable. Probably the issue of roundness and dynamism is not relevant to the group as a whole as Molière presents them to us. Because they are satiric figures, they are necessarily flat and representative, even though they also are the cause of explosive laughter.

Beth Henley, *Am I Blue, pages 1402–1417*

Answers to the Study Questions, pages 1417–1418

(1) Ashbe's actions and speeches set her out as an unusual person, to say the least. Ordinarily, people do not hide under other people's raincoats, nor do they crawl under tables (when sober) to escape the gaze of waitresses. Ashbe's speech demonstrates that she is streetwise and brash, and her comparison of herself with Robin Hood suggests a vivid imagination together with the brashness to carry out her pose. In a real sense, Ashbe is resorting to her poses and her inhibition-free speech in an apparent attempt to find herself and establish her character.

(2) Ashbe's family seems to be in ruins, and this aspect of her life should be taken seriously. Her father is frequently gone, perhaps on business, but it seems that he has become a drunkard and does little to assist her with her life beyond maintaining the dreary and messy apartment to which he occasionally returns. Ashbe's mother has gone entirely, and is now living in Atlanta and is staying with a woman named Martine (speech 339). The implication is that Ashbe is completely on her own. She must therefore carry on and try to establish her identity without any of the supports that traditionally should come from the family.

(3) Ashbe may be fabricating what she says about G. G., but she does succeed in tearing down the woman whom John Polk has a ticket to see. Her motive is not clear, since she has just met John Polk, but it would

seem that she immediately likes him, and does what she can to forestall his going to the house, first by denigrating Myrtle, and then by indicating the danger at the house ("Only two murders and a knifing in its whole history," speech 49). This speech, together with her description of the type of fancy dress ball she would prefer to attend, suggests her aversion to the life which she is being forced to live, and her yearning for something better.

(4) John Polk is a person cut adrift, just like Ashbe. Under pressure to conform in all the areas of his life, he is frustrated and uncertain. He thinks negatively of both going to college and spending his life in the family soybean business. His uncertainty is shown in the facts that he has felt drawn to the ministerial profession, but that he is uncertain about his theological beliefs. To help himself socially, he has joined a fraternity, but he dislikes the boisterousness of the fraternity activities, and he feels that the birthday appointment that his frat brothers gave him with the whore is casting him in a role he does not wish to take. Ashbe notes his qualities of acquiescence and passivity by calling him a "sheep" (speech 257), and he soon recognizes the aptness of her remarks.

(5, 6) For people who have not known each other more than a few minutes, Ashbe and John Polk begin arguing and taunting each other quickly. Rather than dividing them, however, the arguments bring them together. When John Polk offers to leave after she calls him a sheep, she urges him to stay, and describes her words as "friendly criticism" (speech 265). It seems that Ashbe uses her arguments to encourage John Polk to describe his circumstances and feelings. Ashbe, by contrast, volunteers much information about herself in her taunts. John Polk turns Ashbe down in her offer to make love because he says that he likes her—the implication being that he respects her as an individual and not as a sexual object. His suggestion that they dance all night shows that they recognize each other as kindred spirits, who together feel some of the security they have been seeking.

Discussion of the General Questions, page 1418

(1) The plot of *Am I Blue* develops from the conflicts of both Ashbe and John Polk against the circumstances of their lives and families. Both are fighting against loneliness and alienation. The crisis and climax of the plot is the phone call that Ashbe receives from her father (speech 267). We conclude from her conversation that her father is drunk again, and that he is trying to use her to make contact, for some reason, with her mother. After Ashbe hangs up, her vulnerability shows clearly: (She looks at him blankly, her mind far away). From this point the two become more clearly

drawn to each other, as though together they may contend more strongly against the situation and attitudes that have been suppressing them. The resolution of the plot is the immediate security of their friendship.

(2) There are a number of separate techniques in Henley's verbal comedy. The major one is Ashbe's selection of topic material. When she mentions a butcher and a silver pirate, for example, she exhibits a flamboyant and unusual imagination which produces laughter. The technique of understatement also evident, as in the description of Myrtle's acne (speech 71) and the reference to the two murders and a knifing (speech 49). There is also the reversal of what is expected, as in the question of what soft drink to include in rum (speech 148). Throughout, Henley maintains a surface easiness and humor, even though the seriousness of the plight of Ashbe and John Polk is also constantly emerging.

(3) Both Ashbe and John Polk are appealing because they are vulnerable, pleasant, questing characters. John Polk is more realistically presented than Ashbe, whose oddities would make her out of place in most circumstances. Both are more articulate than young people in their positions would probably be normally. They develop as characters because they quickly see the benefits to be gained from continuing their friendship. (John Polk, for example, speaks about the need for being able to speak to a girl the next day.) Both characters may also be seen symbolically or typologically, for both are in the stage of the quest and initiation. John Polk, however, rejects his initiation in favor of continuing his quest for identity with Ashbe.

(4) The major theme in the play concerns the difficulty that young people experience when they have not been able to establish certainty in their lives or when they are alienated from the roles they are expected to fulfill. The immediate effect of the comic mode is to create a surface diversion from the seriousness of the theme, but the language also exposes the uneasiness and uncertainty felt by the major characters. In fact, the dialogue, together with the change of scene to Ashbe's home, finally focuses on the plight of the characters, and hence stresses the thematic point that friendship and communication can help people to face and begin to surmount their difficulties.

(5) Although the French Quarter is frequently an exotic setting suggesting leisurely and pleasant days and ways, in *Am I Blue,* which takes place in some of the less savory parts of the French Quarter at night during a rain in November, the district and its clientèle symbolize the dangers that Ashbe and John Polk are facing. The two murders and the

knifing (speech 48), though they are mentioned only briefly and comically, indicate the menace and brutality that people may escape only when they are certain about themselves and are able to direct themselves elsewhere. The interactions of John Polk and Ashbe with the street folk indicate a certain knowledge of the streets as long as there are no threats. The drunken man vomiting in the street may symbolize the depths that people can reach if they never put their lives together (perhaps like Ashbe's father, who is apparently an alcoholic).

Writing About Comedy, *pages 1418–1423*

Unlike the discussion of writing in the previous chapter, this material does not introduce any new types of essay. Rather, the section on questions for discovering ideas returns to a focus on the traditional elements of drama. Students are referred to the relevant section of Chapter 26 for additional review of these elements. We recommend that you encourage them to read (or reread) this material before they begin to plan and write. In these pages, we discuss specific aspects of plot, structure, character, and language that can be especially appropriate for comedy. Keep in mind, however, that the comedies in this chapter lend themselves to almost any kind of writing assignment.

The sample essay on *A Midsummer Night's Dream* (pages 1421–1422) illustrates how setting, symbolism, and comic structure may be explored at the same time. The essay thus links and considers three separate elements. In making writing assignments, you may want to consider topics that ask students to deal with one, two, or even three elements that are related and work toward a single effect. Once again, however, we suggest that you warn students about the necessity of focus, development of a few key ideas, and selectivity. As with most other writing projects, students will frequently employ the scatter method, introducing numerous observations about many elements in a disorganized manner. You should strive to encourage a selective focus.

Writing Topics about *Comedy: Restoring the Balance,* *page 1423*

(1) The first direction contains enough questions to enable students to develop a fairly complete essay if they do no more than answer them. The problem, of course, is in organizing all the answers and ideas into a coherent whole.

(2) The second topic is a good one because it forces the consideration of the differences between the tragic and comic modes. Students might use examples from other works to reinforce their points about Molière's comic methods. In *Hamlet,* for instance, Ophelia is in a position like Molière's Lucinda. Her father, Polonius, tries to influence her, and her inability to resist, as Lucinda does, finally drives her to madness and suicide (there are, of course, other disastrous influences acting on Ophelia). Similarly, Mabel Pervin of Lawrence's "The Horse Dealer's Daughter" (page 391) has been driven to the point of suicide after losing first her mother and then her father. We may conclude that Meda Roth of Munro's "Meneseteung" (page 211) has been truncated psychologically by her many years of caring for her father. As a result, she is unable to develop an adequate sexual relationship when it is offered to her. With examples like these for contrast, students might be able to work out more clearly the nature of Molière's comic resolution of the effects of the Sganarelle-Lucinda relationship.

(3) Although many of the circumstances of the characters in *Am I Blue* are serious, the play nevertheless causes amusement. The actions of John Polk and the strangeness of Ashbe, such as her use of kool aid, would provoke laughter in an audience. Students will of course describe their own reactions, but the serious underpinning of the comic development makes the play worthy of serious consideration. *Am I Blue* is not simply entertaining.

(4) The fourth question is a big one, most appropriate for a long investigative essay after a term's work. Some of the answers that students may find may be that comic material does not need to be light, that a comic resolution might easily become tragic under the wrong circumstances, that jokes are funny but not essential to comedy, that farce is also not essential and that too much of it might interfere with the seriousness of what happens in comedy. The "edges" between comedy and tragedy can be dealt with only if students introduce comparisons with tragedies, such as *Hamlet,* where many of the situations could turn out well for the

characters if there were not such destructive forces at work. If students turn to this problem, the essay will become even more extensive than if the three comedies alone are treated. The edge between farce and comedy is more readily dealt with within the scope of the plays included in this chapter. The answer is probably one of emphasis; a certain amount of farce and business enhances the happiness and hope that one looks for in comedy. Too much clowning action, on the other hand, will turn anything into a farce.

(5) Suggestions for how to handle this assignment may be found on text pages 1322, 1324, and 1383–1384, where the types of intrigue plot related to the *Commedia dell'Arte* are described. The pattern of lovers being blocked and overcoming the blockers is the type to be explained, and students may bring out important contrasts while explaining the similarities of the situations in the two plays.

(6) The last writing suggestion is designed to give students some of the joy of writing creatively. They might believe that they need to write jokes, and will need assurance that writing jokes and one-liners is not necessary for this assignment. (They are not, indeed, practicing to become comic dramatists.) The essential thing about the assignment is to concentrate on the situation, and to imagine what characters in particular situations and with certain interests might say under the circumstances that the students create. Again, as with all the creative-writing assignments, the critical essays of self-analysis are quite important, so that students may articulate the discoveries they have made about the principles of good comic writing.

Chapter Twenty-nine
Pages 1424–1575

Realistic and Nonrealistic Plays: Varying the Idea of Drama as Imitation

This chapter examines in some detail the differences between realism and nonrealism in drama. Unless you begin teaching drama with plays from this chapter, these should not be totally new concepts to students. Because all dramatic conventions are nonrealistic, students should be familiar with some nonrealistic devices and techniques before they read this material. Most of the plays in Chapter 26, for example, are fairly realistic, whereas *Oedipus the King* and *Death of a Salesman,* both in the *Tragedy* chapter, demonstrate much that renders them unrealistic as opposed to realistic. In this chapter, 29, the plays show varying degrees of realism. *The Sandbox* is farthest away from reality, with *Mulatto* and *A Doll House* on the other end as close to reality as possible. *The Glass Menagerie* is in the middle, with qualities of both realism and nonrealism.

Another way of approaching realistic and nonrealistic drama in class is to discuss the extent to which a play acknowledges or ignores its own fictiveness and the presence of an audience (or reader). Because realistic plays attempt to imitate life as closely as possible, they do not contain devices that call attention to their own existence as plays, nor do they create any direct links with the audience (even though living actors always respond to the reactions they are getting). The ideal realistic play exists in isolation, and we as an audience are the unacknowledged spies watching through the missing "fourth wall." In contrast, nonrealistic plays usually contain devices that emphasize both the theatricality of the moment and the presence of spectators (or readers).

A 1950 filmed version of *The Glass Menagerie* (107 minutes, B/W, starring Jane Wyman, Gertrude Lawrence, Kirk Douglas, and Arthur Kennedy) is available for classroom use. The films may be obtained from many distributors, including Films Inc. (1144 Wilmette Ave., Wilmette,

IL 60091). If you use films or videotapes to help students appreciate the plays, you might remind them that movies are very different from staged plays. In film, directors gain a much broader canvas and the ability to use cinematic effects such as close-ups and quick cuts; these are impossible on the stage. Conversely, film loses live theater's sense of the entire stage action and scenery, and also the intimacy that connects the actors with the audience. See also Chapter 30, on Film.

EDWARD ALBEE, *The Sandbox, pages 1430–1436*

Albee's absurdist play satirizes the middle class, our treatment of old people, and the American way of death. Language and character are especially effective in building the play's satirical thrust. Many of the absurdist and unrealistic techniques are designed to reveal the emptiness of Mommy and Daddy by stripping them down to caricatures. The bare stage and minimal props reinforce the sense of theatricality and illusion. The sandbox turns out to represent the beach and to symbolize the grave. The opening notes imply that the characters are symbolic and representative. Mommy and Daddy are introduced as universals without regional identity. The Young Man is identified as the Angel of Death. Other techniques, like giving cues to technicians and speaking to the audience, have the effect of reminding us that we are dealing with an artifact rather than with reality.

Answers to the Study Questions, page 1436

(1) Mommy identifies the beach to establish setting. The minimal set does not do this. The family has come to the beach to watch Grandma die and to bury her. Death and funeral are conflated into a single, hurried, and cliché-ridden process. Mommy and Daddy await the off-stage *rumble* (death, page 1434) so that they may be rid of Grandma.

(2) Daddy's whining, along with his deference to Mommy, his vagueness, and his questions, defines him as passive and dominated, a "Caspar Milquetoast" type. He is clearly the weaker character. Mommy treats him with firmness, scorn, and condescension. He treats her with fawning admiration and fear.

(3) Grandma's two modes of language—howling nonsense to Mommy and Daddy and speaking articulately to us and the Young Man—embody a nonrealistic technique that allows language to reflect attitude. The howls that Mommy and Daddy get are what they expect of old people; the implication is that they would not hear sense in any event, so that, as far as they are concerned, the old woman might just as well howl. The

second mode places the reader and audience in a parallel position with the Young Man (Death). We thus see Grandma as a character in her own right, unlike Mommy and Daddy.

(4) The Young Man also symbolizes youth and the younger generation. As a Hollywood actor who has not yet been given a name by his studio, he also represents superficiality and loss of identity. His pursuit of physical health and the body beautiful is another symbol of surface concerns and ego-orientation. Grandma treats him intimately and personally, as though Death is as pleasant as Youth. The Young Man treats her respectfully and affectionately.

(5) The "off-stage rumble" (page 1434)is a traditional and trite way on stage and in films of signifying trouble or danger. It is treated exactly that way in the play. The characters recognize it as a trite convention, but they also recognize it as the harbinger of Grandma's death.

(6) Mommy and Daddy react to Grandma's death with clichés about how "happy" Grandma looks, how "brave" they must be, and how they must now "face the future" (page 1435, speeches 72–77). Grandma recognizes their responses as empty, conventional, and trite; by mimicking Mommy and Daddy, she reveals how vapid and self-centered they are.

(7) The catastrophe occurs when Grandma realizes that she really is dying (page 1435, speech 78). The play resolves on a note of acceptance and forgiveness. Grandma praises the "actor" who has played the Angel of Death, and welcomes her own death by forgiving the Angel.

Discussion of the General Questions, page 1436

(1) All these theatrical devices, some being more appropriate for a rehearsal rather than a performance, seem designed to destroy any shreds of realism or verisimilitude, and to remind us that we are dealing with dramatic illusion. These are alienating or distancing devices, designed to push us away from the play and to create objectivity and aesthetic distance.

(2) All the characters are flat, static, representative, and symbolic; the absence of names underscores this representation. Mommy and Daddy, particularly, have been reduced from individuals to functions. They have no names, but only titles—the ones assigned by tiny children, and they symbolize the type of marriage from which all love and intimacy have been drained. To the degree that their relationship contains qualities of middle-class life, they symbolize the vacuity of the middle class. Grandma symbolizes old age and traditional values; her treatment symbolizes the discarding of values and contemporary attitudes toward the old. Albee

seems to view modern middle-class marriage and the family as destructive institutions that force people into dehumanizing molds.

(3) Albee uses repetition to emphasize the formulaic and vacuous lives of Mommy, Daddy, and the Young Man. Daddy's repetition of questions and complaints underscores his inanity and subservience to Mommy. Mommy and Daddy's language is fairly neutral, but Grandma's lines are full of dialect, idiom, and connotative words (fat cow, figgers, lordy) that help us define her and help her define her family. Mommy and Daddy speak in clichés, especially when talking about Grandma's death. Like repetition, the clichés underscore the conventionalized and meaningless pattern that life has become for these characters. There is no sincerity or feeling—just a collection of conventional responses.

(4) The way in which Grandma speaks may illustrate how Albee employs language to shape the work. Grandma suggests, through diction and exaggeration, that her relationship with Mommy and Daddy is terrible. She tells us in almost childish words and rhythms that Mommy and Daddy "fixed a nice place for me under the stove ... gave me an army blanket ... and my own dish" (page 1434, speech 52), thus claiming that she has been treated like a dog. Her words against Mommy also indicate her status as a person decreasing in power and status, for she refers to Mommy as "that big cow" and "that over there," suggesting childish scorn and disgust. Throughout the play, the many exclamations and simple greetings also indicate the stripped-down, elemental humanity with which Albee is dealing. See also study questions 3 and 6.

(5) The play presents three generations in Grandma (old, grandparents), Mommy and Daddy (middle-aged, parents), and the Young Man (youth, the child). Grandma embodies the values and standards of the past, especially in the solid self-sufficiency of the nineteenth century, when the country was still primarily agrarian and the family was a close-knit unit in which people presumably knew each other, worked with each other, and loved and respected each other. Mommy and Daddy apparently reflect people who have been dehumanized by the increasingly consumer-oriented, manipulated culture of radio and television of the late 1950s. The Young Man embodies the innocent and mindless focus on ego and "body beautiful" that Albee saw in the future.

Langston Hughes, *Mulatto*, *pages 1437–1462*

Mulatto is above all a realistic play. The interior is real and the references to the outside world are real. What happens on the outside, in fact, creates the oppressive reality of the inside. The prevailing social structure of the American South of the 1930s is really the antagonist of Robert, the son, and to a lesser degree of Colonel Norwood, the father. This massive social structure of white supremacy is condemnatory, and all its force is brought down on Robert. His fast driving of the Ford, his affront to the woman at the post office, the posse chasing him in the areas near the house, and his suicide at the end of the chase—all these are features of the play's predominant realism.

In light of Hughes's desire to dramatize the real circumstances of African Americans in the deep South during the 1930s, the play, indeed, had to be realistic. Anything unrealistic and impressionistic would have lessened the impact of his critique of white supremacy and his dedication to changing the system. His characters are therefore real, and their inner conflicts and their resistance to changing the status quo are real. The characterizations are real, from the rebellious Robert to the more subservient Billy and Sam. The most realistic of the characters is Cora, who has patiently tried to make the best of things. The final element of realism in this realistic play is Talbot's slapping Cora at the play's end. It is a symbol of suppression, although Cora bears it with the stoic patience she has always possessed. Hughes's implication is that it will be the Coras who will ultimately prevail.

Answers to the Study Questions, page 1462

Act I

1. To say that the children belong to anyone but Cora would be to acknowledge Colonel Norwood's paternity openly. At one point it is stated that all African American children are considered the children of their mothers only, thereby asserting perhaps covertly that all African American women are promiscuous.

2. The Colonel does not permit Sallie's bags to be carried out the front door because to do so would put her on an equal footing with him. The use of the front door is therefore unthinkable for him.

3. Robert's idea is that he has a right to claim both Norwood's paternity and name, and that at a future time he could inherit the property. Higgins and Norwood find such an attitude impossible and unacceptable because Robert is a "yellow" mulatto and has no rights at all.

4. Colonel Norwood wants no schooling available to the African Americans in his area or on his plantation. His thought is clearly that education would be a means by which blacks could justify claiming equal

rights with whites. He therefore advises Sallie to develop her cooking and cleaning skills, and to forget about education.

5. Talbot, representing the brute power by which Norwood rules, is the overseer who takes on the unpleasant task of keeping the blacks on the plantation in line. He is, of course frequently involved in the corporal punishment of blacks. Because he does not enter until late in the play his presence is an offstage threat, but his removal from the action also enables the domestic drama in the Norwood household to develop in intensity.

6. Higgins reports on Robert's insistence on being treated with the same fairness a white would be, i.e., to have his money returned, to make those behind him wait while he returns the broken package, etc. Robert, by his assertiveness, frightens the white clerk and then resists being thrown out of the post office. Higgins also says that Robert drives in a way which does not show sufficient deference to white drivers and pedestrians.

7. Higgins adopts the apparent attitude of white men of his class and place toward women of color, namely that these women exist for the sexual pleasure of white men and for the bearing of "yellow" children. In no way does Higgins ever believe that women of color are the equals of white women, who alone are to be treated with respect and who are the only ones fit to become the wives of white men.

8. Colonel Norwood's previous kindness toward Robert ceased once the child called him "papa" in public, and he probably wouldn't have accepted such an action privately either. The beating seems to have created considerable resentment in Robert, but it does not appear to have frightened him enough to cause him to be publicly cautious.

9. The Colonel has apparently decided not to continue Robert's education but to put him to work in the fields. Cora's general fear is that the Colonel will punish all the people of color on the plantation, and she fears that the Colonel will refuse to permit Sallie to go back to school.

Act II. Scene I.

10. For Colonel Norwood, the issue is control. As a man who has "never had trouble" with his "colored folks," he doesn't want to lose that authority. He expects gratitude for all he's done for those whom he terms "Cora's children," and he refuses to be pushed by Robert into acknowledging paternity for Robert or any other child. Yet the Colonel is being lenient to some degree, for he is willing to let Robert leave the plantation instead of being put to work in the fields. For Robert the issues are his determination to be acknowledged as Norwood's son and to be treated

and allowed to act like any normal man, with all legally guaranteed rights and privileges. In addition, he resents Norwood's attitude toward Cora.

11. As the Colonel explains it (speech 35), Robert's dilemma is that he is acknowledged and respected by neither the whites nor the African Americans. He belongs to neither group, and as a result he dislikes both groups. Because of this confrontation, the Colonel orders Robert off the plantation and even out of the state.

12. Robert believes that Norwood will not use the gun, and that beneath his white hostility of blacks Norwood believes he has obligations toward his mulatto children. There is both irony and pathos in the disparity between Norwood's verbal aggressiveness and dismissiveness toward Robert and the history of care (for that time and place) he has shown and continues to show by not carrying through on all his threats.

13. Talbot and the storekeeper immediately organize a hunt for Robert, with the obvious intention of lynching him if they find him. Robert realizes that he has virtually no chance to escape. Perhaps the fact that he refuses to run out the back (where he would not be seen by the whites) indicates his resignation to the fact that the only outcome of the situation, later if not sooner, is that he will be captured.

14. Cora's long speech serves to give us some sense of the life of a woman of color living in her circumstances in the South of her time. Her long sexual servitude to Norwood, and her own mother's apparent welcoming of her daughter's protected position, makes clear that supplying sexual services and household care was the only way for such women to survive. Clearly she has labored and schemed to protect her children, to get them educated and away from the South. Although such plans have doomed her to an old age without her children near her, the sacrifice was worth it to her. With Norwood's death and her son's imminent tragedy her servitude has ended, but she breaks emotionally and delivers the speech in a state of apparent dissociation which echoes the double life she has had to live. In such a state she makes her long pain and suffering clear as she could not have done had she remained fully lucid and in touch with reality.

Act II. Scene 2.

15. The undertaker and his companion return us brutally to the real world after the glimpse of Cora's broken state. Their insensitivity to Cora and their obvious enjoyment of their planned lynching deepen Hughes's rendering of the tragedy of African American life in the South during the time of the play.

16. The old ways of the South constituted virtual slavery for African Americans despite their alleged freedom after the Civil War. Clearly all African American women had to be sexually available to any white man who wanted them, and there was no redress for any person of color, black or white, after any kind of wrong.

17. Cora's second monologue tells us more about Colonel Norwood, making it clear that although he followed the "old ways" overtly, there was a side to him which found them repulsive. But clearly he was not strong enough to go against the mores of his time and place, and, quite possibly, had he done so he would have lost everything he had and become as much of an outsider as Robert was.

18. Robert kills himself in Cora's room. There are a number of reasons for which Talbot slaps Cora. First, he is frustrated because she has helped her son elude the rope. Second, his blow is a brutal way of showing her that she and Robert have not scored a victory by foiling the mob's intentions. Third, the slap symbolically represents the continuation of white supremacy over blacks.

General Questions:

1. The play contains may details about the plantations and the customs of the South because those details are peculiar to that time and place. Even though such conditions continued well up to the civil rights movement, some twenty-five or thirty years later, they are unknown to a new generation of Americans. The richness of detail here helps ground the play in reality, and keeps its meanings accessible to any reader or audience.

2. The front door symbolizes an open and acknowledged expression of the importance of those who can use it, and the insignificance and subservience of those who cannot. The incident in the post office shows how the caste system worked outside of Norwood's house, just as the front door shows how it worked inside that house. By insisting on equal treatment, and by inconveniencing whites standing in line behind him, Robert was violating all the customs of the state. And in driving the Ford fast and refusing to yield to white drivers and pedestrians, once again, he was displaying his insistence that he be treated as an equal.

3. Norwood is in some ways a pathetic figure because he cannot be who and what he really is. He observes the customs of his time and place openly, but in the privacy of his own home he breaks them in many ways. Participating in a lynching, but being sick afterward and killing the dogs which had hunted human prey; having both a white wife and an African

American mistress (perfectly acceptable), but then installing the mistress as the only woman in his house for all the years after the death of his wife (not acceptable); fathering mulatto children, but then educating them. In all these ways Norwood is unusual and, perhaps, doomed. Clearly, beneath his authoritarian and often verbally threatening exterior, there is far more fondness for his children and a far greater moral sensibility than his status enables him to acknowledge.

4. Robert is clearly very like his father in that he is, when young, assertive and willing to use his obvious good looks and intelligence to demand what he wants from the world. But he displays a tragic (and perhaps youthful) idealism which makes him blind to the realities of the world which has bred him but from which he has been away too long. In great measure he brings about his own destruction—inevitable, perhaps, granted the depths of self hatred he clearly expresses.

5. Cora is a truly pathetic figure, for she has been powerless all her life except for whatever power her sexual appeal to Norwood has given her. Using that power has clearly necessitated that she sacrifice any individual desires she herself may have had, but her careful use of her position has enabled her to give her children all the advantages that could have been available to children of mixed race in America of the 1930s. She seems aware that Norwood is a man of greater kindness that he often displays, and has some fondness for him despite their master-slave relationship. But in her two speeches we get both a picture of her life and of his, of her personality and of his, and we see, as she dissociates herself from reality, that the life-long stilling of her own emotional needs has quite suddenly, under the terrible shock of Norwood's death and the impending death of her son, driven her into a final emotional state in which painful reality has no further hold on her.

6. Granted the time and the place and the personalities of the persons involved, it appears unlikely that the play could have ended any way but tragically. The conclusion clearly shows Hughes' intention: to expose and attack the racial tragedy which America was living and which was headed to burst onto the stage of history and remain there for many decades. W. E. B. DuBois's comment that the major issue of the twentieth century in America would be the issue of color is clearly demonstrated by Hughes' play.

Henrik Ibsen, *A Doll House, pages 1466–1516*

Time has not dated this play or made it irrelevant. To the contrary, Ibsen anticipates recent concerns with identity crises, role playing, the rights of women, and the fulfillment of human potential. In teaching the play, there is a tendency to focus on the themes at the expense of other elements. Ibsen's ideas are important and attractive; they inform every aspect of the play. At the same time, other elements such as character, language, structure, and symbolism are worthy of class discussion; they all work together to shape the play's impact and meaning.

The play is carefully structured to build up to the climactic confrontation between Nora and Torvald (pages 1509–1515). Anxiety about money permeates the entire drama. With the appearance of Krogstad, tension increases considerably, and continues to rise until the catastrophe. Nora faces an expanding nest of dilemmas: Will Torvald find out about the loan and the forgery? What will happen when he finds out? What will happen to the marriage? Torvald's self-centered diatribe (pages 1509–1510, speeches 222–242) and the subsequent discussion answer these questions and comprise the catastrophe and resolution.

It is tempting to claim that the only puppet figure in the story is Nora, the doll living in her dollhouse. Certainly the doll-like role playing and make believe that she assumes is imposed by everything that society can bring to bear on a woman. The close of Ibsen's play makes it clear, however, that Nora is not the only doll. Torvald is as badly in need of education and self-fulfillment as Nora. Their role playing has failed to create for them the adult characters that could make them complete human beings. Interestingly, the play closes just as this educational phase of their lives is starting.

A Doll House, which has been extensively produced since the 1960s, is available in two 1973 films, both in color. One (106 minutes, available on videotape) was directed by Joseph Losey and stars Jane Fonda and Trevor Howard. The other (105 minutes) was directed by Patrick Garland and stars Claire Bloom and Sir Anthony Hopkins. More recently, Juliet Stephenson has done the starring role in a performance that was aired on public television in 1993.

Answers to the Study Questions, pages 1516–1517

(1) The opening stage direction indicates that the Helmer family is middle-class and reasonably well-off. Adjectives like *comfortably* and *tastefully* as well as the specific pieces of furniture names contribute to this impression. The stage direction also indicates that it is winter; throughout the play, the warmth inside the apartment contrasts with the cold of the Norwegian winter outside.

(2) Ibsen sets the tone and nature of the relationship early in the play

when Nora sneaks a macaroon and then lies about sweets to Torvald (page 1469, speech 63). The pattern of behavior is more appropriate for a parent-child relationship than for a husband and wife. Torvald often acts out the parental role. In Act 2, he tells Nora that she can make as much noise as she pleases since he will not hear her in the study (page 1466, speech 139). Nora understands the dynamics of the relationship; she tells Rank that "being with Torvald is a little like being with papa" (page 1491, speech 239). Torvald's paternalistic and superior attitude toward Nora is reflected in the terms of endearment he uses: *my little lark, my little squirrel, my little spendthrift.* Such phrases diminish and dehumanize Nora, and remind her of her inferior position. The repetition of *my* suggests that Torvald has objectified Nora and turned her into his possession—a common enough assumption of many men who accept a male-dominated view of the world. The repetition of *little* similarly indicates Torvald's perception of Nora as an object of no real significance. Nora's reference to herself as *we skylarks and squirrels* (page 1469, speech 49) and her flattery of Torvald's male ego (*some clever man*, page 1478, speech 287) suggests that she is aware of the situation, has come to terms with it, and is able to function within it.

(3) Torvald's pompous statements about borrowing (page 1467–1468, speeches 16, 22) indicate his tendency to moralize and to assume conventionally proper and acceptable positions that will make him appear good and responsible. Other instances of such posturing are found in his attitude toward unsavory cases (page 1490, speech 114), fear of losing face (page 1490, speech 115), working with Krogstad (page 1485, speech 478), and even Nora's decorating the Christmas tree (page 1469, speech 73). Torvald's moral posturing reflects his sexist and paternalistic attitudes, his concern with appearances, the degree to which he is trapped by background and society, and the role that he and society have successfully imposed on Nora. He is, in fact, pompous and sententious.

(4) The Helmers have spent years struggling to maintain appearances with too little money. Torvald has doled out the household funds carefully; Nora has scrimped in order to maintain a middle-class home and pay off the debt to Krogstad. Money is thus an abiding concern, especially for Nora. As the play opens, she sees a change in their financial situation (and a release from the burden of the debt) through Torvald's new job and big salary as director of the bank. She thinks that their "hard times are over" and that Torvald is "going to have a big salary and earn lots and lots of money" (page 1467, speech 13).

(5) Mrs. Linde's arrival (page 1470) is the first complication of the

play. Christine seems to be a striking contrast to Nora. She made an unhappy marriage for money and has had difficulty supporting herself since her husband's death. In contrast, Nora's life seems comfortable and her marriage loving. We discover, however, that Nora has her own burdens—the loan and the need to save and earn secretly to pay it back. In the course of the play, Nora moves progressively closer to Mrs. Linde's initial status. Ironically, Mrs. Linde moves in the other direction, toward an honest and equal union with Krogstad. At the end, the women have almost exchanged positions. Christine will find stability and security with Krogstad, while Nora will struggle alone to become a whole person. Nora's success in getting Christine a position at the bank ironically places her in jeopardy. Torvald gives her Krogstad's position. Krogstad, in turn, pressures Nora with threats of exposure to get him a better position.

(6) Ibsen uses both stage directions (movement, expression, tone) and dialogue to indicate that Krogstad (the second complication) is a threat to Nora (page 1475). Mrs. Linde starts, trembles, and turns away. Nora steps toward him and speaks in a strained, low voice. At this point in the play, Krogstad is symbolically linked with winter, sickness, and cold; when he goes into the study, Nora quickly stirs up the fire in the stove (warmth against coldness).

(7) The children's scene (page 1479) is significant for three reasons: (1) it shows us the happy domestic world of game playing that is threatened by Nora's crime, Krogstad's knowledge, and Torvald's conventional attitudes; (2) it identifies Nora as another child as she talks and plays hide-and-seek with her children; (3) it significantly expands the image of the Doll house and stands as a metaphor for life in the Helmer household. Nora's games with her little dolly children (page 1479, speech 312) are metaphorically parallel to the roles and games that Nora and Torvald play in their marriage.

(8) Nora's secret pride is that she saved Torvald's life by borrowing the money to pay for the year in Italy. Nora tells Christine Linde this to show that she has known troubles (page 1473, speech 179). Ibsen also hints at the crime here when Christine points out that "a wife cannot borrow without her husband's consent." The crime is forgery; Nora forged her father's signature on the bond with Krogstad (pages 1482, speech 401). Ironically, Nora's crime duplicates the crime that ruined Krogstad originally. Nora's motives transcend law; she forged the name in order to spare her father and save her husband (page 1483, speech 416) Krogstad points out that "the law cares nothing about motives" (page 1483, speech 413). At

the close of Act 1, Nora is faced with the probability that Krogstad will reveal the forgery and the loan—Nora's secret joy and pride—to Torvald.

(9) In Act 1, the Christmas tree is placed in the middle of the room and decorated with candles, flowers, and other ornaments (page 1483). At the opening on Act 2 (the next day), the tree is stripped of its ornaments and has burnt-down candle-ends on its disheveled branches (page 1486); it has also been shoved into the corner by the piano. The stripped tree and its displacement from the center of the room symbolize the erosion of Nora's happiness, the growth of anxiety, and the mounting threats to her carefully patterned life.

(10) Here, as elsewhere, Nora's references to herself as *your little squirrel* and *your skylark* (page 1464) indicate that she is consciously playing a role for Torvald. Nora offers to play her role to the hilt ("I will sing for you, dance for you") if Torvald will let Krogstad keep his post in the bank. Nora's awareness of the role that Torvald expects her to enact leads her to attempt to manipulate him. For additional discussion of role playing, see question 2 above and question 4 in the "General Questions."

(11, 14) Torvald's claim that he is "man enough to take everything on himself" (page 1491, speech 135) conforms to Nora's hope for a wonderful thing. Nora anticipates with both dread and longing that Torvald will assume full responsibility for the loan and the forgery. She asks Christine to witness that the act was solely hers in the event that "someone ... wanted to take all the responsibility, all the blame" (page 1498, speech 337). At the close of Act 2, Nora is waiting for this wonderful thing (page 1501 , speech 423). The thought of such an act of self-sacrifice never occurs to Torvald. Nora explains her hope for this wonderful thing in detail after Torvald's failure to measure up to her heroic ideal (page 1514, speech 340 ff.).

(12) While Torvald is Nora's husband-lover-father figure, Dr. Rank is her companion and friend. She talks to Rank about all sorts of things that she never mentions to Torvald. The flirtation (touching Rank, showing him the stockings) is motivated partly by Nora's desire to control him and partly by her need for money; she almost asks him for the necessary cash (page 1493, speech 209). Nora feels safe playing with Rank; she considers herself his equal (or perhaps his superior). When Rank admits his love for Nora (page 1494, speech 214), he changes the basis of the relationship and makes it impossible for Nora to go on. She can accept Rank's love and maintain her own sense of conventional morality so long as he does not tell her about it, but once the profession of love has been made, Nora has no choice but to reject it, along with him.

(13) The tarantella occurs at the close of Act 2, after Krogstad has made his threats and left the letter in the mailbox. The violence of the dance symbolizes Nora's mounting desperation. Torvald suggests that she is dancing as if her life depended on it and she replies, "So it does." The dance, linked to the poisonous bite of the tarantula, suggests that the poison of fear and deceit is eating away at Nora's life. Ironically Rank, who plays the piano for the dance, is also being destroyed by secret internal poisons.

(15, 16) Christine rejected Krogstad about ten years earlier out of a sense of duty to her helpless mother and two little brothers (page 1502, speech 21). Krogstad's prospects seemed hopeless, and Christine had to marry wealth. She suggests a union with Krogstad at this point as a kind of mutual redemption; she has faith in his real character and she needs something to work for (page 1502, speech 47). Unlike the Helmer's marriage, this will be a union of equals based on mutual need, understanding, honesty, and self-knowledge. Christine eventually decides that this same honesty and knowledge is necessary for the Helmers. Although she had originally planned to have Krogstad recall his letter, she decides that is must be read by Torvald so that the unhappy secret will be disclosed and the Helmers can have a complete understanding between them (page 1503, speech 77).

(17) Neither Torvald nor Nora is significantly moved by Rank's imminent death. Nora, who already knew about it, is preoccupied with Krogstad's letter and her hope/fear that Torvald will save her. Torvald's lack of concern reflects his consistent focus on himself and his own needs. At this moment, he is far more interested in Nora as a sexual object than he is in any news about Rank; he sees both Rank's visit and the news about the death as an intrusion.

(18) Torvald reacts to Krogstad's letter with rage, indignation, and fear for his own position. He condemns Nora and accuses her of destroying his happiness and future. His concern is completely focused on himself, his own reputation, appearance, and standing in the community (notice Torvald's frequent use of first-person pronouns here). Far from acting with the love and selfless heroism that Nora had imagined, Torvald plans to appease Krogstad and maintain appearances (page 1510, speech 242). Nora begins to see Torvald and her marriage clearly for the first time. The stage directions here (*steadily, questioningly*) indicate Nora's progressively greater understanding of Torvald and alienation from him.

(19) As a result of the experience, Nora has fully realized that her life with Torvald has been without substance, communication, or meaning (page 1512). She realizes that she has been Torvald's doll-wife (page 1512,

speech 286, the speech that explains the title) rather than a fulfilled individual. She understands that she must try to educate herself, to comprehend the world, to learn what she can about God and religion, to get to the "bottom" of things, and to fulfill her duties to herself despite the demands of husband, family, and social conventions and restrictions. She also sees that Torvald is an incomplete person who needs to seek his own education and self-knowledge.

Discussion of the "General Questions", page 1517

(1, 2) Almost all the elements are realistic. One of the less realistic aspects that deserves discussion is Ibsen's use of coincidence. Perhaps the least realistic element is Ibsen's symbolism. The Christmas tree and the tarantella are discussed above (questions 9 and 13). Rank symbolizes hereditary corruption and death. The macaroons become a symbol of Nora's doll-like relationship with Torvald. The children's presents (sword, doll, horse) symbolize the perpetuation of traditional and conventional sex-linked roles. The locked mailbox serves as an emblem of Nora's (and women's) second-class status in society and marriage. Nora's clothing is also employed symbolically. The fisher-girl costume evokes the south, Italy, freedom, and Nora's saving of Torvald. When she wraps this costume in black (her shawl and Torvald's domino, page 1485, speech 221), this "southern energy " is transformed into a symbol of death. The final change of costume (from party clothes to severe daytime dress) and the slamming of the door make concrete Nora's emotional and conceptual shift away from Torvald, marriage, family, and convention, and toward self-fulfillment. You might also ask students to consider Ibsen's symbolic use of time. The play moves inexorably toward midnight. Act 1 occurs during the day; Act 2 begins in daylight, but it grows dark during Nora's conversation with Rank. Act 3 begins at night and ends near midnight.

(3) Ibsen clearly wants us to see Nora as a victim, protagonist, and heroine, rather than a villain. He creates a situation in which Nora is trapped by convention, law, and custom. (Who is the villain or antagonist of the play? It seems to be Krogstad at first. Can we finally conclude that Torvald is the antagonist? Society?) Nora's abandonment of husband and children in the light of her duties to herself is intended to be taken as necessary, if not admirable. Audiences and students have not always seen it this way; traditional values can lead many to view Nora's departure as scandalous. Indeed, Ibsen was forced to write an alternative ending to forestall unauthorized tampering with the play. In this alternative ver-

sion, Torvald forces Nora to look upon her sleeping children and she collapses in tears, agreeing to remain in the home as a wife and mother. Ibsen considered this ending a disgusting travesty and advised theatrical producers not to use it. As a spur to class discussion, you can tell students about this alternative ending and ask them which they prefer. In order to elicit the best discussion, you should press students to explain and defend their choices.

(4) Role playing is linked to the idea of the doll house and the doll-like existence of the characters. For most of her life, Nora has happily taken the role of doll-child and doll-wife that her father, Torvald, and society have cast her in, and she has accepted the part willingly and has done a fine job with it. She has, in fact, done so well that she has taken financial responsibilities on herself, and as a result she has saved her husband's life. At the start of the play she seems to be childish and empty-headed, but we soon learn that she is a strong adult who is aware of the conflict between her expected role as an object for display and her real role as the bulwark of the family. At the close of the play, the adult in her has emerged, and she finally articulates her knowledge that her home has been a playroom, that she has been a doll-wife, and that her children have been little more than her own dolls (page 1512, speech 286). The servants keep the doll house running smoothly; Nora contends that they know how to run the home much better than she does. Torvald is perhaps the most interesting doll, partly because he has no awareness of the role imposed on him by background, heredity, and society. Unlike Nora, Torvald had no sense that he is acting out the role he has been conditioned to play. Nevertheless, Nora concludes that his life is as incomplete and doll-like as hers; he unconsciously follows a set of rules and roles as constricting and dehumanizing as those that have controlled Nora's life.

(5) Torvald is concerned with appearances and reputation rather than substance. This is evident throughout the play just about every time he opens his mouth. Examples are his version of the public image of the family, his own self-importance, his patronizing attitudes toward Nora, his inability to abide even the slightest hint of venality in others, and his holier-than-thou refusal to accept Krogstad back at the bank. Particularly telling in the discovery scene is that he does not ask Nora for any explanations, but immediately fulminates against her, disavows her as mother of their children, and generally reads her out of the human race. His utter emptiness and hypocrisy are shown in his quick delight once he learns that Krogstad will not inform further on Nora, and also in his pompous forgiveness of her, as though he will once again let her into his royal favor.

(6) Inherited or hereditary corruption (disease, evil, immorality) is an idea that fascinated Ibsen; he explored it at length in other plays, most notably in *Ghosts.* In *A Doll House,* the idea is applied to Nora, Krogstad, and Rank. Torvald asserts that Nora inherited her corruption and amorality from her father and might pass it on to her children (see pages 1442, speech 50, and 1485, speech 1555). Both Rank and Torvald contend that Krogstad is morally corrupted and that he may be infecting his own sons (pages 1450, speech 251, and 1460, speech 478). Rank is the most explicit symbol of corrupted blood; he is dying of the diseases he inherited from his morally and physically corrupted father (page 1462, speech 38).

(7) Ibsen's ideas about marriage, growth, and self-fulfillment are expressed partly by Christine Linde in conversation with Krogstad, but mostly by Nora at the close of the play. Christine has achieved a great deal of self-knowledge; she seeks some sort of fulfillment with Krogstad. Nora comes to realize that her own education and development as a complete person are more important than husband, marriage, children, law, religion, or convention. At the same time, she begins to question the validity of forces such as religion and law that have guided her life. Although Nora is the only character who acts in a radically untraditional manner on the basis of these realizations, Ibsen makes clear that all the characters locked into the system them prevailing need to develop themselves as human beings. Nora, for example, claims that Torvald needs to reshape his view of their lives as individuals, just as she is hoping to do. Her final words concern the idea of changing, and she seems to be hoping at the end for real changes to occur that would turn their "life together" into "real wedlock" (page 1516, speech 380). Thus, in terms of the play's themes, and in terms of the structure of the play, Nora's decision to leave and seek her improvement is a comedic improvement for the better. This has not prevented generations of readers and theater-goers from being shocked by her abandonment of marriage and children. The question may not be resolved in class discussion, but it should provoke heated argument.

(8) The three concluding essay subjects are designed to encourage students to take a position and then develop it and defend it with reference to the text of *A Doll House*. Probably students will take the position that the play is "something in between." A good argument can be made that the characters change for the better. And the conclusion may be interpreted as being affirmative, largely because all the major characters come to recognize their situations clearly whereas they do not possess that vision when the play opens.

Tennessee Williams, *The Glass Menagerie, pages 1518–1568*

This play combines realistic and nonrealistic techniques in a fairly even balance to produce a highly effective portrait of the Wingfield family. Many of the play's nonrealistic devices are discussed by Williams in the production notes (pages 1520–1521). In teaching the play, you can focus class discussion on each of these elements. All of Williams's nonrealistic devices heighten the fact that the play is a work of art, a construction. This, of course, is in keeping with the idea of a memory play.

The other primary focus for class discussion is the characters. They all live in fantasy worlds or pursue dreams that are doomed to fail. Amanda seeks release in her romanticized memories of Blue Mountain. She plans marriage or a business career for a daughter who is so reclusive that she can barely speak to strangers, let alone function effectively in the world at large. Laura takes shelter in a fantasy world built on old phonograph records and a collection of glass figurines. Tom, the would-be poet, dreams of a life of adventure based on the movies—his mode of escape from the apartment and the warehouse. Even Jim, "the most realistic character in the play," embodies failure. He has not fulfilled the promise he showed in high school, and it is clear that his dream of jumping from the warehouse to an executive position by way of night courses in public speaking and radio engineering is overly optimistic.

The Glass Menagerie is produced often by both professional and amateur groups. A 1973 color production first done for TV is available commercially (100 minutes), directed by Anthony Harvey and starring Katharine Hepburn, Sam Waterston, Joanna Miles, and Michael Moriarty. The virtue of this production is that it was specially adapted for TV by Williams himself; in addition, the production marked the first time that Hepburn had acted on TV. There is another notable color version (1987) directed by Paul Newman and starring Joanne Woodward, John Malkovich, Karen Allen, and James Naughton. A 1950 version starring Jane Wyman is also available.

Answers to the Study Questions, pages 1568–1569

(1) The setting defines a world of poverty, deprivation, and desperation. Key adjectives are ***warty, overcrowded, lower middle-class, dark, grim, narrow***, and ***sinister***. The alleys symbolize dead ends, confusion, and entrapment—the world that Tom wants to escape. The fire escape represents both the squalor of the Wingfields and also a way out.

(2) The fifth character—the missing father—is present in his often illuminated photograph, dressed in his World War I uniform. This absentee figure parallels Tom's appearance on stage in the uniform of a merchant sailor. The father and son both attempt to escape by abandoning the family. Amanda remarks that Tom's attitudes and behavior are similar to those of his father (Scene 4, speech 63, page 1536). Tom also compares himself to his father, claiming that he is following in his father's footsteps (Scene 7, speech 323, the last in the play).

(3) Amanda describes her genteel past in Blue Mountain, and her success with Gentlemen Callers, in scene 1 (speeches 14, 16, and 29, pages 1524, 1525). These memories come up several times in the play (Scene 5, speech 101; Scene 6, speech 19, pages 1543, 1547), contrasting with the decay and poverty of life in Saint Louis. Amanda's habitual retreat to the past and her repetition of these memories is indicated by the way Tom and Laura react to the story; they have heard it all many times before, but Laura insists that Tom "let her tell it" because "she loves to tell it" (Scene 1, speeches 18, 20, page 1524).

(4, 5) Laura was unable to deal with her own fear, shyness, and insecurity at Rubicam's. She became ill during the first typing test and stopped going to class thereafter (Scene 2, speech 16, page 1527). Laura's failure provokes a crisis for Amanda and leads to the central crisis of the play. Amanda refuses to face the reality of Laura's incapacities; she sees two possible futures for Laura—business or marriage. Either would make Laura secure and save her from becoming the barely tolerated maiden lady that burdens many families. Because Laura fails at business, Amanda turns her attention and energy to getting a Gentleman Caller. This evokes the image of Jim, the one boy that Laura admired (from afar) in high school. This image and memory of Jim foreshadows his visit in the last scene. Amanda's plan to marry off Laura is impracticable because of Laura's insecurity, withdrawal, and inability to deal with social situations.

(6) The argument in Scene 3 highlights the central concerns of the two characters. Amanda is worried about survival of the family and, more particularly, Laura's future; she accuses Tom of being self-centered and trying to run away from his responsibilities. Tom considers himself self-sacrificing. He is disgusted with his life at home and at the warehouse and he wants to escape from the apartment and the Continental Shoemakers, and go in search of adventure. He claims that he has given up all his dreams to support the family. Laura is spotlighted throughout the argument (scene 3, speech 2.3 S.D., page 1530) because Williams wants to

emphasize the impact of this conflict on her feelings and future. Amanda's concerns and Tom's ultimate decision to leave both have a pronounced effect on Laura.

(8) Scene 5 contains the announcement (annunciation) of the impending visit of Jim, the Gentleman Caller. Amanda sees Jim as a potential husband for Laura; she goes to extraordinary lengths to present Laura and the family in the best light. Her expectations are unreasonable and unrealistic; she cannot or will not see Laura's limitations. Tom is a good deal more realistic; he observes that "lots of fellows meet girls whom they don't marry" (Scene 5, speech 82, page 1542) and he is aware that Laura is crippled, different, and peculiar: "She lives in a world of her own—a world of little glass ornaments" (Scene 5, speech 132 , page 1544). Laura is terrified by the ideal of a Gentleman Caller. Moreover, she becomes almost totally incapacitated when she discovers that the Caller is Jim O'Connor; she refuses to answer the door or sit at the table, and she seeks refuge in her old phonograph records (Scene 6, speech 59, page 1549). She behaves this way partly because of her shyness and inability to function with people and partly because Jim, since high school, has embodied her secret fantasy of having a boy friend.

(9) The unicorn symbolizes Laura (as does the whole glass menagerie). Like Laura, the unicorn is unique, isolated, peculiar, different, fragile. The broken unicorn (missing its horn) is ironically more normal; Laura observes that the "horn was removed to make him feel less—freakish. Now he will feel more at home with the other horses" (Scene 7, speech 262, page 1518). This may symbolize Laura's momentary emergence from fantasy to reality and her normal interaction with Jim. Laura's giving Jim the broken unicorn as a *souvenir* represents the end of Laura's hopes. In both a real and symbolic sense, Jim carries Laura's potential for a normal life away with him. After she gives him the souvenir, she crouches beside the victrola to *wind it up*.

(10, 11) Tom, as narrator in the present, indicates that he escaped from the apartment and the warehouse, and "traveled around a great deal" (Scene 7, speech 323, page 1567). He has not, however, escaped from memory, guilt, or Laura. Laura and Amanda face a bleak existence in Saint Louis. Although Amanda ends the play comforting Laura, the extinguished candles suggest the end of hope.

Discussion of the "General Questions," page 1569

(1) The nonrealistic aspects of this play include the setting, lighting,

music, screen devices, use of a narrator, direct address to the audience, and the idea of the play as memory. Each of these will lend itself well to class discussion and/or writing assignments. There is, of course, no "right" answer to which is the most effective; all contribute to the total impact and meaning of the play. Williams probably incorporated the screen device to provide thematic focus for scenes or parts of scenes. It focuses our attention on the major idea or event of the particular scene that is taking place at the moment—the sights along with the sounds that define the period and culture of the Wingfields.

(2) Amanda, as protagonist, battles against poverty and abandonment in a vain (and heroic?) attempt to sustain genteel values, hold the family together, and provide for Laura's future. Tom, as protagonist, struggles for artistic expression and escape from his tedious and troubled life in the apartment and the warehouse. Laura, as the most passive character, is also the most difficult to cast as protagonist. One might argue, however, that her scene with Jim, the climax of the play, embodies her struggle to gain a normal life.

Unfortunately, all the central characters fail. Amanda and Laura are abandoned by Tom and Jim. Tom finds that he cannot escape the past. Tom is the only character who learns or gains self-knowledge in the play. In a larger context, both religion and the American Dream of adventure (Tom) or upward mobility (Jim) fail. Tom travels, but he achieves neither the artistic fulfillment nor the Hollywood-inspired adventure that he craves. Jim's failure to live up to his high-school potential suggests that he, too, is destined to remain trapped (in the warehouse, the past, marriage, unfulfilled dreams). The religious imagery that runs through the play ironically highlights the failures; Tom is not reborn; Amanda fails as a mother; the annunciation leads to a disaster instead of a miracle; Laura blows the candles out.

To deal with the harshness of life as they face it in the play, Amanda escapes into her memories of an idealized Southern past of plantations and genteel society. Laura seeks refuge in her fantasy world of the glass menagerie and the phonograph records left behind by her father. Tom escapes by going to the movies where he can experience adventure vicariously.

(3) This distinction is discussed in the sample essay (pages 1572–1573). Tom as character strives for escape, adventure, and self-expression. Tom as narrator understands that one can never escape from the past, memories, or guilt.

(4) Laura's crippled foot is a visual representation of her crippled spirit.

This, in turn, accounts for her shyness, withdrawal, and inability to cope with the world at large. Williams uses Laura's high-school memories, the episode at Rubicam's, and her initial reaction to Jim's arrival to illustrate her limitations. The glass menagerie is part of her fantasy world; she constantly retreats to this world of old records and glass figurines. The fragility of the glass also symbolizes her fragility.

(5) In using *The Glass Menagerie* as a writing assignment, you might ask students to focus on either Amanda's laughable or her admirable qualities. For a longer essay, have students deal with both. Amanda's pretensions toward gentility, her idealization of the past, and her unrealistic assessment of Laura. These are pitiable and laughable. Her fierce attempts to provide for Laura's future, however, are heroic and admirable. Williams seems to want to leave us with the latter image at the close of the play. When Amanda silently comforts Laura, *her silliness is gone and she has dignity and tragic beauty* (Scene 7, line 322.3, S. D., page 1568).

(6) Jim is realistic in the sense that he is the most nearly normal person in the play, "an emissary from the world of reality." He is an optimistic and energetic would-be achiever who is concerned mostly with himself and his own dreams. Jim's goals (an executive position, a perfect marriage) reflect the American Dream of self-improvement and upward mobility; they are more normal (acceptable) than Tom's dreams of artistic expression and escape. Even so, they are almost as unreachable as Tom's. Jim's momentary interest in Laura probably grows out of the fact that she remembers his high-school glory days. His realism is qualified by the fact that Tom (Williams) uses him as a symbol of "the long-delayed but always expected something that we live for."

(7) Tom focuses on the geopolitical and economic social background of the dramatized events twice (see pages 1522, 1540). In each instance, the relative calm and ignorance of the United States is contrasted with the growing chaos in Europe. The contrast—and Tom's retrospective awareness of it—might suggest a number of considerations for discussion or writing: a–the self-absorption of the Wingfields parallels national blindness; b–Laura's fantasy world parallels the national fantasy of approaching peace and prosperity; c–Tom's memories of Saint Louis represent a mid-point between Amanda's idealized Southern past and the impending disaster of World War II.

(8) Like *A Doll House*, this play contains a wealth of symbolism. Writing assignments can be geared to a specific type or specific line of symbolism. The two symbolic characters are Jim and Malvolio the Magi-

cian (Scene 4, speech 9, page 1533). Symbolic places include the alley, fire escape, Guernica, Blue Mountain, the Paradise Dance Hall, and the warehouse. Symbolic actions include Laura's polishing the glass figurines, playing the Victrola, and the two instances in which glass figures are broken (Scene 3, line 38.1 S.D., and Scene 7, speech 249.1 S.D., pages 1532, 1562). Symbolic objects and images include the photograph, blue roses, the unicorn and the glass menagerie, movies, and the coffin. The diffuse line of religious imagery and symbolism relates to all three central figures. Malvolio's escape from the coffin suggests resurrection or an escape from death (Lazarus); both are linked to Tom's desire to escape. The *Ave Maria* ironically celebrates Amanda as a mother. The Paradise Dance Hall—across the alley from the apartment—embodies a false heaven (reflecting the national blindness) in contrast to the hellish life of the Wingfields. The *annunciation* and the candles give Laura a religious aura that heightens her pathos and isolation.

Writing About Realistic and Nonrealistic Drama, *pages 1570–1574*

This material surveys approaches to planning and writing essays about realistic and/or nonrealistic aspects of plays. Again, the primary focus is on the relative realism or nonrealism of the element and the degree to which this, in turn, affects the impact and meaning of the play.

In developing (or having students develop) a writing project that engages the issue of realism or nonrealism, you have the option of calling for a relatively simple or a somewhat more complex essay. At the simplest level, you might ask students to select an aspect or element of a play and support an assertion that it is realistic (or nonrealistic). Such an essay might demonstrate the realism of one of Ibsen's characters or the nonrealsim of the lighting in *The Glass Menagerie*. At a more complex level, you can ask students to discuss both the realism (or nonrealism) of a specific element and the effect thus produced. This is the more difficult but more rewarding assignment; it will help students learn much about the play at hand.

Writing Topics for *Realistic and Nonrealistic Drama*, *pages 1574–1575*

(1) None of the figures represents what could be called models of family stability. The closest are the Helmers at the beginning of the play.

At first they seem stable, and the husband-wife-children pattern seems in order, but things disintegrate quickly once the couple starts discussing the truth with each other. Mommy and Daddy are also somewhat stable, but their relationship seems more like that of children than of adults. (Is Albee suggesting something here?) The Wingfield family is of course split apart and is in the process of splitting even more apart. Family in *The Glass Menagerie* is presented as a network of contradictory desires and hopes, which are embodied in the ongoing conflict between Tom and Amanda. From Tom's perspective, family is also a trap. Poverty complicates the dynamics of the family considerably; it motivates Amanda's desperate efforts to secure Laura's future and it keeps Tom trapped in the warehouse. Personality is shaped by the past (Amanda's memories, Jim's high-school achievements, Tom's memories), dreams, and physical form (Laura's crippled foot). Colonel Norwood is at heart not a bad sort, and he has been the idol of Robert's childhood heart. The Colonel is prevented from normal family relationships, however, because of his social, economic, and racial position.

Normality of course implies a judgment based on what is happening today. By such a standard, the normal family is the Wingfields, whereas the other families may represent an ideal more honored with words than with actuality. But with a relationship like that of Mommy and Daddy, who could ever want the ideal to become real?

(2) The question of comparable settings will require the technique of comparison-contrast (Appendix B). Students will need to analyze the opening stage-setting descriptions, and they should also consider how the settings figure into the action of the play, such as the sandbox, the exercising young man, or the screened images and statements. Though the properties are all realistic, the way in which they are put together suggests their function in the absurdist and memory play context. Of great interest would be the statements that students might make about the effects of staging on audience perceptions. Is photographic staging necessary? Can a play work as well in an abstract or convention-loaded stage?

(3) This topic is considered in this manual in question 1 of the study questions and question 1 of the general questions (please refer to text pages 1568 and 1569).

(4) For beginning an essay on symbolism in *Mulatto*, please see the discussion of general question 2 (text page 1463).

(5) Although economics and the need for feminine independence are applicable to all the plays in the chapter to at least some degree, the subject is perhaps best applied to *A Doll House*. Hardly a page does not contain some reference to the financial circumstances of the Helmer household, and Nora's yearning to be free is to her the same as to be free of debt. It is clear that the root of all their ills was their early financial difficulty and Nora's borrowing to pay for Helmer's rehabilitation in Italy. The same applies to a feminist essay. The early parts of *A Doll House* are almost a textbook case in the need for female freedom, and the final act contains one of the best confrontation of wife and husband over the issue of female identity.

(6) Students may pick their own topics in addition to the ones suggested in direction 6. What is important is that they create scenes of different levels of reality. It would be satisfactory for many of the same speeches to be duplicated in either version, so long as the realistic or unrealistic context is maintained.

Chapter Thirty
Pages 1576–1598

Film: Drama on the Silver and Color Screens

This chapter was added in the third edition at the request of a number of instructors who have used films in their courses. At the present time the seeing of films has been totally revolutionized by the existence of videotapes and VCRs. Virtually the entire corpus of films, right from the very beginning to the last six months, is available for classroom use. The problem in studying films is hence not so much availability but rather being able to choose from the plethora of existing films. One needs only to enter a typical videotape rental outlet to conclude that the problems of teaching films today did not exist as recently as ten years ago.

In teaching film you may go as far as time may allow. The "Thumbnail History" of film (pages 1576–1577) is intended as no more than a hasty outline which includes only the most essential details. You might carry this as far as you class's interests will allow. More to the point of a course in literature including film, the discussions of *Stage Plays and Film, The Aesthetics of Film*, and *The Techniques of Film* (pages 1577–1582) are of major interest, especially the sections on visual, action, and sound techniques.

Since a discussion of film is designed to increase understanding of film literature and techniques, it is appropriate to stress what students should look for in a film. Here you might rely on those students who have had experience in taking photographs. Almost everyone has snapped a picture, but few have ever done so in accordance with artistic principles. A discussion might raise the question of what can be achieved by a closeup, or by a longshot. Why take one or the other? Which type do students prefer? What is the effect of a longshot in which the entire body is included? What is the effect of a photograph of a person standing underneath a tree, with the tree dwarfing that person? Is it good or bad to have an object, say a tree branch, in the foreground of a picture? With a discussion developing out of questions like these, you can make a number of points about photographic technique.

Invariably you will find that some of your students will have used either motion picture or (more likely) videotape cameras. They might thus be able to describe the differences between stationary and motion photography. How much time should be devoted to photographing a single person? Why should a running camera be shifted from one point to another slowly rather than rapidly? How should a zoom lens be used? Perhaps a description might be made (and illustrated, if possible) of a home movie—usually taken with appalling technique—and this description might be contrasted with the description of a professionally photographed film. Such contrasts are effective in helping students recognize basic problems, and solutions, of motion-picture photography.

There are many other aspects of film technique, and you may devote as much or as little time to them as you find desirable. Probably the most important additional element to stress, however, is *montage* or editing. Students knowing about the possible results of editing can see a film with confidence and develop informed responses to it.

Orson Welles and Herman J. Mankiewicz: Shot 71 from the shooting script of *Citizen Kane, pages 1583–1586*

Students would of course benefit from discussing this passage after having seen the entire film. A videocassette copy of *Citizen Kane* is readily available for use if your department or your audio-visual service has any budget at all for rentals. The updated and revised fiftieth anniversary edition of the film has been released in videocassette and is available for rental at most video stores (Turner Home Entertainment. Catalogue No. 6261).

Answers to the Study Questions, page 1587

(1) The scene follows Kane's political loss in the gubernatorial election. Jedediah enters with the obvious purpose of declaring that he wishes to end his immediate associations with Kane. In effect, the scene is a major showdown between the two men, although there is a final one later when Kane rewrites Jedediah's damnatory review of the operatic performance given by Kane's wife. The opening words indicate that the two men have been the closest of friends, for Kane says "I thought I heard somebody knock" (line 2). This is a criticism of Jedediah's formality, for we may assume that he never had to knock before to see Kane. Jedediah's speeches show the cause of his unhappiness: Kane cannot accept objective criticism and advice, because he takes everything personally. Jedediah is frustrated with this situa-

tion, and asks for a transfer, which Kane reluctantly grants, while corroborating Jedediah's judgment in the scene's last speech (line 31).

(2) The reason for the title might be debated. Kane certainly is an American tycoon, and his self-indulgence with his own money ultimately leads all his friends and associates to desert him, thus illustrating the perils of wealth. The reason for the choice of *Citizen* as the title, however, may be taken as an ironic commentary on Kane's life. This scene demonstrates how Kane conceptualizes his role as a citizen: If he can't control things, he will either lose or not participate. This is not the position most citizens are in; hence the irony.

(3) If one is accustomed to straight-on, eye-level photography, the camera angles from below exaggerate the height and distance of the characters' heads, thus emphasizing both their size and suggesting their general significance as symbols as well as characters. The use of light and shadow suggests that even in open conversation (light) there is still an immense amount of thought, feeling, and motivation that are obscured (shadow). The theme of the movie is that Kane is a riddle and an enigma, and the development consists of the attempt to explain him. Thus, the use of camera and light in this scene fit right into the story and structure of the film.

Arthur Laurents, A Scene from *The Turning Point*, *pages 1587–1592*

There are two major films which have succeeded because of their use of ballet. One is *The Red Shoes* (1948), in which the ballet ultimately becomes the heroine's story. The other is *The Turning Point,* in which the ballet scenes are included as aspects of the developing story. The feature dances are by Michael Baryshnikov and Leslie Browne. The concluding credit unit, in which Leslie Browne dances to the music of a Chopin Etude, is one of the best ballet sequences ever to have been put on film.

Answers to the Study Questions, pages 1592–1593

(1) The argument, boiling over as the women whack each other, indicates that their friendship is stronger than the pent-up resentments and jealousies they have allowed to fester over the years. Emma makes the confession that she "had to have" the ballet years before, and therefore she would have said anything to get it, including giving false advice to Deedee about her marriage. Once this admission is made, Deedee can put away all her self doubts, because Emma has in effect recognized that Deedee was a superb dancer.

(2) The last ten speeches add nothing to the conflict and reconciliation that has just occurred between the two women. In fact the conclusion suggests, as they "walk in opposite directions," that the reconciliation may not be complete. In the finished film, the scene ends logically, without including what is in effect an anti-climax.

(3) If the scene had remained in the bar, it would have made the purse-whacking impossible, for presumably someone nearby would have tried to stop the two women. By moving outside to the plaza Emma and Deedee have the privacy to shout at each other loudly and vent their anger completely. This kind of fidelity to realism would be impossible on stage, unless, of course, the stage scene were established as the open, empty, darkened plaza. Obviously, film, with its many scenes and shots, provides for many possibilities that stage plays cannot possess.

(4) There are a number of changes from script to film. The elevator becomes a stairway, and afterward there is a second hallway along which the two women walk. The plaza is the same, but the women are first seen arguing and throwing things from above at a distance. When their battle-scene develops, they are seen closely, and at the fountain they are filmed from the waist up. In this way the visual presentation complements their emotional reconciliation. When the whacking ends in the film, it is laughter and not exhaustion that ends it, and thereby the reconciliation takes place within a mood of emotional release and merriment. Students may be able to suggest additional changes, but a major one is that a number of verbal variations may be noted, which may have been introduced directly by the actresses, Shirley MacLaine and Anne Bancroft. Students might wish to discuss the freedom that film actors seem to possess.

Writing About Film, *pages 1593–1597*

A major decision here is for students to select a suitable topic. The easiest path to follow is to focus on normal literary topics like character development, a major idea, structure, and so on. As long as students rely on references to film action and dialogue, they will be on safe ground for whatever conclusions they make. References to non-literary techniques like facial expression, camera angles, and lighting and shading are much harder for students to interpret with confidence. Even so, they should make a beginning approach. Obviously, the more that students study film techniques, the more reliable will be their references. If students are experienced with film, they might choose to concentrate on purely cinematic as opposed to literary matters, but many students—and instructors—will feel more secure if they emphasize the literary.

A common problem for students writing about a film is shortness of memory. Use of a videocassette, and the re-running of a particular scene, can help in this regard. Also, however, a well-kept journal is essential here, for once a student begins writing there may be no further opportunity to verify details in the film.

As a preliminary, students may benefit from a number of exercises to help them in their understanding of film. Some useful hints might be these:

a. For a film or TV show, determine how your understanding of a particular character is influenced by cinematic techniques (camera angles and views, lighting, setting), acting techniques (facial expressions, tones of voice, actions, "body language"), and costumes and makeup.

b. Observe a chase scene in a film or TV show, and determine the effects of camera techniques on your responses to the chase. (There is a hilarious chase scene in *What's Up, Doc?* [1972], in which Barbra Streisand and Ryan O'Neill are pursued through the streets and steps of San Francisco.)

c. For any film or TV show, record all unusual or noteworthy uses of the camera or of lighting. If any scene especially affected you, determine those elements that contributed to the effect.

d. Consider the uses of silence, sound effects, and music in a scene or series of scenes. What is the relationship between the dramatic situations and sound? Does sound help make a happy scene happier? A tense one more tense? A dangerous one more dangerous? A threatening one sinister? A scary one frightening? etc.

Writing Topics for *Film: Drama on the Silver and Color Screens, pages 1597–1598*

(1) A good technique for this topic might be the use of montage. It would not be necessary to discuss details for the entire film, however, but might be most effective if followed through two or three sequences of action. The same would apply if the student were to discuss camera technique, the use of closeups or longshots, and so on.

(2) This topic requires the full examination of just about everything that goes into the makeup of a particular scene. The scene itself, therefore, will not need to be long, because the problem here will be in coming to a stop.

(3) Although this is a creative-writing topic, it would be appropriate only after students have already spent a little time in analyzing and discussing film techniques and the relationship of dramatic to film presentations. The perspective that students should bring to the assignment is that of the director, giving directions to actors in order to realize a conception of a particular scene. Topics abound in the daily papers, and even more topics might be found in the weekly newsmagazines that stuff the racks near grocery checkout counters.

Appendix D
Pages 1650–1663

Critical Approaches Important in the Study of Literature

Needless to say, pursuing the subject of critical study is an occupation in itself. The materials in this chapter are designed to do no more than introduce students to the existence of the various critical approaches. You may therefore wish to augment the chapter with a detailed set of materials for their consideration. The best place to start is the recent book by Charles E. Bressler, *Literary Criticism: An Introduction to Theory and Practice* (Englewood Cliffs: Prentice Hall, 1994). This book goes over all the ground in great detail. It is highly recommended. Especially significant about Bressler's book are the sixteen pages of bibliography, beginning on page 185, which is extensive, well detailed, and up to date. The bibliography lists at least 225 books, an overwhelming number for any student getting interested in literary approaches. Bressler bases his illustrative discussions on three works that are also included in the fourth edition of *Literature: An Introduction to Reading and Writing.* These are Glaspell's *Trifles,* Browning's *My Last Duchess,* and Hawthorne's *Young Goodman Brown..*

As an abbreviated bibliography, the following books, most of which Bressler lists, might be useful.

- Bloom, Harold, and Paul de Man, Jacques Derrida, Geoffrey H. Hartman, and J. Hillis Miller, *Deconstruction and Criticism* (New York: Continuum, 1988).
- Brooks, Cleanth, and Robert Penn Warren. *Understanding Poetry.* New York: Holt, 1928.
- Calahan, James M. and David B. Downing. *Practicing Theory in Introductory Literature Courses.* Urbana: National Council of teachers of English, 1991.

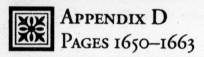

- Donovan, Josephine, ed., *Feminist Literary Criticism: Explorations in Theory*. Lexington: Kentucky UP, 1975.
- Hirsch, David H., *The Deconstruction of Literature: Criticism After Auschwitz*. Hanover: Brown UP, 1991.
- Richards, I. A., *Practical Criticism*. New York: Harcourt, 1929.
- Scholes, Robert. *Structuralism in Literature: An Introduction*. New Haven: Yale UP, 1974.
- Tompkins, Jane P., ed., *Reader-Response Criticism From Formalism to Post-Structuralism. Baltimore: Johns Hopkins UP, 1980.*